Collins
Primary illustrated Dictionary

Published by Collins
An imprint of HarperCollins Publishers
Westerhill Road
Bishopbriggs
Glasgow G64 2QT

Second Edition 2015

10 9 8 7 6 5

© HarperCollins Publishers 2010, 2015

PB ISBN 978-0-00-757875-7
HB ISBN 978-0-00-812690-2

Collins® is a registered trademark of
HarperCollins Publishers Limited

www.collinsdictionary.com
www.collins.co.uk/childrensreference

Typeset by Davidson Publishing Solutions

Printed and Bound by Printing Express Ltd,
Hong Kong

Entered words that we have reason to believe
constitute trademarks have been designated
as such. However, neither the presence nor
absence of such designation should be regarded
as affecting the legal status of any trademark.

The contents of this publication are believed
correct at the time of printing. Nevertheless the
publisher can accept no responsibility for errors
or omissions, changes in the detail given or for
any expense or loss thereby caused.

HarperCollins does not warrant that any
website mentioned in this title will be provided
uninterrupted, that any website will be error
free, that defects will be corrected, or that the
website or the server that makes it available
are free of viruses or bugs. For full terms and
conditions please refer to the site terms
provided on the website.

A catalogue record for this book is available
from the British Library.

If you would like to comment on any aspect
of this book, please contact us at the given
address or online.
E-mail: dictionaries@harpercollins.co.uk
🐦 @Collins4Parents

Acknowledgements
We would like to thank those authors and
publishers who kindly gave permission for
copyright material to be used in the Collins
Corpus. We would also like to thank Times
Newspapers Ltd for providing valuable data.

Contents

Using this dictionary

A dictionary helps you to find out what a word means and how to spell it correctly. The words in a dictionary are arranged in alphabetical order.

How to find a word

An **alphabet line** has been printed at the side of each page, and the letter in the blue box tells you which letter the words on that page begin with. So if you want to find the word **maximum**, use the alphabet line to look for words beginning with **m**.

At the top of each page there is a **guide word**. On a left-hand page the guide word tells you the first word on the page. On a right-hand page the guide word tells you the last word on the page. This means that when you open your dictionary, you can see straight away if you are at the right place. For example, if you are looking up **maximum**, you know that it must come on the pages with the guide words **marvel** and **maze**, because the words in the dictionary always come in alphabetical order.

When you think you have the right page, look at the headwords until you find the word you want.

Finding your way around the dictionary

① The **alphabet line** shows the first letter of the word.

② The **guide word** shows the first word on the page if it is a left-hand page and the last word on the page if it is a right-hand page.

③ The **headword** is the word you are looking up.

④ After the headword there can be **other forms** of the word, such as plural nouns, verb tenses, and comparative and superlative adjectives.

⑤ The **part of speech** tells you what type of word the headword is, such as a noun, verb, adjective, adverb, or pronoun.

⑥ The **definition** tells you what the word means.

⑦ Sometimes there is an **example** to show how the word is used.

⑧ If the headword has more than one meaning, each meaning has a different **number**.

⑨ A **pronunciation** shows you how to say a difficult word.

⑩ Some entries have a **related word**, such as a noun, adjective, or adverb made from the headword.

⑪ A **word history** tells you where a word originally came from.

⑫ **Synonyms**, or words that you can use instead, are given for some words.

⑬ **Antonyms**, or words that have the opposite meaning, are given for some words.

maze

material materials
NOUN **1** cloth
2 anything from which something else can be made • artists' **materials**

maternal
ADJECTIVE **1** used to describe things relating to a mother • My **maternal** grandfather was Welsh.
2 A woman who is **maternal** has strong motherly feelings.

maternity
ADJECTIVE relating to or involving pregnant women and childbirth • The baby was born in the **maternity** wing of the hospital.

mathematics
NOUN the study of numbers, quantities and shapes
mathematical ADJECTIVE
mathematically ADVERB
mathematician NOUN

maths
NOUN an abbreviation of mathematics

matinee matinees
Said "**mat**-i-nay" NOUN an afternoon performance at a theatre or cinema

matrix matrices
Said "**may**-trix, **may**-tri-sees" NOUN In mathematics, a **matrix** is a set of numbers or letters set out in rows and columns.

matt
ADJECTIVE dull rather than shiny • Mum painted the front door **matt** green.

matter matters, mattering, mattered
NOUN **1** a task or situation that you have to attend to • We will have to discuss the **matter** with the head teacher.
SYNONYMS: affair, business, subject
2 any substance • The scientists explored how **matter** behaves at high temperatures.
VERB **3** If something **matters**, it is important.
PHRASE **4** If you ask **What's the matter?**, you want to know what is wrong.

mattress mattresses
NOUN a large, flat, spongy pad that is put on a bed to make it comfortable to sleep on

mature matures, maturing, matured
VERB **1** When a child or other young animal **matures**, it becomes an adult.
ADJECTIVE **2** fully grown or developed
maturely ADVERB   maturity NOUN

maul mauls, mauling, mauled
VERB If an animal **mauls** someone, they savagely attack and badly injure them.

mauve
Rhymes with "stove" NOUN OR ADJECTIVE a light purple colour

maximum
ADJECTIVE **1** The **maximum** amount is the most that is possible or allowed. • The **maximum** score for this question is five marks.
ANTONYM: minimum
NOUN **2** the most that is possible or allowed • Pupils are allowed a **maximum** of two pounds to spend on the school trip.
ANTONYM: minimum

may
VERB **1** If something **may** happen, it is possible that it will happen.
2 If you **may** do something, you are allowed to do it.

May
NOUN the fifth month of the year. **May** has 31 days.
[probably from the Roman goddess Maia]

maybe
ADVERB If you think there is a possibility that something will happen, but you are not sure, you use **maybe**. • **Maybe** we will be allowed to go to the cinema tonight.

mayonnaise
NOUN a thick salad dressing made with egg yolks and oil

mayor mayors
NOUN someone who has been elected to represent the people of a town at official functions

maze mazes
NOUN a system of complicated passages which it is difficult to find your way through

a
b
c
d
e
f
g
h
i
j
k
l
m
n
o
p
q
r
s
t
u
v
w
x
y
z

243

5

Using this dictionary

Other features of this dictionary

- Some headwords can be spelt in more than one way.

> **medieval**; also spelt **mediaeval**
>
> **age** ages, ageing or aging, aged

- Sometimes definitions include a label, such as FORMAL, INFORMAL, or TRADEMARK. This tells you a little more about the word or how it is used.

> **mum** mums
>
> NOUN INFORMAL mother

- Sometimes a photo or an illustration is included.

> **mollusc** molluscs
>
> NOUN an animal with a soft body and no backbone. Snails, slugs, clams and mussels are all **molluscs**.
>
>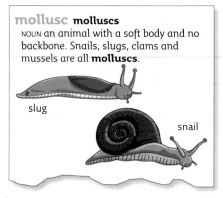
>
> slug
>
> snail

- Grammar and spelling tips provide extra information on the spelling or use of words.

> **different**
>
> ADJECTIVE If one thing is **different** from another, it is not like it.
>
> ✏ There are two *es* in *different*.

- Some definitions tell you where to find more information at another headword.

> **convex**
>
> ADJECTIVE A **convex** surface bulges outwards, rather than being level or curving inwards.
> *See* **concave**

Extra help for you

Word Wizard is a special section at the back of this book to help you with your writing. It contains information on things like parts of speech, prefixes, suffixes, and punctuation. It also tells you how you can improve your spelling. There are interesting facts about where some words come from. It even has information on shapes, numbers, fractions, and angles, along with pictures.

The Earth and Space is a fact-filled section with colourful pictures. This is where to look if you want to know more about the Solar System, the Earth, the Moon, the continents, and the world's mountains, rivers, and oceans. There are also pages showing you the flags of some of the nations of the world.

Aa

a an

ADJECTIVE **A** and **an** are used when you talk about one of something. **A** is used when the next sound is a consonant: *a car*, *a dog*. **An** is used when the next sound is a vowel (a, e, i, o or u): *an apple*, *an elephant*.

abacus abacuses

NOUN a frame with beads that slide along rods, used for counting
[from Greek *abax* meaning board covered with sand for doing sums on]

abandon abandons, abandoning, abandoned

VERB If you **abandon** someone or something, you leave them or give them up for good. • He **abandoned** all hope of catching the train on time.

abbey abbeys

NOUN a church with buildings attached to it in which monks or nuns live

abbreviation abbreviations

NOUN a short form of a word or phrase • N is an **abbreviation** for North.

abdomen abdomens

NOUN the front part of your body below your chest, containing your stomach and intestines
abdominal ADJECTIVE

ability abilities

NOUN If you have **ability**, you have the intelligence and skill to do things.

able

ADJECTIVE If you are **able** to do something, you can do it.
ANTONYM: unable

abnormal

ADJECTIVE not normal or usual
abnormally ADVERB

aboard

PREPOSITION OR ADVERB If you are **aboard** a plane or a ship you are on it.

Aborigine Aborigines

NOUN someone descended from the people who were living in Australia before the European settlers arrived

about

PREPOSITION OR ADVERB **1** If you talk or write **about** a particular thing, you say things that are to do with that subject. • *a book* **about** *London*
2 You say **about** in front of a number to show it is not exact. • **about** *two o'clock*
PHRASE **3** If you are **about to** do something, you are just going to do it. • He was **about to** leave.

above

PREPOSITION OR ADVERB If one thing is above another, it is higher up. • *The plane was flying* **above** *the clouds.*
ANTONYM: below

abroad

ADVERB If you go **abroad**, you go to another country.

abscess abscesses

NOUN a painful swelling on the body, which contains pus

abseil abseils, abseiling, abseiled

VERB If you **abseil** down a rock face, you use ropes to go down it.

absent

ADJECTIVE If you are **absent** from a place, you are not there.
ANTONYM: present

absolute

ADJECTIVE **1** total and complete • **absolute** *darkness*
2 having total power • *an* **absolute** *ruler*

absolutely

ADVERB If you are **absolutely** sure about something, you are completely sure of it.

absorb absorbs, absorbing, absorbed

VERB If something **absorbs** liquid or gas, it soaks it up. • *Plants* **absorb** *moisture from the soil.*

absorbent

ADJECTIVE If something is **absorbent**, it soaks up liquids easily.

abstract

ADJECTIVE **1** An **abstract** idea is based on thoughts and ideas rather than on real objects or happenings, for example *bravery* and *happiness*.
2 Abstract art uses shapes rather than images of people or objects.

an abstract painting

3 In grammar, **abstract** nouns refer to qualities or ideas, rather than physical objects, for example *happiness*.
See **noun**

absurd

ADJECTIVE Something that is **absurd** is stupid or ridiculous.

abuse **abuses, abusing, abused**

Said "ab-**yooss**" NOUN **1** cruel treatment of someone
2 rude and unkind remarks
Said "ab-**yooz**" VERB **3** To **abuse** someone is to treat them cruelly.
4 If you **abuse** someone, you speak to them in a rude and insulting way.

abysmal

ADJECTIVE very bad
abysmally ADVERB

academic **academics**

ADJECTIVE **1 Academic** work is done in school, college and university.
NOUN **2** someone who teaches or does research in a college or university

academy **academies**

NOUN **1** a school or college, usually one that specializes in a particular subject
● the Royal **Academy** of Arts
2 an organization of scientists, writers, artists or musicians

accelerate **accelerates, accelerating, accelerated**

VERB To **accelerate** is to speed up.
ANTONYM: decelerate

acceleration

NOUN the rate at which the speed of something increases

accent **accents**

NOUN a way of pronouncing a language
● She had an Australian **accent**.

accept **accepts, accepting, accepted**

VERB **1** If you **accept** something, you say yes to it or you take it from someone.
● She **accepted** our invitation to the party.
2 If you **accept** a situation, you realize that it cannot be changed. ● I **accepted** that I would have to work hard before my exams.

acceptable

ADJECTIVE satisfactory

access

NOUN If you have **access** to a place, you may enter it. If you have **access** to a thing, you may use it.

accessible

ADJECTIVE **1** easy to reach or to see
● The beach was **accessible** by a narrow path.
2 Books that are **accessible** are easy to understand.

accident **accidents**

NOUN **1** something that happens suddenly or unexpectedly, causing people to be hurt or killed
PHRASE **2** Something that happens **by accident** has not been planned.
● We met **by accident** in the supermarket.

accidental

ADJECTIVE Something that is **accidental** has not been planned.
accidentally ADVERB

acknowledge

accommodation
NOUN a place where you can live, work or sleep

accompany **accompanies, accompanying, accompanied**
VERB **1** If you **accompany** someone, you go with them.
2 If you **accompany** a singer, you play an instrument while they sing.

accomplice **accomplices**
NOUN a person who helps someone else to commit a crime

accomplish **accomplishes, accomplishing, accomplished**
VERB If you **accomplish** something, you succeed in doing it.

according to
PREPOSITION If something is true **according to** a particular person, that person says that it is true. ● *According to* my grandad, *that castle is haunted.*

account **accounts, accounting, accounted**
NOUN **1** a written or spoken report of something
2 money that you keep at a bank
PHRASE **3 On account of** means because of. ● *He couldn't play football, on account of a sore throat.*
VERB **4** To **account for** something is to explain it. ● *The bad weather accounts for the cancellation of the barbecue.*

accountant **accountants**
NOUN someone whose job is to look after the financial affairs of people and companies

accumulate **accumulates, accumulating, accumulated**
VERB If things **accumulate**, or if you **accumulate** things, they collect over a period of time. ● *While they were away, a large pile of letters accumulated on the doormat.*
accumulation NOUN

accurate
ADJECTIVE absolutely correct
accuracy NOUN

accuse **accuses, accusing, accused**
VERB If you **accuse** someone of doing something wrong, you say they have done it.
accusation NOUN

ace **aces**
NOUN **1** In a pack of cards, the **ace** is a card with a single symbol on it.
2 In tennis, an **ace** is a serve that the other player is unable to return.
ADJECTIVE **3** INFORMAL good or skilful ● *an ace squash player*

ache **aches, aching, ached**
NOUN **1** a continuous, dull pain
VERB **2** If a part of your body **aches**, you feel a continuous, dull pain there.

achieve **achieves, achieving, achieved**
VERB If you **achieve** something, you are successful at doing it or at making it happen.

> The *i* comes before the *e* in *achieve*.

acid **acids**
NOUN **1** a chemical substance. Strong **acids** can damage skin, cloth and metal, for example sulphuric **acid**. Other **acids**, such as those found in citrus fruit and vinegar, are harmless.
ANTONYM: alkali
ADJECTIVE **2** If something has an **acid** taste, it tastes sharp or bitter.
ANTONYM: alkaline
[from Latin *acidus* meaning sour]

acid rain
NOUN rain that has been polluted by the burning of fossil fuels, such as coal and oil

acknowledge **acknowledges, acknowledging, acknowledged**
VERB **1** If you **acknowledge** a fact or a situation, you admit that it is true.
2 If you **acknowledge** someone, you show that you have seen and recognized them, by waving or saying *hello*.
3 If you **acknowledge** a message or a letter, you tell the person who sent it that you have received it.

9

A
B
C
D
E
F
G
H
I
J
K
L
M
N
O
P
Q
R
S
T
U
V
W
X
Y
Z

acne

NOUN a skin disease that causes spots on the face and neck. **Acne** is common among teenagers.

acorn acorns

NOUN a nut that grows on oak trees

acquaintance acquaintances

NOUN someone you know slightly but not well

acre acres

NOUN a unit for measuring land. One acre is equal to 4840 square yards or about 4047 square metres.

acrobat acrobats

NOUN an entertainer who performs difficult gymnastic acts
[from Greek *akrobates* meaning someone who walks on tiptoe]
acrobatic ADJECTIVE
acrobatics PLURAL NOUN

acronym acronyms

NOUN a word made up of the initial letters of a phrase • *NATO is an **acronym**, and stands for North Atlantic Treaty Organization.*

across

PREPOSITION OR ADVERB **1** If you go **across** a place, you go from one side of it to the other. • *We walked **across** Hyde Park.*
2 Something that is situated **across** a road or river is on the other side of it.

act acts, acting, acted

VERB **1** If you **act**, you do something. • *We have to **act** quickly in an emergency.*
2 If you **act** in a particular way, you behave in that way. • *You're **acting** like a baby.*
3 If you **act** in a play or film, you play a role in it.
NOUN **4** a single thing someone does • *The rescue was a brave **act**.*
5 An **Act** of Parliament is a law passed by the government.
6 Stage plays are divided into parts called **acts**.

action actions

NOUN **1** something you do for a particular purpose
2 a physical movement, such as jumping

active

ADJECTIVE **1** Someone who is **active** moves around a lot or does a lot of things.
2 In grammar the **active**, or the **active** voice, is the form of the verb in which the subject of the sentence is the person or thing doing the action, rather than having it done to them. For example, the sentence *The dog bit Ben* is in the **active** voice. In the passive voice the subject is acted upon: *Ben was bitten by the dog.*
ANTONYM: passive

activity activities

NOUN **1** a situation in which a lot of things are happening at the same time • *There was a great deal of **activity** in the hall as we got ready for the school play.*
2 something you do for pleasure, such as gymnastics or music

actor actors

NOUN a man or woman whose job is performing in plays or films

actress actresses

NOUN a woman whose profession is acting

actual

ADJECTIVE real, rather than imaginary or guessed at • *You guessed I was eleven – my **actual** age is twelve.*
actually ADVERB

acute

ADJECTIVE **1** severe or intense • *She had an **acute** pain in her arm.*
2 In mathematics, an **acute** angle measures less than 90 degrees.
3 Someone who is **acute** is intelligent.

AD

ADJECTIVE You use AD in dates to show the number of years after the birth of Jesus Christ.
[an abbreviation of the Latin *Anno Domini* meaning the year of Our Lord]

adapt adapts, adapting, adapted

VERB **1** If you **adapt** to something, you get used to it.
2 If you **adapt** something, you change it so that it can be used in a new way.

adaptable

ADJECTIVE If you are **adaptable**, you change

easily in a new situation or to suit new circumstances.

add adds, adding, added

VERB **1** If you **add** something to a number of things, you put it with those things.
● *Each girl added more wood to the pile.*
2 If you **add** numbers together, or **add** them up, you work out the total. ● *Two and three added together are five (2 + 3 = 5).*

adder

adders

NOUN a small, poisonous snake

addiction

addictions

NOUN If you have an **addiction** to something, you cannot stop doing it or wanting it.

addition additions

NOUN **1** the process of adding two or more numbers together
2 something that is added to something else ● *The addition of sugar would improve the taste of these plums.*

additional

ADJECTIVE extra or more

additive additives

NOUN something that is added to something else, such as food

address addresses, addressing, addressed

NOUN **1** Your **address** is the number of the house where you live, together with the name of the street and the town or village.
VERB **2** If someone **addresses** a letter to you, they write your name and address on it.
3 If you **address** a group of people, you speak to them formally.

 There are two *d*s and two *ss* in *address*.

adenoids

PLURAL NOUN small lumps of flesh at the back of the throat

adequate

ADJECTIVE just enough for what is needed
SYNONYMS: enough, satisfactory, sufficient

adhesive adhesives

NOUN **1** a substance used to stick things together, such as glue
ADJECTIVE **2** If something is **adhesive**, it sticks to other things.

adjective adjectives

NOUN a word that adds to the description of a noun. For example, *large* and *old* are both **adjectives**.

adjust adjusts, adjusting, adjusted

VERB **1** If you **adjust** something, you change its position or alter it in some other way. ● *She adjusted her pillow to make herself more comfortable.*
2 If you **adjust** to a new situation, you get used to it.
adjustment NOUN

administration administrations

NOUN the work of managing and supervising an organization

admiral admirals

NOUN a senior officer in the navy

admire admires, admiring, admired

VERB If you **admire** someone or something, you respect and approve of them.
admirer NOUN

admission admissions

NOUN **1** If you are allowed **admission** to a place, you may go into it.
2 If you make an **admission**, you confess to something or agree that it is true.

admit admits, admitting, admitted

VERB **1** If you **admit** something, you agree that it is true.
2 If you **admit** to something, you agree that you did something you shouldn't have done.
3 To **admit** someone or something to a place is to allow them to enter it.

admittance

NOUN the right to enter somewhere ● *There will be no admittance to the party after eight o'clock.*

adolescent **adolescents**
NOUN a young person who is no longer a child, but is not yet an adult
[from Latin *adolescere* meaning to grow up]
adolescence NOUN

adopt **adopts, adopting, adopted**
VERB If someone **adopts** a child, they take them into their family as their son or daughter by a legal process.
[from Latin *adoptare* meaning to choose for oneself]

adorable
ADJECTIVE loveable and attractive

adore **adores, adoring, adored**
VERB If you **adore** someone, you feel deep love and admiration for them.
adoration NOUN

adult **adults**
NOUN a mature and fully developed person or animal

advance **advances, advancing, advanced**
VERB **1** To **advance** is to move forward.
NOUN **2** An **advance** is progress in something. ● *There have been many scientific **advances** in the past century.*
PHRASE **3** If you do something **in advance** of something, you do it beforehand. ● *We booked our holiday well **in advance**.*

advanced
ADJECTIVE If something is **advanced**, it is at a high level, or ahead in development or progress. ● *The children in the top group do **advanced** maths exercises.*

advantage **advantages**
NOUN **1** a benefit, or something that puts you in a better position ● *The **advantage** of e-mail is that it is quicker than the post.*
PHRASE **2** If you **take advantage** of someone, you treat them unfairly for your own benefit.
3 If you **take advantage** of something, you make use of it.

adventure **adventures**
NOUN something that is exciting, and perhaps even dangerous

adverb **adverbs**
NOUN a word that tells you how, when, where or why something happens or something is done. For example, she walked *slowly*, he came *yesterday*, they live *here*.
[from Latin *adverbium* meaning added word]

advert
NOUN an abbreviation for *advertisement*

advertise **advertises, advertising, advertised**
VERB If you **advertise** something, you tell people about it in a newspaper, on a poster or on TV.

advertisement **advertisements**
NOUN a notice in a newspaper, on a poster or on TV about a job or things for sale

advice
NOUN a suggestion from someone about what you should do

The noun *advice* ends in *ce*.

advisable
ADJECTIVE If it is **advisable** to do something, it is a sensible thing to do and will probably give the results that you want. ● *It is **advisable** to wear a helmet when cycling.*

advise **advises, advising, advised**
VERB If you **advise** someone to do something, you tell them you think they should do it.

The verb *advise* ends in *se*.

aerial **aerials**
NOUN **1** a piece of wire for receiving television or radio signals
ADJECTIVE **2** happening in the air
● *We watched the **aerial** displays at the RAF airshow.*

aero-
PREFIX to do with the air, for example **aero**plane
[from Greek *aer* meaning air]

aerobics
NOUN a type of fast physical exercise that increases the oxygen in your blood and

A B C D E F G H I J K L M N O P Q R S T U V W X Y Z

strengthens your heart and lungs
aerobic ADJECTIVE

aeroplane aeroplanes
NOUN a vehicle with wings and engines
that enable it to fly

aerosol aerosols
NOUN a small, metal container in which
liquid is kept under pressure so that it
can be forced out as a spray

affair affairs
NOUN **1** an event or series of events
• *The wedding was a happy **affair**.*
2 If something is your own **affair**, then
it is your concern only.

affect affects, affecting, affected
VERB When something **affects** someone or
something, it causes them to change.
• *Computers **affect** our lives in many ways.*

affection
NOUN a feeling of love and fondness for
someone
affectionate ADJECTIVE

affluent
ADJECTIVE People who are **affluent** have a
lot of money and possessions.

afford affords, affording, afforded
VERB **1** If you can **afford** something, you
have enough money to pay for it.
2 If you can **afford** to relax, you feel you
have done enough work for the moment,
and have time to take things easy.

afloat
ADVERB If something or someone is **afloat**,
they are floating.

afraid
ADJECTIVE **1** If you are **afraid**, you are
frightened.
SYNONYM: scared
2 If you are **afraid** something might
happen, you worry that it might happen.

after
PREPOSITION OR ADVERB **1** later than a particular
time, date or event • *She left just **after**
breakfast.* • *Soon **after**, he went to work.*
PREPOSITION **2** If you come **after** someone or
something, you are behind them and
following them. • *They ran **after** her.*

afternoon afternoons
NOUN the part of the day between twelve
noon and about six o'clock

afterwards
ADVERB after an event or time • *We went
swimming, and **afterwards** we had an ice
cream.*

again
ADVERB happening one more time • *The
film was so good that we went to see it
again.*
SYNONYM: once more

against
PREPOSITION **1** touching and resting on
• *He leaned the ladder **against** the wall.*
2 in opposition to • *France played **against**
England.*

age ages, ageing or aging, aged
NOUN **1** The **age** of something or someone
is the number of years they have lived or
existed.
2 a particular period in history • *the Iron
Age*
PLURAL NOUN **3** INFORMAL **Ages** means a very
long time. • *He's been talking for **ages**.*
VERB **4** To **age** is to grow old or to appear
older.

> Ageing and aging are both correct
> spellings.

agency agencies
NOUN an organization or business that
provides special services • *detective
agency* • *advertising **agency***

agenda agendas
NOUN a list of items to be discussed at a
meeting

agent agents
NOUN **1** someone who does business or
arranges things for other people • *a travel
agent*
2 someone who works for their country's
secret service

**aggravate aggravates,
aggravating, aggravated**
VERB **1** If you **aggravate** something,
you make it worse.

A
B
C
D
E
F
G
H
I
J
K
L
M
N
O
P
Q
R
S
T
U
V
W
X
Y
Z

2 INFORMAL If you **aggravate** someone, you annoy them.
aggravating ADJECTIVE aggravation NOUN

aggressive
ADJECTIVE full of hostility and violence
• *Some breeds of dog are more* **aggressive** *than others.*
SYNONYMS: belligerent, hostile

agile
ADJECTIVE able to move quickly and easily
• *He is as* **agile** *as a cat.*
agilely ADVERB agility NOUN

agitated
ADJECTIVE worried and anxious
agitation NOUN

ago
ADVERB in the past • *She bought her flat three years* **ago**.

agony
NOUN very great physical or mental pain
SYNONYMS: suffering, torment

agree agrees, agreeing, agreed
VERB **1** If you **agree** with someone, you have the same opinion as they do.
2 If you **agree** to do something, you say you will do it.

agreeable
ADJECTIVE **1** pleasant or enjoyable
2 If you are **agreeable** to something, you are willing to allow it or to do it.
agreeably ADVERB

agreement agreements
NOUN If you reach an **agreement** with one or more people, you make a decision with them or come to an arrangement with them.

agriculture
NOUN farming

ahead
ADVERB **1** in front • *He looked* **ahead** *as he cycled down the road.*
2 more advanced than someone or something else • *Some countries are* **ahead** *of others in space travel.*
3 in the future • *I can't think that far* **ahead**.

aid aids
NOUN **1** money, equipment or services provided for people in need
2 something that makes a job easier
• *The whiteboard is a useful teaching* **aid**.

ailment ailments
NOUN a minor illness

aim aims, aiming, aimed
VERB **1** If you **aim** at something, you point a weapon at it.
2 If you **aim** to do something, you are planning to do it.
SYNONYMS: intend, mean
NOUN **3** Your **aim** is what you intend to achieve. • *The* **aim** *of the jumble sale is to raise money for charity.*
SYNONYMS: goal, objective

aimless
ADJECTIVE If you are **aimless**, you have no clear purpose or sense of direction.
aimlessly ADVERB

air
NOUN **1** the mixture of oxygen and other gases that we breathe and that forms the earth's atmosphere
2 the space around things or above the ground • *The balloons floated up into the* **air**.
3 used to refer to travel in aircraft
• *My uncle often travels by* **air**.

air conditioning
NOUN a way of keeping cool, fresh air in a building

aircraft
NOUN any vehicle that can fly

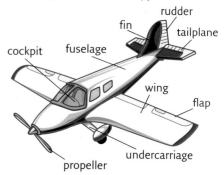

cockpit fuselage fin rudder tailplane wing flap undercarriage propeller

air force air forces
NOUN the part of a country's armed services that fights using aircraft

airline airlines
NOUN a company that provides air travel

airmail
NOUN the system of sending letters and parcels by air • *He sent letters from Hong Kong to Britain by* **airmail**.

airport airports
NOUN a place where people go to catch aeroplanes

airtight
ADJECTIVE If something is **airtight**, no air can get in or out.

aisle aisles
NOUN a long, narrow gap that people can walk along between rows of seats or shelves • *The ticket collector was coming down the* **aisle**.

ajar
ADJECTIVE A door or window that is **ajar** is slightly open.

alarm alarms, alarming, alarmed
NOUN **1** a feeling of fear and worry • *The cat sprang back in* **alarm**.
2 an automatic device used to warn people of something • *The burglar* **alarm** *went off accidentally.*
VERB **3** If something **alarms** you, it makes you worried and anxious.

album albums
NOUN **1** a CD, cassette or record with a number of songs on it
2 a book in which you keep a collection of things, such as photographs or stamps

alcohol
NOUN the name for drinks such as beer, wine and spirits

alert alerts, alerting, alerted
ADJECTIVE **1** If you are **alert**, you are paying full attention to what is happening.
SYNONYMS: vigilant, watchful
VERB **2** If you **alert** someone to a problem or danger, you warn them of it.

algebra
NOUN a branch of mathematics in which symbols and letters are used to represent unknown numbers

alias aliases
NOUN a false name

alibi alibis
NOUN If you have an **alibi**, you have evidence proving you were somewhere else when a crime was committed.

alien aliens
NOUN **1** In science fiction, an **alien** is a creature from outer space.
ADJECTIVE **2** Something that is **alien** to you seems strange because it is not part of your normal experience. • *The desert is an* **alien** *environment to many people.*
[from Latin *alienus* meaning foreign]

alight alights, alighting, alighted
ADJECTIVE **1** Something that is **alight** is burning.
VERB **2** If something **alights** somewhere, it lands there.
3 If someone **alights** from a vehicle, they get out of it.

alike
ADJECTIVE **1** Things that are **alike** are very similar in some way.
ADVERB **2** If people or things are treated **alike**, they are treated the same.

alive
ADJECTIVE If someone or something is **alive**, they are living.

alkali alkalis
NOUN a chemical substance sometimes used in cleaning materials. **Alkalis** can neutralize acids.
ANTONYM: acid
alkaline ADJECTIVE

all
ADJECTIVE, NOUN OR ADVERB **1** the whole of something • *She told us* **all** *about it.*
• *He ate* **all** *the chocolate.*
ADVERB **2** also used to show that both sides in a game or contest have the same score • *The final score was three points* **all**.

Allah
PROPER NOUN the Muslim name for God

a b c d e f g h i j k l m n o p q r s t u v w x y z

A
B
C
D
E
F
G
H
I
J
K
L
M
N
O
P
Q
R
S
T
U
V
W
X
Y
Z

allege **alleges, alleging, alleged**
VERB If you **allege** that something is true, you say it's true, but you cannot prove it.

allergy **allergies**
NOUN If you have an **allergy** to something, it makes you ill to eat or touch it.
allergic ADJECTIVE

alley **alleys**
NOUN a narrow street or passageway between buildings

alliance **alliances**
NOUN a group of countries, organizations or people who have similar aims and who work together to achieve them

alligator **alligators**
NOUN a large, scaly reptile, similar to a crocodile
[from Spanish *el lagarto* meaning lizard]

alliteration
NOUN the use of several words together that begin with the same letter or sound. For example, *the slithery snake slid silently across the sand.*

allotment **allotments**
NOUN a piece of land that people rent to grow fruit and vegetables on

allow **allows, allowing, allowed**
VERB If someone **allows** you to do something, they let you do it.

all right
ADJECTIVE **1** If something is **all right**, it is satisfactory, but not especially good.
• *Do you like mushrooms? They're* ***all right***.
2 If someone is **all right**, they are safe and not harmed.
3 You say **all right** if you agree to something. • *Will you help?* ***All right***.

ally **allies**
NOUN a person or a country that helps and supports another
SYNONYMS: friend, partner

almond **almonds**
NOUN an oval edible nut, cream in colour

almost
ADVERB very nearly • *I have* ***almost*** *as many points as you.*
SYNONYMS: just about, practically

alone
ADJECTIVE not with other people or things

along
PREPOSITION **1** moving forward • *We strolled* ***along*** *the road.*
2 from one end of something to the other • *The cupboards stretched* ***along*** *the wall.*

alongside
PREPOSITION OR ADVERB next to something • *We tied our boat* ***alongside*** *the jetty.*

aloud
ADVERB When you read **aloud**, you read so that people can hear you.

alphabet **alphabets**
NOUN all the letters used to write words in a language. The letters of an **alphabet** are written in a special order.

alphabetical
ADJECTIVE If something is in **alphabetical** order, it is arranged according to the letters of the alphabet.
alphabetically ADVERB

already
ADVERB If you have done something **already**, you did it earlier. • *Josh has* ***already*** *gone to bed.*

also
ADVERB in addition to something that has just been mentioned • *I bought an ice cream, and I* ***also*** *bought a drink.*

altar **altars**
NOUN a holy table in a church or temple

alter **alters, altering, altered**
VERB If something **alters**, or if you **alter** it, it changes.

alternate **alternates, alternating, alternated**
Said "ol-**ter**-nut" ADJECTIVE **1** If something happens on **alternate** days, it happens on one in every two days.
Said "ol-ter-nayt" VERB **2** If two things **alternate**, they regularly happen one after the other.

alternative **alternatives**
NOUN something you can do or have instead of something else ● *Is there an **alternative** to meat on the menu?*

although
CONJUNCTION in spite of the fact that ● *He wasn't well-known in America, **although** he had made a film there.*

altitude **altitudes**
NOUN height above sea level ● *The mountain range reaches an **altitude** of 1330 metres.*

altogether
ADVERB **1** completely or entirely ● *The car got slower, then stopped **altogether**.* **2** in total – used of amounts ● *I have two cats and two dogs. That's four pets **altogether**.*

aluminium
NOUN a silvery-white, lightweight metal

always
ADVERB **1** all the time ● *He's **always** late.* **2** forever ● *I'll **always** remember this day.*

a.m.
a.m. is used to show times in the morning
[an abbreviation of the Latin *ante meridiem* meaning before noon]

am
VERB a present tense of **be**

amateur **amateurs**
NOUN someone who does something without being paid for it ● *He began playing football as an **amateur**, but now he is a professional.*

amaze **amazes, amazing, amazed**
VERB If something **amazes** you, it surprises you very much.
SYNONYMS: astonish, astound
amazement NOUN

amazing
ADJECTIVE If something is **amazing**, it is very surprising.
amazingly ADVERB

ambassador **ambassadors**
NOUN a person sent to a foreign country as the representative of their own government

amber
NOUN **1** a hard, yellowish-brown substance from trees, used in making jewellery
NOUN OR ADJECTIVE **2** an orange-brown colour

ambiguous
ADJECTIVE If something is **ambiguous**, it can have more than one meaning.
ambiguously ADVERB **ambiguity** NOUN

ambition **ambitions**
NOUN If you have an **ambition** to do something, you want very much to do it.

amble **ambles, ambling, ambled**
VERB If you **amble**, you walk along in a slow, relaxed way.

ambulance **ambulances**
NOUN a vehicle for taking sick and injured people to hospital

ambush **ambushes, ambushing, ambushed**
NOUN **1** a surprise attack
VERB **2** If one group of people **ambushes** another, they hide and lie in wait, and then make a surprise attack.

ammonia
NOUN a strong-smelling, colourless liquid or gas, often used in cleaning substances

ammunition
NOUN anything that can be fired from a gun or other weapon, for example bullets and shells

amoeba **amoebas** or **amoebae**
NOUN a tiny living organism that has only one cell. An **amoeba** reproduces by dividing into two.

among or **amongst**
PREPOSITION **1** surrounded by **2** in the company of ● *He was **among** friends.* **3** between more than two ● *The money will be divided **among** seven charities.*

amount **amounts**
NOUN how much there is of something ● *You need a large **amount** of flour for this recipe.*

amphibian amphibians
NOUN a creature that lives partly on land and partly in water, for example a frog or a newt
amphibious ADJECTIVE

frog   newt

amplify amplifies, amplifying, amplified
VERB If you **amplify** a sound, you make it louder.
amplifier NOUN

amputate amputates, amputating, amputated
VERB If a surgeon **amputates** part of the body, such as an arm or a leg, they cut it off.
amputation NOUN

amuse amuses, amusing, amused
VERB **1** If something **amuses** you, you think it is funny.
2 If you **amuse** yourself, you find things to do that stop you from being bored.
amused ADJECTIVE   **amusing** ADJECTIVE

amusement amusements
NOUN **1** the feeling you have when you think that something is funny or you have pleasure
2 a mechanical device used for entertainment, at a fair for example
3 Amusements are ways of passing the time pleasantly.

an
ADJECTIVE **An** is used instead of *a* in front of words that begin with the vowels a, e, i, o, or u. • *an apple* • *an egg*

anaemia
NOUN a medical condition in which there are too few red cells in the blood. It makes you feel tired and look pale.
anaemic ADJECTIVE

anaesthetic anaesthetics; also spelt anesthetic
NOUN a substance that stops you feeling pain. A general **anaesthetic** stops you from feeling pain in the whole of your body by putting you to sleep. A local **anaesthetic** makes just one part of your body go numb.

anagram anagrams
NOUN a word or phrase formed by changing the order of the letters of another word or phrase. For example, *draw* is an **anagram** of *ward* and *dear* is an **anagram** of *read.*

analogue
ADJECTIVE An **analogue** watch or clock shows the time with pointers that move round a dial.
ANTONYM: digital

analogy analogies
NOUN a comparison between two things that are similar in some ways

analyse analyses, analysing, analysed
VERB If you **analyse** something, you investigate it carefully to understand it or to find out what it consists of.

anatomy anatomies
NOUN the study of the structure of bodies, both animal and human, to find out how they work
anatomical ADJECTIVE

ancestor ancestors
NOUN a member of your family who lived many years ago • *He could trace his **ancestors** back 700 years.*
[from Latin *antecessor* meaning one who goes before]

anchor anchors, anchoring, anchored
NOUN **1** a heavy, hooked object at the end of a chain. It is dropped from a boat into the water to keep the boat from floating away.
VERB **2** If you **anchor** something, you hold it down firmly.

ancient
ADJECTIVE Things that are **ancient** existed or happened a very long time ago.
ANTONYM: modern

and
CONJUNCTION You use **and** to link two or more parts of a sentence together. ● *Let's go to the cinema **and** then have pizza.*

anecdote **anecdotes**
NOUN a short, sometimes entertaining story about a person or an event

angel **angels**
NOUN a being who, some people believe, lives in heaven and acts as a messenger for God
[from Greek *angelos* meaning messenger]

anger
NOUN the strong feeling you get about something unfair or cruel
SYNONYMS: fury, rage, wrath

angle **angles**
NOUN **1** the distance between two lines at the point where they join together. **Angles** are measured in degrees.
● *an **angle** of 90 degrees*
2 the direction from which you look at something ● *He painted pictures of the garden from all **angles**.*

angry **angrier, angriest**
ADJECTIVE very annoyed
SYNONYMS: furious, cross

anguish
NOUN great suffering

animal **animals**
NOUN any living being that is not a plant

animation **animations**
NOUN a way of making films using drawings that appear to move when you watch them
animated ADJECTIVE

ankle **ankles**
NOUN the joint that connects your foot to your leg

annihilate **annihilates, annihilating, annihilated**
VERB If someone or something **annihilates**

someone or something else, they destroy them completely.
annihilation NOUN

anniversary **anniversaries**
NOUN a date that is remembered because something special happened on that date in a previous year ● *We celebrated Mum and Dad's twelfth wedding **anniversary**.*

announce **announces, announcing, announced**
VERB If you **announce** something, you tell people about it publicly or officially.
● *They **announced** the team on Friday morning.*
SYNONYM: make known
announcement NOUN

annoy **annoys, annoying, annoyed**
VERB If someone or something **annoys** you, they make you angry or impatient.
SYNONYMS: bother, irritate
annoyance NOUN

annual **annuals**
ADJECTIVE **1** happening once a year ● *our **annual** sports day*
NOUN **2** a book that is published once a year for children

anonymous
ADJECTIVE If something is **anonymous**, nobody knows who is responsible for it.
● *The charity received an **anonymous** donation.*

anorak **anoraks**
NOUN a warm, waterproof jacket, usually with a hood
[an Eskimo word]

anorexia
NOUN a psychological illness in which the person refuses to eat
[from Greek *an* + *orexis* meaning no appetite]

another
ADJECTIVE OR PRONOUN one more person or thing

answer **answers, answering, answered**
VERB **1** If you **answer** someone, you reply to them in speech or writing.
NOUN **2** the reply you give when you

a
b
c
d
e
f
g
h
i
j
k
l
m
n
o
p
q
r
s
t
u
v
w
x

२५

A B C D E F G H I J K L M N O P Q R S T U V W X Y Z

answer someone • *I received an **answer** to my letter.*
3 a solution to a problem

ant ants
NOUN **Ants** are small insects that live in large groups.

antagonize antagonizes, antagonizing, antagonized
VERB If you **antagonize** someone, you upset them and make them feel angry.

Antarctic
NOUN the area around the South Pole

antelope antelopes
NOUN a hoofed animal, similar to a deer

antenna antennae or antennas
NOUN **1** one of the two long, thin parts attached to the head of an insect or other animal, which it uses to feel with. The plural is **antennae**.
2 In Australian, New Zealand and American English, an **antenna** is a radio or television aerial. The plural is **antennas**.

anthem anthems
NOUN usually a song of celebration, and sometimes a religious song

anther anthers
NOUN the part of the stamen in a flower where the pollen matures

anthology anthologies
NOUN a collection of writings by various authors, published in one book
[from Greek *anthologia* meaning flower gathering]

anti-
PREFIX against or opposite • *an **anti**malaria tablet*
ANTONYM: pro-

antibiotic antibiotics
NOUN a drug or chemical used in medicine to kill bacteria and cure infections

anticipate anticipates, anticipating, anticipated
VERB If you **anticipate** an event, you are expecting it and are getting prepared for it.
anticipation NOUN

anticlimax anticlimaxes
NOUN If something is an **anticlimax**, it disappoints you because it is not as exciting as you expected, or because it occurs after something that was more exciting.

anticlockwise
ADJECTIVE OR ADVERB
moving in the opposite direction to the hands of a clock
ANTONYM: clockwise

antidote antidotes
NOUN a chemical substance that works against the effects of a poison

antique antiques
NOUN an object from the past that is collected because of its value or beauty

antiseptic
ADJECTIVE Something that is **antiseptic** can kill some germs.

antler antlers
NOUN **Antlers** are the branched horns on the top of a male deer's head.

antonym antonyms
NOUN a word that means the opposite of another word • *Happy is the **antonym** of sad.*

anxiety anxieties
NOUN nervousness or worry

anxious
ADJECTIVE **1** If you are **anxious**, you are nervous or worried.
2 If you are **anxious** to do something, you very much want to do it. • *She was **anxious** to pass her ballet exam.*

any
ADJECTIVE OR PRONOUN **1** one, some or several • *Have you **any** sausages?*
2 even the smallest amount or even one • *She can't eat nuts of **any** kind.*
3 no matter which or what • *I'm so thirsty, **any** drink will do.*

anybody
PRONOUN any person

anyhow

ADVERB **1** in any case ● *It's still early, but I'm going to bed **anyhow***.
2 in a careless way ● *They were all shoved in **anyhow***.

anyone

PRONOUN any person ● *I won't tell **anyone***.

anything

PRONOUN any object, event, situation or action ● *Can you see **anything**?*

anyway

ADVERB in any case ● *It's raining, but I'm going out **anyway***.

anywhere

ADVERB in, at or to any place ● *Can you see him **anywhere**?* ● *We haven't got **anywhere** to play.*

apart

ADVERB OR ADJECTIVE **1** When something is **apart** from something else, there is a space or a distance between them. ● *The gliders landed about seventy metres **apart***.
ADVERB **2** If you take something **apart**, you separate it into pieces.

apartment apartments

NOUN a set of rooms for living in, usually on one floor of a building

ape apes, aping, aped

NOUN **1** a large animal similar to a monkey, but without a tail. **Apes** include chimpanzees and gorillas.
VERB **2** If you **ape** someone's speech or behaviour, you imitate it.

apex apexes or apices

NOUN The **apex** of something is its pointed top. ● *the **apex** of a cone*
SYNONYM: vertex

apex

apologize apologizes, apologizing, apologized; also spelt apologise

VERB When you **apologize** to someone, you say you are sorry for something you have said or done.
apology NOUN

apostrophe apostrophes

NOUN **1** a punctuation mark (') used to show that one or more letters have been missed out of a word, for example *he's* for *he is*

2 Apostrophes are also used with -s at the end of a noun to show that what follows belongs to or relates to the noun. If the noun already has an -s at the end, for example because it is plural, the **apostrophe** comes after the s. For example, *my brother's books* (one brother), *my brothers' books* (more than one brother).

apparatus

NOUN the equipment used for a particular task ● *The firefighters wore breathing **apparatus***.

apparent

ADJECTIVE **1** An **apparent** situation seems to exist, although you cannot be certain of it.
2 clear and obvious ● *It was **apparent** they would get on well together.*
apparently ADVERB

appeal appeals, appealing, appealed

VERB **1** If you **appeal** for something, you make an urgent request for it. ● *The police **appealed** for witnesses to come forward.*
2 If something or someone **appeals** to you, you find them attractive or interesting.
NOUN **3** a formal or serious request ● *an **appeal** for funds to help people in need*

appear appears, appearing, appeared

VERB **1** When something **appears**, it moves from somewhere you could not see to somewhere you can see it. ● *The sun **appeared** from behind the clouds.*
2 If something **appears** to be a certain way, it seems or looks that way.

appearance appearances

NOUN **1** Someone's or something's **appearance** is the way they look to other people.
2 If a person makes an **appearance** in a film or a show, they take part in it.

3 The **appearance** of something is the time it begins to exist.

appendicitis

NOUN a painful illness in which a person's appendix becomes infected

appendix **appendices** or **appendixes**

NOUN **1** Your **appendix** is a small, closed tube forming part of your digestive system. **2** extra information that comes at the end of a book

🖉 When *appendix* means the body part, the plural is *appendixes*. When it means the part of a book, the plural is *appendices*.

appetite **appetites**

NOUN a desire to eat
[from Latin *appetere* meaning to desire]

appetizing

ADJECTIVE When food is **appetizing**, it looks or smells good and you want to eat it.

applause

NOUN the sound of people clapping to show their enjoyment or approval of something

apple **apples**

NOUN a round fruit with smooth skin and firm white flesh

appliance **appliances**

NOUN any machine in your home that you use to do a job like cleaning or cooking. For example, a toaster is a kitchen **appliance**.

application **applications**

NOUN If you make an **application** for something, you make a formal request, usually in writing.

apply **applies, applying, applied**

VERB **1** If you **apply** for something, you ask for it formally, usually by writing a letter. ● *My brother is **applying** for jobs.*
2 If you **apply** something to a surface, you put it on or rub it into the surface.
● *She **applied** sun cream to her face.*
3 If you **apply** yourself to a task, you give it all of your attention.

appoint **appoints, appointing, appointed**

VERB If a person **appoints** someone to a job or position, they formally choose them for it. ● *The teacher **appointed** Sunita as team captain.*

appointment **appointments**

NOUN an arrangement you have with someone to meet them

appreciate **appreciates, appreciating, appreciated**

VERB If you **appreciate** something that someone has done for you, you are grateful to them for it.

apprehensive

ADJECTIVE If you are **apprehensive** about something, you feel worried and unsure about it.

apprentice **apprentices**

NOUN someone who works with another person for a length of time to learn that person's job or skill

approach **approaches, approaching, approached**

VERB If you **approach** something, you come near or nearer to it.

appropriate

ADJECTIVE suitable or acceptable for a particular situation

approval

NOUN If you ask for **approval** for something that you want to do, you ask for agreement with your plans.

approve **approves, approving, approved**

VERB **1** If you **approve** of something or someone, you think they are acceptable or good.
SYNONYMS: favour, like
2 If someone **approves** a plan or idea, they agree to it. ● *The council **approved** plans for the new swimming pool.*
SYNONYMS: agree to, permit

approximate

ADJECTIVE near but not exactly right ● *What was the **approximate** time you arrived?*

apricot apricots
NOUN a small, soft, yellowish-orange fruit

April
NOUN the fourth month of the year. **April** has 30 days.

apron aprons
NOUN a piece of clothing worn over the front of normal clothing to protect it

aquarium aquaria or aquariums
NOUN a glass tank filled with water in which fish and other aquatic animals or plants are kept

aquatic
ADJECTIVE An **aquatic** animal or plant lives in water.

aqueduct aqueducts
NOUN a bridge with many arches, which carries a water supply over a valley

arable
ADJECTIVE **Arable** land is used for growing crops.

arc arcs
NOUN **1** a smoothly curving line
2 In geometry, an **arc** is a section of the circumference of a circle.

arcade arcades
NOUN a covered passageway where there are shops or market stalls

arch arches, arching, arched
NOUN **1** a structure that has a curved top, supported on either side by a pillar or wall
VERB **2** If something **arches**, or if you **arch** it, it forms a curved line or shape.
• The cat **arched** its back.

archaeology; also spelt **archeology**
NOUN the study of the past by digging up and examining the remains of things such as buildings, tools, and pots
[from Greek *arkhaios* meaning ancient]

archbishop archbishops
NOUN a bishop of the highest rank in a Christian Church • the **Archbishop** of Canterbury

archery
NOUN a sport in which people shoot at a target with a bow and arrow

architect architects
NOUN a person who designs buildings

architecture
NOUN the art or practice of designing buildings

arctic
NOUN **1** The **Arctic** is the region north of the Arctic Circle.
ADJECTIVE **2** very cold indeed • You need specially warm clothes for **arctic** conditions.

are
VERB a present tense of **be**

area areas
NOUN **1** a particular part of a place, country, or the world • a built-up **area** of the city
SYNONYMS: district, region, zone
2 the measurement of a flat surface
• The **area** of the playground is 1500 square metres (1500 m²).

arena arenas
NOUN a place where sports and other public events take place
[from Latin *harena* meaning sand, because of the sandy centre of an amphitheatre where gladiators fought]

aren't
VERB a contraction of *are not*

argue argues, arguing, argued
VERB **1** If you **argue** with someone about something, you disagree with them about it, sometimes in an angry way.
2 If you **argue** that something is true, you give reasons why you think that it is.

A
B
C
D
E
F
G
H
I
J
K
L
M
N
O
P
Q
R
S
T
U
V
W
X
Y
Z

argument **arguments**
NOUN a talk between people who do not agree

arid
ADJECTIVE **Arid** land is very dry because there has been very little rain.
ANTONYM: fertile

arise **arises, arising, arose, arisen**
VERB When something such as an opportunity or a problem **arises**, it begins to exist.

aristocrat **aristocrats**
NOUN someone whose family has a high social rank, and who has a title such as Lord or Lady
aristocratic ADJECTIVE   **aristocracy** NOUN

arithmetic
NOUN the part of mathematics that is to do with the addition, subtraction, multiplication and division of numbers [from Greek *arithmos* meaning number]
arithmetical ADJECTIVE
arithmetically ADVERB

arm **arms, arming, armed**
NOUN **1** the part of your body between your shoulder and your wrist
PLURAL NOUN **2 Arms** are weapons used in a war.
VERB **3** If a country **arms** itself, it prepares for war.

armada **armadas**
NOUN a large fleet of warships • *The Spanish Armada was the fleet sent to destroy the English in 1588.*

armchair **armchairs**
NOUN a large chair with a support on each side for your arms

armistice **armistices**
NOUN In war, an **armistice** is an agreement to stop fighting.

armour
NOUN **1** In the past, **armour** was metal clothing worn for protection in battle.
2 In modern warfare, tanks are often referred to as **armour**.

army **armies**
NOUN a large group of soldiers who are trained to fight on land

aroma **aromas**
NOUN a strong, pleasant smell [a Greek word meaning spice]
aromatic ADJECTIVE

around
PREPOSITION **1** situated at various points in a place or area • *There are several post boxes around the town.*
2 from place to place inside an area • *We walked around the stalls at the summer fair.*
3 surrounding or encircling a place or object • *We were sitting around the table.*
4 at approximately the time or place mentioned • *The jumble sale began around noon.*

arrange **arranges, arranging, arranged**
VERB **1** If you **arrange** to do something, or **arrange** something for someone, you make plans for it or make it possible. • *I arranged to meet him later.* • *Dad arranged a trip to the circus for us.*
2 If you **arrange** objects, you set them out in a particular way. • *We arranged the books in alphabetical order.*

array **arrays**
NOUN **1** a large number of different things displayed together
2 a mathematical way of grouping. For example, 3 × 2 is shown as ::: and 2 × 3 is shown as ::.

arrest **arrests, arresting, arrested**
VERB **1** If the police **arrest** someone, they take them to a police station because they believe they may have committed a crime.
NOUN **2** An **arrest** is the act of arresting someone.

arrive **arrives, arriving, arrived**
VERB **1** When you **arrive** at a place, you reach it at the end of your journey.
2 When you **arrive** at a decision you make up your mind.
arrival NOUN

arrogant
ADJECTIVE **Arrogant** people behave as if they are better than other people.

arrow **arrows**
NOUN a long, thin weapon with a sharp point at one end, shot from a bow

arsenal **arsenals**
NOUN a place where weapons and ammunition are stored or produced

arsenic
NOUN a strong, dangerous poison that can kill

arson
NOUN the crime of deliberately setting fire to something, especially a building

art **arts**
NOUN **1** the creation of objects, such as paintings and sculptures, that are thought to be beautiful or that express a particular idea ● *He wanted to take* **art** *classes to learn how to draw and paint well.*
2 **Art** is also used to refer to the objects themselves. ● *We saw lots of interesting paintings and sculptures at the* **art** *exhibition.*
3 something that needs special skills or ability ● *I would like to master the* **art** *of sewing.*

artery **arteries**
NOUN the tubes that carry blood from your heart to the rest of your body
See **vein**
arterial ADJECTIVE

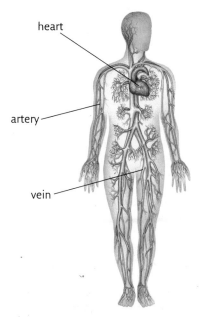

heart

artery

vein

arthritis
NOUN a condition in which the joints in someone's body become painful, and sometimes swollen
arthritic ADJECTIVE

article **articles**
NOUN **1** a piece of writing in a newspaper or magazine
2 a particular item ● *an* **article** *of clothing*

artificial
ADJECTIVE Something **artificial** is created by people rather than occurring naturally.
ANTONYM: natural

artillery
NOUN **1** **Artillery** consists of large, powerful guns and rockets.
2 The **artillery** is the branch of an army that uses these weapons.

artist **artists**
NOUN a person who draws or paints or produces other works of art

as
CONJUNCTION **1** at the same time that
● *We watched television* **as** *we ate our sandwiches.*
2 because ● **As** *I like school I get there early.*
PHRASE **3** You use **as if** or **as though** when you are giving an explanation for something. ● *Shane walked past* **as if** *he didn't know me.*

ascend **ascends, ascending, ascended**
VERB FORMAL If someone or something **ascends**, they move or lead upwards.
● *We* **ascended** *the stairs to the second floor.*
ANTONYM: descend

ash **ashes**
NOUN the grey or black powdery remains of anything that has been burnt ● *We put the* **ashes** *from the bonfire on the compost heap.*

ashamed
ADJECTIVE **1** If you are **ashamed**, you feel embarrassed or guilty.
2 If you are **ashamed** of someone, you feel embarrassed to be connected with them.

a
b
c
d
e
f
g
h
i
j
k
l
m
n
o
p
q
r
s
t
u
v
w
x
y
z

ashore

ADVERB If someone or something comes **ashore**, they come on to the land from the sea or a river.

aside

ADVERB If you move something **aside**, you move it to one side. • *She closed the book and laid it* ***aside***.

ask asks, asking, asked

VERB **1** If you **ask** someone something, you put a question to them.
2 If you **ask** someone to do something, you tell them you want them to do it. • *We* ***asked*** *him to do his card trick.*
3 If you **ask** for something, you say you would like to have it. • *She* ***asked*** *for a drink of water.*
4 If you **ask** someone to come or go somewhere, you invite them there.

asleep

ADJECTIVE If you are **asleep**, your eyes are closed and your whole body is resting.

aspect aspects

NOUN one of many ways of seeing or thinking about something

aspirin aspirins

NOUN **1** a white drug used to relieve pain, fever and colds
2 a small white tablet of this drug

ass asses

NOUN another word for **donkey**

assassinate assassinates, assassinating, assassinated

VERB If someone **assassinates** an important person, they murder them.
assassination NOUN

assault assaults

NOUN a violent attack on someone
[from Latin *assalire* meaning to leap upon]

assemble assembles, assembling, assembled

VERB **1** If people **assemble**, they gather together. • *We* ***assembled*** *in the playground to watch the display.*
2 If you **assemble** something, you fit the parts of it together. • *It took us ages to* ***assemble*** *the model car.*

assembly assemblies

NOUN a group of people who have gathered together for a meeting

assess assesses, assessing, assessed

VERB If you **assess** something, you consider it carefully and make a judgement about it. • *She tried to* ***assess*** *how much further they had to walk.*
SYNONYMS: judge, size up

asset assets

NOUN **1** If someone or something is an **asset**, they are useful or helpful. • *He's an* ***asset*** *to the school.*
2 The **assets** of a person or a company are all the things they own that could be sold to raise money.

assignment assignments

NOUN a job you are given to do

assist assists, assisting, assisted

VERB If you **assist** someone, you help them to do something.

assistant assistants

NOUN someone who helps another person to do their job

associate associates, associating, associated

VERB **1** If you **associate** with someone, you spend time with them.
2 If you **associate** one thing with another, you make a connection between them.

association associations

NOUN **1** an organization for people who have similar interests, jobs or aims
2 An **association** between two things is a link you make in your mind between them.

assorted

ADJECTIVE **Assorted** things are a mixture of various sorts of something. They may be different colours, sizes and shapes.

assortment assortments

NOUN a group of similar things that are different sizes, shapes and colours • *There was an amazing* ***assortment*** *of toys in the shop.*

assume **assumes, assuming, assumed**
VERB **1** If you **assume** that something is true, you believe it, even if you have not thought carefully about it.
2 If you **assume** responsibility for something, you decide to do it. • I **assumed** responsibility for feeding the hamster.

assure **assures, assuring, assured**
VERB If you **assure** someone of something, you say something to make them less worried about it. • I **assured** him that I wouldn't be late.

asterisk **asterisks**
NOUN a symbol (*) used in writing and printing to draw attention to something that is explained somewhere else, usually at the bottom of the page

asteroid **asteroids**
NOUN one of the large number of very small planets that move around the sun between the orbits of Jupiter and Mars

asthma
NOUN a disease of the chest that causes wheezing and difficulty in breathing [from Greek *azein* meaning to breathe hard]
asthmatic ADJECTIVE

astonish **astonishes, astonishing, astonished**
VERB If something **astonishes** you, it surprises you very much.
astonished ADJECTIVE **astonishing** ADJECTIVE **astonishingly** ADVERB **astonishment** NOUN

astrology
NOUN the study of the sun, moon and stars in the belief that their movements can influence people's lives

astronaut **astronauts**
NOUN a person who operates a spacecraft [from Greek *astron* meaning star and *nautes* meaning sailor]

astronomy
NOUN the scientific study of stars and planets
astronomer NOUN

at
PREPOSITION **1** where someone or something is • John waited for me **at** the bus stop.
2 the direction something is going in • I threw the snowball **at** my brother.
3 when something happens • The party starts **at** six o'clock.

ate
VERB the past tense of **eat**

atheist **atheists**
NOUN someone who does not believe in any form of God

athlete **athletes**
NOUN a person who is very good at sport and who takes part in sporting competitions

athletics
NOUN sporting events such as running, long jump and discus

Atlantic
NOUN the ocean that separates North and South America from Europe and Africa

atlas **atlases**
NOUN a book of maps [from the giant *Atlas* in Greek mythology, who supported the sky on his shoulders]

atmosphere **atmospheres**
NOUN **1** gases that surround a planet
2 the general mood of a place • There was a friendly **atmosphere** at the party.

atom **atoms**
NOUN the smallest part of an element that can take part in a chemical reaction

atrocity **atrocities**
NOUN an extremely shocking and cruel act

attach **attaches, attaching, attached**
VERB If you **attach** something to something else, you join or fasten the two things together.

attachment **attachments**
NOUN **1** a feeling of love and affection for someone
2 a file attached to an e-mail

a
b
c
d
e
f
g
h
i
j
k
l
m
n
o
p
q
r
s
t
u
v
w
x
y
z

attack attacks, attacking, attacked

VERB **1** If someone **attacks** another person or animal, they use violence in order to hurt or kill them. • *The lion attacked the zebra in order to kill it for food.*

2 In a game such as football or hockey, players **attack** to get the ball into a position from which a goal can be scored.

NOUN **3** violent, physical action against someone

attempt attempts, attempting, attempted

VERB **1** If you **attempt** to do something, you try to do it.

NOUN **2** the act of trying to do something • *He made a brave **attempt** to help.*

attend attends, attending, attended

VERB **1** If you **attend** school, church or hospital, you go there regularly.

2 If you **attend** an event, you are present at it.

attend to

VERB If you **attend to** something, you deal with it. • *We should **attend to** our homework before going to the park.*

attendant attendants

NOUN someone whose job is to help people in a place such as a museum or shop

attention

NOUN the thought or care that you give to someone or something • *I paid a lot of **attention** to my homework.*

attentive

ADJECTIVE When you are **attentive**, you pay close attention.

attentively ADVERB

attic attics

NOUN a room at the top of a house immediately below the roof

attitude attitudes

NOUN the way you think about someone or something • *I'm not going in that shop again. I don't like their **attitude**.*

attract attracts, attracting, attracted

VERB **1** If something **attracts** people, it interests them and makes them want to go to it.

2 If someone **attracts** you, you like them and are interested in them.

3 When magnetic materials are **attracted** to a magnet, they are pulled towards it.

attraction attractions

NOUN **1** If you feel an **attraction** for someone, you like them very much.

2 somewhere people like to visit for interest or pleasure, such as a fun fair or a stately home

3 A force of **attraction** pulls magnetic materials towards a magnet.

attractive

ADJECTIVE **1** Someone who is **attractive** is good-looking or has an exciting personality.

2 If something is **attractive**, it is interesting.

aubergine aubergines

NOUN a dark purple, pear-shaped vegetable. It is also called an eggplant.

auburn

ADJECTIVE a red-brown hair colour

auction auctions, auctioning, auctioned

NOUN **1** a public sale in which goods are sold to the person who offers the highest price

VERB **2** to sell something in an auction

audible

ADJECTIVE If something is **audible**, you can hear it.

audience audiences

NOUN **1** the group of people who are watching or listening to a performance

2 a private or formal meeting with an important person ● *The winners of the bravery awards had an* **audience** *with the Queen.*

audition **auditions**
NOUN a short performance by an actor or musician, so that a director can decide whether they are suitable for a part in a play or a film, or for a place in an orchestra

auditorium **auditoriums** or **auditoria**
NOUN the part of a theatre or concert hall where the audience sits

August
NOUN the eighth month of the year. **August** has 31 days.

aunt **aunts**
NOUN Your **aunt** is the sister of your mother or father, or the wife of your uncle.

author **authors**
NOUN The **author** of a book is the person who wrote it.

authority **authorities**
NOUN **1** the power to tell other people what to do ● *The teacher had the* **authority** *to give me detention.*
2 an organization that controls public interests ● *the local health* **authority**
3 Someone who is an **authority** on something, knows a lot about it.

authorize **authorizes, authorizing, authorized**
VERB If someone **authorizes** something, they give official permission for it.
authorization NOUN

auto-
PREFIX **1** self or same ● **auto**biography
2 self-propelling ● **auto**matic car

autobiography **autobiographies**
NOUN an account of someone's life that they have written themselves
autobiographical ADJECTIVE

autograph **autographs**
NOUN the signature of a famous person

[from Greek *auto* meaning self and *graphos* meaning written]

automatic **automatics**
ADJECTIVE **1** An **automatic** machine is programmed to perform tasks without needing a person to operate it.
NOUN **2** a car in which the gears change automatically as the car's speed changes

autumn **autumns**
NOUN the season between summer and winter, when the leaves fall off the trees ● *I love the golden colours of the trees in* **autumn***.*

available
ADJECTIVE **1** If something is **available**, it is easy to get or to buy.
2 A person who is **available** is ready for work or free to talk to.

avalanche **avalanches**
NOUN a huge mass of snow and ice that falls down a mountainside

avenue **avenues**
NOUN a street, especially one with trees along it

average **averages**
NOUN **1** a result obtained by adding several amounts together and then dividing the total by the number of different amounts ● *If I shared 36 sweets between four children, the* **average** *would be nine sweets per child.*
ADJECTIVE **2** standard or usual ● *The* **average** *teenager is interested in pop music.*
SYNONYMS: normal, ordinary, typical
PHRASE **3** You say **on average** when mentioning what usually happens in a situation. ● *Men are,* **on average**, *taller than women.*

aviary **aviaries**
NOUN a large cage or group of cages in which birds are kept

aviation
NOUN the science of flying aircraft

avocado **avocados**
NOUN a pear-shaped fruit with dark green skin, soft greenish-yellow flesh, and a large stone

a
b
c
d
e
f
g
h
i
j
k
l
m
n
o
p
q
r
s
t
u
v
w
x
y
z

avoid avoids, avoiding, avoided

VERB **1** If you **avoid** someone or something, you keep away from them. • *To avoid him, she went home the other way.* **2** If you **avoid** doing something, you make an effort not to do it.

SYNONYMS: dodge, shirk

awake

ADJECTIVE Someone who is **awake** is not sleeping.

award awards, awarding, awarded

NOUN **1** a prize or certificate for doing something well

VERB **2** If someone **awards** you something, they give it to you formally or officially. • *He was awarded the prize for fastest runner.*

aware

ADJECTIVE **1** If you are **aware** of something, you know about it. **2** If you are **aware** of something, you can see, hear, smell or feel it.

away

ADVERB **1** moving from a place • *I saw them walk away from the house.* **2** at a distance from a place • *The nearest supermarket is 12 kilometres away.* **3** in its proper place • *He put his CDs away.* **4** not at home, school or work • *My friend's been away from school for a week.*

awe

NOUN FORMAL a feeling of great respect mixed with amazement, and sometimes slight fear • *Looking up at the mountains, we felt a sense of awe.*

awful

ADJECTIVE very unpleasant or very bad • *Isn't the weather awful?*

SYNONYMS: dreadful, terrible

awkward

ADJECTIVE **1** difficult to deal with • *an awkward situation* **2** clumsy and uncomfortable • *The large bag was awkward to carry.* [from Old Norse *ofugr* meaning turned the wrong way]

axe axes

NOUN a tool with a handle and a sharp blade, used for chopping wood

axis axes

NOUN **1** an imaginary line through the middle of something, around which it moves • *The earth turns on its axis.* **2** one of the two sides of a graph

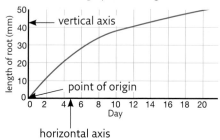

Line graph of seed growth

vertical axis

point of origin

horizontal axis

length of root (mm)

Day

axle axles

NOUN the long bar that connects a pair of wheels on a vehicle

Bb

babble **babbles, babbling, babbled**
VERB If someone **babbles**, they talk in a quick and confused way that is difficult to understand.

baboon **baboons**
NOUN an African monkey with a pointed face, large teeth and a long tail

baby **babies**
NOUN a child in the first year or two of its life

baby-sit **baby-sits, baby-sitting, baby-sat**
VERB If you **baby-sit** for someone, you look after their children while they are out.

bachelor **bachelors**
NOUN a man who has never been married

back **backs, backing, backed**
ADVERB **1** When people or things move **back**, they move in the opposite direction to the one they are facing.
2 When you go **back** to a place or situation, you return to it. ● *She went* ***back*** *to sleep.*
NOUN **3** the rear part of your body
ADJECTIVE **4** The **back** parts of something are the ones at the rear. ● *the dog's* ***back*** *legs*
VERB **5** If a building **backs** on to something, the back of it faces in that direction.

backbone **backbones**
NOUN the column of linked bones along the middle of the back of a human and other vertebrates

background **backgrounds**
NOUN **1** the things in a picture or scene that are less noticeable than the main things

2 the kind of home you come from, and your education and experience

backstroke
NOUN a style of swimming movement on your back

backward
ADJECTIVE If you take a **backward** look, you look behind you.

backwards
ADVERB **1** If you move **backwards**, you move to a place behind you.
2 If you do something **backwards**, you do it opposite to the usual way. ● *He told them to count* ***backwards*** *from 20 to 5.*

bacon
NOUN meat from the back or sides of a pig, which has been salted or smoked

bacteria
PLURAL NOUN very tiny organisms that can cause disease
[from Greek *bakterion* meaning little rod; some bacteria are rod-shaped]
bacterial ADJECTIVE

bad **worse, worst**
ADJECTIVE **1** **Bad** things are harmful or upsetting. ● *I have some* ***bad*** *news.*
SYNONYMS: distressing, grave, terrible
2 not enough or of poor quality ● *We thought the film was very* ***bad***.
3 **Bad** food is not fresh.
SYNONYMS: rotten, decayed

badge **badges**
NOUN a piece of plastic or metal with a design or message on it that you can pin to your clothes

badger **badgers, badgering, badgered**
NOUN **1** a nocturnal mammal that has a white head with two black stripes on it
VERB **2** If you **badger** someone, you keep asking them questions or pestering them to do something.

badly **worse, worst**
ADVERB **1** not well, poorly ● *The script was* ***badly*** *written.*
2 seriously ● *She was* ***badly*** *hurt in the accident.*

A
B
C
D
E
F
G
H
I
J
K
L
M
N
O
P
Q
R
S
T
U
V
W
X
Y
Z

badminton

NOUN a game in which two or four players use rackets to hit a feathered object, called a shuttlecock, over a high net

bag **bags**

NOUN a container for carrying things in [From Old Norse *baggi* meaning bundle]

baggage

NOUN Your **baggage** is all the suitcases, holdalls and bags that you take with you when you travel.

bagpipes

PLURAL NOUN a musical instrument played by squeezing air out of a leather bag and through pipes

baguette **baguettes**

NOUN a long, thin French loaf of bread

bail **bails**

NOUN **1** In cricket, the **bails** are the two small pieces of wood placed on top of the stumps to form the wicket.
2 a sum of money paid to a court to allow an accused person to go free until the time of the trial • *The accused man was released on **bail**.*

bait **baits, baiting, baited**

NOUN **1** a small amount of food placed on a hook, or in a trap, to attract and catch a fish or wild animal
VERB **2** If you **bait** a hook or a trap, you put some food on it to catch a fish or wild animal.

bake **bakes, baking, baked**

VERB **1** When you **bake** food, you cook it in an oven without using extra liquid or fat.
2 If you **bake** earth or clay, you heat it until it becomes hard.

baker **bakers**

NOUN a person who makes and sells bread and cakes

balance **balances, balancing, balanced**

VERB **1** When someone or something **balances**, they remain steady and do not fall over.
2 used in mathematics when weighing and comparing two weights. If two weights are equal, they **balance**.
NOUN **3** the state of being upright and steady • *She lost her **balance** and fell.*
4 the amount of money in someone's bank account

balcony **balconies**

NOUN **1** a platform on the outside of a building, with a wall or railing round it
2 an area of upstairs seats in a theatre or cinema

bald **balder, baldest**

ADJECTIVE A **bald** person has little or no hair on their head.
[from Middle English *ballede* meaning having a white patch]

bale **bales, baling, baled**

NOUN **1** a large bundle of something, such as paper or hay, tied tightly
VERB **2** If you **bale** water from a boat, you remove it using a container; also spelt **bail**.

ball **balls**

NOUN **1** a round object used in games such as tennis, soccer, and hockey
2 The **ball** of your foot or thumb is the rounded part where your toes join your foot or your thumb joins your hand.

ballad **ballads**

NOUN **1** a long song or poem that tells a story
2 a slow, romantic pop song

ballerina **ballerinas**

NOUN a female ballet dancer

ballet

NOUN a type of artistic dancing based on precise steps
[from Italian *balletto* meaning little dance]

balloon **balloons**

NOUN **1** a small bag made of thin rubber that you blow into until it becomes larger. **Balloons** are often used as party decorations.
2 a large, strong bag filled with gas or hot air, that travels through the air carrying passengers in a basket underneath it • *They went on a hot air **balloon** flight over the city.*

ballpoint ballpoints
NOUN a pen with a small, metal ball at the writing point

bamboo
NOUN a tall tropical grass with hard, hollow stems used for making furniture

ban bans, banning, banned
VERB **1** If you **ban** something, you forbid it to be done.
SYNONYMS: forbid, prohibit
NOUN **2** If there is a **ban** on something, it is not allowed.

banana bananas
NOUN a long, curved fruit with a yellow skin

band bands
NOUN **1** a group of musicians who play jazz or pop music together
2 a group of people who share a common purpose
3 a narrow strip of something used to hold things together • She tied her hair back with an elastic **band**.

bandage bandages
NOUN a strip of cloth wrapped round a wound to protect it

bang bangs, banging, banged
NOUN **1** a sudden, short, loud noise
2 a hard, painful bump against something
VERB **3** If you **bang** something, you hit it or put it down violently so that it makes a loud noise.
4 If you **bang** a part of your body against something, you accidentally bump it.

banish banishes, banishing, banished
VERB **1** If someone is **banished**, they are sent away and never allowed to return.
2 If you **banish** something from your thoughts, you try not to think about it.
banishment NOUN

banister banisters
NOUN a rail supported by posts up the side of a staircase

banjo banjos or banjoes
NOUN a musical instrument, like a small guitar with a round body

bank banks, banking, banked
NOUN **1** a business that looks after people's money
2 the raised ground along the edge of a river or lake
VERB **3** If you **bank on** something happening, you rely on it. • I know we said we'd go swimming, but don't **bank on** it.

banner banners
NOUN **1** a long strip of cloth with a message or slogan on it • We saw **banners** advertising the fair.
ADJECTIVE **2** A **banner** headline is a headline printed right across the page of a newspaper.

banquet banquets
NOUN a grand, formal dinner, often followed by speeches
[from Old French banquet, originally meaning little bench]

baptism baptisms
NOUN the ceremony in which someone has water sprinkled on them, or they are immersed in water, as a sign that they have become a Christian

baptize baptizes, baptizing, baptized; also spelt **baptise**
VERB When a church official **baptizes** someone, they sprinkle water on them, or immerse them in water, as a sign that they have become a Christian.

bar bars, barring, barred
NOUN **1** a long, straight piece of metal
VERB **2** If you **bar** someone's way, you stop them going somewhere by standing in front of them.
NOUN **3** a counter or room where alcoholic drinks are served
4 a piece of something made in a rectangular shape • a **bar** of soap

barbecue barbecues
NOUN **1** a grill with a charcoal fire on which you cook food, usually outdoors
2 an outdoor party where you eat food cooked on a **barbecue**
[from a Caribbean word meaning framework]

barber barbers
NOUN a man who cuts men's hair

bar chart bar charts
NOUN a kind of graph where the information is shown in rows or bars

Goals scored by United

bar code bar codes
NOUN a pattern of lines and numbers on something that is for sale, so that the price can be read by a machine

bare barer, barest
ADJECTIVE **1** If a part of your body is **bare**, it is not covered by any clothing. • **bare** *feet*
SYNONYMS: naked, uncovered
2 If something is **bare**, it is not covered or decorated with anything. • **bare** *wooden floors*
3 The **bare** minimum, or the **bare** essentials, means the very least that is needed.

barely
ADVERB If you **barely** manage to do something, you only just succeed in doing it.

bargain bargains, bargaining, bargained
NOUN **1** an agreement in which two people or groups discuss and agree what each will do, pay or receive
2 something that is sold at a low price and that is good value • *The apples are a* **bargain** *at this price.*
VERB **3** When people **bargain** with each other, they discuss and agree terms about what each will do, pay or receive.

barge barges, barging, barged
NOUN **1** a boat with a flat bottom used for carrying heavy loads, especially on canals
VERB **2** INFORMAL If you **barge** into a place, you push into it in a rough or rude way.

bark barks, barking, barked
VERB **1** When a dog **barks**, it makes a short, loud noise, once or several times.
NOUN **2** the tough material that covers the outside of a tree

barley
NOUN a cereal that is grown for food and is also used for making beer and whisky

bar mitzvah
NOUN A Jewish boy's **bar mitzvah** is a ceremony that takes place on his 13th birthday, after which he is regarded as an adult.

barn barns
NOUN a large farm building used for storing crops or animal food
[from Old English *beren* meaning barley room]

barnacle barnacles
NOUN a small shellfish that fixes itself to rocks and to the bottom of boats

barometer barometers
NOUN an instrument that measures air pressure and shows when the weather is changing

barrel barrels
NOUN **1** a wooden container with rounded sides and flat ends
2 The **barrel** of a gun is the long tube through which the bullet is fired.

barricade barricades, barricading, barricaded
NOUN **1** a temporary barrier put up to stop people getting past
VERB **2** If you **barricade** yourself inside a room or building, you put something heavy against the door to stop people getting in.
[from Old French *barriquer* meaning to block with barrels]

barrier barriers
NOUN a fence or wall that prevents people or animals getting from one area to another

barrister barristers
NOUN a lawyer who is qualified to represent people in the higher courts

barrow barrows

NOUN **1** another word for **wheelbarrow**
2 a large cart from which fruit or other goods are sold in the street

base bases, basing, based

NOUN **1** the lowest part of something
• *The waves crashed at the **base** of the cliffs.*
2 The **base** of a triangle or a square-shaped pyramid is the bottom.
3 a place where part of an army, navy or air force works from
VERB **4** If you **base** one thing on another, you develop from it. • *She **based** the film on a true story.*
5 If you are **based** somewhere, you live there or work from there. • *My dad is **based** in Cardiff, but spends a lot of time abroad.*

baseball

NOUN a team game played with a bat and a ball. It is popular in the USA.

basement basements

NOUN a room or set of rooms below the level of the street • *My aunt lives in the **basement** of our house.*

basic

ADJECTIVE **1** The **basic** aspects of something are the most necessary ones. • *The **basic** ingredients of bread are flour, yeast and water.*
2 having only the essentials, and no extras or luxuries
basically ADVERB

basin basins

NOUN **1** a round, wide container which is open at the top
2 A river **basin** is a bowl of land from which water runs into the river.

basis bases

NOUN If something is the **basis** of something else, it is the main principle on which it is based, and from which other points and ideas can be developed.

bask basks, basking, basked

VERB If you **bask** in hot weather, you lie in the sun and enjoy the warmth.

basket baskets

NOUN a container made of thin strips of wood or metal woven together
• *a shopping **basket***

basketball

NOUN a game in which two teams try to score goals by throwing a large ball through one of two circular nets that are suspended high up at each end of the **basketball** court

bass basses

NOUN **1** a man with a very deep singing voice
ADJECTIVE **2** In music, a **bass** instrument produces a very deep sound. • *a **bass** guitar*

bassoon bassoons

NOUN a large woodwind instrument

bat bats, batting, batted

NOUN **1** a specially shaped piece of wood with a handle, used for hitting a ball in games such as table tennis or cricket
2 a small animal like a mouse with leathery wings. **Bats** fly at night and sleep hanging upside down.
VERB **3** If you are **batting** in cricket, baseball or rounders, it is your turn to hit the ball.

batch batches

NOUN A **batch** of things is a group of things that are all the same or are being dealt with at the same time. • *They delivered the first **batch** of books at the start of term.*

bath baths

NOUN a long container that you fill with water and sit in to wash yourself

bathe bathes, bathing, bathed

VERB When you **bathe** in a sea, river or lake, you swim or play there.

bathroom bathrooms

NOUN a room with a bath or shower, a washbasin and often a toilet in it

a
b
c
d
e
f
g
h
i
j
k
l
m
n
o
p
q
r
s
t
u
v
w
x
y
z

baton batons
NOUN **1** a light, thin stick that a conductor uses to direct an orchestra or choir
2 a short stick passed from one runner to another at the changeover in a relay race

battalion battalions
NOUN an army unit consisting of three or more companies

batter batters, battering, battered
NOUN **1** a mixture of flour, eggs and milk, used to make pancakes, or to coat food before frying it
VERB **2** When someone or something **batters** someone or something, they hit them many times. • *The waves* **battered** *the sides of the ship.*

battery batteries
NOUN a device for storing energy and producing electricity, for example in a torch or a car

battle battles
NOUN a fight between armed forces, or a struggle between two people or groups with different aims

battlefield battlefields
NOUN a place where a battle has been fought or is being fought

battlements
PLURAL NOUN the top part of a castle where there are openings through which arrows or guns could be fired

battleship battleships
NOUN a large fighting ship carrying powerful guns

bawl bawls, bawling, bawled
VERB If someone **bawls**, they shout or cry loudly.

bay bays, baying, bayed
NOUN **1** part of the coastline where the land curves
2 a space or an area used for a particular purpose • *a loading* **bay**
3 a tree with dark green leaves. The leaves are used for flavouring food.
VERB **4** When a dog or a wolf **bays**, it makes a deep, howling sound.

PHRASE **5** If you keep something **at bay**, you stop it hurting you. • *Try eating an orange to keep a cold* **at bay**.

bayonet bayonets
NOUN a sharp blade that can be fixed to the end of a rifle

bazaar bazaars
NOUN **1** an area with many small shops and stalls, especially in Eastern countries
2 a sale to raise money for charity
• *a Christmas* **bazaar**
[from Persian *bazar* meaning market]

BC
ADJECTIVE You use **BC** to show the dates before the birth of Jesus Christ. It is an abbreviation for *before Christ*.

be am, is, are; being; was, were; been
VERB **1** You can use **be** with the present participle of other verbs. • *Look! I* **am** *riding on my own!*
2 You can also use **be** to say that something will happen. • *I will* **be** *nine in November.*
3 You use **be** to say more about something or somebody. • *His name* **is** *Tom.*

beach beaches
NOUN an area of sand or pebbles beside the sea

beacon beacons
NOUN In the past, a **beacon** was a light or fire on a hill, which acted as a signal or warning.

bead beads
NOUN **1** a small, shaped piece of glass, stone or wood with a hole through the middle. **Beads** are strung together with others to make necklaces or bracelets.
2 a drop of liquid • **beads** *of perspiration*

beak beaks
NOUN the hard part of a bird's mouth that sticks out. It is used for pecking up food and for carrying things such as twigs.

beam beams, beaming, beamed
NOUN **1** a long, thick bar of wood or metal, especially one that supports a roof
2 a band of light that shines from something such as a torch or the sun
VERB **3** If you **beam**, you smile broadly.

bean beans

NOUN the seed or pod of a plant, eaten as a vegetable or used for other purposes
• *runner* **beans** • *coffee* **beans** • *soya* **beans**

bear bears, bearing, bore, borne

NOUN **1** a large, strong, wild mammal with thick fur and sharp claws • *polar* **bear**
• *grizzly* **bear**

VERB **2** If someone or something **bears** something, they carry it or support its weight. • *The ice wasn't thick enough to* **bear** *their weight.*

3 If something **bears** a mark or typical feature, it has it. • *The room* **bore** *all the signs of a violent struggle.*

4 If you **bear** something difficult, you accept it and are able to deal with it.
• *The loneliness was hard to* **bear**.

beard beards

NOUN the hair that grows on the lower part of a man's face

beast beasts

NOUN **1** an old-fashioned word for a large, wild animal

2 INFORMAL If you call someone a **beast**, you mean that they are cruel or spiteful.

beat beats, beating, beat, beaten

VERB **1** If someone or something **beats** someone or something else, they hit them hard and repeatedly. • *The rain was* **beating** *against the window.*

2 If you **beat** someone in a race or game, you defeat them or do better than them.

3 When your heart **beats**, it pumps blood with a regular rhythm.

NOUN **4** the main rhythm of a piece of music or poetry

beautiful

ADJECTIVE very attractive or pleasing
SYNONYM: lovely

beauty beauties

NOUN **1** the quality of being beautiful
• *the* **beauty** *of the stars on a clear night*
2 The **beauty** of an idea or a plan is what makes it attractive or worth doing.
• *The* **beauty** *of going in September is that the sea will be warmer for swimming.*

beaver beavers

NOUN a mammal with a big, flat tail and webbed hind feet. **Beavers** build dams.

because

CONJUNCTION **1 Because** is used with other words to give the reason for something.
• *I went home* **because** *I was tired.*
PHRASE **2 Because of** is used with a noun that gives the reason for something.
• *I had to stay late* **because of** *detention.*

beckon beckons, beckoning, beckoned

VERB If you **beckon** to someone, you make a sign to them with your hand, asking them to come to you.

become becomes, becoming, became, become

VERB If someone or something **becomes** something else, they start feeling or being that thing. • *I* **became** *more and more angry.*
[from Old English *becuman* meaning to happen]

bed beds

NOUN **1** a piece of furniture that you lie on when you sleep
2 an area of ground in a garden which has been dug and prepared for planting
3 The **bed** of the sea or a river is the bottom of it.

bedraggled

ADJECTIVE If a person or animal is **bedraggled**, they are wet, dirty and messy.

bedroom bedrooms

NOUN a room for sleeping in

bedtime bedtimes

NOUN the time when you go to bed

bee bees

NOUN a winged insect that makes honey. Many types of **bee** live in large groups.

beech beeches

NOUN a tree with a smooth, grey trunk and shiny leaves

A
B
C
D
E
F
G
H
I
J
K
L
M
N
O
P
Q
R
S
T
U
V
W
X
Y
Z

beef

NOUN the meat of a cow, bull or ox

beehive **beehives**

NOUN a specially designed structure in which bees are kept so that their honey can be collected

been

VERB the past participle of **be**

beer **beers**

NOUN an alcoholic drink made from malt and flavoured with hops

beetle **beetles**

NOUN a flying insect with hard wings that cover its body when it is not flying [from Old English *bitan* meaning to bite]

beetroot **beetroots**

NOUN a round, dark red root vegetable

before

ADVERB, PREPOSITION OR CONJUNCTION If something happens **before**, it happens earlier than something else. ● *Can I see you* ***before*** *you go?*

ANTONYM: after

beg **begs, begging, begged**

VERB **1** When people **beg**, they ask for food or money, because they are very poor.
2 If you **beg** someone to do something, you ask them very anxiously to do it.
● *David* ***begged*** *his dad to take him to the cinema.*

began

VERB the past tense of **begin**

begin **begins, beginning, began, begun**

VERB If you **begin** something, you start it.

beginner **beginners**

NOUN someone who has just started to learn something

SYNONYM: learner

beginning **beginnings**

NOUN The **beginning** of something is when or where it starts.

begun

VERB the past participle of **begin**

behalf

PHRASE If you do something **on behalf of** someone or something, you do it for them or in their name. ● *We did the sponsored swim* ***on behalf of*** *various charities.*

behave **behaves, behaving, behaved**

VERB **1** If you **behave** in a particular way, you act in that way. ● *He knew that he'd* ***behaved*** *badly.*
2 If you **behave** yourself, you act correctly or properly.

behind

PREPOSITION **1** at the back of ● *The moon disappeared* ***behind*** *a cloud.*
2 supporting someone ● *The whole school was* ***behind*** *him in the competition.*
ADVERB **3** If you stay **behind**, you remain after other people have gone.
4 If you leave something **behind**, you do not take it with you.

beige

ADJECTIVE a cream-brown colour

being

VERB the present participle of **be**

belch **belches, belching, belched**

VERB **1** If you **belch**, you make a sudden noise in your throat because air has risen up from your stomach.
2 If something **belches** smoke or fire, it sends it out in large amounts. ● *Smoke* ***belched*** *from the factory chimneys.*
NOUN **3** the noise you make when you belch

belief **beliefs**

NOUN If you have a **belief** in something, you are certain that it is right or true.

believe believes, believing, believed
VERB **1** If you **believe** that something is true, you think that it is true.
2 If you **believe** someone, you accept that they are telling the truth.

bell bells
NOUN **1** a cup-shaped metal object with a piece inside it called a clapper that hits the side and makes a ringing sound
2 an electrical device that you can ring or buzz to get attention

bellow bellows, bellowing, bellowed
VERB If a human or other animal **bellows**, they shout very loudly or make a very loud, deep noise like a roar.

belly bellies
NOUN the part of your body, especially your stomach, that holds and digests food

belong belongs, belonging, belonged
VERB **1** If something **belongs** to you, it is yours and you own it.
2 If you **belong** to a group, you are a member of it.
3 If something **belongs** in a particular place, that is where it should be. • *That book **belongs** on the top shelf.*

belongings
PLURAL NOUN Your **belongings** are all the things that you own.

below
PREPOSITION OR ADVERB **1** If something is **below** something else, it is in a lower position. • *We could hear music coming up from the flat two floors **below**.*
ANTONYM: above
2 If something is **below** a particular amount or level, it is less than it.
• ***below** average rainfall*
ANTONYM: above

belt belts
NOUN a strip of leather or cloth that you fasten round your waist to hold your trousers or skirt up

bench benches
NOUN a long seat that two or more people can sit on

bend bends, bending, bent
VERB **1** When you **bend** something, you use force to make it curved or angular.
2 When you **bend**, you move your head and shoulders forwards and downwards.
• *I **bent** over to pick up my glasses.*
NOUN **3** a curved part of something
• *a **bend** in the road*

beneath
PREPOSITION OR ADVERB FORMAL underneath

benefit benefits, benefiting, benefited
NOUN **1** the advantage that something brings to people • *the **benefit** of a good education*
VERB **2** If you **benefit** from something, it helps you. • *He'll **benefit** from some extra tuition.*
[from Latin *benefactum* meaning good deed]

bent
ADJECTIVE curved or twisted out of shape

bereaved
ADJECTIVE FORMAL You say that someone is **bereaved** when a close relative of theirs has recently died.
bereavement NOUN

berry berries
NOUN a small, round fruit that grows on bushes or trees

berserk
ADVERB If somebody goes **berserk**, they lose control of themselves and become extremely violent.
[from Icelandic *berserkr* meaning a Viking who wore a shirt made from the skin of a bear and who worked himself into a mad frenzy before going into battle]

berth berths
NOUN **1** a space in a harbour where a ship stays when it is being loaded or unloaded
2 In a boat or caravan, a **berth** is a bed.
PHRASE **3** If you give someone or something **a wide berth**, you avoid them because they are unpleasant or dangerous.

beside
PREPOSITION If one thing is **beside** another thing, it is next to it.

a
b
c
d
e
f
g
h
i
j
k
l
m
n
o
p
q
r
s
t
u
v
w
x
y
z

A
B
C
D
E
F
G
H
I
J
K
L
M
N
O
P
Q
R
S
T
U
V
W
X
Y
Z

besides
ADVERB also or in addition to

best
ADJECTIVE **1** the superlative of *good* and *well*
• *That was one of the **best** films I've ever seen.*
ANTONYM: worst
ADVERB **2** The thing that you like **best** is the thing that you prefer to everything else.

bet **bets, betting, bet**
VERB If you **bet** on the result of an event, you will win money if what you bet on happens and lose money if it does not.

betray **betrays, betraying, betrayed**
VERB If you **betray** someone who trusts you, you tell people something secret about them.

better
ADJECTIVE **1** the comparative of *good* and *well* • *I am feeling **better** today.*
2 If you are **better** after an illness, you are no longer ill.
SYNONYM: cured

between
PREPOSITION OR ADVERB **1** If something is **between** two other things, it is situated or happens in the space or time that separates them. • *He was head teacher **between** 1989 and 2000.*
2 A relationship or a difference **between** two people or two things is one that involves them both. • *the difference **between** frogs and toads*

beware
VERB If you tell someone to **beware** of something, you are warning them that it might be dangerous or harmful.

bewilder **bewilders, bewildering, bewildered**
VERB If something **bewilders** you, it confuses and muddles you so that you can't understand.
bewilderment NOUN

beyond
PREPOSITION **1** If something is **beyond** a certain place, it is on the other side of it.

• ***Beyond** the mountains was the secret valley.*
2 If something is **beyond** you, you cannot do it or understand it.

bi-
PREFIX added to a word to mean two or twice. For example, someone who is **bi**lingual can speak two languages.

bib **bibs**
NOUN a piece of cloth or plastic put under a baby's chin to protect its clothes from stains

Bible **Bibles**
NOUN the sacred book of the Christian religion • *I read about Noah and the Ark in the **Bible**.*

bibliography **bibliographies**
NOUN a list of books or articles

bicycle **bicycles**
NOUN a two-wheeled vehicle that you ride by pushing two pedals with your feet

bid **bids, bidding, bid**
VERB If you **bid** for something, you offer to buy it for a certain sum of money.
• *He **bid** for an old bike at the auction.*

big **bigger, biggest**
ADJECTIVE large or important
ANTONYMS: small, tiny, little

bike **bikes**
NOUN an abbreviation for *bicycle*

bikini **bikinis**
NOUN a small, two-piece swimming costume worn by women

bilingual
ADJECTIVE involving or using two languages
• ***bilingual** street signs*
[from Latin *bis* meaning two and *lingua* meaning tongue]

bill **bills**
NOUN **1** a written statement of how much is owed for goods or services • *a phone **bill***
2 a formal statement of a proposed new law that is discussed and then voted on in Parliament
3 A **bill** can be a piece of paper money.
• *a dollar **bill***
4 A bird's **bill** is its beak.

billiards

NOUN a game in which a long stick called a cue is used to move balls on a table

billion **billions**

NOUN a thousand million • *You can write one **billion** like this: 1,000,000,000.*

billow **billows, billowing, billowed**

VERB **1** When things made of cloth **billow**, they swell out and flap slowly in the wind. **2** When smoke or cloud **billows**, it spreads upwards and outwards. NOUN **3** a large wave

billy goat **billy goats**

NOUN a male goat

bin **bins**

NOUN a container, especially one that you put rubbish in

binary

ADJECTIVE The **binary** system is a number system used when working with computers. It uses only two digits, 0 and 1.

bind **binds, binding, bound**

VERB **1** If you **bind** something, you tie rope or string round it so that it is held firmly. **2** If you **bind** a wound, you wrap bandages round it. **3** When a book is **bound**, the pages are joined together and a cover is put on.

bingo

NOUN a game in which players aim to match the numbers that someone calls out with the numbers on the card they have been given

binoculars

PLURAL NOUN an instrument with lenses for both eyes, which you look through in order to see objects far away • *They used **binoculars** for bird watching.*

biodegradable

ADJECTIVE **Biodegradable** materials can be broken down naturally, and so they are not dangerous to the environment.

biography **biographies**

NOUN the history of someone's life, written by someone else

biology

NOUN the study of living things [from Greek *bios* + *logos* meaning life study]

birch **birches**

NOUN a tall, deciduous tree with thin branches and thin bark

bird **birds**

NOUN an egg-laying animal with feathers, two wings, two legs and a beak

birth **births**

NOUN Your **birth** was when you were born.

birthday **birthdays**

NOUN Your **birthday** is the anniversary of the date on which you were born.

birthmark **birthmarks**

NOUN a mark on your skin that has been there since you were born

biscuit **biscuits**

NOUN a small, flat cake that is crisp and usually sweet

bisect **bisects, bisecting, bisected**

VERB to divide a line or an area in half

bishop **bishops**

NOUN a high-ranking clergyman in some Christian Churches

bison

NOUN a large, hairy animal, related to cattle, with a large head and shoulders. **Bison** used to be very common on the prairies in North America, but they are now almost extinct.

bit **bits**

VERB **1** the past tense of **bite** • *She **bit** into the toast.* NOUN **2** A **bit** of something is a small amount of it. PHRASE **3** INFORMAL A **bit** means slightly or to a small extent. • *That's **a bit** difficult.*

bitch bitches
NOUN a female dog

bite bites, biting, bit, bitten
VERB If you **bite** something, you cut into it with your teeth.

bitter bitterest
ADJECTIVE **1** A **bitter** taste is sharp and unpleasant.
2 A **bitter** wind is extremely cold.
3 If you are **bitter** about something, you feel angry and resentful.

bizarre
ADJECTIVE very strange and weird
SYNONYMS: odd, peculiar

black blacker, blackest
NOUN OR ADJECTIVE the darkest possible colour, like the sky at night when there is no light

blackberry blackberries
NOUN a small, soft black fruit that grows on brambles

blackbird blackbirds
NOUN a common European bird, the male of which has black feathers and a yellow beak

blackboard blackboards
NOUN a dark-coloured board in a classroom, which teachers write on using chalk

blackcurrant blackcurrants
NOUN **Blackcurrants** are very small, dark, purple fruits that grow in bunches on bushes.

black hole black holes
NOUN the empty space made by the collapse of a star

bladder bladders
NOUN the part of your body where urine is held until it leaves your body

blade blades
NOUN **1** the sharp part of a knife, axe or saw
2 a single piece of grass

blame blames, blaming, blamed
VERB If someone **blames** a person for something bad that has happened, they believe that person caused it.
SYNONYM: accuse

blank blanker, blankest
ADJECTIVE **1** Something that is **blank** has nothing on it. ● a **blank** sheet of paper
2 If you look **blank**, your face shows no feeling or interest.

blanket blankets
NOUN a large rectangle of thick cloth that is put on a bed to keep people warm [from Old French *blancquete* meaning little white thing]

blare blares, blaring, blared
VERB to make a loud, unpleasant noise ● The radio **blared** from the flat below.

blast blasts, blasting, blasted
VERB **1** When people **blast** a hole in something, they make a hole with an explosion. ● They're using dynamite to **blast** away rocks.
NOUN **2** a big explosion, especially one caused by a bomb

blaze blazes, blazing, blazed
NOUN **1** a large, hot fire
VERB **2** If something **blazes**, it burns or shines brightly. ● The fire **blazed** in the fireplace.

blazer blazers
NOUN a kind of jacket, often in the colours of a school or sports team

bleach bleaches, bleaching, bleached
NOUN **1** a chemical that is used to make material white or to clean thoroughly and kill germs
VERB **2** If you **bleach** material or hair, you make it white, usually by using a chemical.

bleak bleaker, bleakest
ADJECTIVE **1** If a place is **bleak**, it is cold, bare and exposed to the wind. ● a **bleak** mountain top
2 If a situation is **bleak**, it is bad and seems unlikely to improve.

bleat bleats, bleating, bleated
VERB When sheep or goats **bleat**, they make a high-pitched cry.

bleed bleeds, bleeding, bled
VERB When you **bleed**, you lose blood as

A B C D E F G H I J K L M N O P Q R S T U V W X Y Z

a result of an injury. ● *My hand **bled** a lot after I cut it.*

blend **blends, blending, blended**
VERB **1** When you **blend** substances, you mix them together to form a single substance. ● ***Blend** the butter with the sugar.*
2 When colours or sounds **blend**, they combine in a pleasing way.

bless **blesses, blessing, blessed** or **blest**
VERB When a priest **blesses** people or things, he or she asks God to give his protection to them.
[from Old English *bloedsian* meaning to sprinkle with sacrificial blood]

blew
VERB the past tense of **blow**

blind **blinds, blinding, blinded**
ADJECTIVE **1** Someone who is **blind** cannot see.
VERB **2** If something **blinds** you, it stops you seeing, either for a short time or permanently.
NOUN **3** a roll of cloth or paper that you pull down over a window to keep out the light

blindfold **blindfolds**
NOUN a strip of cloth tied over someone's eyes to stop them seeing

blink **blinks, blinking, blinked**
VERB When you **blink**, you close your eyes quickly for a moment.

bliss
NOUN a state of complete happiness
blissful ADJECTIVE **blissfully** ADVERB

blister **blisters**
NOUN a small bubble on your skin containing watery liquid, caused by a burn or rubbing

blizzard **blizzards**
NOUN a heavy snowstorm with strong winds

bloated
ADJECTIVE Something that is **bloated** is much larger than normal, often because there is a lot of liquid or gas inside it.

block **blocks, blocking, blocked**
NOUN **1** a large building containing flats or offices
2 In a town, a **block** is an area of land with streets on all its sides.
3 a large, rectangular, three-dimensional piece of something
VERB **4** If someone or something **blocks** a road or channel, they put something across it so that nothing can get through.
SYNONYM: obstruct

block capitals
PLURAL NOUN large upper-case letters. THESE ARE BLOCK CAPITALS.

block graph **block graphs**
NOUN another name for **bar chart**

blog **blogs, blogging, blogged**
NOUN **1** a person's online diary that they put on the internet so that other people can read it
VERB **2** If you **blog** about something, you write about it in a blog. ● *He **blogs** about cooking and restaurants.*

blonde **blondes**
ADJECTIVE **1** **Blonde** hair is pale yellow in colour. The spelling **blond** is used when referring to men.
NOUN **2** A **blonde** or **blond** is a person with pale yellow hair.

blood
NOUN the red liquid that is pumped by the heart round the bodies of human beings and other vertebrates

bloodstream
NOUN the flow of blood through your body

bloodthirsty
ADJECTIVE Someone who is **bloodthirsty** enjoys using or watching violence.

bloom **blooms, blooming, bloomed**
NOUN **1** a flower on a plant
VERB **2** When a plant **blooms**, it produces flowers.

blossom **blossoms, blossoming, blossomed**
NOUN **1** all the flowers that appear on a tree before the fruit

VERB **2** When a tree **blossoms**, it produces flowers.

blot blots
NOUN a mark made by a drop of liquid, especially ink

blouse blouses
NOUN a light shirt, worn by a girl or a woman

blow blows, blowing, blew, blown
VERB **1** When the wind **blows**, the air moves.
2 If you **blow**, you send a stream of air from your mouth.
3 If you **blow** your nose, you force air out of it through your nostrils in order to clear it.
NOUN **4** If you receive a **blow**, someone or something hits you.

blow up
VERB **1** If something **blows up**, it is destroyed by an explosion.
2 If you **blow up** a balloon or a tyre, you fill it with air.

blubber
NOUN the layer of fat beneath the skin of animals such as whales and seals that protects them from the cold

blue bluer, bluest
ADJECTIVE OR NOUN the colour of the sky on a clear, sunny day

bluebell bluebells
NOUN a woodland plant with blue, bell-shaped flowers

bluff bluffs, bluffing, bluffed
NOUN **1** an attempt to make someone believe that you will do something when you do not really intend to do it
VERB **2** If you are **bluffing**, you are trying to make someone believe that you are in a strong position when you are not.
[from Dutch *bluffen* meaning to boast]

blunder blunders, blundering, blundered
NOUN **1** a silly mistake
VERB **2** If you **blunder**, you make a silly mistake.

blunt blunter, bluntest
ADJECTIVE **1** A **blunt** object has a rounded point or edge, rather than a sharp one.
● *My pencil was **blunt** so I could not write with it.*
2 If you are **blunt**, you say exactly what you think, without trying to be polite.
SYNONYMS: outspoken, straightforward

blur
NOUN If something is a **blur**, you can't see it clearly. ● *The mountain was a **blur** through the mist.*

blurb blurbs
NOUN the description of a book printed on the back cover

blurt out blurts out, blurting out, blurted out
VERB If you **blurt out** something, you say it suddenly, after trying to keep it a secret.

blush blushes, blushing, blushed
VERB If you **blush**, your face becomes red, because you are embarrassed or ashamed.
[from Old English *blyscan* meaning to glow]

boa boas
NOUN a large snake that kills its prey by coiling round it and crushing it

boar boars
NOUN **1** a male wild pig
2 a male domestic pig used for breeding

board boards, boarding, boarded
NOUN **1** a long, flat piece of wood
2 a flat piece of wood, plastic or cardboard, which is used for a particular purpose ● *a chess**board*** ● *a surf**board***
3 the group of people who control a company or organization ● *My mum is on the **board** of governors.*
4 the meals provided when you stay in a hotel or guesthouse ● *The price includes full **board**.*
VERB **5** If you **board** a ship or aircraft, you get on it or in it.
PHRASE **6** If you are **on board** a ship or aircraft, you are on it or in it.

🖉 Do not confuse *board* with *bored*.

boarder **boarders**
NOUN **1** a pupil who lives at school during term
2 a lodger

boast **boasts, boasting, boasted**
VERB If you **boast**, you talk proudly about what you have or what you can do.
SYNONYM: brag

boat **boats**
NOUN a small vehicle for travelling across water

body **bodies**
NOUN **1** Your **body** is all of you, from your head to your feet.
2 You can say **body** when you mean just the main part of a human or other animal, not counting head, arms and legs.

bodyguard **bodyguards**
NOUN a person employed to protect someone

bog **bogs**
NOUN an area of wet, spongy ground

boil **boils, boiling, boiled**
VERB **1** When a hot liquid **boils**, or when you **boil** it, it starts to bubble and to give off steam.
2 When you **boil** food, you cook it in boiling water.

boiler **boilers**
NOUN a piece of equipment that burns fuel to provide hot water

boisterous
ADJECTIVE Someone who is **boisterous** is noisy and lively.
SYNONYMS: loud, rowdy
boisterously ADVERB

bold **bolder, boldest**
ADJECTIVE **1** brave or confident • *He was* **bold** *enough to ask for her autograph.*
2 clear and noticeable • *The sign was painted in* **bold** *colours.*
[from Old Norse *ballr* meaning dangerous or terrible]

bollard **bollards**
NOUN a short, thick post used to stop vehicles from entering a road

bolt **bolts, bolting, bolted**
NOUN **1** a metal object that screws into a nut and is used to fasten things together

bolt   nut

VERB **2** If you **bolt** one thing to another, you fasten them together using a bolt.
• *They* **bolted** *the chair to the floor.*
3 If you **bolt** a door or window, you slide a metal bar across in order to fasten it.

bomb **bombs, bombing, bombed**
NOUN **1** a container filled with material that explodes when it hits something or when it is set off by a timer
VERB **2** If you **bomb** something, you attack it with a bomb.
[from Greek *bombos* meaning a booming sound]

bond **bonds**
NOUN a close relationship between people
• *the* **bond** *between mothers and babies*

bone **bones**
NOUN the hard parts that form the framework of a person's or animal's body

bonfire **bonfires**
NOUN a large fire made outdoors, to burn rubbish or to celebrate something
[from *bone* + *fire* – bones were used as fuel in the Middle Ages]

bonnet **bonnets**
NOUN **1** the metal cover over a car's engine
2 a baby's or woman's hat tied under the chin

bonus **bonuses**
NOUN **1** an amount of money added to a person's usual pay
2 a good thing that you get in addition to something else

bony bonier, boniest

ADJECTIVE **Bony** people or animals are very thin, with not much flesh covering their bones.

book books, booking, booked

NOUN **1** a number of pages held together inside a cover

VERB **2** When you **book** something, you arrange to have it or use it at a particular time. • *Mum **booked** two rooms at the hotel.*

bookcase bookcases

NOUN a piece of furniture where you keep books

booklet booklets

NOUN a small book with a paper cover

boom booms, booming, boomed

NOUN **1** a deep, echoing sound

2 a fast increase in something • *There has been a **boom** in the sale of sun cream this summer.*

VERB **3** If something **booms**, it makes a loud booming sound. • *We heard the foghorn **boom** in the distance.*

boomerang boomerangs

NOUN a curved, wooden missile that can be thrown so that it returns to the thrower. **Boomerangs** were traditionally used as weapons by Australian Aborigines.

boost boosts, boosting, boosted

VERB If someone **boosts** something, they improve or increase it. • *The teacher **boosted** Juliet's confidence when she praised her story.*

boot boots

NOUN **1** strong shoes that come up over your ankle, and sometimes your calf

2 the covered space in a car, usually at the back, for carrying things in

booth booths

NOUN **1** a small, partly-enclosed area • *a telephone **booth***

2 a stall where you can buy things, for example at a market or a fair

border borders

NOUN **1** the dividing line between two countries

2 a strip or band round the edge of something

3 flower beds round the edges of a garden

borderline borderlines

NOUN If someone or something is on the **borderline**, they are on the division between two different categories.

bore bores, boring, bored

VERB **1** If something **bores** you, you find it dull and uninteresting.

2 If you **bore** a hole in something, you make it using a tool such as a drill.

3 the past tense of **bear**

NOUN **4** someone or something that bores you

bored

ADJECTIVE If you are **bored**, you are miserable because you have nothing interesting to do.

Do not confuse *bored* with *board*.

boring

ADJECTIVE dull and uninteresting

ANTONYM: interesting

born

VERB When an animal such as a human baby is **born**, it comes out of its mother's body and starts to live.

borrow borrows, borrowing, borrowed

VERB If you **borrow** something that belongs to someone else, they let you have it for a period of time. • *I **borrowed** a book from my friend.*

boss bosses, bossing, bossed

NOUN **1** Someone's **boss** is the person in charge of the place where they work.

VERB **2** If someone **bosses** you, they keep telling you what to do.

bossy bossier, bossiest

ADJECTIVE If you are **bossy**, you like to order other people around.

botany

NOUN the study and classification of plants

both

ADJECTIVE OR PRONOUN **Both** is used when saying something about two things or two people. • *You can **both** come to my party.*

bother bothers, bothering, bothered

VERB **1** If you don't **bother** to do something, you don't do it because it takes too much effort or it's not important.
2 If something **bothers** you, you are worried about it.
3 If you are not **bothered** about something, you don't care about it.
4 If you **bother** someone, you interrupt them when they are busy.
NOUN **5** trouble, fuss or difficulty • *Mum's having a bit of **bother** with the car.*

bottle bottles, bottling, bottled

NOUN **1** a glass or plastic container for keeping liquids in
VERB **2** If you **bottle** something, you put it in a bottle to store it.

bottom bottoms

NOUN **1** the lowest part of something • *It sank to the **bottom** of the pond.*
2 Your **bottom** is the part of your body that you sit on.

bottomless

ADJECTIVE If something is **bottomless**, it has no bottom or it is very deep.

bough boughs

Rhymes with "cow" NOUN a large branch of a tree

bought

VERB the past tense and past participle of **buy**

🖉 Do not confuse *bought* with *brought*.

boulder boulders

NOUN a large, rounded rock

bounce bounces, bouncing, bounced

VERB When an object **bounces**, it springs back from something after hitting it.
• *The ball **bounced** high off the ground.*

bound bounds, bounding, bounded

ADJECTIVE **1** If you say that something is **bound** to happen, you mean that it is certain to happen. • *He's **bound** to find out.*
NOUN **2** a large leap
VERB **3** When humans or other animals **bound**, they move quickly with large leaps.

boundary boundaries

NOUN the limit of an area

bouquet bouquets

NOUN an attractively arranged bunch of flowers

bout bouts

NOUN **1** something that lasts for a short period of time • *I had a **bout** of flu.*
2 a boxing or wrestling match

boutique boutiques

NOUN a small shop that sells fashionable clothes

bow bows, bowing, bowed

Rhymes with "now" VERB **1** When you **bow**, you bend your body or lower your head as a sign of respect or greeting.
NOUN **2** the movement you make when you **bow**
3 the front part of a ship
Rhymes with "low" NOUN **4** a knot with two loops and two loose ends • *The ribbon was tied in a **bow**.*
5 a long, thin piece of wood with horsehair strings stretched along it, used to play some stringed instruments, such as the violin and the cello
6 a long, flexible piece of wood used for shooting arrows

bowel bowels

NOUN the tubes leading from your stomach, through which waste passes before it leaves your body
[from Latin *botellus* meaning little sausage]

bowl bowls, bowling, bowled

NOUN **1** a round container with a wide, uncovered top, used for holding liquid or for serving food • *a **bowl** of soup*

2 the hollow, rounded part of something
• *a toilet **bowl***
VERB **3** When you **bowl** in cricket and rounders, you throw the ball towards the batsman.

bowling
NOUN a game in which you roll a heavy ball down a narrow track towards a set of wooden objects called pins, and try to knock them down

bowls
NOUN a game in which the players try to roll large wooden balls as near as possible to a small ball

box **boxes, boxing, boxed**
NOUN **1** a container with a firm base and sides, and usually a lid
VERB **2** If someone **boxes**, they fight according to special rules.

boxer **boxers**
NOUN **1** a person who boxes
2 a medium-sized, smooth-haired dog with a flat face

Boxing Day
NOUN the day after Christmas Day

boy **boys**
NOUN a male child

boyfriend **boyfriends**
NOUN Someone's **boyfriend** is the man or boy with whom they are having a romantic relationship.

bra **bras**
NOUN a piece of underwear worn by a woman to support her breasts

brace **braces, bracing, braced**
NOUN **1** an object fixed to something to straighten or support it • *I wore a **brace** on my teeth for two years.*
PLURAL NOUN **2** **Braces** are elastic straps worn over the shoulders to hold trousers up.
VERB **3** If you **brace** yourself, you stiffen your body to steady yourself. • *We **braced** ourselves as the bus went round the corner.*
4 If you **brace** yourself for something unpleasant, you prepare yourself to deal with it.

bracelet **bracelets**
NOUN a chain or band worn around someone's wrist as an ornament
[from Old French *bracel* meaning little arm]

bracken
NOUN a plant like a large fern that grows on hills and in woods

bracket **brackets**
NOUN a pair of written marks, ( ), { } or [ ], placed round a word or sentence that is not part of the main text, or to show that the items inside the **brackets** belong together

brag **brags, bragging, bragged**
VERB If you **brag**, you boast about something.

Braille
NOUN a system of printing for blind people in which letters are represented by raised dots that can be felt with the fingers

brain **brains**
NOUN the organ inside your head that controls your body and enables you to think and feel

brainstorm **brainstorms**
NOUN **1** a clever idea that you think of suddenly
2 If you have a **brainstorm**, you become confused and cannot think clearly.

brainy **brainier, brainiest**
ADJECTIVE clever and good at learning things

brake **brakes, braking, braked**
NOUN **1** a device for making a vehicle stop or slow down
VERB **2** When drivers **brake**, they make a

vehicle stop or slow down by using its brakes.

bramble **brambles**
NOUN a wild, trailing bush with thorns, which produces blackberries

branch **branches, branching, branched**
NOUN **1** part of a tree that grows out from the trunk
2 A **branch** of a business or organization is one of its offices or shops.
VERB **3** A road that **branches** off from another road splits off from it to lead in a different direction.

brand **brands**
NOUN a particular kind or make of something

brandy
NOUN a strong, alcoholic drink, often drunk after a meal
[from Dutch *brandewijn* meaning burnt wine]

brass
NOUN OR ADJECTIVE **1** a yellow-coloured metal made from copper and zinc
2 In an orchestra, the **brass** section consists of instruments such as trumpets and trombones.

brave **braver, bravest; braves, braving, braved**
ADJECTIVE **1** A **brave** person is willing to do dangerous things and does not show any fear.
SYNONYMS: courageous, daring
VERB **2** If you **brave** an unpleasant or dangerous situation, you face up to it in order to do something. • We **braved** the snow to go to the party.
[from Italian *bravo* meaning courageous or wild]

brawl **brawls, brawling, brawled**
NOUN **1** a rough fight
VERB **2** When people **brawl**, they take part in a rough fight.

bread
NOUN a very common food made from flour, and baked in an oven

breadth **breadths**
NOUN the distance between two sides of something • I can swim the **breadth** of the pool.
See **width**

break **breaks, breaking, broke, broken**
VERB **1** When an object **breaks**, or when you **break** it, it becomes damaged or separates into pieces.
2 If you **break** a rule or promise, you fail to keep it.
3 To **break** a record means to do better than the previous recorded best. • She **broke** the record for the long jump.
NOUN **4** a short period during which you rest or do something different

break down
VERB When a machine or a vehicle **breaks down**, it stops working.

break up
VERB When schools **break up**, the term ends. • We **break up** on Thursday.

breakable
ADJECTIVE easy to break

breakdown **breakdowns**
NOUN If there is a **breakdown** in a system, it stops working.

breakfast **breakfasts**
NOUN the first meal of the day

breast **breasts**
NOUN A woman's breasts are the two soft, fleshy parts on her chest, which produce milk after she has had a baby.

breast-feed **breast-feeds, breast-feeding, breast-fed**
VERB If a woman **breast-feeds** her baby, she feeds it with milk from her breasts.

breath **breaths**
NOUN **1** the air you take into your lungs and let out again when you breathe • He took a deep **breath** before jumping into the pool.
PHRASE **2** If you are **out of breath**, you are breathing with difficulty after doing something energetic.

breathe breathes, breathing, breathed

VERB When you **breathe**, you take air into your lungs and let it out again.

breathless

ADJECTIVE If you are **breathless**, you are breathing very fast or with difficulty.
● I was **breathless** after running to catch the bus.
breathlessly ADVERB
breathlessness NOUN

breed breeds, breeding, bred

NOUN **1** a particular type of animal. For example, an Alsatian is a **breed** of dog.
VERB **2** Someone who **breeds** animals or plants keeps them in order to produce more animals or plants with particular qualities. ● He used to **breed** dogs for the police.
3 When animals **breed**, they produce young.
SYNONYM: reproduce

breeze breezes

NOUN a gentle wind
breezy ADJECTIVE

brewery breweries

NOUN a place where beer is made, or a company that makes beer

bribe bribes, bribing, bribed

NOUN **1** a gift or money given to an official to persuade them to allow you to do something
VERB **2** If someone **bribes** someone else, they give them a bribe.

brick bricks

NOUN a rectangular block of baked clay used in building

bride brides

NOUN a woman who is getting married or who has just got married

bridegroom bridegrooms

NOUN a man on or near his wedding day

bridesmaid bridesmaids

NOUN a woman or girl who helps a bride on her wedding day

bridge bridges

NOUN **1** a structure built over a river, road or railway so that vehicles and people can cross
2 a card game for four players

bridle bridles

NOUN a set of straps round a horse's head and mouth, which the rider uses to control the horse

brief briefer, briefest; briefs, briefing, briefed

ADJECTIVE **1** Something that is **brief** lasts only a short time. ● We only had time for a **brief** visit.
VERB **2** When you **brief** someone on a task, you give them all the necessary instructions or information about it.

briefcase briefcases

NOUN a small, flat case for carrying papers

bright brighter, brightest

ADJECTIVE **1** strong and startling ● a **bright** light
SYNONYMS: brilliant, dazzling
2 clever ● That's a **bright** idea.
SYNONYMS: intelligent, quick

brighten brightens, brightening, brightened

VERB If something **brightens**, it becomes brighter.

brighten up

VERB If you **brighten up** something, you make it look brighter and more attractive.

brilliant

ADJECTIVE **1** A **brilliant** person is extremely clever.
2 INFORMAL Something that is **brilliant** is extremely good or enjoyable.
3 A **brilliant** colour or light is extremely bright.

brim brims

NOUN **1** the wide part of a hat that sticks outwards from the head
2 If a container is filled to the **brim**, it is filled right to the top.

bring brings, bringing, brought

VERB If you **bring** something or someone

with you when you go to a place, you take them with you.

bring up

VERB When someone **brings up** children, they look after them while they grow up.

brink

NOUN **1** the edge of a deep hole, cliff or ravine

PHRASE **2** If you are **on the brink** of something, you are about to do it.

• *They were on the brink of discovering a cure for the common cold.*

brisk brisker, briskest

ADJECTIVE **1** quick and energetic • *a brisk walk*

2 If someone's manner is **brisk**, it shows that they want to get things done quickly and efficiently.

briskly ADVERB **briskness** NOUN

bristle bristles, bristling, bristled

NOUN **1 Bristles** are strong animal hairs used to make brushes.

VERB **2** If the hairs on an animal's body **bristle**, they rise up because it is frightened.

bristly ADJECTIVE

brittle

ADJECTIVE An object that is **brittle** is hard but breaks easily.

broad broader, broadest

ADJECTIVE **1** A **broad** river is wide.

2 The **broad** outline of a story gives the main points, but no details.

broadband

NOUN a digital system for sending data to and from televisions, computers and telephones • *What is the broadband speed like here?*

broadcast broadcasts, broadcasting, broadcast

NOUN **1** a programme or announcement on radio or television

VERB **2** When someone **broadcasts** something, they send it out by radio waves, so that it can be seen on television or heard on radio.

broccoli

NOUN a vegetable with green stalks and green or purple flower buds

brochure brochures

NOUN a booklet that gives information about a product or a service • *holiday brochure*

broke

VERB **1** the past tense of **break**

ADJECTIVE **2** If you are **broke**, you have no money.

broken

ADJECTIVE A **broken** object is damaged in some way.

bronchitis

NOUN an illness in which the tubes connecting your windpipe to your lungs become infected, making you cough

brontosaurus brontosauruses

NOUN a very large, plant-eating dinosaur

bronze

NOUN a yellowish-brown metal that is a mixture of copper and tin

brooch brooches

Rhymes with "coach" NOUN a piece of jewellery with a pin at the back for attaching to clothes

brood broods, brooding, brooded

NOUN **1** a family of baby birds

VERB **2** If you **brood** about something, you are worried about it and can't stop thinking about it.

brook brooks

NOUN a stream

broom brooms

NOUN a long-handled brush

brother brothers

NOUN Your **brother** is a boy or man who has the same parents as you.

brother-in-law brothers-in-law

NOUN Someone's **brother-in-law** is the brother of their husband or wife, or their sister's husband.

a
b
c
d
e
f
g
h
i
j
k
l
m
n
o
p
q
r
s
t
u
v
w
x
y
z

brought

VERB the past tense and past participle of **bring**

🖊 Do not confuse *brought* with *bought*.

brown **browner, brownest**

ADJECTIVE OR NOUN the colour of earth or wood

Brownie **Brownies**

NOUN a junior member of the Girl Guides

bruise **bruises, bruising, bruised**

NOUN **1** a purple mark that appears on your skin after something has hit it
VERB **2** If something **bruises** you, it hits you so that a bruise appears on your skin.

brunette **brunettes**

NOUN a girl or a woman with dark brown hair

brush **brushes, brushing, brushed**

NOUN **1** an object with bristles. There are **brushes** for cleaning things, painting or tidying your hair.

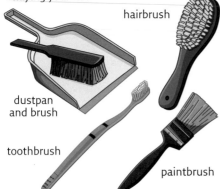

hairbrush

dustpan and brush

toothbrush

paintbrush

VERB **2** If you **brush** something, you clean it or tidy it with a brush.

Brussels sprout **Brussels sprouts**

NOUN a vegetable that looks like a tiny cabbage

brutal

ADJECTIVE **Brutal** behaviour is violent and cruel.

brutally ADVERB **brutality** NOUN

bubble **bubbles, bubbling, bubbled**

NOUN **1** a ball of air in a liquid
VERB **2** When a liquid **bubbles**, bubbles form in it.

buck **bucks, bucking, bucked**

NOUN **1** the male of various animals, including deer and rabbits
VERB **2** If a horse **bucks**, it jumps into the air with all four feet off the ground.

bucket **buckets**

NOUN a deep, round container with an open top and a handle

buckle **buckles, buckling, buckled**

NOUN **1** a fastening on the end of a belt or strap
VERB **2** If you **buckle** a belt or strap, you fasten it.
3 If metal **buckles**, it crumples up.

bud **buds**

NOUN a small, tight swelling on a tree or plant, which develops into a flower or leaf

Buddhist

NOUN someone who follows the religious teachings of Buddha, who taught in India in the fifth century. **Buddhists** believe that the way to end suffering is by overcoming our desires.

Buddhism NOUN

budgerigar **budgerigars**

NOUN a small, brightly-coloured pet bird. **Budgerigars** originated in Australia. [an Australian Aboriginal name, from *budgeri + gar* meaning good cockatoo]

budget **budgets, budgeting, budgeted**

NOUN **1** a plan showing how much money will be available and how it will be spent
VERB **2** If you **budget** for something, you plan how you use your money carefully, so as to be able to afford what you want.

buffalo **buffaloes**

NOUN **1** a wild animal like a large cow with long curved horns
2 another word for **bison**

buffet buffets

NOUN **1** a café at a station or on a train **2** a meal at which people serve themselves

bug bugs, bugging, bugged

NOUN **1** a small insect, especially one that causes damage
2 an infection or virus that makes you ill
3 a small error in a computer programme that stops it working properly
VERB **4** If a place is **bugged**, tiny microphones are hidden there to pick up what people are saying.

build builds, building, built

VERB If you **build** something, you make it from all its parts.

builder builders

NOUN a person whose job is to build buildings

building buildings

NOUN a structure with walls and a roof

bulb bulbs

NOUN **1** the glass part of an electric lamp
2 an onion-shaped root from which a flower or plant grows. Tulips and daffodils are grown from **bulbs**.
[from Greek *bolbos* meaning onion]

bulge bulges, bulging, bulged

VERB **1** If something **bulges**, it swells out.
NOUN **2** a lump on a normally flat surface

bulk bulks

NOUN **1** a large mass of something
PHRASE **2** If you buy something **in bulk**, you buy it in large quantities.

bulky bulkier, bulkiest

ADJECTIVE Something that is **bulky** is large and heavy and sometimes difficult to move.

bull bulls

NOUN the male of some animal species including cattle, elephants and whales

bulldozer bulldozers

NOUN a powerful tractor with a broad blade in front, which is used for moving earth or knocking things down

bullet bullets

NOUN a small piece of metal fired from a gun

bulletin bulletins

NOUN a short news report on radio or television

bullion

NOUN gold or silver bars

bullock bullocks

NOUN a young male bull that is reared for meat

bully bullies, bullying, bullied

NOUN **1** someone who uses their strength or power to hurt or frighten other people
VERB **2** If someone **bullies** you into doing something, they make you do it by using force or threats.
[a sixteenth-century word meaning fine fellow or hired ruffian]

bump bumps, bumping, bumped

VERB **1** If you **bump** into something, you knock into it accidentally.
NOUN **2** a soft noise made by something knocking into something else
3 a raised, uneven part of a surface
SYNONYMS: bulge, lump

bumper bumpers

NOUN a bar on the front or back of a vehicle that protects it if it bumps into something

bumpy bumpier, bumpiest

ADJECTIVE Something that is **bumpy** has a rough, uneven surface. • *a **bumpy** road*

bun buns

NOUN a small, round bread roll or cake

bunch bunches

NOUN a group of things together • *a **bunch** of flowers*

bundle bundles, bundling, bundled

NOUN **1** a number of things tied together or wrapped up in a cloth
VERB **2** If you **bundle** someone or something somewhere, you push them there quickly and roughly.

bungalow bungalows

NOUN a one-storey house
[from Hindi *bangla* meaning house]

a
b
c
d
e
f
g
h
i
j
k
l
m
n
o
p
q
r
s
t
u
v
w
x
y
z

bunk **bunks**

NOUN a bed fixed to a wall in a ship or caravan

bunk beds

PLURAL NOUN two beds fixed together, one above the other

buoy **buoys**

NOUN a floating object anchored to the bottom of the sea, marking a channel or warning of danger

buoyancy

NOUN Something that has **buoyancy** is able to float in liquid or in the air.

buoyant

ADJECTIVE **1** Something that is **buoyant** is able to float.
2 Someone who is **buoyant** is lively and cheerful.

burden **burdens**

NOUN a heavy load

burger **burgers**

NOUN a flat fried cake of meat, vegetables or cheese, served in a bread roll

burglar **burglars**

NOUN someone who breaks into buildings and steals things
burgle VERB

burn **burns, burning, burned** or **burnt**

VERB **1** If something is **burning**, it is on fire.
2 To **burn** something means to damage or destroy it with fire.
3 People often **burn** fuel, such as coal, to keep warm.
NOUN **4** A **burn** is an injury caused by fire or by something hot.

✏️ You can write either *burned* or *burnt* as the past form of *burn*.

burqa **burqas**; also spelt **burka**

Said "**bur**-ka" NOUN a long garment worn by some Muslim women in public, covering everything except the eyes

burrow **burrows, burrowing, burrowed**

NOUN **1** a tunnel or hole in the ground dug by a small animal

VERB **2** When an animal **burrows**, it digs a burrow.

burst **bursts, bursting, burst**

VERB **1** When something **bursts**, or when you **burst** it, it splits open suddenly.
2 When you **burst** into a room, you enter suddenly and with force.
NOUN **3** A **burst** of something is a sudden short period of it. • *a **burst** of applause*

bury **buries, burying, buried**

VERB **1** If you **bury** something, you put it in a hole in the ground and cover it with earth.
2 If something is **buried** under something, it is covered by it. • *My trainers were **buried** under a pile of clothes.*

bus **buses**

NOUN a large motor vehicle that carries passengers
[from Latin *omnibus* meaning for all]

bush **bushes**

NOUN **1** a large plant, smaller than a tree and with a lot of woody branches
2 In Australia and South Africa, an uncultivated area outside a town or city is called the **bush**.
3 In New Zealand, the **bush** is land covered by rainforest.

bushy **bushier, bushiest**

ADJECTIVE **Bushy** hair or fur grows very thickly. • *My dad has **bushy** eyebrows.*

business **businesses**

NOUN **1** work relating to the buying and selling of goods and services
2 an organization that produces or sells goods, or provides a service
SYNONYMS: company, firm, organization

busker **buskers**

NOUN someone who sings or plays music in public places for money

bus stop **bus stops**

NOUN a place where the bus stops regularly for passengers to get on or off, usually marked with a sign

busy **busier, busiest**

ADJECTIVE **1** If you are **busy**, you are doing something and are not free to do

anything else. ● *She was too **busy** to come to the cinema with us.*
2 A **busy** place is full of people doing things or moving about.

but

CONJUNCTION **1** used to introduce an idea that is opposite to what has gone before ● *I love cooking, **but** I hate washing up afterwards.*
2 used when you apologize for something ● *Sorry, **but** I can't come to play tomorrow.*
PREPOSITION **3** except ● *There was nothing to eat **but** potatoes.*

butcher butchers

NOUN a shopkeeper who prepares and sells meat

butter

NOUN a soft, fatty food made from cream, which is spread on bread and used in cooking

buttercup buttercups

NOUN a wild plant with bright yellow flowers

butterfly butterflies

NOUN a type of insect with large, colourful wings. **Butterflies** develop from caterpillars.

buttocks

PLURAL NOUN Your **buttocks** are the part of your body that you sit on.
[from Old English *buttuc* meaning rounded slope]

button buttons, buttoning, buttoned

NOUN **1** a small, hard round object sewn on to clothing such as shirts ● *My new jeans fasten with **buttons** instead of a zip.*
2 a small object on a piece of equipment that you press to make it work ● *You must*
push the **button** down to switch the video on.
VERB **3** If you **button** a garment, you fasten it using its buttons.

buy buys, buying, bought

VERB If you **buy** something, you get it by paying money for it.

buzz buzzes, buzzing, buzzed

VERB If something **buzzes**, it makes a humming sound, like a bee.

buzzer buzzers

NOUN a device that makes a buzzing sound. **Buzzers** are used to attract attention. ● *I pressed the door **buzzer** but nobody was home.*

by

PREPOSITION **1** used to show who or what has done something ● *The announcement was made **by** the head teacher.*
2 used to show how something is done ● *He cheered us up **by** taking us to the cinema.*
3 next to or near to ● *They live **by** the park.*
4 before a particular time ● *We should finish **by** tea time.*
PREPOSITION OR ADVERB **5** going past ● *We drove **by** her house.*

bypass bypasses

NOUN a road that takes traffic around the edge of a town instead of through the middle ● *The centre of town is much quieter since they built the **bypass**.*

byte bytes

NOUN a unit of storage in a computer

Cc

cab **cabs**
NOUN **1** a taxi
2 The **cab** is where the driver sits in a lorry, bus or train.

cabbage **cabbages**
NOUN a large, green, leafy vegetable

cabin **cabins**
NOUN **1** a room in a ship where a passenger sleeps
2 a small wooden house, usually in the country

cabinet **cabinets**
NOUN **1** a small cupboard • *a medicine cabinet*
2 The **cabinet** in a government is a group of ministers who advise the leader and decide policies.

cable **cables**
NOUN **1** a strong, thick rope or chain
2 a bundle of wires with a rubber covering, which carries electricity

cable television
NOUN a television service that comes through underground wires

cactus **cacti** or **cactuses**
NOUN a thick, fleshy plant that grows in deserts. **Cactuses** are usually covered in spikes.

cadet **cadets**
NOUN a young person being trained in the armed forces or police

café **cafés**
NOUN a place where you can buy light meals and drinks
[from the French *café* meaning coffee or coffee house]

caffeine; also spelt **caffein**
NOUN a chemical in coffee and tea that makes you more active

cage **cages**
NOUN a box or room made with bars, in which birds or animals are kept
caged ADJECTIVE

cake **cakes, caking, caked**
NOUN **1** a sweet food made from eggs, flour, butter and sugar
2 a block of a hard substance such as soap
VERB **3** If something is **caked**, it becomes covered with a solid layer of something else. • *My shoes were **caked** in mud.*

calamity **calamities**
NOUN something terrible that happens, causing destruction and misery • *The earthquake was a terrible **calamity**.*
SYNONYMS: disaster, catastrophe

calcium
*Said "**kal**-see-um"* NOUN a soft white mineral found in bones and teeth and in some foods. Milk and cheese are good sources of **calcium**.

calculate **calculates, calculating, calculated**
VERB If you **calculate** something, you work it out, usually by doing some arithmetic. • *We **calculated** how much money we had raised from the sponsored walk.*
[from Latin *calculus* meaning stone or pebble, which the Romans used for counting]

calculation **calculations**
NOUN something that you think about carefully and work out mathematically, or that you do on a machine such as a calculator

calculator **calculators**
NOUN a small electronic machine used for doing mathematical calculations

calendar **calendars**
NOUN a chart, usually organized month by month, showing the date of each day in a particular year • *We marked the end of term on the **calendar** in red.*

calf **calves**
NOUN **1** a young cow
2 Your **calves** are the backs of your legs between your knees and ankles.

call **calls, calling, called**
VERB **1** If you **call** someone or something a particular name, that is their name.
● *I will **call** my dog Spot.* ● *That type of machine is **called** a combine harvester.*
2 If you **call** someone, you telephone them.
3 If you **call** someone, you shout their name loudly.
NOUN **4** A **call** is a shout or a cry. ● *We heard a **call** for help.*

call off
VERB If something is **called off** it is cancelled. ● *The party was **called off**.*

call on
VERB If you **call on** someone, you pay them a short visit.

calm **calmer, calmest**
ADJECTIVE **1** Someone who is **calm** is quiet and does not show any worry or excitement.
2 If the sea is **calm**, the water is not moving very much.

calorie **calories**
NOUN The amount of energy that food gives you is measured in **calories**.

came
VERB the past tense of **come**

camel **camels**
NOUN a large mammal with either one or two humps on its back. **Camels** live in hot desert areas and are used for carrying people and things.

camera **cameras**
NOUN a piece of equipment used for taking photographs or for filming

camouflage **camouflages, camouflaging, camouflaged**
NOUN **1** a way of avoiding being seen by having the same colour or appearance as the surroundings
VERB **2** To **camouflage** something is to hide it by giving it the same colour or appearance as its surroundings.

camp **camps, camping, camped**
NOUN **1** a place where people live in tents or stay in tents for a holiday
VERB **2** If you **camp**, you stay in a tent.
NOUN **3** a collection of buildings for soldiers or prisoners
camper NOUN

campaign **campaigns, campaigning, campaigned**
VERB When people **campaign**, they take action in order to achieve something.
● *She **campaigned** against the export of live animals.*
campaign NOUN

can **could; cans**
VERB **1** If someone says you **can** do something, you are allowed to do it.
2 If you **can** do something, you are able to do it. ● *I **can** say "hello" in French.*
NOUN **3** a metal container, often sealed, with food or drink inside

canal **canals**
NOUN a long, narrow, man-made stretch of water

canary **canaries**
NOUN a yellow songbird

cancel **cancels, cancelling, cancelled**
VERB If you **cancel** something that has been arranged, you stop it from happening. ● *They **cancelled** the school trip.*

cancer **cancers**
NOUN a serious disease in which abnormal cells in a part of the body increase rapidly, causing growths

candidate candidates
NOUN a person who is being considered for a job

candle candles
NOUN a stick of hard wax with a piece of string called a wick through the middle. You light the wick to produce a flame.

cane canes
NOUN **1** the long, hollow stem of a plant such as bamboo
2 strips of **cane** used for weaving baskets and other containers
3 a long, narrow stick used to support plants

canine canines
ADJECTIVE **1** relating to dogs
NOUN **2** a **canine** is one of the pointed teeth near the front of the mouth in humans and some animals

cannibal cannibals
NOUN a person who eats human flesh

cannon cannons or cannon
NOUN a large gun, usually on wheels, which fires heavy iron balls

cannot
VERB the same as *can not*

canoe canoes
NOUN a small, narrow boat that you row using a paddle
canoeing NOUN canoeist NOUN

can't
VERB a contraction of *cannot*

canteen canteens
NOUN a place to eat in a school or workplace

canvas canvases
NOUN **1** strong, heavy cloth used for making things such as sails and tents
2 a piece of **canvas** on which an artist does a painting

canyon canyons
NOUN a narrow river valley with steep sides

cap caps
NOUN **1** a soft, flat hat, often with a peak at the front

2 a bottle top
3 a small explosive used in toy guns

capable
ADJECTIVE **1** If you are **capable** of doing something, you are able to do it.
2 Someone who is **capable** is able to do something well.

capacity capacities
NOUN the maximum amount that something can hold or produce • *The arena has a seating capacity of two thousand.*

capital capitals
NOUN **1** The **capital** of a country is the city where the government meets. • *Paris is the capital of France.*
2 A **capital**, or a **capital** letter, is a larger, upper-case letter used at the beginning of a sentence or a name: **C**arol, **T**im.

capsize capsizes, capsizing, capsized
VERB If a boat **capsizes**, it turns upside down.

capsule capsules
NOUN **1** a small container with medicine inside, which you swallow
2 the part of a spacecraft in which astronauts travel
[from Latin *capsula* meaning little box]

captain captains
NOUN **1** the officer in charge of a ship or aeroplane
2 the leader of a sports team

caption captions
NOUN a title printed underneath a picture or a photograph

captive captives
NOUN someone who is locked up and kept prisoner

capture captures, capturing, captured
VERB If someone **captures** someone or something, they take them prisoner.

car cars
NOUN **1** a four-wheeled road vehicle with an engine and room to carry a few passengers

2 a railway carriage used for a particular purpose • *the buffet* **car**

caravan caravans
NOUN **1** a vehicle pulled by a car in which people live or spend their holidays
2 a group of people and animals travelling together, usually across a desert

carbohydrate carbohydrates
NOUN a substance that gives you energy. It is found in foods like sugar and bread.

carbon
NOUN a chemical found in coal, diamonds and graphite. All living things contain **carbon**.

carbon dioxide
NOUN the gas that human beings and other animals breathe out

carbon footprint carbon footprints
NOUN the amount of carbon monoxide produced by a person, company or country

card cards
NOUN **1** a piece of stiff paper or plastic with a message or information on it
• *birthday* **card** • *credit* **card**
2 When you play **cards**, you play a game using special playing **cards**.
3 strong, stiff paper

cardboard
NOUN thick, stiff paper, which is stronger than card

cardigan cardigans
NOUN a knitted jacket that fastens up the front

care cares, caring, cared
VERB **1** If you **care** about something or someone, you are concerned about them and interested in them.
2 If you **care** for a person or an animal, you look after them.
NOUN **3** worry or trouble • *She didn't have a* **care** *in the world.*
4 If you do something with **care**, you concentrate very hard on it so that you don't make mistakes. • *He wrote the*
telephone number down with great **care**.
PHRASE **5** If you **take care of** a person or an animal, you look after them. • *Shakira said she would* **take care of** *the hamsters while we were on holiday.*

career careers
NOUN Your **career** is the series of jobs you have in life, often in the same occupation. • *a teaching* **career**

careful
ADJECTIVE acting sensibly and with care
ANTONYM: careless
carefully ADVERB

careless
ADJECTIVE not paying attention to what you are doing
SYNONYMS: slapdash, sloppy
carelessly ADVERB **carelessness** NOUN

caretaker caretakers
NOUN a person who looks after a large building such as a school

cargo cargoes
NOUN goods carried on a ship or plane

Caribbean
Said "carib-**ee**-un" NOUN **1** short for the **Caribbean** Sea, which lies between the West Indies and South America
ADJECTIVE **2** to do with the **Caribbean** Sea or the islands in it • *I love* **Caribbean** *food.*

carnation carnations
NOUN a plant with thin leaves and scented white, pink or red flowers

carnival carnivals
NOUN a public festival with music, processions and dancing

carnivore carnivores
NOUN an animal that eats meat
carnivorous ADJECTIVE

carol carols
NOUN a religious song sung at Christmas time

carpenter carpenters
NOUN a person who makes and repairs wooden things
carpentry NOUN

carpet carpets

NOUN a thick floor covering usually made of material like wool

carriage carriages

NOUN **1** one of the separate sections of a passenger train

2 an old-fashioned vehicle for carrying passengers, usually pulled by horses

Carroll diagram Carroll diagrams

NOUN a way of sorting and displaying information in the form of a grid

Walk	Do not walk	
③ Fiona Sophie Poppy	③ John Gavin Anita	Travel less than 1km
④ Kay Rabi Aaran Rajeev	④ Nina Mark George Krishna	Travel 1km or more

How Class 4 travel to school

carrot carrots

NOUN a long, thin, orange-coloured root vegetable

carry carries, carrying, carried

VERB **1** If you **carry** something, you hold it and take it somewhere.

2 When a vehicle **carries** people, they travel in it.

3 If people or animals **carry** a germ or a disease, they can pass it on to others.

4 If a sound **carries** it can be heard a long way off. ● *Their voices* **carried** *across the valley.*

cart carts

NOUN a vehicle with wheels, used for carrying things and usually pulled by horses or cattle

carton cartons

NOUN a cardboard or plastic container

cartoon cartoons

NOUN **1** a humorous drawing in a newspaper, comic or magazine

2 a film in which all the characters and scenes are drawn

cartridge cartridges

NOUN **1** a tube containing a bullet and an explosive substance, used in guns

2 a small plastic container filled with ink that you put in a pen or a printer

cartwheel cartwheels

NOUN an acrobatic movement in which you lift both arms in the air then throw yourself sideways on to one hand, swinging your body around in a circle with your legs straight until you land on your feet again

carve carves, carving, carved

VERB If you **carve** something, you shape it or slice it with a knife.

cascade cascades, cascading, cascaded

NOUN **1** a small waterfall or group of waterfalls flowing down a rocky hillside

VERB **2** When water **cascades**, it flows very fast down a hillside or over rocks.

case cases

NOUN **1** a box for keeping or carrying things in

2 a particular situation or event ● *a bad* **case** *of measles*

3 A crime that the police are investigating is called a **case**.

cash

NOUN money in notes and coins

cashier cashiers

NOUN the person who deals with money in a place such as a shop or a bank

casserole casseroles

NOUN **1** a stew made with meat, vegetables or fish that is baked in the oven

2 a dish with a lid, which is used for cooking

cast casts, casting, cast

NOUN **1** all the people who act in a play or film

2 an object made by pouring a liquid such as plaster into a container and leaving it to harden

VERB **3** If an object **casts** a shadow on to a place, it makes a shadow fall there.

castaway **castaways**
NOUN someone who has been shipwrecked but manages to survive on a lonely shore or an island

castle **castles**
NOUN a large building with walls or ditches round it to protect it from attack
[from Latin *castellum* meaning small fort]

casual
ADJECTIVE **1** happening by chance and without planning • *I made a* **casual** *remark.*
2 **Casual** clothes are suitable for informal occasions.

casualty **casualties**
NOUN a person killed or injured in an accident or a war • *There were many* **casualties** *after the motorway crash.*

cat **cats**
NOUN a small, furry mammal with whiskers, a tail and sharp claws, often kept as a pet

catalogue **catalogues**
NOUN a list of things, such as the goods you can buy from a company, the objects in a museum, or the books in a library • *I ordered my trainers from a mail order* **catalogue**.

catastrophe **catastrophes**
NOUN a terrible disaster
catastrophic ADJECTIVE

catch **catches, catching, caught**
VERB **1** If you **catch** an object that is moving through the air, you grasp it with your hands.
2 If you **catch** a person or animal, you capture them. • *The police* **caught** *the thief.*
3 If you **catch** a bus, train or plane, you get on it and travel somewhere.
4 If you **catch** a cold or a disease, you become ill with it.
NOUN **5** a hook that fastens or locks a door or window

catching
ADJECTIVE If a disease or illness is **catching** it spreads very quickly. • *Measles is* **catching**.

catchy **catchier, catchiest**
ADJECTIVE Something that is **catchy**, such as a tune, is pleasant and easy to remember.

category **categories**
NOUN a group of things that have something in common

caterpillar **caterpillars**
NOUN the larva of a butterfly or moth. **Caterpillars** look like small, coloured worms and feed on plants.

cathedral **cathedrals**
NOUN an important church with a bishop in charge of it • *Canterbury* **Cathedral**

Catholic **Catholics**
ADJECTIVE OR NOUN a Roman **Catholic**, or belonging to that religion

cattle
PLURAL NOUN cows and bulls kept by farmers

caught
VERB the past tense of **catch**

cauldron **cauldrons**
NOUN a large, round metal cooking pot, especially one that sits over a fire
[from Latin *caldarium* meaning hot bath]

cauliflower **cauliflowers**
NOUN a large, round, white vegetable surrounded by green leaves

cause **causes, causing, caused**
VERB **1** To **cause** something means to make it happen.
NOUN **2** The **cause** of something is the thing that makes it happen. • *The* **cause** *of the explosion was a gas leak.*

cautious
ADJECTIVE Someone who is **cautious** acts carefully in order to avoid danger or disappointment.

cavalry
NOUN The **cavalry** is the part of an army that fights on horseback or in armoured vehicles such as tanks.

cave **caves, caving, caved**
NOUN a large hole in the side of a cliff or under the ground

a b c d e f g h i j k l m n o p q r s t u v w x y z

cave in

VERB If a roof **caves in**, it collapses inwards.

caveman or **cavewoman**

cavemen or **cavewomen**

NOUN **Cavemen** and **cavewomen** were people who lived in caves in prehistoric times.

cavity **cavities**

NOUN a small hole in something solid

• *There were **cavities** in his back teeth.*

CD

NOUN an abbreviation for *compact disc*

CD-ROM

NOUN a way of storing video, sound or text on a compact disc that can be played on a computer. **CD-ROM** is an abbreviation for *compact disc read-only memory*.

cease **ceases, ceasing, ceased**

VERB **1** If something **ceases**, it stops.

2 If you **cease** doing something, you stop doing it.

ceiling **ceilings**

NOUN the roof inside a room

celebrate **celebrates, celebrating, celebrated**

VERB If you **celebrate** something, you do something special and enjoyable because of it. • *We felt like **celebrating** the end of exams.*

celebration NOUN

celebrity **celebrities**

NOUN a famous person

celery

NOUN a vegetable with long, pale green stalks

cell **cells**

NOUN **1** In biology, a **cell** is the smallest part of an animal or plant that can exist by itself. Humans, animals and plants are made up of millions of **cells**.

2 a small room in a prison or police station where a prisoner is locked up

nucleus

cell membrane

cellar **cellars**

NOUN a room underneath a building

cello **cellos**

*Said "**chel**-oh"* NOUN a large, stringed musical instrument that you play sitting down

cellist NOUN

Celsius

NOUN a scale for measuring temperature in which water freezes at 0 degrees (0 °C) and boils at 100 degrees (100 °C) [named after Anders *Celsius* (1701–1744) who invented it]

cement

NOUN a grey powder that is mixed with sand and water to make concrete

cemetery **cemeteries**

NOUN an area of land where dead people are buried

census **censuses**

NOUN an official survey of the population of a country

cent **cents**

NOUN In some countries a **cent** is a unit of currency.

centenary **centenaries**

NOUN the hundredth anniversary of something

centigrade

NOUN another word for **Celsius**

centimetre **centimetres**

NOUN a unit of length (cm). One **centimetre** is equal to ten millimetres (mm).

centipede **centipedes**

NOUN a long, thin creature with many pairs of legs [from Latin *centum* + *pedes* meaning a hundred feet]

central

ADJECTIVE **1** Something **central** is in the middle.

2 An idea that is **central** is the main idea.

central heating

NOUN a heating system in which water or air is heated and passed round a building through pipes and radiators

centre centres
NOUN **1** the middle of an object or area
2 a building where people go for activities, meetings, or help • *We played badminton at the sports **centre**.*

century centuries
NOUN a period of one hundred years

ceramic ceramics
Said "ser-**ram**-ic" NOUN **1** a hard material made by baking clay at very high temperatures
PLURAL NOUN **2 Ceramics** is the art of making objects out of clay.

cereal cereals
NOUN **1** a food made from grain, often eaten with milk for breakfast
2 a plant that produces edible grain, such as wheat, oats, barley and rye

ceremony ceremonies
NOUN a formal event such as a wedding or prizegiving

certain
ADJECTIVE **1** If you are **certain** about something, you are sure it is true. • *She is **certain** she wants to be a vet.*
2 You use **certain** to refer to a particular person, place or thing. • *I like **certain** animals, for example cats and dogs.*

certainly
ADVERB without any doubt • *"Will you be at the party?" "I **certainly** will."*

certificate certificates
NOUN an official piece of paper that proves that something took place • *a birth **certificate***

chaffinch chaffinches
NOUN a small European bird with black and white wings

chain chains
NOUN **1** a number of metal rings linked together in a line
2 a number of things in a series or connected to each other • *a **chain** of shops* • *a **chain** of events*

chair chairs
NOUN a seat for one person to sit on, with a back and four legs

chalet chalets
NOUN a small wooden house with a sloping roof, especially found in mountain areas or holiday camps

chalk
NOUN a soft, white rock. Small sticks of **chalk** are used for writing or drawing on a blackboard.
chalky ADJECTIVE

challenge challenges, challenging, challenged
NOUN **1** something new and exciting that needs a lot of effort • *Learning how to cook is a new **challenge** for me.*
VERB **2** If someone **challenges** you, they suggest that you compete with them. • *She **challenged** me to a game of table tennis.*

challenging
ADJECTIVE If you find something **challenging**, you find it quite difficult.

chameleon chameleons
NOUN a lizard that is able to change the colour of its skin to match the colour of its surroundings
[from Greek *khamai* + *leon* meaning ground lion]

champagne champagnes
NOUN a sparkling white wine made in France

champion champions
NOUN a person who wins a competition

championship championships
NOUN a competition to find the best player or players of a particular sport

chance chances
NOUN **1** how possible or likely something is • *I think we've got a good **chance** of winning.*
2 an opportunity to do something • *This is your **chance** to be a TV star!*
3 a possibility that something dangerous or unpleasant may happen
PHRASE **4** Something that happens **by chance** happens unexpectedly, without being planned.

a
b
c
d
e
f
g
h
i
j
k
l
m
n
o
p
q
r
s
t
u
v
w
x
y
z

63

chancellor chancellors
NOUN the head of government in some European countries

Chancellor of the Exchequer
NOUN the government minister in charge of finance and taxes in Britain

change changes, changing, changed
NOUN **1** money you get back when you pay for something with more money than it costs
VERB **2** When something **changes**, or you **change** it, it becomes different. • *The wind **changed** direction.*

channel channels
NOUN **1** a wavelength on which television programmes are broadcast. It can also be the television station itself.
2 a passage for water or other liquid
3 The **Channel**, or the English **Channel**, is the stretch of sea between England and France.

chaos
NOUN a state of complete disorder
• *The demonstration ended in **chaos**.*
chaotic ADJECTIVE

chapel chapels
NOUN **1** a section of a church or cathedral with its own altar
2 a type of small church

chapter chapters
NOUN one of the parts into which a book is divided

character characters
NOUN **1** all the qualities that make a person or a place special • *She has a gentle **character**.*
2 The **characters** in a film, play or book are the people in it.

characteristic characteristics
NOUN **1** a special quality about a person, place or thing
ADJECTIVE **2** typical of a place or person
• *Noise and traffic fumes are **characteristic** of cities.*

charades
NOUN a party game where one team guesses what the other team is acting out

charcoal
NOUN burnt wood used as a fuel.
Charcoal is also used for drawing.

charge charges, charging, charged
VERB **1** If someone **charges** you money, they ask you to pay for something you have bought or received.
2 rush forward • *She **charged** into the room.*
PHRASE **3** If you are **in charge of** someone or something, you are responsible for them. • *I left him **in charge of** the shop while I went out.*

chariot chariots
NOUN a two-wheeled open vehicle pulled by horses in ancient times

charity charities
NOUN **1** an organization that raises money to help people in need
2 money or other help given to people in need

charm charms, charming, charmed
NOUN **1** something you wear for good luck
2 the quality of being attractive and pleasant
VERB **3** If you **charm** someone, you use your charm to please them.

chart charts
NOUN a diagram or table showing information

chase chases, chasing, chased
VERB If you **chase** someone, you run after them or follow them in order to catch them or make them leave a place.

chat chats, chatting, chatted
NOUN **1** a friendly talk with someone
VERB **2** When people **chat**, they talk to each other in a friendly way about things that are not very important.
chatty ADJECTIVE

chatroom chatrooms
NOUN an internet site where users have discussions using e-mail

chatter chatters, chattering, chattered
VERB **1** When people **chatter**, they talk about unimportant things.

2 If your teeth **chatter**, they knock together and make a clicking noise because you are cold.

chauffeur **chauffeurs**
NOUN a person whose job is to drive another person's car • *He had a* **chauffeur** *to drive him everywhere.*

cheap **cheaper, cheapest**
ADJECTIVE **1** Something that is **cheap** costs very little money.
2 Cheap sometimes means of poor quality.
cheaply ADVERB

cheat **cheats, cheating, cheated**
VERB If someone **cheats** in a game or exam, they break the rules in order to do better.

check **checks, checking, checked**
VERB **1** If you **check** something, you examine it to make sure that everything is all right. • **Check** *your work carefully when you finish.*
NOUN **2** an inspection to make sure that everything is all right
3 Checks are different coloured squares that form a pattern.

checkout **checkouts**
NOUN the place in a supermarket where you pay for your goods

cheek **cheeks**
NOUN **1** Your **cheeks** are the sides of your face below your eyes.
2 speech or behaviour that is rude and disrespectful • *Their grandparents won't stand any* **cheek** *from them.*
cheeky ADJECTIVE   **cheekily** ADVERB

cheer **cheers, cheering, cheered**
VERB When people **cheer**, they shout loudly and happily. • *We* **cheered** *our team when they won.*

cheerful
ADJECTIVE A **cheerful** person is happy.
cheerfully ADVERB

cheese **cheeses**
NOUN a solid savoury food made from milk

cheetah **cheetahs**
NOUN a wild mammal like a large cat with black spots, mainly found in Africa [from Sanskrit *citra* + *kaya* meaning speckled body]

chef **chefs**
NOUN a head cook in a restaurant or hotel
[from French *chef* meaning head]

chemical **chemicals**
NOUN **1** a substance made by the use of chemistry • *Dangerous* **chemicals** *should be handled carefully.*
ADJECTIVE **2** involved in chemistry or using chemicals • *a* **chemical** *reaction*

chemist **chemists**
NOUN a shop that sells medicines and cosmetics

chemistry
NOUN the scientific study of substances and the ways in which they change when they are combined

cheque **cheques**
NOUN a printed piece of paper that people can use to pay for things

cherry **cherries**
NOUN a small, juicy fruit with a red, yellow or black skin and a hard stone in the centre

chess
NOUN a game played on a board with 64 squares. Each player has 16 pieces.

chest **chests**
NOUN **1** the front part of your body between your shoulders and your waist
2 a large wooden box used for storing things

chestnut **chestnuts**
NOUN **1** a reddish-brown nut that grows inside a prickly, green outer covering
2 the tree that produces these nuts
ADJECTIVE **3** Something that is **chestnut** is reddish-brown in colour.

a
b
c
d
e
f
g
h
i
j
k
l
m
n
o
p
q
r
s
t
u
v
w
x
y
z

chew chews, chewing, chewed
VERB When you **chew** something, you use your teeth to break it up in your mouth before swallowing it.

chewing gum
NOUN a kind of sweet that you chew for a long time, but which you do not swallow

chick chicks
NOUN a young bird

chicken chickens
NOUN a bird kept on a farm for its eggs and meat; also the meat of this bird

chickenpox
NOUN an illness that causes a fever and blister-like spots to appear on the skin

chief chiefs
NOUN **1** the leader of a group or organization
ADJECTIVE **2** main or most important

chilblain chilblains
NOUN a sore, itchy swelling on a finger or toe, which causes discomfort in cold weather

child children
NOUN **1** a young person who is not yet an adult
SYNONYMS: kid, youngster
2 Someone's **child** is their son or daughter.

childhood childhoods
NOUN Your **childhood** is the time when you are a child.

childish
ADJECTIVE If someone is **childish**, they are not acting in an adult way.
ANTONYM: adult
childishly ADVERB

childminder childminders
NOUN a person who is paid to look after children while their parents are at work

children
PLURAL NOUN the plural of **child**

chill chills, chilling, chilled
VERB **1** When you **chill** something, you make it cold. • *Chill the orange juice before you drink it.*
NOUN **2** a feverish cold
3 a feeling of cold • *the chill of early morning*

chilli chillies
NOUN the red or green seed pod of a type of pepper that has a very hot, spicy taste

chilly chillier, chilliest
ADJECTIVE **1** **Chilly** weather is rather cold.
2 If people behave in a **chilly** way, they are not very friendly.

chime chimes, chiming, chimed
VERB **1** When a bell **chimes**, it makes a clear ringing sound.
NOUN **2** **Chimes** are a set of bells or other objects that make ringing sounds.

chimney chimneys
NOUN a pipe above a fireplace or furnace through which smoke from the fire can escape

chimpanzee chimpanzees
NOUN a small ape with dark fur that lives in forests in Africa

chin chins
NOUN the part of your face below your mouth

china
NOUN plates, cups, saucers and other dishes that are made from fine clay

chink chinks
NOUN **1** a small, narrow opening • *a chink in the fence*
2 a small ringing sound, like glasses touching each other

chip chips, chipping, chipped
NOUN **1** **Chips** are thin strips of fried potato.
2 a tiny piece of silicon inside a computer, which is used to form electronic circuits • *computer chips*
VERB **3** If you **chip** an object, you break a small piece off it.

chirp chirps, chirping, chirped
VERB When a bird **chirps**, it makes a short, high-pitched sound.

chisel chisels, chiselling, chiselled

NOUN **1** a tool with a long metal blade and a sharp edge at the end. **Chisels** are used for cutting and shaping wood, stone or metal.

VERB **2** If you **chisel** wood, stone or metal, you cut or shape it using a chisel.

chlorine

NOUN a poisonous greenish-yellow gas with a strong, unpleasant smell. It is used to disinfect water and to make bleach.

chocolate chocolates

NOUN a sweet food made from cocoa beans [from Aztec *xococ + atl* meaning bitter water]

choice choices

NOUN **1** a range of different things that are available to choose from

SYNONYMS: range, variety

2 something that you choose • *You made a good **choice** when you bought this book.*

choir choirs

NOUN a group of singers, for example in a church

choke chokes, choking, choked

VERB If you **choke** on something, it prevents you from breathing properly. • *He **choked** on a fish bone.*

cholesterol

NOUN a substance found in all animal fats, tissues and blood

choose chooses, choosing, chose, chosen

VERB If you **choose** something, you decide to have it or do it.

SYNONYMS: pick, select

chop chops, chopping, chopped

VERB **1** If you **chop** something, you cut it with quick, heavy strokes using an axe or a knife. • *Mum **chopped** the logs for firewood.*

NOUN **2** a small piece of pork or lamb that contains a bone • *We had **chops** and broccoli for dinner.*

choppy

ADJECTIVE When the sea or a stretch of water is **choppy**, there are a lot of waves on it because it is windy.

chopstick chopsticks

NOUN **Chopsticks** are a pair of thin sticks used for eating Chinese and Japanese food.

choral

*Said "**kor**-al"* ADJECTIVE for a choir

chord chords

NOUN a group of three or more musical notes played together

chore chores

NOUN an uninteresting job that has to be done

chorus choruses

NOUN **1** a part of a song that is repeated after each verse
2 a large group of singers

chose

VERB the past tense of **choose**

chosen

VERB **1** the past participle of **choose**
2 When you are **chosen**, you are picked to do something. • *I was **chosen** for the volleyball team.*

christen christens, christening, christened

VERB When a priest **christens** someone, they name them in a ceremony where water is poured over their head as a sign that they are a member of the Christian church.

christening NOUN

Christian Christians

NOUN a person who believes in Jesus Christ and his teachings

Christianity NOUN

Christmas Christmases

NOUN a Christian festival held on December 25th to celebrate the birth of Jesus Christ

chrome

*Said "**krome**"* NOUN metal plated with chromium, a hard, silver-grey metal

A
B
C
D
E
F
G
H
I
J
K
L
M
N
O
P
Q
R
S
T
U
V
W
X
Y
Z

chromosome **chromosomes**
Said "krome-uh-soam" NOUN the part of a cell in living things that contains the genes that determine what characteristics the animal or plant will have

chronic
ADJECTIVE lasting a very long time or never stopping • *He suffers from* ***chronic*** *hay fever.*

chronological
ADJECTIVE arranged in the order in which things happened • *Tell me the whole story in* ***chronological*** *order.*
chronologically ADVERB

chrysalis **chrysalises**
NOUN a butterfly or moth when it is developing from being a caterpillar to being a fully grown adult

chrysanthemum
chrysanthemums
NOUN a plant with large, brightly-coloured flowers

chuckle **chuckles, chuckling, chuckled**
VERB When you **chuckle**, you laugh quietly.

chunk **chunks**
NOUN a thick piece of something
SYNONYMS: hunk, lump, piece

church **churches**
NOUN a building where Christians go for religious services and worship

churchyard **churchyards**
NOUN an area of land around a church, often used as a graveyard

churn **churns, churning, churned**
NOUN **1** a container used for making milk or cream into butter
VERB **2** When you **churn** something, you stir it vigorously, for example when making milk into butter.

churn out
VERB If you **churn out** something, you produce it quickly in large numbers.
• *They* ***churned out*** *hundreds of leaflets advertising the dance.*

chutney
NOUN a strong-tasting, thick sauce made from fruit, vinegar and spices

cider
NOUN an alcoholic drink made from apples

cigar **cigars**
NOUN a roll of dried tobacco leaves, which people smoke

cigarette **cigarettes**
NOUN a thin tube of paper containing tobacco, which people smoke

cinder **cinders**
NOUN **Cinders** are small pieces of burnt material left after something such as wood or coal has burned.

cinema **cinemas**
NOUN a place where people go to watch films

circle **circles, circling, circled**
NOUN **1** a regular, two-dimensional round shape. Every point on the edge is the same distance from the centre.
VERB **2** to move around in a circle
• *Seagulls* ***circled*** *overhead.*
circular ADJECTIVE

circuit **circuits**
NOUN **1** the path of an electric current
2 a racecourse
3 A training **circuit** is a course of physical activities.

circulation **circulations**
NOUN **1** the movement of blood around a body
2 the number of copies of a newspaper or magazine that are sold each time it is issued

circumference
circumferences
NOUN **1** the outer line or edge of a circle
2 The length of this line is also called the **circumference**.

circumference

circumstance **circumstances**
NOUN The **circumstances** of a situation or event are the conditions that affect

what happens. • *He did well under difficult circumstances*.

circus circuses
NOUN a travelling show performed in a large tent, with performers such as clowns and acrobats

cistern cisterns
NOUN a tank in which water is stored, such as in the roof of a house, or above a toilet

citizen citizens
NOUN The **citizens** of a country or city are the people who live in it or belong to it.

citrus fruit citrus fruits
NOUN **Citrus fruits** are juicy, sharp-tasting fruits such as oranges, lemons and grapefruit.

city cities
NOUN a large town where many people live and work

civil
ADJECTIVE **1** relating to the citizens of a place
2 Someone who is **civil** is polite.

civilian civilians
NOUN a person who is not in the armed forces

civilization civilizations; also spelt **civilisation**
NOUN **1** a large group of people with a high level of organization and culture
• *We're learning about the ancient **civilizations** of Greece, Rome and Egypt.*
2 a highly developed and organized way of life

civilized; also spelt **civilised**
ADJECTIVE **1** A **civilized** society is one with a highly developed social organization and a comfortable way of life.
2 A **civilized** person is polite and reasonable.

civil war civil wars
NOUN a war between groups of people who live in the same country

claim claims, claiming, claimed
VERB **1** If you **claim** that something is the case, you say that it is so.

2 If you **claim** something, you ask for it because you believe you have a right to it.

clamber clambers, clambering, clambered
VERB If you **clamber** somewhere, you climb there with difficulty. • *We **clambered** over the rocks to get to the beach.*

clammy clammier, clammiest
ADJECTIVE unpleasantly damp and sticky
• *The weather was very **clammy**.*

clamp clamps, clamping, clamped
NOUN **1** a device that holds something firmly in place
VERB **2** When you **clamp** one thing to another, you fasten them together with a clamp.

clan clans
NOUN a group of families related to each other by being descended from the same ancestor

clang clangs, clanging, clanged
VERB When something made of metal **clangs**, or when you **clang** it, it makes a loud, ringing sound.

clank clanks, clanking, clanked
VERB When something **clanks**, it makes a loud, metallic sound.

clap claps, clapping, clapped
VERB **1** When you **clap**, you hit your hands together loudly to show that you have enjoyed something or that you approve of something.
NOUN **2** a sudden loud noise of thunder

clarify clarifies, clarifying, clarified
VERB If you **clarify** something, you make it clear and easier to understand.
clarification NOUN

clarinet clarinets
NOUN a woodwind instrument with a straight tube and a single reed in its mouthpiece

clarity
NOUN The **clarity** of something is its clearness. • *The **clarity** of the water made me think it was very clean.*

clash clashes, clashing, clashed
VERB **1** Colours or ideas that **clash** are so different that they do not go together. • *Debbie's red shirt **clashed** with her green shorts.*
2 If one event **clashes** with another, they happen at the same time, so you cannot go to both.
3 If people **clash** with each other, they fight or argue.

clasp clasps, clasping, clasped
VERB **1** If you **clasp** something, you hold it tightly.
NOUN **2** a fastening such as a hook or a catch

class classes
NOUN **1** a group of pupils or students taught together, or a lesson that they have together
2 A **class** of people or things is a group of them of a particular type. • *Beetles and ants belong to different **classes** of insect.*
SYNONYMS: group, kind, type

classic
ADJECTIVE Something described as **classic** is considered a high quality example of something. • *He has a **classic** car.*

classical
ADJECTIVE **1** traditional in style and content • *classical ballet*
2 Classical music is serious music thought to be of lasting value.

classify classifies, classifying, classified
VERB to arrange things into groups with something in common • *We **classified** the foods into three groups: fruits, vegetables and meats.*
classification NOUN

classroom classrooms
NOUN a room in a school where lessons take place

clatter clatters, clattering, clattered
VERB **1** When things **clatter**, they hit each other with a loud, rattling noise.
NOUN **2** a loud noise made by hard things hitting against each other • *There was a great **clatter** when the waitress dropped the tray.*

clause clauses
NOUN In grammar, a **clause** is a group of words with a subject and a verb, which may be a complete sentence or part of a sentence.

claw claws, clawing, clawed
NOUN **1** An animal's **claws** are the hard, curved nails at the end of its feet.
2 The **claws** of a crab or a lobster are the two jointed parts at the end of the leg, used for holding things.
VERB **3** 3 If an animal claws something, it digs its claws into it

clay
NOUN a type of earth that is soft and sticky when wet and hard when baked dry. It is used to make pottery and bricks.

clean cleaner, cleanest; cleans, cleaning, cleaned
ADJECTIVE **1** free from dirt or unwanted marks
VERB **2** to remove dirt from something

clear clearer, clearest; clears, clearing, cleared
ADJECTIVE **1** easy to understand, see or hear • *The instructions on the packet were very clear.*
2 easy to see through • *a **clear** liquid*
VERB **3** To **clear** unwanted things from a place is to remove them. • *We **cleared** the dirty dishes from the table.*
4 If you **clear** a fence or other obstacle, you jump over it without touching it.
clearly ADVERB

clear up
VERB When you **clear up** a place, you tidy it and put things away.

clench clenches, clenching, clenched
VERB **1** When you **clench** your fist, you curl your fingers up tightly.
2 When you **clench** your teeth, you squeeze them together tightly, either in pain or in anger.

clerk **clerks**
NOUN a person who keeps records or accounts in an office, bank or law court

clever **cleverer, cleverest**
ADJECTIVE **1** intelligent and quick to understand things
SYNONYMS: bright, intelligent, smart
2 very effective or skilful • *We came up with a **clever** plan.*

cliché **clichés**
NOUN an idea or phrase that is no longer effective because it has been used so much. For example, *in this day and age* and *over the moon*.

click **clicks, clicking, clicked**
VERB **1** When something **clicks** or when you **click** it, it makes a short snapping sound.
NOUN **2** a sound of something clicking

client **clients**
NOUN someone who pays a professional person or company for a service

cliff **cliffs**
NOUN a high area of land with a very steep side, usually next to the sea

cliffhanger **cliffhangers**
NOUN a very exciting or frightening situation, usually in a television or radio serial, where you are left not knowing what is going to happen next

climate **climates**
NOUN the general weather conditions that are typical of a place

climax **climaxes**
NOUN the most exciting moment of something, usually near the end

climb **climbs, climbing, climbed**
VERB **1** If you **climb** something, such as a tree, mountain or ladder, you move towards the top of it.
2 If you **climb** somewhere, you move there with difficulty. • *We **climbed** over the high wall.*
NOUN **3** a movement upwards • *I was tired after the long **climb** to the top of the hill.*
climber NOUN

cling **clings, clinging, clung**
VERB If you **cling** to something, you hold on to it tightly.

clinic **clinics**
NOUN a place where people go for medical advice or treatment

clip **clips, clipping, clipped**
NOUN **1** a small metal or plastic object used for holding things together
2 a short piece of a film shown by itself
VERB **3** If you **clip** something, you cut bits from it to shape it.

clipboard **clipboards**
NOUN a stiff piece of board or plastic, with a clip at the top to keep papers in place

clippers
PLURAL NOUN a tool used for cutting • *hedge **clippers***

cloak **cloaks, cloaking, cloaked**
NOUN **1** a wide, loose coat without sleeves
VERB **2** If something **cloaks** something else, it covers or hides it. • *The mist **cloaked** the land.*

cloakroom **cloakrooms**
NOUN **1** a room where you can leave coats and luggage for a while
2 a room with toilets and washbasins in a public building

clock **clocks**
NOUN an instrument that measures and shows the time

clockwise
ADVERB in the same direction as the hands on a clock

clockwork
NOUN **1** Toys that move by **clockwork** are wound up with a key.
PHRASE **2** If something goes **like clockwork**, it happens with no problems or delays.

clog **clogs, clogging, clogged**
VERB **1** When something is **clogged**, or when you **clog** something up, it becomes blocked and doesn't work properly or

clone

doesn't allow things to move freely.
• The traffic was **clogging** the roads.
NOUN **2** a shoe made entirely of wood, originally from the Netherlands

clone clones
NOUN an animal or plant that is an identical copy of another animal or plant

close closes, closing, closed; closer, closest
Said "**klohz**" VERB **1** If you **close** something, you move it so that it is no longer open. • He **closed** the door behind him.
2 If a shop or other building **closes** at a certain time, it does not do business after that time.
Said "**klohss**" ADJECTIVE **3** Something that is **close** to something else is near to it.
SYNONYMS: near, nearby
4 People who are **close** are very friendly with each other and know each other well.
5 If the weather is **close**, it is uncomfortably warm and stuffy.
NOUN **6** a street that is closed at one end
• We live in Park **Close**.
closely ADVERB

close-up close-ups
Said "**klohss**-up" NOUN A **close-up** in a film or a photograph is taken at very close range and shows things in great detail.

cloth cloths
NOUN **1** fabric made by a process such as weaving
2 a piece of material used for wiping or protecting things

clothes
PLURAL NOUN things people wear on their bodies

cloud clouds
NOUN **1** a mass of water vapour that is seen as a white or grey patch in the sky
2 A **cloud** of smoke or dust is a mass of it floating in the air.

cloudy cloudier, cloudiest
ADJECTIVE **1** full of clouds • The sky was **cloudy**.
SYNONYMS: dull, overcast

2 difficult to see through • a **cloudy** liquid
SYNONYM: murky

clover
NOUN a small plant with leaves made up of three similar parts

clown clowns
NOUN a circus performer who wears funny clothes and make-up and does silly things to make people laugh

club clubs
NOUN **1** a group of people with similar interests, who meet regularly. The place where they meet is also called a **club**.
• a youth **club**
2 a team that competes in sports competitions

clue clues
NOUN something that helps solve a problem or mystery • Police have found **clues** to the robbery.

clueless
ADJECTIVE INFORMAL If you say that someone is **clueless**, you think they are stupid and not able to do things properly.

clump clumps
NOUN a small group of things growing or standing close together • a **clump** of trees

clumsy clumsier, clumsiest
ADJECTIVE moving awkwardly and carelessly
SYNONYMS: awkward, ungainly
clumsily ADVERB

clung
VERB the past tense and past participle of **cling**

cluster clusters, clustering, clustered
NOUN **1** a group of things together
• There is a **cluster** of houses by the lake.
VERB **2** If people **cluster** together, they stay together in a close group.
[from Old English clyster meaning bunch of grapes]

clutch clutches, clutching, clutched
VERB If you **clutch** something, you hold it tightly or seize it.

clutter clutters, cluttering, cluttered
NOUN **1** an untidy mess
VERB **2** Things that **clutter** a place fill it and make it untidy.

coach coaches, coaching, coached
NOUN **1** a large bus that takes passengers on long journeys
2 a section of a train that carries passengers
VERB **3** If someone **coaches** you, they help you to get better at a sport or a subject.
SYNONYMS: instruct, train
NOUN **4** someone who coaches a person or sports team

coal
NOUN a hard, black rock taken from under the ground and burned as a fuel

coarse coarser, coarsest
ADJECTIVE **1** Something that is **coarse** is rough in texture.
2 Someone who is **coarse** talks or behaves in a rude, offensive way.
coarsely ADVERB **coarseness** NOUN

coast coasts, coasting, coasted
NOUN **1** the edge of the land where it meets the sea
VERB **2** If a vehicle **coasts** somewhere, it moves there with the engine switched off. • *The car coasted quietly down the hill.*
coastal ADJECTIVE

coastguard coastguards
NOUN an official who watches the sea near a coast to get help for sailors when they need it

coat coats, coating, coated
NOUN **1** a piece of outdoor clothing with sleeves, which you wear over other clothes
2 An animal's **coat** is the fur or hair on its body.
3 A **coat** of paint or varnish is a layer of it.
VERB **4** If you **coat** something, you cover it with a thin layer of something. • *We coated the biscuits with chocolate.*

coating coatings
NOUN a thin layer of something spread over a surface

coax coaxes, coaxing, coaxed
VERB If you **coax** someone to do something, you persuade them gently to do it.

cobble cobbles
NOUN **Cobbles** or cobblestones are stones with a rounded surface that were used in the past for making roads.

cobra cobras
NOUN a type of large poisonous snake from Africa and Asia

cobweb cobwebs
NOUN the very thin net that a spider spins to catch insects

cock cocks
NOUN an adult male chicken, or any other male bird

cockerel cockerels
NOUN a young cock

cockle cockles
NOUN a type of small, edible shellfish

Cockney Cockneys
NOUN someone who was born in the East End of London

cockpit cockpits
NOUN **1** the area in a plane where the pilot sits in control
2 the driver's compartment in a racing car

cockroach cockroaches
NOUN a large, dark-coloured insect often found in dirty rooms
[from Spanish *cucaracha*]

cocky cockier, cockiest
ADJECTIVE INFORMAL If you are **cocky**, you are sure of yourself and sometimes rather cheeky.

cocoa
NOUN **1** a brown powder made from the seeds of a tropical tree and used for making chocolate
2 a hot drink made from this powder

a
b
c
d
e
f
g
h
i
j
k
l
m
n
o
p
q
r
s
t
u
v
w
x
y
z

coconut **coconuts**
NOUN a very large nut with white flesh, milky juice, and a hard hairy shell

cocoon **cocoons**
NOUN a silky covering over the larvae of moths and some other insects

cod
NOUN a large, edible fish

🖉 The plural of *cod* is *cod*.

code **codes**
NOUN **1** a system of replacing the letters or words in a message with other letters or words, so that nobody can understand the message unless they know the system ● *They wrote messages in **code**.*
2 a group of numbers and letters used to identify something ● *the telephone **code** for Falmouth*

coeducation
NOUN **Coeducation** is a system where girls and boys are taught together at the same school.
coeducational ADJECTIVE

coffee
NOUN **1** a powder made by roasting and grinding the beans of the **coffee** plant
2 a hot drink made from **coffee**

coffin **coffins**
NOUN a box in which a dead body is buried or cremated

cog **cogs**
NOUN a wheel with teeth, which turns another wheel or part of a machine

coil **coils, coiling, coiled**
NOUN **1** a length of rope or wire wound into a series of loops
2 A single loop is also called a **coil**.
VERB **3** If something **coils**, or if you **coil** it, it winds into a series of loops.
● *The snake **coiled** around the branch.*

coin **coins, coining, coined**
NOUN **1** a small metal disc used as money
VERB **2** If you **coin** a word or a phrase, you invent it.

coinage
NOUN the coins that are used in a particular country

coincide **coincides, coinciding, coincided**
VERB When two things **coincide**, they happen at the same time. ● *Auntie's visit **coincided** with my birthday.*

coincidence **coincidences**
NOUN what happens when two or more things occur at the same time by chance

coke
NOUN a grey fuel produced from coal

cola **colas**
NOUN a sweet, brown fizzy drink, like Coca-Cola

colander **colanders**
NOUN a bowl-shaped container with holes in it, used for washing or draining food

cold **colder, coldest; colds**
ADJECTIVE **1** If something is **cold**, it has a very low temperature.
2 If the weather is **cold**, the air temperature is very low.
NOUN **3** a minor illness that makes you sneeze and cough, and sometimes gives you a sore throat

cold-blooded
ADJECTIVE **1** A **cold-blooded** animal has a body temperature that changes according to the surrounding temperature.
2 Someone who is **cold-blooded** does not show any pity.
cold-bloodedly ADVERB

coleslaw
NOUN a salad of chopped cabbage and other vegetables in mayonnaise

collaborate **collaborates, collaborating, collaborated**
VERB When people **collaborate**, they work together to produce something. ● *The two schools **collaborated** to produce a play.*
collaboration NOUN **collaborator** NOUN

collage **collages**
NOUN a picture made by sticking pieces of paper or cloth on to a surface

collapse **collapses, collapsing, collapsed**
VERB **1** If something such as a building **collapses**, it falls down suddenly.
2 If a person **collapses**, they fall down suddenly because they are ill.

collapsible
ADJECTIVE A **collapsible** object can be folded flat when it is not in use.
• **collapsible** chairs

collar **collars**
NOUN **1** the part around the neck of something, such as a coat or shirt
2 a leather band round the neck of a dog or cat

colleague **colleagues**
NOUN A person's **colleagues** are the people they work with.

collect **collects, collecting, collected**
VERB **1** If you **collect** things, you gather them together for a special purpose or as a hobby.
2 If you **collect** someone or something from a place, you call there and take them away. • We **collected** Ali from school.
3 When things **collect** in a place, they gather there over a period of time. • Dust **collects** in corners.

collection **collections**
NOUN **1** a group of things you have gathered over a period of time • a stamp **collection**
2 the organized collecting of money, for example for charity, or the money collected

collective noun **collective nouns**
NOUN a noun that refers to a group of people or things. For example, a flock, a herd, and a shoal are all **collective nouns**.

college **colleges**
NOUN a place where students study after they have left school

collide **collides, colliding, collided**
VERB If a moving object **collides** with

something, it hits it. • They **collided** with each other as they rushed through the door.

collision **collisions**
NOUN A **collision** is when a moving object hits something.
SYNONYM: crash

colon **colons**
NOUN **1** the punctuation mark (:). It is used to introduce a list, a quotation or an explanation of a statement. • We need to buy several things: bread, milk, fruit and toothpaste.
2 part of your intestine

colonel **colonels**
NOUN an army officer with a fairly high rank

colony **colonies**
NOUN **1** a country that is controlled by another country
2 a group of people or animals living together

colossal
ADJECTIVE very large indeed
[from Greek kolossos meaning huge statue]

colour **colours**
NOUN the appearance something has as a result of reflecting light • Red, blue and yellow are the primary **colours**.

colour blind
ADJECTIVE Someone who is **colour blind** is not able to see the difference between certain colours.

colourful
ADJECTIVE **1** Something that is **colourful** has a lot of different colours or bright colours.
ANTONYMS: dull, colourless
2 A **colourful** story is very exciting and interesting.
ANTONYMS: dull, boring

colourless
ADJECTIVE **1** without colour
2 dull and uninteresting

colt **colts**
NOUN a young male horse

column **columns**
NOUN **1** a tall, solid, upright cylinder, especially one supporting part of a building

a
b
c
d
e
f
g
h
i
j
k
l
m
n
o
p
q
r
s
t
u
v
w
x
y
z

2 In a newspaper or magazine, a **column** is a vertical section of writing.
3 a group of people or vehicles moving in a long line

coma comas
NOUN a state of deep unconsciousness

comb combs, combing, combed
NOUN **1** a flat object with long, thin, pointed parts, which you use for tidying your hair
VERB **2** When you **comb** your hair, you tidy it with a comb.

combat combats, combating, combated
NOUN **1** fighting • *In the Falklands War many soldiers had to take part in armed **combat**.*
VERB **2** If someone **combats** something, they try to stop it happening. • *We need new ways to **combat** crime.*

combination combinations
NOUN **1** a mixture of things • *Fatima won the competition through a **combination** of skill and determination.*
2 a series of numbers or letters used to open a special lock

combine combines, combining, combined
VERB If you **combine** things, you mix them together. • ***Combine** the butter and sugar, then add the eggs.* • *The book **combines** adventure and mystery.*

combine harvester combine harvesters
NOUN a large machine used on farms to cut, sort and clean grain

combustion
NOUN the process of burning

come comes, coming, came
VERB **1** If you **come** to a place, you move or arrive there.
2 If something **comes** to a particular point, it reaches that point. • *The water **came** up to her waist.*
3 When a particular time **comes**, it happens. • *Spring **came** early this year.*

comedian comedians
NOUN an entertainer whose job is to make people laugh

comedy comedies
NOUN a play, film, or television programme that is intended to make people laugh

comet comets
NOUN an object that travels around the sun leaving a bright trail behind it [from Greek *kometes* meaning long-haired]

comfort comforts, comforting, comforted
NOUN **1** the state of being pleasantly relaxed
2 a feeling of relief from worry or unhappiness • *It's a **comfort** to me to know that they are safe.*
VERB **3** If you **comfort** someone, you make them less worried or unhappy.

comfortable
ADJECTIVE **1** If you are **comfortable**, you are at ease and relaxed.
2 Something that is **comfortable** makes you feel relaxed. • *a **comfortable** chair*
comfortably ADVERB

comic comics
NOUN **1** a magazine that contains stories told in pictures
ADJECTIVE **2** funny • *a **comic** song*

comma commas
NOUN the punctuation mark (,). It can show a short pause, or it can separate items in a list or words in speech marks from the rest of the sentence.

command commands, commanding, commanded
NOUN **1** an order to do something
VERB **2** If you **command** someone to do something, you order them to do it.

commemorate commemorates, commemorating, commemorated
VERB If you **commemorate** something, you do something special to show that you remember it. • *On Remembrance Day we **commemorate** all the people who died in the two World Wars.*

comment comments, commenting, commented
NOUN **1** a remark about something
VERB **2** If you **comment** on something, you make a remark about it.

commentary **commentaries**

NOUN a description of an event that is broadcast on radio or television while the event is happening • The **commentary** on the match was on the radio.

commentator **commentators**

NOUN someone who gives a radio or television commentary

commerce

NOUN the buying and selling of goods

commercial **commercials**

NOUN **1** an advertisement on television or radio

ADJECTIVE **2** **Commercial** activities involve producing large amounts of goods to sell and make money.

commit **commits, committing, committed**

VERB When someone **commits** a crime or sin, they do it. • The police know who **committed** the burglary.

committee **committees**

NOUN a group of people who make decisions on behalf of a larger group

common **commoner, commonest; commons**

ADJECTIVE **1** Something that is **common** exists in large numbers or happens often.

NOUN **2** an area of grassy land where everyone can go

ADJECTIVE **3** If something is **common** to two or more people, they all have it or use it. • We had a **common** interest in butterflies.

PHRASE **4** If two things or people have something **in common**, they both have it. • Sarah and I have a lot **in common**.

common noun **common nouns**

NOUN **Common nouns** name things in general. They begin with lower-case letters: girl, boy, animal, picture. See **noun**

common sense

NOUN knowing how to behave sensibly in any situation

Commonwealth

NOUN The **Commonwealth** is a group of countries that used to be ruled by Britain.

commotion

NOUN a lot of noise and excitement

communal

ADJECTIVE shared by a group of people • The shop had **communal** changing rooms.

communicate **communicates, communicating, communicated**

VERB When people **communicate**, they exchange information, usually by talking or writing to each other.

communication **communications**

NOUN **1** the act of exchanging information, usually by talking, writing or, in the case of animals, making sounds • the **communication** of ideas

PLURAL NOUN **2** **Communications** are electrical or radio systems that allow people to broadcast or communicate information.

communion

NOUN **1** a Christian religious service in which people share holy bread and wine **2** the sharing of thoughts and feelings

community **communities**

NOUN all the people living in a particular area

commuter **commuters**

NOUN a person who has to travel a long way to work every day

compact

ADJECTIVE Something that is **compact** takes up very little space, or no more space than is necessary.

compact disc **compact discs**

NOUN a music or video recording in the form of a small plastic disc

companion **companions**

NOUN someone you travel or spend time with

company **companies**

NOUN **1** a business that sells goods or provides a service

comparative

2 If you have **company**, you have a friend or visitor with you.

PHRASE **3** If you **keep someone company**, you spend time with them.

comparative comparatives

ADJECTIVE **1** You use **comparative** to show that something is true only when compared with something else.

NOUN **2** In grammar, the **comparative** is the form of an adjective or adverb that shows an increase in size, quality or amount. It is usually formed by adding *-er* to a word, for example, *bigger*, *faster*, or by putting *more* before the word, for example, *more difficult*.

compare compares, comparing, compared

VERB When you **compare** things, you see in what ways they are different or similar. • *We **compared** our hair to see whose was longest.*

comparison comparisons

NOUN When you make a **comparison**, you consider two things together and decide in what ways they are different or similar.

compartment compartments

NOUN **1** a section of a railway carriage
2 one of the separate sections of something such as a bag or a box

compass compasses

NOUN **1** an instrument with a magnetic needle that always points north. You use a **compass** to find your way.

PLURAL NOUN **2 Compasses** are a hinged instrument for drawing circles.

compassion

NOUN pity and sympathy for someone who is suffering

compassionate ADJECTIVE

compass point compass points

NOUN one of the 32 marks on the dial of a compass that show direction • *North, south, east and west are **compass points**.*

compel compels, compelling, compelled

VERB **1** If you **compel** someone to do something, you force them to do it.

ADJECTIVE **2** A **compelling** story or event is extremely interesting.

3 A **compelling** argument or reason makes you believe that something is true.

compensate compensates, compensating, compensated

VERB **1** To **compensate** someone means to give them money to replace something that has been lost or damaged.

2 If one thing **compensates** for another, it cancels out the bad effects of it. • *The trip to Disneyland **compensated** for her long illness.*

compete competes, competing, competed

VERB **1** If you **compete** in a contest or game, you take part in it.

2 If you **compete**, you try to do better than others.

competent

ADJECTIVE Someone who is **competent** at something can do it satisfactorily. • *He is a **competent** nurse.*

competition competitions

NOUN an event in which people take part to find out who is the best at something

compile compiles, compiling, compiled

VERB When you **compile** information, you collect it and put it together.

complain complains, complaining, complained

VERB **1** If you **complain**, you say that you are not happy about something. • *The neighbours **complained** about the noise.*

2 If you **complain** of pain or illness, you say that you have it.

complaint NOUN

complement complements, complementing, complemented

VERB **1** If one thing **complements** another, the two things go well together. • *Her piano music **complements** the poem.*

NOUN **2** In grammar, a **complement** is a word or phrase that gives information about the subject or object of a sentence. For example, in the sentence *Rover is a dog*, *is a dog* is the **complement**.

🖉 Do not confuse *complement* with *compliment*.

complete **completes, completing, completed**

VERB **1** If you **complete** something, you finish it. • *She has just completed her third short story.*

ADJECTIVE **2** If something is **complete**, none of it is missing.

completely

ADVERB totally

SYNONYM: utterly

complex **complexes**

ADJECTIVE **1 Complex** things have many different parts and are hard to understand.

NOUN **2** a group of buildings used for a particular purpose, such a sports **complex**

complexion **complexions**

NOUN the quality of the skin on your face

complicated

ADJECTIVE Something that is **complicated** is hard to understand.

complication **complications**

NOUN something that makes a situation more difficult to deal with

compliment **compliments**

NOUN If you pay someone a **compliment**, you tell them you admire or like something about them.

🖉 Do not confuse *compliment* with *complement*.

component **components**

NOUN The **components** of something are the parts it is made of.

compose **composes, composing, composed**

VERB **1** If you **compose** a piece of music, a letter, or a speech, you write it.

2 If something is **composed** of particular things or people, it is made up of them.

composer **composers**

NOUN someone who writes music

composition **compositions**

NOUN **1** a piece of music or writing

2 the things that something is made up of

compost

NOUN a mixture of rotted plants and manure that gardeners add to the soil to help plants grow

compound word **compound words**

NOUN a word with a single meaning, but made up of two or more words. For example, *gingerbread*, *housework* and *teapot* are all **compound words**.

comprehend **comprehends, comprehending, comprehended**

VERB If you **comprehend** something, you understand it.

comprehensive **comprehensives**

ADJECTIVE **1** Something that is **comprehensive** includes everything that you need to know.

NOUN **2** a school where children of all abilities are taught together

comprehensively ADVERB

compress **compresses, compressing, compressed**

VERB If you **compress** something, you squeeze it or shorten it. • *She compressed her story into one page.*

compromise **compromises, compromising, compromised**

NOUN **1** an agreement in which people accept less than they really wanted

VERB **2** When people **compromise**, they settle for less than they really wanted.

compulsory

ADJECTIVE If something is **compulsory**, you have to do it.

computer **computers**

NOUN an electronic machine that stores information and makes calculations

computerize **computerizes, computerizing, computerized**; also spelt **computerise**

VERB When a system or process is

a
b
c
d
e
f
g
h
i
j
k
l
m
n
o
p
q
r
s
t
u
v
w
x
y
z

computerized, such as train timetables or bank accounts, the work is done by computers.

comrade comrades
NOUN a companion, especially in battle

con cons, conning, conned
VERB **1** If someone **cons** you, or you are **conned**, you are tricked into doing something. • *He **conned** me into buying the tickets.*
NOUN **2** a trick that makes you believe or do something that you would not normally believe or do

concave
ADJECTIVE A **concave** surface curves inwards, rather than being level or bulging outwards.
ANTONYM: convex

concave   convex

conceal conceals, concealing, concealed
VERB If you **conceal** something, you hide it.

conceited
ADJECTIVE Someone who is **conceited** is too proud of their appearance or abilities.
SYNONYMS: bigheaded, self-important

conceive conceives, conceiving, conceived
VERB **1** If you can't **conceive** of something, you can't imagine it or believe it. • *He couldn't **conceive** of anything more fun than surfing.*
2 If you **conceive** something such as a plan, you think of it and work out how it could be done. • *Alex **conceived** the idea while eating his lunch.*
3 When a woman **conceives**, she becomes pregnant.

concentrate concentrates, concentrating, concentrated
VERB **1** If you **concentrate** on something, you give it all your attention. • *I need to **concentrate** on my homework.*

2 When something is **concentrated** in one place, it is all there rather than in several places. • *The shops were **concentrated** in the town centre.*

concentrated
ADJECTIVE A **concentrated** liquid has been made stronger by having water removed from it. • *concentrated* orange juice

concentration concentrations
NOUN **1** the ability to give your full attention to something you do or hear
2 A **concentration** of something is a large amount of it in one place.

concept concepts
NOUN an abstract or general idea

conception conceptions
NOUN the idea you have of something

concern concerns, concerning, concerned
NOUN **1** worry about something or someone
2 If something is your **concern**, it is your duty or responsibility.
VERB **3** If something **concerns** you or if you are **concerned** about it, it worries you.
concerned ADJECTIVE

concerning
PREPOSITION You use **concerning** to show what something is about. • *an article **concerning** fox hunting*

concert concerts
NOUN a public performance by musicians

concession concessions
NOUN If you make a **concession**, you agree to let someone have or do something.

concise
ADJECTIVE giving all the necessary information using as few words as possible • *a **concise** explanation*
SYNONYMS: brief, short
concisely ADVERB

conclude concludes, concluding, concluded
VERB **1** If you **conclude** something, you

examine the facts and decide what your opinion is. • We **concluded** that the letter was a fake.

2 When you **conclude** something, you finish it.

conclusion conclusions
NOUN **1** the end of something

2 a final decision about something • We wanted to go for a swim in the sea, but we came to the **conclusion** that it was too cold.

concrete
NOUN **1** a building material made by mixing cement, sand and water

ADJECTIVE **2** real and physical, rather than abstract • He had no **concrete** evidence.

concussion
NOUN damage to the brain caused by a blow or a fall, which causes confusion, sickness or unconsciousness

concussed ADJECTIVE

condemn condemns, condemning, condemned
VERB **1** If you **condemn** something, you say it is bad and unacceptable.

2 If someone is **condemned** to a punishment, they are given it. • The burglar was **condemned** to five years in prison.

condensation
NOUN a coating of tiny drops of liquid formed on a cold surface by steam or vapour

condense condenses, condensing, condensed
VERB **1** If you **condense** a piece of writing or a speech, you shorten it.

2 When a gas or vapour **condenses**, it changes into a liquid.

condition conditions
NOUN **1** the state someone or something is in • The antique clock was still in good **condition**.

2 something that must happen in order for something else to be possible • I can go swimming on Saturday on the **condition** that I do my homework first.

conduct conducts, conducting, conducted
Said "**kon**-duct" NOUN **1** behaviour
Said "kon-**duct**" VERB **2** When you **conduct** an activity, you carry it out.

3 When someone **conducts** an orchestra, a band or a choir, they direct it in a piece of music.

4 If something **conducts** heat or electricity, heat or electricity can pass along it. • Copper **conducts** electricity well.

conductor conductors
NOUN **1** someone who conducts an orchestra or choir

2 someone who moves round a bus or train selling and checking tickets

3 a substance that conducts heat or electricity

cone cones
NOUN **1** a regular three-dimensional shape with a circular base and a point at the top

2 the fruit of a fir or pine tree

conference conferences
NOUN a meeting at which formal discussions take place

confess confesses, confessing, confessed
VERB If you **confess** to something, you admit that you did it.

confession confessions
NOUN **1** If you make a **confession**, you admit that you have done something wrong.

SYNONYM: admission

2 the act of confessing something, especially as a religious act, where people confess their sins to a priest

confetti
NOUN small pieces of coloured paper thrown over the bride and groom at a wedding [from Italian confetto meaning a sweet]

confide confides, confiding, confided
VERB If you **confide** in or to someone, you tell them a secret.

a
b
c
d
e
f
g
h
i
j
k
l
m
n
o
p
q
r
s
t
u
v
w
x
y
z

confidence

NOUN **1** If you have **confidence** in someone, you feel you can trust them.
2 Someone who has **confidence** is sure of their own abilities or qualities.

confident

ADJECTIVE **1** If you are **confident** about something, you are sure it will happen the way you want it to.
2 Someone who is **confident** is very sure of themselves and their own abilities.
confidently ADVERB

confidential

ADJECTIVE **Confidential** information is meant to be kept secret.

confine confines, confining, confined

VERB **1** If someone **confines** you to a place, you can't leave it. • *The doctor* **confined** *Debbie to bed for two weeks as she had pneumonia.*
2 If you **confine** yourself to doing something, you do only that thing. • *On their trip abroad, they* **confined** *themselves to drinking bottled water.*

confirm confirms, confirming, confirmed

VERB **1** If you **confirm** something, you say or show that it is true. • *The teacher* **confirmed** *that we had all passed our spelling test.*
2 If you **confirm** an arrangement or appointment, you say it is definite.
• *Dad* **confirmed** *our holiday booking.*

confiscate confiscates, confiscating, confiscated

VERB If someone **confiscates** something, they take it away from someone as a punishment.
[from Latin *confiscare* meaning to seize for the public treasury]
confiscation NOUN

conflict conflicts, conflicting, conflicted

NOUN **1** disagreement and argument
2 a war or battle
VERB **3** When two ideas or interests **conflict**, they are different and it seems impossible for them both to be true.

conform conforms, conforming, conformed

VERB **1** If you **conform**, you behave the way people expect you to.
2 If something **conforms** to a law or to someone's wishes, it does what is required or wanted.
conformist NOUN OR ADJECTIVE

confront confronts, confronting, confronted

VERB **1** If you are **confronted** with a problem or task, you have to deal with it.
2 If you **confront** someone, you meet them face to face, especially when you are going to fight or argue with them.

confrontation confrontations

NOUN a serious dispute between two people or groups of people who come face to face

confuse confuses, confusing, confused

VERB **1** If you **confuse** two people or things, you mix them up and are not sure which is which.
2 If you **confuse** someone, you make them uncertain about what is happening or what to do.
confusion NOUN

congested

ADJECTIVE **1** When a road is **congested**, it is so full of traffic that normal movement is impossible.
2 If your nose is **congested**, it is blocked and you cannot breathe properly.
congestion NOUN

congratulate congratulates, congratulating, congratulated

VERB If you **congratulate** someone, you say that you're pleased about something good that has happened to them, or praise them for something they have done. • *He* **congratulated** *us on winning the competition.*
congratulations NOUN

congregation congregations

NOUN the people attending a service in a church

congruent

ADJECTIVE In mathematics, things that are **congruent** are exactly the same size and shape, and would fit exactly on top of each other. • **congruent** *triangles*

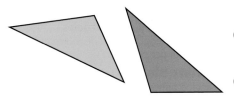

conifer **conifers**

NOUN any type of evergreen tree that produces cones
coniferous ADJECTIVE

conjunction **conjunctions**

NOUN In grammar, a **conjunction** is a word that links two other words or two clauses, such as *and*, *but*, *or*, *while* and *that*. For example: "I love bacon *and* eggs." "I'm happy, *but* my brother is not".

conjurer **conjurers**

NOUN someone who entertains people by doing magic tricks

conker **conkers**

NOUN a brown nut from a horse chestnut tree

connect **connects, connecting, connected**

VERB **1** If you **connect** two things, you join them together.
2 If one thing or person is **connected** with another, there is a link between them.

connection **connections**

NOUN **1** the point where two things are joined together
2 If you make a **connection** at a station or airport, you continue your journey by catching another train, bus or plane.
• *Our train was late, so we missed our* **connection***.*

connective **connectives**

NOUN a word that connects phrases, clauses or words together
See **conjunction**

conquer **conquers, conquering, conquered**

VERB **1** If you **conquer** something difficult or dangerous, you succeed in controlling it. • *She* **conquered** *her fear of spiders.*
2 to take control of a country by force
conqueror NOUN

conscience

NOUN the part of your mind that tells you what is right or wrong

conscientious

ADJECTIVE Someone who is **conscientious** takes great care over their work.
conscientiously ADVERB

conscious

ADJECTIVE **1** Someone who is **conscious** is awake, rather than asleep or unconscious.
2 If you are **conscious** of something, you are aware of it.
3 A **conscious** action or effort is done deliberately.

consecutive

ADJECTIVE **1** **Consecutive** events or periods of time happen one after the other. • *We had eight* **consecutive** *days of rain.*
2 **Consecutive** numbers follow each other in order. For example, 1, 2, 3, 4 are **consecutive** numbers.
consecutively ADVERB

consent **consents, consenting, consented**

NOUN **1** permission to do something
2 agreement between two or more people
• *By common* **consent** *we went to France for the holiday.*
VERB **3** If you **consent** to something, you agree to do it or allow it to happen.

consequence **consequences**

NOUN result or effect

conservation

NOUN the preservation of the environment
conservationist NOUN OR ADJECTIVE

conservative **conservatives**

NOUN **1** a member or supporter of the **Conservative** Party in Britain
ADJECTIVE **2** Someone who is **conservative** does not like change or new ideas.

a
b
c
d
e
f
g
h
i
j
k
l
m
n
o
p
q
r
s
t
u
v
w
x
y
z

3 A **conservative** estimate or guess is a cautious or moderate one.

conservatory conservatories

NOUN a room with glass walls and a glass roof in which plants are kept

conserve conserves, conserving, conserved

VERB **1** If you **conserve** a supply of something, you make it last as long as possible. • *I switched off my torch to* **conserve** *the battery.*
2 If you **conserve** something, you keep it as it is and do not change it. • *We should* **conserve** *this old building.*

consider considers, considering, considered

VERB If you **consider** something, you think about it carefully.

considerable

ADJECTIVE A **considerable** amount of something is a lot of it.

considerate

ADJECTIVE Someone who is **considerate** thinks of other people's needs and feelings.

consideration considerations

NOUN **1** careful thought about something
2 something that should be thought about when you are planning or deciding something
3 Someone who shows **consideration** pays attention to the needs and feelings of other people.

consist consists, consisting, consisted

VERB Something that **consists** of certain things is made up of them. • *This bread* **consists** *of flour, yeast and water.*

consistent

ADJECTIVE Something that is **consistent** does not change.

console consoles, consoling, consoled

Said "kon-sole" VERB **1** If you **console** someone who is unhappy, you comfort them and cheer them up.
Said "**kon**-sole" NOUN **2** a panel with switches or knobs for operating a machine

consonant consonants

NOUN all the letters of the alphabet that are not vowels

conspicuous

ADJECTIVE If something is **conspicuous**, you can see or notice it very easily.

conspiracy conspiracies

NOUN an illegal plan made in secret by a group of people

constable constables

NOUN a police officer of the lowest rank

constant

ADJECTIVE **1** Something that is **constant** happens all the time or is always there. • *We could hear the* **constant** *sound of the waves pounding the shore.*
2 If an amount or level is **constant**, it stays the same.

constellation constellations

NOUN a group of stars

constipated

ADJECTIVE Someone who is **constipated** finds it difficult to empty their bowels. [from Latin *constipare* meaning to press together]

constipation NOUN

constitution constitutions

NOUN **1** The **constitution** of a country is the system of laws and principles by which it is governed.
2 Your **constitution** is your health.

construct constructs, constructing, constructed

VERB If you **construct** something, you build or make it.

construction constructions

NOUN **1** the process of building or making something
2 something built or made

constructive

ADJECTIVE helpful • *The tennis coach made some* **constructive** *comments about my backhand.*

consult consults, consulting, consulted

VERB **1** If you **consult** someone, you ask for their opinion or advice.

2 If you **consult** a book or map, you look at it for information.
consultation NOUN

consultant consultants
NOUN an experienced doctor who specializes in one type of medicine
• a **consultant** heart surgeon

consume consumes, consuming, consumed
VERB **1** If you **consume** something, you eat or drink it.
2 To **consume** fuel or energy is to use it up.

consumer consumers
NOUN someone who buys things or uses services • magazines aimed at teenage **consumers**

consumption
NOUN The **consumption** of fuel or food is the using of it, or the amount used. • The **consumption** of ice cream rises in hot weather.

contact contacts, contacting, contacted
NOUN **1** If you are in **contact** with someone, you talk or write to them regularly. • I am in **contact** with a pen pal in France.
2 When things are in **contact**, they are touching each other.
VERB **3** If you **contact** someone, you telephone them or write to them.

contact lens contact lenses
NOUN small plastic lenses that you put in your eyes instead of wearing glasses, to help you see better

contagious
ADJECTIVE A **contagious** disease can be caught by touching people or things infected with it. • Measles is **contagious**.

contain contains, containing, contained
VERB **1** If a substance **contains** something, that thing is a part of it.
2 The things a box or room **contains** are the things inside it.

container containers
NOUN something that you keep things in, such as a box or a jar

contaminate contaminates, contaminating, contaminated
VERB If dirt, chemicals or radiation **contaminate** something, they make it impure and harmful.
contamination NOUN

contemplate contemplates, contemplating, contemplated
VERB **1** If you **contemplate**, you think very carefully about something. • She **contemplated** what she would do at the weekend.
2 If you **contemplate** something, you look at it for a long time.

contemporary
ADJECTIVE **1** produced or happening now
2 A **contemporary** work is one that was written at the time of the events it describes.

contempt
NOUN If you treat someone with **contempt**, you show no respect for them at all.

content
Said "kon-**tent**" ADJECTIVE **1** If you are **content**, you are happy and satisfied with your life.
2 If you are **content** to do something, you are willing to do it.

contents
Said "**kon**-tents" PLURAL NOUN **1** The **contents** of something like a box or a cake are the things in it.
2 The **contents** page of a book tells you what is in it.

contest contests
NOUN a competition or game

contestant contestants
NOUN someone who takes part in a competition
SYNONYMS: competitor, player

context contexts
NOUN The **context** of a word or sentence is the words or sentences that come before and after it, which help to make the meaning clear.

a
b
c
d
e
f
g
h
i
j
k
l
m
n
o
p
q
r
s
t
u
v
w
x
y
z

continent continents

NOUN **1** a very large area of land, such as Africa or Asia
2 In Britain, the mainland of Europe is sometimes called the **Continent**.
[from Latin *terra continens* meaning continuous land]

continental

ADJECTIVE In Britain, **continental** means on, belonging to or typical of the mainland of Europe. ● *continental breakfast*

continual

ADJECTIVE happening again and again
● *Mum had a **continual** stream of phone calls.*

continue continues, continuing, continued

VERB **1** If you **continue** to do something, you keep doing it.
2 If something **continues**, it does not stop.
3 You say something **continues** when it starts again after stopping. ● *She paused for a moment, then **continued**.*

continuous

ADJECTIVE happening all the time without stopping ● *The television made a **continuous** buzzing noise.*

contour contours

NOUN **1** The **contour** of something is its general shape or outline.
2 On a map, a **contour** is a line joining points of equal height.

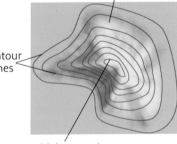

low ground

contour lines

high ground

contract contracts, contracting, contracted

Said "**con**-trakt" NOUN **1** a legal agreement about the sale of something or work done for money ● *He was given a two-year* **contract**.
Said "con-**trakt**" VERB **2** When something **contracts**, it gets smaller or shorter.
● *Metals **contract** with cold and expand with heat.*
ANTONYM: expand

contraction contractions

NOUN a shortened form of a word or words, often marked by an apostrophe ● *"I've"* is a **contraction** of "I have".

contradict contradicts, contradicting, contradicted

VERB If you **contradict** someone, you say that what they have just said is wrong.
contradiction NOUN

contrary

ADJECTIVE **1** **Contrary** ideas, opinions or attitudes are completely different from each other.
PHRASE **2** **On the contrary** is used to contradict something that has just been said.

contrast contrasts, contrasting, contrasted

Said "**con**-trast" NOUN **1** a great difference between things ● *the **contrast** between town and country*
Said "con-**trast**" VERB **2** If you **contrast** things, you describe or emphasize the differences between them.

contribute contributes, contributing, contributed

VERB **1** If you **contribute** to something, you do something to make it successful.
● *Everyone **contributed** to the class project.*
2 If you **contribute** money to something, you help to pay for it. ● *We **contributed** some money to the appeal for the homeless.*
SYNONYMS: donate, give
contribution NOUN

control controls, controlling, controlled

NOUN **1** If you have **control** over something,

you are able to make it work the way you want it to.

2 The **controls** on a machine are the knobs or other devices used to work it.

VERB **3** If someone **controls** a country or an organization, they make the decisions about how it is run.

4 If someone **controls** something such as a machine, they make it work the way they want it to.

PHRASE **5** If something is **out of control**, nobody has any power over it. • *The fire was out of control.*

controversial

ADJECTIVE Something that is **controversial** causes a lot of discussion and argument, because many people disapprove of it. • *The film was controversial.*

convalescent **convalescents**

NOUN someone who is resting while recovering from an illness

convenient

ADJECTIVE If something is **convenient**, it is easy to use or it makes something easy to do. • *It's convenient living close to the bus stop.*

convenience NOUN

convent **convents**

NOUN **1** a building where nuns live
2 a school run by nuns

conventional

ADJECTIVE Someone who is **conventional** thinks or behaves in an ordinary and accepted way.

converge **converges, converging, converged**

VERB When things meet or join at a particular place, they **converge**. • *The roads converge after three kilometres.*

convergence NOUN

conversation **conversations**

NOUN When people have a **conversation**, they talk to each other.

convert **converts, converting, converted**

VERB **1** If you **convert** something, it changes from one thing to another.

• *Dad converted the loft into a workshop.*

2 If someone **converts** you, they persuade you to change your religious or political beliefs.

3 In mathematics, **convert** means to change a number from one form to another. These are equal to each other. For example, you can **convert** a fraction to a decimal ($1/2 = 0.5$).

convex

ADJECTIVE A **convex** surface bulges outwards, rather than being level or curving inwards.

See **concave**

ANTONYM: concave

convey **conveys, conveying, conveyed**

VERB **1** If someone **conveys** people or things to a place, they take them there.
2 If you **convey** information, ideas or feelings, you tell people about them.

conveyor belt **conveyor belts**

NOUN a moving strip used in factories for moving objects along

convict **convicts, convicting, convicted**

Said "kon-**vikt**" VERB **1** If a law court **convicts** someone of a crime, it says they are guilty of it.

Said "**kon**-vikt" NOUN **2** someone serving a prison sentence

convince **convinces, convincing, convinced**

VERB If you **convince** someone of something, you persuade them to do it or that it is true. • *I convinced mum and dad to let me go on the school trip.*

convoy **convoys**

NOUN a group of ships or vehicles travelling together

cook **cooks, cooking, cooked**

VERB **1** When you **cook**, you prepare food for eating by boiling, baking or frying it.

NOUN **2** a person whose job is to prepare food

cooker **cookers**

NOUN an apparatus for cooking food

cookery

NOUN the art of preparing and cooking food

cookie cookies

NOUN **1** a sweet biscuit • *a chocolate cookie*
2 a small file placed on a user's computer by a website • *This website uses cookies.*

cool cooler, coolest; cools, cooling, cooled

ADJECTIVE **1** Something **cool** has a low temperature but is not cold.
2 If you are **cool** in a difficult situation, you stay calm.
VERB **3** When something **cools**, it becomes less warm.

cooperate cooperates, cooperating, cooperated

VERB **1** When people **cooperate**, they work or act together.
2 If you **cooperate**, you do what someone asks you to do.

cooperative cooperatives

ADJECTIVE **1** A **cooperative** person does what they are asked to do willingly and cheerfully.
NOUN **2** a business or organization run by the people who work for it, and who share its profits

coordinates

PLURAL NOUN a pair of numbers or letters that tell you exactly where a point is on a grid, map or graph

cop cops

NOUN INFORMAL a policeman

cope copes, coping, coped

VERB If you **cope**, you are able to do something even if the circumstances are difficult. • *I managed to cope with my homework and with looking after my little brother at the same time.*

copper

NOUN a soft, reddish-brown metal

copy copies, copying, copied

NOUN **1** something made to look like something else • *a copy of a famous painting*

2 A **copy** of a book, newspaper or record is one of many identical ones produced at the same time. • *a copy of today's newspaper*
VERB **3** If you **copy** what someone does, you do the same thing.
4 If you **copy** something, you make a copy of it.

copyright copyrights

NOUN If someone has the **copyright** on a piece of writing or music, it cannot be copied or performed without their permission.

coral corals

NOUN a hard substance that forms in the sea from the skeletons of tiny animals called **corals**

cord cords

NOUN **1** strong, thick string
2 electrical wire covered in rubber or plastic

corduroy

NOUN heavy, ribbed cloth made of cotton

core cores

NOUN the most central part of an object or place • *an apple core* • *the earth's core*

cork corks

NOUN **1** a soft, light substance that forms the bark of a Mediterranean tree
2 a piece of **cork** pushed into the end of a bottle to close it

corkscrew corkscrews

NOUN a device for pulling corks out of bottles

corn

NOUN **1** crops such as wheat and barley **2** the seeds of these crops

corner corners, cornering, cornered

NOUN **1** the point where two sides or edges of something meet • *The TV was in the corner of the room.*
See **vertex**

VERB **2** If someone **corners** a person or animal, they get them into a place they can't escape from. • *The police cornered the thief.*

cornet cornets

NOUN a small, brass instrument used in brass and military bands

coronation coronations

NOUN the ceremony at which a king or queen is crowned

coroner coroners

NOUN an official who investigates the deaths of people who have died in a violent or unusual way

corporal corporals

NOUN an officer of low rank in the army or air force

corporal punishment

NOUN punishing of people by beating them

corps

Said "**kor**" NOUN part of an army with special duties • *the Medical Corps*

corpse corpses

NOUN a dead body

correct corrects, correcting, corrected

ADJECTIVE **1** If something is **correct**, there are no mistakes in it.

VERB **2** If you **correct** something that is wrong, you make it right. • *She corrected my maths homework.*
correction NOUN

correspond corresponds, corresponding, corresponded

VERB **1** If one thing **corresponds** with another, it is similar to it or it matches it in some way.

2 If numbers or amounts **correspond**, they are the same.
3 When people **correspond**, they write to each other.

correspondence

NOUN **1** letters or the writing of letters **2** If there is a **correspondence** between two things, there is a similarity between them.

correspondent correspondents

NOUN a newspaper, radio or television reporter

corridor corridors

NOUN a passage in a building or train [from Old Italian *corridore* meaning place for running]

corrode corrodes, corroding, corroded

VERB When something **corrodes**, it is eaten away. When iron and steel are **corroded**, rust is formed.
corrosion NOUN **corrosive** ADJECTIVE

corrugated

ADJECTIVE **Corrugated** metal or cardboard has parallel folds to make it stronger.

corrupt corrupts, corrupting, corrupted

ADJECTIVE **1** People who are **corrupt** act dishonestly or illegally in return for money or power.
SYNONYM: dishonest

VERB **2** If you **corrupt** someone, you make them dishonest.
3 If a bug in a computer spoils files, it **corrupts** them.
corruption NOUN

cosmetics

PLURAL NOUN lipstick, face powder and other make-up

cosmic

ADJECTIVE belonging to or relating to the whole universe

cosmos

NOUN the universe

A
B
C
D
E
F
G
H
I
J
K
L
M
N
O
P
Q
R
S
T
U
V
W
X
Y
Z

cost **costs, costing, cost**
NOUN **1** the amount of money needed to buy, do or make something
VERB **2** You use **cost** to talk about the amount of money you have to pay for things. • *You can't have that – it costs too much.*

costume **costumes**
NOUN **1** a set of clothes worn by an actor
2 the clothing worn in a particular place or during a particular period

cosy **cosier, cosiest**
ADJECTIVE warm and comfortable

cot **cots**
NOUN a small bed for a baby, with bars or panels round it to stop the baby falling out

cottage **cottages**
NOUN a small house, especially in the country

cotton
NOUN **1** cloth made from the soft fibres of the **cotton** plant • *a cotton shirt*
2 thread used for sewing • *a needle and cotton*

couch **couches**
NOUN a long, soft piece of furniture for sitting or lying on

cough **coughs, coughing, coughed**
VERB When you **cough**, you force air out of your throat with a sudden harsh noise.

could
VERB **1** the past tense of **can**
2 You use **could** to say that something might happen or might be true. • *It could rain later.*
3 You use **could** when you are asking for something politely. • *Could you tell me the way to the station, please?*

couldn't
VERB a contraction of *could not*

council **councils**
NOUN a group of people elected to look after something, especially the affairs of a town, district or county

counsel **counsels, counselling, counselled**
NOUN **1** advice
VERB **2** If someone **counsels** people, they give them advice about their problems.

count **counts, counting, counted**
VERB **1** When you **count**, you say all the numbers in order up to a particular number.
2 If you **count**, or **count** up, all the things in a group, you add them up to see how many there are.
3 If you can **count** on someone or something, you can rely on them. • *You can count on me to help.*
PHRASE **4** If you **keep count** of something, you keep a record of how often it happens. • *Who's keeping count of the score?*
5 If you **lose count** of something, you cannot remember how often it has happened.

counter **counters**
NOUN **1** a long, flat surface in a shop, over which goods are sold
2 a small, flat, round object used in board games

counterfeit **counterfeits, counterfeiting, counterfeited**
Said "**kown**-ter-fit" ADJECTIVE
1 **Counterfeit** things are not genuine, but have been made to look genuine in order to deceive people. • *counterfeit money*
VERB **2** If someone **counterfeits** something, they make an exact copy of it in order to trick people.

countless
ADJECTIVE too many to count

country **countries**
NOUN **1** one of the political areas the world is divided into
2 land away from towns and cities • *It is peaceful living in the country.*

countryside
NOUN land away from towns and cities

county **counties**

NOUN a region with its own local government ● *The* **county** *of Lincolnshire is in the east of England.*

couple **couples**

NOUN **1** two people who are married or having a romantic relationship
2 A **couple** of things or people means two of them, or not very many.

couplet **couplets**

NOUN two lines of poetry together that usually rhyme

coupon **coupons**

NOUN **1** a piece of printed paper that entitles you to pay less than usual for something
2 a form you fill in to ask for information or to enter a competition

courage

NOUN the quality shown by people who do things that they know are dangerous or difficult ● *She showed great* **courage** *in her efforts to save them from the burning house.*
courageous ADJECTIVE
courageously ADVERB

courgette **courgettes**

NOUN a vegetable that looks like a small green marrow

courier **couriers**

NOUN **1** someone employed by a travel company to look after people on holiday
2 someone employed to deliver letters and parcels quickly

course **courses**

NOUN **1** a series of lessons or lectures
2 a piece of land where races take place or golf is played
3 the route something such as a ship or a river takes ● *The captain changed* **course** *to avoid the storm.*
4 one of the parts of a meal ● *The first* **course** *was soup.*
PHRASE **5** If you say **of course**, you are showing that you are absolutely sure about something. ● *Of course she wouldn't do a thing like that.*

court **courts**

NOUN **1** a place where legal matters are decided by a judge and jury or a magistrate. The judge and jury or magistrate can also be referred to as the **court**. ● *He is due to appear in* **court** *next week.* ● *The* **court** *awarded him ten thousand pounds in compensation.*
2 a place where a game such as tennis or badminton is played
3 the place where a king or queen lives and works

courteous

ADJECTIVE **Courteous** behaviour is polite and considerate.
courteously ADVERB

courtyard **courtyards**

NOUN a flat area of ground surrounded by buildings or walls

cousin **cousins**

NOUN Your **cousin** is the child of your uncle or aunt.

cove **coves**

NOUN a small bay on the coast

cover **covers, covering, covered**

VERB **1** If you **cover** something, you put something else over it to protect it or hide it.
2 If something **covers** something else, it forms a layer over it.
3 If you **cover** a particular distance, you travel that distance.
4 If you **cover** a subject, you discuss it in a lesson, course or book. ● *We* **covered** *the Vikings in today's lesson.*
NOUN **5** something put over an object to protect it or keep it warm
6 The **cover** of a book or magazine is its outside.
7 **Cover** is trees, rocks or other places where you can shelter or hide. ● *When it started raining they ran for* **cover**.

coverage

NOUN The **coverage** of something in the news is the reporting of it. ● *There was complete* **coverage** *of the Wimbledon finals on television.*

A
B
C
D
E
F
G
H
I
J
K
L
M
N
O
P
Q
R
S
T
U
V
W
X
Y
Z

cow cows
NOUN a large female mammal kept on farms for its milk and meat

coward cowards
NOUN a person who is easily frightened and avoids dangerous situations
cowardly ADJECTIVE cowardice NOUN

cowboy cowboys
NOUN a man employed to look after cattle in America

coy coyer, coyest
ADJECTIVE If someone behaves in a **coy** way, they pretend to be shy and modest.

crab crabs
NOUN a crustacean with four pairs of legs, two claws, and a flat, round body covered by a shell

crack cracks, cracking, cracked
VERB **1** If something **cracks**, or if something **cracks** it, it becomes damaged, with lines appearing on its surface.
2 If you **crack** a joke, you tell it.
3 If you **crack** a problem or code, you solve it.
NOUN **4** one of the lines appearing on something when it cracks
5 a narrow gap • *My ring fell into a **crack** in the pavement.*

cracker crackers
NOUN **1** a thin, crisp biscuit that is often eaten with cheese
2 a paper-covered tube that pulls apart with a bang, and usually has a toy and paper hat inside

crackle crackles, crackling, crackled
VERB **1** something **crackles**, it makes a series of short sharp sounds • *The bonfire started to **crackle** as the flames grew higher.*
NOUN **2** a short sharp sound

cradle cradles, cradling, cradled
NOUN **1** a box-shaped bed for a baby
VERB **2** If you **cradle** something in your arms or hands, you hold it there carefully.

craft crafts
NOUN **1** an activity that needs skill with the hands, such as weaving, carving or pottery
2 a boat, plane or spacecraft

craftsman or **craftswoman**
craftsmen or **craftswomen**
NOUN a person who makes things skilfully with their hands
craftsmanship NOUN

crafty craftier, craftiest
ADJECTIVE **Crafty** people get what they want by tricking other people in a clever way.
SYNONYMS: cunning, wily

crag crags
NOUN a steep, rugged rock or peak

cram crams, cramming, crammed
VERB If you **cram** people or things into a place, you put more in than there is room for. • *I **crammed** my dirty washing into the washing machine.*

cramp cramps
NOUN pain caused when muscles contract

cramped
ADJECTIVE If a room or a building is **cramped**, it is not big enough for the people or things in it.

crane cranes, craning, craned
NOUN **1** a machine that moves heavy things by lifting them in the air
2 a large bird with a long neck and long legs
VERB **3** If you **crane** your neck, you extend your head in a particular direction to see or hear something better.

crash **crashes, crashing, crashed**
NOUN **1** an accident in which a moving vehicle hits something and is damaged
2 a sudden, loud noise
VERB **3** If a vehicle **crashes**, it hits something and is badly damaged.

crate **crates**
NOUN a large box used for transporting or storing things

crater **craters**
NOUN a wide hole in the ground caused by something hitting it or by an explosion
● *The surface of the moon has many **craters**.*
[from Greek *krater* meaning mixing-bowl]

crave **craves, craving, craved**
VERB If you **crave** something, you want it very much. ● *I **craved** a bar of chocolate.*
craving NOUN

crawl **crawls, crawling, crawled**
VERB **1** When you **crawl**, you move forward on your hands and knees.
2 When an insect or vehicle **crawls** somewhere, it moves there very slowly.

crayon **crayons**
NOUN a coloured pencil or a stick of coloured wax

craze **crazes**
NOUN something that is very popular for a short time

crazy **crazier, craziest**
ADJECTIVE INFORMAL **1** very strange or foolish
2 If you are **crazy** about something or someone, you like them very much.

creak **creaks, creaking, creaked**
VERB **1** If something **creaks**, it makes a harsh sound when it moves or when you stand on it.
NOUN **2** a harsh, squeaking noise
creaky ADJECTIVE

cream **creams**
NOUN **1** a thick, yellowish-white liquid taken from the top of milk
2 a substance that you can rub into your skin to make it soft or protect it
ADJECTIVE **3** a yellowish-white colour

crease **creases, creasing, creased**
NOUN **1** an irregular line that appears on cloth or paper when it is crumpled
2 a straight line on something that has been pressed or folded neatly
● *Dad ironed a sharp **crease** in his best trousers.*
VERB **3** If you **crease** something, you make lines appear on it.

create **creates, creating, created**
VERB If someone **creates** something, they cause it to happen or exist.
creation NOUN

creative
ADJECTIVE **Creative** people are good at inventing and developing new ideas.

creature **creatures**
NOUN any living thing that is not a plant

crèche **crèches**
NOUN a place where small children are looked after while their parents are working
[from old French *crèche* meaning crib or manger]

credit **credits**
NOUN **1** a system where you pay for something in small amounts, regularly over a period of time
2 praise given to you for good work
PLURAL NOUN **3 Credits** are the list of people who helped make a film, record or television programme.
PHRASE **4** If your bank account is **in credit**, you have money in it.

credit card **credit cards**
NOUN a plastic card that allows someone to buy goods on credit rather than paying with cash

creek **creeks**
NOUN a narrow inlet where the sea comes a long way into the land

creep **creeps, creeping, crept**
VERB If you **creep** somewhere, you move there quietly and slowly.

creepy **creepier, creepiest**
ADJECTIVE strange and frightening ● *The film was **creepy**.*
SYNONYMS: eerie, spooky

a
b
c
d
e
f
g
h
i
j
k
l
m
n
o
p
q
r
s
t
u
v
w
x
y
z

A
B
C
D
E
F
G
H
I
J
K
L
M
N
O
P
Q
R
S
T
U
V
W
X
Y
Z

cremate **cremates, cremating, cremated**
VERB If someone is **cremated** when they die, their body is burned instead of buried.

crematorium **crematoriums** or **crematoria**
NOUN a building in which people are cremated

crescent **crescents**
NOUN a curved shape that is wider in the middle than at the ends, like a new moon

cress
NOUN a plant with small, strong-tasting leaves, used in salads

crest **crests**
NOUN **1** the highest part of a hill or wave **2** a tuft of feathers on top of a bird's head **3** a special sign of something, such as a school or other organization

crevice **crevices**
NOUN a narrow crack or gap in rock

crew **crews**
NOUN The **crew** of a ship, aeroplane or spacecraft are the people who operate it.

cricket **crickets**
NOUN **1** an outdoor game played by two teams, who take turns at scoring runs by hitting a ball with a bat **2** a small, jumping insect that produces sounds by rubbing its wings together

cried
VERB the past tense and past participle of **cry**

crime **crimes**
NOUN an action for which you can be punished by law

criminal **criminals**
NOUN **1** someone who has committed a crime
ADJECTIVE **2** involving or related to crime

crimson
NOUN OR ADJECTIVE dark, purplish-red

crinkle **crinkles, crinkling, crinkled**
VERB **1** If something **crinkles**, it becomes slightly creased or folded.
NOUN **2** a small crease or fold

cripple **cripples, crippling, crippled**
VERB If someone is **crippled** by something, they are injured so severely that they can never move properly again.
crippling ADJECTIVE

crisis **crises**
NOUN a serious or dangerous situation
• The food **crisis** was caused by drought.

crisp **crisper, crispest; crisps**
ADJECTIVE **1** pleasantly fresh and firm
• **crisp** lettuce leaves
NOUN **2** a thin slice of potato that has been fried until it is hard and crunchy

critic **critics**
NOUN **1** someone who writes reviews of books, films, plays or musical performances for newspapers or magazines **2** a person who criticizes someone or something publicly

critical
ADJECTIVE **1** A **critical** time or situation is a very important and serious one when things must be done correctly. **2** If the state of a sick or injured person is **critical**, they are in danger of dying. **3** Someone who is **critical** judges people and things very severely.

criticism **criticisms**
NOUN **1** spoken or written disapproval of someone or something **2** A **criticism** of a book, film or play is an examination of its good and bad points.

criticize **criticizes, criticizing, criticized**; also spelt **criticise**
VERB If you **criticize** someone or something, you say what you think is wrong with them.

croak **croaks, croaking, croaked**
VERB **1** When animals and birds **croak**, they make harsh, low sounds.
NOUN **2** a harsh, low sound
croaky ADJECTIVE

crochet **crochets, crocheting, crocheted**
Said "**kroh**-shay" NOUN **1** a kind of knitting done with a hooked needle and cotton or wool

VERB **2** If you **crochet**, you use a hooked needle and wool or cotton to make lacy material for things such as clothes and shawls.

crockery
NOUN things you use for eating and drinking, such as plates, cups, bowls and saucers

crocodile crocodiles
NOUN a large, scaly, meat-eating reptile that lives in tropical rivers
[from Greek *krokodeilos* meaning lizard]

crocus crocuses
NOUN **Crocuses** are yellow, purple or white flowers that grow in early spring.

crook crooks
NOUN **1** a criminal
2 The **crook** of your arm or leg is the soft, inside part of your elbow or your knee.
3 a long stick with a hooked end used by shepherds

crooked
ADJECTIVE **1** bent or twisted
2 dishonest

crop crops, cropping, cropped
NOUN **1** plants such as wheat and potatoes that are grown for food
2 the plants collected at harvest time
• *They gather two crops of rice a year.*
VERB **3** If you **crop** something such as your hair, you cut it very short.

cross crosses, crossing, crossed; crosser, crossest
VERB **1** If you **cross** something, such as a room or a road, you go to the other side of it.
2 Lines or roads that **cross** meet and go across each other.
3 If you **cross** your arms, legs or fingers, you put one on top of the other.
NOUN **4** a mark or a shape like + or ×
ADJECTIVE **5** Someone who is **cross** is rather angry.

cross out
VERB If you **cross out** words on a page, you draw a line through them.

cross-country
NOUN the sport of running across open countryside, rather than on roads or a track

crossing crossings
NOUN **1** a place where you can cross the road, a railway or a river
2 a journey by ship to a place across the sea

crossroads
NOUN a place where two roads meet and cross each other

cross-section cross-sections
NOUN **1** the flat part of something that you see when you cut straight through it to see inside • *We looked at cross-sections of kiwi fruit and oranges.*

2 a typical sample of people or things • *We interviewed a cross-section of teenagers.*

crossword crosswords
NOUN a word puzzle in which you work out answers to clues and write them in a grid

crouch crouches, crouching, crouched
VERB If you **crouch**, you lower your body with your knees bent.

crow crows, crowing, crowed
NOUN **1** a large black bird that makes a loud, harsh sound
VERB **2** When a cock **crows**, it makes a series of loud sounds, usually early in the morning.

crowbar crowbars
NOUN a heavy, iron bar used as a lever or for forcing things open

crowd crowds, crowding, crowded
NOUN **1** a large group of people gathered together

a
b
c
d
e
f
g
h
i
j
k
l
m
n
o
p
q
r
s
t
u
v
w
x
y
z

95

A
B
C
D
E
F
G
H
I
J
K
L
M
N
O
P
Q
R
S
T
U
V
W
X
Y
Z

VERB **2** When people **crowd** around someone or something, they gather closely together around them.

crown crowns, crowning, crowned
NOUN **1** a circular ornament made of gold or jewels, which a king or queen wears on their head
VERB **2** When a king or queen is **crowned**, a crown is put on their head and they are officially made king or queen.

crucial
ADJECTIVE Something that is **crucial** is very important.

crucify crucifies, crucifying, crucified
VERB When a person is **crucified** they are tied or nailed to a cross and left there to die.
crucifixion NOUN

crude cruder, crudest
ADJECTIVE **1** rough and simple • *a **crude** shelter made of old boxes*
2 rude and vulgar

cruel crueller, cruellest
ADJECTIVE **Cruel** people deliberately cause pain or distress to other people or to animals.
SYNONYMS: brutal, unkind
cruelly ADVERB   **cruelty** NOUN

cruise cruises, cruising, cruised
NOUN **1** a holiday in which you travel on a ship and visit places
VERB **2** When a vehicle **cruises**, it moves at a constant, moderate speed.

crumb crumbs
NOUN a very small piece of bread or cake

crumble crumbles, crumbling, crumbled
VERB When something **crumbles**, or when you **crumble** it, it breaks into small pieces.

crumple crumples, crumpling, crumpled
VERB If you **crumple** paper or cloth, you squash it so that it is full of creases and folds.

crunch crunches, crunching, crunched
VERB If you **crunch** something, you crush it noisily, for example between your teeth or under your feet.

crusade crusades
NOUN **1** In the Middle Ages, the **Crusades** were a number of expeditions to Palestine by Christians who were attempting to recapture the Holy Land from the Muslims.
2 a long and determined attempt to achieve something
[from Spanish *cruzar* meaning to take up the cross]
crusader NOUN

crush crushes, crushing, crushed
VERB **1** If you **crush** something, you squeeze it hard until its shape is destroyed. • *He **crushed** the empty can.*
2 If you **crush** against someone or something, you press hard against them. • *We **crushed** against each other in the crowded bus.*

crust crusts
NOUN **1** the hard outside part of a loaf
2 a hard layer on top of something
• *the earth's **crust***

crustacean crustaceans
Said "krus-**tay**-shun" NOUN an animal with a hard outer shell and several pairs of legs, which usually lives in water
• *Crabs, lobsters and shrimps are **crustaceans**.*

crutch crutches
NOUN a support like a long stick that you lean on if you have injured your leg or foot • *I was on **crutches** while my ankle healed.*

cry cries, crying, cried
VERB **1** When you **cry**, tears come from your eyes because you are unhappy or hurt.
2 If you **cry** something, you shout it or say it loudly.
NOUN **3** a shout or other loud sound made with your voice

crypt crypts
NOUN an underground room beneath a church, usually used as a burial place

crystal crystals
NOUN **1** a piece of a mineral that has formed naturally into a regular shape
2 a type of transparent rock, used in jewellery
3 a type of very high quality glass
crystalline ADJECTIVE

cub cubs
NOUN **1** the young of some wild animals
• *a fox* **cub** • *a lion* **cub**
2 The **Cubs** is an organization for young boys before they join the Scouts.

cube cubes
NOUN a solid shape with six square faces that are all the same size

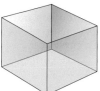

cubic
ADJECTIVE **1** shaped like a cube
2 used to describe volume when you measure height, width and depth
• *a* **cubic** *metre*

cubicle cubicles
NOUN a small enclosed area in a place such as a sports centre or a shop, where you can dress and undress

cuboid cuboids
NOUN a rectangular, three-dimensional box shape. A **cuboid** has six faces, all of which are rectangles.

cuckoo cuckoos
NOUN a grey bird with a two-note call. **Cuckoos** lay their eggs in other birds' nests.

cucumber cucumbers
NOUN a long, thin, green vegetable that is eaten raw

cud
NOUN food that has been chewed and digested more than once by cows, sheep or other animals that have more than one stomach

cuddle cuddles, cuddling, cuddled
VERB **1** If you **cuddle** someone, you hold them closely in your arms as a way of showing your affection.
NOUN **2** If you give someone a **cuddle**, you cuddle them.
cuddly ADJECTIVE

cuff cuffs
NOUN the end part of a sleeve, especially a shirt sleeve

cul-de-sac cul-de-sacs
NOUN a road that does not lead to any other roads because one end is blocked off
[from French *cul + de + sac* meaning bottom of the bag]

culprit culprits
NOUN someone who has done something harmful or wrong

cult cults
NOUN **1** a small religious group, especially one that is considered strange
ADJECTIVE **2** very popular or fashionable among a particular group of people
• *It became a* **cult** *film.*

cultivate cultivates, cultivating, cultivated
VERB When someone **cultivates** land, they grow crops on it.
cultivation NOUN

culture cultures
NOUN the ideas, customs and art of a particular society

cunning
ADJECTIVE A **cunning** person or plan achieves things in a clever way, often by deceiving people.
SYNONYMS: crafty, sly, wily

cup cups, cupping, cupped
NOUN **1** a small, round container with a handle, which you drink from
2 a large metal container with two handles, which is given as a prize
VERB **3** If you **cup** your hands, you put them together to make a shape like a cup.

cupboard cupboards
NOUN **1** a piece of furniture with doors and shelves

2 a very small room for storing things in • *The broom is in the* **cupboard** *under the stairs.*

curator **curators**
NOUN the person in a museum or art gallery in charge of its contents

curb **curbs, curbing, curbed**
VERB If you **curb** something, you keep it within limits. • *You must* **curb** *your spending on comics.*

curdle **curdles, curdling, curdled**
VERB When milk **curdles**, it turns sour.

cure **cures, curing, cured**
VERB **1** If a doctor **cures** someone of an illness, they help them get better.
NOUN **2** something that heals or helps someone to get better
VERB **3** If someone **cures** meat or fish, they smoke it to give it flavour and preserve it.

curfew **curfews**
NOUN a rule or a law stating that people must stay indoors between particular times at night

curiosity **curiosities**
NOUN **1** the desire to know something or about many things
2 something unusual and interesting

curious
ADJECTIVE **1** Someone who is **curious** wants to know more about something.
SYNONYMS: inquisitive, nosy
2 Something that is **curious** is unusual or difficult to understand.
SYNONYMS: strange, peculiar

curl **curls, curling, curled**
NOUN **1** **Curls** are lengths of hair shaped in tight curves and circles.
2 a curved or spiral shape • *A* **curl** *of smoke rose from the chimney.*
VERB **3** If something **curls**, it moves in a curve or spiral. • *Smoke* **curled** *up the chimney.*
curly ADJECTIVE

currant **currants**
NOUN a small, dried grape. **Currants** are often used in cakes and puddings.

currency **currencies**
NOUN A country's **currency** is its coins and banknotes.

current **currents**
NOUN **1** a steady continuous flowing movement of water or air
NOUN **2** An electric **current** is a flow of electricity through a wire or circuit.
ADJECTIVE **3** Something that is **current** is happening now. • **current** *fashion trends*

curriculum **curriculums** or **curricula**
NOUN the different courses taught at a school or university

curry **curries**
NOUN an Indian dish made with hot spices

curse **curses, cursing, cursed**
NOUN **1** an evil spell • *She said the old house had a* **curse** *on it.*
VERB **2** If you **curse**, you swear because you are angry.

cursor **cursors**
NOUN a sign on a computer monitor that shows where the next letter or symbol is

curtain **curtains**
NOUN a hanging piece of material that can be pulled across a window

curtsy **curtsies, curtsying, curtsied**
NOUN **1** a little bobbing bow to show respect • *I made a little* **curtsy** *to the Queen.*
VERB **2** the action of making a curtsy

curve **curves, curving, curved**
NOUN **1** a smooth, gradually bending line

VERB **2** When something **curves**, it moves in a curve or has the shape of a curve. • *The lane* **curved** *to the right.*
curved ADJECTIVE

cushion **cushions, cushioning, cushioned**
NOUN **1** a soft object that you put on a seat to make it more comfortable
VERB **2** When something **cushions** something else, it reduces its effect. • *The pile of leaves* **cushioned** *his fall.*

custard
NOUN a sweet, yellow sauce made from milk and eggs

custody
NOUN **1** If someone has **custody** of a child, they have the legal right to keep it and look after it.
PHRASE **2** Someone who is **in custody** is being kept in prison until they can be tried in a court.
[from Latin *custos* meaning a guard]
custodial ADJECTIVE

custom **customs**
NOUN something that people usually do
• the **custom** of decorating the house for Christmas

customary
ADJECTIVE usual

customer **customers**
NOUN a person who buys things from a shop or firm

customs
NOUN the place at a border, airport or harbour where you declare any goods that you are bringing into the country

cut **cuts, cutting, cut**
VERB **1** If you **cut** something, you use a pair of scissors, a knife or another sharp tool to mark it or remove parts of it.
2 If you **cut** yourself, you injure yourself with a sharp object.
NOUN **3** a mark made with a knife or a sharp tool
4 a reduction in something • *There were lots of price **cuts** during the sales.*

cutlery
NOUN knives, forks and spoons

cycle **cycles, cycling, cycled**
NOUN **1** a bicycle
2 a series of events that is repeated again and again • the **cycle** of the seasons
VERB **3** When you **cycle**, you ride a bicycle.
cyclist NOUN

cyclone **cyclones**
NOUN a violent wind that blows in a spiral like a corkscrew

cygnet **cygnets**
NOUN a young swan

cylinder **cylinders**
NOUN **1** a hollow or solid shape with straight sides and equal circular faces
See **prism**
2 the part of an engine that the piston moves in
cylindrical ADJECTIVE

cymbal **cymbals**
NOUN a circular brass plate used as a percussion instrument. **Cymbals** are clashed together or hit with a stick.
See **percussion**

a
b
c
d
e
f
g
h
i
j
k
l
m
n
o
p
q
r
s
t
u
v
w
x
y
z

Dd

dabble dabbles, dabbling, dabbled
VERB If you **dabble** in something, you work or play at it without being seriously involved in it.

dad or **daddy** dads or daddies
NOUN INFORMAL Your **dad** or your **daddy** is your father.

daffodil daffodils
NOUN a plant with yellow, trumpet-shaped flowers that blooms in spring

daft dafter, daftest
ADJECTIVE silly and not very sensible

dagger daggers
NOUN a weapon like a short knife

daily
ADJECTIVE occurring every day

dainty daintier, daintiest
ADJECTIVE very delicate and pretty

dairy dairies
NOUN **1** a shop or company that supplies milk and milk products
2 In New Zealand, a **dairy** is a small shop selling groceries.
ADJECTIVE **3 Dairy** products are foods made from milk, such as butter, cheese, cream and yogurt.

daisy daisies
NOUN a small, wild flower with a yellow centre and small, white petals
[from Old English *deagesege* meaning day's eye, because the daisy opens in the daytime and closes at night]

Dalmatian Dalmatians
NOUN a large, smooth-haired white dog with black or brown spots

dam dams
NOUN a barrier built across a river to hold back water

damage damages, damaging, damaged
VERB If you **damage** something, you harm or spoil it.

damp damper, dampest
ADJECTIVE slightly wet
dampness NOUN

damson damsons
NOUN **1** a small, blue-black plum
2 the tree that damsons grow on

dance dances, dancing, danced
VERB **1** When you **dance**, you move around in time to music.
NOUN **2** a series of rhythmic movements that you do in time to music
3 a social event where people dance with each other

dandelion dandelions
NOUN a wild plant with yellow flowers that form a ball of fluffy seeds
[from Old French *dent de lion* meaning lion's tooth, referring to the shape of the leaves]

dandruff
NOUN small, loose scales of dead skin in someone's hair

danger dangers
NOUN the possibility that someone may be harmed or killed
SYNONYMS: peril, risk

dangerous
ADJECTIVE If something is **dangerous**, it is likely to cause hurt or harm. ● *It is **dangerous** to walk close to the edge of the cliff.*
SYNONYMS: unsafe, hazardous
dangerously ADVERB

dangle dangles, dangling, dangled
VERB When something **dangles**, or when you **dangle** it, it swings or hangs loosely.
● *We sat by the pool and **dangled** our legs in the water.*

dappled
ADJECTIVE marked with patches of a different or darker shade ● *The lawn was **dappled** with the shadows of the leafy trees.*

dare dares, daring, dared
VERB **1** If you **dare** to do something, you have the courage to do it.
2 If you **dare** someone to do something, you challenge them to do it. ● *I **dare** you to ask him his name.*
[from Old English *durran* meaning to venture or to be bold]

daredevil daredevils
NOUN a person who enjoys doing dangerous things

daring
ADJECTIVE **1** bold and willing to take risks
NOUN **2** the courage required to do things that are dangerous
daringly ADVERB

dark darker, darkest
ADJECTIVE **1** If it is **dark**, there is not enough light to see properly.
2 Dark colours have a lot of black, grey or brown tones in them.
dark NOUN

darken darkens, darkening, darkened
VERB If something **darkens**, it becomes darker than it was before. ● *The sky **darkened** as the storm approached.*

darkness
NOUN being dark

darling darlings
NOUN You call someone **darling** if you love them or like them very much.

darn darns, darning, darned
VERB **1** When you **darn** a hole in a garment, you mend it with crossing stitches.
NOUN **2** A **darn** is the part of a garment that has been darned.

dart darts, darting, darted
NOUN **1** a small, pointed arrow
2 Darts is a game in which the players throw **darts** at a round board divided into numbered sections.
VERB **3** If you **dart** somewhere, you move there quickly and suddenly.

dash dashes, dashing, dashed
VERB **1** If you **dash** somewhere, you rush there.
NOUN **2** the punctuation mark (–) which may be used instead of brackets

dashboard dashboards
NOUN the instrument panel in a car

data
NOUN information, usually in the form of facts or statistics

Data is really a plural word, but is usually used as a singular word: *Customer data is stored here.*

database databases
NOUN a collection of information stored in a computer

date dates
NOUN **1** a particular day or year that can be named ● *What is your **date** of birth?*
2 If you have a **date**, you have an appointment to meet someone.
3 a small, brown, sticky fruit with a stone inside. **Dates** grow on palm trees.

daughter daughters
NOUN Someone's **daughter** is their female child.

dawdle dawdles, dawdling, dawdled
VERB If you **dawdle**, you are slow about doing something or going somewhere.
● *Don't **dawdle**, we have to be there in ten minutes.*

dawn dawns
NOUN the time in the morning when light first appears in the sky

day days
NOUN **1** the time taken between one midnight and the next. There are 24 hours in one **day**.

2 the period of light between sunrise and sunset

daydream daydreams, daydreaming, daydreamed

NOUN **1** pleasant thoughts about things that you would like to happen

VERB **2** When you **daydream**, you drift off into a daydream.

daylight

NOUN the part of the day when it is light

daytime

NOUN the part of the day when it is light

daze

PHRASE If you are **in a daze**, you are confused and bewildered.

dazzle dazzles, dazzling, dazzled

VERB If a bright light **dazzles** you, it blinds you for a moment.

dazzling ADJECTIVE

de-

PREFIX added to some words to mean removal or reversal of something • *She debugged the computer program.* • *We had to defrost the windscreen before leaving.*

dead

ADJECTIVE **1** no longer living

2 no longer functioning • *The phone went dead.*

ADVERB **3** precisely or exactly • *We arrived dead on eight o'clock.*

deadly deadlier, deadliest

ADJECTIVE **1** likely or able to cause death • *a deadly disease*

ADVERB OR ADJECTIVE **2** used to emphasize how serious or unpleasant something is • *deadly dangerous* • *deadly serious*

deaf deafer, deafest

ADJECTIVE **Deaf** people are unable to hear anything or unable to hear well.

deafening

ADJECTIVE A **deafening** sound is so loud that you cannot hear anything else.

deal deals, dealing, dealt

NOUN **1** an agreement or arrangement, especially in business

VERB **2** If you **deal** with something, you do what is necessary to sort it out.

3 When you **deal** cards, you give them out to the players.

PHRASE **4 A good deal** *or* **a great deal** of something is a lot of it.

dear dearer, dearest

NOUN **1** You call someone **dear** as a sign of affection.

ADJECTIVE **2** Something that is **dear** is very expensive.

3 You use **dear** at the beginning of a letter, with the name of the person you are writing to. • *Dear Sunita.*

death deaths

NOUN the end of the life of a human being or other animal or plant

debate debates, debating, debated

NOUN **1** argument or discussion

2 a formal discussion in which opposing views are expressed

VERB **3** When people **debate** something, they discuss it in a formal way.

debit card debit cards

NOUN a plastic card that allows someone to buy goods using the money in their bank account

debris

NOUN fragments or rubble left after something has been destroyed • *After the eruption, volcanic debris was found scattered for miles.*

debt debts

NOUN a sum of money that someone owes

debut debuts

NOUN a performer's first public appearance

decade decades

NOUN a period of ten years

decaffeinated

ADJECTIVE **Decaffeinated** coffee or tea has had most of the caffeine removed.

decathlon decathlons

NOUN an athletic competition in which competitors take part in ten different events

decay decays, decaying, decayed

VERB When things **decay**, they rot or go bad.

deceased

ADJECTIVE FORMAL A **deceased** person is someone who has recently died.

deceit

NOUN behaviour that makes people believe something to be true that is not true

deceive deceives, deceiving, deceived

VERB If you **deceive** someone, you make them believe something that is not true.

December

NOUN the twelfth month of the year. **December** has 31 days.

decent

ADJECTIVE honest and respectable

deception deceptions

NOUN **1** something that is intended to trick or deceive someone
2 the act of deceiving someone

deceptive

ADJECTIVE likely to make people believe that something is true when it is not

decide decides, deciding, decided

VERB If you **decide** to do something, you choose to do it, usually after thinking about it carefully.
SYNONYM: make up one's mind
decision NOUN

deciduous

ADJECTIVE **Deciduous** trees lose their leaves in the autumn every year.

decimal decimals

ADJECTIVE **1** A **decimal** system involves counting in units of ten.
NOUN **2** A **decimal**, or **decimal** fraction, is a fraction in which a dot, called a decimal point, separates the whole numbers on the left from tenths, hundredths and thousandths on the right. For example, 0.5 represents $5/10$ (or $1/2$); 0.05 represents $5/100$ (or $1/20$).

decision decisions

NOUN a choice or judgement that is made about something

decisive

ADJECTIVE **1** A **decisive** person is able to make decisions quickly.
2 having an important influence on the result of something • *The first goal was a **decisive** moment in the match.*

deck decks

NOUN a downstairs or upstairs area on a bus or ship

declare declares, declaring, declared

VERB **1** If you **declare** something, you say it firmly and forcefully.
SYNONYMS: announce, proclaim, state
2 FORMAL If something is **declared**, it is announced publicly. • *War was **declared** in 1939.*

decline declines, declining, declined

VERB **1** If something **declines**, it becomes smaller or weaker. • *The number of students has **declined** this year.*
2 If you **decline** something, you politely refuse to accept it or do it.

decode decodes, decoding, decoded

VERB If you **decode** a coded message, you convert it into ordinary language.

decompose decomposes, decomposing, decomposed

VERB If something **decomposes**, it rots after it dies.

decorate decorates, decorating, decorated

VERB **1** If you **decorate** something, you make it more attractive by adding things to it.
2 If you **decorate** a room or building, you paint or wallpaper it.

decoy decoys

NOUN something used to lead a person or animal into a trap

decrease decreases, decreasing, decreased

VERB If something **decreases**, or if you **decrease** it, it becomes less. • *The number of children in the class **decreased** rapidly.*

a
b
c
d
e
f
g
h
i
j
k
l
m
n
o
p
q
r
s
t
u
v
w
x
y
z

decree decrees, decreeing, decreed

NOUN **1** an official order by the government, church or the rulers of a country

VERB **2** If someone **decrees** something, they announce formally that it will happen.

dedicate dedicates, dedicating, dedicated

VERB **1** If you **dedicate** yourself to something, you give your time and energy to it.

2 If you **dedicate** a book or piece of music to someone, you say that it is written for them.

deduct deducts, deducting, deducted

VERB If you **deduct** an amount from a total, you take it away.

deed deeds

NOUN **1** something that is done • a good **deed**

2 an important piece of paper or document that an agreement is written on

deep deeper, deepest

ADJECTIVE **1** going a long way down from the surface • a **deep** hole

2 great or intense • **deep** affection

3 a low sound • a **deep** voice

deer

NOUN a large, fast-running, graceful mammal with hooves, that lives wild in parts of Britain and other countries. Male **deer** have antlers.

deface defaces, defacing, defaced

VERB If you **deface** something, you damage its appearance in some way.
• The gang **defaced** the walls with spray paint.

defeat defeats, defeating, defeated

VERB **1** If you **defeat** someone or something, you win a victory over them, or cause them to fail.

NOUN **2** the state of being beaten or of failing • The team was downhearted after its **defeat**.

defect defects, defecting, defected

NOUN **1** a fault or flaw in something

VERB **2** If someone **defects**, they leave their own country or organization and join an opposing one.

defection NOUN **defector** NOUN

defective

ADJECTIVE Something that is **defective** is not perfect or has something wrong with it.

defence defences

NOUN **1** something that protects you against attack • She carried an alarm as a **defence** against muggers.

2 A country's **defences** are its armed forces and its weapons.

defend defends, defending, defended

VERB **1** If you **defend** someone or something, you protect them from harm or danger.

2 If you **defend** a person or their ideas, you argue in support of them.

defendant defendants

NOUN a person in a court of law who is accused of a crime

defer defers, deferring, deferred

VERB If you **defer** something, you put off doing it until later.

defiant

ADJECTIVE If you are **defiant**, you behave in a way that shows you are not willing to obey someone.

defiance NOUN **defiantly** ADVERB

deficient

ADJECTIVE lacking in something

deficiency NOUN

define defines, defining, defined

VERB If you **define** something, you say what it is or what it means.

definite

ADJECTIVE **1** clear and unlikely to be changed • We must arrange a **definite** date for the party.

2 true rather than being someone's guess or opinion

There is no a in definite.

definitely
ADVERB OR EXCLAMATION certainly; without doubt
• I am **definitely** going on holiday next week.

definition definitions
NOUN a statement explaining the meaning of a word or an idea

deflate deflates, deflating, deflated
VERB If you **deflate** something, such as a tyre or balloon, you let all the air or gas out of it.
ANTONYMS: inflate, blow up

deforestation
NOUN the cutting down or the destruction of all the trees in an area

deformed
ADJECTIVE disfigured or abnormally shaped

defrost defrosts, defrosting, defrosted
VERB **1** If you **defrost** frozen food, you let it thaw out.
2 If you **defrost** a freezer or refrigerator, you remove the ice from it.

defuse defuses, defusing, defused
VERB **1** If someone **defuses** a bomb, they remove its fuse or detonator so that it cannot explode.
2 If you **defuse** a dangerous or tense situation, you make it less dangerous or tense.

defy defies, defying, defied
VERB If you **defy** a person or a law, you openly refuse to obey.

degree degrees
NOUN **1** a unit of measurement for temperatures, angles, and longitude and latitude, written as ° after a number • The temperature was 20 °C. • A right angle is a ninety-**degree** angle.
2 an amount of a feeling or quality • As captain you have a high **degree** of responsibility.
3 a university qualification gained after completing a course of study there

dehydrated
ADJECTIVE If someone is **dehydrated**, they are weak or ill because they have lost too much water from their body.

deity deities
NOUN a god or goddess

dejected
ADJECTIVE If you are **dejected**, you are sad and gloomy.
dejection NOUN

delay delays, delaying, delayed
VERB **1** If you **delay** doing something, you put it off until later.
SYNONYM: postpone
2 If something **delays** you, it makes you late or slows you down.
NOUN **3** If there is a **delay**, something does not happen until later than planned or expected.

delete deletes, deleting, deleted
VERB If you **delete** something written, you cross it out or remove it.

deliberate
ADJECTIVE **1** done on purpose or planned in advance
2 slow and careful in speech and action
• **deliberate** movements
deliberately ADVERB

delicate
ADJECTIVE **1** light and attractive • a **delicate** perfume
2 fragile and needing to be handled carefully • a **delicate** china cup
3 precise or sensitive • **delicate** instruments
delicately ADVERB

delicatessen delicatessens
NOUN a shop selling unusual or imported foods

delicious
ADJECTIVE **Delicious** food or drink has an extremely pleasant taste.
SYNONYMS: delectable, scrumptious

delight delights, delighting, delighted
NOUN **1** great pleasure or joy
VERB **2** If something **delights** you, or if you are **delighted** by it, it gives you a lot of pleasure.
delighted ADJECTIVE

A
B
C
D
E
F
G
H
I
J
K
L
M
N
O
P
Q
R
S
T
U
V
W
X
Y
Z

delinquent delinquents
NOUN a young person who commits minor crimes
delinquency NOUN

delirious
ADJECTIVE **1** unable to speak or act in a rational way because of illness or fever **2** wildly excited and happy
deliriously ADVERB

deliver delivers, delivering, delivered
VERB **1** If you **deliver** something to someone, you take it and give it to them. **2** If someone **delivers** a baby, they help the woman who is giving birth.

delta deltas
NOUN a triangular piece of land at the mouth of a river where it divides into separate streams

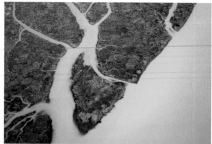

deluge deluges
NOUN a sudden, heavy downpour of rain

demand demands, demanding, demanded
VERB **1** If you **demand** something, you ask for it forcefully.
NOUN **2** If there is **demand** for something, a lot of people want to buy it or have it.

democracy democracies
NOUN a system of government in which the people choose their leaders by voting for them in elections
democratic ADJECTIVE

demolish demolishes, demolishing, demolished
VERB If someone **demolishes** a building, they knock it down.
demolition NOUN

demon demons
NOUN a devil or an evil spirit

demonstrate demonstrates, demonstrating, demonstrated
VERB **1** If you **demonstrate** something to somebody, you show them how to do it or how it works. **2** If people **demonstrate**, they march or gather together to show that they oppose or support something.

demonstration demonstrations
NOUN **1** If someone gives a **demonstration**, they show how to do something or how something works. **2** a march or a gathering of people to show publicly what they think about something

den dens
NOUN **1** a home or hiding place of a wild animal **2** a special place where you can do what you want without being disturbed

denial denials
NOUN **1** A **denial** of something is a statement that it is untrue. **2** The **denial** of a request is the refusal to grant it.

denim denims
NOUN strong, cotton cloth used for making clothes, especially jeans
[from French *serge de Nîmes*, meaning serge (a type of cloth) from Nîmes]

denominator denominators
NOUN In mathematics, the **denominator** is the bottom number of a fraction.

dense denser, densest
ADJECTIVE **1** Something that is **dense** contains a lot of things or people in a small area. ● *We cut our way through the **dense** forest.* **2** difficult to see through ● *The **dense** fog prevented us from enjoying the view over the hills.*
densely ADVERB

density densities
NOUN **1** thickness **2** the proportion of mass to volume

dent dents, denting, dented

VERB **1** If you **dent** something, you damage its surface by hitting it.

NOUN **2** a hollow in the surface of something

dental

ADJECTIVE to do with teeth

dentist dentists

NOUN a person who is qualified to treat people's teeth

dentures

PLURAL NOUN false teeth

deny denies, denying, denied

VERB **1** If you **deny** something, you say that it is not true.

2 If you are **denied** something, you are refused it.

deodorant deodorants

NOUN a substance used to hide or prevent the smell of sweat on your body

depart departs, departing, departed

VERB When you **depart**, you leave.

departure NOUN

department departments

NOUN one of the sections into which a large shop or an organization is divided

department store department stores

NOUN a very large shop divided into departments, each selling different types of goods

depend depends, depending, depended

VERB **1** If one thing **depends** on another, it is influenced by it. • *The cooking time* ***depends*** *on the size of the potato.*

2 If you **depend** on someone or something, you trust them and rely on them.

dependable

ADJECTIVE If someone is **dependable**, you can trust them to be helpful, sensible and reliable.

depict depicts, depicting, depicted

VERB If you **depict** someone or something, you paint, draw or describe them.

deport deports, deporting, deported

VERB If someone is **deported** from a country they are sent out of it, either because they have no right to be there, because they have done something wrong or because they did not ask permission to be there.

deposit deposits, depositing, deposited

VERB **1** If you **deposit** something, you put it down or leave it somewhere.

NOUN **2** a sum of money given in part payment for goods or services

depot depots

NOUN **1** a place where supplies of food or equipment are stored until they are needed

2 A bus **depot** is a bus station.

depressed

ADJECTIVE sad and gloomy

depression depressions

NOUN **1** a state of mind in which someone feels unhappy and has no energy or enthusiasm for anything

2 a hollow in the ground or on any other surface

3 a time when there is a lot of unemployment and poverty

deprive deprives, depriving, deprived

VERB If you **deprive** someone of something, you take it away from them or prevent them from having it.

depth depths

NOUN **1** the measurement or distance between the top and bottom of something, or the back and front of something • *The* ***depth*** *of the swimming pool at the deep end is 1.5 m.*

PHRASE **2 In depth** means thoroughly. • *We studied the poem* ***in depth***.

deputy deputies

NOUN a person who helps someone in their job and acts on their behalf when they are away

derail derails, derailed, derailing

VERB If a train is **derailed**, it comes off the railway tracks.

derivation derivations
NOUN The **derivation** of something is where it has come from.

derive derives, deriving, derived
VERB **1** FORMAL If you **derive** something from someone or something, you get it from them. ● He **derives** great pleasure from music.
2 If something is **derived** from something else, it comes from that thing. ● His name is **derived** from a Greek word.

descant descants
NOUN **1** The **descant** to a tune is another tune played at the same time but at a higher pitch.
ADJECTIVE **2** A **descant** musical instrument plays the highest notes in a range of instruments. ● a **descant** recorder

descend descends, descending, descended
VERB If someone or something **descends**, they move downwards. ● We **descended** to the basement in the lift.
ANTONYM: ascend

descendant descendants
NOUN A person's **descendants** are all the people in later generations who are related to them.

describe describes, describing, described
VERB If you **describe** someone or something, you say what they are like.

desert deserts, deserting, deserted
Said "dez-ert" NOUN **1** an area of land, usually in a hot region, that has almost no water, rain, trees or plants ● the Sahara **Desert**

Said "de-**zert**" VERB **2** If someone **deserts** you, they leave you and no longer help or support you.

deserted
ADJECTIVE A **deserted** building or place is one that people have left and never come back to.

deserve deserves, deserving, deserved
VERB If you **deserve** something, you earn it or have a right to it.

design designs, designing, designed
VERB **1** If you **design** something new, you plan what it should be like.
NOUN **2** a drawing from which something can be built or made
3 a decorative pattern of lines or shapes

desire desires, desiring, desired
VERB **1** If you **desire** something, you want it.
NOUN **2** a strong feeling of wanting something
SYNONYMS: longing, want, wish

desk desks
NOUN a piece of furniture with a flat or sloping top, which you sit at to write, read or work

desktop
ADJECTIVE small enough to be used at a desk ● a **desktop** computer

desolate
ADJECTIVE **1** deserted and bleak ● a **desolate** mountain top
2 lonely, very sad, and without hope
desolation NOUN

despair despairs, despairing, despaired
NOUN **1** a total loss of hope
VERB **2** If you **despair**, you lose hope.

desperate
ADJECTIVE **1** If you are **desperate**, you are in such a bad situation that you will try anything to change it.
2 A **desperate** situation is extremely dangerous or serious.

despicable

ADJECTIVE Something that is **despicable** is nasty, cruel or evil.

despise despises, despising, despised

VERB If you **despise** someone or something, you have a very low opinion of them.

despite

PREPOSITION If you do something **despite** some difficulty, you manage to do it anyway.

dessert desserts

NOUN a sweet food that you eat at the end of a meal

destination destinations

NOUN the place you are going to

destined

ADJECTIVE meant to happen ● *They were* **destined** *to meet.*

destiny destinies

NOUN Your **destiny** is your fate: the things that will happen to you in the future.

destitute

ADJECTIVE without money or possessions, and therefore in great need
destitution NOUN

destroy destroys, destroying, destroyed

VERB If you **destroy** something, you damage it so much that it is completely ruined.
SYNONYMS: demolish, ruin, wreck
destruction NOUN

destructive

ADJECTIVE Something that is **destructive** can cause great damage, harm or injury.
SYNONYM: damaging

detach detaches, detaching, detached

VERB If you **detach** something, you remove or unfasten it.
detachable ADJECTIVE

detached

ADJECTIVE separate or standing apart ● *It was a* **detached** *house, standing alone at the top of the hill.*

detail details

NOUN **1** an individual fact or feature of something ● *I remember every* **detail** *of that film.*
PLURAL NOUN **2 Details** about something are information about it. For example, your **details** might be your name and address.

detain detains, detaining, detained

VERB If you **detain** someone, you keep them from going somewhere or doing something.

detect detects, detecting, detected

VERB If you **detect** something, you notice or find it. ● *X-rays can* **detect** *broken bones.*

detective detectives

NOUN a person, usually a police officer, whose job is to investigate crimes

detector detectors

NOUN an instrument used to detect the presence of something ● *a metal* **detector**

detention

NOUN **1** a form of punishment in which a pupil is made to stay in school for extra time when other children do not have to **2** arrest or imprisonment

deter deters, deterring, deterred

VERB If you **deter** someone from doing something, you persuade them not to do it or try to stop them in some way.

detergent detergents

NOUN a chemical substance used for washing or cleaning things

deteriorate deteriorates, deteriorating, deteriorated

VERB If something **deteriorates**, it gets worse.
deterioration NOUN

determination

NOUN a great strength and will to do something

determined

ADJECTIVE having your mind firmly made up ● *She was* **determined** *to pass her exams.*

A
B
C
D
E
F
G
H
I
J
K
L
M
N
O
P
Q
R
S
T
U
V
W
X
Y
Z

deterrent deterrents
NOUN something that prevents people from doing something, usually by making them afraid to do it • We have a car alarm as a **deterrent** to car thieves.

detest detests, detesting, detested
VERB If you **detest** someone or something, you dislike them intensely.
[from Latin detestari meaning to curse]
detestable ADJECTIVE

detonate detonates, detonating, detonated
VERB If someone **detonates** a bomb or mine, they cause it to explode.
detonation NOUN   detonator NOUN

detour detours
NOUN If you make a **detour** on a journey, you go by a longer or less direct route.

devastate devastates, devastating, devastated
VERB A place that has been **devastated** has been severely damaged or destroyed.
devastation NOUN

develop develops, developing, developed
VERB **1** When something **develops**, it grows or becomes more advanced.
2 If you **develop** photographs or film, you produce a visible image from them.

development developments
NOUN gradual growth or progress • There have been great **developments** in technology over the past fifty years.

device devices
NOUN a machine or tool that is used for a particular purpose

devil devils
NOUN an evil spirit

devious
ADJECTIVE **Devious** people behave in an underhand, nasty and secretive way.

devise devises, devising, devised
VERB If you **devise** something, you invent it or design it.

devoted
ADJECTIVE very loving and loyal

devour devours, devouring, devoured
VERB **1** If you **devour** food, you eat it quickly and greedily.
2 If one creature **devours** another, it eats it.
3 If you **devour** a book, you read it very quickly.

devout
ADJECTIVE very deeply religious

dew
NOUN drops of moisture that form on the ground and other cool surfaces at night

diabetes
NOUN a condition in which a person has too much sugar in their blood
diabetic NOUN OR ADJECTIVE

diagnose diagnoses, diagnosing, diagnosed
VERB If someone **diagnoses** an illness or problem, they identify what is wrong.

diagonal diagonals
NOUN **1** a straight line that slopes from one corner of a shape to another
ADJECTIVE **2** in a slanting direction
• a **diagonal** line
[from Greek diagonios meaning from angle to angle]

diagram diagrams
NOUN a drawing that shows or explains something • Carroll or Venn **diagram**

dial dials, dialling, dialled
NOUN **1** the part of a clock or meter where the time or a measurement is shown
VERB **2** If you **dial** a telephone number, you press the buttons to select the number you want.

dialect dialects
NOUN the form of a language spoken in a particular area

dialogue dialogues
NOUN In a novel, play or film, **dialogue** is conversation.

diameter
diameters
NOUN the length of a straight line drawn across a circle through its centre

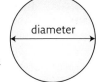
diameter

diamond **diamonds**
NOUN **1** a precious stone made of pure carbon
2 a shape with four straight sides of equal length that are not at right angles to each other
See **rhombus**

diarrhoea
NOUN an illness that attacks your bowels so that you can't stop going to the lavatory

diary **diaries**
NOUN a notebook with a separate space or page for each day of the year

dice **dices, dicing, diced**
NOUN **1** a small cube with dots on each of its six faces
VERB **2** If you **dice** food, you cut it into small cubes.

dictate **dictates, dictating, dictated**
VERB **1** If you **dictate** something, you say it or read it aloud for someone else to write down.
2 If you **dictate** to someone, you give them orders in a bossy way.
dictation NOUN

dictionary **dictionaries**
NOUN a book in which words are listed alphabetically and their meanings explained

did
VERB the past tense of **do**

didgeridoo **didgeridoos**
NOUN an Australian wind instrument made from a long, hollowed-out piece of wood

didn't
VERB a contraction of *did not*

die **dies, dying, died**
VERB **1** When humans, other animals or plants **die**, they stop living.
2 When something **dies**, **dies away** or **dies down**, it becomes less intense and disappears. • *The wind* ***died down***.

diesel **diesels**
NOUN **1** a heavy fuel used in trains, buses and lorries
2 a vehicle with a diesel engine

diet **diets**
NOUN **1** the food you usually eat
2 If you are on a **diet**, you eat only certain foods for health reasons or to lose weight.

difference **differences**
NOUN **1** the way in which things are unlike each other
2 the amount by which one number is less than another
3 a change in someone or something

different
ADJECTIVE If one thing is **different** from another, it is not like it.

There are two *es* in *different*.

difficult
ADJECTIVE **1 Difficult** things are not easy to do, understand or solve.
2 Someone who is **difficult** behaves in an unreasonable way.

difficulty **difficulties**
NOUN a problem

dig **digs, digging, dug**
VERB **1** If you **dig**, you make a hole in earth or sand, especially with a spade.
2 If you **dig** something, you poke it.

digest **digests, digesting, digested**
VERB To **digest** food means to break it down in the gut so that it can be easily absorbed and used by the body.
digestible ADJECTIVE

digit **digits**
Said "**dij**-it" NOUN **1** a written symbol for any of the numbers from zero (0) to nine (9) • *A two-**digit** number: 46.*
2 a finger or toe

a
b
c
d
e
f
g
h
i
j
k
l
m
n
o
p
q
r
s
t
u
v
w
x
y
z

111

digital

ADJECTIVE **Digital** instruments, such as watches, have changing numbers instead of a dial with hands.

ANTONYM: analogue

dignified

ADJECTIVE **Dignified** people are calm, and behave in a way that other people admire and respect.

dilemma dilemmas

NOUN a situation where you have to choose between two alternatives that are equally difficult or unpleasant

diligent

ADJECTIVE hard-working and showing care

diligently ADVERB   diligence NOUN

dilute dilutes, diluting, diluted

VERB If you **dilute** a liquid, you add water or another liquid to it to make it weaker.

dim dimmer, dimmest; dims, dimming, dimmed

ADJECTIVE **1** lacking in brightness and badly lit

VERB **2** If lights **dim**, or are **dimmed**, they become less bright.

dimension dimensions

NOUN The **dimensions** of something are its measurements or its size.

diminish diminishes, diminishing, diminished

VERB If something **diminishes**, or you **diminish** it, it reduces in size or importance.

diminutive diminutives

ADJECTIVE **1** very small

NOUN **2** You can make **diminutives** by adding the suffixes -kin, -let or -ette to other words. For example lambkin, piglet, diskette.

dimple dimples

NOUN a small hollow in someone's cheek or chin

din

NOUN a very loud and unpleasant noise

dine dines, dining, dined

VERB FORMAL When you **dine**, you eat dinner in the evening.

dinghy dinghies

NOUN a small boat that is rowed, sailed or powered by an outboard motor

dingo dingoes

NOUN an Australian wild dog

dingy dingier, dingiest

ADJECTIVE shabby and dirty to look at

dinner dinners

NOUN the main meal of the day, eaten either in the evening or in the middle of the day

dinosaur dinosaurs

NOUN a large reptile that lived in prehistoric times

[from Greek deinos + sauros meaning fearful lizard]

dip dips, dipping, dipped

VERB **1** If you **dip** something into a liquid, you lower it in and take it out again quickly.

2 If something **dips**, it slopes downwards or goes below a certain level. • The road **dipped** suddenly.

NOUN **3** a downward slope or hollow

• There was a **dip** in the road.

4 a quick swim

5 a savoury mixture for eating, in which you dip crisps, crackers or vegetables

diploma diplomas

NOUN a certificate that is awarded to a student who has successfully completed a course of study

diplomat diplomats

NOUN an official who negotiates with another country on behalf of his or her own country

diplomatic
ADJECTIVE If you are **diplomatic**, you are tactful and say and do things without offending people.

direct directs, directing, directed
ADVERB **1** If you go **direct** to a place, you go straight there. ● *This train goes direct to Paris.*
ADJECTIVE **2** If someone's speech or behaviour is **direct**, they are honest and say what they mean.
SYNONYMS: frank, open, straightforward
VERB **3** If you **direct** someone to a place, you show them how to get there.
4 Someone who **directs** a film or play decides the way it is made and performed.

direction directions
NOUN **1** the way that someone or something is moving or pointing
PLURAL NOUN **2** instructions that tell you how to do something or how to get somewhere

director directors
NOUN **1** a senior manager of a company
2 the person who decides how a film or play is made and performed

directory directories
NOUN a book that gives lists of information, such as people's names, addresses and telephone numbers

dirt
NOUN **1** any unclean substance such as mud, dust or stains
2 earth or soil

dirty dirtier, dirtiest
ADJECTIVE **1** marked or covered with dirt
SYNONYMS: filthy, grubby, mucky
2 unfair or dishonest

dis-
PREFIX added to some words to make them mean the opposite. For example, **dis**contented means not content.

disability disabilities
NOUN a condition or illness that limits the way in which someone can use their body

disabled
ADJECTIVE **Disabled** people have an illness or injury that can restrict their way of life.
disable VERB

disadvantage disadvantages
NOUN something that makes things difficult

disagree disagrees, disagreeing, disagreed
VERB **1** If you **disagree** with someone, you have a different opinion or view from them.
2 If you **disagree** with an action or proposal, you believe it is wrong.

disagreeable
ADJECTIVE unpleasant or unhelpful and unfriendly ● *The woman was very disagreeable and did not even offer to help.*

disappear disappears, disappearing, disappeared
VERB **1** If someone or something **disappears**, they go where they cannot be seen or found.
2 If something **disappears**, it stops existing or happening.

disappoint disappoints, disappointing, disappointed
VERB If someone or something **disappoints** you, they fail to live up to what you expected.

disapprove disapproves, disapproving, disapproved
VERB If you **disapprove** of something or someone, you believe they are wrong or bad.
disapproval NOUN   disapproving ADJECTIVE

disaster disasters
NOUN **1** a very bad accident, such as an earthquake or a plane crash
SYNONYMS: calamity, catastrophe
2 a complete failure ● *The party was a disaster.*

disc discs; also spelt disk
NOUN **1** anything with a flat, circular shape, such as a compact **disc**

2 a storage device used in computers
• *Please insert a **disc** into the drive.*

discard discards, discarding, discarded
VERB If you **discard** something, you throw it away because it is of no use to you anymore.

discharge discharges, discharging, discharged
VERB **1** If a doctor **discharges** someone from hospital, they allow them to leave.
2 If something **discharges** or is **discharged**, it is given or sent out.
• *Cars **discharge** exhaust fumes into the atmosphere.*

disciple disciples
NOUN a follower of someone or something
[from Latin *discipulus* meaning pupil]

discipline disciplines, disciplining, disciplined
NOUN **1** making people obey rules, by training them and by punishing them when they break the rules
2 the ability to behave and work in a controlled way
VERB **3** If a parent **disciplines** a child, they punish them.

disc jockey disc jockeys
NOUN someone who introduces and plays pop records on the radio or at a night club

disco discos
NOUN a party or a club where people go to dance to pop music

discomfort
NOUN slight pain or worry

disconnect disconnects, disconnecting, disconnected
VERB If you **disconnect** something, you detach it from something else or break its connection.

discontinue discontinues, discontinuing, discontinued
VERB If you **discontinue** something, you stop doing it.

discount discounts
NOUN a reduction in the price of something

discourage discourages, discouraging, discouraged
VERB **1** If you **discourage** someone, you take away their enthusiasm for doing something.
2 If you **discourage** someone from doing something, you try to persuade them not to do it.
discouraging ADJECTIVE
discouragement NOUN

discover discovers, discovering, discovered
VERB If you **discover** something, you find it or learn about it for the first time.
• *She **discovered** that they'd escaped.*

discreet
ADJECTIVE If you are **discreet**, you keep private things to yourself and can be trusted with a secret.
discretion NOUN

discriminate discriminates, discriminating, discriminated
VERB **1** If you **discriminate** between people, you treat them differently – often unfairly – because of their race, religion or gender.
2 If you are **discriminating**, you can recognise differences between things and use your judgement to make choices.
discrimination NOUN

discus discuses
NOUN a flat, circular weight that athletes throw in a competition

discuss discusses, discussing, discussed
VERB When people **discuss** something, they talk about it in detail.
discussion NOUN

disease diseases
NOUN an illness that affects human beings, other animals or plants

disgrace disgraces, disgracing, disgraced
NOUN **1** something unacceptable
• *Tidy your room – it's a **disgrace**.*

disorder

VERB 2 If you **disgrace** yourself, you do something that others disapprove of.

disgruntled
ADJECTIVE If you are **disgruntled**, you are cross and discontented about something.

disguise disguises, disguising, disguised
VERB **1** If you **disguise** yourself, you change your appearance so that people will not recognize you.
NOUN **2** something you wear or a change you make to your appearance so that people will not recognize you

disgust disgusts, disgusting, disgusted
NOUN **1** a very strong feeling of dislike and loathing
VERB **2** If you **disgust** someone, you make them feel a strong sense of dislike and disapproval.
disgusting ADJECTIVE

dish dishes
NOUN **1** a shallow container for cooking or serving food
2 a particular kind of food, or food cooked in a particular way ● a vegetarian **dish**

disheartened
ADJECTIVE If you are **disheartened**, you feel disappointed.

dishonest
ADJECTIVE not truthful or fit to be trusted
dishonestly ADVERB

dishwasher dishwashers
NOUN a machine that washes crockery, cutlery, pots and pans

disinfectant disinfectants
NOUN a chemical substance that kills germs

disintegrate disintegrates, disintegrating, disintegrated
VERB If an object **disintegrates**, it breaks into many pieces and so is destroyed.
disintegration NOUN

disk
NOUN another spelling of **disc**

dislike dislikes, disliking, disliked
VERB If you **dislike** something or someone, you think they are unpleasant.

dislocate dislocates, dislocating, dislocated
VERB If you **dislocate** a bone in your body, you put it out of its usual position by accident.

disloyal
ADJECTIVE not loyal

dismal
ADJECTIVE depressing and bleak ● It was a **dismal** day, with rain pouring down and cold winds blowing.

dismantle dismantles, dismantling, dismantled
VERB If you **dismantle** something, you take it apart.

dismay dismays, dismaying, dismayed
VERB **1** If something **dismays** you, it worries and alarms you.
NOUN **2** a feeling of fear and worry

dismiss dismisses, dismissing, dismissed
VERB **1** If you **dismiss** something, you decide that it is not important enough for you to think about.
2 If someone is **dismissed**, they are told to leave a place or leave their job. ● She **dismissed** the class.

dismount dismounts, dismounting, dismounted
VERB to get off a horse or a bicycle

disobey disobeys, disobeying, disobeyed
VERB If you **disobey** the rules, you break them. If you **disobey** a person, you refuse to do as they say.
disobedience NOUN **disobedient** ADJECTIVE

disorder disorders
NOUN **1** a state of untidiness
2 lack of organization
3 an illness ● a stomach **disorder**
disorderly ADJECTIVE

a b c d e f g h i j k l m n o p q r s t u v w x y z

115

disorganized; also spelt **disorganised**

ADJECTIVE Someone or something that is **disorganized** is muddled, confused or badly prepared.

dispatch **dispatches, dispatching, dispatched**

VERB **1** If you **dispatch** someone or something to a particular place, you send them there for a particular reason.

NOUN **2** an official message

dispensary **dispensaries**

NOUN a place where medicines are prepared and given out

dispersal

NOUN The **dispersal** of something is its spreading or scattering out in many directions.

disperse **disperses, dispersing, dispersed**

VERB If someone **disperses** people, they send them away.

display **displays, displaying, displayed**

NOUN **1** an arrangement of things designed to attract people's attention • *a firework* ***display***

VERB **2** If you **display** something, you put it on show.

3 If you **display** an emotion, you behave in a way that shows how you feel.

disposable

ADJECTIVE **Disposable** things are designed to be thrown away after they have been used.

dispose **disposes, disposing, disposed**

VERB If you **dispose** of something, you get rid of it. • *We* ***disposed*** *of our litter carefully.*

disprove **disproves, disproving, disproved**

VERB If you **disprove** something, you show that it is not true.

dispute **disputes, disputing, disputed**

NOUN **1** an argument

VERB **2** If you **dispute** a fact or theory, you say that it is incorrect or untrue.

disqualify **disqualifies, disqualifying, disqualified**

VERB If someone **disqualifies** someone from a competition or activity, they officially stop them from taking part in it.

• *The team was* ***disqualified*** *from the competition for cheating.*

disregard **disregards, disregarding, disregarded**

VERB **1** If you **disregard** someone or something, you take no notice of them.

NOUN **2** If you show **disregard** for something, you show that you do not care for it.

disrespect

NOUN contempt or lack of respect

disrespectful ADJECTIVE

disrupt **disrupts, disrupting, disrupted**

VERB If you **disrupt** something, you break it up or throw it into confusion.

• *Rain* ***disrupted*** *the school's sports day.* [from Latin *dirumpere* meaning to smash to pieces]

disruption NOUN **disruptive** ADJECTIVE

dissatisfied

ADJECTIVE not pleased or contented

dissatisfaction NOUN

dissect **dissects, dissecting, dissected**

VERB When you **dissect** a plant or part of the body of an animal, you cut it up carefully so that you can examine it closely.

dissolve **dissolves, dissolving, dissolved**

VERB If you **dissolve** something, or if something **dissolves** in a liquid, it mixes with the liquid and becomes part of it.

distance **distances**

NOUN **1** The **distance** between two points is the amount of space between them.

2 the fact of being far away • *My friend's house is a great* ***distance*** *from mine.*

distant

ADJECTIVE far away in space or time
● a **distant** planet

distil distils, distilling, distilled

VERB When you **distil** a liquid, you purify it by boiling it and condensing the vapour.

distinct

ADJECTIVE **1** If one thing is **distinct** from another, there is an important difference between them. ● *The word "chest" has two* **distinct** *meanings.*
2 If something is **distinct**, you can hear, smell, see or sense it clearly.

distinction distinctions

NOUN **1** a difference between two things
2 a quality of excellence and superiority
● *a woman of* **distinction**
3 the highest level of achievement in an examination

distinctive

ADJECTIVE If something is **distinctive**, it has a special quality that makes it recognisable. ● *Peppermint has a* **distinctive** *smell.*

distinguish distinguishes, distinguishing, distinguished

VERB **1** If you can **distinguish** one thing from another, you can see or understand the difference between them.
2 If you can **distinguish** something, you can see, hear or taste it. ● *I heard shouting but couldn't* **distinguish** *the words.*

distort distorts, distorting, distorted

VERB **1** If you **distort** something, you twist it out of shape.
2 If you **distort** an argument or the truth, you alter the facts to suit yourself.

distract distracts, distracting, distracted

VERB If you **distract** someone, you take their attention away from what they are doing.
distraction NOUN

distress distresses, distressing, distressed

NOUN **1 Distress** is suffering caused by pain or sorrow.

VERB **2** If something **distresses** you, it causes you to be upset or worried.

PHRASE **3** If someone or something is **in distress**, they are in danger and need help.

distribute distributes, distributing, distributed

VERB **1** If you **distribute** things, you hand them out or deliver them.
2 If you **distribute** something, you share it among a number of people.

district districts

NOUN an area of a town or country

distrust distrusts, distrusting, distrusted

VERB **1** If you **distrust** someone, you are suspicious of them because you are not sure whether they are honest.
NOUN **2** suspicion
distrustful ADJECTIVE **distrustfully** ADVERB

disturb disturbs, disturbing, disturbed

VERB If you **disturb** someone, you interrupt their peace or privacy.
disturbance NOUN

disused

ADJECTIVE If something is **disused**, it is neglected or no longer used.
disuse NOUN

ditch ditches

NOUN a channel cut into the ground at the side of a road or field

dive dives, diving, dived

VERB **1** If you **dive**, you plunge head first into deep water.
2 If something or someone **dives**, they move suddenly and quickly. ● *The birds* **dived** *to catch the insects.*

diver divers

NOUN **1** a person who uses breathing apparatus to swim or work under water
2 a person who takes part in diving competitions
3 a bird that catches its food by diving into water

diverse

ADJECTIVE If things are **diverse**, they show a wide range of differences. ● *There was a* **diverse** *collection of paintings in the gallery.*

diversion diversions

NOUN **1** an alternative road you can use if the main one is blocked
2 something that takes your attention away from what you are doing
divert VERB

divide divides, dividing, divided

VERB **1** When you **divide** something, or when it divides, it separates into two or more parts. • We **divided** the cake into six equal slices.
ANTONYM: multiply
2 If something **divides** two areas, it forms a barrier between them. • A tall hedge **divided** the two gardens.
3 If you **divide** a larger number by a smaller number, or into a smaller number, you calculate how many times the larger number contains the smaller number.
• Thirty-five **divided** by five is seven $(35 \div 5 = 7)$. Six **divided** into three is two.
ANTONYM: multiply

divine

ADJECTIVE having the qualities of a god or goddess

divisible

ADJECTIVE A number that is **divisible** can be divided by another number. • 8, 20, 46 and 166 are all **divisible** exactly by two.

division

NOUN the process of dividing numbers or things

divorce divorces, divorcing, divorced

VERB When married couples **divorce**, they end their marriage legally.

Diwali

NOUN a Hindu festival of light, celebrated in the autumn

DIY

NOUN the activity of making or repairing things yourself. **DIY** is an abbreviation for do-it-yourself.

dizzy dizzier, dizziest

ADJECTIVE If you feel **dizzy**, you feel that you are losing your balance and are about to fall.

do does, doing, did, done

VERB **1** If you **do** something, you get on and finish it. • I've **done** my homework.
2 You can use **do** with other verbs.
• **Do** you like ice cream?
3 If you ask people what they **do**, you want to know what their job is.

docile

ADJECTIVE A **docile** person or other animal is calm and unlikely to cause any trouble.

dock docks

NOUN an enclosed space in a harbour where ships go to be loaded, unloaded or repaired

doctor doctors

NOUN a person who is qualified in medicine and treats people who are ill

document documents, documenting, documented

NOUN **1** a piece of paper that provides an official record of something
VERB **2** If you **document** something, you make a detailed record of it.

documentary documentaries

NOUN a radio or television programme, or a film, that gives information about real events

dodge dodges, dodging, dodged

VERB If you **dodge** something, you move suddenly to avoid being seen, hit or caught.

dodgy

ADJECTIVE INFORMAL dangerous, risky or unreliable

doe does

NOUN a female deer, rabbit or hare

does

Said "**duz**" VERB a present tense of **do**

doesn't

VERB a contraction of does not

dog dogs

NOUN a mammal that is often kept as a pet or used to guard or hunt things

dole doles, doling, doled

VERB If you **dole** something out, you give a certain amount of it to each individual in a group.

doll **dolls**
NOUN a toy that looks like a baby or a person

dollar **dollars**
NOUN a unit of money in the USA, Australia, Canada, New Zealand and some other countries. A **dollar** is worth 100 cents.

dolphin **dolphins**
NOUN a mammal that lives in the sea

dome **domes**
NOUN a rounded roof

domestic
ADJECTIVE involving or concerned with the home and family
● *Dogs and cats are often kept as domestic pets.*

dominant
ADJECTIVE most powerful or important

dominate **dominates, dominating, dominated**
VERB **1** If someone or something **dominates** a situation or an event, they are the most powerful or important thing in it.
2 If one person **dominates** another, they have power and control over them. [from Latin *dominari* meaning to be lord over]

domino **dominoes**
NOUN a small, rectangular block marked with two groups of spots on one side, used for playing the game called **dominoes**

donate **donates, donating, donated**
VERB If you **donate** something, you give it, especially to a charity.

done
VERB the past participle of **do**

donkey **donkeys**
NOUN an animal like a horse, but smaller and with longer ears

donor **donors**
NOUN someone who donates something, such as a blood **donor** or someone who gives to charity

don't
VERB a contraction of *do not*

doodle **doodles, doodling, doodled**
NOUN **1** a drawing done when you are thinking about something else or when you are bored
VERB **2** When you **doodle**, you draw doodles.

doomed
ADJECTIVE If someone or something is **doomed** to an unhappy or unpleasant experience, they are certain to suffer it.

door **doors**
NOUN a swinging or sliding panel for opening or closing the entrance to something

dormitory **dormitories**
NOUN a large bedroom where several people sleep

dormouse **dormice**
NOUN a mammal, like a large mouse, with a furry tail

dose **doses**
NOUN a measured amount of a medicine or drug

dot **dots, dotting, dotted**
NOUN **1** a very small, round mark, such as a full stop or a decimal point
VERB **2** When things **dot** a place or an area they are scattered all over it. ● *The hillside was **dotted** with trees.*
PHRASE **3** If you arrive somewhere **on the dot**, you arrive at exactly the right time.

double **doubles, doubling, doubled**
ADJECTIVE **1** twice the usual size
2 consisting of two parts
VERB **3** If something **doubles**, or if you **double** it, it becomes twice as large. ● *The number of pupils has **doubled** over the last year.*
NOUN **4** Your **double** is someone who looks exactly like you.

a
b
c
d
e
f
g
h
i
j
k
l
m
n
o
p
q
r
s
t
u
v
w
x
y
z

double bass
double basses

NOUN a very large stringed instrument • *My brother plays the* **double bass** *in a jazz band.*

doubt **doubts, doubting, doubted**

VERB If you **doubt** something, you think that it is probably not true or possible. • *I* **doubt** *if I'll be allowed to go to the party.*

doubtful

ADJECTIVE uncertain or unlikely

doubtless

ADVERB certainly; without any doubt

dough

NOUN a mixture of flour and water used to make bread, pastry or biscuits

doughnut **doughnuts**

NOUN a ring of sweet dough cooked in hot fat

dove **doves**

NOUN a bird of the pigeon family that makes a soft, cooing sound

down

PREPOSITION OR ADVERB **1** towards the ground, towards a lower level, or in a lower place

ADVERB **2** If you put something **down**, you place it on a surface.

3 If an amount of something goes **down**, it decreases. • *The water level in the river has gone* **down**.

NOUN **4** the tiny, soft feathers on baby birds

downcast

ADJECTIVE If you are **downcast**, you feel sad and without hope.

downhill

ADVERB down a slope

download **downloads, downloading, downloaded**

VERB When you **download** a program from a disk or from the internet, you move it into a file on your own computer.

downpour **downpours**

NOUN a very heavy shower of rain

downstairs

ADVERB **1** If you go **downstairs**, you go towards the ground floor.

ADJECTIVE **2** on a lower floor

doze **dozes, dozing, dozed**

VERB When you **doze**, you sleep lightly for a short period.

dozen **dozens**

NOUN OR ADJECTIVE A **dozen** or a **dozen** things are twelve of them.

Dr

NOUN an abbreviation for *Doctor*

drab

ADJECTIVE plain, dull and unattractive

draft **drafts**

NOUN an early plan for a story, a book, a letter or a speech that you are going to write

drag **drags, dragging, dragged**

VERB If you **drag** a heavy object somewhere, you pull it there slowly and with difficulty.

dragon **dragons**

NOUN In stories and legends, **dragons** are large, fire-breathing, lizard-like creatures with claws and leathery wings.

dragonfly **dragonflies**

NOUN a colourful insect that is often found near water

drain **drains, draining, drained**

NOUN **1** a pipe that carries water or sewage away from a place, or an opening in a surface that leads to the pipe

VERB **2** If you **drain** something, or if it **drains**, liquid flows out of it or off it.

drake **drakes**

NOUN a male duck

drama **dramas**

NOUN **1** a serious play for the theatre, television or radio

2 You can refer to the exciting aspects of a situation as **drama**.

dramatic
ADJECTIVE Something **dramatic** is very exciting, interesting and impressive.

drank
VERB the past tense of **drink**

drape drapes, draping, draped
VERB If you **drape** a piece of material over something, you hang it loosely.

drastic
ADJECTIVE A **drastic** course of action is very severe and is usually taken urgently.

draught draughts
Said "draft" NOUN **1** a current of cold air
PLURAL NOUN **2 Draughts** is a game for two people, played on a chessboard with round pieces.
draughty ADJECTIVE

draw draws, drawing, drew, drawn
VERB **1** When you **draw** something, you use a pen or pencil to make a picture of it.
2 If you **draw** the curtains, you pull them so that they cover or uncover the window.
NOUN **3** the result of a game or competition in which both sides have the same score, so nobody wins

draw lots
PHRASE If you **draw lots**, you decide who will do something by a method that depends on chance, such as taking names out of a hat.

drawback drawbacks
NOUN a problem that upsets a plan • One **drawback** of eating too much chocolate is that you feel sick.

drawer drawers
NOUN part of a desk or other piece of furniture that is shaped like a box and slides in and out

drawing drawings
NOUN a picture made with a pencil, pen or crayon

drawing pin drawing pins
NOUN a short nail with a broad flat top. You pin papers to a board by pressing a drawing pin through them with your thumb.

dread dreads, dreading, dreaded
VERB If you **dread** something, you feel very worried and frightened about it.

dreadful
ADJECTIVE very bad or unpleasant • The weather has been **dreadful** this week.
SYNONYMS: atrocious, awful, terrible

dreadlocks
PLURAL NOUN a hairstyle where the hair is grown long and twisted into tightly curled strands

dream dreams, dreaming, dreamed or **dreamt**
NOUN **1** a series of events that you experience in your mind while asleep
2 a hope or ambition that you often think about because you would very much like it to happen
VERB **3** When you **dream**, you see events in your mind while you are asleep.

You can write either *dreamed* or *dreamt* as the past form of *dream*.

dreary drearier, dreariest
ADJECTIVE extremely dull and boring

drenched
ADJECTIVE soaking wet

dress dresses, dressing, dressed
NOUN **1** a piece of clothing worn by women and girls, made up of a top and skirt joined together
2 Dress is used to describe clothing or costumes in general, such as national **dress** or fancy **dress**.
VERB **3** When you **dress**, you put on your clothes.
4 When you **dress** a wound, you clean it and treat it.

dress up
VERB When you **dress up**, you put on clothes that make you look like something else. • Let's **dress up** as witches for the party.

dressing dressings
NOUN **1** a bandage or plaster to put on a wound

2 a mixture of oils and spices that can be added to salads and other dishes to heighten the flavour

dressing gown **dressing gowns**
NOUN a long, warm garment, usually worn over night clothes

drew
VERB the past tense of **draw**

dribble **dribbles, dribbling, dribbled**
VERB **1** If a person or animal **dribbles**, saliva trickles from their mouth.
2 In sport, when you **dribble** a ball, you move it along by repeatedly tapping it with your foot or a stick.

drift **drifts, drifting, drifted**
VERB **1** When something **drifts**, it is carried along by the wind or by water.
2 When people **drift**, they move aimlessly from one place or one activity to another.
NOUN **3** snow or sand piled up by the wind
4 INFORMAL the general meaning of something

drill **drills, drilling, drilled**
NOUN **1** a tool for making holes
2 a routine exercise or routine training
VERB **3** If you **drill** a hole, you make a hole using a drill.

drink **drinks, drinking, drank, drunk**
VERB **1** When you **drink** a liquid, you take it into your mouth and swallow it.
NOUN **2** A **drink** is an amount of liquid for drinking.

drip **drips, dripping, dripped**
VERB **1** When liquid **drips**, it falls in small drops.
2 When an object **drips**, drops of liquid fall from it. ● Stop that tap **dripping**.
NOUN **3** a drop of liquid that is falling

drive **drives, driving, drove, driven**
VERB **1** When someone **drives** a vehicle, they operate it and control its movements.
2 If something **drives** a machine, it supplies the power that makes it work.
NOUN **3** a journey in a vehicle

4 a private road that leads from a public road to a person's house
driver NOUN

drizzle
NOUN light rain

drone **drones, droning, droned**
VERB **1** If something **drones**, it makes a low, continuous humming noise.
NOUN **2** a continuous, low, dull sound
3 a male bee

drool **drools, drooling, drooled**
VERB If someone **drools**, saliva drips from their mouth continuously.

droop **droops, drooping, drooped**
VERB If something **droops**, it hangs or sags downwards with no strength or firmness.

drop **drops, dropping, dropped**
VERB **1** If you **drop** something, you let it fall.
2 If something **drops**, it falls straight down.
3 If the level or the amount of something **drops**, it becomes less.
NOUN **4** a very small, round quantity of liquid
5 the distance between the top and the bottom of something ● There was a fifty-metre **drop** to the river below.

drought **droughts**
NOUN a long period during which there is no rain

drove
VERB the past tense of **drive**

drown **drowns, drowning, drowned**
VERB When someone **drowns**, or when they are **drowned**, they die because they have gone under water and cannot breathe.

drowsy **drowsier, drowsiest**
ADJECTIVE feeling sleepy

drug **drugs**
NOUN **1** a chemical used by the medical profession to treat people with illnesses or diseases
2 a substance that some people smell, smoke, inject or swallow because of its

stimulating or calming effects. **Drugs** can be harmful to health and may be illegal.

drum drums

NOUN **1** a musical instrument consisting of a skin stretched tightly over a round frame **2** an object or container shaped like a **drum** • *an oil **drum***

drunk drunker, drunkest

VERB **1** the past participle of **drink**

ADJECTIVE **2** If someone is **drunk**, they have consumed too much alcohol.

dry drier or dryer, driest; dries, drying, dried

ADJECTIVE **1** Something that is **dry** is not wet, and contains no water or liquid.

VERB **2** When you **dry** something, or when it **dries**, liquid is removed from it.

dual

ADJECTIVE having two parts, functions or aspects • *This is a **dual**-purpose room – it is both the office and the spare bedroom.*

dual carriageway dual carriageways

NOUN a road with several lanes in each direction

dubious

ADJECTIVE **1** not entirely honest, safe or reliable

2 doubtful • *I felt **dubious** about the idea.*

dubiously ADVERB

duchess duchesses

NOUN a woman who has the same rank as a duke, or who is a duke's wife or widow

duck ducks, ducking, ducked

NOUN **1** a bird that lives in water and has webbed feet and a large flat bill

VERB **2** If you **duck**, you move your head quickly downwards in order to avoid being hit by something.

3 If you **duck** someone, you push them under water for a very short time.

duckling ducklings

NOUN a young duck

due

ADJECTIVE expected to happen or arrive • *The train is **due** at eight o'clock.*

duel duels

NOUN a fight arranged between two people

duet duets

NOUN a piece of music sung or played by two people

dug

VERB the past tense of **dig**

duke dukes

NOUN a nobleman with a rank just below that of a prince

dull duller, dullest

ADJECTIVE **1** not interesting • *I thought the story was rather **dull**.*

2 not bright, sharp or clear • *a **dull** day*

dumb dumber, dumbest

ADJECTIVE **1** unable to speak • *She was so shocked that she was momentarily struck **dumb**.*

2 INFORMAL stupid

dumbfounded

ADJECTIVE If you are **dumbfounded**, you are so shocked or surprised about something that you cannot speak.

dummy dummies

NOUN **1** a rubber or plastic teat given to a baby to suck to keep it happy

2 an imitation or model of something that is used for display • *I first saw the jacket on a **dummy** in a shop window.*

dump dumps, dumping, dumped

VERB **1** If you **dump** something somewhere, you put it there in a careless way.

NOUN **2** a place where rubbish is left

3 INFORMAL You refer to a place as a **dump** when it is unattractive and unpleasant to live in.

dune dunes

NOUN a hill of sand near the sea or in the desert

dung

NOUN body waste excreted by large animals

dungarees

PLURAL NOUN trousers that have a bib covering the chest and straps over the shoulders

[named after *Dungri* in India, where dungaree material was first made]

dungeon dungeons

NOUN an underground prison

dunk dunks, dunking, dunked

VERB If you **dunk** something, you dip it into water or some other liquid for a short time.

duo duos

NOUN any two people who do something together, especially a pair of musical performers

duplicate duplicates, duplicating, duplicated

Said "**dyoo**-pli-kayt" VERB **1** If someone **duplicates** something, they make an exact copy of it.

Said "**dyoo**-pli-kut" NOUN **2** something that is identical to something else, or an exact copy

duplication NOUN

durable

ADJECTIVE Things that are **durable** are very strong and last a long time.

duration

NOUN the length of time during which something happens or exists

during

PREPOSITION happening throughout a particular time or while something else is going on • *We had an ice cream during the interval.*

dusk

NOUN the time just before nightfall when it is not completely dark

dust dusts, dusting, dusted

NOUN **1** dry, fine, powdery material such as particles of earth, dirt or pollen

VERB **2** When you **dust** furniture or other objects, you remove dust from them using a duster.

3 If you **dust** a surface with something powdery, you cover it lightly with that substance. • *Dust the top of the cake with icing sugar.*

dustbin dustbins

NOUN a large container for rubbish

duster dusters

NOUN a cloth for dusting things

dusty dustier, dustiest

ADJECTIVE covered with dust

duty duties

NOUN **1** Your **duty** is what you should do because it is part of your job or because it is expected of you.

PHRASE **2** When workers are **on duty**, they are at work.

duvet duvets

NOUN a large bed cover filled with feathers or similar material, which you use instead of sheets and blankets

DVD DVDs

NOUN a type of compact disc that can store large amounts of video and sound information. **DVD** is an abbreviation for *digital video* or *versatile disc*.

dwarf dwarfs, dwarfing, dwarfed

NOUN **1** a person or thing that is smaller than average

VERB **2** If one thing **dwarfs** another, it is so much bigger that it makes it look very small. • *The mountains dwarfed the village.*

dwindle dwindles, dwindling, dwindled

VERB If something **dwindles**, it becomes smaller or weaker. • *Their supplies of firewood dwindled.* • *As it got later the light dwindled.*

dye dyes, dyeing, dyed

VERB **1** If you **dye** something, you change its colour by soaking it in a special liquid.

NOUN **2** a substance used to change the colour of something such as cloth or hair

dying

VERB the present participle of **die**

dyke **dykes**; also spelt **dike**

NOUN a thick wall or barrier that prevents a river or the sea from flooding the land

dynamic

ADJECTIVE A **dynamic** person is full of energy, ambition and new ideas.

dynamite

NOUN a powerful explosive

dynamo **dynamos**

NOUN a device that uses movement to produce electricity. A **dynamo** can be used for lighting bicycle lamps.

dynasty **dynasties**

NOUN a series of rulers of a country, all belonging to the same family

dyslexia

NOUN a certain type of difficulty with reading and writing

dyslexic ADJECTIVE OR NOUN

Ee

each

ADJECTIVE OR PRONOUN every one of a group

eager

ADJECTIVE If you are **eager**, you are keen to do something.

SYNONYM: enthusiastic

eagerly ADVERB

eagle **eagles**

NOUN a large bird of prey

ear **ears**

NOUN Your **ears** are the parts of your body on either side of your head, with which you hear sounds.

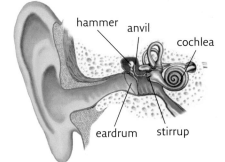

hammer anvil

cochlea

eardrum stirrup

earache

NOUN a pain in your ear

early **earlier, earliest**

ADJECTIVE OR ADVERB **1** before the arranged or expected time

ADJECTIVE **2** near the beginning of something ● *I like to go for a walk in the **early** morning.*

earn **earns, earning, earned**

VERB **1** If you **earn** money, you receive it in return for work that you do.

2 If you **earn** something such as praise, you receive it because you deserve it.

A B C D **E** F G H I J K L M N O P Q R S T U V W X Y Z

earnest

ADJECTIVE If you are **earnest** about something, you are very serious about it.
earnestly ADVERB

earnings

PLURAL NOUN the money or payment that you receive for working

earphone **earphones**

NOUN a very small speaker worn in your ear so you can listen to a radio or MP3 player

earring **earrings**

NOUN a piece of jewellery that you wear on your ear

earth

NOUN **1** The **earth** is the planet we live on. **2** another word for **soil**

earthquake **earthquakes**

NOUN a violent shaking of the ground caused by movement of the earth's crust

earthworm **earthworms**

NOUN a worm that lives in the soil

earwig **earwigs**

NOUN a small, brown insect with pincers at the tail end of its body

ease **eases, easing, eased**

VERB **1** When something **eases**, it becomes less difficult or intense. • *The rain **eased** as the dark clouds were blown away.*
NOUN **2** a lack of difficulty or trouble • *She finished her homework with **ease**.*
VERB **3** If you **ease** something, you move it gently and slowly. • *He **eased** himself into the chair.*

easel **easels**

NOUN an upright frame that supports a picture that someone is painting

easily

ADVERB If you do something **easily**, you do it without difficulty.

east

NOUN one of the four main points of the compass. The sun rises in the **east**. The abbreviation for **east** is E.

Easter

NOUN a Christian religious festival celebrating Christ's return to life after his death
[from Old English *Eostre*, a goddess whose festival was at the spring equinox]

eastern

ADJECTIVE in or from the east

easy **easier, easiest**

ADJECTIVE If something is **easy**, you can do it without difficulty.

eat **eats, eating, ate, eaten**

VERB When you **eat** food, you chew it and swallow it.

ebb **ebbs, ebbing, ebbed**

VERB When the sea or the tide **ebbs**, it goes out.

ebony

NOUN a hard, dark-coloured wood

e-book **e-books**

NOUN a book for reading on an electronic device

eccentric

ADJECTIVE Someone **eccentric** has habits or opinions that other people think are odd or peculiar.
eccentricity NOUN   **eccentrically** ADVERB

echo **echoes, echoing, echoed**

NOUN **1** the repeat of a sound caused by the sound being reflected off a surface
VERB **2** When a sound **echoes**, it is reflected off a surface so that it can be heard again. • *Their cries **echoed** back from the mountain.*

eclipse **eclipses**

NOUN An **eclipse** of the sun happens when the moon passes between the sun and the earth and part or all of the sun is hidden from view.

ecology

NOUN the relationship between living

things and their environment, or the study of this relationship
ecological ADJECTIVE **ecologically** ADVERB **ecologist** NOUN

economical

ADJECTIVE If you are **economical**, you are not wasteful with money or things.
economically ADVERB

economics

NOUN the system of organizing the money, production and trade of a country, region or group

economy **economies**

NOUN The **economy** of a country or region is the way in which the industries, banks and businesses are organized to make money.
economist NOUN

ecosystem **ecosystems**

NOUN the relationship between plants and animals and their environment

ecstasy

NOUN a feeling of extreme happiness
ecstatic ADJECTIVE

eczema

NOUN a skin disease that makes the skin rough and itchy

edge **edges**

NOUN the part along the side or end of something

edible

ADJECTIVE Things that are **edible** are safe to eat.

edit **edits, editing, edited**

VERB **1** If you **edit** a piece of writing, you correct it.
2 If you **edit** a film or a television programme, you select different parts of it and arrange them in a particular order.

edition **editions**

NOUN An **edition** of a book or newspaper is one or all of the copies printed at one time.

editor **editors**

NOUN **1** someone who is responsible for the contents of a newspaper or magazine

2 someone who edits a piece of writing, a film or a television programme

editorial **editorials**

NOUN an article in a newspaper or magazine which expresses the opinion of the editor

educate **educates, educating, educated**

VERB If you **educate** someone about something, you teach them so that they learn about it.

education

NOUN When you receive an **education**, you gain knowledge and understanding through learning.
educational ADJECTIVE **educationally** ADVERB

eel **eels**

NOUN a long, thin fish shaped like a snake

eerie **eerier, eeriest**

ADJECTIVE strange and frightening ● *There was an **eerie** silence after the thunderstorm.*

effect **effects**

NOUN **1** something that happens as a result of something else ● *The **effects** of global warming are now becoming clear.*
2 the impression something makes ● *The **effect** of the moonlight in the mist was eerie.*

effective

ADJECTIVE If something is **effective**, it works well and gives the results that were intended.
effectively ADVERB

efficient

ADJECTIVE capable of doing something well, without wasting time or energy
efficiently ADVERB **efficiency** NOUN

effort **efforts**

NOUN the physical or mental energy needed to do something

effortless

ADJECTIVE done easily and without much effort
effortlessly ADVERB

eg or **e.g.**

Eg means *for example*.

A
B
C
D
E
F
G
H
I
J
K
L
M
N
O
P
Q
R
S
T
U
V
W
X
Y
Z

egg **eggs**

NOUN **1** a rounded object produced by female birds, reptiles, fish and insects. The young animal develops in the **egg** until it is ready to hatch.
2 a hen's **egg** used as food

Eid

Said "**eed**" NOUN a festival at the end of the Muslim fast of Ramadan

eight

NOUN **Eight** is the number 8.
eighth NOUN OR ADJECTIVE

eighteen

NOUN **Eighteen** is the number 18.
eighteenth NOUN OR ADJECTIVE

eighty

NOUN **Eighty** is the number 80.
eightieth NOUN OR ADJECTIVE

either

ADJECTIVE, PRONOUN OR CONJUNCTION **1** You use **either** to refer to each of two possible alternatives. • *You can **either** come with me or stay here.*
ADJECTIVE **2** You use **either** to refer to both of two things. • *There were fields on **either** side of the road.*

eject **ejects, ejecting, ejected**

VERB If you **eject** someone or something, you push or send them out of something with force. • *They **ejected** the children from the cinema because they were making too much noise.*
ejection NOUN

elaborate

ADJECTIVE having many different parts, often very detailed or complicated
elaborately ADVERB **elaboration** NOUN

elastic

NOUN rubber material that stretches when you pull it, and returns to its original shape when you let it go

elated

ADJECTIVE very happy or excited

elbow **elbows**

NOUN the joint where your arm bends in the middle

elder

ADJECTIVE Your **elder** brother or sister is older than you.

elderly

ADJECTIVE Someone who is **elderly** is old.

eldest

ADJECTIVE If you are the **eldest** in a family, you are the oldest.

elect **elects, electing, elected**

VERB If you **elect** someone, you choose them as your representative by voting for them.

election **elections**

NOUN When there is an **election**, people choose someone to represent them by voting for them.
[from Latin *eligere* meaning to select]

electric

ADJECTIVE powered or produced by electricity
electrical ADJECTIVE

electrician **electricians**

NOUN a person whose job it is to install and repair electrical equipment

electricity

NOUN a form of energy that provides power for heating, lighting and machines
[from Greek *elektron* meaning amber. In early experiments, scientists rubbed amber in order to get an electrical charge]

electrocute **electrocutes, electrocuting, electrocuted**

VERB If someone **electrocutes** themselves, they accidentally kill themselves or injure themselves badly by touching a strong electric current.
electrocution NOUN

electronic

ADJECTIVE An **electronic** device contains transistors or silicon chips that control an electric current. • *Computers and televisions are examples of **electronic** devices.*
electronically ADVERB

electronic mail

NOUN the sending of messages and documents from one computer to another

elegant

ADJECTIVE attractive and graceful
elegantly ADVERB **elegance** NOUN

element **elements**

NOUN **1** a part of something that combines with others to make a whole **2** In chemistry, an **element** is a substance that is made up of only one atom.
3 The **elements** are the weather, especially when it is bad.

elephant **elephants**

NOUN a very large mammal with a long trunk, large ears, thick skin and ivory tusks

eleven

NOUN **Eleven** is the number 11.
eleventh NOUN OR ADJECTIVE

elf **elves**

NOUN a small, mischievous creature in fairy stories

eligible

ADJECTIVE If you are **eligible** for something, you are suitable or have the right qualifications. • *You are **eligible** to enter the under-twelves competition.*
eligibility NOUN

eliminate **eliminates, eliminating, eliminated**

VERB If you **eliminate** something or someone, you get rid of them.

ellipse **ellipses**

NOUN a regular oval shape

elm **elms**

NOUN a tall tree with broad leaves

else

ADJECTIVE **1** besides or as well as • *What **else** do you see?*
PHRASE **2 Or else** means otherwise. • *You'd better hurry, **or else** you'll miss the bus.*

elsewhere

ADVERB If you do something **elsewhere**, you do it in another place.

e-mail **e-mails**; also spelt **email**

NOUN **1** the short form for **electronic mail**

2 When you send an **e-mail**, you send a message from one computer to another.

embark **embarks, embarking, embarked**

VERB **1** When you **embark**, you go on to a ship at the start of your journey.
2 When you **embark** on a project, you start it.

embarrass **embarrasses, embarrassing, embarrassed**

VERB If you **embarrass** someone, you make them feel ashamed or awkward.

There are two *r*s and two *ss* in *embarrass*.

embarrassed ADJECTIVE
embarrassing ADJECTIVE
embarrassment NOUN

embassy **embassies**

NOUN the building in which an ambassador and his or her staff work

emblem **emblems**

NOUN an object or a design representing an organization or a country

embrace **embraces, embracing, embraced**

VERB If you **embrace** someone, you put your arms round them to show your affection for them.

embroider **embroiders, embroidering, embroidered**

VERB If you **embroider** fabric, you sew a decorative design on to it.
embroidery NOUN

embryo **embryos**

NOUN an unborn animal, such as a human being, in the very early stages of development

emerald **emeralds**

NOUN **1** a bright-green precious stone
NOUN OR ADJECTIVE **2** bright green

emerge **emerges, emerging, emerged**

VERB If you **emerge** from somewhere, you come out from it.
emergence NOUN

emergency **emergencies**
NOUN an unexpected and serious situation that must be dealt with quickly

emigrate **emigrates, emigrating, emigrated**
VERB If you **emigrate**, you leave your native country and go to live permanently in another one.
ANTONYM: immigrate
emigration NOUN

eminent
ADJECTIVE If someone is **eminent**, they are well known and respected for what they do.
eminently ADVERB

emit **emits, emitting, emitted**
VERB If something **emits** light, sound, heat or smell, it produces it or lets it out.
emission NOUN

emotion **emotions**
NOUN a strong feeling, such as love or fear
emotional ADJECTIVE

emperor **emperors**
NOUN a male ruler of an empire

emphasis **emphases**
NOUN the special importance or stress put on something ● *When you read out the poem, you must put* **emphasis** *on the important words.*

emphasize **emphasizes, emphasizing, emphasized**; also spelt **emphasise**
VERB If you **emphasize** something, you make it look or sound more important than the things around it. ● *He* **emphasized** *the word by underlining it.*

empire **empires**
NOUN a group of countries controlled by one ruler ● *The Roman* **Empire** *covered many lands.*
[from Latin *imperium* meaning rule]

employ **employs, employing, employed**
VERB If you **employ** someone, you pay them to work for you.

employee **employees**
NOUN someone who works for someone else

employer **employers**
NOUN the person or company that someone works for

employment
NOUN the state of having a paid job

empress **empresses**
NOUN **1** a female ruler of an empire
2 the wife or widow of an emperor

empty **emptier, emptiest; empties, emptying, emptied**
ADJECTIVE **1** having nothing or nobody inside
VERB **2** If you **empty** something, you remove the contents.
emptiness NOUN

emu **emus**
NOUN a large, Australian bird that can run fast but cannot fly

enable **enables, enabling, enabled**
VERB If you **enable** something to happen, you make it possible. ● *The ramp* **enables** *people in wheelchairs to use the library.*

enchanted
ADJECTIVE If you are **enchanted** by something or someone, you are fascinated or charmed by them. ● *The audience were* **enchanted** *by her dancing.*

encircle **encircles, encircling, encircled**
VERB If you **encircle** someone or something, you surround them completely.

enclose **encloses, enclosing, enclosed**
VERB **1** If you **enclose** something with a letter, you put it in the same envelope.
2 If you **enclose** an object or area, you surround it with something solid. ● *They* **enclosed** *the garden with a strong fence.*
enclosed ADJECTIVE

encore **encores**
NOUN an extra item at the end of a performance, when the audience asks for more
[from French *encore* meaning again]

encounter encounters,
encountering, encountered

VERB **1** If you **encounter** someone or something, you meet them or are faced with them. • *Did you encounter any problems?*

NOUN **2** a meeting, especially when it is difficult or unexpected

encourage encourages,
encouraging, encouraged

VERB If you **encourage** someone, you give them the confidence to do something.

encouraging ADJECTIVE

encouragement NOUN

encyclopedia encyclopedias; also
spelt **encyclopaedia**

NOUN a book or set of books that gives information about a number of different subjects

end ends, ending, ended

NOUN **1** The **end** of something is the furthest point of it.

2 The **end** of an event is the last part of it.

VERB **3** When something **ends**, it finishes.

endanger endangers,
endangering, endangered

VERB If someone **endangers** something, they cause it to be in a dangerous or harmful situation.

endangered ADJECTIVE

endeavour endeavours,
endeavouring, endeavoured

VERB If you **endeavour** to do something, you try very hard to do it.

ending endings

NOUN The **ending** of something is when it finishes.

endless

ADJECTIVE Something that is **endless** has, or seems to have, no end. • *His endless chatter was very boring.*

endlessly ADVERB

endure endures, enduring, endured

VERB **1** If you **endure** someone or something unpleasant, you put up with them.

2 If something **endures**, it continues or lasts.

enduring ADJECTIVE

enemy enemies

NOUN Your **enemy** is someone who is very much against you and may wish to harm you.

energetic

ADJECTIVE full of energy

SYNONYMS: active, lively

energy energies

NOUN **1** the physical strength needed to do active things • *He is saving his energy for next week's race.*

2 the power that makes things move, light up, make a sound or get hotter
• *electrical energy* • *nuclear energy*

engage engages, engaging,
engaged

VERB **1** If you **engage** in an activity, you take part in it.

2 If you **engage** someone to do something, you pay them to do it.

engaged

ADJECTIVE **1** If two people are **engaged**, they have agreed to marry each other.

2 If someone or something is **engaged**, they are busy. • *Every time I tried to telephone you, your number was engaged.*

engine engines

NOUN **1** the part of a vehicle that produces the power to make it move

2 the large vehicle that pulls a railway train

engineer engineers

NOUN a person trained in designing and building machinery and electrical devices, or roads and bridges

engineering

NOUN the job of designing and building machinery and electrical devices

engrave engraves, engraving,
engraved

VERB If you **engrave**, you cut letters or designs into a hard surface with a tool.
• *He engraved the stone with an unusual design.*

engraving NOUN

a
b
c
d
e
f
g
h
i
j
k
l
m
n
o
p
q
r
s
t
u
v
w
x
y
z

A
B
C
D
E
F
G
H
I
J
K
L
M
N
O
P
Q
R
S
T
U
V
W
X
Y
Z

enjoy **enjoys, enjoying, enjoyed**
VERB **1** If you **enjoy** something, it gives you pleasure.
2 If you **enjoy yourself**, you are happy and have fun.
enjoyable ADJECTIVE   enjoyment NOUN

enlarge **enlarges, enlarging, enlarged**
VERB When you **enlarge** something, you make it bigger.
enlargement NOUN

enormous
ADJECTIVE very large in size or amount
SYNONYMS: vast, huge, massive

enough
ADJECTIVE OR ADVERB as much or as many as is necessary ● *Do you have **enough** money to buy that?*

enquire **enquires, enquiring, enquired**
VERB If you **enquire** about something or someone, you ask for information about them.

enrol **enrols, enrolling, enrolled**
VERB If you **enrol** for something, such as a course or a society, you register to join or become a member of it.

ensure **ensures, ensuring, ensured**
VERB If you **ensure** that something happens, you make certain that it happens. ● *I will **ensure** that I arrive on time.*

enter **enters, entering, entered**
VERB **1** To **enter** a place means to go into it.
2 If you **enter** a competition, you take part in it.
3 If you **enter** something in a diary or a list, you write it down.

enterprise **enterprises**
NOUN **1** something new and exciting that you try to do
2 a large business or company
enterprising ADJECTIVE

entertain **entertains, entertaining, entertained**
VERB If you **entertain** someone, you do something to amuse them.

enthusiasm
NOUN If you show **enthusiasm** for something, you show much interest and excitement.

enthusiastic
ADJECTIVE If you are **enthusiastic** about something, you are very keen on it and talk or behave in an excited and eager way that shows how much you like it.
enthusiastically ADVERB

entire
ADJECTIVE whole, complete ● *The **entire** class went on the trip.*

entirely
ADVERB wholly and completely ● *My sister and I are **entirely** different.*

entrance **entrances**
NOUN the doorway or gate to a building or area

entry **entries**
NOUN **1** the act of entering a place ● *No **entry** after 11 p.m.*
2 something you write in order to take part in a competition ● *Send your **entry** to the address below.*
3 something written in a diary or list ● *the **entry** for March 23 in her diary*

envelope **envelopes**
NOUN the paper cover in which you put a letter

envious
ADJECTIVE If you are **envious**, you wish you could have what someone else has.
enviously ADVERB

environment **environments**
NOUN **1** Your **environment** is your surroundings, especially the conditions in which you live or work.
2 the natural world around us ● *Many people are keen to preserve the **environment**.*

There is an *n* before the *m* in *environment*.

132

envy **envies, envying, envied**
VERB If you **envy** someone, you wish that you had what they have.

epidemic **epidemics**
NOUN an outbreak of a disease that takes place in one area, spreading quickly and affecting many people

epilepsy
NOUN a condition of the brain that causes fits and periods of unconsciousness
epileptic NOUN OR ADJECTIVE

episode **episodes**
NOUN **1** one of the programmes in a serial on television or radio
2 an event or period of time, especially one that is important or unusual

epitaph **epitaphs**
NOUN words about a person who has died, usually found on their gravestone

equal **equals, equalling, equalled**
ADJECTIVE **1** being the same in size, number or amount
VERB **2** In mathematics, the symbol (=) stands for **equals**. The numbers before it equal the numbers after it. For example, 3 + 3 = 6.

equally
ADVERB to the same extent or in the same amounts • *We shared the sweets **equally** between the three of us.*

equation **equations**
NOUN a mathematical number sentence stating that two amounts or values are the same • *3 + 6 = 9 is an **equation** because what is on the left equals what is on the right.*

equator
NOUN an imaginary line drawn round the middle of the earth, lying halfway between the north and south poles
See **tropic**
equatorial ADJECTIVE

equilateral
ADJECTIVE An **equilateral** triangle has sides that are all the same length, and angles that are all the same size.

equinox **equinoxes**
NOUN one of the two days in the year when the day and night are of equal length. The spring **equinox** occurs in March and the autumn **equinox** in September.
[from Latin *aequinoctium* meaning equal night]

equip **equips, equipping, equipped**
VERB If you **equip** yourself, you collect together everything that you need to do a particular thing.

equipment
NOUN all the things that are needed or used for a particular job or activity
• *camping **equipment***

equivalent **equivalents**
ADJECTIVE **1** equal in use, size, value or effect
2 In mathematics, **equivalent** means of equal value. Fractions can be **equivalent** if they are of equal value, for example $^2/_4 = ^1/_2$. Different forms can be **equivalent**, for example 0.5 = $^1/_2$ = 50%.
NOUN **3** Something that has the same use, size, value or effect as something else.
• *One metre is the **equivalent** of 1.094 yards.* • *An example of **equivalent** fractions is $^2/_4 = ^1/_2$.*

erase **erases, erasing, erased**
VERB If you **erase** writing, you rub it out.

erect **erects, erecting, erected**
VERB If you **erect** something, you put it up or construct it. • *They **erected** the tent in the garden.*

errand **errands**
NOUN If you run an **errand** for someone, you go a short distance to do a job for them, such as taking a message or fetching something.

erratic
ADJECTIVE not following a regular pattern
• *His attendance at school was **erratic**.*
erratically ADVERB

a
b
c
d
e
f
g
h
i
j
k
l
m
n
o
p
q
r
s
t
u
v
w
x
y
z

A
B
C
D
E
F
G
H
I
J
K
L
M
N
O
P
Q
R
S
T
U
V
W
X
Y
Z

error errors
NOUN a mistake, or something that is wrong

erupt erupts, erupting, erupted
VERB **1** When a volcano **erupts**, it throws out a lot of hot lava and ash.
2 When a situation **erupts**, it begins suddenly and violently. • *A family row erupted*.

escalator escalators
NOUN a mechanical, moving staircase

escape escapes, escaping, escaped
VERB **1** If you **escape** from someone or something, you succeed in getting away from them.
2 If you **escape** something unpleasant or difficult, you succeed in avoiding it. • *She was lucky to escape serious injury*.
NOUN **3** If you make an **escape** from somewhere, you manage to get away.

escort escorts, escorting, escorted
NOUN **1** a person or vehicle that travels with another in order to protect or guide them
VERB **2** If you **escort** someone, you go with them somewhere, especially in order to protect or guide them. • *I will escort you round the new buildings*.

Eskimo Eskimos
NOUN a member of a group of people who live in North America, Greenland and eastern Siberia. Eskimos who come from North America and parts of Greenland are called Inuits.

especially
ADVERB You say **especially** to show that something applies more to one thing, person or situation than to others. • *It is always cold at the top of the mountain, especially when the wind is blowing*.

espionage
NOUN the act of spying to get secret information, especially to find out military or political secrets
[from French *espionner* meaning to spy]

essay essays
NOUN a short piece of writing on a particular subject, especially one written as an exercise by a student

essential essentials
ADJECTIVE **1** Something that is **essential** is absolutely necessary.
NOUN **2** something that is very important or necessary

establish establishes, establishing, established
VERB **1** If you **establish** something, you set it up and keep it going.
2 If you **establish** a fact, you confirm that it is definitely correct.
established ADJECTIVE **establishment** NOUN

estate estates
NOUN **1** a large area of land in the country, owned by one person or organization
2 an area of land that has been developed for housing or industry
• *a housing estate*

estate agent estate agents
NOUN a person who works for a company that sells houses and land

estimate estimates, estimating, estimated
Said "**ess**-ti-mayt" VERB **1** If you **estimate** an amount or quantity, you calculate it approximately. • *They estimated that the trip would take around three hours*.
Said "**ess**-ti-mit" NOUN **2** an approximate calculation of an amount or quantity
• *The final cost was twice the original estimate*.

estuary estuaries
NOUN the wide part of a river near where it joins the sea, and where fresh water mixes with salt water

etc.
a written abbreviation for *et cetera*

et cetera
Et cetera means *and so on* or *and similar things*.
[from Latin, meaning and others]

eternal
ADJECTIVE lasting forever, or seeming to last forever
SYNONYMS: endless, everlasting, perpetual
eternally ADVERB

ethnic

ADJECTIVE connected with a particular racial group of people ● *There were many different **ethnic** groups in the school.*
[from Greek *ethnos* meaning race]
ethnically ADVERB

EU

NOUN an abbreviation for *European Union*

euro euros

NOUN the unit of currency used in many countries in Europe, including Germany, France, Italy, Ireland, Spain and the Netherlands

euthanasia

NOUN causing someone to die painlessly and gently, so that they do not suffer during an incurable illness
[from Greek *eu* meaning well and *thanatos* meaning death]

evacuate evacuates, evacuating, evacuated

VERB If people **evacuate**, or are **evacuated**, they move from somewhere dangerous to a place of safety. ● *The police **evacuated** shoppers from a store after a bomb scare.*
evacuee NOUN

evaluate evaluates, evaluating, evaluated

VERB If you **evaluate** something, you assess its quality or value.
evaluation NOUN

evaporate evaporates, evaporating, evaporated

VERB When a liquid **evaporates**, it gradually changes from a liquid into a gas or vapour.
[from Latin *vapor* meaning steam]
evaporation NOUN

even

ADJECTIVE **1** An **even** number is one that can be divided into two equal halves, such as two, four and six.
ANTONYM: odd
2 An **even** surface is level, smooth and flat.
3 An **even** measurement or rate stays at about the same level. ● *Keep the cooker at an **even** temperature.*
ADVERB **4 Even** is used to say that something is greater in degree than something else. ● *He was speaking **even** more slowly than usual.*
PHRASE **5 Even if** or **even though** are used to introduce something that is surprising in relation to the rest of the sentence. ● *She did not say anything, **even though** she had been left out again.*

evening evenings

NOUN the part of the day between the end of the afternoon and the time you go to bed

event events

NOUN **1** something that happens, especially when it is unusual or important
SYNONYMS: happening, incident, occurrence
2 an organized activity, such as a sports match or a concert

eventually

ADVERB in the end ● *It was a long way, but we got there **eventually**.*

ever

ADVERB at any time in the past or future ● *That's the biggest dog I've **ever** seen.*

evergreen evergreens

NOUN An **evergreen** is a plant that does not lose its leaves in the winter.

every

ADJECTIVE **1 Every** is used to refer to all the members of a group or all the parts of something. ● ***Every** shop in the town was closed.*
2 Every is also used to indicate that something happens at regular intervals. ● *The clock strikes **every** hour.*
PHRASE **3** If something happens **every other** day or week, it happens on alternate days or weeks. ● *Practice sessions are held **every other** week.*

a
b
c
d
e
f
g
h
i
j
k
l
m
n
o
p
q
r
s
t
u
v
w
x
y
z

A
B
C
D
E
F
G
H
I
J
K
L
M
N
O
P
Q
R
S
T
U
V
W
X
Y
Z

everybody
PRONOUN every person

everyone
PRONOUN all the people in a group

everything
PRONOUN all or the whole of something

everywhere
ADVERB in many or most places

evict evicts, evicting, evicted
VERB To **evict** someone means to officially force them to leave a place they are occupying.
eviction NOUN

evidence
NOUN **1** anything that causes you to believe that something is true or exists **2** the information used in a court of law to try to prove something

evident
ADJECTIVE If something is **evident**, it is clear and obvious.
evidently ADVERB

evil evils
NOUN **1 Evil** is used to refer to all the wicked or bad things that happen in the world.
ADJECTIVE **2** Someone or something **evil** is very bad and causes harm to people.

evolution
NOUN a process that takes place over many generations. During this time, living things slowly change as they adapt to different environments.
evolutionary ADJECTIVE

evolve evolves, evolving, evolved
VERB When living things **evolve**, they gradually change and develop into different forms. • *Many people believe that man **evolved** from apes.*

ewe ewes
NOUN a female sheep

ex-
PREFIX former • *the **ex**-prime minister*

exact
ADJECTIVE If something is **exact**, it is accurately measured or made.
exactly ADJECTIVE

exaggerate exaggerates, exaggerating, exaggerated
VERB If you **exaggerate**, you make something seem better, worse, bigger or more important than it really is.

> There are two *g*s but only one *r* in *exaggerate*.

exaggeration NOUN

exam exams
NOUN an official test that aims to find out your knowledge in a subject • *a science exam*

examination examinations
NOUN **1** the full word for **exam**
2 If someone makes an **examination** of something, they look at it very carefully.

examine examines, examining, examined
VERB **1** If you **examine** something, you inspect it carefully.
2 If a doctor **examines** you, he or she checks your body to find out how healthy you are.
examiner NOUN

example examples
NOUN **1** something that is typical of a particular group of things
SYNONYMS: sample, specimen
2 Someone who is an **example** to others is worth imitating.
PHRASE **3** You use **for example** to give an example of something you are talking about. • *large mammals, **for example** whales*
[from Latin *exemplum* meaning pattern]

exasperate exasperates, exasperating, exasperated
VERB If someone or something **exasperates** you, they annoy and frustrate you.
exasperating ADJECTIVE **exasperation** NOUN

excavate **excavates, excavating, excavated**
VERB When someone **excavates**, they remove earth from the ground by digging. When archaeologists **excavate** objects, they carefully uncover remains in the ground to discover information about the past. ● *They found some interesting Roman artefacts while they were **excavating**.*
excavation NOUN **excavator** NOUN

exceed **exceeds, exceeding, exceeded**
VERB If something **exceeds** a particular amount, it is greater than that amount.

excel **excels, excelling, excelled**
VERB If someone **excels** in something, they are very good at doing it.

excellent
ADJECTIVE very good indeed
SYNONYMS: first-rate, outstanding, superb
excellence NOUN

except
PREPOSITION apart from or not including someone or something ● *Everyone laughed **except** Ben.*

exception **exceptions**
NOUN somebody or something that is not included in a general rule ● *All my family are musicians, with the **exception** of my father.*

exceptional
ADJECTIVE If someone or something is **exceptional**, they are unusual or remarkable in some way. For example, they may be very clever or have special talents.
exceptionally ADVERB

excerpt **excerpts**
NOUN a short piece of writing, music or film that is taken from a longer piece

excess **excesses**
NOUN too much of something

excessive
ADJECTIVE more than is needed or allowed
excessively ADVERB

exchange **exchanges, exchanging, exchanged**
VERB If you **exchange** something for something else, you replace it with something. ● *I took the shoes back to the shop and **exchanged** them for another pair.*

excite **excites, exciting, excited**
VERB If something **excites** you, it makes you feel very happy and enthusiastic.
excited ADJECTIVE **excitedly** ADVERB
exciting ADJECTIVE **excitement** NOUN

exclaim **exclaims, exclaiming, exclaimed**
VERB When you **exclaim**, you cry out suddenly or loudly because you are excited or shocked.
exclamation NOUN

exclamation mark **exclamation marks**
NOUN a punctuation mark (!) used in writing to show a strong feeling

exclude **excludes, excluding, excluded**
VERB If you **exclude** someone from a place or activity, you prevent them from entering or taking part.
ANTONYM: include
exclusion NOUN

exclusive
ADJECTIVE **1** available to a small group of rich or privileged people
2 belonging to a particular person or group only ● *Our group will have **exclusive** use of the pool.*
exclusively ADVERB

excruciating
ADJECTIVE extremely painful
excruciatingly ADVERB

excursion **excursions**
NOUN a short journey or outing

excuse **excuses, excusing, excused**
Said "ex-**kyooss**" NOUN **1** a reason you give to explain why something has been done, has not been done, or will not be done
Said "ex-**kyooz**" VERB **2** If you **excuse** someone's behaviour, you give reasons for why they behaved in that way.
PHRASE **3** You say **excuse me** to try to catch somebody's attention or to apologize for an interruption.

A
B
C
D
E
F
G
H
I
J
K
L
M
N
O
P
Q
R
S
T
U
V
W
X
Y
Z

execute executes, executing, executed

VERB To **execute** somebody means to kill them as a punishment for a crime.
execution NOUN

executive executives

NOUN a person who works at a senior level in a company

exercise exercises, exercising, exercised

NOUN **1** any activity that you do in order to get fit or stay healthy
2 a piece of work that you do for practice
VERB **3** When you **exercise**, you do activities that help you to get fit and stay healthy.

exert exerts, exerting, exerted

VERB If you **exert** yourself, you make a great deal of effort to do something.

exhale exhales, exhaling, exhaled

VERB When you **exhale**, you breathe out.
ANTONYM: inhale

exhaust exhausts, exhausting, exhausted

VERB **1** If something **exhausts** you, it makes you very tired.
NOUN **2** the pipe that carries the gas or steam out of the engine of a vehicle
exhaustion NOUN

exhausted

ADJECTIVE If you are **exhausted**, you are very tired.

exhibit exhibits, exhibiting, exhibited

VERB **1** If someone **exhibits** something, they put it on show for others to see, especially in a gallery or museum.
NOUN **2** something that is put on show for others to see, especially in a gallery or museum

exhibition exhibitions

NOUN a public display of works of art, products or skills

exile exiles, exiling, exiled

NOUN **1** a person who is not allowed to live in their own country

VERB **2** If someone is **exiled**, they are sent away from their own country, usually as a punishment.

exist exists, existing, existed

VERB If something **exists**, it is in the world as a real thing.
existence NOUN

exit exits, exiting, exited

NOUN **1** a doorway through which you can leave a public place
ANTONYM: entrance
2 If you make an **exit**, you leave a place.
ANTONYM: entrance
VERB **3** If you **exit** a place, you leave it.

exotic

ADJECTIVE If something is **exotic**, it is unusual and interesting, usually because it comes from another country.

expand expands, expanding, expanded

VERB If something **expands**, or if you **expand** it, it becomes larger.
expansion NOUN

expanse expanses

NOUN a large area of something such as the sky or land

expect expects, expecting, expected

VERB **1** If you **expect** something to happen, you believe that it will happen.
2 If you are **expecting** someone, you are waiting for them to arrive.
3 If you **expect** something, you believe that you ought to get it or have it. • *I'm expecting you to help me.*
expectation NOUN

expedition expeditions

NOUN **1** an organized journey made for a special purpose, often to explore
2 the party of people who go on an expedition • *The expedition set out through the rainforest.*

expel expels, expelling, expelled

VERB **1** If someone **expels** a person from a school or club, they tell them officially to leave because they have behaved badly.
2 If a gas or liquid is **expelled** from a place, it is forced out of it.

expulsion NOUN

expense expenses

NOUN the amount of money it costs to do something or buy something • *They could not afford the expense of the school trip.*

expensive

ADJECTIVE If something is **expensive** it costs a lot of money.

expensively ADVERB

experience experiences, experiencing, experienced

NOUN **1** all the things that you have done or that have happened to you
2 something that you do or something that happens to you, especially something new or unusual
VERB **3** If you **experience** something, it happens to you or you are affected by it.
• *We had never experienced this kind of holiday before.*

experiment experiments, experimenting, experimented

NOUN **1** a scientific test that aims to prove or discover something
VERB **2** If you **experiment** with something or on something, you do a scientific test to prove or discover something about it.

experimentation NOUN
experimental ADJECTIVE
experimentally ADVERB

expert experts

NOUN a person who is very skilled at something or who knows a lot about a particular subject

SYNONYMS: authority, specialist
expertly ADVERB

expire expires, expiring, expired

VERB If something **expires**, it comes to an end and you can no longer use it.

explain explains, explaining, explained

VERB If you **explain** something, you give information about it or reasons for it so that it can be understood.

SYNONYMS: clarify, make clear
explanatory ADJECTIVE

explanation explanations

NOUN An **explanation** explains something.

explode explodes, exploding, exploded

VERB If something such as a bomb **explodes**, it bursts with great force.

explosion NOUN   **explosive** ADJECTIVE

exploit exploits, exploiting, exploited

Said "ex-**ploit**" VERB **1** If somebody **exploits** a person or a situation, they take advantage of them for their own ends.

Said "**ex**-ploit" NOUN **2** something daring or interesting that somebody has done

explore explores, exploring, explored

VERB If you **explore** a place, you travel around it to discover what it is like.

exploration NOUN   **exploratory** ADJECTIVE
explorer NOUN

explosive explosives

ADJECTIVE **1** If something is **explosive**, it is likely to explode.
NOUN **2** something that can cause an explosion

export exports, exporting, exported

Said "ex-**port**" VERB **1** If someone **exports** goods, they sell them to another country.

Said "**ex**-port" NOUN **2 Exports** are goods that are sold to another country.

expose exposes, exposing, exposed

VERB **1** If you **expose** something, you uncover it so that it can be seen.
2 If a person is **exposed** to something dangerous, they are put in a situation that might harm them. • *The patients were isolated so that no one else would be exposed to the disease.*

exposure exposures

NOUN **1** the harmful effect of the weather on the body if a person is outside too long without any protection
2 a single photograph on a film

a
b
c
d
e
f
g
h
i
j
k
l
m
n
o
p
q
r
s
t
u
v
w
x
y
z

express **expresses, expressing, expressed**
VERB **1** When you **express** an idea or feeling, you show what you think or feel by saying or doing something. • She **expressed** her gratitude by giving me a hug.
ADJECTIVE **2** very fast • an **express** train

expression **expressions**
NOUN **1** Your **expression** is the look on your face that shows what you are thinking or feeling.
2 The **expression** of ideas or feelings is the act of showing them through words, actions or art.
3 An **expression** is a phrase with a special meaning, such as nosy parker.
expressive ADJECTIVE

exquisite
ADJECTIVE Something that is **exquisite** is extremely beautiful and pleasing.

extend **extends, extending, extended**
VERB If you **extend** something, you make it longer or bigger.

extension **extensions**
NOUN **1** a room or building that is added on to an existing building
2 an additional telephone connected to the same line as another telephone

extensive
ADJECTIVE **1** covering a large area • The gardens are **extensive**.
2 very great in effect • After the storm the house required **extensive** repairs.
extensively ADVERB

extent **extents**
NOUN The **extent** of something is its length or the area it covers.

exterior **exteriors**
NOUN the outside of something

exterminate **exterminates, exterminating, exterminated**
VERB To **exterminate** people or animals means to kill them deliberately.
extermination NOUN

external
ADJECTIVE existing or happening on the outside of something • The **external** walls of the house need painting.

extinct
ADJECTIVE **1** An **extinct** species of animal or plant is no longer in existence.
2 An **extinct** volcano is no longer likely to erupt.
extinction NOUN

extinguish **extinguishes, extinguishing, extinguished**
VERB If you **extinguish** a light or fire, you put it out.

extra
ADJECTIVE OR ADVERB more than is usual, necessary or expected
SYNONYMS: added, additional, further

extract **extracts, extracting, extracted**
Said "ex-**trakt**" VERB **1** If you **extract** something from a place you get it out, often by force. • The dentist had to **extract** my loose tooth.
Said "**ex**-trakt" NOUN **2** a small section taken from a book or a piece of music

extraordinary
ADJECTIVE very unusual or surprising
SYNONYMS: exceptional, remarkable
extraordinarily ADVERB

extraterrestrial
ADJECTIVE If something is **extraterrestrial**, it happens or exists beyond the earth's atmosphere.

extravagant
ADJECTIVE spending or costing more money than is reasonable or affordable
extravagantly ADVERB **extravagance** NOUN

extreme **extremes**
ADJECTIVE **1** very great in degree or intensity • **extreme** cold
NOUN **2** the furthest point or edge of something
3 the highest or furthest degree of something • You experience **extremes** of temperature in the desert, where it is very cold at night and very hot during the day.
extremely ADVERB

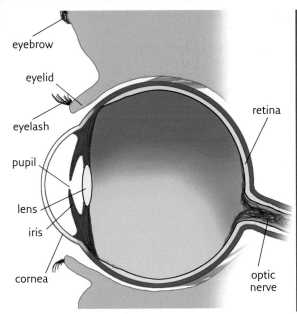

eyebrow

eyelid

eyelash

pupil

lens

iris

cornea

retina

optic nerve

The **pupil** is a hole that changes size to control the amount of light that enters the eye. When it is light the pupil is small and when it is dark the pupil is large.

The **iris** is the coloured part of the eye.

The **cornea** is a clear, tough covering over the iris and pupil that helps protect the eye and begins focusing the light.

The **lens** bends the rays of light coming into the eye so that they fall on the back of the eye.

The back of the eye is called the **retina**, and this is where the light rays are focused.

The **optic nerve** connects the retina to the brain.

a
b
c
d
e
f
g
h
i
j
k
l
m
n
o
p
q
r
s
t
u
v
w
x
y
z

eye **eyes, eyeing** or **eying, eyed**
NOUN **1** the parts of your body with which you see
VERB **2** To **eye** something means to look at it. ● They **eyed** each other's new shoes with interest.

eyebrow **eyebrows**
NOUN Your **eyebrows** are the lines of hair that grow on the ridges of bone above your eyes. ● She raised her **eyebrows** in surprise when she saw her dad's new hat.

eyelash **eyelashes**
NOUN Your **eyelashes** are the hairs that grow on the edges of your eyelids.

eyelid **eyelids**
NOUN Your **eyelids** are the folds of skin that cover your eyes when they are closed. ● I was so tired that my **eyelids** started to droop.

eyesight
NOUN the ability to see ● His **eyesight** is not very good, so he wears glasses.

eyewitness **eyewitnesses**
NOUN someone who has seen something happen and can describe it, especially an accident or a crime ● The police appealed for any **eyewitnesses** to the crash to come forward.

Ff

fable fables
NOUN a story intended to teach a moral lesson ● the **fable** of the tortoise and the hare

fabric fabrics
NOUN cloth ● Silk is a delicate **fabric**.

fabulous
ADJECTIVE **1** wonderful or very impressive **2 Fabulous** creatures are only found in legends or fairy tales.

face faces, facing, faced
NOUN **1** the front part of your head, from your chin to your forehead
2 a surface or side of something ● We could see the north **face** of the mountain.
VERB **3** If you **face** something or someone, you are opposite them and look in their direction.
4 If you **face** in a certain direction, you look there.

facility facilities
NOUN a piece of equipment or a service that is provided for a particular purpose ● The school has excellent sports **facilities**.

fact facts
NOUN **1** a piece of information that is true, or something that has actually happened
PHRASE **2 In fact** and **as a matter of fact** mean actually or really and are used for emphasis. ● **As a matter of fact**, I do like the idea.

factor factors
NOUN **1** something that affects an event or situation ● One of the main **factors** in our success was our strong team.
SYNONYMS: element, part
2 The **factors** of a number are the whole numbers that will divide exactly into it.

● Two and five are **factors** of 10: $2 \times 5 = 10$, $10 \div 5 = 2$, $10 \div 2 = 5$.

factory factories
NOUN a building or group of buildings where goods are made in large quantities

factual
ADJECTIVE If something is **factual**, it has actually happened.
factually ADVERB

fade fades, fading, faded
VERB When something **fades**, it slowly becomes less bright or less loud. ● The colour has **faded** from my favourite T-shirt.

Fahrenheit
Said "**fa**-ren-hite" NOUN the temperature scale that has the freezing point for water at 32 °F and the boiling point at 212 °F
See **Celsius**

fail fails, failing, failed
VERB **1** If you **fail** to do something, you do not succeed in doing it.
ANTONYM: succeed
2 If you **fail** an exam, your marks are too low and you do not pass.
3 If someone or something **fails** to do something that they should have done, they do not do it. ● The bomb **failed** to explode.
PHRASE **4 Without fail** means definitely or regularly. ● He plays football every Sunday **without fail**.

failure failures
NOUN **1** a lack of success in doing something ● Her attempt to win the race ended in **failure**.
2 an unsuccessful person, thing or action

faint fainter, faintest; faints, fainting, fainted
ADJECTIVE **1** A sound, colour or feeling that is **faint** is not strong or intense. ● Their voices grew **fainter** as they moved away.
2 If you feel **faint**, you feel dizzy and unsteady. ● I was feeling **faint**, so I sat down.
VERB **3** If you **faint**, you lose consciousness for a short time.
faintly ADVERB

fair fairer, fairest; fairs

ADJECTIVE **1** Something that is **fair** seems reasonable to most people.
2 If the weather is **fair** it is fine.
3 quite good or moderate • *I think I have a* **fair** *chance of passing my exams.*
4 People who are **fair** have light-coloured hair.
NOUN **5** a form of entertainment that takes place outside, with stalls, games and rides
fairly ADVERB **fairness** NOUN

fairground fairgrounds

NOUN an open piece of ground where fairs are held

fairly

ADVERB quite or rather • *My room's* **fairly** *small.*

fairy fairies

NOUN In stories, **fairies** are small, supernatural creatures with magical powers.

fairy tale fairy tales

NOUN a story of magical events

faith faiths

NOUN **1** If you have **faith** in someone, you trust them.
2 a religious belief

faithful

ADJECTIVE If you are **faithful** to someone or something, you are loyal and continue to support them. • *He is one of my most* **faithful** *friends.*
faithfully ADVERB

fake fakes, faking, faked

NOUN **1** an imitation of something, made to trick people into thinking that it is genuine
ADJECTIVE **2** imitation and not genuine • *The coat was made of* **fake** *fur.*
VERB **3** If you **fake** a feeling, you pretend that you are experiencing it. • *I* **faked** *illness to avoid the games lesson.*

fall falls, falling, fell, fallen

VERB **1** If someone or something **falls**, or **falls** over, or **falls** down, they drop towards the ground. • *The snow* **fell** *all day, covering the fields and trees.*

2 to become lower or less • *The temperature usually* **falls** *at night.*
3 If you **fall ill**, you become ill.
4 If you **fall asleep**, you begin to sleep.
5 If you **fall in love**, you begin to love someone.
6 If you **fall out** with someone, you disagree and quarrel with them.
NOUN **7** If you have a **fall**, you fall over.

false

ADJECTIVE **1** untrue or incorrect
2 not real or genuine, but intended to seem real • *Grandad has* **false** *teeth.*
falsely ADVERB

fame

NOUN the state of being very well known

familiar

ADJECTIVE **1** well-known or easy to recognize • *The room was full of* **familiar** *faces.*
ANTONYM: unfamiliar
2 If you are **familiar with** something, you know it or understand it well. • *He was very* **familiar with** *the local area.*
ANTONYM: unfamiliar

family families

NOUN a group of people who are related to each other, especially parents and their children

family tree family trees

NOUN a diagram that shows how different members of a family are related to each other

famine famines

NOUN a serious shortage of food that may cause many deaths
[from Latin *fames* meaning hunger]

famished

ADJECTIVE very hungry

famous

ADJECTIVE very well-known
famously ADVERB

fan fans, fanning, fanned

NOUN **1** If you are a **fan** of something or someone famous, you like them very much.
2 a hand-held or mechanical device that moves air to make it cooler

A
B
C
D
E
F
G
H
I
J
K
L
M
N
O
P
Q
R
S
T
U
V
W
X
Y
Z

VERB **3** If you **fan** yourself, you cool the air around you with a fan.

fancy fancies, fancying, fancied; fancier, fanciest
VERB **1** If you **fancy** something, you want to have it.
ADJECTIVE **2** highly decorated and special

fancy dress
NOUN clothing worn for a party at which people dress up to look like a particular character or animal

fang fangs
NOUN a long, sharp tooth

fantastic
ADJECTIVE **1** wonderful and very pleasing
SYNONYM: marvellous
2 strange or unusual, like a fantasy
[from Greek *phantasia* meaning imagination]
fantastically ADVERB

fantasy fantasies
NOUN an imaginative story that is unlikely to happen in real life

far farther or further, farthest or furthest
ADVERB **1** a long distance away
ANTONYMS: near, close
ADJECTIVE **2** You can use **far** to ask questions about distance. • *How far is the nearest supermarket?*
ANTONYMS: near, close

fare fares
NOUN the amount that you pay to travel on a bus, train or plane

farewell
EXCLAMATION goodbye

far-fetched
ADJECTIVE unlikely to be true

farm farms, farming, farmed
NOUN **1** an area of land and buildings, used for growing crops or raising animals
VERB **2** If someone **farms** land, they plant crops or keep animals there.
farming NOUN

farmer farmers
NOUN someone who looks after a farm

fascinate fascinates, fascinating, fascinated
VERB If something **fascinates** you, it interests and attracts you.
fascinating ADJECTIVE

fashion fashions
NOUN a style of dress or way of behaving that is popular at a particular time
fashionable ADJECTIVE fashionably ADVERB

fast faster, fastest; fasts, fasting, fasted
ADJECTIVE OR ADVERB **1** If something is **fast**, or is happening **fast**, it is happening quickly or with great speed. • *Our car is very fast.*
2 If a clock is **fast**, it shows a time that is ahead of the real time.
PHRASE **3** If you are **fast asleep**, you are in a deep sleep.
VERB **4** If you **fast**, you eat no food for a period of time, usually for religious reasons.

fasten fastens, fastening, fastened
VERB If you **fasten** something, you close it or attach it firmly to something else.
fastener NOUN fastening NOUN

fat fatter, fattest
ADJECTIVE **1** having a lot of flesh on the body
NOUN **2** the greasy, white substance that animals and humans have under their skin. It is used to store energy and helps to keep them warm.
3 the greasy or oily substance from animals and plants that is used in cooking

fatal
ADJECTIVE A **fatal** accident or illness causes someone's death.
fatally ADVERB

fate fates
NOUN **1** a power that some people believe controls events
2 Someone's **fate** is what becomes of them.

father fathers
NOUN a male parent

father-in-law **fathers-in-law**
NOUN the father of someone's husband or wife

fatigue
NOUN extreme tiredness

fault **faults, faulting, faulted**
NOUN **1** a mistake or something wrong with the way something is made
2 If something bad is your **fault**, you are to blame for it.
VERB **3** If you **fault** someone or something, you find something wrong with them.
• *You can't* ***fault*** *his piano playing.*
faultless ADJECTIVE

faulty
ADJECTIVE If something is **faulty**, there is something wrong with it.

favour **favours, favouring, favoured**
NOUN **1** If you do someone a **favour**, you do something to help them.
VERB **2** If you **favour** someone or something, you prefer them to others.

favourite **favourites**
ADJECTIVE **1** Your **favourite** person or thing is the one you like best. • *Peaches are my* ***favourite*** *fruit.*
NOUN **2** Someone's **favourite** is the person or thing they like best. • *I like all sports, but soccer is my* ***favourite***.

fawn **fawns**
NOUN **1** a young deer
NOUN OR ADJECTIVE **2** a light-brown colour

fax **faxes, faxing, faxed**
NOUN **1** a machine that sends and receives documents electronically along a telephone line
2 a document sent in this way
VERB **3** If you **fax** a document, you send it electronically along a telephone line.

fear **fears, fearing, feared**
NOUN **1** the feeling of worry you have when you think that you are in danger or that something bad might happen
VERB **2** If you **fear** someone or something, you are afraid of them.

fearful
ADJECTIVE If you are **fearful** of someone or something, you are afraid of them.
fearfully ADVERB

fearless
ADJECTIVE If you are **fearless**, you are brave and have no fear.
fearlessly ADVERB

fearsome
ADJECTIVE frightening or terrible

feast **feasts**
NOUN a large and special meal for many people

feat **feats**
NOUN a difficult and impressive achievement

feather **feathers**
NOUN A bird's **feathers** are the light, soft growths covering its body.

feature **features**
NOUN **1** a particular part or characteristic of something that is interesting or important
PLURAL NOUN **2** Your **features** are your eyes, nose, mouth and other parts of your face.
• *Your* ***features*** *are similar to your mother's.*

February
NOUN the second month of the year.
February usually has 28 days, but has 29 days in a leap year.

✐ There is an *r* after the *b* in *February*.

fed
VERB the past participle of **feed**

fed up
ADJECTIVE INFORMAL unhappy or bored • *I'm* ***fed up*** *with this rainy weather.*

fee **fees**
NOUN a charge or payment for a job, service or activity

feeble **feebler, feeblest**
ADJECTIVE weak, with no strength or power

feed **feeds, feeding, fed**
VERB **1** If you **feed** a person or animal,

you give them food. • *She **feeds** the pigeons every day.*

2 When an animal or baby **feeds**, it eats. • *These insects **feed** on wood.*

3 If you **feed** something into a machine, you put it in there. • *They **fed** the information into a computer.*

feel **feels, feeling, felt**

VERB **1** If you **feel** an emotion or sensation, you experience it. • *I **felt** very happy on my birthday.*

2 If you **feel** something, you touch it. • *The doctor **felt** my forehead.*

PHRASE **3** If you **feel like** doing something, you want to do it.

feeler **feelers**

NOUN **Feelers** are long, thin antennae on the heads of some insects, used to sense things around them.

feeling **feelings**

NOUN **1** an emotion • *Finishing my homework gave me a **feeling** of satisfaction.*

2 a physical sensation • *I had a **feeling** of pins and needles in my foot.*

3 Your **feelings** about something are your general attitudes or thoughts about it.

feet

PLURAL NOUN the plural of **foot**

feline

ADJECTIVE relating to the cat family, or catlike • *The dancer moved with **feline** grace.*

felt

VERB **1** the past tense and past participle of **feel**

NOUN **2** a thick cloth made by pressing short threads together

female **females**

NOUN **1** a person or animal that belongs to the gender that can have babies or young

ADJECTIVE **2** concerning or relating to females

[from Latin *femina* meaning woman]

feminine

ADJECTIVE relating to women or considered to be typical of women

fence **fences**

NOUN a wooden or wire barrier between two areas of land

ferment **ferments, fermenting, fermented**

VERB When beer, wine or fruit **ferments**, a chemical change takes place and alcohol is often produced.

fern **ferns**

NOUN a plant with long, feathery leaves and no flowers

ferocious

ADJECTIVE violent and fierce

ferociously ADVERB   **ferocity** NOUN

ferret **ferrets**

NOUN a small mammal that can be trained to hunt rabbits or rats

ferry **ferries, ferrying, ferried**

NOUN **1** a boat that carries people and vehicles across short stretches of water • *We took the **ferry** across to France.*

VERB **2** If someone **ferries** people or goods somewhere, they transport them there, usually on a short, regular journey. • *A fleet of buses **ferried** people to the concert.*

fertile

ADJECTIVE **1** If soil is **fertile** it can produce strong, healthy plants.

2 If a human or other animal is **fertile**, they are able to have babies or young.

fertility NOUN

fertilize **fertilizes, fertilizing, fertilized**; also spelt **fertilise**

VERB **1** When an egg is **fertilized**, the process of reproduction has begun. • *Pollen **fertilizes** the female part of a plant.*

2 When you **fertilize** land, you put manure or chemicals on to it to help the growth of plants.

fertilizer; also spelt **fertiliser** NOUN

festival **festivals**

NOUN **1** an organized series of events and performances • *The film **festival** at Cannes in France is very famous.*

2 a time when something special is celebrated • *Harvest festival is in the autumn.*

fetch fetches, fetching, fetched
VERB If you **fetch** something, you go to where it is and bring it back. • *She fetched a towel from the bathroom.*

fête fêtes; also spelt **fete**
Said "*fayt*" NOUN an outdoor event with games, displays and goods for sale • *The school fête was a big success.*
[from the French *feste* meaning feast]

feud feuds, feuding, feuded
Said "*fyood*" NOUN **1** a long-running and bitter quarrel, especially between families
VERB **2** When people **feud**, they quarrel over a long period of time.

fever fevers
NOUN If you have a **fever**, your temperature is higher than usual because you are ill.

feverish
ADJECTIVE If you are **feverish**, you have a higher body temperature than usual.
feverishly ADVERB

few fewer, fewest
ADJECTIVE OR NOUN not many or a small number of things or people • *I saw him a few moments ago.*

Use *fewer* to talk about things that can be counted and *less* for things that can't be counted: *fewer apples; less time.*

fiancé fiancés
Said "*fee-on-say*" NOUN A woman's **fiancé** is the man to whom she is engaged to be married.
[from Old French *fiancer* meaning to promise or betroth]

fiancée fiancées
Said "*fee-on-say*" NOUN A man's **fiancée** is the woman to whom he is engaged to be married.
[from Old French *fiancer* meaning to promise or betroth]

fiasco fiascos
Said "*fee-ass-koh*" NOUN When something is a **fiasco**, it fails completely, especially in a ridiculous or disorganized way.

fib fibs, fibbing, fibbed
VERB If you **fib** about something, you tell a small lie about it.

fibre fibres
NOUN **1** a thin thread of a substance used to make cloth • *Many fabrics today are made from artificial fibres.*
2 a part of plants that can be eaten but not digested by your body • *Fibre is good for your digestive system.*

fickle
ADJECTIVE If you are **fickle**, you keep changing your mind about what you want.

fiction
NOUN stories about imaginary people and events
ANTONYM: non-fiction
fictional ADJECTIVE

fiddle fiddles, fiddling, fiddled
VERB **1** If you **fiddle** with something, you keep touching it and playing with it in a restless way.
NOUN **2** another word for **violin**

fidget fidgets, fidgeting, fidgeted
VERB If you **fidget**, you keep changing your position or making small restless movements because you are nervous or bored.
fidgety ADJECTIVE

field fields
NOUN **1** an area of land where crops are grown or animals are kept
2 an area of land where sports are played • *a football field*
3 a particular subject or area of interest

fiend fiends
Said "*feend*" NOUN **1** a devil or evil spirit
2 a very wicked or cruel person

fierce fiercer, fiercest
ADJECTIVE very aggressive or intense • *a fierce dog* • *fierce competition*
fiercely ADVERB

A
B
C
D
E
F
G
H
I
J
K
L
M
N
O
P
Q
R
S
T
U
V
W
X
Y
Z

fiery **fierier, fieriest**

ADJECTIVE If you are **fiery**, you show great anger, energy or passion in what you do.

fifteen

NOUN **Fifteen** is the number 15.

fifteenth NOUN OR ADJECTIVE

fifth

NOUN OR ADJECTIVE The **fifth** or the **fifth** thing in a series is the one counted as number five.

fifty

NOUN **Fifty** is the number 50.

fiftieth NOUN OR ADJECTIVE

fig **figs**

NOUN a very sweet fruit that is full of seeds and can be eaten dried

fight **fights, fighting, fought**

VERB **1** When people **fight**, they take part in a battle, a boxing match, or in some other attempt to hurt or kill someone.
2 If you **fight** something, or if you fight against it, you try in a determined way to stop it happening. ● *I've* **fought** *all my life against cruelty to animals.*
NOUN **3** a situation in which people hit or try to hurt each other
SYNONYMS: battle, conflict

figurative

ADJECTIVE If you use a word or expression in a **figurative** sense, you use it for effect, with a more abstract or imaginative meaning than its usual one. For example, you could write about a person as if he or she was a bird. ● *He flew down the stairs.* ● *She perched on a chair.*

figure **figures**

NOUN **1** a written number ● *He wrote the* **figures** *down and then added them up.*
2 Your **figure** is the shape of your body.
3 a diagram or table in a book or a magazine

figure of speech **figures of speech**

NOUN an expression, such as a metaphor or a simile, where the words should not be taken literally. *She was as cold as ice* (simile). *The road was a ribbon of moonlight* (metaphor).

file **files, filing, filed**

NOUN **1** a box or folder in which papers are kept
2 In computing, a **file** is a set of related data with its own name. ● *He copied the* **file** *on to a floppy disk.*
3 a tool with rough surfaces, used for smoothing and shaping hard materials
VERB **4** When someone **files** something, they put it in its correct place with others that are similar. ● *They* **filed** *the students' papers alphabetically.*
5 When a group of people **file** somewhere, they walk one behind the other in a line. ● *The children* **filed** *out of the school.*
PHRASE **6** If people walk **in single file**, they walk one behind the other.

fill **fills, filling, filled**

VERB **1** If you **fill** something, or if it **fills** up, it becomes full. ● *The arena soon began to* **fill** *up.*
2 If something **fills** a space, there is very little room left. ● *The water* **filled** *the jug.*

fill in

VERB If you **fill in** a form, you write information in the spaces on it.

filling **fillings**

NOUN **1** the mixture inside a sandwich, cake or pie
2 a small amount of metal or plastic that a dentist puts into a hole in a tooth

film **films, filming, filmed**

NOUN **1** a series of moving pictures that can be shown in a cinema or on television
2 a strip of thin plastic that you use in a camera to take photographs
3 a very thin layer of powder or liquid ● *A* **film** *of dust covered every surface.*

VERB **4** If you **film** someone or something, you use a camera to take moving pictures of them.

filter filters, filtering, filtered

NOUN **1** a device that allows some substances, lights or sounds to pass through it, but not others ● *The suntan cream acted as a **filter** against the harmful rays of the sun.*

VERB **2** If you **filter** something, you pass it through a filter to remove tiny particles from it.

filtration NOUN

filthy filthier, filthiest

ADJECTIVE very dirty

fin fins

NOUN a flat object on the body of a fish that helps it to swim and keep its balance *See* **fish**

final finals

ADJECTIVE **1** The **final** thing in a series is the last one, or the one that happens at the end. ● *the **final** chapter of a book*
2 A decision that is **final** cannot be changed or questioned. ● *The judges' decision is **final**.*
NOUN **3** The **final** is the last game or contest in a series, that decides the overall winner.

finalist finalists

NOUN someone who takes part in the final of a competition

finally

ADVERB **1** If something **finally** happens, it happens after a long delay. ● ***Finally**, he answered the phone.*
SYNONYMS: at last, eventually
2 You use **finally** to introduce the last point or topic. ● ***Finally**, I would like to thank everyone for coming.*
SYNONYMS: in conclusion, lastly

finance finances, financing, financed

NOUN **1** **Finance** describes affairs to do with money.
VERB **2** If someone **finances** something, they provide the money for it.

find finds, finding, found

VERB **1** If you **find** someone or something, you see them or discover where they are. ● *He eventually **found** the book under his bed.*
2 If you **find** something, you know it from experience. ● *I **find** that air travel tires me.*

find out

VERB If you **find out** something, you learn or discover something. ● *He wants to **find out** what really happened.*

fine finer, finest; fines

ADJECTIVE **1** Something that is **fine** is very good or very beautiful.
2 If something is **fine** it is satisfactory or suitable. ● *That outfit is **fine** for the party.*
3 If you are **fine**, you are well and happy.
4 **Fine** sand or powder is made up of very small particles.
5 When the weather is **fine**, it is bright and sunny.
NOUN **6** a sum of money that must be paid as a punishment

finger fingers

NOUN one of the four long structures at the end of your hands that you use to feel and hold things

fingernail fingernails

NOUN the hard coverings at the ends of your fingers

fingerprint fingerprints

NOUN the unique marks made by the tip of your fingers when you touch something

finish finishes, finishing, finished

VERB **1** When you **finish** something, you do the last part of it and complete it.
2 When something **finishes**, it ends. ● *The film **finished** at eight o'clock.*
NOUN **3** The **finish** of something is the last part of it. ● *There was a very exciting **finish** to the match.*
SYNONYMS: close, conclusion, end

fir firs

NOUN an evergreen tree with thin, needle-like leaves and cones

A
B
C
D
E
F
G
H
I
J
K
L
M
N
O
P
Q
R
S
T
U
V
W
X
Y
Z

fire fires, firing, fired
NOUN **1** the flames produced when something burns
2 a mass of burning material • *We lit a fire on the beach.*
3 a device that uses electricity, coal, gas or wood to heat a room
VERB **4** If someone **fires** a gun, they shoot a bullet. • *He fired the gun into the air.*
5 INFORMAL If an employer **fires** someone, that person loses their job.
PHRASE **6** If something is **on fire**, it is burning.

fire brigade fire brigades
NOUN the organization that has the job of putting out fires

fire engine fire engines
NOUN a vehicle used by firefighters to help them put out fires

fire escape fire escapes
NOUN an emergency exit or staircase for use if there is a fire

fire extinguisher fire extinguishers
NOUN a device that contains water or foam that is sprayed on to fires to put them out

firefighter firefighters
NOUN a person whose job is to put out fires

fireplace fireplaces
NOUN the opening beneath a chimney where a fire can be lit

fireproof
ADJECTIVE If something is **fireproof**, it is resistant to fire.

firework fireworks
NOUN a small object that produces coloured sparks or smoke when lit

firm firmer, firmest; firms
ADJECTIVE **1** Something that is **firm** is fairly hard and does not change shape very much when it is pressed. • *I like sleeping on a firm mattress.*
2 A **firm** grasp or push is strong or controlled. • *His handshake was firm and confident.*
3 Someone who is **firm** behaves in a fairly strict way and will not change their mind.

NOUN **4** a business that sells or produces something • *an engineering firm*

first firsts
ADJECTIVE OR ADVERB **1** happening, coming or done before all the others • *Andrea came first in the 100 metres race.*
NOUN **2** the person or thing that happens or comes before all the others • *I was the first to arrive.*
ADJECTIVE **3** the most important • *Her painting won first prize.*
ADVERB **4** for the first time • *They first met in 1995.*
PHRASE **5** You use **at first** to refer to what happens to start with, or what happens at the beginning of something.

first aid
NOUN simple treatment given as soon as possible to a person who is injured or who suddenly becomes ill

first class
ADJECTIVE Something that is **first class** is of the highest quality or standard.

first person
NOUN In grammar, the **first person** refers to yourself when you are speaking or writing. It is expressed as I or me.
• *William wrote his story in the first person.*

fish fishes, fishing, fished
NOUN **1** an animal with a tail and fins that lives in water

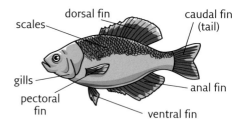

scales
dorsal fin
caudal fin (tail)
gills
pectoral fin
ventral fin
anal fin

VERB **2** If you **fish**, you try to catch fish.

🖉 The plural of the noun *fish* can be either *fish* or *fishes*, but *fish* is more common.

fishing NOUN

fisherman fishermen
NOUN someone who catches fish for a living or as a sport

fist fists
NOUN a hand with the fingers curled tightly towards the palm

fit fits, fitting, fitted; fitter, fittest
VERB **1** If something **fits**, it is the right shape or size for a particular person or position. • *There is now a computer that **fits** into your pocket.*
2 If you **fit** something, you put it securely in place. • *We need to **fit** a new pane of glass in the broken window.*
3 If something **fits** a particular situation, person or thing, it is suitable or appropriate.
NOUN **4** A **fit** of laughter, coughing, rage, or panic is a sudden, uncontrolled outburst of it. • *They collapsed in a **fit** of laughter.*
5 If someone has a **fit**, they lose consciousness and their body makes uncontrollable movements. • *epileptic **fit***
ADJECTIVE **6** Someone who is **fit** is healthy and physically strong.
fitness NOUN

five
NOUN **Five** is the number 5.

fix fixes, fixing, fixed
VERB **1** If you **fix** something somewhere, you attach it there securely. • *He **fixed** the clock to the wall.*
2 If you **fix** something that is broken, you repair it.
SYNONYM: mend

fixture fixtures
NOUN **1** a sports event that takes place on a particular date
2 an object such as a cupboard or a bath that is fixed in position in a building

fizz fizzes, fizzing, fizzed
VERB When something **fizzes** it makes a hissing or bubbling sound.

fizzy fizzier, fizziest
ADJECTIVE A **fizzy** drink has a gas called carbon dioxide in it to make it bubbly.

flag flags
NOUN a piece of cloth that has a particular colour or design, and is used as the symbol of a country or as a signal

flake flakes, flaking, flaked
NOUN **1** a small, thin piece of something
• *Flakes of rust came off the old bicycle.*
VERB **2** When something such as paint **flakes**, small, thin pieces of it come off.
flaky ADJECTIVE   **flaked** ADJECTIVE

flame flames
NOUN a hot, bright stream of burning gas
• *The **flames** of the fire flickered.*

flamingo flamingos or flamingoes
NOUN a long-legged wading bird with pink feathers and a long neck

flammable
ADJECTIVE likely to catch fire and burn easily

flan flans
NOUN a flat, open tart that can be sweet or savoury

flannel flannels
NOUN **1** a small square of towelling, used for washing yourself. In Australian English it is called a *washer*.
2 a lightweight woollen fabric

flap flaps, flapping, flapped
VERB **1** If something **flaps**, or if you **flap** it, it moves quickly up and down or from side to side. • *The flag was **flapping** in the wind.*
NOUN **2** a loose piece of something, such as cloth or plastic, that is attached at one edge • *a cat **flap***

flare flares, flaring, flared
NOUN **1** a device that produces a brightly coloured flame, used especially as an emergency signal
VERB **2** If a fire **flares**, it suddenly burns much more vigorously.

flash flashes, flashing, flashed
NOUN **1** a sudden, short burst of light
• *There was a **flash** of lightning in the middle of the storm.*
VERB **2** If a light **flashes**, or if you **flash** it, it shines suddenly and briefly. • *The light*

flask

A
B
C
D
E
F
G
H
I
J
K
L
M
N
O
P
Q
R
S
T
U
V
W
X
Y
Z

from the lighthouse **flashed** in the night.
3 If something **flashes**, it moves or happens very quickly. • A car **flashed** past the window.

flask flasks
NOUN a special bottle used for keeping drinks hot or cold, and for carrying around with you. It is an abbreviation for vacuum flask or Thermos flask.

flat flats; flatter, flattest
NOUN **1** a set of rooms for living in. A **flat** is part of a larger building. • We live in a block of **flats**.
ADJECTIVE **2** Something that is **flat** is level and smooth.
3 A **flat** tyre or ball has not got enough air in it.
4 A **flat** battery has lost its electrical charge.

flatten flattens, flattening, flattened
VERB If you **flatten** something, you make it flat or flatter.

flatter flatters, flattering, flattered
VERB If you **flatter** someone, you praise them in an exaggerated way, either to please them or to persuade them to do something. • When she **flatters** me I know she wants me to do something for her.
flattering ADJECTIVE   flattery NOUN

flaunt flaunts, flaunting, flaunted
VERB If you **flaunt** something, you show it off to others.

flavour flavours, flavouring, flavoured
NOUN **1** the taste of food and drink • This cheese has a very strong **flavour**.
VERB **2** If you **flavour** food, you add something to it to give it a particular taste. • You can **flavour** the pasta sauce with herbs.

flaw flaws
NOUN a fault or weakness in something
flawed ADJECTIVE   flawless ADJECTIVE

flax
NOUN a plant that is used for making rope and cloth

flea fleas
NOUN a small, wingless, jumping insect that feeds on blood

fleece fleeces
NOUN A sheep's **fleece** is its coat of wool.

fleet fleets
NOUN a group of ships or vehicles owned by the same organization, or travelling together

flesh
NOUN the soft part of your body between the bones and the skin
fleshy ADJECTIVE

flew
VERB the past tense of **fly**

flex flexes, flexing, flexed
NOUN **1** a length of wire covered in plastic, that carries electricity to an appliance
VERB **2** If you **flex** your muscles, you bend and stretch them.

flexible
ADJECTIVE Something that is **flexible** can be bent easily without breaking.
flexibility NOUN

flick flicks, flicking, flicked
VERB **1** If you **flick** something, you move it sharply with your finger. • He **flicked** through the pages of the book to find where he was up to.
NOUN **2** a sudden, quick movement or sharp touch with the finger • The cat gave a sudden **flick** of its tail.

flicker flickers, flickering, flickered
VERB If a light or a flame **flickers**, its brightness comes and goes.

flies
PLURAL NOUN the plural of **fly**

flight flights
NOUN **1** a journey made by aeroplane
2 the action of flying or the ability to fly
3 A **flight** of stairs or steps is a row of them.
4 the action of running away • The girl took **flight** when she saw the big dog.

152

flight attendant flight attendants
NOUN a person who looks after the passengers on an aeroplane

flimsy flimsier, flimsiest
ADJECTIVE made of something very thin and easily damaged • *The shelter they made in the garden was very **flimsy**.*

flinch flinches, flinching, flinched
VERB If you **flinch**, you make a sudden, small movement in fear or pain. • *She **flinched** when the dentist's drill started.*
SYNONYMS: cringe, wince

fling flings, flinging, flung
VERB If you **fling** something somewhere, you throw it there using a lot of force. • *He **flung** his shoes into the corner.*

flint flints
NOUN a very hard, grey-black stone used for building

flip flips, flipping, flipped
VERB If you **flip** something, you turn it over quickly. • *He **flipped** open the book to start his homework.*

flipper flippers
NOUN one of the flat limbs of an animal like a penguin or seal that they use for swimming

float floats, floating, floated
VERB 1 Something that **floats** is supported by liquid. • *A branch **floated** down the river.*
2 If something **floats** in the air, it hangs in the air or moves slowly through it. • *A leaf **floated** on the breeze.*
NOUN 3 an object attached to a fishing line to keep the hook floating in the water
4 an amount of money that a shop or stall keeps for change

flock flocks, flocking, flocked
NOUN 1 a group of birds, sheep or goats
VERB 2 If people **flock** somewhere, they go there in large numbers.

flood floods, flooding, flooded
NOUN 1 If there is a **flood**, a large amount of water covers an area that is usually dry.
2 A **flood** of something is a large amount of it occurring suddenly. • *There was a **flood** of letters after the programme.*
VERB 3 If water **floods** an area that is usually dry, or if the area **floods**, it becomes covered with water. • *He left the tap running and **flooded** the kitchen.*

floodlight floodlights
NOUN a very powerful outdoor light that is used to illuminate sports fields and public buildings

floor floors
NOUN 1 the part of a room that you walk on
2 one of the levels in a building • *Our flat is on the fifth **floor** of the building.*

flop flops, flopping, flopped
VERB 1 If someone or something **flops**, they fall loosely and heavily. • *He **flopped** down on to the sofa when he got home.*
2 INFORMAL If something **flops**, it fails. • *The play **flopped** after it had some bad reviews.*

florist florists
NOUN a person or shop selling flowers

flour
NOUN a white or brown powder made by grinding grain. It is used for making bread, cakes and pastry.

flourish flourishes, flourishing, flourished
VERB Something that **flourishes** develops or grows successfully or healthily.
[from Latin *florere* meaning to flower]

flow flows, flowing, flowed
VERB 1 If something **flows** somewhere, it moves there in a steady and continuous manner. • *The river **flows** south from the town.*
NOUN 2 A **flow** of something is a steady, continuous movement of it. • *There is a constant **flow** of traffic down the main road.*

flow chart flow charts
NOUN a diagram that shows the sequence of steps and choices that lead to various results and courses of action

a
b
c
d
e
f
g
h
i
j
k
l
m
n
o
p
q
r
s
t
u
v
w
x
y
z

flower **flowers, flowering, flowered**
NOUN **1** the part of a plant that grows at the end of a stem. It carries the reproductive parts of the plant from which the fruit and seeds develop.

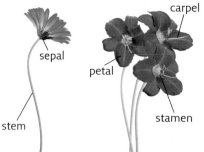

VERB **2** When a plant **flowers**, its flowers open.

flown
VERB the past participle of **fly**

flu
NOUN an abbreviation of *influenza*. **Flu** is an illness similar to a bad cold, but more serious.

fluent
ADJECTIVE Someone who is **fluent** in a foreign language can speak it correctly and without hesitation.
fluently ADVERB

fluff
NOUN soft, light, woolly threads or fibres bunched together

fluffy **fluffier, fluffiest**
ADJECTIVE soft and woolly

fluid **fluids**
NOUN a liquid • *Drink plenty of* **fluids** *in hot weather.*

fluke **flukes**
NOUN an accidental success • *It must be a* **fluke** *that I did so well in my exams.*

fluorescent
ADJECTIVE **1** When something is **fluorescent**, it gives out its own light when another light is shone on it.
2 A **fluorescent** light is in the form of a tube that shines with a harsh, bright light.

fluoride
NOUN a chemical mixture that is often added to drinking water and to toothpaste because it is thought to prevent tooth decay

flush **flushes, flushing, flushed**
VERB **1** If you **flush**, your face goes red.
2 If you **flush** a toilet or something such as a pipe, you force water through it to clean it.

flute **flutes**
NOUN a musical wind instrument in the shape of a long tube with holes along it. You play it by blowing over a hole near one end while holding it sideways to your mouth.

flutter **flutters, fluttering, fluttered**
VERB If something **flutters**, it flaps or waves with small, quick movements. • *I felt the bird* **flutter** *in my hands.*

fly **flies, flying, flew, flown**
NOUN **1** an insect with two pairs of wings
VERB **2** When a bird, insect or aircraft **flies**, it moves through the air. • *The bird* **flew** *away.*
3 If you **fly** somewhere, you travel there in an aircraft.
flying ADJECTIVE OR NOUN **flyer** NOUN

flyover **flyovers**
NOUN a bridge that takes one road over the top of another one

foal **foals**
NOUN a young horse

foam **foams, foaming, foamed**
NOUN **1** a mass of tiny bubbles • *The bubble bath produced a lot of* **foam**.
VERB **2** When something **foams**, it forms a mass of small bubbles. • *The powder* **foamed** *in the washing machine.*

focus **focuses, focusing, focused** or **focusses, focussing, focussed**
VERB **1** If you **focus** your eyes or a camera on something, you adjust your eyes or the camera so that the image is clear. • *She* **focused** *her eyes on the ball.*
2 If you **focus** on a particular topic, you concentrate on it.

PHRASE 3 If an image is **in focus**, the edges of the image are clear and sharp. If it is **out of focus**, the edges are blurred. [from Latin *focus* meaning hearth, which was seen as the centre of a Roman home]

✎ You can spell the inflections of *focus* with one *s* or two *ss* in the middle but the spellings with one *s* are much more common: *focuses*, *focusing*, *focused*.

fodder
NOUN food given to horses and cattle

foe **foes**
NOUN If someone is your **foe**, they are your enemy.

foetus **foetuses**; also spelt **fetus**
NOUN A **foetus** is an unborn child or other animal in the womb.

fog
NOUN a thick mist caused by tiny drops of water in the air

foil **foils, foiling, foiled**
VERB **1** If you **foil** someone's attempt at something, you prevent it from succeeding. • *The policeman* **foiled** *the robbery.*
NOUN **2** thin, paper-like sheets of metal used to wrap food

fold **folds, folding, folded**
VERB **1** If you **fold** something, you bend it so that one part lies over another. • *He* **folded** *the letter and put it back in the envelope.*
NOUN **2** a crease or bend in paper or cloth

folder **folders**
NOUN a thin piece of folded cardboard used for keeping papers together

foliage
NOUN the leaves of plants

folk
PLURAL NOUN **1** people • *These are the* **folk** *I was telling you about.*
ADJECTIVE **2** **Folk** music and art are traditional or typical of the people of a particular area. • *My dad likes Irish* **folk** *music.*

folklore
NOUN the traditional stories and beliefs of a community

follow **follows, following, followed**
VERB **1** If you **follow** someone or something, you move along behind them. • *We* **followed** *him up the steps.*
2 If you **follow** a path or a sign, you go somewhere using the path or sign to direct you. • *I* **followed** *the signs to the dining room.*
3 If you **follow** instructions or advice, you do what you are told.
4 If you **follow** an explanation or the plot of a story, you understand each stage of it.
follower NOUN

fond **fonder, fondest**
ADJECTIVE If you are **fond** of someone or something, you like them.

font **fonts**
NOUN **1** a large, stone bowl in a church that holds the water for baptisms
2 a style of printed writing. There are many **fonts** to choose from, such as: Helvetica, Times, Courier or Frutiger.

food **foods**
NOUN what people and other animals eat

food chain **food chains**
NOUN a series of living things that are linked together because each one feeds on another in the chain

fool **fools, fooling, fooled**
NOUN **1** someone who is silly and is not sensible
VERB **2** If you **fool** someone, you deceive or trick them. • *Don't be* **fooled** *by his appearance.*

foolish
ADJECTIVE stupid or silly

foolproof
ADJECTIVE If something is **foolproof**, it cannot fail.

foot **feet**
NOUN **1** the part of your body at the end of your leg

a
b
c
d
e
f
g
h
i
j
k
l
m
n
o
p
q
r
s
t
u
v
w
x
y
z

2 the part of something that is farthest from the top • *The hotel was at the* **foot** *of the mountain.*

3 a unit of length equal to 12 inches or about 30.5 centimetres

football **footballs**

NOUN **1** a game such as soccer and American **football**, in which the ball can be kicked and two teams try to score goals

2 a ball used in these games

footballer NOUN

foothold **footholds**

NOUN a place where you can put your foot when climbing

footpath **footpaths**

NOUN a path for people to walk on, especially in the countryside

footprint **footprints**

NOUN the mark made by a foot on the ground

footstep **footsteps**

NOUN the sound made by someone's feet when they are walking • *They heard* **footsteps** *in the corridor.*

for

PREPOSITION **1** to be used by or given to a particular person • *I bought a present* **for** *my brother.*

2 **For** is used when explaining the reason, cause or purpose of something. • *I'm going shopping* **for** *a pair of shoes.*

3 You use **for** to show a distance, time or quantity. • *I have been waiting here* **for** *ages.*

4 If you are **for** something, you support it. • *My parents are all* **for** *the new school.* ANTONYM: against

forbid **forbids, forbidding, forbade, forbidden**

VERB If someone **forbids** you to do something, they order you not to do it.

forbidden ADJECTIVE

force **forces, forcing, forced**

VERB **1** If you **force** someone to do something, you make them do it.

NOUN **2** violence or great strength

• *He used a lot of* **force** *to pull the wall down.*

3 an organized group of people, especially soldiers or police • *The police* **force** *helped to maintain order at the football match.*

4 a push or pull. **Forces** are measured in newtons.

forceful ADJECTIVE **forcefully** ADVERB

forecast **forecasts, forecasting, forecast or forecasted**

NOUN **1** A **forecast** says what is likely to happen. • *the weather* **forecast**

VERB **2** If you **forecast** an event, you say what is likely to happen. • *We* **forecast** *that we would win the game.*

foreground **foregrounds**

NOUN In a picture, the **foreground** is the part that seems nearest to you.

forehead **foreheads**

NOUN the area at the front of your head, above your eyebrows and below your hair

foreign

ADJECTIVE belonging to or involving a country that is not your own • *It is useful to learn a* **foreign** *language.*

foreigner NOUN

forest **forests**

NOUN a large area of trees growing close together

forever

ADVERB permanently or continually

forfeit **forfeits, forfeiting, forfeited**

VERB If you **forfeit** something, you have to give it up as a penalty.

forgave

VERB the past tense of **forgive**

forge **forges, forging, forged**

NOUN **1** a place where a blacksmith works making metal goods by hand

VERB **2** If someone **forges** metal, they hammer and bend it into shape while it is hot.

3 Someone who **forges** money, documents or paintings makes illegal copies of them.

forgery forgeries
NOUN **1** the crime of making false copies of something
2 an illegal false copy of something

forget forgets, forgetting, forgot, forgotten
VERB If you **forget** something, you do not remember it.
forgetful ADJECTIVE

forgive forgives, forgiving, forgave, forgiven
VERB If you **forgive** someone who has done something wrong, you stop being angry with them.

fork forks
NOUN **1** an instrument with prongs on the end of a handle, used for eating food or for digging earth
2 If there is a **fork** in a road or river, it divides into two or more parts.

forlorn
ADJECTIVE If you are **forlorn**, you are unhappy and lonely.

form forms, forming, formed
NOUN **1** a particular type or kind of something • *Running is a **form** of exercise.*
2 the shape or pattern of something • *Cut out your paper in the **form** of a star.*
3 a class in school
4 a piece of paper with questions and spaces where you fill in your answers
VERB **5** If you **form** something, you make it or give it a particular shape. • *Please all stand up and **form** a circle.*
6 If something **forms**, it develops or comes into existence. • *The puddles **formed** on the pavement after the rain.*

formal
ADJECTIVE **1** **Formal** speech, writing or behaviour is correct and serious, rather than relaxed and friendly. • *At the prizegiving everyone wore **formal** clothes.*
ANTONYM: informal
2 A **formal** action or event is an official one that follows accepted rules.
ANTONYM: informal
formally ADVERB

format formats
NOUN the way something is arranged and presented • *The **format** of the book is easy to follow.*

formation formations
NOUN **1** the start or creation of something
2 the pattern or shape of something

former
ADJECTIVE **1** happening or existing before now, or in the past • *The **former** tennis champion presented the trophy to the new champion.*
2 **Former** refers to the first of two things mentioned. • *Exams and coursework are both important, but the **former** must take priority this term.*
formerly ADVERB

formula formulae or formulas
NOUN a group of letters, numbers or symbols that stand for a mathematical or scientific rule

fort forts
NOUN a strong, fortified building built for defence

fortify fortifies, fortifying, fortified
VERB If someone **fortifies** a building, they make it stronger against attack.

fortnight fortnights
NOUN a period of two weeks

fortress fortresses
NOUN a very strong and well-protected castle or town

fortunate
ADJECTIVE lucky
fortunately ADVERB

fortune fortunes
NOUN **1** luck
2 a lot of money

forty
NOUN **Forty** is the number 40.
fortieth NOUN OR ADJECTIVE

forward forwards
ADVERB **1** If you move something **forward**, you move it towards the front.
NOUN **2** In a game like hockey or football, a **forward** is someone in an attacking position.

fossil **fossils**

NOUN the remains or impression of an animal or plant from a previous age, which has been preserved in rock

fossilize VERB

foster **fosters, fostering, fostered**

VERB If someone **fosters** a child, they look after the child for a period in their home, but do not become his or her legal parent.

foster child NOUN   **foster home** NOUN

foster parent NOUN

fought

VERB the past tense of **fight**

foul **fouler, foulest; fouls**

ADJECTIVE **1** very unpleasant, especially because it is dirty or obscene • *There was a* **foul** *smell coming from the drains.*

NOUN **2** In sport, a **foul** is an action that breaks the rules.

found **founds, founding, founded**

VERB **1** the past tense and past participle of **find**

2 If someone **founds** an organization or company, they create it. • *He* **founded** *the charity ten years ago.*

foundation **foundations**

NOUN **1** the basic ideas on which something is based • *A good education is the* **foundation** *for a successful life.*

PLURAL NOUN **2** The **foundations** of a building are the layer of concrete or bricks below the ground on which it is built.

NOUN **3** the founding of something

fountain **fountains**

NOUN an ornamental structure in which a jet of water is forced into the air by a pump

fountain pen **fountain pens**

NOUN a pen that has a nib which is supplied with ink from a container inside the pen

four

NOUN **Four** is the number 4.

fourth NOUN OR ADJECTIVE

fourteen

NOUN **Fourteen** is the number 14.

fourteenth NOUN OR ADJECTIVE

fowl **fowls**

NOUN a bird, such as chicken or duck, that is kept or hunted for its meat or eggs

fox **foxes**

NOUN a wild mammal that looks like a dog and has reddish-brown fur and a thick tail

foyer **foyers**

*Said "***foy***-ay"* NOUN a large entrance hall just inside the main doors of a cinema, hotel or public building

fraction **fractions**

NOUN **1** In mathematics, a **fraction** is a part of a whole number.

2 a tiny proportion or amount of something

fracture **fractures, fracturing, fractured**

NOUN **1** a crack or break in something, especially a bone

VERB **2** If something **fractures**, or if you **fracture** it, it breaks. • *She* **fractured** *her arm while playing netball.*

fragile

ADJECTIVE easily broken or damaged

fragility NOUN

fragment **fragments**

NOUN a small piece or part of something • *There were* **fragments** *of glass on the floor after I dropped the vase.*

fragmentation NOUN

fragmented ADJECTIVE

fragrant

ADJECTIVE Something that is **fragrant** smells sweet or pleasant.

frail **frailer, frailest**
ADJECTIVE weak or fragile
frailty NOUN

frame **frames, framing, framed**
NOUN **1** the structure surrounding a door, window or picture
VERB **2** If you **frame** a picture, you make a frame for it.

framework **frameworks**
NOUN a structure that forms a support or frame for something • *wooden shelves on a steel **framework***

frantic
ADJECTIVE If you are **frantic**, you behave in a wild, desperate way because you are anxious or frightened.
frantically ADVERB

fraud **frauds**
NOUN the crime of getting money by deceit

fraught
ADJECTIVE **1** If a situation is **fraught**, it is full of potential problems or difficulties.
2 If someone is **fraught**, they are tense and upset.

frayed
ADJECTIVE If material is **frayed**, the edges are worn and ragged.

freak **freaks**
NOUN **1** A **freak** is someone whose appearance or behaviour is very unusual.
ADJECTIVE **2** A **freak** event is very unusual.
• *We had a **freak** storm in the middle of the summer.*

freckle **freckles**
NOUN a small, light-brown spot on someone's skin, especially their face
freckled ADJECTIVE

free **freer, freest; frees, freeing, freed**
ADJECTIVE **1** If something is **free**, you can have it without paying for it.
2 Someone who is **free** is no longer a prisoner.
3 If someone is **free**, they are not busy.
• *Are you **free** on Saturday afternoon?*
VERB **4** If you **free** someone or something that is trapped, you release them.

freedom
NOUN If you have the **freedom** to do something, you are free to do it.

free verse
NOUN poetry that does not use patterns of rhyme or rhythm

freeway **freeways**
NOUN In Australia, South Africa and the USA, a **freeway** is a road for fast-moving traffic.

freeze **freezes, freezing, froze, frozen**
VERB **1** When a liquid **freezes**, or when something **freezes** it, it becomes solid because it is very cold.
2 If you **freeze** food, you make it very cold to preserve it.
3 If you **freeze**, you suddenly stop moving because there is danger.
ADJECTIVE **4** You say you are **freezing** when you are very cold.

freezer **freezers**
NOUN a refrigerator in which you can store food for a long time at very low temperatures

freight
NOUN goods moved by lorries, ships or other transport

frenzy **frenzies**
NOUN If someone is in a **frenzy**, their behaviour is wild and uncontrolled.
frenzied ADJECTIVE

frequency **frequencies**
NOUN **1** The **frequency** of an event is how often it happens.
2 The **frequency** of a sound or radio wave is the rate at which it vibrates.

frequency table **frequency tables**
NOUN a chart where you write down how often something happens

frequent
ADJECTIVE If something happens at **frequent** intervals, it happens often.
frequently ADVERB

fresh **fresher, freshest**
ADJECTIVE **1** Something that is not old or

used. ● *We put **fresh** towels out for the guests.*

2 Fresh food has been made or picked recently, and is not tinned or frozen.

3 Fresh water is water that is not salty. ● *The water in a river or lake is **fresh** water.*

freshwater

ADJECTIVE A **freshwater** animal lives in a river, lake or pool and not in the sea.

fret frets, fretting, fretted

VERB **1** If you **fret** about something, you worry about it.

NOUN **2** The **frets** on a stringed instrument, such as a guitar, are the metal ridges across its neck.

friction

NOUN **1** the force that slows things down and can stop them from moving

2 Friction between people is disagreement and quarrels. ● *There was a lot of **friction** between the two families.*

Friday Fridays

NOUN the sixth day of the week, coming between Thursday and Saturday [from Old English *Frigedæg* meaning Freya's day, the Norse goddess of love]

fridge fridges

NOUN a short form of *refrigerator*

friend friends

NOUN someone you know well and like, but who is not related to you

friendly friendlier, friendliest

ADJECTIVE A **friendly** person is kind and pleasant to others.

friendship friendships

NOUN the state of being friends with someone ● *Her **friendship** means a lot to me.*

fright

NOUN a sudden feeling of fear

frighten frightens, frightening, frightened

VERB If something or someone **frightens** you, they make you afraid.

frightened ADJECTIVE   frightening ADJECTIVE

frill frills

NOUN a strip of material with a lot of folds

in it, that is attached to something as decoration

fringe fringes

NOUN **1** the hair that hangs over a person's forehead ● *She had a long **fringe** that almost covered her eyes.*

2 a decoration on clothes and other objects, consisting of a row of hanging threads ● *There is a **fringe** along the bottom of the curtains.*

fringed ADJECTIVE

frivolous

ADJECTIVE Someone who is **frivolous** behaves in a silly or light-hearted way, especially when they should be serious or sensible.

frivolously ADVERB   frivolity NOUN

frizzy frizzier, frizziest

ADJECTIVE **Frizzy** hair has tight, wiry curls.

frog frogs

NOUN a small, amphibious animal with long back legs

frolic frolics, frolicking, frolicked

VERB When children and other young animals **frolic**, they run around and play in a lively way. ● *In the spring, the lambs **frolic** in the fields.*

from

PREPOSITION **1 From** tells you where someone or something started. ● *The river flows **from** the north.*

2 If you take something **from** an amount, you reduce the amount by that much. ● *If you take five **from** 20 you are left with 15.*

3 You use **from** to state the range of something. ● *Lunchtime is **from** 12 o'clock to 1 o'clock.*

front fronts

NOUN **1** the part of something that faces forward ● *a jacket with buttons down the front*

ADJECTIVE **2** The **front** part of something is the part that is furthest forward. ● *I like to sit in the **front** seats of the cinema.*

NOUN **3** In a war, the **front** is the place where two armies are fighting.

4 At the seaside, the **front** is the road or promenade that runs alongside the beach.

frontier frontiers

NOUN a border between two countries
- *Their passports were checked at the **frontier**.*

frost frosts

NOUN powdery, white ice that forms on the ground when the temperature outside falls below freezing

frosty frostier, frostiest

ADJECTIVE When it is **frosty**, the temperature outside falls below freezing and powdery, white ice forms on the ground.

froth froths, frothing, frothed

NOUN **1** a mass of small bubbles on the surface of a liquid
VERB **2** If a liquid **froths**, small bubbles appear on its surface.
frothy ADJECTIVE

frown frowns, frowning, frowned

VERB **1** If you **frown**, you move your eyebrows closer together and wrinkle your forehead, usually because you are annoyed, worried or puzzled.
NOUN **2** an expression on the face of someone who is frowning

froze

VERB the past tense of **freeze**

frozen

VERB **1** the past participle of **freeze**
ADJECTIVE **2** If you say you are **frozen**, you mean you have become very cold.

fruit fruits

NOUN the part of a plant that develops after the flower has been fertilized, that contains the seeds. Apples, oranges and bananas are all **fruit**.
[from Latin *fructus* meaning produce or benefit]

frustrate frustrates, frustrating, frustrated

VERB **1** If something **frustrates** you, it prevents you doing what you want and makes you upset.
2 If you **frustrate** something, such as a plan, you prevent it. • *They deliberately **frustrated** my attempts to do my homework.*
frustrated ADJECTIVE   frustrating ADJECTIVE
frustration NOUN

fry fries, frying, fried

VERB When you **fry** food, you cook it in a pan containing hot fat.

fudge

NOUN a soft, brown sweet made from butter, milk and sugar

fuel fuels

NOUN a substance such as coal, gas, oil or wood that is burned to provide heat or power

fugitive fugitives

NOUN someone who is running away or hiding, especially from the police

fulfil fulfils, fulfilling, fulfilled

VERB **1** If you **fulfil** a promise, you keep it.
2 If something **fulfils** you, it gives you satisfaction.
fulfilling ADJECTIVE   fulfilment NOUN

full fuller, fullest

ADJECTIVE **1** Something that is **full** contains as much as it is possible to hold. • *The bus was **full** so we had to wait for the next one.*
ANTONYM: empty
2 to the greatest possible extent • *The radio was playing at **full** volume.*
3 complete or whole • *I will tell you the **full** story later.*
ADVERB **4** completely or wholly • *Turn the taps **full** on.*
fullness NOUN   fully ADVERB

full stop full stops

NOUN the punctuation mark (.) used at the end of a sentence and after an abbreviation or initial

full-time
ADJECTIVE If you have a **full-time** job, you work for the whole of each normal working week.

fumble **fumbles, fumbling, fumbled**
VERB If you **fumble**, you feel or handle something clumsily. • *I **fumbled** with the door handle because it was so dark.*

fume **fumes, fuming, fumed**
PLURAL NOUN **1 Fumes** are unpleasant-smelling gases and smoke that are sometimes poisonous, and are produced by burning and by some chemicals.
VERB **2** If something **fumes**, it produces smoke or gas.
3 If you **fume**, you are very angry.

fun
NOUN **1** pleasant, enjoyable and light-hearted activity • *Let's have some **fun**!*
ADJECTIVE **2** If someone or something is **fun**, you enjoy being with them or you enjoy doing it. • *She is always **fun** to be with.*
PHRASE **3** If you **make fun** of someone or something, you tease them or make jokes about them.

function **functions, functioning, functioned**
VERB **1** If a thing **functions**, it works as it should.
NOUN **2** The **function** of someone or something is their purpose or the work they are supposed to do.
functional ADJECTIVE

fund **funds**
NOUN an amount of money that is collected for a particular purpose

fundamental
ADJECTIVE If something is **fundamental**, it is basic and necessary. • *You must understand the **fundamental** rules of the game before you can progress.*

funeral **funerals**
NOUN a ceremony for the burial or cremation of someone who has died

fungus **fungi** or **funguses**
NOUN an organism, such as a mushroom or mould, that does not have flowers or leaves
fungal ADJECTIVE

funnel **funnels**
NOUN **1** an open cone that narrows to a tube, and is used to pour substances into containers **2** a metal chimney on a ship or steam engine

funny **funnier, funniest**
ADJECTIVE **1** causing amusement or laughter • *He told us a **funny** story.*
SYNONYMS: amusing, comical, humorous
2 strange or puzzling • *We could hear a **funny** noise.*
SYNONYMS: odd, peculiar

fur
NOUN the thick hair that grows on the bodies of many animals • *Polar bears have white **fur**.*
furry ADJECTIVE

furious
ADJECTIVE extremely angry
furiously ADVERB

furnace **furnaces**
NOUN a very large, hot oven used for heating glass and melting metal

furnish **furnishes, furnishing, furnished**
VERB If you **furnish** a house or a room, you put furniture into it.

furniture
NOUN movable objects such as tables, chairs and wardrobes that you need inside a building • *bedroom **furniture***

furrow **furrows**
NOUN a shallow, straight channel dug into the earth by a plough

further **furthest**
ADJECTIVE OR ADVERB another word for *farther*
See **far**

Gg

furtive
ADJECTIVE secretive, sly and cautious
furtively ADVERB

fury
NOUN violent or extreme anger
[from Latin *furia* meaning madness]

fuse **fuses, fusing, fused**
NOUN **1** a safety device in an electrical plug or appliance, consisting of a piece of wire that melts to stop the electric current if a fault occurs
VERB **2** When an electrical appliance **fuses**, it stops working because the fuse has melted to protect it.

fuss **fusses, fussing, fussed**
NOUN **1** unnecessarily anxious or excited behaviour
VERB **2** If someone **fusses**, they behave with unnecessary anxiety and concern for unimportant things.

fussy **fussier, fussiest**
ADJECTIVE If you are **fussy**, you worry too much about unnecessary details.

future **futures**
NOUN **1** the period of time after the present
● *He is already making plans for his **future**.*
ADJECTIVE **2** relating to or occurring at a time after the present
PHRASE **3** **In future** means from now on.
● *Be more careful **in future**.*

fuzzy **fuzzier, fuzziest**
ADJECTIVE **1** soft and fluffy
2 If a picture is **fuzzy**, it is not clear.

gadget **gadgets**
NOUN a small mechanical device or tool

gain **gains, gaining, gained**
VERB **1** If you **gain** something, you get more of it or get something you didn't have before. ● *She was pleased when she began to **gain** better marks.*
2 If a clock or watch **gains** time, it starts telling a later time than it is.
● *I think my watch has **gained** five minutes. It says five past one and the clock says one o'clock.*

gala **galas**
NOUN a special, public celebration or performance ● *a swimming **gala***

galaxy **galaxies**
NOUN a huge group of stars that extends over millions of kilometres

Our galaxy, the Milky Way

gale **gales**
NOUN an extremely strong wind

gallant
ADJECTIVE brave and honourable
gallantly ADVERB **gallantry** NOUN

galleon **galleons**
NOUN a large Spanish sailing ship in the sixteenth and seventeenth centuries

gallery **galleries**
NOUN a building where paintings and other works of art are shown

gallon **gallons**
NOUN a measure of liquid that is equal to eight pints or 4.55 litres

gallop **gallops, galloping, galloped**
VERB When a horse **gallops**, it runs very fast, so that during each stride all four feet are off the ground at the same time.

gallows
NOUN a framework on which criminals used to be hanged

gamble **gambles, gambling, gambled**
VERB When someone **gambles**, they bet money on the result of a contest or race.

game **games**
NOUN **1** an activity with a set of rules that is played by individuals or teams against each other
2 a term for wild birds and animals that are hunted for food or sport, such as pheasant or boar

gammon
NOUN cured meat from a pig, similar to bacon but usually in thicker and larger slices

gander **ganders**
NOUN a male goose

gang **gangs, ganging, ganged**
NOUN **1** a group of people who join together for some purpose, for example to commit a crime
VERB **2** INFORMAL If people **gang up** on you, they join together to oppose you. ● *The children finally **ganged up** on the bully.*

gangster **gangsters**
NOUN a violent criminal who is a member of a gang

gangway **gangways**
NOUN **1** a space left between rows of seats, for example in a train or cinema, for people to walk through
2 a movable passenger bridge between a ship and the shore

gaol
NOUN OR VERB another spelling of **jail**

gap **gaps**
NOUN a space between two things or a hole in something solid ● *He was just able to squeeze through the **gap** in the hedge.*

gape **gapes, gaping, gaped**
VERB **1** If you **gape**, you stare with your mouth wide open.
2 If something **gapes**, it is wide open.

garage **garages**
NOUN **1** a building in which you can keep a car
2 a place where cars are repaired or where petrol is sold

garbage
NOUN In American English, **garbage** is rubbish, especially waste from a kitchen.

garden **gardens**
NOUN an area of land next to a house, with plants, trees and grass

gardener **gardeners**
NOUN a person who looks after a garden as a job or as a hobby

gargle **gargles, gargling, gargled**
VERB When you **gargle**, you rinse the back of your throat by putting some liquid in your mouth and making a bubbling sound without swallowing the liquid.

gargoyle **gargoyles**
NOUN a stone carving below the roof of an old building, in the shape of an ugly person or animal

garlic
NOUN the small, white bulb of an onion-like plant that has a strong taste and smell and is used in cooking

garment **garments**
NOUN an item of clothing

gas **gases**
NOUN a substance that is not a liquid or a solid. Air is a mixture of **gases**. The bubbles in fizzy lemonade contain a **gas** called carbon dioxide.

A
B
C
D
E
F
G
H
I
J
K
L
M
N
O
P
Q
R
S
T
U
V
W
X
Y
Z

gasp gasps, gasping, gasped
VERB If you **gasp**, you quickly draw in your breath through your mouth because you are surprised or in pain.

gate gates
NOUN a barrier that can be opened or shut and is used to close off the entrance to a field, garden or path

gateau gateaux
NOUN a rich, layered cake with cream in it [from French *gâteau* meaning cake]

gather gathers, gathering, gathered
VERB **1** If you **gather** things, you collect or pick them. • *I gathered some flowers from the garden.*
2 When people **gather**, they come together in a group. • *We gathered at my house before we went to the party.*
3 If you **gather** information, you learn it, often from hearing or reading about it. • *I gather you passed your exams.*

gathering gatherings
NOUN a meeting of people who gather together for a particular purpose

gauge gauges, gauging, gauged
VERB **1** If you **gauge** something, you estimate or work out how much of it there is or how much is required.
NOUN **2** an instrument used for measuring • *The fuel gauge shows that we need more petrol.*

gauze
NOUN a thin, cotton cloth, often used for bandages

gave
VERB the past tense of **give**

gaze gazes, gazing, gazed
VERB If you **gaze** at something, you look steadily at it for a long time. • *We gazed up at the stars.*

gazelle gazelles
NOUN a small antelope found in Africa and Asia

gear gears
NOUN **1** The **gears** in a car or on a bicycle are a set of cogs that work together to send power to the wheels.
2 the clothes or equipment that you need for an activity • *climbing gear*

geese
PLURAL NOUN the plural of **goose**

gel gels
NOUN a smooth, soft, jelly-like substance • *hair gel*

gem gems
NOUN a jewel or precious stone

gender genders
NOUN The **gender** of a person or animal is whether they are male or female.

gene genes
Said "**jeen**" NOUN one of the parts of the chromosomes found inside the cells of an organism. Offspring inherit **genes** from their parents.
genetic ADJECTIVE **genetically** ADVERB

general generals
ADJECTIVE **1** relating to the whole of something or to most things in a group • *There has been a general improvement in your work.*
2 including or involving a range of different things • *There was a general knowledge quiz at the end of term.*
NOUN **3** an army officer of very high rank
PHRASE **4** **In general** is used to indicate that a statement is true in most cases, or that it applies to most people or things. • *In general, people take their holidays over the summer.*
generally ADVERB

general election general elections
NOUN an election in which people vote for who they want to represent them in the national parliament

generate generates, generating, generated
VERB If someone or something **generates** something else, they produce or create it.

a
b
c
d
e
f
g
h
i
j
k
l
m
n
o
p
q
r
s
t
u
v
w
x
y
z

A
B
C
D
E
F
G
H
I
J
K
L
M
N
O
P
Q
R
S
T
U
V
W
X
Y
Z

• *They built a new power station to* **generate** *more electricity.*

generation generations

NOUN **1** all the people of a similar age • *the younger* **generation**
2 the length of time that it takes for children to grow up and have children of their own • *The next* **generation** *will see a lot more changes.*

generator generators

NOUN a machine that produces electricity from another form of energy, such as wind or water power

generous

ADJECTIVE A **generous** person gives or shares what they have, especially time or money.
generously ADVERB

genie genies

NOUN a magical being that obeys the wishes of the person who controls it
• *Aladdin rubbed his magic lamp and the* **genie** *appeared.*
[from Arabic *jinni* meaning demon]

genitals

PLURAL NOUN The **genitals** are the reproductive organs. The technical name is **genitalia**.

genius geniuses

NOUN a highly intelligent, creative or talented person • *a mathematical* **genius**

gentle gentler, gentlest

ADJECTIVE Someone or something that is **gentle** is mild and calm. • *A* **gentle** *breeze blew across the field.*
ANTONYMS: violent, rough

gentleman gentlemen

NOUN **1** a man who is polite and well-educated
2 a polite way of referring to any man

genuine

ADJECTIVE real and exactly what it appears to be • *It's a* **genuine** *diamond.*

geography

NOUN the study of the physical features of the earth, its countries, climate and people
geographical ADJECTIVE

geology

NOUN the study of the earth's structure, especially the layers of rock and soil that make up the surface of the earth
geological ADJECTIVE **geologist** NOUN

geometry

NOUN that part of mathematics that deals with lines, angles, curves and shapes

geranium geraniums

NOUN a plant with bright red, pink or white flowers

gerbil gerbils

NOUN a small rodent with long back legs that is often kept as a pet

germ germs

NOUN a very small organism that can cause disease

germinate germinates, germinating, germinated

VERB When a seed **germinates**, it starts to grow.
germination NOUN

gesture gestures, gesturing, gestured

NOUN **1** a movement of your hands or head that suggests a message or feeling • *She made an angry* **gesture** *with her fist.*
VERB **2** If you **gesture**, you move your hands or head in order to communicate a message or feeling. • *She* **gestured** *to me to come over.*

get gets, getting, got

VERB **1** If you **get** something, you fetch it or receive it. • *He* **got** *his report on the last day of term.*
2 If you **get** a bus, you travel on it.
3 If you **get** a meal ready, you prepare it.
4 If you **get** someone to do something for you, you persuade them to do it.
5 If you **get** a joke, you understand it.
6 If you **get** ill, you become ill.
7 If you **get** to a place, you arrive there.

geyser **geysers**

NOUN a natural spring out of which hot water and steam gush in spurts. There are many geysers in Iceland and New Zealand.

[from Old Norse *geysa* meaning to gush]

ghastly **ghastlier, ghastliest**

ADJECTIVE extremely horrible and unpleasant

ghost **ghosts**

NOUN the spirit of a dead person that appears to someone who is still alive • *She believes she saw a **ghost** in the old house.*

giant **giants**

NOUN **1** a huge person in a myth or legend

ADJECTIVE **2** much larger than other similar things • *There was a **giant** Christmas tree in the town centre.*

giddy **giddier, giddiest**

ADJECTIVE If you feel **giddy**, you feel unsteady on your feet, usually because you are ill.

giddily ADVERB   **giddiness** NOUN

gift **gifts**

NOUN **1** something that you give someone as a present

2 a natural skill or ability • *He has a **gift** for acting.*

gifted

ADJECTIVE If you are **gifted**, you have special talents. • *She is a **gifted** musician.*

gigantic

ADJECTIVE extremely large • *She was keen to ride on the **gigantic** big wheel.*

SYNONYMS: huge, massive, enormous

giggle **giggles, giggling, giggled**

VERB If you **giggle**, you laugh in a nervous, quiet way.

gill **gills**

NOUN the organs on the sides of a fish that it uses for breathing

gimmick **gimmicks**

NOUN something that is not really necessary, but is unusual and used to attract interest • *The new shop needed a **gimmick** to attract customers.*

gimmicky ADJECTIVE

gin

NOUN a strong, colourless alcoholic drink made from grain and juniper berries

ginger

NOUN **1** a plant root with a hot, spicy flavour, used in cooking

ADJECTIVE **2** bright orangey-brown

Gipsy

NOUN another spelling of **Gypsy**

giraffe **giraffes**

NOUN a large African mammal with a very long neck, long legs and yellowish skin with dark patches

girder **girders**

NOUN a strong metal or concrete beam used in building

girl **girls**

NOUN a female child

girlfriend **girlfriends**

NOUN Someone's **girlfriend** is the woman or girl with whom they are having a romantic relationship.

give **gives, giving, gave, given**

VERB **1** If you **give** something to someone, you hand it to them or provide it for them.

a
b
c
d
e
f
g
h
i
j
k
l
m
n
o
p
q
r
s
t
u
v
w
x
y
z

• *Please would you* **give** *me back the book I lent to you?*
2 If you **give** a party, you host it.
3 Give can be used to express an action.
• **give** *a speech* • **give** *the door a push*
PHRASE **4** If something **gives way**, it collapses.

glacier glaciers
NOUN a huge, frozen river of slow-moving ice

glad gladder, gladdest
ADJECTIVE happy or pleased

gladiator gladiators
NOUN In ancient Rome, **gladiators** were slaves trained to fight in arenas to provide entertainment.

glance glances, glancing, glanced
VERB **1** If you **glance** at something, you look at it quickly. • *He* **glanced** *at his watch.*
NOUN **2** a quick look

gland glands
NOUN an organ in your body which produces and releases special chemicals. Some **glands** help to get rid of waste products from your body. Sweat **glands** are small **glands** in your skin that produce sweat.
glandular ADJECTIVE

glare glares, glaring, glared
VERB **1** If you **glare** at someone, you look at them angrily.
NOUN **2** a hard, angry look

glass glasses
NOUN **1** the hard, transparent substance that windows and bottles are made of
2 a container made of glass, from which you can drink • *a* **glass** *of water*

glasses
PLURAL NOUN two lenses in a frame, that some people wear over their eyes to improve their eyesight

glaze glazes, glazing, glazed
NOUN **1** a smooth, shiny surface on pottery or food
VERB **2** If you **glaze** pottery or food, you cover it with a glaze.

3 If someone **glazes** a window, they fit a sheet of glass into the window frame.

gleam gleams, gleaming, gleamed
VERB **1** If something **gleams**, it shines and reflects light. • *He polished the silver teapot until it* **gleamed***.*
NOUN **2** a pale, shining light • *There was a* **gleam** *of light at the end of the dark tunnel.*

glide glides, gliding, glided
VERB **1** If you **glide**, you move smoothly.
• *The skater* **glided** *across the ice.*
2 When birds or aeroplanes **glide**, they float on air currents.

glider gliders
NOUN an aeroplane without an engine, that flies by floating on air currents

glimmer glimmers, glimmering, glimmered
NOUN **1** a faint, unsteady light • *There was a* **glimmer** *of light ahead.*
VERB **2** If something **glimmers**, it produces a faint, unsteady light.

glimpse glimpses, glimpsing, glimpsed
NOUN **1** a brief sight of something
VERB **2** If you **glimpse** something, you see it briefly. • *They* **glimpsed** *a rare bird through the trees.*

glisten glistens, glistening, glistened
VERB If something **glistens**, it shines or sparkles. • *The frost* **glistened** *in the moonlight.*

glitter glitters, glittering, glittered
VERB **1** If something **glitters**, it shines in a sparkling way. • *The diamond* **glittered** *in the sunlight.*
NOUN **2** sparkling light

gloat gloats, gloating, gloated
VERB If you **gloat**, you cruelly show how pleased you are about your own success or someone else's failure.

global
ADJECTIVE to do with the whole world
• *Pollution of the atmosphere is a* **global** *concern.*

global warming
NOUN an increase in the world's overall temperature, believed to be caused by a thinning of the ozone layer

globe globes
NOUN **1** the earth, the planet you live on
2 a sphere fixed to a stand, with a map of the world on it
global ADJECTIVE

gloom
NOUN **1** darkness or dimness ● *I could not see in the **gloom** of the forest.*
2 a feeling of unhappiness or despair

gloomy gloomier, gloomiest
ADJECTIVE **1** Something that is **gloomy** is dull and dark, and sometimes depressing.
● *It was a **gloomy** winter day.*
2 If you are **gloomy**, you are unhappy.
gloomily ADVERB

glorious
ADJECTIVE beautiful and splendid ● *We were lucky to have **glorious** weather while we were on holiday.*

glory glories
NOUN something considered splendid or admirable ● *They enjoyed the **glory** of their son's success.*

gloss
NOUN a bright shine on a smooth surface

glossary glossaries
NOUN a list of explanations of specialist words, usually found at the back of a book

glossy glossier, glossiest
ADJECTIVE smooth and shiny ● *This new shampoo makes my hair **glossy**.*

glove gloves
NOUN **Gloves** cover your hands and keep them warm or give them protection.

glow glows, glowing, glowed
VERB **1** If something **glows**, it shines with a dull, steady light.

NOUN **2** a dull, steady light
3 a strong feeling of pleasure or happiness

glucose
NOUN a natural sugar found in plants and produced in the bodies of animals, including humans, to give them energy

glue glues, gluing or glueing, glued
NOUN **1** a substance used for sticking things together
VERB **2** If you **glue** one object to another, you stick them together using glue.
● *She **glued** the picture into her book.*

glutton gluttons
NOUN a person who eats too much
gluttony NOUN

gnarled
ADJECTIVE If something is **gnarled** it is old, twisted and rough. ● *There is a big, **gnarled** tree in the churchyard.*

gnash gnashes, gnashing, gnashed
VERB If you **gnash** your teeth, you make a noise with them by grinding them together because you are angry or upset.

gnat gnats
NOUN a tiny flying insect that bites

gnaw gnaws, gnawing, gnawed
VERB If someone or something **gnaws** at something, they chew and bite at it repeatedly. ● *The hamster **gnawed** at the bars of its cage.*

gnome gnomes
NOUN a tiny old man in fairy stories, who usually lives underground

go goes, going, went, gone
VERB **1** If you **go** somewhere, you walk, move or travel there.
2 If something **goes** well, it is a success.
3 If you **go**, you start to move. ● *When you hear the whistle, **go** as fast as you can.*
4 If something **goes** somewhere, it leads there. ● *This road **goes** to the centre of town.*
5 If something **goes**, it works properly. ● *My watch doesn't **go** any more.*
6 become ● *This fruit has **gone** bad.*

NOUN **7** an attempt or a turn at doing something

VERB **8** disappear • *The mist has **gone**.*

9 If you are **going** to do something, you will do it.

go down

VERB **1** If you **go down** with an illness, you catch it.

2 If something **goes down** well, people like it. If it **goes down** badly, they do not like it.

go off

VERB **1** If you **go off** someone or something, you stop liking them.

2 If a bomb **goes off**, it explodes.

3 If food **goes off**, it becomes unsafe and has begun to decompose.

go on

VERB **1** If you **go on** doing something, you continue to do it.

2 If you **go on** about something, you keep talking about it in a rather boring way.

3 If something is **going on**, it is happening.

go through

VERB If you **go through** an unpleasant event, you experience it.

goal goals

NOUN **1** In games like football and hockey, the **goal** is the space into which the players try to get the ball to score a point.

2 In games like football and hockey, if a player scores a **goal**, they get the ball into the **goal**.

3 something that you hope to achieve • *Our **goal** is to raise as much money as possible for charity.*

goat goats

NOUN an animal similar to a sheep, with shaggy hair, a beard and horns

gobble gobbles, gobbling, gobbled

VERB **1** If you **gobble** food, you eat it very quickly.

2 When a turkey **gobbles**, it makes a loud gurgling sound.

goblet goblets

NOUN a kind of drinking cup or glass

goblin goblins

NOUN a small, ugly and mischievous creature found in fairy stories

god gods

PROPER NOUN **1** God is the being worshipped by Christians, Jews and Muslims as the creator and ruler of the world.

NOUN **2** any of the beings that are believed in many religions to have power over an aspect of the world • *Mars was the Roman **god** of war.*

goddess goddesses

NOUN a female god

godparent godparents

NOUN someone who agrees, at a child's christening, to be responsible for their religious upbringing

goggles

PLURAL NOUN special glasses that fit closely round your eyes to protect them • *I usually wear **goggles** when I go swimming.*

go-kart go-karts

NOUN a small motorized vehicle that can be raced

gold

NOUN **1** a valuable, yellow-coloured metal, used for making jewellery and as an international currency

ADJECTIVE **2** made of gold • *a **gold** necklace*

golden

ADJECTIVE gold in colour or made of gold

goldfish

NOUN a small, orange fish, often kept as a pet in a bowl or pond

golf

NOUN a game in which players use special clubs to hit a ball into holes that are spread out over a large area of grassy land

gondola
gondolas
NOUN a long, narrow boat used on the canals in Venice. **Gondolas** are propelled by using a long pole.

gone
VERB the past participle of **go**

gong gongs
NOUN a flat, circular piece of metal that is hit with a hammer to make a loud sound, often as a signal for something • *They sounded the **gong** for dinner.*

good better, best
ADJECTIVE **1** pleasant or enjoyable • *The weather turned out to be **good**.*
2 of a high quality • *The food was very **good**.*
3 sensible or valid • *The rain gives me a **good** reason for staying at home.*
4 well-behaved • *Have the children been **good**?*
PHRASE **5 For good** means forever.

goodbye
GREETING You say **goodbye** when you are leaving someone or ending a telephone conversation.

goodness
NOUN the quality of being good and kind

good night
GREETING You say **good night** to someone when you are leaving them at night.

goods
PLURAL NOUN things that are bought and sold in a shop or warehouse

google googles, googling, googled
VERB If you **google** a person or thing, you search the internet for information about them.

goose geese
NOUN a fairly large bird, with webbed feet and a long neck

gooseberry gooseberries
NOUN a round, green berry that grows on a bush and has a sharp taste

gore gores, goring, gored
NOUN **1** the blood from a wound
VERB **2** If an animal **gores** someone, it wounds them by sticking a horn or tusk into them.

gorge gorges, gorging, gorged
NOUN **1** a deep, narrow valley
VERB **2** If you **gorge** yourself, you eat a lot of food greedily.

gorgeous
ADJECTIVE extremely pleasant or attractive • *a **gorgeous** dress*

gorilla gorillas
NOUN a very strong, large ape, that lives in family groups

gory gorier, goriest
ADJECTIVE involving a lot of blood and violence • *a **gory** film*

gosling goslings
NOUN a young goose

gospel gospels
NOUN one of the four books in the New Testament that describe the life and teachings of Jesus Christ

gossip gossips, gossiping, gossiped
NOUN **1** informal conversation, often about people's private affairs
VERB **2** If you **gossip**, you talk informally with someone, especially about other people.

got
VERB the past tense of **get**

gouge gouges, gouging, gouged
VERB If you **gouge** something out, you scoop it out forcefully with a pointed object. • *She **gouged** a hole in the apple with a knife.*

govern governs, governing, governed
VERB When someone **governs** something, they rule or control it, especially a country or state.

a
b
c
d
e
f
g
h
i
j
k
l
m
n
o
p
q
r
s
t
u
v
w
x
y
z

A
B
C
D
E
F
G
H
I
J
K
L
M
N
O
P
Q
R
S
T
U
V
W
X
Y
Z

government **governments**
NOUN The **government** is the group of people who officially control a country.

There is an *n* before the *m* in *government*.

governor **governors**
NOUN **1** someone who controls or helps to run a state or organization
2 In Australia, New Zealand and other commonwealth countries the **Governor** represents the British King or Queen.

GP **GPs**
NOUN an abbreviation of *general practitioner*. A **GP** is a doctor who treats all kinds of illnesses, and sends people to a specialist if necessary.

grab **grabs, grabbing, grabbed**
VERB If you **grab** something, you take it or pick it up quickly and roughly. • *He* **grabbed** *a sandwich before running for the bus.*

grace **graces**
NOUN **1** an elegant and attractive way of moving
2 a short prayer before or after a meal
3 a pleasant and kind way of behaving

graceful
ADJECTIVE If you are **graceful**, you move in a smooth and elegant way.
gracefully ADVERB

gracious
ADJECTIVE kind, polite and pleasant • *He always acts in a* **gracious** *and thoughtful manner.*
graciously ADVERB

grade **grades, grading, graded**
VERB **1** If someone **grades** things, they judge them according to their quality.
NOUN **2** the mark that you get in an exam

gradient **gradients**
NOUN a slope or the steepness of a slope • *The* **gradient** *of this hill means it will be difficult to climb.*

gradual
ADJECTIVE happening or changing slowly over a long period of time • *Her spelling*

showed **gradual** *improvement.*
gradually ADVERB

graduate **graduates**
NOUN someone who has a degree from a university or college

graffiti
NOUN slogans or drawings scribbled on walls

grain **grains**
NOUN **1** a cereal plant, such as wheat, that is grown and harvested for food
2 a seed from a cereal plant such as wheat or rice
3 a tiny, hard particle of something • *I have got* **grains** *of sand in my shoes from walking on the beach.*
4 the natural pattern of lines in a piece of wood, made by the fibres in it

gram **grams**
NOUN a unit of mass and weight (g). There are one thousand **grams** in a kilogram (kg).

grammar
NOUN the rules of a language that state how words can be combined to form sentences

grand **grander, grandest**
ADJECTIVE splendid or impressive

grandad **grandads**
NOUN INFORMAL grandfather

grandchild **grandchildren**
NOUN Someone's **grandchildren** are the children of their son or daughter.

granddaughter **granddaughters**
NOUN Someone's **granddaughter** is the daughter of their son or daughter.

grandfather **grandfathers**
NOUN Your **grandfather** is your father's father or your mother's father.

grandmother **grandmothers**
NOUN Your **grandmother** is your father's mother or your mother's mother.

grandparent **grandparents**
NOUN Your **grandparents** are the parents of your father or mother.

grandson grandsons
NOUN Someone's **grandson** is the son of their son or daughter.

granite
NOUN a very strong, hard rock often used in building

granny grannies
NOUN INFORMAL grandmother

grant grants, granting, granted
NOUN **1** an amount of money that an official body gives to someone for a particular purpose ● *He was given a **grant** to go to university.*
VERB **2** If you **grant** something to someone, you allow them to have it.
● *I will **grant** you a wish.*

grape grapes
NOUN a small, green or purple fruit that grows in bunches on vines. **Grapes** are eaten raw or used to make wine.

grapefruit grapefruits
NOUN a large, round, yellow citrus fruit

graph graphs
NOUN a diagram that gives information about how two sets of numbers and measurements are related

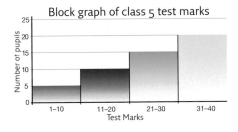
Block graph of class 5 test marks

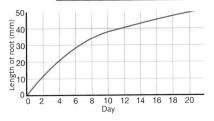
Line graph of seed growth

graphic graphics
ADJECTIVE **1** A **graphic** description is very detailed and clear.
PLURAL NOUN **2 Graphics** are drawings, designs and diagrams. ● *computer **graphics***

grasp grasps, grasping, grasped
VERB **1** If you **grasp** something, you hold it firmly. ● *He **grasped** both my hands.*
2 If you **grasp** an idea, you understand it. ● *She finally **grasped** the answer.*

grass grasses
NOUN the common green plant that grows on lawns and in parks

grasshopper grasshoppers
NOUN an insect with long back legs that it uses for jumping and making a high-pitched sound

grate grates, grating, grated
VERB **1** If you **grate** food, you shred it into small pieces by rubbing it against a tool called a grater.
NOUN **2** a framework of metal bars in a fireplace for holding coal or wood
● *A wood fire burned in the **grate**.*

grateful
ADJECTIVE If you are **grateful** for something, you feel thankful for it. ● *I'm **grateful** to you for your help.*
SYNONYM: appreciative
gratefully ADVERB

gratitude
NOUN If you show **gratitude** to someone for something, you are thankful.
SYNONYMS: thankfulness, appreciation

grave graves; graver, gravest
NOUN **1** a place where a dead person is buried
ADJECTIVE **2** FORMAL very serious ● *We are in **grave** danger.*

gravel
NOUN small stones used for making roads and paths

graveyard graveyards
NOUN a place where people are buried, usually in a churchyard

a
b
c
d
e
f
g
h
i
j
k
l
m
n
o
p
q
r
s
t
u
v
w
x
y
z

A
B
C
D
E
F
G
H
I
J
K
L
M
N
O
P
Q
R
S
T
U
V
W
X
Y
Z

gravity
NOUN the force that pulls things down towards the earth

gravy
NOUN a brown sauce made from meat juices

graze grazes, grazing, grazed
VERB **1** When animals **graze**, they eat grass that is growing. • *The cows grazed in the field.*
2 If something **grazes** a part of your body, it scrapes against it, injuring you slightly.
NOUN **3** a slight injury caused by something scraping against your skin

grease greases, greasing, greased
NOUN **1** a substance used for oiling machines
2 animal fat used in cooking
VERB **3** If you **grease** something, you put grease on it. • *Lightly grease a baking tray.*

great greater, greatest
ADJECTIVE **1** very large in size, amount or degree • *She had great difficulty in staying awake.*
2 very important • *a great artist*
3 very good • *That's a great idea.*

greedy greedier, greediest
ADJECTIVE Someone who is **greedy** wants more of something than is necessary or fair.
greedily ADVERB

green greener, greenest; greens
ADJECTIVE OR NOUN **1** a colour between yellow and blue on the spectrum. Grass and leaves are usually **green**.
NOUN **2** a smooth, flat area of grass • *We played cricket on the village green.*

greengrocer greengrocers
NOUN a shopkeeper who sells fruit and vegetables

greenhouse greenhouses
NOUN a glass building in which people grow plants that need to be kept warm

greenhouse effect
NOUN the gradual increase in the temperature of the earth's atmosphere because the heat absorbed from the sun is not able to escape

greet greets, greeting, greeted
VERB If you **greet** someone, you say something friendly and welcoming to them when you meet them.

greeting greetings
NOUN the words or actions that you use when you meet someone

grenade grenades
NOUN a small bomb that can be thrown by hand
[from Spanish *granada* meaning pomegranate, which is a similar shape to a grenade]

grew
VERB the past tense of **grow**

grey greyer, greyest
ADJECTIVE OR NOUN the colour of ashes or of clouds on a rainy day

grid grids
NOUN a pattern of lines crossing each other to form squares

grief
NOUN extreme sadness

grieve grieves, grieving, grieved
VERB If you **grieve** you are very sad, especially because someone has died.

grill grills, grilling, grilled
NOUN **1** the part of a cooker where food is cooked by heat from above • *Place the fish under a hot grill.*
VERB **2** If you **grill** food, you cook it under or over direct heat. • *We grilled the chicken on the barbecue.*

grim grimmer, grimmest
ADJECTIVE If a situation or piece of news is **grim**, it is very unpleasant and worrying.
grimly ADVERB

grimace grimaces
NOUN a twisted facial expression that shows disgust or pain

grime

NOUN thick dirt that gathers on the surface of something

grimy ADJECTIVE

grin grins, grinning, grinned

VERB **1** If you **grin**, you have a broad smile.

NOUN **2** a broad smile

grind grinds, grinding, ground

VERB **1** If you **grind** something, you crush it into a fine powder. ● *He ground the mud into the carpet.*

2 If you **grind** your teeth, you rub your upper and lower teeth together.

PHRASE **3** If something **grinds to a halt**, it slows down and stops.

grip grips, gripping, gripped; grips

VERB **1** If you **grip** something, you hold it firmly. ● *He gripped his mother's hand tightly.*

NOUN **2** a handle on a bat or racket ● *The grip on his tennis racket needed repairing.*

gristle

NOUN the tough, rubbery part of meat that is difficult to eat

groan groans, groaning, groaned

VERB **1** If you **groan**, you make a long, low sound of pain, unhappiness or disapproval.

NOUN **2** the sound you make when you groan

grocer grocers

NOUN a person who runs a shop that sells all kinds of food and household supplies

groceries

PLURAL NOUN the goods that you buy in a grocer's shop

groove grooves

NOUN a deep line cut into a surface

grooved ADJECTIVE

grope gropes, groping, groped

VERB If you **grope** for something, you feel for it with your hands because you cannot see it.

gross grosser, grossest

ADJECTIVE **1** extremely bad ● *I made a gross error on my exam paper.*

2 Gross language or behaviour is very rude.

3 The **gross** amount of something is its total, without anything taken away. For example, the **gross** weight of something is the total weight, including the weight of its container.

4 unpleasantly fat or ugly

grotesque

ADJECTIVE **1** exaggerated and absurd

2 very strange and ugly

grotesquely ADVERB

grotto grottoes or grottos

NOUN a small cave that people visit because it is attractive

ground grounds

NOUN **1** the surface of the land ● *They sat on the ground.*

2 an area of land, especially land that is used for a particular purpose ● *a football ground*

PLURAL NOUN **3** The **grounds** of a large building are the garden or area of land that surrounds it. ● *We camped in the grounds of the stately home.*

4 FORMAL The **grounds** for something are the reason for it. ● *I had grounds to believe that he was telling the truth.*

VERB **5** the past tense and past participle of *grind*

group groups, grouping, grouped

NOUN **1** a number of things or people that are linked in some way ● *a small group of friends*

VERB **2** When things or people **group** together, they are linked in some way. ● *We grouped together for the school photograph.*

grovel grovels, grovelling, grovelled

VERB If you **grovel**, you behave in an unpleasantly humble way towards someone you think is important. [from Middle English *on grufe* meaning lying on your belly]

grow grows, growing, grew, grown

VERB **1** When someone or something **grows**, it gets bigger or increases. ● *Children grow at different rates.*

2 When people **grow** plants, they plant them and look after them.

A
B
C
D
E
F
G
H
I
J
K
L
M
N
O
P
Q
R
S
T
U
V
W
X
Y
Z

3 You use **grow** to say that someone or something gradually changes into a different state. • *He's **growing** old.*

grow up
VERB When a child **grows up**, they become an adult.

growl growls, growling, growled
VERB **1** When an animal **growls**, it makes a low rumbling sound, usually because it is angry.
NOUN **2** the sound an animal makes when it growls

grown-up grown-ups
NOUN an adult

growth
NOUN The process by which something develops to its full size.

grub grubs
NOUN **1** a worm-like creature that is the young of some insects, after it has hatched but before it becomes an adult **2** INFORMAL food

grubby grubbier, grubbiest
ADJECTIVE rather dirty • *That shirt looks a bit **grubby**.*

grudge grudges
NOUN If you have a **grudge** against someone, you resent them because they have harmed or upset you in the past.

gruelling
ADJECTIVE difficult and exhausting • *It was a long and **gruelling** race.*

gruesome
ADJECTIVE shocking and horrible • *The film was unsuitable for the children because it was so **gruesome**.*

gruff gruffer, gruffest
ADJECTIVE If someone's voice is **gruff**, it sounds rough and unfriendly.
gruffly ADVERB

grumble grumbles, grumbling, grumbled
VERB **1** If you **grumble**, you complain in a bad-tempered way.
NOUN **2** a bad-tempered complaint

grumpy grumpier, grumpiest
ADJECTIVE bad-tempered and fed-up • *She is often **grumpy** in the morning.*
grumpily ADVERB

grunt grunts, grunting, grunted
VERB **1** If a person or a pig **grunts**, they make a short, low, gruff sound.
NOUN **2** the sound a person or a pig makes when they grunt

guarantee guarantees, guaranteeing, guaranteed
NOUN **1** a promise by a company to do something, especially to replace or repair a product free of charge within a given time period if it develops a fault • *This television has a five-year **guarantee**.*
VERB **2** If something or someone **guarantees** something, they promise that it will happen. • *I **guarantee** that after all your hard work the day will be a success.*

guard guards, guarding, guarded
VERB **1** If you **guard** a person or object, you watch them carefully, either to protect them or to stop them from escaping.
NOUN **2** a person whose job is to guard a person, object or place

guardian guardians
NOUN someone who has been legally appointed to look after a child, but is not the child's parent

guerrilla guerrillas; also spelt **guerilla**
NOUN a member of a small, unofficial army fighting an official army

guess guesses, guessing, guessed
VERB **1** If you **guess** something, you form an opinion about it without knowing all the relevant facts. • *She **guessed** that he was probably older than her.*
NOUN **2** an attempt to give an answer or opinion about something without knowing all the relevant facts • *If you don't know the answer, have a **guess**.*

guest guests
NOUN someone who has been invited to stay at your home or attend an event

guide guides, guiding, guided
NOUN **1** someone who shows you round places, or leads the way through difficult country
VERB **2** If you **guide** someone somewhere, you lead them there.

guidebook guidebooks
NOUN a book that gives information about a place

guillotine guillotines
NOUN **1** In the past, the **guillotine** was a machine used for beheading people, especially in France.
2 a piece of equipment with a long, sharp blade, used for cutting paper [named after Joseph-Ignace *Guillotin*, who first recommended the guillotine as a way of executing people]

guilt
NOUN **1** the unhappy feeling of having done something wrong
2 Someone's **guilt** is the fact that they have done something wrong. • *After hearing the evidence, the jury felt that his* **guilt** *was clear.*

guilty guiltier, guiltiest
ADJECTIVE If you are **guilty** of doing something wrong, you did it.
guiltily ADVERB

guinea pig guinea pigs
NOUN **1** a small, furry mammal without a tail, often kept as a pet
2 a person used to try something out
• *You will be a* **guinea pig** *in this experiment.*

guitar guitars
NOUN a musical instrument with six strings and a long neck

gulf gulfs
NOUN a very large bay

gull gulls
NOUN a sea bird with long wings, white and grey or black feathers, and webbed feet

gullible
ADJECTIVE If someone is **gullible**, they are easily tricked.

gulp gulps, gulping, gulped
VERB **1** If you **gulp** food or drink, you swallow large quantities of it quickly and noisily.
NOUN **2** a large quantity of food or drink swallowed quickly and noisily

gum gums
NOUN **1** Your **gums** are the firm flesh in which your teeth are set.
2 a soft, flavoured substance that people chew but do not swallow
3 glue

gumboot gumboots
NOUN a wellington boot

gumtree gumtrees
NOUN a eucalyptus or other tree that produces gum

gun guns
NOUN a weapon that fires bullets or shells

gunpowder
NOUN a powder that explodes when it is lit. It is used for making things such as fireworks.

gurdwara gurdwaras
NOUN a Sikh place of worship

gust gusts
NOUN a sudden rush of wind • *A* **gust** *of wind blew his hat off.*

gutter gutters
NOUN the edge of a road next to the pavement, where rain collects and flows away

gym gyms
NOUN a hall or room for sports and exercise. It is short for *gymnasium*.

a
b
c
d
e
f
g
h
i
j
k
l
m
n
o
p
q
r
s
t
u
v
w
x
y
z

gymkhana gymkhanas
Said "jim-**kah**-na" NOUN a competition in which people take part in horse-riding contests

gymnasium gymnasiums
NOUN a room with special equipment for physical exercises

gymnastics
NOUN physical exercises, especially ones using equipment such as bars and ropes

Gypsy Gypsies; also spelt Gipsy
NOUN a member of an ethnic group scattered across most countries of Europe, the Middle East and the Americas. They migrated from north-west India in the 9th century and still have a nomadic lifestyle, although some are settled on sites and in houses. The **Gypsy** language is Romani.
[from *Egyptian* because in the 16th century they were thought to have come from Egypt]

Hh

habit habits
NOUN something that you do often or regularly

habitat habitats
NOUN the natural home of a plant or animal

hack hacks, hacking, hacked
VERB If you **hack** at something, you cut it using rough strokes.

had
VERB the past participle of **have**

haddock
NOUN an edible sea fish

hadn't
VERB a contraction of *had not*

haggard
ADJECTIVE A person who is **haggard** looks very tired and ill.

haggis haggises
NOUN a Scottish dish made of the minced internal organs of a sheep, boiled together with oatmeal and spices in a skin

haggle haggles, haggling, haggled
VERB If you **haggle** with someone, you argue with them about the price of something.

haiku haiku
NOUN a short, Japanese verse form in 17 syllables

hail hails, hailing, hailed
NOUN **1** frozen rain
VERB **2** When it is **hailing**, frozen rain is falling.

hailstone hailstones
NOUN a drop of frozen rain

hair **hairs**
NOUN one of the large number of fine threads that grow on your head and body. **Hair** grows on the bodies of some other animals.

haircut **haircuts**
NOUN the cutting of someone's hair and the style into which it is cut

hairdresser **hairdressers**
NOUN a person who is trained to cut and style hair

hairstyle **hairstyles**
NOUN the way in which your hair is arranged or cut

hairy **hairier, hairiest**
ADJECTIVE covered in a lot of hair

hajj
NOUN the pilgrimage to Mecca that every Muslim must make at least once in their life, if they are healthy and wealthy enough to do so
[from Arabic *hajj* meaning pilgrimage]

halal; also spelt **hallal**
NOUN meat from animals that have been killed according to Muslim law

half **halves**
NOUN OR ADJECTIVE **1** one of two equal parts that make up a whole. It can be written as $^1/_2$. • *the second* **half** *of the match* • *My cup is only* **half** *full.*
ADVERB **2** You can use **half** to say that something is only partly true. • *I* **half** *expected to see the teacher walk in.*
PHRASE **3 Half past** refers to a time that is thirty minutes after a particular hour.
• **half past** *twelve*

halfway
ADVERB If something is **halfway** between two points or two times, it is at the middle point between them.

hall **halls**
NOUN **1** the room just inside the front entrance of a house that leads into the other rooms
2 a large room or building for public events • *a school* **hall**

hallo
EXCLAMATION OR GREETING another spelling of **hello**

Halloween
NOUN **Halloween** is October 31st. In the past people thought that ghosts and witches would be about on this night, and it is now celebrated by children dressing up, often as ghosts and witches.

hallucinate **hallucinates, hallucinating, hallucinated**
VERB If someone **hallucinates**, they imagine that they see strange things, for example because they are ill.

halo **haloes** or **halos**
NOUN a circle of light around something, especially the head of a holy person in a picture

halt **halts, halting, halted**
VERB **1** When someone or something **halts**, they stop. • *They* **halted** *a short distance from the house.*
PHRASE **2** When something **comes to a halt**, it stops.

halter **halters**
NOUN a strap fastened round a horse's head so that it can be led easily

halve **halves, halving, halved**
VERB If you **halve** something, you divide it into two equal parts.

ham
NOUN meat from the hind leg of a pig

hamburger **hamburgers**
NOUN a flat disc of minced meat, fried and eaten in a bread roll
[named after *Hamburg* in Germany, the city where they were first made]

hammer **hammers, hammering, hammered**
NOUN **1** a tool consisting of a heavy piece of metal at the end of a handle, used for hitting nails into things
VERB **2** If you **hammer** something, you hit it repeatedly with a hammer.

hammock **hammocks**
NOUN a piece of net or canvas hung between two supports and used as a bed

hamper **hampers, hampering, hampered**

NOUN **1** a large basket with a lid, used for carrying food

VERB **2** If something **hampers** you, it makes it difficult for you to do what you are trying to do. ● *The bad weather **hampered** their expedition.*

hamster **hamsters**

NOUN a small, furry rodent, often kept as a pet

hand **hands, handing, handed**

NOUN **1** the part of your body at the end of your arm, below the wrist

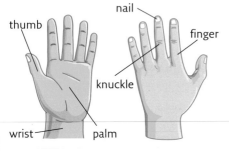

nail
thumb
finger
knuckle
wrist
palm

2 The **hands** of a clock or watch are the pointers that indicate what time it is.

3 In a game of cards, a **hand** is the set of cards dealt to each player.

VERB **4** If you **hand** something to someone, you pass it to them.

PHRASE **5** If you **give a hand**, you help someone to do something.

6 If you do something **by hand**, you do it using your hands rather than a machine.

7 If something gets **out of hand**, it becomes beyond your control.

handbag **handbags**

NOUN a small bag, usually carried by a woman

handcuffs

PLURAL NOUN two strong metal rings joined by chains that are locked round a prisoner's wrists

handful **handfuls**

NOUN **1** A **handful** of something is the amount of it you can hold in your hand.

2 a small number or quantity of something ● *Only a **handful** of people were invited to the party.*

handicap **handicaps**

NOUN **1** a physical or mental disability

2 a disadvantage, or anything that makes it more difficult to do something

handicapped ADJECTIVE

handicraft **handicrafts**

NOUN an activity that involves making things with your hands, such as pottery or knitting

handkerchief **handkerchiefs**

NOUN a small square of fabric used for blowing your nose

handle **handles, handling, handled**

NOUN **1** the part of a tool, bag, cup or other object that you hold in order to pick it up or use it ● *door **handle***

VERB **2** If you **handle** an object, you hold it or touch it with your hands.

3 If you **handle** something, you deal with it successfully. ● *She **handled** the stress of the examination very well.*

handlebars

PLURAL NOUN the bars with handles that are used to steer a bicycle

handset **handsets**

NOUN The **handset** of a telephone is the part that you speak into and listen with.

handsome

ADJECTIVE very attractive in appearance

handstand **handstands**

NOUN the act of balancing upside down on your hands, with your feet in the air

handwriting

NOUN Someone's **handwriting** is their style of writing with a pen or pencil.

handy **handier, handiest**

ADJECTIVE If something is **handy**, it is useful or conveniently near.

hang **hangs, hanging, hung** or **hanged**

VERB **1** If you **hang** something on a hook, nail or line, or if it **hangs** there, it is attached so that it does not touch the ground. ● *His jacket **hung** from a hook on the door.*

hardy

2 To **hang** someone means to kill them by suspending them by a rope around the neck.

✏️ When *hang* means to kill someone by suspending them by a rope, the past tense and past participle are **hanged**.

hang about or **hang around**
VERB INFORMAL If you **hang about** or **hang around** somewhere, you stay or wait there. • *Although he had left, he still hung around outside his old school.*

hang on
VERB **1** If you **hang on** to something, you hold it tightly or keep it.
2 INFORMAL If you **hang on**, you wait.

hang up
VERB If you **hang up** when you are speaking on the phone, you put down the receiver and end the call.

hangar **hangars**
NOUN a large building where aircraft are kept

hanger **hangers**
NOUN a piece of shaped wood, plastic or wire for hanging up clothes

hang-glider **hang-gliders**
NOUN a glider that is made for one or two people who hang below the frame in a harness

Hanukkah or **Chanukah**
NOUN an eight-day Jewish festival of lights

haphazard
ADJECTIVE not organized or planned • *He piled the books up in a haphazard way.*
haphazardly ADVERB

happen **happens, happening, happened**
VERB **1** When something **happens**, it occurs or takes place.
2 If you **happen** to do something, you do it by chance. • *I happened to notice he'd dropped his glove.*

happiness
NOUN a feeling of great contentment or pleasure

happy **happier, happiest**
ADJECTIVE **1** full of contentment or joy
ANTONYMS: miserable, sad
2 If you are **happy** with something, you are satisfied with it.
ANTONYM: dissatisfied
3 If you are **happy** to do something, you are willing to do it.
ANTONYM: reluctant
happily ADVERB

harass **harasses, harassing, harassed**
VERB If someone **harasses** you, they annoy or trouble you continually.
harassed ADJECTIVE

harbour **harbours**
NOUN a protected area of deep water where boats can be moored

hard **harder, hardest**
ADJECTIVE OR ADVERB **1** requiring a lot of effort • *The sponsored walk was hard work.*
2 with a lot of force • *I kicked the ball very hard.*
ADJECTIVE **3** difficult
4 not easy to bend or break

hard disk **hard disks**
NOUN a part of a computer that holds a large amount of information

harden **hardens, hardening, hardened**
VERB If something **hardens** it becomes hard or gets harder. • *The glue took a long time to harden.*

hardly
ADVERB only just • *I could hardly believe it.*

hardship
NOUN a time or situation of suffering and difficulty

hardware
NOUN **1** tools and equipment for use in the home and garden
2 computer machinery rather than computer programs

hardy **hardier, hardiest**
ADJECTIVE tough and able to bear cold and difficult conditions

hare hares
NOUN an animal like a large rabbit, but with longer ears and legs

harm harms, harming, harmed
VERB **1** If someone **harms** someone or something, they injure or damage them.
SYNONYM: hurt
NOUN **2** injury or damage
SYNONYM: hurt

harmful
ADJECTIVE having a bad effect on something
• Too much sun can be **harmful** to your skin.
harmfully ADVERB

harmless
ADJECTIVE safe to use or be near
harmlessly ADVERB

harmonica harmonicas
NOUN a small musical instrument played by moving it across the lips and blowing and sucking air through it. Also called a mouth organ.

harmony harmonies
NOUN **1** a state of peaceful agreement and cooperation • The neighbours lived in **harmony**.
2 In music, **harmony** is the pleasant combination of two or more notes played at the same time.

harness harnesses, harnessing, harnessed
NOUN **1** a set of straps fastened round an animal to control it or attach it to something, such as a horse to a cart
VERB **2** If you **harness** an animal, you put a harness on it.
3 If someone **harnesses** something, they control it so that they can use it. • The windmills **harnessed** the power of the wind.

harp harps
NOUN a musical instrument consisting of a triangular frame with vertical strings that you pluck with your fingers
harpist NOUN

harpoon harpoons
NOUN a barbed spear attached to a rope, thrown or fired from a gun and used for catching whales or large fish

harsh harsher, harshest
ADJECTIVE **1 Harsh** living conditions or climates are rough and unpleasant.
SYNONYMS: hard, severe, tough
2 Harsh actions or remarks are unkind and show no sympathy.
harshly ADVERB harshness NOUN

harvest harvests
NOUN the act of gathering a crop, or the time when this is done
[from Old German herbist meaning autumn]

has
VERB part of the verb have

hasn't
VERB a contraction of has not

hassle hassles, hassling, hassled
NOUN **1** INFORMAL Something that is a **hassle** is difficult or causes trouble. • Organizing the school trip is always a **hassle**.
VERB **2** If you **hassle** someone, you annoy them by repeatedly asking them to do something.

hasty hastier, hastiest
ADJECTIVE done quickly and without preparation • Do not give a **hasty** answer.

hat hats
NOUN a covering for the head

hatch hatches, hatching, hatched
VERB **1** When an egg **hatches**, or when a bird or a reptile **hatches** from an egg, the shell breaks open and the young bird or reptile comes out.
NOUN **2** an opening in a wall where food can be passed through

hatchback hatchbacks
NOUN a car with a door at the back that opens upwards

hatchet hatchets
NOUN a small axe

hate hates, hating, hated
VERB If you **hate** someone or something, you dislike them very much.

hateful
ADJECTIVE very nasty and detestable

hatred
NOUN an extremely strong feeling of dislike

haul hauls, hauling, hauled
VERB If you **haul** something somewhere, you pull it with great effort.

haunt haunts, haunting, haunted
VERB If a ghost **haunts** a place, it is seen or heard there regularly.
haunting ADJECTIVE

haunted
ADJECTIVE Somewhere that is **haunted** is visited often by a ghost. • *People believe that the house on the hill is* ***haunted***.

have has, having, had
VERB **1** If you **have** something, it belongs to you or you possess it.
2 If you **have** something such as a cold or an accident, you feel or experience it.
3 If you **have** something such as lunch or a letter, you take or get it.
4 If you **have** something such as a haircut, you cause it to be done.
PHRASE **5** If you **have to** do something, you must do it. • *I* ***have to*** *clean my room before I go out.*
VERB **6 Have** can be used with other verbs to form the past tense. • *I* ***have*** *already read that book.*

haven't
VERB a contraction of *have not*

havoc
NOUN disorder and confusion • *The bad weather played* ***havoc*** *with our plans.*

hawk hawks
NOUN a bird of prey with short, rounded wings and a long tail

hay
NOUN grass that has been cut and dried and is used to feed animals

hay fever
NOUN an allergy to pollen and grass, causing sneezing and watering eyes

haystack haystacks
NOUN a large, firmly-built pile of hay, usually covered and left out in the open

hazard hazards
NOUN something that could be dangerous to you • *The pollution in the city centre is a health* ***hazard***.

haze
NOUN If there is a **haze**, it is difficult to see clearly because there is moisture or smoke in the air.

hazel hazels
NOUN **1** a small tree with edible nuts
ADJECTIVE **2** a green-brown colour • *He has* ***hazel*** *eyes.*

hazy hazier, haziest
ADJECTIVE dim or vague • ***hazy*** *sunshine* • *a* ***hazy*** *memory*

he
PRONOUN **He** is used to refer to a man, boy or male animal that has already been mentioned.

head heads, heading, headed
NOUN **1** the part of your body that has your eyes, brain and mouth in it
2 the top or front of something, or the most important end of it • *We went to the* ***head*** *of the queue.*
3 When you toss a coin, the side called **heads** is the one with the **head** on it.
4 In an organization or group of people, the **head** is the main person in charge.
VERB **5** If you **head** something, you lead it. • *She* ***headed*** *the expedition to the North Pole.*
6 If you **head** somewhere, you go in that direction or towards something. • *We* ***headed*** *to the canteen for lunch.*
7 If you **head** a ball, you hit it with your head. • *He* ***headed*** *the ball into the goal.*

headache headaches
NOUN a pain in your head

heading headings
NOUN a piece of writing that is written or printed at the top of a page

headlight headlights
NOUN the large, powerful lights on the front of a motor vehicle

headline headlines
NOUN The **headline** of a newspaper is the heading printed in big, bold letters on the front page at the top of an article.

a
b
c
d
e
f
g
h
i
j
k
l
m
n
o
p
q
r
s
t
u
v
w
x
y
z

183

headphones

NOUN a pair of small speakers that you wear over your ears to listen to a radio, a television or a stereo without other people hearing

headquarters

NOUN the main place from which an organization is run

head teacher **head teachers**

NOUN the teacher who is in charge of a school

heal **heals, healing, healed**

VERB If a cut or a wound **heals**, it gets better. • *The cut on my leg* **healed** *quickly.*

health

NOUN the condition of someone's body and mind • *I felt in very good* **health** *after our holiday.*

healthy **healthier, healthiest**

ADJECTIVE **1** Someone who is **healthy** is fit and well, and is not suffering from any illness. • *She goes to the gym to stay* **healthy**.
2 Something that is **healthy** is good for you. • *You should try and eat a* **healthy** *diet.*

heap **heaps, heaping, heaped**

NOUN **1** an untidy pile of things
VERB **2** If you **heap** things, you pile them up.

hear **hears, hearing, heard**

VERB **1** When you **hear** sounds, you are aware of them because they reach your ears. • *We could* **hear** *the waves crashing on the beach.*
2 When you **hear** from someone, they write to you or phone you.

hearing

NOUN **1** the ability to hear
2 If someone gives you a **hearing**, they let you give your point of view and listen to you.

hearse **hearses**

NOUN a large car that carries the coffin at a funeral

heart **hearts**

NOUN **1** the organ in your chest that pumps the blood around your body

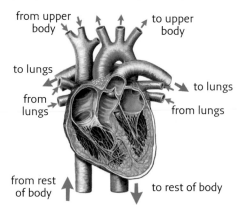

from upper body — to upper body
to lungs
from lungs — to lungs
from lungs
from rest of body — to rest of body

2 Your **heart** is also thought of as the centre of your emotions and feelings. • *When his hamster died it broke his* **heart**.
3 the most central or important part of something • *It is always busy in the* **heart** *of the city.*
4 courage
5 a curved shape like this ♥, or a playing card with this shape on it
PHRASE **6** If you learn something **by heart**, you learn it so that you know it from memory.

heart attack **heart attacks**

NOUN a serious medical condition in which someone's heart suddenly beats irregularly or stops completely

hearth **hearths**

Said "**harth**" NOUN the floor of a fireplace

heat **heats, heating, heated**

NOUN **1** warmth or the quality of being hot • *the fierce* **heat** *of the sun*
2 a contest or race in a competition that decides who will compete in the final
VERB **3** When you **heat** something, you warm it.

heater **heaters**

NOUN a device used to produce heat in order to warm a place, such as a room or a car

heath
NOUN a large open area of land covered in rough grass or heather, with very few trees

heather
NOUN a plant with small purple or white flowers that grows wild on hills and moorland

heave heaves, heaving, heaved
VERB If you **heave** something, you lift, push or throw it with a lot of effort.

heaven
NOUN In some religions, **heaven** is the place where God lives and where good people go when they die.

heavy heavier, heaviest
ADJECTIVE **1** Something that is **heavy** weighs a lot.
2 You use **heavy** to talk about how much something weighs. • How **heavy** is the baby?

Hebrew
Said "**hee**-broo" NOUN an ancient language that is now spoken in Israel by the Jewish people

hectare hectares
NOUN a unit for measuring an area of land, equal to 10,000 square metres or about 2.471 acres

hectic
ADJECTIVE involving a lot of rushed activity • She leads a very **hectic** life.

he'd
a contraction of he had or he would

hedge hedges
NOUN a row of bushes along the edge of a garden, field or road

hedgehog hedgehogs
NOUN a small, brown mammal with sharp spikes covering its back

heel heels
NOUN **1** the back part of your foot, below your ankle
2 the part on the bottom at the back of a shoe or sock

heifer heifers
NOUN a young cow that has not yet had calves

height heights
NOUN **1** a measurement from the bottom to the top of someone or something
2 a high position or place • He's afraid of **heights**.
3 the highest or most important part of something • He's at the **height** of his success.

heir heirs
NOUN the person who is entitled to inherit someone's property or title • the **heir** to the throne

held
VERB the past tense of **hold**

helicopter helicopters
NOUN an aircraft with rotating blades instead of wings, that enable it to take off vertically

helium
NOUN a gas that is lighter than air. It is sometimes used to fill party balloons.

he'll
a contraction of he will or he shall

hell
NOUN **1** In some religions, **hell** is the place where the Devil lives and where wicked people are sent to be punished when they die.
2 INFORMAL If you say that something is **hell**, you mean that it is very unpleasant.

hello
EXCLAMATION OR GREETING You say **hello** when you meet someone or answer the telephone.

helmet helmets
NOUN a hard hat that you wear to protect your head

help helps, helping, helped
VERB **1** If you **help** someone, you make something easier or better for them.
NOUN **2** assistance • Thanks for your **help**.

185

helpful
ADJECTIVE If you are **helpful**, you cooperate with others and support them.
helpfully ADVERB

helping **helpings**
NOUN a portion of food at a meal

helpless
ADJECTIVE If you are **helpless**, you are unable to protect yourself or do anything useful.
helplessly ADVERB

hem **hems, hemming, hemmed**
NOUN **1** The **hem** of a garment is the edge of it that has been folded up and stitched in place.
VERB **2** If you **hem** a garment, you make a hem on it.

hemisphere **hemispheres**
NOUN one half of the earth or a sphere

hen **hens**
NOUN **1** a female chicken
2 any female bird

heptagon **heptagons**
NOUN a flat shape with seven flat sides

her
PRONOUN OR ADJECTIVE **1** refers to a woman, girl or female animal that has already been mentioned • *I like Amy. I often play with **her**.*
2 shows that something belongs to a particular female • *Mum is going to wear **her** blue jumper.*

heraldry
NOUN the study of coats of arms

herb **herbs**
NOUN a plant whose leaves are used as a medicine or to flavour food

herbivore **herbivores**
NOUN an animal that eats only plants
herbivorous ADJECTIVE

herd **herds, herding, herded**
NOUN **1** a large group of animals grazing together • *a **herd** of cattle*
VERB **2** If you **herd** animals or people, you make them move together as a group.
• *The teachers **herded** the children on to the bus.*

here
ADVERB at, to or in the place where you are

hereditary
ADJECTIVE passed on to a child from a parent

heritage
NOUN The **heritage** of a country is all its traditions, customs and art that have been passed from one generation to another.

hermit **hermits**
NOUN someone who prefers to live a simple life alone and far from other people, often for religious reasons

hero **heroes**
NOUN **1** the main male character in a book, film or play
2 a person who is admired because they have done something brave or good

heroine **heroines**
NOUN the main female character in a book, play or film

heron **herons**
NOUN a wading bird with very long legs and a long beak and neck

herring **herrings**
NOUN a silvery fish that lives in large shoals in northern seas

hers
PRONOUN refers to something that belongs or relates to a woman, girl or other female animal

herself
PRONOUN refers to the same woman, girl or female animal who does an action and is affected by it • *She pulled **herself** up.*

he's
a contraction of *he is* or *he has*

hesitate **hesitates, hesitating, hesitated**
VERB If you **hesitate**, you pause or show uncertainty.

hexagon **hexagons**
NOUN a flat shape with six straight sides
hexagonal ADJECTIVE

hibernate **hibernates, hibernating, hibernated**
VERB Animals that **hibernate** spend the winter in a state like a deep sleep.
hibernation NOUN

hiccup **hiccups, hiccupping, hiccupped**; also spelt **hiccough**
NOUN **1** short, uncontrolled sounds in your throat
VERB **2** When you **hiccup**, you suffer from hiccups.

hide **hides, hiding, hid, hidden**
VERB **1** If you **hide** something, you put it where it cannot be seen, or prevent it from being discovered. ● *He **hid** his disappointment.*
2 If you **hide**, you go somewhere where you cannot be seen or found easily.

hideous
ADJECTIVE extremely ugly or unpleasant
hideously ADVERB

hieroglyphics
Said "hy-ro-**gliff**-iks" PLURAL NOUN ancient Egyptian writing that uses pictures instead of words. It involves over 700 picture signs.

high **higher, highest**
ADJECTIVE **1** **High** refers to how much something measures from the bottom to the top. ● *The statue was three metres **high**.*
ADJECTIVE OR ADVERB **2** a long way above the ground ● *He jumped **high** into the air.*
3 great in degree, quantity or intensity ● *There were **high** winds before the storm.*

highlight **highlights, highlighting, highlighted**
NOUN **1** the most interesting part of something ● *The **highlight** of the week was our trip to the cinema.*
VERB **2** If you **highlight** a point or a problem, you emphasize it.

high-rise
ADJECTIVE **High-rise** buildings are very tall.

highway **highways**
NOUN a main road

hijab **hijabs**; also spelt **hejab**
Said "hi-**jab**" NOUN a veil worn by some Muslim women in public, covering the hair and the chest

hijack **hijacks, hijacking, hijacked**
VERB If someone **hijacks** a plane or other vehicle, they take control of it unlawfully and by force.
hijacker NOUN

hike **hikes, hiking, hiked**
VERB **1** If you **hike**, you go for a long walk across country.
NOUN **2** a long and demanding walk

hilarious
ADJECTIVE very funny

hill **hills**
NOUN a high, rounded piece of ground

hilt **hilts**
NOUN the handle of a knife or sword

him
PRONOUN refers to a man, boy or male animal that has already been mentioned ● *Let's invite Ben. I really like **him**.*

himself
PRONOUN refers to the same man, boy or male animal that does an action and is affected by it ● *He pushed **himself** to the front of the crowd.*

hind **hinds**
NOUN **1** a female deer
ADJECTIVE **2** The **hind** legs of an animal are its back legs.

hinder **hinders, hindering, hindered**
VERB If you **hinder** someone or something, you get in their way and make it difficult for them to do what they want to do.

A
B
C
D
E
F
G
H
I
J
K
L
M
N
O
P
Q
R
S
T
U
V
W
X
Y
Z

Hindu **Hindus**

NOUN a person who believes in Hinduism, an Indian religion that has many gods and involves the belief that people have another life on earth after death

hinge **hinges**

NOUN the movable joint that attaches a door or window to its frame

hint **hints, hinting, hinted**

NOUN **1** an indirect suggestion ● *He dropped* **hints** *about his birthday present.*
2 a helpful piece of advice
VERB **3** If you **hint** that something is true, you suggest it indirectly. ● *The teacher* **hinted** *that they had all done well in the tests.*

hip **hips**

NOUN Your **hips** are the joints and the bony parts at the top of your thigh and below your waist.

hippopotamus **hippopotamuses** or **hippopotami**

NOUN a large, African mammal with thick, wrinkled skin and short legs, that lives near rivers

hire **hires, hiring, hired**

VERB **1** If you **hire** something, you pay money to use it for a period of time.
PHRASE **2** Something that is **for hire** is available for people to hire. ● *There are bicycles* **for hire** *down by the beach.*

his

PRONOUN refers to something that belongs or relates to a man, boy or other male animal

hiss **hisses, hissing, hissed**

VERB If someone or something **hisses**, they make a long s sound.

historic

ADJECTIVE important in the past, or likely to be seen as important in the future

historical

ADJECTIVE occurring in the past, or relating to the study of the past

history **histories**

NOUN **1** the study of the past

2 the set of facts that are known about a place or subject ● *There was a leaflet on the* **history** *of the stately home.*
[from Greek *historein* meaning to narrate a story]

hit **hits, hitting, hit**

VERB **1** If you **hit** someone or something, you strike or knock them with force.
2 If something **hits** you, it affects you suddenly and forcefully. ● *The answer suddenly* **hit** *me.*
NOUN **3** If someone or something is a big **hit**, they are a great success.
4 the action of hitting something

hitch **hitches, hitching, hitched**

VERB **1** If you **hitch** something, you tie it up using a loop.
2 INFORMAL If you **hitch** somewhere, you travel by getting lifts from passing vehicles.
NOUN **3** a slight problem of difficulty ● *Their plans went ahead without a* **hitch**.

hitchhike **hitchhikes, hitchhiking, hitchhiked**

VERB to travel by getting lifts from passing vehicles

hive **hives**

NOUN **1** a beehive
2 A place that is a **hive** of activity is very busy.

hoard **hoards, hoarding, hoarded**

VERB **1** If you **hoard** things, you save them even though they may no longer be useful.
NOUN **2** a store of things that has been saved or hidden

hoarse **hoarser, hoarsest**

ADJECTIVE A **hoarse** voice sounds rough and unclear.
hoarsely ADVERB

hoax **hoaxes**

NOUN a trick or an attempt to deceive someone ● *The bomb scare was a* **hoax**.

hobby **hobbies**

NOUN something that you do for enjoyment in your spare time

hockey
NOUN a game in which two teams use long sticks with curved ends to try to hit a small ball into the other team's goal

hockey stick

hoe hoes
NOUN a long-handled gardening tool with a small, square blade, used to remove weeds and break up the soil

Hogmanay
NOUN New Year's Eve and its celebrations in Scotland

hoist hoists, hoisting, hoisted
VERB If someone **hoists** something, they lift it, especially using ropes and pulleys, a crane or other machinery.

hold holds, holding, held
VERB **1** If you **hold** something, you carry it or keep it in place, usually with your hands or arms.
2 If you **hold** a meeting or a party, you arrange it and cause it to happen.
3 If you **hold** someone responsible for something, you decide that they did it.
4 If something **holds** a certain amount, it can contain that amount. • *This jug **holds** a litre of water.*
5 If you **hold** something, you possess it. • *She **holds** the world long jump record.*
NOUN **6** the part of a ship or aircraft where cargo or luggage is stored
7 If someone has a **hold** over you, they have power over you.
8 If you keep a **hold** on something, you hold it securely.

hole holes
NOUN an opening or hollow space in something

Holi
NOUN a Hindu festival celebrated in spring

holiday holidays
NOUN **1** a period of time spent away from home for enjoyment
2 a day when people do not go to work or school because of a national festival
• *In Britain, Christmas Day is always a **holiday**.*

hollow hollows, hollowing, hollowed
ADJECTIVE **1** Something that is **hollow** has a hole or space inside it.
ANTONYM: solid
NOUN **2** a small valley or sunken place
VERB **3** If you **hollow** something out, you make it hollow. • *We **hollowed** out the pumpkin to make a lantern for Halloween.*

holly
NOUN an evergreen tree or shrub with spiky leaves. It often has red berries in winter.

hologram holograms
NOUN a three-dimensional picture made by laser beams

holster holsters
NOUN a holder for a hand gun, worn at the side of the body or under the arm

holy holier, holiest
ADJECTIVE Something that is **holy** relates to God or to a particular religion.

home homes
NOUN **1** the building or place in which you live
2 A nursing **home** is a building in which elderly or ill people live and are looked after.
3 the place where you feel you belong

homeless
ADJECTIVE Someone who is **homeless** has nowhere to live.
homelessness NOUN

home page home pages
NOUN the first page you see on a website, which tells you about the site and has links to the information or services provided

homesick
ADJECTIVE If you are **homesick**, you are unhappy because you are away from your home and family. • *I enjoyed my exchange trip to Germany, but I did feel **homesick** sometimes.*

homework

NOUN school work given to pupils to be done at home

homograph **homographs**

NOUN one of a group of words spelt in the same way but with different meanings, such as *saw* (meaning a tool for cutting) and *saw* (the past tense of *see*)

homonym **homonyms**

NOUN one of a group of words that are pronounced or spelt in the same way but have different meanings; for example *eight* and *ate*, or *bank* (meaning a slope) and *bank* (meaning a place where you keep your money)

homophone **homophones**

NOUN one of a group of words with different meanings that are pronounced in the same way but spelt differently. *Write* and *right* are **homophones**.

honest

NOUN If you are **honest**, you can be trusted to tell the truth.

SYNONYMS: trustworthy, truthful

honestly ADVERB

honey

NOUN a sweet, edible, sticky substance made by bees

honeycomb

honeycombs

NOUN a wax structure made with six-sided cells by bees for storing honey

honeymoon **honeymoons**

NOUN a holiday for a newly married couple after their wedding

honour **honours, honouring, honoured**

NOUN **1** An **honour** is an award given to someone for something they have done.
2 If you feel that it is an **honour** to do something, you feel proud or privileged to do it.
VERB **3** If you **honour** someone, you give them special praise or attention, or an award.

hood **hoods**

NOUN **1** a loose covering for the head, usually part of a coat or jacket
2 In American English, the **hood** of a car is the cover over the engine at the front.

hoof **hooves** or **hoofs**

NOUN the hard, bony part of the feet of horses, cattle and deer

hook **hooks, hooking, hooked**

NOUN **1** a curved piece of metal or plastic that is used for catching things or for holding things up
VERB **2** If you **hook** one thing on to another, you attach it there using a hook.
• He **hooked** the caravan to the car.

hooligan **hooligans**

NOUN a destructive and violent young person

hooliganism NOUN

hoop **hoops**

NOUN a large wooden, metal or plastic ring

hoot **hoots, hooting, hooted**

VERB **1** If a car horn **hoots**, it makes a loud, honking noise.
2 If someone **hoots**, they make a long *oo* sound like an owl or a car horn.
• We all **hooted** with laughter at his joke.

hop **hops, hopping, hopped**

VERB **1** If you **hop**, you jump on one foot.
2 When animals such as kangaroos, birds or insects **hop**, they jump with two or more feet together.

hope **hopes, hoping, hoped**

VERB **1** If you **hope** that something will happen, you want or expect it to happen.
NOUN **2** the wish or expectation that things will go well in the future

hopeful

ADJECTIVE If you are **hopeful** about something, you hope it will turn out well.

hopefully ADVERB

hopeless

ADJECTIVE **1** You say something is **hopeless** when it is very bad and you do not feel it can get any better.
2 unable to do something well • *I'm* **hopeless** *at art.*

hopelessly ADVERB

horde **hordes**
NOUN a large group or number of people or other animals

horizon **horizons**
NOUN the distant line where the sky seems to touch the land or sea

horizontal
ADJECTIVE flat and level with, or parallel to the ground
horizontally ADVERB

horn **horns**
NOUN **1** a warning device on a vehicle that makes a loud noise
2 one of the hard, pointed things that grow from the head of a cow or goat

hornet **hornets**
NOUN **1** a type of very large wasp
PHRASE **2** A situation described as **a hornet's nest** is very difficult to deal with and likely to cause trouble.

horoscope **horoscopes**
NOUN a prediction about what is going to happen to someone, based on the position of the stars when they were born

horrible
ADJECTIVE disagreeable and unpleasant

horrific
ADJECTIVE If something is **horrific**, it horrifies people.

horrify **horrifies, horrifying, horrified**
VERB If someone or something **horrifies** you, they make you feel disgusted and shocked.

horror
NOUN a strong feeling of alarm caused by something very unpleasant

horse **horses**
NOUN a large mammal with a mane and tail, that people can ride

horse chestnut **horse chestnuts**
NOUN a large tree with flowers and shiny, brown nuts known as conkers

horsepower
NOUN a unit used for measuring how powerful an engine is

horseshoe **horseshoes**
NOUN a U-shaped piece of iron that is nailed to the bottom of a horse's hoof to protect it

hose **hoses**
NOUN a long, flexible tube through which liquid or gas can be passed • *a garden* **hose**

hospitable
ADJECTIVE If you are **hospitable**, you are friendly, welcoming and generous to others.

hospital **hospitals**
NOUN a place where sick people are looked after by doctors and nurses

host **hosts, hosting, hosted**
NOUN **1** the person who gives a party or organizes an event, and who welcomes and looks after the guests
2 a large number of things • *There was a* **host** *of things to do at the fair.*
VERB **3** If you **host** an event, you organize it and act as the host.

hostage **hostages**
NOUN a person who is illegally held prisoner and threatened with injury or death unless certain demands are met by other people

hostel **hostels**
NOUN a large house where people can stay cheaply for a short time • *a youth* **hostel**

hostile
ADJECTIVE If someone is **hostile** to you, they behave in an unfriendly aggressive way towards you.

hot **hotter, hottest**
ADJECTIVE **1** having a high temperature
2 having a burning taste caused by spices

hotel **hotels**
NOUN a building where people stay, paying for their room and meals

hound **hounds**
NOUN a dog, especially one used for hunting or racing

hour **hours**
NOUN a period of 60 minutes
[from Greek *hora* meaning season or time of day]

a
b
c
d
e
f
g
h
i
j
k
l
m
n
o
p
q
r
s
t
u
v
w
x
y
z

house **houses**

NOUN a building where people live

household **households**

NOUN **1** all the people who live as a group in a house or flat

PHRASE **2** Someone who is **a household name** is very well known.

householder NOUN

housewife **housewives**

NOUN a married woman who does not have a paid job, but instead looks after her home and children

housework

NOUN all the work done in the home, like the cleaning and cooking

hover **hovers, hovering, hovered**

VERB When a bird, insect or aircraft **hovers**, it stays in the same position in the air.

hovercraft **hovercraft** or **hovercrafts**

NOUN a vehicle that can travel over water or land supported by a cushion of air

how

ADVERB used to ask about, explain or refer to the way something is done ● **How** did you get so dirty?

however

ADVERB **1** You use **however** when you are adding a comment that contrasts with what has just been said. ● He is very chatty and seems confident. **However**, he is quite shy.

2 You use **however** to say that something makes no difference to a situation. ● **However** hard she tried, nothing seemed to work.

howl **howls, howling, howled**

VERB **1** If someone or something **howls**, they make a long, loud wailing noise such as that made by a dog or a baby when it is upset.

NOUN **2** a long, loud wailing noise

hub **hubs**

NOUN **1** the centre part of a wheel

2 the most important or active part of a place or organization

huddle **huddles, huddling, huddled**

VERB **1** If you **huddle** up, or are **huddled**, you are curled up with your arms and legs close to your body.

2 When people or animals **huddle** together, they sit or stand close to each other, often for warmth.

hug **hugs, hugging, hugged**

VERB If you **hug** someone, you put your arms round them and hold them close to you, usually to comfort them or to show affection.

huge

ADJECTIVE extremely large in amount, size or degree ● The party was a **huge** success.

SYNONYMS: enormous, gigantic, vast

hull **hulls**

NOUN The **hull** of a ship is the main part of its body that sits in the water.

hum **hums, humming, hummed**

VERB **1** If something **hums**, it makes a continuous, low noise.

2 If you **hum**, you sing with your lips closed.

NOUN **3** a continuous, low noise

human **humans**

ADJECTIVE **1** relating to or concerning people ● We are all part of the **human** race.

NOUN **2** a person

[from Latin homo meaning man]

human being **human beings**

NOUN a person

humane

ADJECTIVE showing kindness and sympathy towards others

humaneness NOUN   **humanely** ADVERB

humanity

NOUN **1** the human race

2 Someone who shows **humanity** is kind and sympathetic.

humble **humbler, humblest**

ADJECTIVE A **humble** person is modest and thinks that they have very little value.

humbly ADVERB

humid
ADJECTIVE If the weather is **humid**, the air feels damp, heavy and warm.
humidity NOUN

humiliate **humiliates, humiliating, humiliated**
VERB If you **humiliate** someone, you make them feel ashamed or appear stupid to other people.
humiliation NOUN

humour **humours, humouring, humoured**
NOUN **1** the quality of being funny
2 the ability to be amused by certain things • *She's got a peculiar sense of* **humour**.
VERB **3** If you **humour** someone, you try to please them, so that they will not become upset.

hump **humps**
NOUN a small, rounded lump or mound • *a camel's* **hump**

hunch **hunches, hunching, hunched**
VERB **1** If you **hunch** your shoulders, you raise them and push them forward, bending forward slightly.
2 If you have a **hunch** about something, you have an idea that something will happen.

hundred **hundreds**
NOUN A **hundred** is the number 100.
hundredth NOUN OR ADJECTIVE

hung
VERB the past tense and past participle of **hang**

hunger
NOUN the need or desire to eat

hungry **hungrier, hungriest**
ADJECTIVE If you are **hungry**, you need or want food.
hungrily ADVERB

hunt **hunts, hunting, hunted**
VERB **1** If you **hunt** for something, you search for it.
2 When people **hunt**, they chase and kill wild animals for food or sport.
NOUN **3** the act of searching for something • *The neighbours joined in the* **hunt** *for the missing cat.*

hurdle **hurdles**
NOUN **1** one of the frames or barriers that you jump over in an athletics race called **hurdles** • *She knocked over the last* **hurdle**, *but still managed to win the race.*
2 a problem or difficulty • *Several* **hurdles** *had to be overcome before the school play could go ahead.*

hurl **hurls, hurling, hurled**
VERB If you **hurl** something, you throw it with great force.

hurricane **hurricanes**
NOUN a very violent storm with strong winds

eye – may be 100 km wide

wind will spin at 50 to 200 kph

The sun heats the ocean making a spiral of clouds and wind. The centre of a hurricane is called the eye.

A
B
C
D
E
F
G
H
I
J
K
L
M
N
O
P
Q
R
S
T
U
V
W
X
Y
Z

hurry hurries, hurrying, hurried

VERB **1** If you **hurry** somewhere, you go there quickly.

2 If you **hurry** someone or something, or if you tell someone to **hurry** up, you try to make something happen more quickly.

PHRASE **3** If you are **in a hurry** to do something, you want to do it quickly. If you do something **in a hurry**, you do it quickly.

hurt hurts, hurting, hurt

VERB **1** If you **hurt** yourself or someone else, you injure or cause physical pain to yourself or someone else.

2 If a part of your body **hurts**, you feel pain there.

3 If you **hurt** someone, or **hurt** their feelings, you upset them by being unkind towards them.

ADJECTIVE **4** If you are **hurt**, you are injured.

5 If you feel **hurt**, you are upset because of someone's unkindness towards you.

• *She was **hurt** that they did not invite her to the party.*

[from Old French *hurter* meaning to knock against]

hurtle hurtles, hurtling, hurtled

VERB If someone or something **hurtles**, they move along very fast in an uncontrolled way. • *The car **hurtled** along the bumpy road.*

husband husbands

NOUN A woman's **husband** is the man she is married to.

hustle hustles, hustling, hustled

VERB **1** If you **hustle** someone, you make them move by pushing and jostling them.

2 hurry

hut huts

NOUN a small house or shelter

hutch hutches

NOUN a wooden box with wire mesh at one side, in which small pets can be kept

hydrant hydrants

NOUN a pipe connected to the main water supply of a town and used for emergencies

hydraulic

ADJECTIVE operated by water or other fluid that is under pressure

hydroelectric

ADJECTIVE **Hydroelectric** power is electricity produced from the energy of moving water.

hydrogen

NOUN a colourless gas that is the lightest and most common element in the world. **Hydrogen**-filled balloons explode because this gas is very flammable.

hyena hyenas; also spelt hyaena

*Said "high-**ee**-na"* NOUN a wild, dog-like animal found in Africa and Asia, that hunts in packs

[from Greek *huaina* meaning hog]

hygiene

*Said "**hy**-jeen"* NOUN the state of being clean and free of germs

hymn hymns

NOUN a Christian song in praise of God

hyphen hyphens

NOUN a punctuation mark (-) used to join together words or parts of words, as in *left-handed*

hypocrite hypocrites

NOUN someone who pretends to have certain views and beliefs that are different from their actual views and beliefs

hypocritical ADJECTIVE hypocrisy NOUN

hypothermia

NOUN a condition in which a person is very ill because their body has been extremely cold for a long time • *After spending the night stuck on the mountain, the climbers had **hypothermia**.*

Ii

I

PRONOUN A speaker or writer uses **I** to refer to themselves.

ice

NOUN water that has frozen solid

iceberg **icebergs**

NOUN a large mass of ice floating in the sea [from Dutch *ijsberg* meaning ice mountain]

ice cream **ice creams**

NOUN a very cold, sweet, creamy food

ice skate **ice skates**

NOUN a boot with a metal blade on the bottom, that you wear to move around on ice

ice-skate VERB

icicle **icicles**

NOUN a piece of ice shaped like a pointed stick, that hangs down from a surface

icing

NOUN a sweet covering for a cake or biscuits

icon **icons**

NOUN **1** a picture on a computer screen representing a program that can be activated by moving the cursor over it

2 a holy picture of Christ, the Virgin Mary or a saint

ICT

NOUN an abbreviation of *Information and Communication Technology*. **ICT** is the use of computers, telephones, television and radio to store, organize and give out information.

icy **icier, iciest**

ADJECTIVE **1** Something that is **icy** is very cold. ● *We tried to shelter from the **icy** wind.* **2** An **icy** road has ice on it.

icily ADVERB

I'd

a contraction of *I had* or *I would*

idea **ideas**

NOUN **1** a plan or possible course of action **2** an opinion or belief **3** If you have an **idea** of something, you have a general but not a detailed knowledge of it. ● *Could you give me an **idea** of the cost?*

ideal

ADJECTIVE The **ideal** person or thing for a particular purpose is the best possible one.

identical

ADJECTIVE exactly the same ● *They are **identical** twins.*

identification

NOUN a document, such as a driving licence or passport, that states who you are

identify **identifies, identifying, identified**

VERB If you **identify** someone or something, you recognise and name them.

identifiable ADJECTIVE

identity **identities**

NOUN the things that make you who you are

idiom **idioms**

NOUN a group of words that, when used together, mean something different from when the words are used individually. For example, *It rained cats and dogs.*

A
B
C
D
E
F
G
H
I
J
K
L
M
N
O
P
Q
R
S
T
U
V
W
X
Y
Z

idiot **idiots**
NOUN someone who is stupid or foolish

idiotic
ADJECTIVE very stupid
idiotically ADVERB

idle **idler, idlest**
ADJECTIVE **1** If you are **idle**, you are doing nothing.
2 Machines or factories that are **idle** are not being used.
3 lazy
idleness NOUN   **idly** ADVERB

idol **idols**
NOUN a famous person who is loved and admired by fans

i.e.
i.e. means *that is.* • *Please meet me in three days' time, **i.e.** on Sunday.*
[from Latin *id est* meaning that is]

if
CONJUNCTION **1** on condition that • *You can watch TV **if** you do your homework first.*
2 whether • *I asked him **if** he could come to the party.*

igloo **igloos**
NOUN a dome-shaped house built out of blocks of snow by the Inuit or Eskimo people [from *igdlu*, an Inuit word meaning house]

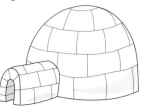

ignite **ignites, igniting, ignited**
VERB If you **ignite** something, or it **ignites**, you set it on fire or it catches fire.
[from Latin *ignis* meaning fire]

ignorant
ADJECTIVE If you are **ignorant** of something, you do not know about it.

ignore **ignores, ignoring, ignored**
VERB If you **ignore** someone or something, you do not take any notice of them.

iguana **iguanas**
NOUN a large, tropical lizard

il-
PREFIX You add **il-** to the beginning of a word to mean that it is not something. For example, **il**legal means not legal, and **il**legible means not legible.

I'll
a contraction of *I will* or *I shall*

ill
ADJECTIVE unhealthy or sick
SYNONYM: unwell
[from Norse *illr* meaning bad]

illegal
ADJECTIVE If something is **illegal** it is forbidden by the law.
SYNONYMS: criminal, unlawful
illegally ADVERB

illegible
ADJECTIVE Writing that is **illegible** is unclear and very difficult to read.
ANTONYM: legible
illegibly ADVERB

illegitimate
ADJECTIVE If something is **illegitimate** it is not allowed by law, or is not accepted as fair by most people.
illegitimacy NOUN

illiterate
ADJECTIVE unable to read or write
ANTONYM: literate

illness **illnesses**
NOUN **1** the state or experience of being ill
2 a particular disease • *Flu is a common **illness** during the winter months.*

illogical
ADJECTIVE An **illogical** feeling or action is not reasonable or sensible.
ANTONYM: logical
illogically ADVERB

illuminate **illuminates, illuminating, illuminated**
VERB If you **illuminate** something, you shine light on to it so that it is easier to see, or you decorate it with lights.

illumination illuminations
NOUN one of the coloured lights put up to decorate a town, especially at Christmas

illusion illusions
NOUN **1** an idea that you think is true, but is not • *We were under the **illusion** that this was going to be an easy project.*
2 something that seems to be there but does not really exist

illustrate illustrates, illustrating, illustrated
VERB **1** If you **illustrate** a book, you help to explain its meaning by putting in pictures and diagrams.
2 If you **illustrate** a point when you are speaking, you make its meaning clearer, often by giving examples.

illustration illustrations
NOUN a picture or a diagram that helps to explain something

illustrator illustrators
NOUN someone who produces the pictures that go into books

I'm
a contraction of *I am*

im-
PREFIX You add **im-** to the beginning of a word to mean not something. For example, something that is **im**movable cannot be moved, and something that is **im**perfect is not perfect.

image images
NOUN a picture or photograph

imagery
NOUN The **imagery** of a poem or book is the words that are used to produce a picture in the mind of the reader.

imaginary
ADJECTIVE Something that is **imaginary** exists only in your mind, not in real life.
ANTONYM: real

imagination imaginations
NOUN If you show **imagination**, you have the ability to form ideas and pictures in your mind.

imaginative
ADJECTIVE If you are **imaginative**, you find

it easy to create new and exciting ideas in your mind.
ANTONYM: unimaginative
imaginatively ADVERB

imagine imagines, imagining, imagined
VERB If you **imagine** something or someone, you create a picture of them in your mind.

imam
NOUN a person who leads a group in prayer in a mosque

imitate imitates, imitating, imitated
VERB If you **imitate** someone or something, you copy them.
SYNONYM: mimic

imitation imitations
NOUN a copy of something else

immature
ADJECTIVE **1** Something that is **immature** is not fully grown or developed.
ANTONYM: mature
2 An **immature** person does not behave in a sensible way.
ANTONYM: mature
immaturely ADVERB   **immaturity** NOUN

immediately
ADVERB If something happens **immediately**, it happens at once.

immense
ADJECTIVE very large
SYNONYMS: huge, vast
immensely ADVERB   **immensity** NOUN

immerse immerses, immersing, immersed
VERB **1** If you **immerse** something, you cover it completely with liquid.
2 If you **immerse** yourself in an activity, you become completely occupied with it.
immersion NOUN

immigrant immigrants
NOUN someone who has come to live in a country from another country

immigrate immigrates, immigrating, immigrated
VERB If someone **immigrates**, they come

a b c d e f g h i j k l m n o p q r s t u v w x y z

to live permanently in a country that is not their own.

ANTONYM: emigrate

immobile

ADJECTIVE If something or someone is **immobile**, they are not moving.

immobility NOUN

immoral

ADJECTIVE If someone is **immoral**, they do not follow most people's standards of acceptable behaviour.

immorality NOUN

immortal

ADJECTIVE **1** Someone or something that is **immortal** is famous and will be remembered for a long time.

2 Something that is **immortal** will last forever.

immortality NOUN

immune

ADJECTIVE If you are **immune** to a particular disease, you cannot catch it.

immunity NOUN

immunize

immunizes, immunizing, immunized

VERB If a doctor **immunizes** you against a disease, they give you an injection so that you are protected from the disease.

immunization NOUN

impact **impacts**

NOUN **1** The **impact** of one object on another is the force with which it hits it.

2 If something has an **impact** on a situation or person, it has a strong effect on them.

[from Latin *impactus* meaning pushed against]

impartial

ADJECTIVE If you are **impartial** about something, you are fair and unbiased.

ANTONYM: partial

impartially ADVERB

impatient

ADJECTIVE If you are **impatient**, you become annoyed easily because you do not want to wait for someone or something.

ANTONYM: patient

impatiently ADVERB impatience NOUN

imperfect

ADJECTIVE Something that is **imperfect** has faults.

imperfectly ADVERB imperfection NOUN

imperial

ADJECTIVE **1** relating to an empire, emperor or empress

2 The **imperial** system of measurement is a system that uses inches, feet and yards, ounces and pounds, and pints and gallons.

impersonal

ADJECTIVE Something that is **impersonal** makes you feel that individuals and their feelings do not matter.

impersonally ADVERB

impersonate **impersonates, impersonating, impersonated**

VERB If you **impersonate** someone, you pretend to be that person.

impersonation NOUN
impersonator NOUN

impertinent

ADJECTIVE If you are **impertinent**, you are disrespectful and rude to someone.

import **imports, importing, imported**

Said "im-**port**" VERB **1** If someone **imports** something, they buy it or bring it in from another country.

ANTONYM: export

Said "**im**-port" NOUN **2 Imports** are goods brought into one country from another country.

ANTONYM: export

important

ADJECTIVE **1** Something that is **important** is very valuable, necessary or significant.

2 An **important** person has a lot of influence or power.

impose imposes, imposing, imposed
VERB If someone **imposes** something on someone, they force it on them.

imposing
ADJECTIVE If someone or something is **imposing**, they look impressive and important.

impossible
ADJECTIVE Something that is **impossible** cannot happen or cannot be done.
impossibly ADVERB   **impossibility** NOUN

imposter imposters
NOUN An **imposter** is someone who pretends to be someone else, usually for devious reasons.

impractical
ADJECTIVE If someone or something is **impractical**, they are not sensible or realistic. ● *It is **impractical** to camp in this wet weather.*
ANTONYM: practical

impress impresses, impressing, impressed
VERB **1** If you **impress** someone, you cause them to admire or respect you.
2 If you **impress** something on someone, you make sure that they understand it and remember it.

impression impressions
NOUN **1** An **impression** of someone or something is a vague idea or feeling that you have about them. ● *I have the **impression** that I've met you before.*
2 a mark made by pressing ● *You leave an **impression** when you press a coin into Plasticine then take it away.*
3 an imitation of a person, animal or thing

impressive
ADJECTIVE If someone or something is **impressive**, it causes you to admire or respect it.
impressively ADVERB

imprison imprisons, imprisoning, imprisoned
VERB If someone **imprisons** another person, they put them in prison or lock them up somewhere.
imprisonment NOUN

improbable
ADJECTIVE not probable or likely to happen
ANTONYM: probable
improbably ADVERB   **improbability** NOUN

improve improves, improving, improved
VERB If something **improves**, or if you **improve** it, it gets better.
improvement NOUN

improvise improvises, improvising, improvised
VERB **1** If you **improvise** something, you make or do something without planning it in advance, and with whatever materials are available. ● *In order to save money the children **improvised** their costumes for the school play.*
2 When musicians or actors **improvise**, they make up the music or words as they go along.
improvised ADJECTIVE   **improvisation** NOUN

impudent
ADJECTIVE If you are **impudent**, you are rude and insolent.
impudently ADVERB   **impudence** NOUN

impulse impulses
NOUN If you have an **impulse** to do something, you have a strong urge to do it immediately.
impulsive ADJECTIVE

in
PREPOSITION OR ADVERB **1** at or inside
● *The cow was **in** the field.*
2 into ● *They went **in** the house.*
3 during ● *It snows **in** winter.*

in-
PREFIX You add **in-** to the beginning of a word to mean not something. For example, **in**accurate means not accurate, and **in**accessible means not accessible.

inability inabilities
NOUN If you have an **inability** to do something, you cannot do it.
ANTONYM: ability

inaccessible
ADJECTIVE If something is **inaccessible**, it is very difficult or impossible to reach.
ANTONYM: accessible

A
B
C
D
E
F
G
H
I
J
K
L
M
N
O
P
Q
R
S
T
U
V
W
X
Y
Z

inaccurate
ADJECTIVE If something is **inaccurate**, it is incorrect.
ANTONYM: accurate

inadequate
ADJECTIVE If something is **inadequate**, there is not enough of it, or it is not good enough for a particular purpose.
ANTONYM: adequate

inanimate
ADJECTIVE not alive. For example, rocks and furniture are **inanimate**.

inaudible
ADJECTIVE If something is **inaudible**, it cannot be heard.
ANTONYM: audible

incapable
ADJECTIVE Someone who is **incapable** of doing something is not able to do it.
ANTONYM: capable

incendiary
ADJECTIVE An **incendiary** device is designed to set fire to things.

incense
NOUN a spicy substance that gives off a sweet smell when it is burned

incessant
ADJECTIVE If something is **incessant**, it continues without stopping. ● *The sound of the rain on the windows was **incessant**.*
incessantly ADVERB

inch **inches**
NOUN a unit of length equal to about 2.54 centimetres
[from Latin *uncia* meaning twelfth part; there are twelve inches in a foot]

incident **incidents**
NOUN an event or occurrence, especially an unusual one

incidentally
ADVERB If something happens **incidentally**, it happens along with something else, as a minor part of it.

incinerate **incinerates, incinerating, incinerated**
VERB If you **incinerate** something, you burn it until only ashes are left.
incineration NOUN

incisor **incisors**
NOUN Your **incisors** are the sharp teeth at the front of your mouth, used for biting and cutting food.

inclination **inclinations**
NOUN If you have an **inclination** to do something, you want to do it.

incline **inclines, inclining, inclined**
Said "in-**klyn**" VERB **1** If you are **inclined** to do something, you often do it or you would like to do it.
Said "**in**-klyn" NOUN **2** a slope

include **includes, including, included**
VERB If one thing **includes** another, the second thing is part of the first thing.
● *Meals are **included** in the price at this hotel.*
ANTONYM: exclude

inclusive
ADJECTIVE When something is **inclusive**, it includes everything and nothing is left out. ● *The price for the meal was **inclusive**, so Gran had nothing extra to pay for our milkshakes.*

incognito
ADVERB If someone is **incognito**, they are in disguise.
[from Latin *in* + *cognitus* meaning not known]

income **incomes**
NOUN the money a person earns

incomplete
ADJECTIVE Something that is **incomplete** is not complete or finished.
ANTONYM: complete

incongruous
ADJECTIVE If something is **incongruous** in a particular place or situation, it seems unsuitable and out of place.
incongruously ADVERB

inconsiderate
ADJECTIVE If you are **inconsiderate**, you do not consider the needs or feelings of others.
ANTONYM: considerate

inconspicuous

ADJECTIVE If someone or something is **inconspicuous**, they are not noticeable or obvious, and cannot easily be seen.
ANTONYM: conspicuous
inconspicuously ADVERB

inconvenient

ADJECTIVE If something is **inconvenient**, it is awkward and causes difficulties. • *an inconvenient time to call*
ANTONYM: convenient
inconveniently ADVERB

incorporate incorporates, incorporating, incorporated

VERB If someone **incorporates** one thing into another thing, they include the first thing so that it becomes part of the second.

incorrect

ADJECTIVE Something that is **incorrect** is wrong or untrue.
ANTONYM: correct

increase increases, increasing, increased

VERB **1** If something **increases**, or if you **increase** it, it becomes larger in number, level or amount. • *Her dad **increased** her pocket money.*
ANTONYM: decrease
NOUN **2** a rise in the number, level or amount of something • *There has been an **increase** in the number of children walking to school.*
ANTONYM: decrease

incredible

ADJECTIVE totally amazing or impossible to believe
SYNONYM: unbelievable

incubate incubates, incubating, incubated

Said "**in**-kyoo-bayt" VERB When eggs **incubate**, or a bird **incubates** them, they are kept warm until they hatch.

incubator incubators

NOUN a piece of hospital equipment in which sick or weak newborn babies are kept warm and safe

incurable

ADJECTIVE If someone has an **incurable** disease, they cannot be cured.
ANTONYM: curable

indebted

ADJECTIVE If you are **indebted** to someone, you are very grateful to them.

indecent

ADJECTIVE Something that is **indecent** is shocking or rude.
ANTONYM: decent
indecently ADVERB   indecency NOUN

indecisive

ADJECTIVE If someone is **indecisive**, they find it difficult to make up their mind.
ANTONYM: decisive

indeed

ADVERB **1** You use **indeed** to emphasize a point that you are making. • *The cake was very good **indeed**.*
2 You use **indeed** to show that you agree with something. • *"Are you going to the party?" "**Indeed** I am."*

indefinite

ADJECTIVE If something is **indefinite**, it is vague and unclear.
ANTONYM: definite

indefinitely

ADVERB If something goes on **indefinitely**, there is no clear time when it will finish and it can go on for an unlimited time.

indent indents, indenting, indented

VERB If you **indent** a paragraph when you write, you start the first line further to the right, away from the margin.

independent

ADJECTIVE **1** If you are **independent**, you are able to do things yourself and do not need help from other people.
2 free and not controlled by anyone
independently ADVERB
independence NOUN

indestructible

ADJECTIVE If something is **indestructible**, it cannot be destroyed.

indicate *indicates, indicating, indicated*

VERB **1** If you **indicate** something to someone, you point it out or show it to them.

2 If the driver of a vehicle **indicates**, they give a signal to show which way they are going to move or turn. • *The cyclist indicated that he was turning right.*

indicator *indicators*

NOUN **1** something that tells you what something is like or what is happening

2 A car's **indicators** are the lights at the front and back that are used to show when it is turning left or right.

indifferent

ADJECTIVE If you are **indifferent** to something, you have no interest in it.
indifferently ADVERB **indifference** NOUN

indigestion

NOUN a pain you get when you have difficulty digesting food

indignant

ADJECTIVE If you are **indignant** about something, you are angry about it because you think it is unfair.
indignantly ADVERB

indigo

ADJECTIVE deep blue or violet

indirect

ADJECTIVE If something happens in an **indirect** way, it does not happen in a straightforward way.
ANTONYM: direct
indirectly ADVERB

indispensable

ADJECTIVE absolutely necessary; essential

indistinct

ADJECTIVE not clear
ANTONYM: distinct
indistinctly ADVERB

individual *individuals*

ADJECTIVE **1** relating to one particular person or thing • *Each child in the class gets individual attention.*

2 single or separate • *Each sweet in the*
packet comes in an **individual** wrapper.

NOUN **3** a person, different from any other person • *We should treat people as individuals.*

indoor

ADJECTIVE happening inside a building
• *The hotel has an indoor swimming pool.*

indoors

ADVERB If something happens **indoors**, it takes place inside a building.

indulge *indulges, indulging, indulged*

VERB **1** If you **indulge** in something, you allow yourself to do it because you enjoy it.

2 If you **indulge** someone, you allow them to have or do what they want.
indulgence NOUN

industrial

ADJECTIVE to do with the work and processes involved in making things in factories

industrious

ADJECTIVE If you are **industrious**, you work hard.
industriously ADVERB

industry *industries*

NOUN **1** the work involved in making things in factories

2 all the people and processes involved in manufacturing a particular thing • *My dad works in the computer industry.*
[from Latin *industria* meaning diligence or hard work]

inedible

ADJECTIVE If something is **inedible**, it is too unpleasant or poisonous to eat.

inefficient

ADJECTIVE badly organized, wasteful and slow
inefficiently ADVERB **inefficiency** NOUN

inevitable

ADJECTIVE certain to happen

inexpensive

ADJECTIVE not costing much

inexplicable

ADJECTIVE If something is **inexplicable**,

you cannot explain it.
inexplicably ADVERB

infamous
Said "in-fum-uss" ADJECTIVE Someone or something that is **infamous** is well known for their bad qualities.
SYNONYM: notorious

infant **infants**
NOUN a baby or very young child [from Latin *infans* meaning unable to speak]

infantry
NOUN In an army, the **infantry** are soldiers who fight on foot rather than in tanks or on horses.

infatuated
ADJECTIVE If you are **infatuated** with someone, you are so much in love with them that you cannot think reasonably about them.
infatuation NOUN

infect **infects, infecting, infected**
VERB If someone or something **infects** another person or animal, they pass a disease on to them.

infection **infections**
NOUN an illness caused by germs

infectious
ADJECTIVE Something that is **infectious** spreads from one person to another.
• *Measles is an **infectious** disease.*

infer **infers, inferring, inferred**
VERB If you **infer** that something is happening or is correct, you work it out from the details you already have.
inference NOUN

inferior
ADJECTIVE Something that is **inferior** is not as good as something else of a similar kind. • *The trainers were of **inferior** quality.*
inferiority NOUN

inferno **infernos**
NOUN a huge and fierce fire

infertile
ADJECTIVE **1** **Infertile** soil is of poor quality and plants cannot grow well in it.

2 A person, animal or plant that is **infertile** is unable to reproduce.

infested
ADJECTIVE If something is **infested**, it is full of pests, like insects, rats or fleas.

infinite
ADJECTIVE If something is **infinite**, it is endless and without limits.
infinitely ADVERB

infinitive **infinitives**
NOUN the base form of a verb. An **infinitive** often has "to" in front of it, for example *to be* or *to see*.

infirm
ADJECTIVE If someone is **infirm**, they are weak because they are ill or old.
infirmity NOUN

infirmary **infirmaries**
NOUN a hospital

inflammable
ADJECTIVE An **inflammable** material burns easily.

inflammation
NOUN painful redness or swelling of a part of the body

inflate **inflates, inflating, inflated**
VERB If you **inflate** something, you put air or a gas such as helium into it to make it swell.
inflatable ADJECTIVE

inflation
NOUN a general increase in the price of goods and services in a country

inflexible
ADJECTIVE If someone or something is **inflexible**, they cannot be bent or altered.

inflict inflicts, inflicting, inflicted
VERB If you **inflict** something unpleasant on someone, you make them suffer it.

influence influences, influencing, influenced
VERB If you **influence** someone or something, you have an effect on what they do or what happens.

influential
ADJECTIVE Someone who is **influential** is important and can influence people or events.
[from Latin *influentia* meaning power flowing from the stars]

influenza
NOUN FORMAL flu

inform informs, informing, informed
VERB If you **inform** somebody about something, you let them know about it.

informal
ADJECTIVE relaxed and casual
informally ADVERB

information
NOUN knowledge about something ● *He used the encyclopedia to find more* **information**.

information technology
NOUN the storage and communication of information using computers

informative
ADJECTIVE Something that is **informative** gives you information.

infuriate infuriates, infuriating, infuriated
VERB If someone or something **infuriates** you, they make you very angry.
infuriating ADJECTIVE

ingenious
Said "in-**jeen**-yuss" ADJECTIVE Something that is **ingenious** is clever and involves new ideas.
ingeniously ADVERB

ingratitude
NOUN If you show **ingratitude**, you show a lack of care or thanks for something that has been done for you.
ANTONYM: gratitude

ingredient ingredients
NOUN **Ingredients** are the things that something is made from, especially in cookery.

inhabit inhabits, inhabiting, inhabited
VERB If you **inhabit** a place, you live there.

inhabitant inhabitants
NOUN If you are an **inhabitant** of a place, you live there.

inhale inhales, inhaling, inhaled
VERB When you **inhale** something, you breathe it in.
inhalation NOUN

inherit inherits, inheriting, inherited
VERB **1** If you **inherit** money or property, you receive it from someone who has died.
2 If you **inherit** a feature or quality from a parent or ancestor, you are born with it.
● *Her children have* **inherited** *her love of sport.*
inheritance NOUN   **inheritor** NOUN

inhospitable
ADJECTIVE **1** If you are **inhospitable**, you are unwelcoming to people who visit you.
2 An **inhospitable** place is an unpleasant and difficult place to live in.

inhuman
ADJECTIVE **1** not human or not behaving like a human
2 extremely cruel

initial initials
Said "in-**nish**-ul" NOUN **1** one of the capital letters that begin each word of a name
ADJECTIVE **2** first or at the beginning
initially ADVERB

initiative
Said "in-**nish**-ut-iv" NOUN If you show **initiative**, you have the ability to see what needs to be done and do it, without relying on others.

inject injects, injecting, injected
VERB If a doctor or nurse **injects** you, they use a needle and syringe to put medicine into your body.
[from Latin *in* + *jacere* meaning to throw into]

injure injures, injuring, injured
VERB If you **injure** someone, you hurt or harm them in some way.

injury injuries
NOUN damage to part of a person's or animal's body

injustice
NOUN If someone suffers **injustice**, they are treated unfairly.

ink
NOUN the coloured liquid used for writing or printing

inland
ADJECTIVE OR ADVERB If a place is **inland**, it is away from the coast.

inlet inlets
NOUN a narrow bay or channel of water that goes inland from the sea, a lake or a river

inmate inmates
NOUN someone who lives in an institution, such as a prison

inn inns
NOUN a small, old country pub or hotel

inner
ADJECTIVE contained inside a place or object ● The **inner** tube of my front tyre has a puncture.

innings
NOUN In cricket, an **innings** is a period of time when a particular team is batting.

innocent
ADJECTIVE not guilty of a crime or of doing something wrong
ANTONYM: guilty
innocently ADVERB **innocence** NOUN

innovation innovations
NOUN a completely new idea, product or way of doing things

inoculate inoculates, inoculating, inoculated
VERB If a doctor or nurse **inoculates** you, they give you an injection to protect you from catching a particular disease.
inoculation NOUN

input inputs, inputting, input
NOUN **1** Your **input** is your contribution and what you put into something. ● The class project requires **input** from everyone.
2 In computing, **input** is information that is fed into a computer.
VERB **3** To **input** information into a computer means to feed it in.

inquest inquests
NOUN an official inquiry to find out what caused a person's death

inquire inquires, inquired, inquiring; also spelt **enquire**
VERB If you **inquire** about something, you ask for information about it.

inquiry inquiries
NOUN **1** an official investigation
2 a question or a request for information

inquisitive
ADJECTIVE Someone who is **inquisitive** is keen to find out about things.
inquisitively ADVERB **inquisitiveness** NOUN

insane
ADJECTIVE Someone or something **insane** is mad.
insanely ADVERB **insanity** NOUN

inscription inscriptions
NOUN the words that are carved or engraved on something such as a monument, gravestone or coin, or written in the front of a book

insect insects
NOUN a small animal with six legs and no backbone, with its skeleton on the outside. **Insects** often have wings, for example beetles, butterflies and grasshoppers.
[from Latin *insectum* meaning animal that has been cut into, because the bodies of many insects are divided into parts]

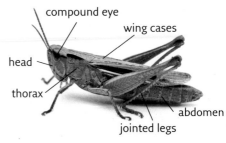

compound eye
wing cases
head
thorax
abdomen
jointed legs

insecticide insecticides
NOUN a poisonous chemical used to kill insects

insecure
ADJECTIVE **1** If you feel **insecure**, you lack confidence and feel worried.
2 If something is **insecure**, it is not fixed properly.
insecurity NOUN

inseparable
ADJECTIVE **1** If people are **inseparable**, they are always together. • *The three of them are such good friends, they're inseparable.*
2 If things are **inseparable**, they cannot be parted.

insert inserts, inserting, inserted
VERB If you **insert** an object into something, you put it inside. • *He inserted the key into the lock.*

inside insides
ADVERB, PREPOSITION OR ADJECTIVE **1 Inside** means in something. • *an inside pocket* • *I waited inside the house.*
ANTONYM: outside
NOUN **2** The **inside** of something is the part that is surrounded by the main part, and is often hidden. • *I painted the inside of the shed.*
ANTONYM: outside
PHRASE **3 Inside out** means with the inside part facing outwards. • *Her umbrella blew inside out.*
PLURAL NOUN **4** Your **insides** are the parts within your body that cannot be seen.

🖉 Do not use *of* after *inside* when it is a preposition. It is correct to say *I waited inside the shop*, not *I waited inside of the shop.*

insight insights
NOUN If you show **insight** into a problem, you show a deep and accurate understanding of it.

insignificant
ADJECTIVE small and unimportant
insignificantly ADVERB
insignificance NOUN

insist insists, insisting, insisted
VERB If you **insist** on something, you demand it forcefully. • *As it was already dark, she insisted on giving us a lift home.*

insistent
ADJECTIVE If you are **insistent**, you insist on having or doing something.
insistence NOUN

insolent
ADJECTIVE very rude and showing no respect
insolently ADVERB **insolence** NOUN

insoluble
ADJECTIVE **1** impossible to solve
2 unable to dissolve

insomnia
NOUN difficulty in sleeping
insomniac NOUN

inspect inspects, inspecting, inspected
VERB If you **inspect** something, you examine or check it carefully.

inspector inspectors
NOUN **1** someone in authority whose job it is to inspect things
2 a rank of police officer

inspire inspires, inspiring, inspired
VERB If someone or something **inspires** you, they give you new ideas, confidence and enthusiasm.
inspired ADJECTIVE **inspiration** NOUN

install installs, installing, installed
VERB If you **install** something, you put it in place so that it is ready to be used.
installation NOUN

instalment instalments
NOUN **1** If you pay for something in **instalments**, you pay small amounts of money regularly over a period of time.
2 one of the parts of a story or television series

instance instances
NOUN **1** a particular example or occurrence of something
PHRASE **2** You use **for instance** to give an example of something you are talking about. • *In some countries, for instance in Spain, many shops are closed at lunchtime.*

instant instants
NOUN **1** a moment or short period of time

ADJECTIVE **2** immediate and without delay
● *The book was an **instant** success.*
instantly ADVERB

instead
ADVERB If you do one thing **instead** of another, you do the first thing and not the second thing. ● *They took the stairs **instead** of the lift.*

instinct **instincts**
NOUN a natural tendency to do something in a particular way ● *Her **instincts** told her to run away as quickly as possible.*

institute **institutes**
NOUN an organization set up for a purpose, such as teaching or research

institution **institutions**
NOUN a large, important organization, such as a university or bank

instruct **instructs, instructing, instructed**
VERB **1** If you **instruct** someone to do something, you tell them to do it.
2 If someone **instructs** you in a subject or skill, they teach you about it.
instructor NOUN **instructive** ADJECTIVE

instruction **instructions**
NOUN If you follow an **instruction**, you do what someone tells you to do.

instrument **instruments**
NOUN **1** a tool that is used to do a particular job
2 an object, such as a piano or guitar, that you play to make music

insufficient
ADJECTIVE not enough for a particular purpose ● *There is **insufficient** flour to make two cakes.*

insulate **insulates, insulating, insulated**
VERB If you **insulate** something, you cover it with materials such as foam or plastic to stop heat or electricity passing out of it.
insulation NOUN **insulator** NOUN

insulin
NOUN a substance that controls the level of sugar in your blood

insult **insults, insulting, insulted**
Said "in-**sult**" VERB **1** If you **insult** someone, you offend them by being rude to them.
Said "**in**-sult" NOUN **2** a rude remark that offends someone
insulting ADJECTIVE

insurance
NOUN an amount of money paid on a regular basis to a company that, in return, will pay you money if you have an accident or need medical treatment

intact
ADJECTIVE If something is **intact**, it is complete and undamaged.

integer **integers**
NOUN a whole number. For example, 2 is an **integer** but $2\frac{1}{2}$ is not.

integrate **integrates, integrating, integrated**
VERB If a person **integrates** into a group, they become a part of it.

integrity
NOUN the quality of being honest and trustworthy

intellectual
ADJECTIVE involving thought, ideas and understanding ● *an **intellectual** exercise, like learning French*

intelligence
NOUN Your **intelligence** is your ability to understand and learn things.

intelligent
ADJECTIVE clever and able to understand things easily
intelligently ADVERB

intend **intends, intending, intended**
VERB If you **intend** to do something, you decide or plan to do it.

intense
ADJECTIVE very great in strength or amount
● ***intense** heat*
intensely ADVERB **intensity** NOUN

intensive
ADJECTIVE If something is **intensive**, it

involves a lot of energy or effort over a short time.
intensively ADVERB

intention intentions
NOUN an idea or a plan of what you mean to do • *He had every **intention** of working hard that day.*

intentional
ADJECTIVE If something is **intentional**, it is done on purpose.
intentionally ADVERB

inter-
PREFIX You add **inter-** to a word to mean between or among two or more people or things. • ***inter**-school competitions* • ***inter**national travel*

interactive
ADJECTIVE If a computer is **interactive**, it allows two-way communication between itself and the person using it, so that information can pass in both directions.

intercept intercepts, intercepting, intercepted
VERB If you **intercept** someone or something as they move from one place to another, you stop them reaching their destination.
interception NOUN

intercom intercoms
NOUN a device that people use to communicate with each other if they are in different rooms

interest interests, interesting, interested
NOUN **1** a thing you enjoy doing
2 Interest is an extra payment that you receive if you have invested money, or an extra payment that you make if you have borrowed money.
VERB **3** If something **interests** you, you want to know more about it.

interfere interferes, interfering, interfered
VERB **1** If you **interfere** in a situation, you try to influence it, although it does not concern you.
2 If you **interfere** with a plan, you get in the way of it.

interior interiors
NOUN **1** the inside part of something • *the **interior** of the building*
ADJECTIVE **2** inside • *the **interior** walls*

interjection interjections
NOUN a word or phrase spoken suddenly to expresses an emotion, such as surprise, excitement or anger. For example, *Help!* is an **interjection**.

intermediate
ADJECTIVE An **intermediate** stage occurs in the middle, between two others. • *This dance class is for beginners. The next one is at **intermediate** level.*

internal
ADJECTIVE happening on, or part of, the inside of something • *Your lungs are **internal** organs.*

international
ADJECTIVE involving different countries • *This is an important **international** match.*

internet or **Internet**
NOUN a worldwide system where people communicate using computers

interpret interprets, interpreting, interpreted
VERB **1** If you **interpret** something, you decide what it means. • *I tried to **interpret** his painting.*
2 If you **interpret** what someone is saying, you immediately translate it into another language.
interpretation NOUN **interpreter** NOUN

interrogate interrogates, interrogating, interrogated
VERB If you **interrogate** someone, you question them in great detail.
interrogation NOUN **interrogator** NOUN

interrupt interrupts, interrupting, interrupted
VERB If you **interrupt** someone, you start talking while they are talking.
interruption NOUN

intersect intersects, intersecting, intersected
VERB When two roads **intersect**, they cross each other.

intersection **intersections**

NOUN **1** a point where two roads cross over each other

2 the point where lines, arcs or sets cross each other

point of intersection

interval **intervals**

NOUN a short break during a play, concert or performance

intervene **intervenes, intervening, intervened**

VERB If you **intervene** in a situation, you step in, usually to sort out an argument or quarrel.

intervention NOUN

interview **interviews, interviewing, interviewed**

NOUN **1** a formal meeting where someone is asked questions

VERB **2** When someone **interviews** you, they ask you questions, usually in order to find out if you are suitable for something in particular.

intestine **intestines**

NOUN the part of your digestive system that carries food from your stomach. Your **intestines** are long tubes folded up inside your abdomen.

intestinal ADJECTIVE

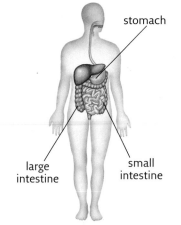

stomach

large intestine

small intestine

intimate

ADJECTIVE **1** If you are **intimate** with someone, you are very friendly with them.

2 Intimate details or thoughts are personal or private.

intimidate **intimidates, intimidating, intimidated**

VERB If you **intimidate** someone, you frighten them in a threatening way. [from Latin *timidus* meaning fearful]

intimidated ADJECTIVE

intimidating ADJECTIVE

intimidation NOUN

into

PREPOSITION **1** If you go **into** something, you go inside it. • Come **into** the house.

2 If you bump or crash **into** something, you bump or crash against it.

intrepid

ADJECTIVE brave and fearless

intrepidly ADVERB

intricate

ADJECTIVE detailed and complicated

intricately ADVERB

intrigue **intrigues, intriguing, intrigued**

VERB If something **intrigues** you, you are fascinated by it and curious about it.

intrigue NOUN   intriguing ADJECTIVE

introduce **introduces, introducing, introduced**

VERB **1** If you **introduce** one person to another, you tell them each other's name so that they can get to know each other.

2 If you **introduce** someone to something, they learn about it for the first time from you. • My friend **introduced** me to water-skiing on holiday.

introduction **introductions**

NOUN a piece of writing at the beginning of a book, that tells you what the book is about

introductory ADJECTIVE

intrude **intrudes, intruding, intruded**

VERB If you **intrude** on someone or something, you disturb them.

intrusion NOUN   intrusive ADJECTIVE

intruder intruders
NOUN a person who forces their way into someone else's property without their consent • *The security guard caught an **intruder** last night.*

intuition intuitions
NOUN the ability to know about something without thinking about it or being able to explain it
intuitive ADJECTIVE   intuitively ADVERB

Inuit Inuits
NOUN an Eskimo who comes from North America or Greenland

invade invades, invading, invaded
VERB If an army **invades** a country, it enters it by force.

invalid invalids
Said "in-va-lid" NOUN **1** someone who is so ill that they need to be looked after by someone else
*Said "in-**val**-id"* ADJECTIVE **2** If something is **invalid**, it cannot be accepted because there is something wrong with it. • *Your ticket is **invalid** for this train service.*

invaluable
ADJECTIVE extremely useful

invasion invasions
NOUN the forceful entering or attacking of a place • *At the end of the match, there was an **invasion** of the pitch by fans.*

invent invents, inventing, invented
VERB **1** If you **invent** something, you are the first person to think of it or make it.
2 If you **invent** a story or an excuse, you make it up.
inventor NOUN   invention NOUN
inventive ADJECTIVE   inventiveness NOUN

inverse
NOUN FORMAL In mathematics, if you turn something upside down or back to front, you have its **inverse**. • *The **inverse** of 23 is 32.*

invert inverts, inverting, inverted
VERB **1** If you **invert** something, you turn it upside down.

2 If you **invert** a fraction, the top number changes places with the bottom number.

invertebrate invertebrates
NOUN an animal without a backbone

inverted commas
NOUN punctuation marks (" ") are used to show where speech begins and ends • *"Good morning!" she cried.*

invest invests, investing, invested
VERB If you **invest** money in something, you try to increase its value, for example by putting it into a bank or building society so that it will gain interest.
investor NOUN   investment NOUN

investigate investigates, investigating, investigated
VERB If someone **investigates** something, they try to find out all the facts about it. • *Police are still **investigating** the accident.*
SYNONYMS: examine, look into, study
investigator NOUN

investigation investigations
NOUN If you conduct an **investigation** into something, you examine it carefully and try to find out the facts about it. • *The disappearance of the money was under **investigation**.*

invincible
ADJECTIVE If something is **invincible**, it cannot be defeated.
invincibly ADVERB   invincibility NOUN

invisible
ADJECTIVE If something is **invisible**, you cannot see it.
invisibly ADVERB   invisibility NOUN

invitation invitations
NOUN a request for someone to come to something, such as a party

invite invites, inviting, invited
VERB If you **invite** someone to an event, you ask them to come to it.

involve involves, involving, involved
VERB **1** If a situation or activity **involves**

something, that thing is a necessary part of it. ● *Being president **involves** a lot of responsibility.*
2 If you **involve** yourself in something, you take part in it. ● *I'm **involved** in the production of the school play.*

ir-

PREFIX a variation of in-, meaning not. For example, **ir**relevant means not relevant, and **ir**replaceable means not replaceable.

irate

ADJECTIVE very angry
irately ADVERB

iris irises

NOUN the coloured part of your eye
[from Greek *iris* meaning rainbow or coloured circle]

iron irons, ironing, ironed

NOUN **1** a hard, dark metal used to make steel
2 an appliance you heat up and press on clothes to remove creases
VERB **3** If you **iron** clothes, you use a hot iron to remove creases from them.
ironing NOUN

irony

NOUN When you use **irony**, you use words, often in a humorous way, to say the opposite of what you really mean.
ironic ADJECTIVE   ironically ADVERB

irrational

ADJECTIVE If you act in an **irrational** way, you show no reason or logic in what you do.
irrationally ADVERB

irregular

ADJECTIVE **1** Something that is **irregular** is not smooth or straight, or does not make a regular pattern.
2 **Irregular** verbs do not follow the usual rules.
irregularly ADVERB   irregularity NOUN

irrelevant

ADJECTIVE If something is **irrelevant**, it has nothing to do with what is being said or discussed.
irrelevance NOUN

irresistible

ADJECTIVE **1** If something is **irresistible**, it cannot be controlled. ● *I had an **irresistible** urge to laugh.*
2 If someone is **irresistible**, they are very attractive.

irresponsible

ADJECTIVE If you do something in an **irresponsible** way, you act thoughtlessly and carelessly.
SYNONYMS: careless, thoughtless
irresponsibly ADVERB
irresponsibility NOUN

irreversible

ADJECTIVE If something is **irreversible**, it cannot be reversed or changed back to the way it was before.
irreversibly ADVERB

irrigate irrigates, irrigating, irrigated

VERB To **irrigate** land is to supply it with water brought through pipes or ditches. ● *In hot, dry countries the land is **irrigated**.* [from Latin *rigare* meaning to moisten]
irrigated ADJECTIVE   irrigation NOUN

irritable

ADJECTIVE If you are **irritable**, you are easily annoyed.
irritably ADVERB

irritate irritates, irritating, irritated

VERB If something **irritates** you, it annoys you.
irritation NOUN

is

VERB a present tense of **be**

Islam

NOUN the Muslim religion, which teaches that there is only one God, Allah, and Mohammed is his prophet

island islands

NOUN a piece of land surrounded by water

isle isles

NOUN a literary word for an island

isn't

VERB a contraction of *is not*

isolate **isolates, isolating, isolated**

VERB **1** If you **isolate** yourself, you separate yourself from other people.
● *I isolated myself in my room.*
2 To **isolate** a sick person or animal means to keep them away from others so that the disease does not spread.
isolated ADJECTIVE isolation NOUN

isosceles

ADJECTIVE An **isosceles** triangle has two sides of the same length and two equal angles.

ISP **ISPs**

NOUN a business that provides access to the internet. **ISP** is an abbreviation for *internet service provider*.

issue **issues**

NOUN **1** an important subject that people are talking about ● *The **issue** of homeless people is important to many people.*
2 a particular newspaper or magazine ● *this week's **issue** of the local paper*

it

PRONOUN **1** used to refer to something that has already been mentioned. **It** can also refer to babies or other animals whose gender is not known. ● *I like that dog. **It** is very friendly.*
2 You use **it** to talk about the weather, time or date. ● ***It**'s been raining all day.*

IT

NOUN an abbreviation of *Information Technology*

italics

PLURAL NOUN letters printed in a particular sloping way. They are often used for emphasis. ● *This writing is in **italics**.*

itch **itches, itching, itched**

VERB **1** When a part of your body **itches**, you have an unpleasant feeling that makes you want to scratch it.
NOUN **2** an unpleasant feeling on your skin that makes you want to scratch it

item **items**

NOUN one of a collection or list of objects
● *Milk is the most important **item** on my shopping list.*

itinerary **itineraries**

NOUN The **itinerary** of a journey is a detailed plan of where to go and what to see along the route.

it's

a contraction of *it is* or *it has*

Do not confuse *it's* with *its*.

its

ADJECTIVE OR PRONOUN **Its** is used to refer to something belonging to things, children or animals that have already been mentioned. ● *The cat won't eat. **Its** bowl needs cleaning.*

Do not confuse *its* with *it's*.

I've

a contraction of *I have*

ivory

NOUN **1** the valuable, creamy-white bone that forms the tusk of an elephant. It is used to make ornaments.
NOUN OR ADJECTIVE **2** creamy-white

ivy

NOUN an evergreen plant that creeps along the ground and up walls

Jj

jab jabs, jabbing, jabbed
VERB **1** If you **jab** something, you poke at it roughly.
NOUN **2** a sharp, sudden poke • *a **jab** in the ribs*
3 INFORMAL an injection • *a measles **jab***

jack jacks
NOUN **1** a piece of equipment for lifting heavy objects, especially for lifting a car when changing a wheel
2 In a pack of cards, a **jack** is a card whose value is between a ten and a queen.

jackal jackals
NOUN a wild animal related to the dog

jacket jackets
NOUN **1** a short coat
2 the paper cover of a book

jackpot jackpots
NOUN the top prize in a gambling game • *He was excited to hear he had won the **jackpot** in the lottery.*

jagged
ADJECTIVE A **jagged** rock has a rough, uneven shape with sharp edges.

jail jails, jailing, jailed or gaol
NOUN **1** a building where people convicted of a crime are locked up
VERB **2** To **jail** someone means to lock them up in a jail.

jam jams, jamming, jammed
NOUN **1** a food made by boiling fruit with sugar
2 a situation where there are so many people or things that it is difficult to move • *There is often a traffic **jam** at that junction.*
VERB **3** If you **jam** something into a place, you squeeze it in. • *He **jammed** his clothes into the suitcase.*

4 If you **jam** something, or if it **jams**, it becomes stuck. • *The coin was **jammed** in the slot.*

January
NOUN the first month of the year. **January** has 31 days.

jar jars, jarring, jarred
NOUN **1** a glass container used for storing food
VERB **2** If something **jars**, you find it unpleasant or annoying.

jargon
NOUN language containing lots of technical words, used by particular groups of people • *Doctors often use **jargon**.*

jaundice
NOUN an illness of the liver, where the skin and the whites of the eyes become yellow

javelin javelins
NOUN a long spear that is thrown in sports competitions

jaw jaws
NOUN **1** the bone in which teeth are set
2 the mouth and teeth of a person or animal

jazz
NOUN a style of popular music with a strong rhythm

jealous
ADJECTIVE If you are **jealous**, you feel envious of others, wanting to have what they have or wanting to be like them.
jealously ADVERB **jealousy** NOUN

jeans
PLURAL NOUN cotton trousers, often made of denim

jeep jeeps
NOUN TRADEMARK a four-wheeled motor vehicle designed for driving over rough ground

jeer jeers, jeering, jeered
VERB **1** If you **jeer** at someone, you insult them in a loud, unpleasant way.
NOUN **2** **Jeers** are rude and insulting remarks.
jeering ADJECTIVE

a
b
c
d
e
f
g
h
i
j
k
l
m
n
o
p
q
r
s
t
u
v
w
x
y
z

jelly jellies
NOUN **1** a clear, sweet food eaten as a dessert
2 a type of clear, set jam • *I like mint jelly with lamb.*

jellyfish jellyfishes
NOUN a sea creature with a clear, soft body and tentacles that may sting

jerk jerks, jerking, jerked
VERB **1** If you **jerk** something, you give it a sudden, sharp pull.
2 If something **jerks**, it moves suddenly and sharply.

jersey jerseys
NOUN a knitted garment for the upper half of the body

jet jets
NOUN **1** an aeroplane that can fly very fast
2 a rush of air, steam or liquid that is forced out under pressure

jetty jetties
NOUN a wide stone wall or wooden platform at the edge of the sea or a river, where boats can be moored

Jew Jews
NOUN a person who practises the religion of Judaism or who is of Hebrew descent
Jewish ADJECTIVE

jewel jewels
NOUN a precious stone, often used to decorate valuable items such as rings or necklaces
jewelled ADJECTIVE

jeweller jewellers
NOUN a person who makes or sells jewellery

jewellery
NOUN the ornaments that people wear, like rings and necklaces

jigsaw jigsaws
NOUN a puzzle that is made up of odd-shaped pieces that must be fitted together to make a picture

jingle jingles
NOUN **1** a short, catchy phrase or rhyme with music, used to advertise something
on radio or television
2 a gentle ringing sound

job jobs
NOUN **1** the work that someone does to earn money
2 anything that has to be done

jockey jockeys
NOUN someone who rides a horse in a race

joey joeys
NOUN a young kangaroo

jog jogs, jogging, jogged
VERB **1** If you **jog**, you run slowly, often for exercise.
2 If you **jog** something, you knock it slightly so that it shakes or moves.
• *My pen slipped when he jogged my arm.*
jogger NOUN **jogging** NOUN

join joins, joining, joined
VERB **1** If you **join** a club, you become a member of it.
2 When two things **join**, or when one thing **joins** another, they come together.
• *The two streams join and form a river.*
SYNONYMS: connect, link

join in
VERB If you **join in** an activity, you take part in it.

joiner joiners
NOUN a person who makes wooden window frames, doors and furniture

joint joints
ADJECTIVE **1** shared by or belonging to two or more people • *The project was a joint effort.*
NOUN **2** a part of your body, such as your elbow or knee, where two bones meet and are able to move together

joke jokes, joking, joked
NOUN **1** something that you say to make people laugh
VERB **2** If you **joke**, you say something amusing or tell a funny story.

jolly jollier, jolliest
ADJECTIVE If you are **jolly**, you are happy and cheerful.

jolt jolts, jolting, jolted
VERB **1** If something **jolts**, it moves or shakes roughly and violently. • *The bus jolted along the bumpy road.*
2 If something or someone **jolts** you, they bump into you clumsily.
NOUN **3** a sudden, jerky movement
4 an unpleasant shock or surprise

jostle jostles, jostling, jostled
VERB If people or animals **jostle**, they push and bump into each other roughly, usually because they are in a crowd.

jot jots, jotting, jotted
VERB If you **jot** something down, you write a quick, brief note.

journal journals
NOUN **1** a magazine that deals with a particular interest
2 a diary where you write what happens each day

journalist journalists
NOUN a person whose job is to gather news and write about it for a newspaper or magazine, or present it on television or radio

journey journeys
NOUN the act of travelling from one place to another

joy joys
NOUN **1** a feeling of great happiness or pleasure
2 something that makes you happy or gives you pleasure • *It was a **joy** to see my friend again.*

joystick joysticks
NOUN **1** a lever in a plane that the pilot uses to control height and direction
2 a lever that controls the cursor on a computer screen, especially in computer games

jubilee jubilees
NOUN a special anniversary of an event such as a coronation • *Queen Elizabeth's Silver **Jubilee** was in 1977.*
[from Hebrew *yobhel* meaning ram's horn, blown during festivals and celebrations to mark the freedom of Hebrew slaves each 50th year, known as the jubilee]

Judaism
NOUN the religion of the Jewish people. It is based on a belief in one God, and draws its laws from the Old Testament.
Judaic ADJECTIVE

judge judges, judging, judged
NOUN **1** the person in a law court who decides how criminals should be punished according to the law
2 the person who chooses the winner of a competition
VERB **3** If a person **judges** someone or something, they act as a judge.
4 If you **judge** someone or something, you decide what they are like.

judgment judgments; also spelt **judgement**
NOUN an opinion that you have after thinking carefully about something

judo
NOUN a sport in which two people try to force each other to the ground using special throwing techniques. It originated in Japan as a form of self-defence.
[from Japanese *ju do* meaning gentleness art]

jug jugs
NOUN a container with a handle and a lip, used for holding and pouring liquids

juggernaut juggernauts
NOUN a large, heavy lorry
[from Hindi *Jagannath*, the name of a huge idol of the god Krishna, which is wheeled through the streets of Puri in India every year]

juggle juggles, juggling, juggled
VERB When someone **juggles** they throw different objects into the air, keeping more than one object in the air at the same time without dropping them.
juggler NOUN

a
b
c
d
e
f
g
h
i
j
k
l
m
n
o
p
q
r
s
t
u
v
w
x
y
z

A
B
C
D
E
F
G
H
I
J
K
L
M
N
O
P
Q
R
S
T
U
V
W
X
Y
Z

juice juices

NOUN the liquid that can be obtained from fruit, vegetables and other food • *orange juice*

juicy juicier, juiciest

ADJECTIVE having a great deal of juice • *The orange was very juicy.*

July

NOUN the seventh month of the year. **July** has 31 days.

jumble jumbles, jumbling, jumbled

NOUN **1** an untidy muddle of things
2 articles for a **jumble** sale
VERB **3** If you **jumble** things, you mix them up untidily.

jumble sale jumble sales

NOUN an event where second-hand items are sold to raise money cheaply, often for charity

jump jumps, jumping, jumped

VERB **1** When you **jump**, you spring off the ground using the muscles in your legs.
2 If someone **jumps**, they make a sudden, sharp movement because they are surprised.

jumper jumpers

NOUN a warm piece of clothing that covers the top part of your body

junction junctions

NOUN a place where roads or railway lines meet or cross

June

NOUN the sixth month of the year. **June** has 30 days.

jungle jungles

NOUN a dense, tropical forest where many trees and other plants grow close together
[from Hindi *jangal* meaning wasteland]

junior

ADJECTIVE **1** A **junior** official or employee holds a lower position in an organization. • *She will be a junior doctor after finishing her training.*
2 younger • *He is the junior of the two brothers.*

junk junks

NOUN **1** old, unwanted or worthless things that are sold cheaply or thrown away
2 a Chinese sailing boat that has a flat bottom and wide sails

junk food

NOUN food that is easy and quick to prepare, or bought ready to eat, but is not always very good for you

jury juries

NOUN a group of people in a court of law who are chosen to listen to the facts about a crime and then decide whether the accused person is guilty or not

just

ADJECTIVE **1** Someone who is **just** is fair.
ADVERB **2** If something has **just** happened, it happened a very short time ago.
3 If you **just** do something, you almost don't do it. • *He just managed to climb the fence.*
4 If something is **just** what you want, it is exactly what you want.

justice

NOUN **1** fairness in the way that people are treated
2 the system of laws created by a community

justify justifies, justifying, justified

VERB If you **justify** what you are doing or saying, you prove or explain why it is reasonable or necessary.
justification NOUN **justifiable** ADJECTIVE

jut juts, jutting, jutted

VERB If something **juts** out, it sticks out beyond a surface or an edge. • *The pier jutted out into the sea.*

juvenile juveniles

ADJECTIVE **1** suitable for or to do with young people
2 childish and rather silly
NOUN **3** a young person not old enough to be considered an adult

Kk

kaleidoscope **kaleidoscopes**
NOUN a toy made of a tube with a hole at one end. When you look through the hole and twist the other end of the tube, you can see a changing pattern of colours.

kangaroo **kangaroos**
NOUN a large, Australian marsupial with very strong back legs that it uses for jumping

karate
NOUN a sport in which people fight each other using only their hands, elbows, feet and legs
[from Japanese *kara* + *te* meaning empty hand]

kayak **kayaks**
NOUN a covered canoe with a small opening for the person sitting in it, originally used by Inuit people

kebab **kebabs**
NOUN pieces of meat or vegetable grilled on a stick
[from Arabic *kabab* meaning roast meat]

keen **keener, keenest**
ADJECTIVE **1** If you are **keen** to do something, or for something to happen, you want very much to do it or for it to happen. • *I was **keen** to meet my cousins from Australia.*
2 If you are **keen** on something or someone, you are fond of them or attracted to them.
3 If your senses are **keen**, you are able to see, hear, taste and smell things very clearly or strongly.

keep **keeps, keeping, kept**
VERB **1** If you **keep** something, you have it and don't give it away. • *I will **keep** this book forever.*
2 If you **keep** an animal, you look after it. • *He **keeps** rabbits.*
3 If you **keep** something somewhere, you store it there. • *I **keep** my bicycle in the garage.*
4 If you **keep** doing something, you do it again and again.
5 If something **keeps** you a certain way, you stay that way because of it. • *The duvet **keeps** me warm.*
6 If you **keep** a promise, you do what you have said you will do.
7 If you **keep** a secret, you do not tell it to anyone else.
NOUN **8** the main tower inside the walls of a castle

keeper **keepers**
NOUN **1** a person whose job is to look after the animals in a zoo
2 a goalkeeper in soccer or hockey • *The **keeper** managed to stop the ball and save the penalty.*

kennel **kennels**
NOUN **1** a small hut for a dog to sleep in
2 A **kennels** is a place where dogs are bred and trained, or looked after when their owners are away.

kept
VERB the past tense and past participle of **keep**

kerb **kerbs**
NOUN the raised edge of a pavement, that separates it from the road • *You must look both ways for traffic before stepping off the **kerb**.*

kernel **kernels**
NOUN the part of a nut that is inside the shell

kestrel **kestrels**
NOUN a type of small hawk

ketchup
NOUN a cold sauce, usually made from tomatoes

a
b
c
d
e
f
g
h
i
j
k
l
m
n
o
p
q
r
s
t
u
v
w
x
y
z

kettle kettles
NOUN a covered container with a spout, in which you boil water

key keys
NOUN **1** a specially shaped piece of metal that fits in a lock, and is turned in order to open the lock
2 The **keys** on a piano or a computer are the buttons that you press in order to operate it.
ADJECTIVE **3 Key** words or sentences are the important ones in a piece of text.
NOUN **4** information arranged in a way that can be used to identify animals, plants and materials. You can use a **key** to help you name an unknown animal, plant or material.

keyboard keyboards
NOUN a set of keys on a piano, typewriter or computer

keyhole keyholes
NOUN the hole in a lock where you put a key

khaki
NOUN OR ADJECTIVE yellowish-brown. Soldiers' uniforms are often made of **khaki** material.
[from Urdu *kaki* meaning dusty]

kick kicks, kicking, kicked
VERB **1** If you **kick** someone or something, you hit them with your foot.
NOUN **2** If you give something a **kick**, you hit it with your foot.
3 INFORMAL If you get a **kick** out of something, you enjoy it very much.

kick off
VERB When a soccer or rugby team **kicks off**, they begin playing.

kid kids, kidding, kidded
NOUN **1** INFORMAL a child
2 a young goat
VERB **3** If you **kid** someone, you tease them and try to make them believe something that isn't true.
SYNONYM: tease

kidnap kidnaps, kidnapping, kidnapped
VERB If someone **kidnaps** someone else, they take them away by force and demand something in exchange for returning them.
[from *kid* + *nap* meaning child stealing; in the 17th century children were kidnapped to work on American plantations]

kidney kidneys
NOUN one of the two organs in your body that remove waste products from your blood

kill kills, killing, killed
VERB If someone **kills** a person, animal or plant, they make them die.

kiln kilns
NOUN an oven for baking china or pottery until it becomes hard and dry

kilo kilos
NOUN a kilogram

kilogram kilograms
NOUN a unit of mass and weight (kg) equal to 1000 grams

kilohertz
NOUN a unit of measurement of radio waves (kHz) equal to 1000 hertz

kilometre kilometres
NOUN a unit of distance (km) equal to 1000 metres

kilowatt kilowatts
NOUN a unit of power (kW) equal to 1000 watts

kilt kilts
NOUN a tartan skirt worn by men as part of Scottish Highland dress

kimono kimonos
NOUN a long, loose garment with wide sleeves and a sash, worn in Japan

kin

PLURAL NOUN Your **kin** are your relatives.

kind **kinder, kindest; kinds**

ADJECTIVE **1** Someone who is **kind** behaves in a caring and helpful way towards other people.

SYNONYM: considerate

NOUN **2** a particular thing of the same type as other things ● *I do not like this **kind** of bread.*

SYNONYMS: sort, class

kindly ADVERB **kindness** NOUN

king **kings**

NOUN a man who is the head of state in a country, and who inherited his position from his parents

kingdom **kingdoms**

NOUN a country that is governed by a king or queen

kingfisher **kingfishers**

NOUN a brightly-coloured bird that lives near water and feeds on fish

kiosk **kiosks**

NOUN a small shop or hut where you can buy newspapers, snacks, and sweets

kipper **kippers**

NOUN a herring that has been dried in smoke to preserve it and give it a special taste

kiss **kisses, kissing, kissed**

VERB **1** When you **kiss** someone, you touch them with your lips in order to show your affection.

NOUN **2** When you give someone a **kiss**, you kiss them.

kit **kits**

NOUN **1** a collection of equipment and clothing that you use for a sport or other activity ● *football **kit***

2 a set of parts that you fit together to make something ● *I got a model aeroplane **kit** for my birthday.*

kitchen **kitchens**

NOUN a room used for cooking and preparing food

kite **kites**

NOUN a light frame covered with paper or cloth, that you fly in the air at the end of a long string

kitten **kittens**

NOUN a very young cat

kiwi **kiwi** or **kiwis**

NOUN **1** a type of bird found in New Zealand. **Kiwis** cannot fly.

2 INFORMAL Someone who comes from New Zealand is called a **kiwi**.

[A Maori word]

kiwi fruit **kiwi fruits**

NOUN a fruit with a brown, hairy skin and green flesh

knack

NOUN an ability to do something easily

knead **kneads, kneading, kneaded**

VERB If you **knead** dough, you press it and squeeze it with your hands before baking it.

knee **knees**

NOUN the joint in your leg between your ankle and your hip

kneel **kneels, kneeling, knelt**

VERB When you **kneel**, or **kneel down**, you bend your legs and lower your body so that one or both knees are touching the ground.

knew

VERB the past tense of **know**

knickers

PLURAL NOUN underpants worn by women and girls

knife **knives**

NOUN a sharp, metal tool used for cutting things

knight **knights, knighting, knighted**

NOUN **1** In medieval times, a **knight** was a nobleman who served his king or lord in battle. ● *King Arthur and the **Knights** of the Round Table*

VERB **2** If a king or queen **knights** a man, they give him the title *Sir* before his name.

[from Old English *cniht* meaning servant]

knit **knits, knitting, knitted**

VERB If you **knit** a piece of clothing, you

make it from wool, using knitting needles or a knitting machine.

knob **knobs**

NOUN a round handle or switch on doors, furniture and machinery

knock **knocks, knocking, knocked**

VERB **1** If you **knock** on something, you hit it hard with your hand to make a noise. • *I knocked on the door when I arrived.*
2 If you **knock** against something, you bump into it.

knocker **knockers**

NOUN a metal lever attached to a door, that you use to knock on the door

knot **knots, knotting, knotted**

NOUN **1** a fastening made by passing one end of a piece of string or fabric through a loop and pulling it tight • *The knot in my laces was so tight that I could not undo it.*

| Overhand knot | Figure 8 knot | Square or reef knot |

2 a hard, round spot on a piece of wood, where a branch grew on the tree
3 a unit for measuring the speed of ships and aircraft
VERB **4** If you **knot** a piece of string, you tie a knot in it.

know **knows, knowing, knew, known**

VERB **1** If you **know** something, you have it clearly in your mind and you do not need to learn it. • *I know how to swim.*
2 If you **know** a person, place or thing, you are familiar with them. • *I've known him for five years.*

knowledge

NOUN all the information and facts that you know • *general knowledge*

knuckle **knuckles**

NOUN one of the joints in your fingers

koala **koalas**

NOUN an Australian marsupial with grey fur and small, tufted ears. **Koalas** live in trees and eat eucalyptus leaves.

Koran or **Qur'an**

NOUN the holy book of Islam
[from Arabic *kara'a* meaning to read]

kosher

ADJECTIVE **Kosher** food has been specially prepared to be eaten according to Jewish law.

Ll

label **labels, labelling, labelled**
NOUN **1** a piece of paper or plastic attached to something and giving information about it ● *The **label** on the bottle told him when to have his medicine.*
VERB **2** If you **label** something, you put a label on it.

laboratory **laboratories**
NOUN a place where scientific experiments are carried out

labour
NOUN **1** hard work
2 In Britain, **Labour**, or the **Labour** Party, is one of the main political parties.

Labrador **Labradors**
NOUN a large dog with short black, golden or chocolate brown hair

labyrinth **labyrinths**
NOUN a complicated series of paths or passages that are difficult to find your way around

lace **laces, lacing, laced**
NOUN **1** a fine, decorated cloth, with a pattern of many holes in it
2 one of the thin pieces of material that are used to fasten shoes
VERB **3** When you **lace** something up, you fix it together by tying a lace.

lack **lacks, lacking, lacked**
NOUN **1** If there is a **lack** of something, there is not enough of it or there is none of it. ● *Despite his **lack** of training, he won the race.*
VERB **2** If someone or something **lacks** something, they do not have it.

lacquer **lacquers**
NOUN thin, clear paint that you put on wood to protect it and make it shiny

ladder **ladders**
NOUN a wooden or metal frame consisting of two long poles with short bars in between. **Ladders** are used for climbing up and down things.

ladle **ladles**
NOUN a long-handled spoon with a deep, round bowl, which you use to serve soup

lady **ladies**
NOUN **1** a polite word for woman
2 In Britain, **Lady** is the title of the wife of a knight or a lord.

ladybird **ladybirds**
NOUN a small, flying beetle with a round body, usually red, patterned with black spots

lag **lags, lagging, lagged**
VERB **1** If a person or a thing **lags** behind, they make slower progress than other people or other things and do not keep up. ● *Don't **lag** behind, or you'll get lost!*
2 If you **lag** pipes or water tanks, you cover them with insulating material to stop heat escaping and prevent freezing.

lager **lagers**
NOUN a kind of light beer

lagoon **lagoons**
NOUN an area of water separated from the sea by reefs or sand

laid
VERB the past tense of **lay**

lain
VERB the past participle of some meanings of *lie* ● *It must have **lain** there for days.*

lair **lairs**
NOUN a place where a wild animal lives

A B C D E F G H I J K L M N O P Q R S T U V W X Y Z

lake **lakes**
NOUN a large area of fresh water surrounded by land

lamb **lambs**
NOUN **1** a young sheep
2 the meat from a lamb

lame
ADJECTIVE **1** Someone who is **lame** has an injured leg and cannot walk easily.
2 A **lame** excuse is unconvincing.
lamely ADVERB **lameness** NOUN

lamp **lamps**
NOUN a device that produces light • *Please turn on the table **lamp** now that it is getting dark.*

lamppost **lampposts**
NOUN a tall column in a street, with a lamp at the top

lance **lances**
NOUN a long spear that was used in the past by soldiers on horseback

land **lands, landing, landed**
NOUN **1** an area of ground • *We camped on the **land** surrounding the castle.*
2 the parts of the earth's surface that are not covered by water
VERB **3** When someone or something **lands** somewhere, they reach the ground after moving through the air.
4 When you **land** somewhere on a plane or a ship, you arrive there.

landing **landings**
NOUN the flat area at the top of a flight of stairs in a building

landlady **landladies**
NOUN a woman who owns a house or small hotel and who lets rooms to people

landlord **landlords**
NOUN **1** a man who owns a house or small hotel and who lets rooms to people
2 a person who looks after a public house
3 someone who owns a large amount of land or houses and lets some of it out in return for rent

landmark **landmarks**
NOUN a noticeable feature in a landscape, that you can use to check your position
• *The tower on the hill is a local **landmark**.*

landscape **landscapes**
NOUN everything you can see when you look across an area of land

lane **lanes**
NOUN **1** a narrow road, especially in the country
2 one of the parallel strips into which a road, a race track or a swimming pool is divided

language **languages**
NOUN a system of words used by a particular group of people to communicate with each other

lantern **lanterns**
NOUN a lamp in a metal frame with glass sides

lap **laps, lapping, lapped**
NOUN **1** the flat area formed by your thighs when you are sitting down
2 one circuit of a running track or racecourse
VERB **3** When water **laps** against something, it gently moves against it in little waves.
4 When an animal **laps** a drink, it uses its tongue to flick the liquid into its mouth.

lapel **lapels**
NOUN the part of the collar that folds back over the front of a jacket or coat

lapse **lapses, lapsing, lapsed**
NOUN **1** a moment of bad behaviour by someone who usually behaves well
2 a period of time that has passed
VERB **3** If you **lapse** into a different way of behaving, you start behaving that way.
• *The class **lapsed** into silence.*
4 If something such as a promise or an agreement **lapses**, it is no longer valid.

laptop **laptops**
NOUN a portable computer small enough to fit on your lap, which is especially useful if you are travelling

lard
NOUN fat from a pig, used in cooking

larder larders
NOUN a room in which you store food, often next to a kitchen

large larger, largest
ADJECTIVE bigger than usual

largely
ADVERB to a great extent ● *It was **largely** a party for his birthday, but we celebrated his sister's exam results too.*

lark larks, larking, larked
NOUN **1** a small, brown bird with a very pleasant song
2 If you do something for a **lark**, you do it in a high-spirited or mischievous way for fun.
VERB **3** If you **lark** about, you enjoy yourself in a high-spirited way.

larva larvae
NOUN an insect after it has hatched from its egg, and before it becomes an adult. A caterpillar is the **larva** of a butterfly.

lasagne
NOUN an Italian dish made with wide, flat sheets of pasta, meat or vegetables and cheese sauce
[from Latin *lasanum* meaning cooking pot]

laser lasers
NOUN **1** a narrow beam of concentrated light produced by a special machine. It is used to cut very hard materials and in some kinds of surgery.
2 the machine that produces the beam of light
[from the first letters of *Light Amplification by Stimulated Emission of Radiation*]

lash lashes, lashing, lashed
NOUN **1** Your **lashes** are the hairs growing on the edge of your eyelids.
VERB **2** If rain **lashes** down, it beats down strongly.
3 If you **lash** things together, you tie them together firmly.

lash out
VERB If you **lash out** at someone you speak to them or strike them harshly.

lasso lassoes or lassos, lassoing, lassoed
NOUN **1** a length of rope looped at one end with a slip-knot, used by cowboys to catch cattle and horses
VERB **2** If you **lasso** an animal, you catch it by throwing the loop of a lasso around its neck.

last lasts, lasting, lasted
ADJECTIVE **1** The **last** person or thing is the one that comes after all the others of the same kind. ● *I was the **last** person to arrive.*
2 The **last** one of a group of things is the only one that remains after all the others have gone. ● *No one wanted the **last** piece of pizza.*
3 The **last** thing or event is the most recent one. ● *The **last** time we went to the beach it rained.*
VERB **4** If something **lasts**, it continues to exist or happen. ● *The sunny weather seems to have **lasted** for ages.*
5 If something **lasts** for a particular time, it remains in good condition for that time.
PHRASE **6** At last means after a long time. ● *The bus arrived **at last**.*

late later, latest
ADVERB OR ADJECTIVE **1** If something or someone is **late**, they arrive after the time that was arranged or expected.
2 If something happens **late**, it happens near the end of something. ● *In the summer it doesn't get dark until **late** in the evening.*

lately
ADVERB If something happened **lately**, it happened recently. ● *We've had a lot of homework **lately**.*

lather
NOUN the frothy foam that you get when you rub soap in water

Latin
NOUN **1** the language of ancient Rome
ADJECTIVE **2** **Latin** peoples and cultures are those of countries such as France, Italy, Spain and Portugal, whose languages developed from Latin.

A
B
C
D
E
F
G
H
I
J
K
L
M
N
O
P
Q
R
S
T
U
V
W
X
Y
Z

latitude latitudes

NOUN The **latitude** of a place is its distance north or south of the equator measured in degrees.

latter

ADJECTIVE OR NOUN **1** You use **latter** to refer to the second of two things you have just mentioned. • *They were eating sandwiches and cakes (the **latter** bought from Mrs Paul's bakery).*

ADJECTIVE **2** The **latter** part of something is the second or later part of it. • *the **latter** stages of the race*

laugh laughs, laughing, laughed

VERB **1** When you **laugh**, you make a noise that shows that you are amused or happy. NOUN **2** the sound you make when you laugh

laughter

NOUN laughing or the sound of people laughing

launch launches, launching, launched

VERB **1** When someone **launches** a ship, they put it into water for the first time. **2** When someone **launches** a rocket, they send it into space.

laundry laundries

NOUN **1** dirty clothes and sheets that are being washed or waiting to be washed **2** a business that washes and irons clothes and sheets

lava

NOUN the very hot, liquid rock that shoots out of a volcano when it erupts, and becomes solid as it cools

lavatory lavatories

NOUN a toilet

lavender

NOUN a small bush with blue flowers that have a strong, pleasant scent

lavish

ADJECTIVE If you are **lavish**, you are very generous with your time, money or gifts.

law laws

NOUN **1** the system of rules developed by the government of a country, that tells people what they are allowed to do **2** one of the rules established by a government, that tells people what they are allowed to do

lawful ADJECTIVE **lawfully** ADVERB

lawn lawns

NOUN a piece of well-kept grass, usually in a park or garden

lawnmower lawnmowers

NOUN a machine for cutting grass

lawyer lawyers

NOUN someone who is trained in the law and who speaks for people in court

lay lays, laying, laid

VERB **1** When you **lay** something somewhere, you place it there. **2** If you **lay** the table, you put things such as knives and forks on the table ready for a meal. **3** When a bird **lays** an egg, an egg comes out of its body.

layer layers

NOUN a single thickness of something underneath or above something else • *There was a thin **layer** of snow on the ground.*

layout layouts

NOUN the pattern in which something is arranged • *The clear **layout** of this book makes it a lot easier to use.*

lazy lazier, laziest

ADJECTIVE If you are **lazy**, you are idle and are unwilling to work.

lazily ADVERB

lead leads, leading, led

Said "leed" VERB **1** If you **lead** someone somewhere, you go in front of them in order to show them the way. **2** If a road or door **leads** somewhere, you can get to that place by following the road or going through the door. **3** If you **lead** in a race or competition, you are at the front. **4** Someone who **leads** a group of people is in charge of them.

NOUN **5** If you take the **lead** in a race or competition, or if you are in the **lead**, you are winning.

6 a length of leather or chain attached to an animal's collar, used for controlling the animal ● *Put the dog on the **lead** when you take him for a walk.*

7 an electric cable for connecting an electrical appliance to a battery or the mains

Said "**led**" NOUN **8** a soft, grey, heavy metal

9 the **lead** in a pencil is the part that makes marks on paper

leader **leaders**

NOUN **1** If you are the **leader** of a group, you are in charge of it.

2 If you are the **leader** in a race or a competition, you are winning.

leaf **leaves**

NOUN **1** a flat structure growing from the stem of a plant. Most plants have green **leaves**.

2 one of the sheets of paper in a book

leafy ADJECTIVE

leaflet **leaflets**

NOUN a piece of paper or thin booklet with information or advertisements

league **leagues**

NOUN a group of people, clubs or countries that have joined together for a particular purpose or because they share a common interest

leak **leaks, leaking, leaked**

VERB **1** If a container or other object **leaks**, it has a hole through which gas or liquid escapes.

NOUN **2** If a container or other object has a **leak**, it has a hole through which gas or liquid escapes.

lean **leans, leaning, leant** or **leaned; leaner, leanest**

VERB **1** When you **lean** in a particular direction, you bend your body in that direction. ● *She **leant** out of the window.*

2 When you **lean** on something, you rest your body against it for support. ● *He was **leaning** on the railing.*

3 If you **lean** something somewhere, you place it there so that its weight is supported. ● *He **leaned** his bike against the wall.*

ADJECTIVE **4** If meat is **lean**, it does not have much fat.

✎ You can write either *leant* or *leaned* as the past form of *lean*.

leap **leaps, leaping, leapt** or **leaped**

VERB **1** If you **leap** somewhere, you jump a long distance or high in the air.

NOUN **2** a jump over a long distance or high in the air

leap year **leap years**

NOUN A **leap year** has 366 days instead of 365, with an extra day in February. It occurs every four years.

learn **learns, learning, learnt** or **learned**

VERB When you **learn** something, you gain knowledge or a skill by practice or by being taught. ● *He's **learning** to play the piano.*

✎ You can write either *learnt* or *learned* as the past form of *learn*.

lease **leases**

NOUN A **lease** is an agreement that lets someone use a house or a flat in return for rent.

least

NOUN **1** the smallest possible amount of something

ADJECTIVE OR ADVERB **2** a superlative form of *little* ● *He ate the **least** amount of food because he felt ill.*

PHRASE **3** You use **at least** to show that you are referring to the minimum amount of something, and that the true amount may be greater. ● *There were **at least** 500 people at the concert.*

leather

NOUN animal skin that has been specially treated so that it can be used to make shoes, clothes, bags and other things

leave **leaves, leaving, left**

VERB **1** When you **leave** a place or person, you go away from them.

2 If you **leave** something somewhere, you let it stay there, or put it there before you go away. • *I* **left** *my bags in the car.*

3 If you **leave** a job or a school, you stop being a part of it.

4 In arithmetic, when you take one number from another, it **leaves** a third number. For example, if you take 2 from 12, it **leaves** 10.

NOUN **5** holiday time • *I'm going to use my* **leave** *to go abroad this year.*

lecture **lectures**

NOUN a formal talk intended to teach people about a particular subject

led

VERB the past tense of **lead**

ledge **ledges**

NOUN a narrow shelf on the side of a cliff or rock face, or on the outside of a building, directly under a window

leek **leeks**

NOUN a long vegetable of the onion family, that is white at one end and has green leaves at the other

left

VERB **1** the past tense of **leave**

NOUN **2** one of the two opposite directions, sides or positions. The **left** is the side of a page that you begin reading on in English.

ANTONYM: right

ADJECTIVE OR ADVERB **3** on or towards the **left** of something • *a cut over his* **left** *eye*

ANTONYM: right

ADJECTIVE **4** If a certain amount of something is **left** or **left over**, it remains when the rest has gone. • *They have two games* **left** *to play.*

leftovers

PLURAL NOUN the bits of uneaten food that are left at the end of a meal

leg **legs**

NOUN **1** one of the long parts of a human or other animal's body that they stand on and walk with

2 The **legs** of a pair of trousers are the parts that cover your legs.

3 The **legs** of a table or chair are the parts that rest on the floor and support it.

4 A **leg** of a journey or a sports match is one part of it. • *The first* **leg** *of the race was very hard work.*

knee, calf, shin, ankle

legacy **legacies**

NOUN property or money that is given to someone in the will of a person who has died

legal

ADJECTIVE relating to the law

legend **legends**

NOUN a very old and popular story

legible

ADJECTIVE Writing that is **legible** is clear enough to be read.

ANTONYM: illegible

legibly ADVERB **legibility** NOUN

legislation

NOUN a law or group of laws made by a government

legitimate

ADJECTIVE If something is **legitimate** it is allowed by law, or is accepted as fair by most people.

legitimately ADVERB

leisure

NOUN time when you do not have to work and can do things that you enjoy

lemon **lemons**

NOUN a yellow citrus fruit with a sour taste

lemonade

NOUN a clear, sweet drink made from lemons, water and sugar. **Lemonade** is often fizzy.

lend lends, lending, lent

VERB **1** If you **lend** something to someone, you let them have it for a period of time.
2 If a person or bank **lends** you money, they give you money and you agree to pay it back later, usually with interest.

length lengths

NOUN **1** The **length** of something is the distance from one end to the other. • *We walked the **length** of the street.*
2 The **length** of an event or activity is the amount of time it continues. • *The film is over two hours in **length**.*

lengthen lengthens, lengthening, lengthened

VERB If you **lengthen** something, you make it longer.
ANTONYM: shorten

lengthy lengthier, lengthiest

ADJECTIVE Something that is **lengthy** lasts for a long time. • *The speech was rather **lengthy**.*

lens lenses

NOUN a thin, curved piece of glass, plastic or other transparent material that makes things appear larger or clearer • *a camera **lens***

lent

VERB the past tense and past participle of **lend**

Lent

NOUN the forty-day period before Easter when some Christians fast or give up something that they enjoy

lentil lentils

NOUN **Lentils** are small, dried, red or brown seeds that are cooked and eaten in soups, stews and curries.

leopard leopards

NOUN a large wild cat, with yellow fur and black or brown spots, found in Africa and Asia

leotard leotards

*Said "**lee**-uh-tard"* NOUN a tight-fitting garment that covers the body rather like a swimming costume, which is worn for dancing or exercise

less

ADJECTIVE OR ADVERB **1** a smaller amount of something, or to a smaller extent • *It is **less** than three weeks until we go back to school.*
ANTONYM: more
2 a comparative form of *little*
PREPOSITION **3** You use **less** to show that one number or amount is to be subtracted from another. • *You can have your pocket money, **less** the money you borrowed last week.*

> Use *less* to talk about things that can't be counted and *fewer* for things that can be counted: *less time; fewer apples.*

lesson lessons

NOUN **1** a fixed period of time during which people are taught something by a teacher
2 an experience that makes you understand something important

let lets, letting, let

VERB **1** If you **let** someone do something, you allow them to do it.
2 If someone **lets** a house or flat that they own, they allow others to use it in return for payment.

lethal

ADJECTIVE Something that is **lethal** can kill you. • *A gun is a **lethal** weapon.*
[from Latin *letum* meaning death]

let's

VERB a contraction of *let us*

letter letters

NOUN **1** a message written on paper and sent to someone, usually through the post
2 one of the written symbols that go together to make words

letter box letter boxes; also spelt letter-box

NOUN **1** an oblong gap in a front door, through which letters are delivered
2 a large, metal container in the street or at a post office, for posting letters

a
b
c
d
e
f
g
h
i
j
k
l
m
n
o
p
q
r
s
t
u
v
w
x
y
z

A
B
C
D
E
F
G
H
I
J
K
L
M
N
O
P
Q
R
S
T
U
V
W
X
Y
Z

lettering
NOUN You use **lettering** to describe writing that is done in a certain way. • *The poster had large black **lettering**.*

lettuce lettuces
NOUN a vegetable with large, green leaves that you eat in salads

leukaemia; also spelt leukemia
Said "loo-**kee**-mee-a" NOUN a serious illness that affects the blood
[from Greek *leukos* meaning white and *haima* meaning blood]

level levels, levelling, levelled
NOUN **1** the height, position or amount of something • *This is the lowest **level** of rainfall for years.*
2 a standard or grade of achievement • *Now that I have passed this piano exam, I will move on to the next **level**.*
SYNONYMS: grade, stage
ADJECTIVE **3** A surface that is **level** is completely flat.
4 If one thing is **level** with another, it is at the same height or position.
VERB **5** If you **level** something, you make it flat.

level crossing level crossings
NOUN a place where traffic is allowed to drive across a railway track

lever levers
NOUN **1** a handle on a machine that you pull in order to make the machine work
2 a bar that you wedge underneath a heavy object and press down on to make the object move

liable
ADJECTIVE **1** Something that is **liable** to happen will probably happen. • *Britain is **liable** to be cold in January.*
2 If someone is **liable** for something such as a crime or a debt, they are legally responsible for it.
liability NOUN

liar liars
NOUN a person who tells lies

liberal
ADJECTIVE **1** If someone is **liberal**, they are tolerant of other people's behaviour and opinions.
2 If you are **liberal** with something, you are generous with it.
liberally ADVERB

liberty
NOUN the freedom to do what you want to do and go where you want to go

librarian librarians
NOUN a person who works in, or is in charge of, a library

library libraries
NOUN a building in which books are kept, especially a public building from which people can borrow books

There is an *r* after the *b* in *library*.

licence licences
NOUN an official document that gives you permission to do, use or own something • *You have to pass a test before you receive a full driving **licence**.*

The noun *licence* ends in *ce*.

license licenses, licensing, licensed
VERB If someone **licenses** an activity, they give official permission for it to be carried out.

The verb *license* ends in *se*.

lichen lichens
Said "**lie**-kun" NOUN a green or greeny-grey mossy growth, found on rocks, trees and walls

lick licks, licking, licked
VERB If you **lick** something, you move your tongue over it. • *I **licked** the stamp and stuck it to the envelope.*

lid lids
NOUN a cover for a box, jar or other container

lie¹ lies, lying, lay, lain
VERB **1** If someone or something **lies** somewhere, they rest there in a flat position.
2 You use **lie** to say where something is or what its position is. • *The village **lies** to the east of the river.*

✎ The past tense of this verb *lie* is *lay*. Do not confuse it with the verb *lay* meaning 'put'.

lie² **lies, lying, lied**

VERB **1** If you **lie**, you say something that you know is not true. ● He **lied** about his age.

NOUN **2** something you say that you know is not true

lieutenant **lieutenants**

Said "lef-**ten**-ant" NOUN a junior officer in the army or navy

life **lives**

NOUN **1** the state of being alive that makes people, animals and plants different from objects

2 your existence from the time you are born until the time you die

lifeboat **lifeboats**

NOUN a boat used for rescuing people who are in danger at sea

life cycle **life cycles**

NOUN the series of changes and developments in the life of a living thing ● *There are several stages in the **life cycle** of a butterfly.*

lifeguard **lifeguards**

NOUN a person whose job is to rescue people who are in difficulty in the sea or in a swimming pool

life jacket **life jackets**

NOUN a sleeveless, inflatable jacket that keeps you afloat in water

lifelike

ADJECTIVE A picture or a sculpture that is **lifelike** looks very real, almost as if it is alive.

SYNONYM: realistic

lifeline **lifelines**

NOUN something that helps you to survive or helps an activity to continue ● *His help was a real **lifeline** to me after I had so many difficulties.*

lifetime **lifetimes**

NOUN the period of time during which you are alive

lift **lifts, lifting, lifted**

VERB **1** If you **lift** something, you move it to a higher position.

NOUN **2** a device that carries people or goods from one floor to another in a building

light **lights, lighting, lighted** or **lit; lighter, lightest**

NOUN **1** the brightness from the sun, moon, fire or lamps, that lets you see things

beam of light

2 a lamp or other device that gives out brightness

ADJECTIVE **3** If it is **light**, there is enough light from the sun to see things.

ANTONYM: dark

4 A **light** colour is pale.

5 A **light** object does not weigh much.

ANTONYM: heavy

VERB **6** If you **light** a fire, you make it start burning.

lighten **lightens, lightening, lightened**

VERB **1** When something **lightens**, it becomes brighter and less dark. ● *After the storm the sky **lightened**.*

2 If you **lighten** a load, you make it less heavy. ● *My case was too heavy, so I **lightened** it by taking out three books.*

lighter **lighters**

NOUN a device for lighting something, such as a fire or a cigarette

lighthouse **lighthouses**

NOUN a tower by the sea, that shines a powerful light to guide ships and warn them of danger

lighting

NOUN The **lighting** in a room or building is the way it is lit.

lightning

NOUN very bright flashes of light you see in the sky, usually during a thunderstorm.

A
B
C
D
E
F
G
H
I
J
K
L
M
N
O
P
Q
R
S
T
U
V
W
X
Y
Z

Lightning is caused by electrical activity in the atmosphere.

light year **light years**
NOUN the distance that light travels in a year, which is about 6 million miles or 9.5 million kilometres

like **likes, liking, liked**
VERB **1** If you **like** someone or something, you find them pleasing.
PREPOSITION **2** If one thing is **like** another, they are similar.

likeable; also spelt **likable**
ADJECTIVE A **likeable** person is pleasant and friendly.

likely **likelier, likeliest**
ADJECTIVE If something is **likely**, it will probably happen or is probably true.

lilac **lilacs**
NOUN **1** a small tree with sweet-smelling clusters of mauve, pink or white flowers
2 a pale mauve colour

lily **lilies**
NOUN a plant with trumpet-shaped flowers of various colours

limb **limbs**
NOUN Your **limbs** are your arms and legs.

lime **limes**
NOUN **1** a small, green, citrus fruit, rather like a lemon
2 a bright green colour
3 a chemical substance used in cement or as a fertiliser

limerick **limericks**
NOUN an amusing nonsense poem of five lines

limit **limits, limiting, limited**
NOUN **1** the largest or smallest amount of something that is possible or allowed
• The speed **limit** on this road is 30 mph.
VERB **2** If you **limit** something, you restrict it to a certain amount or number. • The children were **limited** to two biscuits each.
limited ADJECTIVE

limousine **limousines**
NOUN a large, luxurious car, usually driven by a chauffeur

limp **limps, limping, limped; limper, limpest**
VERB **1** If you **limp**, you walk in an uneven way because you have hurt your leg or foot.
NOUN **2** an uneven way of walking • While her leg was in plaster she walked with a **limp**.
ADJECTIVE **3** Something that is **limp** is soft or weak.

limpet **limpets**
NOUN a small shellfish with a pointed shell, that attaches itself very firmly to rocks

line **lines, lining, lined**
NOUN **1** a long, thin mark
2 a number of people or things that are arranged in a row
3 a long piece of string or wire • a washing **line**
4 a number of words together, for example the **lines** in a play are the words that an actor has to speak • This is my favourite **line** in the poem.
5 a railway or railway track
VERB **6** If people or things **line** something, they make a border or edge along it.
• Crowds **lined** the streets to see the Queen.

linen
NOUN **1** a type of cloth made from a plant called flax
2 household goods made of cloth, such as sheets and tablecloths

liner **liners**
NOUN a large passenger ship that makes long sea journeys

linesman **linesmen**
NOUN an official at a sports match who watches the lines of the field or court and decides if the ball has gone outside them

linger **lingers, lingering, lingered**
VERB If someone or something **lingers**, they stay for a long time. • The smell **lingered** in the kitchen.
lingering ADJECTIVE

linguist **linguists**
NOUN someone who studies foreign languages and can speak them well

lining linings
NOUN any material that is used to line the inside of something • *There is a fleece **lining** in this jacket.*

link links, linking, linked
NOUN **1** one of the rings in a chain
2 a relationship or connection between two things • *There is a **link** between the weather and the clothes we wear.*
3 a physical connection between two things or places • *There is a rail **link** between the two cities.*
VERB **4** If someone or something **links** people, places, or things, they join them together. • *They want to **link** the village to the town with a better road.*

lion lions
NOUN a large member of the cat family that is found in Africa. Male **lions** have long hair on their head and neck, called a mane.

lioness lionesses
NOUN a female lion

lip lips
NOUN Your **lips** are the two outer edges of your mouth.

lipstick lipsticks
NOUN a cosmetic for colouring the lips, usually in the form of a small stick

liquid liquids
NOUN a substance such as water, which is neither a gas nor a solid and which can be poured. A **liquid** always takes the shape of the container it is in.

liquidizer liquidizers
NOUN an electric machine used for making food into liquid • *Dad put strawberries, bananas and milk in the **liquidizer** and mixed us a delicious milkshake.*

liquorice or **licorice**
NOUN **1** a root used to flavour sweets
2 sweets flavoured with liquorice

lisp lisps, lisping, lisped
NOUN **1** Someone who has a **lisp** pronounces the sounds s and z like *th*.
VERB **2** If someone **lisps**, they speak with a lisp.

list lists, listing, listed
NOUN **1** a set of words or items written one after the other • *a shopping **list***
VERB **2** If you **list** a number of things, you write them or say them one after another.

listen listens, listening, listened
VERB **1** If you **listen** to someone, you pay attention to what they are saying.
2 If you **listen** to something, you pay attention to its sound. • *She enjoys **listening** to music.*

lit
VERB the past tense and past participle of **light**

literacy
NOUN the ability to read and write

literally
ADVERB You use **literally** to emphasize that what you are saying is actually true, even though it seems unlikely. • *We **literally** almost died of thirst.*

literate
ADJECTIVE If you are **literate**, you are able to read and write.
literacy NOUN

literature
NOUN Novels, plays and poetry are referred to as **literature**.
[from Latin *litteratura* meaning writing]

litre litres
NOUN a unit for measuring liquid (l) equal to 1000 millilitres or about 1.76 pints

litter litters, littering, littered
NOUN **1** rubbish in the street and other public places
2 baby animals born at the same time to the same mother
VERB **3** If things **litter** a place, they are scattered all over it. • *Paper **littered** the pavement.*

little less, lesser, least
ADJECTIVE **1** small in size or amount • *Stay a **little** longer.*
ANTONYMS: big, large
ADVERB OR PRONOUN **2** not much • *I had very **little** money left.*

a
b
c
d
e
f
g
h
i
j
k
l
m
n
o
p
q
r
s
t
u
v
w
x
y
z

A
B
C
D
E
F
G
H
I
J
K
L
M
N
O
P
Q
R
S
T
U
V
W
X
Y
Z

NOUN **3** A **little** is a small amount or degree of something. • *He showed me a little of his work.*

live lives, living, lived

Rhymes with "give" VERB **1** If someone or something **lives**, they are alive.
2 If you **live** in a place, that is where your home is. • *He lives with his parents.*
3 The way someone **lives** is the kind of life they have. • *We live quite simply.*
Rhymes with "five" ADJECTIVE **4 Live** television or radio is broadcast while the event is taking place.
5 Live animals or plants are alive, rather than dead or artificial.

lively livelier, liveliest

ADJECTIVE full of energy and enthusiasm

liver livers

NOUN a large organ in your body that cleans your blood and stores substances such as vitamins and minerals

living

ADJECTIVE **1** If someone or something is **living**, they are alive.
NOUN **2** Someone who works for a **living**, works to earn the money needed in order to live. • *He makes a living by selling cars.*

liver

living room living rooms

NOUN a room in a house where you sit and relax, doing such things as watching television and reading

lizard lizards

NOUN a reptile with short legs and a tail

llama llamas

NOUN a South American animal that looks rather like a small camel with thick hair and no hump

load loads, loading, loaded

VERB **1** If you **load** a vehicle or container, you put things into it.
2 When you **load** a camera, you put film into it.

NOUN **3** something large or heavy that is being carried • *a tractor with a big load of hay*
4 INFORMAL A **load** of something, or **loads** of something, means a lot of it. • *He's got loads of CDs.*

loaf loaves

NOUN a large piece of bread in a shape that can be cut into slices

loan loans, loaning, loaned

NOUN **1** a sum of money that you borrow
VERB **2** If you **loan** something to someone, you lend it to them.

loathe loathes, loathing, loathed

VERB If you **loathe** someone or something, you feel a very strong dislike for them.
loathing NOUN **loathsome** ADJECTIVE

lobster lobsters

NOUN an edible shellfish with two front claws and eight legs

local locals

ADJECTIVE **1** existing in or belonging to the area where you live • *the local newspaper*
NOUN **2** someone who lives in and comes from a particular area

locality localities

NOUN a small area of a country or a city • *Golden eagles can be seen in certain localities in Scotland.*

locate locates, locating, located

VERB **1** If you **locate** someone or something, you find out where they are.
2 If something is **located** in a place, it is in that place.

location locations

NOUN the place where something is found or where something happens • *She couldn't remember the exact location of the church.*

loch lochs

NOUN In Scottish English, a **loch** is a lake. • *They say there is a monster in Loch Ness.*

lock locks, locking, locked

VERB **1** If you **lock** something, you fasten it with a key.

2 If you **lock** something in a place, you put it there and fasten the lock. • *They locked the money in the safe.*
NOUN **3** a device that prevents something from being opened except with a key • *He heard a key in the lock.*

locker lockers
NOUN a small cupboard for someone's personal belongings, for example in a changing room

locket lockets
NOUN a small piece of jewellery worn on a chain around the neck, which opens so that you can put a small photograph inside

locomotive locomotives
NOUN a railway engine

locust locusts
NOUN an insect like a large grasshopper, that travels in huge swarms and eats crops

loft lofts
NOUN the space immediately under the roof of a house, often used for storing things

log logs
NOUN **1** a thick piece of wood from a branch or trunk of a tree, that has fallen or been cut off
2 an official written account of what happens each day • *The captain wrote each day's events in the ship's log.*

logic
NOUN a way of reasoning that makes sense
logical ADJECTIVE **logically** ADVERB

logo logos
NOUN the special design that is put on all the products of an organization

loiter loiters, loitering, loitered
VERB If you **loiter** in a place, you stand around without going very far or doing very much. • *After school they loitered round the shops.*

lollipop lollipops
NOUN a hard sweet on the end of a stick [from Romani *lolli* meaning red and *pobbel* meaning apple]

lolly lollies
NOUN **1** a lollipop
2 a flavoured ice or ice cream on a stick

lonely lonelier, loneliest
ADJECTIVE **1** If you are **lonely**, you are unhappy because you are alone.
2 A **lonely** place is one that very few people visit.

long longer, longest; longs, longing, longed
ADJECTIVE **1** continuing for a great amount of time • *There had been no rain for a long time.*
ADVERB **2** You use **long** to talk about amounts of time. • *How long is the film?*
ADJECTIVE **3** great in length or distance • *It's a long way home.*
4 You use **long** to talk about the distance that something measures from one end to the other.
PHRASE **5** If something **no longer** happens, it used to happen but does not happen now.
VERB **6** If you **long** for something to happen, or if you **long** to do it, you want it to happen very much.

long division long divisions
NOUN a method of dividing one large number by another one, where you write out all the stages instead of doing them in your head or on a calculator

longitude longitudes
NOUN a position measured in degrees east or west of an imaginary line passing through Greenwich in London

look looks, looking, looked
VERB **1** If you **look** at something, you turn your eyes towards it so that you can see it.
2 If you **look** for someone or something, you try to find them.
3 If you describe the way that something **looks**, you are describing its appearance. • *He looked a bit pale.*
NOUN **4** If you take a **look** at something, you look at it. • *Lucy took a last look in the mirror.*
SYNONYM: glance
5 The **look** on your face is the expression on it.

look after

VERB If you **look after** someone or something, you take care of them.

look forward

VERB If you **look forward** to something, you want it to happen because you think you will enjoy it.

look out

PHRASE You say **look out** to warn someone of danger. • *Look out! There's a car coming.*

lookout lookouts

NOUN **1** someone who is watching for danger, or a place where someone watches for danger

PHRASE **2** If you are **on the lookout** for something, you are watching or waiting for it to happen.

loom looms, looming, loomed

NOUN **1** a machine for weaving cloth

VERB **2** If something **looms** in front of you, it suddenly appears as a tall, unclear and sometimes frightening shape. • *A monster loomed out of the darkness.*

3 If a situation or event is **looming**, it is likely to happen soon and is rather worrying. • *A storm is looming on the horizon.*

loop loops, looping, looped

NOUN **1** a curved or circular shape in something such as a piece of string or wire

VERB **2** If you **loop** rope or string around an object, you place it in a loop around the object. • *He looped the rope over the horse's neck.*

loose looser, loosest

Said "**looss**" ADJECTIVE **1** not firmly held or fixed in place • *a loose tooth*

2 not tight • *a loose jacket*

ADVERB **3** If people or animals break **loose**, or are set **loose**, they are released after they have been held back or tied up.

Do not confuse *loose* with *lose*.

loot loots, looting, looted

VERB **1** If someone **loots** shops and

houses, they steal goods from them, especially during a riot or war.

NOUN **2** stolen money or goods

lopsided

ADJECTIVE Something that is **lopsided** is uneven because one side is different from the other, for example one side is heavier or larger.

lord lords

NOUN In Britain, **Lord** is a title used in front of the names of some men.

lorry lorries

NOUN a large vehicle for transporting goods by road

lose loses, losing, lost

Said "**looz**" VERB **1** If you **lose** something, you cannot find it, or you no longer have it because it has been taken from you.

• *He lost his place in the team.*

2 If you **lose** a fight or an argument, you are beaten.

Do not confuse *lose* with *loose*.

loss losses

NOUN The **loss** of something is the fact of having lost it or of having less of it.

lost

VERB **1** the past tense and past participle of **lose**

ADJECTIVE **2** If you are **lost**, you do not know where you are.

3 If something is **lost**, you cannot find it.

lot lots

NOUN **1** a large amount of something

• *a lot of children*

2 very much or very often • *I miss him a lot.*

3 the whole of something • *He had a whole packet of biscuits and ate the lot.*

lotion lotions

NOUN a liquid that you put on your skin to protect or soften it • *suntan lotion*

lottery lotteries

NOUN a way of raising money by selling tickets and giving prizes to people who have winning tickets, which are selected at random

loud **louder, loudest**
ADJECTIVE A **loud** noise produces a lot of sound.
loudly ADVERB

loudspeaker **loudspeakers**
NOUN a piece of electrical equipment that produces the sound in things such as radios, telephones and CD players

lounge **lounges, lounging, lounged**
NOUN **1** a room in a house, hotel or airport where people can sit and relax
VERB **2** If you **lounge** around, you lean against something or lie around in a lazy way.

louse **lice**
NOUN a small insect that lives on people's bodies

lout **louts**
NOUN a young man who behaves in a rude or aggressive way
loutish ADJECTIVE

love **loves, loving, loved**
VERB **1** If you **love** someone or something, you have strong feelings of affection for them.
2 If you would **love** to do something, you want very much to do it.
NOUN **3** a strong feeling of affection for someone or something
PHRASE **4** If you are **in love** with someone, you feel strongly attracted to them romantically.

lovely **lovelier, loveliest**
ADJECTIVE very beautiful, attractive, pleasant or enjoyable • We had a **lovely** day out.

low **lower, lowest**
ADJECTIVE OR ADVERB **1** Something that is **low** is close to the ground.
ANTONYM: high
ADJECTIVE **2** below average in value or amount • The temperature was **low** for the time of year.
ANTONYM: high

lower **lowers, lowering, lowered**
VERB **1** If you **lower** something, you move it downwards. • She **lowered** the bucket into the well.

ADJECTIVE **2** The **lower** of two things is the bottom one. • the **lower** deck of the bus

lower-case
ADJECTIVE **Lower-case** letters are small letters, not capital letters.

loyal
ADJECTIVE If you are **loyal**, you are firm in your friendship or support for someone or something.

lozenge **lozenges**
NOUN **1** a small sweet with medicine in it, that you can suck if you have a sore throat or a cough
2 a diamond shape, like a rhombus
See **rhombus**

lubricate **lubricates, lubricating, lubricated**
VERB If someone **lubricates** something like a machine, they put oil or grease on to it so that it moves smoothly.
[from Latin lubricus meaning slippery]
lubrication NOUN **lubricant** NOUN

luck
NOUN **1** something that happens by chance • We had good **luck** with the weather. • It was bad **luck** that I lost the game of Monopoly.
PHRASE **2** You say **good luck** to someone when you are wishing them success.

lucky **luckier, luckiest**
ADJECTIVE Someone who is **lucky** has a lot of good luck.
luckily ADVERB

luggage
NOUN Your **luggage** is the bags and suitcases that you take with you when you travel.

lukewarm
ADJECTIVE slightly warm

lull **lulls, lulling, lulled**
NOUN **1** a pause in something, or a short time when it is quiet and calm

a
b
c
d
e
f
g
h
i
j
k
l
m
n
o
p
q
r
s
t
u
v
w
x
y
z

VERB **2** If you **lull** someone, you calm them and make them feel safe.

lullaby **lullabies**
NOUN a song used for sending a baby or child to sleep

lumber **lumbers, lumbering, lumbered**
NOUN **1** wood that has been roughly cut up
VERB **2** If you **lumber** around, you move heavily and clumsily.

luminous
ADJECTIVE Something that is **luminous** glows in the dark without being hot.
luminously ADVERB   **luminosity** NOUN

lump **lumps**
NOUN a solid piece of something

lunar
ADJECTIVE relating to the moon ● The **lunar** *module landed safely on the moon.* [from Latin *luna* meaning moon]

lunch **lunches**
NOUN a meal eaten in the middle of the day

lung **lungs**
NOUN Your **lungs** are the two organs inside your chest that you breathe with.

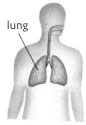

lung

lurch **lurches, lurching, lurched**
VERB **1** If someone or something **lurches**, they make a sudden, jerky movement.
PHRASE **2** If someone leaves you **in the lurch**, they leave you in a difficult or dangerous situation, instead of helping you.

lure **lures, luring, lured**
VERB If you **lure** someone or something, you tempt them into going somewhere or doing something. ● He **lured** the cat back *into the house with some milk.*

lurk **lurks, lurking, lurked**
VERB If someone **lurks** somewhere, they hide there and wait.

lush **lusher, lushest**
ADJECTIVE In a **lush** field or garden, the grass or plants are healthy and growing thickly.

lute **lutes**
NOUN an old-fashioned, stringed musical instrument that is plucked like a guitar

luxury **luxuries**
NOUN **1** great comfort, especially among expensive and beautiful surroundings
2 A **luxury** is something that you would like to have but do not need, and is usually expensive.

lying
VERB the present participle of **lie**

lyrics
PLURAL NOUN The **lyrics** of a song are the words.

A B C D E F G H I J K **L** M N O P Q R S T U V W X Y Z

Mm

macaroni
NOUN short, hollow tubes of pasta
[an Italian word; from Greek *makaria*
meaning food made from barley]

machine **machines**
NOUN a piece of equipment designed to do
a particular job. It is usually powered by
an engine or by electricity. • *a washing
machine*

machine gun **machine guns**
NOUN a gun that works automatically,
firing a continuous stream of bullets very
quickly

machinery
NOUN machines in general • *farm
machinery* • *factory machinery*

mackintosh **mackintoshes**
NOUN a raincoat made from waterproof
cloth

mad **madder, maddest**
ADJECTIVE **1** Someone who is **mad** has a
mental illness that causes them to
behave in strange ways.
2 If you describe someone as **mad**, you
mean that they are very foolish.
3 INFORMAL Someone who is **mad** is angry.
PHRASE **4** If you are **mad about** someone
or something, you like them very much.
• *She had always been **mad about** football.*
madly ADVERB **madness** NOUN

made
VERB the past tense and past participle
of **make**

magazine **magazines**
NOUN a weekly or monthly publication
containing articles and photographs

maggot **maggots**
NOUN the larva of some kinds of fly.

Maggots look like small, fat worms.
maggoty ADJECTIVE

magic
NOUN **1** In fairy stories, **magic** is a special
power that can make impossible things
happen.
2 the art of performing tricks to entertain
people
magical ADJECTIVE

magician **magicians**
NOUN **1** a person who performs tricks that
seem like magic to entertain people
2 In fairy stories, a **magician** is a man
with magic powers.

magistrate **magistrates**
NOUN an official who acts as a judge in a
law court that deals with less serious
crimes

magnet **magnets**
NOUN a piece of iron or steel that attracts
other objects made of iron or steel
towards it.
Magnets can
also push
away, or repel,
other
magnets.

magnetic
ADJECTIVE Something that is **magnetic** is
attracted towards a magnet. Only iron,
steel, nickel and cobalt are **magnetic**.

magnificent
ADJECTIVE extremely beautiful or impressive
SYNONYMS: imposing, splendid
[from Latin *magnificus* meaning great in
deeds]

magnify **magnifies, magnifying,
magnified**
VERB When a microscope or lens
magnifies something, it makes it appear
bigger than it actually is.
magnification NOUN

magnifying glass **magnifying
glasses**
NOUN a glass lens that magnifies things,
making them appear bigger than they
really are

A
B
C
D
E
F
G
H
I
J
K
L
M
N
O
P
Q
R
S
T
U
V
W
X
Y
Z

magpie **magpies**
NOUN a large, black-and-white bird with a long tail

mahogany
NOUN a hard, reddish-brown wood used for making furniture

maid **maids**
NOUN a female servant

maiden name **maiden names**
NOUN the surname a woman had before she married

mail **mails, mailing, mailed**
NOUN **1** the letters and parcels delivered to you by the post office
2 same as **e-mail**
VERB **3** If you **mail** a letter, you send it by post.
4 If you **mail** someone, you send them an e-mail.
[from Old French *male* meaning bag]

maim **maims, maiming, maimed**
VERB To **maim** someone is to injure them very badly for life.
maimed ADJECTIVE

main **mains**
ADJECTIVE **1** most important or largest • *My main interest is music.*
SYNONYMS: chief, major, principal
NOUN **2** The **mains** are the large pipes or cables that carry gas, water or electricity to a building.

mainland
NOUN the main part of a country or continent, not including the islands around it

mainly
ADVERB mostly, chiefly or usually • *We eat mainly vegetarian food.*

maintain **maintains, maintaining, maintained**
VERB **1** If you **maintain** something, you keep it going at a particular rate or level. • *You will need to maintain this level of fitness if you want to take part in the finals.*
2 If you **maintain** a machine or a building, you keep it in good condition.

3 If you **maintain** a belief or an opinion, you have it and state it clearly.

maize
NOUN a tall plant that produces sweetcorn

majesty **majesties**
NOUN **1** You say **His Majesty** when you are talking about a king, and **Her Majesty** when you are talking about a queen.
2 the quality of being dignified and impressive
majestic ADJECTIVE

major **majors**
ADJECTIVE **1** more important or more serious than other things • *She has a major role in the school play.*
ANTONYM: minor
NOUN **2** an army officer of the rank immediately above captain

majority **majorities**
NOUN more than half of a group • *The majority of the passengers became ill.*

make **makes, making, made**
VERB **1** If you **make** something, you create or produce it. • *This is the cake I made yesterday.*
2 If you **make** someone or something do something, you force them to do it or cause it to happen. • *Her mother made her do her homework every night.*
3 If you **make** a promise to do something, you say you will definitely do it.
4 Two amounts added together **make** a sum. • *3 and 5 make 8.*
5 If you **make** a phone call, you use the telephone to speak to someone.
NOUN **6** the name of the product of a particular manufacturer • *What make is your bicycle?*

make-believe
NOUN a fantasy of pretend or imaginary things

make-up
NOUN coloured creams and powders that women and actors put on their faces

malaria
NOUN a serious tropical disease, caught from mosquitoes, that causes fever and shivering

male males
NOUN **1** a person or animal belonging to the gender that cannot have babies
ANTONYM: female
ADJECTIVE **2** concerning or affecting men rather than women
ANTONYM: female

malevolent
Said "mal-**lev**-oh-lent" ADJECTIVE
1 Malevolent people want to cause harm or do evil things.
2 A **malevolent** act is cruel and spiteful.

malfunction malfunctions, malfunctioning, malfunctioned
VERB If a machine **malfunctions**, it fails to work properly.

malicious
ADJECTIVE **Malicious** talk or behaviour is intended to harm someone.

mall malls
NOUN a sheltered place with cafés, shops and restaurants • *a shopping mall*

mallet mallets
NOUN a wooden hammer with a square head

malnutrition
NOUN a condition resulting from not eating enough healthy food or not having enough to eat

mammal mammals
NOUN an animal that gives birth to live babies and feeds its young with milk from the mother's body. Human beings, dogs and whales are all **mammals**.
[from Latin *mamma* meaning breast]
mammalian ADJECTIVE

mammoth mammoths
ADJECTIVE **1** very large indeed
NOUN **2** a huge animal that looked like a hairy elephant with long tusks. **Mammoths** became extinct a long time ago.

man men; mans, manning, manned
NOUN **1** an adult, male human being
ANTONYM: woman
2 Human beings, both male and female, are sometimes referred to as **man**.
• *Primitive man lived in caves.*
VERB **3** If you **man** something, you are in charge of it or you operate it. • *Can you man the bookstall?*

manage manages, managing, managed
VERB **1** If you **manage** to do something, you succeed in doing it even if it is difficult.
• *We managed to find somewhere to sit.*
2 If someone **manages** an organization or business, they are responsible for controlling it.

management
NOUN **1** the controlling and organizing of a business
2 the people who control an organization

manager managers
NOUN a man or woman who is responsible for running a business or organization

mane manes
NOUN long hair growing from the neck of a lion or a horse

manger mangers
NOUN a feeding box in a barn or stable

mangle mangles, mangling, mangled
VERB **1** If you **mangle** something, you crush or twist it out of shape.
NOUN **2** an old-fashioned piece of equipment consisting of two large rollers, for squeezing water out of wet clothes

mango mangoes or mangos
NOUN a sweet yellow fruit that grows in tropical climates

mankind
NOUN used to refer to all human beings
• *Pollution is a threat to mankind.*

manner manners
NOUN **1** the way you do something or behave
PLURAL NOUN **2** If you have good **manners**, you behave very politely.

a b c d e f g h i j k l m n o p q r s t u v w x y z

239

manoeuvre **manoeuvres, manoeuvring, manoeuvred**
Said "man-**noo**-ver" VERB **1** If you **manoeuvre** something into place, you move it there skilfully. • *Mum* **manoeuvred** *the car into the small parking space.*
NOUN **2** A **manoeuvre** is a clever thing that you do or say in order to make something happen the way you want it to.

manor **manors**
NOUN a large country house with land, especially one that was built in the Middle Ages

mansion **mansions**
NOUN a very large house

manslaughter
NOUN the accidental killing of a person

mantelpiece **mantelpieces**
NOUN a shelf over a fireplace

manual **manuals**
ADJECTIVE **1** **Manual** work involves physical strength or skill with your hands, rather than mental skill.
2 **Manual** equipment is operated by hand rather than being automatic or operated by electricity or a motor. • *a* **manual** *whisk*
NOUN **3** a book that tells you how to use a machine • *an instruction* **manual**
[from Latin *manus* meaning hand]
manually ADVERB

manufacture **manufactures, manufacturing, manufactured**
VERB **1** If someone **manufactures** goods, they make them in a factory.
NOUN **2** The **manufacture** of goods is the making of them in a factory.

manure
NOUN animal dung used to improve the soil

manuscript **manuscripts**
NOUN a handwritten or typed copy of a book, play, or piece of music before it is printed
[from Latin *manus* meaning hand and *scribere* meaning to write]

many
ADJECTIVE OR PRONOUN **1** If there are **many** people or things, there are a large number of them.
2 You use **many** to talk about how great a number or quantity is. • *How* **many** *tickets do you need?*

map **maps**
NOUN a detailed drawing of an area of land, showing its shape and features as it would appear if you saw it from above

maple **maples**
NOUN a tree that has large leaves with five points

marathon **marathons**
NOUN a race in which people run 26 miles along roads
[named after *Marathon*, a place from which a messenger ran more than 20 miles to Athens, bringing news of a victory in 490 BC]

marble
NOUN a very hard, cold stone that is often polished to show the coloured patterns in it

march **marches, marching, marched**
NOUN **1** an organized protest in which a large group of people walk somewhere together
VERB **2** When soldiers **march**, they walk with quick regular steps as a group.
NOUN **3** music with a strong beat for marching to

March
NOUN the third month of the year. **March** has 31 days.
[from Latin *Martius* month of Mars, the Roman god of war]

mare **mares**
NOUN an adult female horse

margarine
NOUN a soft substance made from vegetable oil and animal fats, and used like butter

margin **margins**
NOUN **1** the blank space at the top and bottom and on each side of a written or printed page
2 If you win a race or a competition by a large or small **margin**, you win it by a large or small amount.

marina **marinas**
NOUN a harbour for pleasure boats and yachts

marine **marines**
NOUN **1** a soldier who is trained for duties at sea
ADJECTIVE **2** relating to or involving the sea, and the animals and plants that live in the sea

mark **marks, marking, marked**
NOUN **1** a small stain or damaged area on a surface
2 a score given to a student for homework or for an exam
3 a written or printed symbol
VERB **4** If something **marks** a surface, it stains or damages it in some way.
5 When a teacher **marks** a student's work, they decide how good it is and give it a mark.
6 If you **mark** the opposing player in a team game such as hockey or netball, you stay close to them and prevent them from getting the ball.

market **markets, marketing, marketed**
NOUN **1** a place where goods are bought and sold, usually outdoors
VERB **2** If someone **markets** a product, they sell it in an organized way.

marmalade
NOUN a type of jam made from oranges or lemons

maroon
NOUN OR ADJECTIVE dark reddish-purple

marquee **marquees**
NOUN a very large tent used at a fair, a wedding or other outdoor events
[from French, meaning awning]

marriage **marriages**
NOUN **1** the relationship between two people who are married
2 a wedding ceremony

married
VERB **1** the past tense and past participle of **marry**
ADJECTIVE **2** If someone is **married**, they have a husband or a wife.

marrow **marrows**
NOUN a long, thick, green vegetable with cream-coloured flesh

marry **marries, marrying, married**
VERB When two people **marry**, they become partners in a special ceremony.

marsh **marshes**
NOUN an area of land that is permanently wet

marshmallow **marshmallows**
NOUN a soft, spongy sweet, usually pink or white

marsupials **marsupials**
NOUN an animal that carries its young in a pouch. Koalas, kangaroos and wallabies are **marsupials**.
[from Greek *marsupion* meaning purse]

kangaroo

martial
Said "**mar**-shul" ADJECTIVE **Martial** describes anything to do with military matters, war and soldiers.

martial arts
PLURAL NOUN The **martial arts** are techniques of self-defence, such as judo and karate, that come from the Far East.

martyr **martyrs**
NOUN someone who suffers or is killed for their beliefs
martyrdom NOUN

marvel marvels, marvelling, marvelled

VERB **1** If you **marvel** at something, you are filled with amazement and admiration for it. • *We marvelled at the sight of people swimming with the dolphins.*
NOUN **2** something that fills you with surprise and admiration

marvellous

ADJECTIVE wonderful or excellent

marzipan

NOUN a paste made of almonds, sugar and egg. It is put on top of cakes or used to make small sweets.

mascot mascots

NOUN a person, animal or toy that is thought to bring good luck

masculine

ADJECTIVE typical of men, rather than women
ANTONYM: feminine

mask masks, masking, masked

NOUN **1** something you wear over your face for protection or as a disguise
VERB **2** If you **mask** something, you cover it so that it is protected or disguised.

mass masses

NOUN **1** a large amount or heap of something
2 In science, **mass** is the amount of matter in an object. **Mass** is measured in grams (g).
3 A **Mass** is a communion service in a Roman Catholic church.
ADJECTIVE **4** involving or affecting a large number of people

massacre massacres, massacring, massacred

NOUN **1** the killing of a very large number of people in a violent and cruel way
VERB **2** To **massacre** a group of people means to kill them in large numbers in a violent and cruel way.

massage massages, massaging, massaged

VERB **1** If you **massage** someone, you rub

parts of their body in order to help them relax or to relieve pain.
NOUN **2** treatment that involves rubbing parts of the body

massive

ADJECTIVE extremely large
SYNONYMS: huge, vast, enormous

mast masts

NOUN the tall, upright pole that supports the sails of a boat

master masters, mastering, mastered

VERB **1** If you **master** a skill, you learn how to do it well.
NOUN **2** someone who is very skilled at something • *a master of disguise*
3 a male teacher

masterpiece masterpieces

NOUN an excellent painting, novel, film or other work of art that has been made with great skill • *The 'Mona Lisa' is considered a masterpiece.*

mat mats

NOUN **1** a small piece of carpet or other material that is put on floors for protection or decoration
2 a small piece of cloth or other material that is put on a table or other surface to protect it

match matches, matching, matched

NOUN **1** an organized game of football, cricket or some other sport
2 a small, thin wooden stick tipped with a chemical that produces a flame when you strike it against a rough surface. **Matches** are used to light things.
VERB **3** If colours **match**, they go well together. • *My dress matched my shoes.*
4 If you **match** one thing with another, you find the connection between them.

mate mates, mating, mated

NOUN **1** INFORMAL Your **mates** are your friends.
2 The first **mate** on a ship is second in importance after the captain.
VERB **3** When a pair of animals **mate**, they come together in order to breed.

material **materials**
NOUN **1** cloth
2 anything from which something else can be made • artists' **materials**

maternal
ADJECTIVE **1** used to describe things relating to a mother • My **maternal** grandfather was Welsh.
2 A woman who is **maternal** has strong motherly feelings.

maternity
ADJECTIVE relating to or involving pregnant women and childbirth • The baby was born in the **maternity** wing of the hospital.

mathematics
NOUN the study of numbers, quantities and shapes
mathematical ADJECTIVE
mathematically ADVERB
mathematician NOUN

maths
NOUN an abbreviation of mathematics

matinee **matinees**
Said "mat-i-nay" NOUN an afternoon performance at a theatre or cinema

matrix **matrices**
Said "may-trix, may-tri-sees" NOUN In mathematics, a **matrix** is a set of numbers or letters set out in rows and columns.

matt
ADJECTIVE dull rather than shiny • Mum painted the front door **matt** green.

matter **matters, mattering, mattered**
NOUN **1** a task or situation that you have to attend to • We will have to discuss the **matter** with the head teacher.
SYNONYMS: affair, business, subject
2 any substance • The scientists explored how **matter** behaves at high temperatures.
VERB **3** If something **matters**, it is important.
PHRASE **4** If you ask **What's the matter?**, you want to know what is wrong.

mattress **mattresses**
NOUN a large, flat, spongy pad that is put on a bed to make it comfortable to sleep on

mature **matures, maturing, matured**
VERB **1** When a child or other young animal **matures**, it becomes an adult.
ADJECTIVE **2** fully grown or developed
maturely ADVERB **maturity** NOUN

maul **mauls, mauling, mauled**
VERB If an animal **mauls** someone, they savagely attack and badly injure them.

mauve
Rhymes with "stove" NOUN OR ADJECTIVE a light purple colour

maximum
ADJECTIVE **1** The **maximum** amount is the most that is possible or allowed. • The **maximum** score for this question is five marks.
ANTONYM: minimum
NOUN **2** the most that is possible or allowed • Pupils are allowed a **maximum** of two pounds to spend on the school trip.
ANTONYM: minimum

may
VERB **1** If something **may** happen, it is possible that it will happen.
2 If you **may** do something, you are allowed to do it.

May
NOUN the fifth month of the year. **May** has 31 days.
[probably from the Roman goddess Maia]

maybe
ADVERB If you think there is a possibility that something will happen, but you are not sure, you use **maybe**. • **Maybe** we will be allowed to go to the cinema tonight.

mayonnaise
NOUN a thick salad dressing made with egg yolks and oil

mayor **mayors**
NOUN someone who has been elected to represent the people of a town at official functions

maze **mazes**
NOUN a system of complicated passages which it is difficult to find your way through

a
b
c
d
e
f
g
h
i
j
k
l
m
n
o
p
q
r
s
t
u
v
w
x
y
z

me

PRONOUN A speaker or writer uses **me** to refer to himself or herself.

meadow **meadows**

NOUN a field of grass

meagre

ADJECTIVE very small and poor ● *meagre portions*

meal **meals**

NOUN **1** an occasion when people eat
2 the food people eat at meal times

mean **means, meaning, meant; meaner, meanest**

VERB **1** If you ask someone what something **means**, you want them to explain it to you.
2 If you **mean** to do something, you intend to do it.
SYNONYMS: aim, plan
3 If something **means** a lot to you, it is important to you.
ADJECTIVE **4** unkind
5 Someone who is **mean** is unwilling to share with others.
NOUN **6** In mathematics, the **mean** is the average of a set of numbers.

meander **meanders, meandering, meandered**

Said "mee-**and**-er" VERB If a road or river **meanders**, it has a lot of bends in it. [from *Maiandros*, the name of a Greek river]

meaning **meanings**

NOUN The **meaning** of a word, expression or gesture is what it refers to or expresses.
● *Do you know the **meaning** of the proverb "more haste, less speed"?*

meanwhile

ADVERB If something happens, and **meanwhile** something else is happening, the two things are happening at the same time.

measles

NOUN an infectious illness that causes a high temperature and red spots on the skin [from Germanic *masele* meaning spot on the skin]

measure **measures, measuring, measured**

VERB **1** If you **measure** something, you find out the size or amount of it.
NOUN **2** a unit used to measure something
3 a container or an instrument, such as a ruler or a measuring jug, that you use to measure something
4 an action that you take to achieve something

measurement **measurements**

NOUN the result you obtain when you measure something

meat **meats**

NOUN the flesh of animals that people cook and eat

mechanic **mechanics**

NOUN someone whose job is to repair and maintain machines and engines

mechanical

ADJECTIVE **1** to do with machinery. Anything **mechanical** is worked by machinery.
2 If you do something in a **mechanical** way, you do it without thinking about it.
mechanically ADVERB

medal **medals**

NOUN a small piece of decorative metal, often shaped like a large coin and attached to a ribbon, given as an award for bravery or as a prize in sport

meddle **meddles, meddling, meddled**

VERB If you **meddle**, you interfere and try to change things without being asked.

media

PLURAL NOUN You can refer to the television, radio and newspapers as the **media**.

Media is the plural of *medium* but it is becoming more common for it to be used as a singular noun: *The media is obsessed with celebrities.*

median **medians**

NOUN In mathematics, the **median** of a set of numbers is the middle number once the numbers have been arranged in order of size. ● *The **median** of 4, 0, 1, 2, 3 is 2, as 2 is in the middle once they are organized in order.*

medical
ADJECTIVE to do with the treatment of people who are ill

medication **medications**
NOUN a substance that is used to treat illness

medicine **medicines**
NOUN **1** a substance that you take to help cure an illness
2 the care and treatment of ill people

medieval; also spelt **mediaeval**
ADJECTIVE relating to the period between about 1100 AD and 1500 AD, especially in Europe

mediocre
Said "mee-dee-**oh**-ker" ADJECTIVE
Something that is **mediocre** is of average or poor quality or standard. • *We were disappointed by the film – it was* **mediocre**.
mediocrity NOUN

Mediterranean
NOUN **1** the large sea between southern Europe and northern Africa
ADJECTIVE **2** relating to the Mediterranean or the countries adjoining it

medium **mediums** or **media**
ADJECTIVE **1** If something is of **medium** size, it is neither large nor small.
NOUN **2** a means of communicating or expressing something

meek **meeker, meekest**
ADJECTIVE A **meek** person is timid and does what other people say.
meekly ADVERB **meekness** NOUN

meet **meets, meeting, met**
VERB **1** If you **meet** someone, you make an arrangement to go to the same place at the same time as they do. • *Let's* **meet** *at your house before we go out.*
2 If you **meet** someone, you come face-to-face with them or are introduced to them for the first time. • *We* **met** *on our first day at school.*

meeting **meetings**
NOUN **1** an event at which people discuss things or make decisions

2 an occasion when you meet someone by arrangement

megabyte **megabytes**
NOUN a unit of storage in a computer, equal to 1,048,576 bytes

melancholy
ADJECTIVE OR NOUN If you feel **melancholy**, you feel very sad.

melodramatic
ADJECTIVE behaving in an exaggerated, emotional way

melody **melodies**
NOUN a tune
[from Greek *meloidia* meaning singing]

melon **melons**
NOUN a large, juicy fruit with a green or yellow skin and many seeds inside

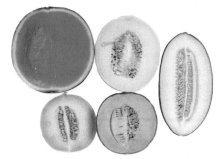

melt **melts, melting, melted**
VERB When something **melts**, or when you **melt** it, it changes from a solid to a liquid because it has been heated.

member **members**
NOUN one of the people or things belonging to a group

membrane **membranes**
NOUN a very thin skin

memorable
ADJECTIVE **Memorable** things or people are likely to be remembered because they are special or unusual.

memorial **memorials**
NOUN a structure built to remind people of a famous person or event • *a war* **memorial**

memorize **memorizes, memorizing, memorized**
VERB If you **memorize** something, you learn it so well that you remember it and can repeat it exactly. • *She memorized all the times tables from 2 to 12 in one week.*

memory **memories**
NOUN **1** your ability to remember things
2 A computer's **memory** is its capacity to store information.

men
PLURAL NOUN the plural of **man**

menace **menaces, menacing, menaced**
NOUN **1** someone or something that is likely to cause harm • *That dog is a menace.*
VERB **2** If someone or something **menaces** you, they threaten to harm you.
menacing ADJECTIVE **menacingly** ADVERB

mend **mends, mending, mended**
VERB If you **mend** something that is broken, you repair or fix it.

menstruate **menstruates, menstruating, menstruated**
VERB When a woman **menstruates**, blood comes from her womb. This normally happens once a month.
menstruation NOUN **menstrual** ADJECTIVE

mental
ADJECTIVE relating to the mind and the process of thinking • *mental arithmetic*

mention **mentions, mentioning, mentioned**
VERB **1** If you **mention** something, you speak or write briefly about it.
NOUN **2** a brief comment about someone or something

menu **menus**
NOUN **1** a list of the food and drink you can buy in a restaurant or café
2 a list of options shown on a computer screen, which the user must choose from

mercenary **mercenaries**
ADJECTIVE **1** Someone who is **mercenary** is mainly interested in getting money.
NOUN **2** a soldier who is paid to fight for a foreign country

merchandise
NOUN goods for buying and selling • *The market stalls were full of all kinds of merchandise.*

merchant **merchants**
NOUN a trader who imports and exports goods

mercury
NOUN a silver-coloured metallic element that is liquid at room temperature. **Mercury** is used in some thermometers.

mercy **mercies**
NOUN If you show **mercy**, you show kindness and forgiveness instead of punishing someone.

merge **merges, merging, merged**
VERB When two things **merge**, they combine or join together to make one thing. • *The two roads merged at the junction.*

meridian **meridians**
NOUN one of the lines on maps or globes, drawn from the North Pole to the South Pole, that help to describe the position of a place

merit **merits, meriting, merited**
NOUN **1** If something has **merit**, it is good or worthwhile.
2 The **merits** of something are its advantages or good qualities. • *I can see now the merits of working hard.*
VERB **3** If something or someone **merits** a particular treatment, they deserve that treatment. • *He merits a place in the team.*

mermaid **mermaids**
NOUN a creature in stories, with a woman's body and a fish's tail instead of legs

merry **merrier, merriest**
ADJECTIVE happy and cheerful
merrily ADVERB

mesh
NOUN threads of wire, plastic or other material twisted together like a net

mess **messes, messing, messed**
NOUN **1** something dirty or untidy
2 something full of problems

mess about or **mess around**
VERB If you **mess about** or **mess around**, you spend time doing silly or casual things. • Stop **messing about** and get on with your work.

mess up
VERB If you **mess up** something, you make it untidy, spoil it or do it badly. • He'd already **messed up** one piece of paper.

message messages
NOUN a piece of information or a request from one person to another

messenger messengers
NOUN someone who takes a message

messy messier, messiest
ADJECTIVE **1** dirty or untidy
2 complicated or confused • He's got himself into a **messy** situation.

met
VERB the past tense and past participle of **meet**

metal metals
NOUN a hard substance such as iron, steel, copper or lead. **Metals** are good conductors of heat and electricity.
metallic ADJECTIVE

metaphor metaphors
NOUN an imaginative way of describing one thing as another thing. For example, if a person is shy and timid, you could describe them as a mouse.

meteor meteors
NOUN a piece of rock or metal moving rapidly through space, that burns very briefly and brightly when it enters the earth's atmosphere

meteorite meteorites
NOUN a piece of rock from space that has landed on earth

meteorology
NOUN the study of the weather
meteorologist NOUN

meter meters
NOUN a device that measures and records something, such as a gas **meter** that records how much gas a household has used

method methods
NOUN a particular way of doing something • Use the **method** I showed you to work out the sum.

methodical
ADJECTIVE **Methodical** people do things in a careful and organized way.
methodically ADVERB

metre metres
NOUN a unit of length (m) equal to 100 centimetres

metric
ADJECTIVE relating to the system of measurement that uses metres, grams and litres

mew mews, mewing, mewed
VERB When a cat **mews**, it makes a short, high-pitched noise.

miaow miaows, miaowing, miaowed
NOUN **1** the noise a cat makes
VERB **2** When a cat **miaows**, it makes a crying sound.

mice
PLURAL NOUN the plural of **mouse**

micro-
PREFIX added to some words to mean very small. For example, a **micro**computer is a very small computer.

microbe microbes
NOUN a very small, living thing that can only be seen through a microscope. **Microbes** can feed, grow and reproduce.

microchip microchips
NOUN a small piece of silicon that has electronic circuits printed on it, and is used in computers and electronic equipment

micro-organism micro-organisms
NOUN a very small organism that can only be seen under a powerful microscope. Some **micro-organisms** are harmful and cause disease. Others, such as yeast, are helpful. Microbes, germs and viruses are sometimes called **micro-organisms**.

microphone
microphones
NOUN a device that is used to record sounds or make them louder

microscope
microscopes
NOUN a piece of equipment that magnifies very small objects so that you can study them • *When the class looked at a leaf through the* **microscope**, *they could see the small veins that they had not been able to see before.*

microscopic
ADJECTIVE too small to be seen without using a microscope

microwave **microwaves**
NOUN a type of oven that cooks food very quickly by radiation

mid-
PREFIX used to form words that refer to the middle part of a place or a period of time • *We had a break* **mid**morning.

midday
NOUN twelve o'clock in the middle of the day

middle **middles**
NOUN **1** The **middle** of something is the part furthest from the edges, ends or surface. • *He stood in the* **middle** *of the room.*
2 The **middle** of an event is the part that comes after the first part and before the last part. • *There was an interval in the* **middle** *of the play.*
ADJECTIVE **3** The **middle** thing in a series is the one with an equal number of things on each side. • *M and N are the* **middle** *letters in the alphabet.*

Middle Ages
NOUN In European history, the **Middle Ages** were the period between about 1100 AD and 1500 AD.

midnight
NOUN twelve o'clock at night

midwife **midwives**
NOUN a nurse who is trained to help women during pregnancy and at the birth of their baby
midwifery NOUN

might
VERB **1** You use **might** to say that something will possibly happen or is possibly true. • *I* **might** *not be back until tomorrow.*
NOUN **2** If you do something with all your **might**, you do it with all your strength and energy.

migraine **migraines**
NOUN a severe headache that makes you feel very ill

migrant **migrants**
NOUN **1** a person who moves from one place to another, usually to find work • **Migrants** *arrived for the fruit-picking season.*
2 a bird, fish or animal that migrates from one part of the world to another • *The spotted flycatcher, a* **migrant** *from Africa, arrives in Britain in May.*

migrate **migrates, migrating, migrated**
VERB **1** If people **migrate**, they move from one place to another, especially to find work.
2 When birds or animals **migrate**, they move at a particular season to a different place, usually to breed or to find new feeding grounds.
migration NOUN **migratory** ADJECTIVE

mild **milder, mildest**
ADJECTIVE Something that is **mild** is gentle, and not very strong or severe. • **mild** *weather*
mildly ADVERB

mildew
NOUN a soft, white fungus that grows on things when they are warm and damp
mildewed ADJECTIVE

mile **miles**
NOUN a unit of distance equal to about 1.6 kilometres

[from Latin *milia passuum* meaning a thousand paces]

mileage mileages
NOUN the distance you have travelled, measured in miles • The **mileage** from home to the hotel was 120 miles.

military
ADJECTIVE to do with the armed forces of a country

milk milks, milking, milked
NOUN **1** the white liquid produced by mammals to feed their young. People drink cows' and goats' milk and make it into butter, cheese and yogurt.
VERB **2** When someone **milks** a cow or other animal, they get milk from it by pulling its udders.

milkman milkmen
NOUN a man who delivers milk to your house

mill mills
NOUN **1** a building where grain is crushed to make flour
2 a factory for making materials such as steel, wool or cotton • a cotton **mill**
3 a small device for grinding something. For example, a pepper **mill** grinds peppercorns.

millennium millennia or millenniums
NOUN a period of 1000 years

milligram milligrams
NOUN a unit of weight (mg). There are 1000 **milligrams** in a gram.

millilitre millilitres
NOUN a unit for measuring liquid (ml). There are 1000 **millilitres** in a litre.

millimetre millimetres
NOUN a unit of length (mm). There are 10 **millimetres** in a centimetre.

million millions
NOUN A **million** is the number 1,000,000.
millionth NOUN OR ADJECTIVE

millionaire millionaires
NOUN someone who has money or property worth at least a million pounds or dollars

mime mimes, miming, mimed
NOUN **1** the use of movements and gestures to express something or to tell a story without using speech
VERB **2** If you **mime** something, you describe or express it using mime.

mimic mimics, mimicking, mimicked
VERB **1** If you **mimic** someone's actions or voice, you imitate them in an amusing way.
NOUN **2** a person who can imitate other people

minaret minarets
NOUN a tall, thin tower on a mosque

minaret

mince minces, mincing, minced
NOUN **1** meat that has been ground into very small pieces
VERB **2** If you **mince** meat, you grind it into very small pieces.

mincemeat
NOUN a sweet mixture of dried fruits used, for example, in mince pies

mind minds, minding, minded
NOUN **1** Your **mind** is your ability to think, together with your memory and all the thoughts you have. • He could still see her face in his **mind**.
PHRASE **2** If you **change your mind**, you change a decision that you have made or an opinion that you have.
VERB **3** If you do not **mind** what happens or what something is like, you do not have a strong preference about it. • I don't **mind** where we go.
4 If you tell someone to **mind** something,

you are warning them to be careful.
• **Mind** that plate, it's hot.
5 If you **mind** something for someone, you look after it for a while.

mindless

ADJECTIVE **1 Mindless** behaviour is stupid and destructive.
2 A **mindless** job or activity is so simple, or repeated so often, that you do not need to think about it at all.
SYNONYM: repetitive

mine mines

PRONOUN **1** something belonging or relating to the person who is speaking or writing • He's a good friend of **mine**.
NOUN **2** a place where deep holes or tunnels are dug under the ground in order to extract minerals • a coal **mine**
3 a bomb hidden in the ground or underwater, that explodes when people or things touch it

minefield minefields

NOUN an area of land or water where explosive mines have been laid

miner miners

NOUN a person who works underground in mines to find and dig out coal, diamonds, gold and other minerals • a coal **miner**

mineral minerals

NOUN small particles that make up different rocks. For example, quartz and diamonds are **minerals**.

mineral water

NOUN water that comes from a natural spring

mingle mingles, mingling, mingled

VERB If things **mingle**, they become mixed together.

mini-

PREFIX used with another word to describe something shorter or smaller than the usual size • a **mini**skirt

miniature

ADJECTIVE a tiny copy of something much larger • I bought a **miniature** version of the Eiffel Tower as a souvenir.

minibus minibuses

NOUN a van with seats in the back, that is used as a small bus

minimum

ADJECTIVE **1** A **minimum** amount of something is the smallest amount that is possible, allowed or needed.
ANTONYM: maximum
NOUN **2** the smallest amount of something that is possible, allowed or needed
ANTONYM: maximum

minister ministers

NOUN **1** a person who is in charge of a particular government department
2 a member of the clergy, especially in a Protestant church
[from Latin minister meaning servant]

ministry ministries

NOUN a government department that deals with a particular area of work • the **Ministry** of Education

mink minks

NOUN a small wild mammal with valuable brown fur

minnow minnows

NOUN a very small, freshwater fish

minor

ADJECTIVE less important or serious than other things • He had a **minor** part in the play.
ANTONYM: major

minority minorities

NOUN less than half of a group of people or things

minstrel minstrels

NOUN a singer and entertainer in medieval times

mint mints

NOUN **1** a plant with strong-smelling leaves used as flavouring in cooking
2 a sweet flavoured with these leaves
3 the place where the official coins of a country are made
ADJECTIVE **4** If something is in **mint** condition, it is like new.

minus

PREPOSITION **1** You use **minus** (–) to show that one number is being subtracted from another. • *Ten **minus** six equals four (10 – 6 = 4).*

ADJECTIVE **2 Minus** before a number means that the number is less than zero. • *There are sometimes temperatures of **minus** 65 °C (–65 °C) in the Arctic.*

minute **minutes**

*Said "**min**-nit"* NOUN **1** a unit of time equal to sixty seconds
2 a short period of time • *See you in a **minute**.*
*Said "my-**nyoot**"* ADJECTIVE **3** extremely small • *A **minute** amount of milk is needed.*

miracle **miracles**

NOUN a surprising and wonderful event, especially one believed to have been caused by God
[from Latin *mirari* meaning to wonder at]

mirage **mirages**

*Said "mi-**rarzh**"* NOUN an image that you can see in the distance in very hot weather, but that does not actually exist

mirror

mirrors

NOUN an object made of glass in which you can see your reflection

mis-

PREFIX added to some words to mean badly or wrongly. For example, **mis**behave means to behave badly, and **mis**calculate means to calculate wrongly.

misbehave **misbehaves, misbehaving, misbehaved**

VERB If someone **misbehaves**, they are naughty or behave badly.
misbehaviour NOUN

miscarriage **miscarriages**

NOUN **1** If a woman has a **miscarriage**, she gives birth to a baby too early, before it is able to survive in the outside world.

2 A **miscarriage** of justice is a wrong decision made by a court, which results in an innocent person being punished.

miscellaneous

*Said "miss-uh-**lay**-nee-uss"* ADJECTIVE A **miscellaneous** group is made up of a mixture of people or things that are different from each other.

mischief

NOUN naughty behaviour, teasing people or playing tricks

mischievous

ADJECTIVE If you are **mischievous**, you enjoy being naughty by teasing or playing tricks on people.
mischievously ADVERB

miser **misers**

NOUN a mean person who enjoys hoarding money, but hates spending it
miserly ADVERB

miserable

ADJECTIVE If you are **miserable**, you are very unhappy.

misery **miseries**

NOUN great unhappiness
SYNONYM: grief

misfire **misfires, misfiring, misfired**

VERB If a plan **misfires**, it goes wrong.

misfit **misfits**

NOUN a person who cannot get on with other people or fit into a group

misfortune **misfortunes**

NOUN an unpleasant occurrence that is regarded as bad luck • *I had the **misfortune** to fall off my bike.*

mishap **mishaps**

*Said "**miss**-hap"* NOUN an accidental or unfortunate happening that is not very serious • *Grandma had a small **mishap** when her hat blew away.*

misjudge **misjudges, misjudging, misjudged**

VERB If you **misjudge** someone or something, you form a wrong or unfair opinion of them.

mislay mislays, mislaying, mislaid
VERB If you **mislay** something, you cannot remember where you put it.

mislead misleads, misleading, misled
VERB If you **mislead** someone, you make them believe something that is not true.

misprint misprints
NOUN a mistake such as a spelling mistake in something that has been printed

miss misses, missing, missed
VERB **1** If you **miss** someone or something, you feel sad because they are no longer with you.
2 If you **miss** a bus, plane or train, you arrive too late to catch it.
3 If you **miss** an event or activity, you fail to attend it. ● *I had to **miss** my piano lesson.*
4 If you **miss** something that you are aiming at, you fail to hit it. ● *The arrow **missed** the target.*
NOUN **5 Miss** is used before the name of a girl or unmarried woman. ● *My teacher this year is **Miss** Weston.*

missile missiles
NOUN **1** a weapon that moves long distances through the air and explodes when it reaches its target ● *nuclear **missiles***
2 any object thrown to harm someone or something

missing
ADJECTIVE Something that is **missing** is lost or not in its usual place. ● *One of my shoes is **missing**.*

mission missions
NOUN **1** a journey made by a military aeroplane or space rocket to carry out a task
2 an important task that has to be done

missionary missionaries
NOUN a Christian who has been sent to a foreign country to work for the Church

misspell misspells, misspelling, misspelt or misspelled
VERB If you **misspell** a word, you spell it wrongly.

mist mists
NOUN many tiny drops of water in the air that make it hard to see clearly

mistake mistakes, mistaking, mistook, mistaken
NOUN **1** If you make a **mistake**, you do something wrong without intending to.
● *There are some spelling **mistakes** in your homework.*
VERB **2** If you **mistake** someone or something for another person or thing, you wrongly think that they are the other person or thing. ● *I **mistook** him for his brother.*

mistletoe
NOUN a plant that grows on trees and has white berries on it

mistook
VERB the past tense of **mistake**

mistreat mistreats, mistreating, mistreated
VERB If you **mistreat** a person or an animal, you treat them badly and make them suffer.

mistress mistresses
NOUN **1** a woman schoolteacher ● *There is a new French **mistress**.*
2 a woman who is in charge of something or someone ● *The dog had run away from its **mistress**.*

mistrust mistrusts, mistrusting, mistrusted
VERB **1** If you **mistrust** someone, you feel that they are not to be trusted.
ANTONYM: trust
NOUN **2** the feeling of not being able to trust someone or something
ANTONYM: trust

misunderstand misunderstands, misunderstanding, misunderstood
VERB If you **misunderstand** someone, you do not properly understand what they say or do. ● *He **misunderstood** the instructions and took the wrong turning.*

misunderstanding misunderstandings
NOUN If people have a **misunderstanding**,

they have a disagreement or a slight quarrel about something.

misuse misuses, misusing, misused
NOUN **1** The **misuse** of something is the incorrect or dishonest use of it.
VERB **2** If you **misuse** something, you use it wrongly or dishonestly.

mix mixes, mixing, mixed
VERB If you **mix** things, you combine them.
mixed up ADJECTIVE

mix up
VERB If you **mix up** things, you get confused.

mixture mixtures
NOUN **1** two or more things mixed together • *They felt a **mixture** of fear and excitement as they climbed the wall.*
2 a substance consisting of two or more other substances that have been mixed together

moan moans, moaning, moaned
VERB **1** If you **moan**, you make a low, miserable sound because you are in pain or unhappy.
2 If you **moan** about something, you complain about it.
NOUN **3** a low cry of pain or unhappiness

moat moats
NOUN a wide, deep ditch around a castle, usually filled with water, to help defend the building

mob mobs, mobbing, mobbed
NOUN **1** a large, disorganized crowd of people
VERB **2** If a group **mobs** someone, they gather closely around them in a disorderly way. • *The fans **mobbed** the band.*

mobile mobiles
ADJECTIVE **1** able to move or be moved easily • *He's much more **mobile** since getting his new wheelchair.*
NOUN **2** short for **mobile phone**
3 an ornament made up of several parts that hang from threads and move in the breeze

mobile phone mobile phones
NOUN a small telephone that you can carry around with you

mock mocks, mocking, mocked
VERB **1** If you **mock** someone, you tease them or try to make them look foolish.
SYNONYMS: laugh at, make fun of
ADJECTIVE **2** not genuine • *The ring is made of **mock** diamonds.*

mode modes
NOUN **1** a particular way of behaving or of doing something
2 In mathematics, the mode is the most popular or most frequently occurring value. • *Of the following numbers – 5, 5, 6, 7, 7, 7, 8 – 7 is the **mode**.*

model models
NOUN OR ADJECTIVE **1** a smaller copy of something that shows what it looks like or how it works in real life • *Mark has a **model** railway in his bedroom.*
NOUN **2** a type or version of a product • *Which **model** of computer did you choose?*
3 a person who wears clothes that are being displayed to possible buyers, or who poses for a photographer or artist
ADJECTIVE **4** A **model** student is an excellent example of a student who is worth copying.

modem modems
NOUN a piece of equipment that links a computer to the telephone system so that data can be sent from one computer to another

moderate moderates, moderating, moderated
*Said "***mod**-er-ut*"* ADJECTIVE **1** A **moderate** amount of something is not too much or too little of it.
2 Moderate ideas and opinions are not extreme.
*Said "***mod**-er-ayt*"* VERB **3** If something **moderates** or is **moderated**, it becomes less extreme. • *He should **moderate** his temper.*
moderately ADVERB

modern
ADJECTIVE new and involving the latest ideas or equipment
[from Latin *modo* meaning just recently]

modest
ADJECTIVE **1** quite small in size or amount • *He inherited a **modest** amount of money.*

2 Modest people do not boast about how clever or how rich they are.

ANTONYM: boastful

modesty NOUN   modestly ADVERB

modify **modifies, modifying, modified**

VERB If you **modify** something, you change it slightly to improve it. • *When he had **modified** his bike, it went much faster.*

module **modules**

NOUN **1** one of the parts which, when put together, form a whole unit or object
2 a part of a spacecraft that can do certain things away from the main body
• *the lunar **module***

moist **moister, moistest**

ADJECTIVE slightly wet, damp

moisten **moistens, moistening, moistened**

VERB If you **moisten** something, you make it slightly wet.

moisture

NOUN tiny drops of water in the air or on the ground

molar **molars**

NOUN Your **molars** are the large teeth at the back of your mouth.

mole **moles**

NOUN **1** a small animal with black fur. **Moles** live in tunnels underground.
2 a dark, slightly-raised spot on your skin

molecule **molecules**

NOUN A **molecule** is made up of two or more atoms held together.

molecular ADJECTIVE

mollusc **molluscs**

NOUN an animal with a soft body and no backbone. Snails, slugs, clams and mussels are all **molluscs**.

slug

snail

molten

ADJECTIVE **Molten** rock or metal has been heated to a very high temperature and has melted to become a thick liquid.
• *When the volcano erupted, **molten** lava flowed down the mountainside.*

moment **moments**

NOUN **1** a very short period of time
• *I paused for a **moment**.*

SYNONYMS: instant, second

2 the point at which something happens • *At that **moment**, the doorbell rang.*

PHRASE **3** If something is happening **at the moment**, it is happening now.

momentum

NOUN the ability that an object has to continue moving as a result of its mass and the speed at which it is already moving

monarchy **monarchies**

NOUN a system in which a queen or king reigns in a country

monastery **monasteries**

NOUN a place where monks live and work [from Latin *monasterium* meaning to live alone]

monastic ADJECTIVE

Monday **Mondays**

NOUN the second day of the week, coming between Sunday and Tuesday [from Old English *Monandæg* meaning moon's day]

money

NOUN the coins and banknotes that you use to buy things

mongrel **mongrels**

NOUN a dog with parents of different breeds

monitor **monitors, monitoring, monitored**

VERB **1** If you **monitor** something, you regularly check its condition and progress.
NOUN **2** a machine used to check or record things
3 the visual display unit of a computer

4 a school pupil chosen to do special duties by the teacher

monk **monks**
NOUN a member of a male religious community

monkey **monkeys**
NOUN an agile animal that has a long tail and climbs trees

mono-
PREFIX having one of something, for example a **mono**rail is a single rail, and a sound that is **mono**tone has only one tone

monologue **monologues**
NOUN a long speech by one person during a play or conversation

monotonous
ADJECTIVE having a regular pattern that is very dull and boring • *a monotonous voice*
monotony NOUN **monotonously** ADVERB

monsoon **monsoons**
NOUN the season of very heavy rain in South-east Asia

monster **monsters**
NOUN **1** a large, imaginary creature that looks very frightening
2 a cruel and frightening person
ADJECTIVE **3** extremely large • *She gave him a monster TV set for his birthday.*
[from Latin *monstrum* meaning omen or warning]

month **months**
NOUN one of the twelve periods that a year is divided into

monthly
ADJECTIVE OR ADVERB happening or appearing once every month

monument **monuments**
NOUN a large structure built to remind people of a famous person or event
[from Latin *monere* meaning to remind]

moo **moos, mooing, mooed**
VERB **1** When cows **moo**, they make a long, deep sound.
NOUN **2** the long, deep sound that cows make

mood **moods**
NOUN the way you are feeling at a particular time

moody **moodier, moodiest**
ADJECTIVE **1** **Moody** people change their mood often and very quickly, seemingly for no reason.
2 depressed and miserable
moodily ADVERB

moon **moons**
NOUN an object that moves round the earth once every four weeks. You see the **moon** as a shining circle or crescent in the sky at night. Some other planets have **moons**.

moonlight
NOUN the light that comes from the moon at night

moor **moors, mooring, moored**
NOUN **1** a high area of open land • *The farmer had flocks of sheep grazing on the **moors**.*
VERB **2** If you **moor** a boat, you attach it to the land with a rope.

moose
NOUN a North American deer or elk, with large, flat antlers

The plural of *moose* is *moose*.

mop **mops, mopping, mopped**
NOUN **1** a tool for washing floors. It has a string or a sponge head at the end of a long handle.
VERB **2** If you **mop** something, you wipe it or clean it up with a mop or a cloth.

mope **mopes, moping, moped**
VERB If you **mope**, you feel miserable and sorry for yourself.

moral **morals**
PLURAL NOUN **1** **Morals** are values based on beliefs that are acceptable to a particular society.
ADJECTIVE **2** relating to beliefs about what is right and wrong • *moral values*
NOUN **3** the lesson taught by a story, that usually tells you that good behaviour is best
morality NOUN **morally** ADVERB

morale

NOUN Your **morale** is the amount of confidence and optimism you feel. • *The **morale** of the school was high.*

morbid

ADJECTIVE If you are **morbid**, you have a great interest in unpleasant things, especially death and illness.
[from Latin *morbus* meaning illness]

more

ADJECTIVE OR PRONOUN **1** a greater number or extent than something else • ***More** than 1500 schools took part in the event.*
ANTONYMS: fewer, less
2 an additional thing or amount of something • *I would like some **more** orange juice.*
ADVERB **3 More** means to a greater degree or extent. • *We can talk **more** later.*
4 You use **more** to show that something is repeated. • *Repeat the exercise once **more**.*
5 You use **more** in front of adjectives and adverbs to form comparatives. • *He did it **more** carefully the second time.*

morning mornings

NOUN **1** the early part of the day, before noon
2 the part of the day between midnight and midday

Morse code

NOUN a code for sending messages by radio signals. Each letter is represented by a series of dots (short sounds) and dashes (longer sounds).

morsel morsels

NOUN a small piece of food

mortal mortals

ADJECTIVE **1** a **mortal** wound causes death
2 unable to live forever and certain to die
NOUN **3** an ordinary person

mortar mortars

NOUN **1** a mixture of sand, water and cement used to hold bricks firmly together
2 a short cannon that fires missiles high into the air

mortgage mortgages

NOUN a loan that people get from a bank or building society in order to buy a house

mortuary mortuaries

NOUN a special room in a hospital where dead bodies are kept before being buried or cremated

mosaic mosaics

NOUN a design made of small, coloured stones, tiles or pieces of coloured glass set into concrete or plaster

Moslem

NOUN OR ADJECTIVE another spelling of **Muslim**

mosque mosques

NOUN a building where Muslims go to worship
[from Arabic *masjid* meaning temple]

mosquito mosquitoes or mosquitos

NOUN a small, flying insect that bites people and animals in order to suck their blood

moss mosses

NOUN a soft, small, green plant that grows on damp soil or stone
mossy ADJECTIVE

most

ADJECTIVE OR PRONOUN **1 Most** of a group of things or people means nearly all of them. • ***Most** people prefer sunny weather.*
2 a larger amount than anyone or anything else • *She has the **most** points.*
ADVERB **3** You use **most** in front of adjectives or adverbs to form superlatives. • *the **most** breathtaking scenery in the world*

motel **motels**
NOUN a hotel for people who are travelling by car, with parking spaces close to the rooms

moth **moths**
NOUN an insect like a butterfly that usually flies at night

mother **mothers**
NOUN Your **mother** is your female parent.

mother-in-law **mothers-in-law**
NOUN the mother of someone's husband or wife

motion **motions**
NOUN movement

motionless
ADJECTIVE If someone or something is **motionless**, they are not moving at all.

motivate **motivates, motivating, motivated**
VERB If you **motivate** someone, you make them determined to do or achieve something.
motivated ADJECTIVE **motivation** NOUN

motive **motives**
NOUN a reason or purpose for doing something

motor **motors**
NOUN a part of a vehicle or machine. The **motor** uses fuel to make the vehicle or machine work
SYNONYM: engine

motorbike **motorbikes**
NOUN a heavy two-wheeled vehicle that is driven by an engine

motorcycle **motorcycles**
NOUN another word for **motorbike**

motorist **motorists**
NOUN a person who drives a car or rides a motorbike

motorway **motorways**
NOUN a wide road built for fast travel over long distances

motto **mottoes** or **mottos**
NOUN a short sentence or phrase that is a rule for good or sensible behaviour. For example, *everything in moderation*.

mould **moulds, moulding, moulded**
VERB **1** If you **mould** a substance, you make it into a particular shape. • *Mould the dough into balls.*
NOUN **2** a container used to make something into a particular shape • *a jelly mould*
3 a soft, grey or green growth that forms on old food or damp walls

mouldy **mouldier, mouldiest**
ADJECTIVE Something that is **mouldy** is covered with mould. • *This old bread had gone mouldy.*

moult **moults, moulting, moulted**
VERB When an animal or bird **moults**, it loses its hair or feathers so that new ones can grow.

mound **mounds**
NOUN **1** a small, man-made hill
2 a large, untidy pile

mount **mounts, mounting, mounted**
VERB **1** If you **mount** a horse or bicycle, you climb onto it.
2 If something **mounts**, it increases in amount. • *The contributions for the tombola were mounting.*
3 If you **mount** a picture or a photograph, you put it in a frame or an album to display it.
NOUN **4** a mountain, especially as part of the name • *Mount Everest is the highest mountain in the world.*

mountain **mountains**
NOUN a very high piece of land with steep sides

mountaineer **mountaineer**
NOUN a person who climbs mountains

mourn **mourns, mourning, mourned**
VERB If you **mourn** for someone who has died, you feel sad and think about them a lot.

mouse **mice**
NOUN **1** a small, furry rodent with a long tail
2 a computer device that you move by hand to control the position of a cursor on the screen

a
b
c
d
e
f
g
h
i
j
k
l
m
n
o
p
q
r
s
t
u
v
w
x
y
z

moustache **moustaches**
NOUN the hair that grows on a man's upper lip

mouth **mouths**
NOUN **1** your lips, or the space behind them where your tongue and teeth are
2 the entrance to a cave or a hole
3 the place where a river flows into the sea

mouthful **mouthfuls**
NOUN the amount of food you put in your mouth • *Don't take such huge **mouthfuls**!*

movable
ADJECTIVE Something that is **movable** can be moved from one place to another.

move **moves, moving, moved**
VERB **1** When you **move** something, or when it **moves**, its position changes.
• *The train began to **move** out of the station.*
2 If you **move** or **move house**, you go to live in a different place.
3 If something **moves** you, it causes you to feel a deep emotion. • *The film **moved** us to tears.*
NOUN **4** a change from one place or position to another, especially in a game
• *It's your **move**.*

movement **movements**
NOUN **1** the action of changing position or moving from one place to another
2 a group of people who act together to try and make something happen • *the animal rights **movement***
3 one of the main parts of a piece of classical music

movie **movies**
NOUN another name for **film**

moving
ADJECTIVE Something that is **moving** makes you feel deep sadness or emotion.
• *a **moving** story*

mow **mows, mowing, mowed, mown**
VERB If you **mow** grass, you cut it with a lawnmower.

MP **MPs**
NOUN someone who has been elected by the people of an area to represent them in Parliament. **MP** is an abbreviation for *Member of Parliament.*

MP3 player **MP3 players**
NOUN a device that plays audio and video files, used for listening to music

Mr
*Said "**miss**-ter"* NOUN **Mr** is used before a man's name when you are speaking to him or talking about him. • *My teacher is called **Mr** Jones.*

Mrs
*Said "**miss**-izz"* NOUN **Mrs** is used before the name of a married woman when you are speaking or referring to her. • *"Good morning, **Mrs** Green."*

Ms
*Said "**miz**"* NOUN **Ms** is used before a woman's name when you are speaking or referring to her. **Ms** does not show whether the woman is married or not.

much
ADVERB **1** You use **much** to indicate the great size, extent or intensity of something. • *He's **much** taller than you.*
2 If something does not happen **much**, it does not happen often. • *He doesn't talk **much**.*
ADJECTIVE OR PRONOUN **3** You use **much** to talk about the size or amount of something. • *There isn't **much** left.*

mud
NOUN wet, sticky earth
muddy ADJECTIVE

muddle **muddles, muddling, muddled**
NOUN **1** a state of disorder or untidiness
VERB **2** If you **muddle** things, you mix them up.
[from Dutch *moddelen* meaning to make muddy]
muddled ADJECTIVE

muesli
NOUN a mixture of cereal flakes, chopped nuts and dried fruit that you can eat with milk for breakfast

muffled
ADJECTIVE A sound that is **muffled** is low or difficult to hear.

mug **mugs, mugging, mugged**
NOUN **1** a large, deep cup

VERB **2** INFORMAL If someone **mugs** you, they attack you in the street in order to steal your money.

mule **mules**
NOUN the offspring of a female horse and a male donkey

multiple **multiples**
ADJECTIVE **1** consisting of many parts or having many uses
NOUN **2** a number that can be divided exactly by another number ● *2, 4, 6, 8, 10 and 12 are all **multiples** of 2.*

multiplication
NOUN the process of multiplying one number by another

multiply **multiplies, multiplying, multiplied**
VERB **1** When you **multiply** one number by another, you calculate the total you would get if you added the first number to itself the number of times shown by the second number. ● *Six **multiplied** by three is 18 (6 × 3 = 18), because 6 + 6 + 6 = 18.*
2 When something **multiplies**, it increases greatly in number or amount.

multitude **multitudes**
NOUN FORMAL a very large number of people or things

mum **mums**
NOUN INFORMAL mother

mumble **mumbles, mumbling, mumbled**
VERB If you **mumble**, you speak very quietly and indistinctly.

mummy **mummies**
NOUN **1** INFORMAL Your **mummy** is your mother.
2 a dead body that was preserved long ago by being rubbed with special oils and wrapped in cloth ● *Mummies have been found in tombs in Egypt.*
[(sense 2) from Persian *mum* meaning wax]

a mummy's coffin from Ancient Egypt

mumps
NOUN a disease that causes painful swelling in the neck

munch **munches, munching, munched**
VERB If you **munch** something, you chew it steadily and thoroughly.

mural **murals**
NOUN a picture painted on a wall

murder **murders, murdering, murdered**
NOUN **1** the deliberate killing of a person
VERB **2** To **murder** someone means to kill them deliberately.
murderer NOUN

murky **murkier, murkiest**
ADJECTIVE dark or dirty and hard to see through ● *murky* water
[from Old Norse *myrkr* meaning darkness]
murk NOUN

murmur **murmurs, murmuring, murmured**
VERB **1** If you **murmur** something, you say it very quietly.
NOUN **2** something someone says that can hardly be heard ● *They spoke in low **murmurs**.*

muscle **muscles**
NOUN Your **muscles** are the bundles of fibres connected to your bones, that enable you to move. [from Latin *musculus* meaning little mouse, because muscles were thought to look like mice]

muscular
Said "**musk**-yoo-lar" ADJECTIVE
1 Muscular people have strong, well-developed muscles.
2 involving or affecting your muscles ● *muscular* pain

museum **museums**
NOUN a public building where interesting or valuable objects are kept and displayed

a b c d e f g h i j k l m n o p q r s t u v w x y z

A
B
C
D
E
F
G
H
I
J
K
L
M
N
O
P
Q
R
S
T
U
V
W
X
Y
Z

mushroom **mushrooms**
NOUN a fungus with a short stem and a round top. Some types of **mushroom** are edible.

music
NOUN **1** the pattern of sounds performed by people singing or playing instruments **2** the written symbols that represent musical sounds

musical **musicals**
ADJECTIVE **1** relating to playing or studying music • *She has considerable musical talent.*
NOUN **2** a play or a film that uses songs and dance to tell the story
musically ADVERB

musician **musicians**
NOUN a person who plays a musical instrument well

Muslim **Muslims**; also spelt **Moslem**
NOUN **1** a person who believes in the Islamic religion and lives according to its rules
ADJECTIVE **2** relating to Islam

mussel **mussels**
NOUN a small, edible shellfish with a black shell

must
VERB **1** If you tell someone that they **must** do something, you make them feel that they ought to do it. • *You must try this pudding – it's delicious.*
2 If something **must** happen, it is very important or necessary that it happens. • *You must be over 15 to see a film with a 15 certificate.*
3 If you think something is very likely, you think it **must** be so. • *You must be Sam's brother.*

mustard
NOUN a spicy-tasting yellow or brown paste made from seeds

mute
ADJECTIVE People or animals that are **mute** do not or cannot speak or make a sound.

mutilate **mutilates, mutilating, mutilated**
VERB **1** If you **mutilate** something, you damage or spoil it.
2 If someone is **mutilated**, they have been very badly cut and injured.

mutiny **mutinies, mutinying, mutinied**
VERB **1** If a group of sailors or soldiers **mutiny**, they rebel against their officers.
NOUN **2** a rebellion against someone in authority
mutineer NOUN

mutter **mutters, muttering, muttered**
VERB If you **mutter**, or if you **mutter** something, you speak very quietly so that it is difficult for people to hear you.

mutton
NOUN the meat of an adult sheep

mutual
Said "**mew**-choo-ul" ADJECTIVE **Mutual** is used to describe something that two or more people give to each other or share. • *My dad and my brother have a mutual love of football.*

muzzle **muzzles, muzzling, muzzled**
NOUN **1** the nose and mouth of an animal
2 a cover or a strap for a dog's nose and mouth to prevent it from biting
3 the open end of a gun where the bullets come out
VERB **4** If you **muzzle** a dog, you put a muzzle on it.

my
ADJECTIVE **My** refers to something belonging to the person who is speaking or writing. • *I ride my bicycle to school every day.*

myself
PRONOUN You use **myself** when you are speaking about yourself. • *I was cross with myself for being so mean.*

mysterious
ADJECTIVE **1** strange and puzzling • *They heard mysterious noises in the night.*
2 If someone is being **mysterious**, they

are being secretive about something.
● *Mum is being very* **mysterious** *about my birthday present.*
mysteriously ADVERB

mystery **mysteries**
NOUN something that is not understood or known about ● *The identity of the burglar remains a* **mystery**.

mystify **mystifies, mystifying, mystified**
VERB If something **mystifies** you, you find it impossible to understand. ● *I am* **mystified** *by the disappearance of my sweater.*

myth **myths**
NOUN a story that was made up long ago to explain natural events and people's religious beliefs

nag **nags, nagging, nagged**
VERB If you **nag** someone, you keep complaining to them or pestering them about something.

nail **nails, nailing, nailed**
NOUN **1** Your **nails** are the thin, hard areas covering the ends of your fingers and toes.
2 a small piece of metal with a sharp point at one end, that you hammer into objects to hold them together
VERB **3** If you **nail** something somewhere, you fix it there using a nail.

naïve
Said "ny-**eeve**" ADJECTIVE If you are **naïve**, you believe that things are easier or less complicated than they really are, usually because of your lack of experience.
naïvely ADVERB

naked
ADJECTIVE not wearing any clothes

name **names, naming, named**
NOUN **1** a word that you use to identify a person, animal, place or thing
VERB **2** When you **name** someone or something, you give them a name.

nameless
ADJECTIVE not having a name or not identified ● *a* **nameless** *terror*

nanny **nannies**
NOUN a person whose job is to look after young children

nap **naps, napping, napped**
NOUN **1** a short sleep
VERB **2** When you **nap**, you have a short sleep.

napkin **napkins**
NOUN a small piece of cloth or paper used

a
b
c
d
e
f
g
h
i
j
k
l
m
n
o
p
q
r
s
t
u
v
w
x
y
z

to wipe your hands and mouth after eating

nappy **nappies**
NOUN a piece of towelling or paper padding worn round a baby's bottom

narrate **narrates, narrating, narrated**
VERB If you **narrate** a story, you tell it.

narrative **narratives**
NOUN a story or an account of events

narrator **narrators**
NOUN the person in a book or a film or in a radio or television broadcast, who tells the story or explains what is happening

narrow **narrower, narrowest; narrows, narrowing, narrowed**
ADJECTIVE **1** Something that is **narrow** measures a small distance from one side to the other. • We walked down a **narrow** passageway.
VERB **2** If something **narrows**, it becomes less wide. • The track **narrowed** ahead.

nasty **nastier, nastiest**
ADJECTIVE very unpleasant
SYNONYMS: unkind, rude, disgusting

nation **nations**
NOUN a country and all the people who live there

national
ADJECTIVE relating to a country or the whole country • He was dressed in the **national** costume.

national anthem **national anthems**
NOUN the official song of a country

nationality **nationalities**
NOUN the fact of being a citizen of a particular nation

native **natives**
ADJECTIVE **1** Your **native** country is the country where you were born.
2 Your **native** language is the language that you first learned to speak.
NOUN **3** A **native** of a place is someone who was born there.

Nativity
NOUN In Christianity, the **Nativity** is the birth of Christ, or the festival celebrating this.

natural
ADJECTIVE **1** normal and to be expected
• It's **natural** to want to do well.
2 existing or happening in nature, rather than caused or made by people • Wool is a **natural** material.
3 If you have a **natural** ability, you are born with it. • She has a **natural** flair for mathematics.
naturally ADVERB

natural history
NOUN the study of animals and plants

nature **natures**
NOUN **1** animals, plants and all the other things in the world that are not made by people
2 the basic quality or character of a person or thing • They liked his warm, generous **nature**.

naughty **naughtier, naughtiest**
ADJECTIVE A child who is **naughty** behaves badly.
naughtiness NOUN

nausea
NOUN a feeling that you are going to be sick
nauseous ADJECTIVE

nautical
ADJECTIVE relating to ships or navigation

naval
ADJECTIVE relating to a navy

navel **navels**
NOUN the small hollow on the front of your body, just below your waist

navigate **navigates, navigating, navigated**
VERB When someone **navigates**, they work out the direction in which a ship, plane or car should go, using maps and sometimes instruments.
navigation NOUN **navigator** NOUN

navy navies
NOUN the part of a country's armed forces that fights at sea

near nearer, nearest; nears, nearing, neared
PREPOSITION OR ADVERB **1** If something is **near** a place, it is a short distance from it.
● *They live in a cottage **near** the river.*
VERB **2** When you are **nearing** a particular place or time, you are approaching it and will soon reach it. ● *The dog began to bark as the visitor **neared** the door.*

nearby
ADJECTIVE OR ADVERB a short distance away

nearly
ADVERB not completely, but almost ● *I've **nearly** finished my homework.*

neat neater, neatest
ADJECTIVE tidy and smart
neatly ADVERB **neatness** NOUN

necessary
ADJECTIVE Something that is **necessary** is needed or must be done. ● *It might be **necessary** to leave quickly.*

🖉 *Necessary has one c and two ss.*

necessity necessities
NOUN **1** the need to do something
2 something that is needed ● *Water is a basic **necessity** of life.*

neck necks
NOUN **1** the part of your body that joins your head to the rest of your body
2 the long, narrow part at one end of a bottle or guitar

necklace necklaces
NOUN a piece of jewellery that a person wears around their neck

nectar
NOUN a sweet liquid produced by flowers and collected by insects

need needs, needing, needed
VERB **1** If you **need** something, you cannot achieve what you want without having it or doing it. ● *I **need** some help with my homework.*

PLURAL NOUN **2** Your **needs** are the things that you need to have.
SYNONYMS: necessities, requirements

needle needles
NOUN **1** a small, thin piece of metal with a hole at one end and a sharp point at the other, used for sewing
2 **Needles** are long, thin pieces of steel or plastic, used for knitting.
3 the sharp part of a syringe that goes into your skin when you have an injection
4 the thin pointer on a dial or compass that moves to show a measurement or bearing
5 Pine **needles** are the sharp, pointed leaves of a pine tree.

needlework
NOUN sewing or embroidery that is done by hand

negative negatives
ADJECTIVE **1** A **negative** answer means no.
ANTONYM: positive
2 A **negative** number is less than zero.
ANTONYM: positive
NOUN **3** the image that is first produced when you take a photograph

neglect neglects, neglecting, neglected
VERB **1** If you **neglect** someone or something, you do not look after them properly. ● *Ben **neglected** his hamster.*
NOUN **2** failure to look after someone or something properly ● *Most of her plants died from **neglect**.*

negotiate negotiates, negotiating, negotiated
VERB When people **negotiate**, they talk about a situation in order to reach an agreement about it.

neigh neighs, neighing, neighed
*Said "**nay**"* VERB **1** When a horse **neighs**, it makes a loud, high-pitched sound through its nose.
NOUN **2** A **neigh** is a loud, high-pitched sound made by a horse.

neighbour neighbours
NOUN someone who lives next door to you or near you

neighbourhood **neighbourhoods**
NOUN Your **neighbourhood** is the area where you live.

neither
CONJUNCTION, ADJECTIVE OR PRONOUN You use **neither** in front of two alternatives to mean not one and not the other. • *He spoke **neither** English nor German.*

neon
NOUN a gas used in glass tubes to make light sources and signs

nephew **nephews**
NOUN Someone's **nephew** is the son of their sister or brother.

nerve **nerves**
NOUN **1** long, thin fibres that send messages between your brain and other parts of your body
2 courage and calm in a difficult situation
3 INFORMAL rudeness or cheek • *She had the **nerve** to answer back to the head teacher.*

nervous
ADJECTIVE easily worried and agitated
nervously ADVERB

nest **nests**
NOUN a structure that birds, insects and other animals make, in which to lay eggs or rear their young

nestle **nestles, nestling, nestled**
*Said "**ness**-sl"* VERB If you **nestle** somewhere, you settle there comfortably, often very close to someone or something else. • *My kitten loves to **nestle** in my lap.*

net **nets**
NOUN **1** short for **internet**
2 material made from threads woven together with small spaces in between
3 a piece of this material used for a particular purpose, for example a fishing **net**

netball
NOUN a game in which two teams of seven players each try to score goals by throwing a ball through a net at the top of a pole

nettle **nettles**
NOUN a wild plant covered with little hairs that sting

network **networks**
NOUN **1** a large number of lines or roads that cross each other at many points
2 a group of computers connected to each other

neutral
ADJECTIVE People who are **neutral** do not support either side in a disagreement or war.

never
ADVERB at no time in the past, present or future • *I've **never** met such a lovely person.*

nevertheless
ADVERB in spite of what has just been said • *I know you're home safely, but **nevertheless** I want you to ring for a lift in future.*

new **newer, newest**
ADJECTIVE **1** recently made, created or discovered • *She's got a **new** film out.*
2 different • *We've got a **new** maths teacher.*

news
NOUN up-to-date information about things that have happened

newsagent **newsagents**
NOUN a person or shop that sells newspapers and magazines

newspaper **newspapers**
NOUN a publication, on large sheets of folded paper, that is produced regularly and contains news and articles

newt **newts**
NOUN a small, amphibious creature with a moist skin, short legs and a long tail

newton newtons
NOUN a unit for measuring force (N)
[named after Sir Isaac *Newton*]

New Year
NOUN the time when people celebrate the start of a year

next
ADJECTIVE **1** The **next** thing, person or event is the one that comes immediately after the present one. ● *We'll catch the **next** train.*
ADVERB **2** You use **next** to refer to an action that follows immediately after the present one. ● *What shall we do **next**?*
3 The **next** place or person is the one nearest to you. ● *She lives in the **next** street.*
PHRASE **4** If one thing is **next to** another, it is at the side of it. ● *She sat down **next to** him.*

nib nibs
NOUN the pointed end of a pen, where the ink comes out

nibble nibbles, nibbling, nibbled
VERB **1** When you **nibble** something, you take small bites of it.
NOUN **2** a small bite of something

nice nicer, nicest
ADJECTIVE pleasant or kind
nicely ADVERB

nickname nicknames
NOUN an informal name for someone or something ● *Red got his **nickname** because of his ginger hair.*
[from Middle English *an ekename* meaning an additional name]

nicotine
NOUN an addictive substance found in tobacco
[named after Jacques *Nicot*, who first brought tobacco to France]

niece nieces
NOUN Someone's **niece** is the daughter of their sister or brother.

night nights
NOUN the time between sunset and sunrise, when it is dark

nightdress nightdresses
NOUN a loose dress that a woman or girl wears to sleep in

nightfall
NOUN the time of day when it starts to get dark

nightingale nightingales
NOUN a small, brown European bird, the male of which sings very beautifully, especially at night

nightmare nightmares
NOUN **1** a frightening dream
2 an unpleasant or frightening situation ● *The whole journey was a **nightmare**.*

nil
NOUN zero or nothing, especially in sports scores ● *At half-time the score was still **nil-nil**.*

nimble nimbler, nimblest
ADJECTIVE able to move quickly and easily
nimbly ADVERB

nine
NOUN **Nine** is the number 9.
ninth NOUN OR ADJECTIVE

nineteen
NOUN **Nineteen** is the number 19.
nineteenth NOUN OR ADJECTIVE

ninety
NOUN **Ninety** is the number 90.
ninetieth NOUN OR ADJECTIVE

nip nips, nipping, nipped
VERB **1** If you **nip** someone or something, you give them a slight pinch or bite.

2 If you **nip** somewhere, you go there quickly. • *I have to **nip** to the shop for some milk.*

NOUN **3** A **nip** is small bite or pinch.

niqab niqabs

Said "ni-**kab**" NOUN a veil worn by some Muslim women in public, covering all the face except the eyes

nitrogen

NOUN a chemical element, usually found as a colourless gas. **Nitrogen** makes up about 78% of the earth's atmosphere.

no

EXCLAMATION **1** You say **no** when you do not want something or do not agree.

ADJECTIVE OR ADVERB **2** none at all or not at all • *He has **no** excuse for his behaviour.*

noble nobler, noblest

ADJECTIVE If someone is **noble**, they are honest and brave, and deserve admiration.

nobody

PRONOUN not a single person • *For a long time **nobody** spoke.*

🖉 Nobody and no one mean the same thing.

nocturnal

ADJECTIVE happening or active at night • *The hedgehog is a **nocturnal** animal.*

nod nods, nodding, nodded

VERB When you **nod** your head, you move it up and down, usually to say yes.

noise noises

NOUN a sound, especially one that is loud or unpleasant

noisy noisier, noisiest

ADJECTIVE making a lot of noise, or full of noise

nomad nomads

NOUN a person who travels from place to place rather than staying in just one • *The Bedouin people in Arabia are **nomads**.*

[from Latin *nomas* meaning wandering shepherd]

nomadic ADJECTIVE

nominate nominates, nominating, nominated

VERB If a person **nominates** someone for a job or position, they formally suggest that they have it.

nomination NOUN

non-

PREFIX not, for example something that is **non**existent does not exist

none

PRONOUN not a single thing or person, or not even a small amount of something • *They asked me for my ideas, but I had **none**.*

non-fiction

NOUN writing dealing with facts and events rather than imaginative storytelling

ANTONYM: fiction

nonsense

NOUN foolish or meaningless words or behaviour

nonsmoking

ADJECTIVE A **nonsmoking** area is a place where smoking is forbidden.

nonstop

ADJECTIVE OR ADVERB continuing without any pauses or breaks

SYNONYM: continuous

noodle noodles

NOUN a kind of pasta shaped into long, thin pieces

noon

NOUN midday

no one or no-one

PRONOUN not a single person • ***No one** goes to that play park any more.*

SYNONYM: nobody

noose nooses

NOUN a loop at the end of a piece of rope, with a knot that tightens when the rope is pulled

nor

CONJUNCTION used after *neither*, or to add emphasis • ***Neither** you **nor** I know the answer.* • *I couldn't afford to go to the fair, and **nor** could my friends.*

normal
ADJECTIVE usual and ordinary

north
NOUN one of the four main points of the compass. If you face the point where the sun rises, **north** is on your left. The abbreviation for **north** is N.

north-east
NOUN, ADVERB OR ADJECTIVE halfway between north and east

northern
ADJECTIVE in or from the north ● *The mountains of **northern** Spain are very beautiful.*

north-west
NOUN, ADVERB OR ADJECTIVE halfway between north and west

nose noses
NOUN the part of your face above your mouth, that you use for smelling and breathing

nostalgia
NOUN a feeling of affection for the past, and sadness that things have changed
nostalgic ADJECTIVE **nostalgically** ADVERB

nostril nostrils
NOUN Your **nostrils** are the two openings in your nose that you breathe through.

nosy nosier, nosiest; also spelt **nosey**
ADJECTIVE **Nosy** people always want to know about other people's business, and like to interfere where they are not wanted.

not
ADVERB used to make a sentence mean the opposite ● *I am **not** very happy.*

note notes
NOUN **1** a short letter
2 You take **notes** to help you remember what has been said.
3 In music, a **note** is a musical sound of a particular pitch, or a written symbol that represents this sound.
4 a piece of paper money ● *a ten-pound note*

notebook notebooks
NOUN a small book for writing notes in

nothing
PRONOUN not a single thing, or not a single part of something

notice notices, noticing, noticed
VERB **1** If you **notice** something, you become aware of it. ● *She **noticed** a bird sitting on the fence.*
NOUN **2** a written announcement
PHRASE **3** If you **take notice of** something, you pay attention to it.

noticeable
ADJECTIVE obvious and easy to see

notify notifies, notifying, notified
VERB If you **notify** someone of something, you officially inform them of it. ● *You must **notify** us of any change of address.*
notification NOUN

notorious
ADJECTIVE well known for something bad ● *a **notorious** criminal*

nought noughts
NOUN the number 0, zero

noun nouns
NOUN a word that refers to a person, thing or idea. Examples of **nouns** are *table, happiness* and *John.*

nourish nourishes, nourishing, nourished
VERB If you **nourish** people or animals, you give them plenty of food.
nourishing ADJECTIVE

nourishment
NOUN the food that your body needs to grow and stay healthy, including vitamins and minerals ● *"Eat your vegetables, they're full of **nourishment**."*

novel novels
NOUN **1** a book that tells a long story about imaginary people and events
ADJECTIVE **2** new and interesting ● *This whole trip has been a **novel** experience.*

novelty novelties
NOUN **1** the quality of being new and interesting

a
b
c
d
e
f
g
h
i
j
k
l
m
n
o
p
q
r
s
t
u
v
w
x
y
z

267

2 something new and interesting

3 a small object sold as a gift or souvenir

November

NOUN the eleventh month of the year. **November** has 30 days.
[from Latin *November* meaning the ninth month]

novice novices

NOUN someone who is not yet experienced at something • *Most of the group are **novices** at horse riding.*

now

ADVERB **1** at the present time or moment
CONJUNCTION **2** as a result or consequence of a particular fact • *Your writing will improve **now** you have a new pen.*

nowhere

ADVERB not anywhere • *There was **nowhere** to hide.*

nozzle nozzles

NOUN a spout fitted onto the end of a pipe or hose to control the flow of liquid or gas

nuclear

ADJECTIVE relating to the energy produced when atoms are split • *We live near a **nuclear** power station.*

nucleus nuclei

*Said "**nyoo**-clee-us" and "**nyoo**-clee-eye"*
NOUN **1** the central part of an atom or a cell

nucleus

an atom

2 the important or central part of something • *We still have the **nucleus** of the team.*

nude nudes

ADJECTIVE **1** If someone is **nude**, they are naked.

NOUN **2** A **nude** is a picture or statue of a naked person.

nudge nudges, nudging, nudged

VERB **1** If you **nudge** someone, you push them gently with your elbow to get their attention or to make them move.
NOUN **2** a gentle push with your elbow

nugget nuggets

NOUN a small rough lump of something, especially gold

nuisance nuisances

NOUN someone or something that is annoying or causing problems

numb

ADJECTIVE unable to feel anything • *I was so cold my hands and feet felt **numb**.*
[from Middle English *nomen* meaning paralysed]

number numbers, numbering, numbered

NOUN **1** a word or symbol used for counting or calculating
2 the series of numbers that you dial when you telephone someone
VERB **3** If you **number** something, you give it a number, usually in a sequence.
• *Please **number** each page you write on.*

numeracy

NOUN the ability to do arithmetic

numeral numerals

NOUN a symbol that is used to represent a number

numerator numerators

NOUN the top number of a fraction. It tells you the number of pieces or parts you are dealing with.

numerical

ADJECTIVE expressed in numbers or relating to numbers • *Please put these pages in **numerical** order.*

numerous

ADJECTIVE Things that are **numerous** exist or happen in large numbers. • *There are **numerous** things to do in a large city.*

nun nuns

NOUN a woman who has taken religious

vows and is a member of a religious community

nurse nurses, nursing, nursed
NOUN **1** a person whose job is to look after people who are ill
VERB **2** If you **nurse** someone, you look after them when they are ill. • *I helped dad to* **nurse** *mum when she had flu.*

nursery nurseries
NOUN **1** a place where young children are looked after when their parents are working
2 a place where plants are grown and sold

nursery rhyme nursery rhymes
NOUN a short poem or song for young children, such as *Little Miss Muffet* and *Jack and Jill*

nursery school nursery schools
NOUN a school for children aged three to five years old

nut nuts
NOUN **1** a fruit with a hard shell that grows on certain trees and bushes

brazil nut

almond

peanut

walnut

2 a piece of metal with a hole in the middle that a bolt screws into

nutrient nutrients
*Said "***new***-tree-unt"* NOUN one of the substances that help plants and animals to grow • *Very heavy rainfall washes valuable* **nutrients** *from the soil.*

nutrition
*Said "new-***trish***-un"* NOUN the food that you eat that helps you to grow and keeps you healthy • *Good* **nutrition** *is vital for healthy development.*

nutritious
ADJECTIVE If food is **nutritious** it helps you to grow and remain healthy. • *Spinach is a very* **nutritious** *vegetable.*

nylon
NOUN a type of strong, artificial fibre used for making, for example, clothes, ropes and brushes • *The rock climbers used brightly coloured ropes made of* **nylon** *to abseil down the rock face.*

a
b
c
d
e
f
g
h
i
j
k
l
m
n
o
p
q
r
s
t
u
v
w
x
y
z

Oo

oak oaks
NOUN a large tree that produces acorns. The **oak** has a hard wood that is often used to make furniture.

oar oars
NOUN a pole with a flat end used to row a boat through water

oasis oases
NOUN a small area in a desert where water and plants are found

oath oaths
NOUN a formal promise, especially a promise to tell the truth in a court of law

oats
PLURAL NOUN a type of grain

obedient
ADJECTIVE If you are **obedient**, you do as you are told.
ANTONYM: disobedient
obediently ADVERB   obedience NOUN

obey obeys, obeying, obeyed
VERB If you **obey** a person or an order, you do what you are told to do.

obituary obituaries
NOUN a piece of writing about the life and achievements of someone who has just died

object objects, objecting, objected
Said "**ob**-jekt" NOUN **1** anything solid that you can touch or see, and that is not alive
• This painting is an **object** of beauty.
2 an aim or purpose • The **object** of the marathon is to raise money.
Said "ob-**jekt**" VERB **3** If you **object** to something, you dislike it, disagree with it or disapprove of it.

objection objections
NOUN If you have an **objection** to something, you dislike it or disagree with it.

oblige obliges, obliging, obliged
VERB **1** If you are **obliged** to do something, you have to do it.
2 If you **oblige** someone, you help them. • He **obliged** us by showing the way.
3 If you are **obliged** to someone, you are grateful to them. • I would be much **obliged** if you could show me where this street is.
obliging ADJECTIVE

oblique
ADJECTIVE An **oblique** line slopes at an angle.

oblong oblongs
NOUN **1** a four-sided shape with four right angles, similar to a square but with two sides longer than the other two
ADJECTIVE **2** shaped like an oblong

obnoxious
ADJECTIVE extremely unpleasant
SYNONYMS: hateful, odious

oboe oboes
NOUN a woodwind instrument that makes a high-pitched sound
[from French *haut bois* meaning literally high wood, a reference to the instrument's pitch]
oboist NOUN

obscene
ADJECTIVE very rude and likely to upset people
obscenely ADVERB   obscenity NOUN

obscure obscures, obscuring, obscured
ADJECTIVE **1** Something **obscure** is difficult to see or to understand.
ANTONYMS: obvious, clear
VERB **2** If something **obscures** something else, it makes it difficult to see or understand. • The moon **obscured** the sun during the eclipse.

observant
ADJECTIVE An **observant** person notices things that are not usually noticed.

observation **observations**
NOUN the act of watching something closely ● *You will need to make careful* **observations** *of the experiment before you do the writing.*
[from Latin *observare* meaning to watch]

observe **observes, observing, observed**
VERB If you **observe** someone or something, you watch them carefully.
observer NOUN

obsession **obsessions**
NOUN If someone has an **obsession** about something or someone, they cannot stop thinking about them.
obsessional ADJECTIVE **obsessed** ADJECTIVE **obsessive** ADJECTIVE

obsolete
ADJECTIVE out of date and no longer used

obstacle **obstacles**
NOUN something that is in your way and makes it difficult for you to do something

obstinate
ADJECTIVE Someone who is **obstinate** is stubborn and unwilling to change their mind.

obstruct **obstructs, obstructing, obstructed**
VERB If something **obstructs** a road or path, it blocks it.

obtain **obtains, obtaining, obtained**
VERB If you **obtain** something, you get it.

obtuse
ADJECTIVE An **obtuse** angle is an angle between 90° and 180°.

115°

obvious
ADJECTIVE easy to see or understand ● *It was* **obvious** *that he didn't know the answer.*
obviously ADVERB

occasion **occasions**
NOUN a time when something happens ● *I met her on several* **occasions**.

 There are two *c*s but only one *s* in *occasion*.

occasional
ADJECTIVE happening sometimes, but not often ● *We go for an* **occasional** *walk in the woods.*
occasionally ADVERB

occupant **occupants**
NOUN the people who live or work in a building

occupation **occupations**
NOUN a job or profession

occupy **occupies, occupying, occupied**
VERB **1** The people who **occupy** a building are the people who live or work there.
2 If something **occupies** you, you spend your time doing it or thinking about it.

occur **occurs, occurring, occurred**
VERB If something **occurs**, it happens.

occur to
VERB If something **occurs to** you, you suddenly think of it or realize it.

ocean **oceans**
NOUN one of the five very large areas of sea in the world

o'clock
ADVERB You use **o'clock** after the number of the hour to say what the time is. ● *We have to be at school by eight* **o'clock**.

octagon **octagons**
NOUN a flat shape with eight straight sides
octagonal ADJECTIVE

octahedron **octahedrons**
NOUN a solid figure with eight identical flat surfaces

octave **octaves**
NOUN the difference in pitch between the first note and the eighth note of a musical scale

October
NOUN the tenth month of the year. **October** has 31 days.
[from Latin *October* meaning the eighth month, as it was the eighth month in the Roman calendar]

a
b
c
d
e
f
g
h
i
j
k
l
m
n
o
p
q
r
s
t
u
v
w
x
y
z

octopus
octopuses
NOUN a sea creature with eight long tentacles that it uses to catch food

odd odder, oddest
ADJECTIVE **1** strange or unusual
2 Odd things do not match each other. • *She always ended up with **odd** socks.*
3 Odd numbers cannot be divided exactly by two. Three and seven are examples of **odd** numbers.
ANTONYM: even

odour odours
NOUN FORMAL a strong smell

of
PREPOSITION **1** consisting of or containing
• *a cup **of** tea*
2 used when talking about things that are characteristic of something
• *a woman **of** great importance*
3 belonging to or connected with
• *a friend **of** Eve*

off
PREPOSITION OR ADVERB **1** used to show movement away from or out of a place
• *They got **off** the bus.*
2 used to show separation or distance from a place • *There are several islands **off** the coast of Britain.*
ADVERB **3** not at work • *He took a day **off**.*
ADVERB OR ADJECTIVE **4** not switched on
• *The television was **off**.*
ADJECTIVE **5** cancelled or postponed
• *The match is **off**.*
6 Food that is **off** is no longer fresh enough to eat, usually tastes unpleasant, and may make you ill.

> Do not use *of* after *off*. It is correct to say *I got off the bus*, not *I got off of the bus*.

offence offences
NOUN **1** a crime • *Burglary is a serious **offence**.*
PHRASE **2** If you **cause offence**, you embarrass or upset someone.
3 If you **take offence**, you feel that someone has been rude or hurtful to you.

offend offends, offending, offended
VERB **1** If you **offend** someone, you upset them.
2 If someone **offends**, they break the law.
offender NOUN

offensive
ADJECTIVE If something is **offensive**, it is rude and upsetting.

offer offers, offering, offered
VERB **1** If you **offer** something to someone, you ask them if they would like it, or say that you are willing to do it. • *I **offered** to wash the car.*
NOUN **2** something that someone says they will give you or do for you

office offices
NOUN **1** a room where people work at desks
2 a place where people can go for information, tickets or other services

officer officers
NOUN a person with a position of authority in the armed forces, the police or a government organization

official
ADJECTIVE approved by the government or by someone in authority
officially ADVERB

offline
ADJECTIVE **1** If a computer is **offline**, it is not connected to the internet.
ADVERB **2** If you do something **offline**, you do it while not connected to the internet.

often
ADVERB happening many times or a lot of the time • *He **often** goes swimming on Sunday.*

ogre ogres
NOUN a cruel, frightening giant in fairy stories

oil oils, oiling, oiled
NOUN **1** a thick, sticky liquid found under rocks that is used for fuel, lubrication and for making plastics and chemicals

A B C D E F G H I J K L M N O P Q R S T U V W X Y Z

2 a thick, greasy liquid made from plants or animal fat • *cooking* **oil**
VERB **3** If you **oil** something, you put oil in it or on it to make it work better. • *This squeaky hinge needs to be* **oiled**.

oily **oilier, oiliest**
ADJECTIVE Something that is **oily** is covered with or contains oil.

ointment **ointments**
NOUN a smooth, thick substance that you put on sore skin to heal it

OK or **okay**
ADJECTIVE all right; fine • *She slipped on the ice but she was* **OK**.

old **older, oldest**
ADJECTIVE **1** having lived or existed for a long time
2 Old is used to give the age of someone or something. • *The baby is six months* **old**.
3 You can use **old** to talk about something that is no longer used or has been replaced by something else. • *I bumped into my teacher from my* **old** *primary school.*

old-fashioned
ADJECTIVE **1** Something **old-fashioned** is out of date and no longer fashionable.
ANTONYM: fashionable
2 If someone is **old-fashioned**, they believe in the values and standards of the past.

olive **olives**
NOUN **1** a small green or black fruit containing a stone. **Olives** are usually pickled and eaten as a snack, or crushed to produce oil for cooking.
ADJECTIVE OR NOUN **2** dark yellowish-green

Olympic Games
Said "ul-**lim**-pic games" NOUN a series of international sporting contests held in a different country every four years [The word *Olympic* comes from *Olympia* in Greece, where games were held in ancient times]

omelette **omelettes**
NOUN a dish made by beating eggs together and cooking them in a flat pan

omit **omits, omitting, omitted**
VERB If you **omit** something, you do not include it. • *She* **omitted** *to mention that her mother could not come.*

omni-
PREFIX added to some words to mean all or everywhere, for example **omni**potent means all-powerful, and **omni**present means present everywhere

omnibus **omnibuses**
NOUN **1** a book containing a collection of stories or articles by the same author or about the same subject
ADJECTIVE **2** An **omnibus** edition of a radio or television series contains two or more episodes that were originally shown separately.

omnivore **omnivores**
NOUN an animal that eats all kinds of food, including meat and plants
omnivorous ADJECTIVE

on
PREPOSITION **1** touching something or attached to it • *We sat* **on** *the seat.*
2 If you are **on** a bus, a plane or a train, you are inside it.
3 If something happens **on** a particular day, that is when it happens.
4 If something is done **on** an instrument or a machine, it is done using it.
5 A book or a talk **on** a particular subject is about that subject.
ADVERB **6** If someone has a piece of clothing **on**, they are wearing it.
ADJECTIVE OR ADVERB **7** If a machine or a switch is **on**, it is working or is in action. • *"Please would you switch the radio* **on**?"

once
ADVERB **1** If something happens **once**, it happens one time only.
2 If something was **once** true, it was true in the past, but is no longer true. • *That ground was* **once** *covered by trees.*
CONJUNCTION **3** If something happens **once** another thing has happened, it happens immediately afterwards. • *I'll do my homework* **once** *I've finished my tea.*
PHRASE **4** If you do something **at once**, you

a
b
c
d
e
f
g
h
i
j
k
l
m
n
o
p
q
r
s
t
u
v
w
x
y
z

do it immediately. • *We must go home* ***at once***.

5 If several things happen **at once**, they all happen at the same time. • *He tried to hold three glasses* ***at once***.

one

NOUN **1 One** is the number 1.

ADJECTIVE **2** When you refer to **one** person or **one** thing, you mean a single person or thing. • *We have* ***one*** *main holiday a year.*

PRONOUN **3 One** refers to a particular person or thing. • *This book was the best* ***one*** *she had read for ages.*

onion onions

NOUN a small, round vegetable with a very strong taste

online

ADJECTIVE **1** If a computer is **online**, it is connected to the internet.

ADVERB **2** If you do something **online**, you do it while connected to the internet.

only

ADVERB **1** You use **only** to show the one thing or person involved. • ***Only*** *one girl was able to complete the race.*

2 You use **only** to make a condition that must happen before something else can happen. • *You will be allowed in* ***only*** *if you have a ticket.*

3 You use **only** to emphasize that something is unimportant or small. • *He's* ***only*** *very young.*

ADJECTIVE **4** If you talk about the **only** thing or person, you mean that there are no others. For example, if you are an **only** child, you have no brothers or sisters.

CONJUNCTION **5** You can use **only** to mean but or except. • *He was very much like you,* ***only*** *with blond hair.*

onomatopoeia

Said "on-uh-mat-uh-**pee**-a" NOUN the use of words that sound like the thing that they represent. *Hiss* and *buzz* are examples of **onomatopoeia**.

onto or on to

PREPOSITION If you put something **onto** an object, you put it on it. • *He threw the pillow* ***onto*** *the bed.*

ooze oozes, oozing, oozed

VERB When a thick liquid **oozes**, it flows slowly. • *The cold mud* ***oozed*** *over her toes.* [from Old English *wos* meaning juice]

opaque

ADJECTIVE If something is **opaque**, it does not let light through, so you cannot see through it. • ***opaque*** *glass windows*

ANTONYM: clear

open opens, opening, opened

ADJECTIVE **1** Something that is **open** is not closed or fastened, allowing things to pass through. • *A light breeze came through the* ***open*** *window.*

2 not enclosed or covered • *At last we were out in the* ***open*** *countryside.*

VERB **3** When you **open** something, or when it **opens**, it is moved so that it is no longer closed. • *She* ***opened*** *the box of chocolates.*

4 When a shop or office **opens**, people are allowed to go in to do business.

5 If you **open** a book, you turn back the cover so that you can read it.

6 If something **opens**, it starts or begins.

ADJECTIVE **7** Someone who is **open** is honest and not secretive.

openly ADVERB

opening openings

NOUN **1** a hole or gap • *There was a small* ***opening*** *in the fence.*

ADJECTIVE **2** coming first • *He sang the* ***opening*** *song in the concert.*

NOUN **3** the first part of a book or film • *I love the* ***opening*** *of that book.*

opera operas

NOUN a play in which the words are sung rather than spoken

operate operates, operating, operated

VERB **1** When you **operate** a machine, you make it work. • *I know how to* ***operate*** *the computer.*

2 When surgeons **operate**, they cut open a person's body to remove or repair a damaged part.

operation operations

NOUN **1** a form of medical treatment in

which a surgeon cuts open a patient's body to remove or repair a damaged part **2** a complex, planned event • *Moving house is going to be quite a difficult* **operation**.

opinion opinions
NOUN a belief or view

opponent opponents
NOUN someone who is against you in an argument or a contest

opportunity opportunities
NOUN a chance to do something

oppose opposes, opposing, opposed
VERB If you **oppose** something or someone, you disagree with them and are against them.

opposing
ADJECTIVE **Opposing** means opposite or very different. • *We managed to be friends even though we had **opposing** points of view.*

opposite opposites
PREPOSITION OR ADVERB **1** If one thing is **opposite** another, it is facing it. • *Our house is **opposite** the park.*
NOUN **2** If people or things are **opposites**, they are completely different from each other.

opposition
NOUN **1** If there is **opposition** to something, there is resistance to it and people oppose it. • *There is a lot of **opposition** to the building of a new road.*
2 In a games or sports event, the **opposition** is the person or team that you are competing against.

opt opts, opting, opted
VERB **1** If you **opt** for something, you choose to do it. • *I **opted** to go to the Gym Club.*
2 If you **opt** out of something, you choose not to do it or be involved with it. • *I **opted** out of football practice.*

optical
ADJECTIVE concerned with vision, light or images

optician opticians
NOUN someone who tests people's eyesight, and makes and sells glasses and contact lenses

optimist optimists
NOUN An **optimist** is a person who is always hopeful that everything will turn out well in the future.
ANTONYM: pessimist
optimism NOUN   **optimistic** ADJECTIVE

option options
NOUN a choice between two or more things

optional
ADJECTIVE If something is **optional**, you can choose whether to do it or not. • *Tennis is* **optional** *at our school.*
ANTONYM: compulsory

or
CONJUNCTION used to link two alternatives or choices • *You need to decide whether to stay* **or** *leave.*

oral
ADJECTIVE **1** spoken rather than written • *Tomorrow we have our French **oral** examination.*
2 to do with your mouth or using your mouth • ***Oral** hygiene is vital for healthy teeth.*
orally ADVERB

orange oranges
NOUN **1** a round citrus fruit that is juicy and sweet and has a thick reddish-yellow skin
ADJECTIVE OR NOUN **2** reddish-yellow
[from Sanskrit *naranga* meaning orange]

orang-utan orang-utans; also spelt orang-utang
NOUN a large ape with reddish-brown hair

orbit orbits, orbiting, orbited
NOUN **1** the curved path followed by an object going round a planet or the sun
VERB **2** If something **orbits** a planet or the sun, it goes round and round it.
• *Our moon **orbits** the earth.*

A B C D E F G H I J K L M N O P Q R S T U V W X Y Z

orchard **orchards**
NOUN a piece of land where fruit trees are grown

orchestra **orchestras**
NOUN a large group of musicians who play musical instruments together

orchid **orchids**
NOUN a type of plant with beautiful and unusual flowers

ordeal **ordeals**
NOUN a very difficult and unpleasant experience

order **orders, ordering, ordered**
NOUN **1** a command given by someone in authority
2 If things are arranged or done in a particular **order**, they are arranged or done in that sequence. • *alphabetical order*
VERB **3** If you **order** someone to do something, you tell them firmly to do it.
4 When you **order** something, you ask for it to be brought or sent to you.

ordinary
ADJECTIVE not special or different in any way

ore **ores**
NOUN rock or earth from which metal can be obtained

organ **organs**
NOUN **1** Your **organs** are parts of your body that have a particular purpose, for example your lungs are the **organs** with which you breathe.
2 a large musical instrument with a keyboard and windpipes through which air is forced to produce a sound

organic
ADJECTIVE **1** **Organic** food is produced without the use of artificial fertilizers or pesticides.
2 produced or found in living things
organically ADVERB

organism **organisms**
NOUN any living animal or plant

organization **organizations**; also spelt **organisation**
NOUN **1** any business or group of people working together for a purpose
2 the act of planning and arranging something

organize **organizes, organizing, organized**; also spelt **organise**
VERB If you **organize** something, you plan and arrange it.

oriental
ADJECTIVE Something that is **oriental** comes from the Far East, which includes countries such as India, China and Japan. • *I like **oriental** food.*

orienteering
NOUN a sport in which people find their way from one place to another in the countryside, using a map and compass

origin **origins**
NOUN the beginning or cause of something • *The **origins** of man have been written about in many books.*

original **originals**
ADJECTIVE **1** the first or earliest • *The **original** owner of this house made lots of alterations.*
2 imaginative and clever • *His paintings are highly **original**.*
NOUN **3** a work of art or a document that is the one that was produced first, and is not a copy
originally ADVERB

ornament **ornaments**
NOUN a small, attractive object that you display in your home or that you wear in order to look attractive

ornithology
NOUN the study of birds
ornithologist NOUN

orphan **orphans**
NOUN a child whose parents are dead

orphanage **orphanages**
NOUN a place where orphans are looked after

ostrich **ostriches**
NOUN the largest bird in the world. **Ostriches** can run fast but cannot fly.

other others

PRONOUN **1** The **other** can mean the second of two things. • *One of the rooms is empty, but the **other** is not.*
ADJECTIVE **2 Other** people or things are different from those already mentioned.
3 The **other** day means a few days ago.

otherwise

ADVERB **1** or else
2 apart from the thing mentioned
• *The food was good, but **otherwise** the party was awful.*

otter otters

NOUN a small, furry animal with a long tail, that lives near water. **Otters** swim well and eat fish.

ought

VERB **1** If you say that someone **ought** to do something, you mean they should do it.
2 If you say that something **ought** to be the case, you mean that you expect it to be the case. • *He **ought** to be here by now.*

ounce ounces

NOUN a unit of weight equal to one-sixteenth of a pound or about 28.35 grams

our

ADJECTIVE belonging to us • ***Our** cat is black.*

ours

PRONOUN belonging to us • *That cat is **ours**.*

ourselves

PRONOUN **Ourselves** is used when talking about a group of people that includes the speaker or writer. • *We didn't hurt **ourselves** too badly.*

out

ADVERB **1** towards the outside of a place or thing • *Take the ice cream **out** of the freezer.*
ADJECTIVE **2** not at home

outbreak outbreaks

NOUN If there is an **outbreak** of something unpleasant, such as war, it suddenly occurs. • *The **outbreak** of the disease made many people unwell.*

outburst outbursts

NOUN a sudden strong expression of emotion, especially anger or violent action • *He apologized for his angry **outburst**.*

outcome outcomes

NOUN a result

outdoor

ADJECTIVE happening or used outside

outdoors

ADVERB If something happens **outdoors**, it takes place outside in the open air.

outer

ADJECTIVE The **outer** parts of something are the parts furthest from the centre. • *the **outer** doors*

outer space

NOUN everything beyond the earth's atmosphere

outfit outfits

NOUN a set of clothes • *I bought a new **outfit** for the party.*

outgoing

ADJECTIVE Someone who is **outgoing** is friendly and not shy. • *She is always fun to be with as she has such an **outgoing** personality.*

outgrow outgrows, outgrowing, outgrew, outgrown

VERB **1** If you **outgrow** a piece of clothing, you grow too big to wear it. • *I've already **outgrown** my best jeans.*
2 If you **outgrow** a way of behaving, you stop behaving that way because you are older and more mature.

outing outings

NOUN a trip made for pleasure

outlaw outlaws, outlawing, outlawed

VERB **1** If someone **outlaws** something, they ban it.
NOUN **2** In the past, an **outlaw** was a criminal.

outlet outlets

NOUN **1** a hole or pipe through which water or air can flow away

a
b
c
d
e
f
g
h
i
j
k
l
m
n
o
p
q
r
s
t
u
v
w
x
y
z

2 a shop that sells goods made by a particular manufacturer

outline outlines, outlining, outlined

NOUN **1** The **outline** of something is its shape.

VERB **2** If you **outline** a plan or idea, you give brief details of it.

outlook outlooks

NOUN **1** Your **outlook** is your general attitude towards life. ● *His outlook on life is always positive.*

2 The **outlook** of a situation is the way it is likely to develop. ● *The outlook for the weather over the next few days is not very good.*

outnumber outnumbers, outnumbering, outnumbered

VERB If there is more of one group than of another, the first group **outnumbers** the second. ● *Boys outnumber girls in our class.*

outpatient outpatients

NOUN someone who receives treatment in hospital without staying overnight

output outputs

NOUN **1** the amount of something produced by a person or organization

2 The **output** of a computer is the information that it produces.

outrage outrages, outraging, outraged

VERB **1** If something **outrages** you, it angers and shocks you.

NOUN **2** a feeling of anger and shock

3 something very shocking or violent

outrageous ADJECTIVE   **outrageously** ADVERB

outright

ADJECTIVE **1** total and complete ● *She made an outright refusal to come with us.*

ADVERB **2** completely, totally ● *Smoking in the building has been banned outright.*

outside

NOUN **1** The **outside** of something is the part that surrounds or encloses the rest of it. ● *We wandered around the outside of the house.*

ADVERB, ADJECTIVE OR PREPOSITION **2** not inside

NOUN **3** not included in something ● *The building will be closed outside school hours.*

> 🖉 Do not use *of* after *outside* when it is a preposition. It is correct to say *I met her outside the school*, not *I met her outside of the school*.

outskirts

PLURAL NOUN the parts around the edge of a city or town ● *Our home is on the outskirts of a large town.*

outspoken

ADJECTIVE **Outspoken** people give their opinions openly, even if they shock other people.

outstanding

ADJECTIVE extremely good

outwit outwits, outwitting, outwitted

VERB If you **outwit** someone, you use your intelligence or a clever trick to defeat them or get the better of them.

oval ovals

NOUN **1** a shape similar to a circle, but wider in one direction than the other

ADJECTIVE **2** shaped like an oval

[from Latin *ovalis* meaning egg-shaped]

oven ovens

NOUN the part of a cooker that you use for baking or roasting food

over overs

PREPOSITION **1** directly above something or covering it ● *She hung the picture over the fireplace.* ● *He put his hands over his eyes.*

2 A view **over** an area is a view across it. ● *I love the view over the lake to the mountains.*

3 If something happens **over** a period of time, it happens during that period. ● *I went to New Zealand over Christmas.*

ADVERB **4** If an amount of something is left **over**, that amount remains.

5 If you lean **over**, you bend your body in a particular direction. ● *He leant over to*

open the door of the car.
6 If something rolls or turns **over**, it moves so that its other side is facing upwards.

ADJECTIVE **7** Something that is **over** is completely finished.

NOUN **8** In cricket, an **over** is a series of six balls bowled by one bowler.

over-

PREFIX too much, or to too great an extent. For example, if fruit is **over**ripe, it is too ripe, and if someone **over**eats, they eat too much.

overall

ADJECTIVE OR ADVERB taking into account all the parts or aspects of something
• *Overall, the project has been a success.*

overalls

PLURAL NOUN a piece of clothing that you wear to protect your other clothes when you are working

overboard

ADVERB If you fall **overboard**, you fall over the side of a ship into the water.

overcast

ADJECTIVE When the sky is **overcast**, it is covered by thick cloud.

overcoat **overcoats**

NOUN a thick, warm coat

overcome **overcomes, overcoming, overcame, overcome**

VERB **1** If you **overcome** a problem or a feeling, you manage to deal with it or control it.

2 If you are **overcome**, you are affected by strong emotions. • *They were overcome with happiness.*

3 If you are **overcome** by fumes, gas or smoke, for example, you are made unconscious by them.

overcrowded

ADJECTIVE If a place is **overcrowded**, there are too many things or people in it.

overdue

ADJECTIVE If someone or something is **overdue**, they are late. • *The train is now overdue.*

overflow **overflows, overflowing, overflowed**

VERB If a liquid **overflows**, it spills over the edge of its container. If a river **overflows**, it flows over its banks.

overgrown

ADJECTIVE If a place is **overgrown**, it is thickly covered with plants and weeds.

overhaul **overhauls, overhauling, overhauled**

VERB **1** If you **overhaul** something, you examine and check it carefully, and repair any faults.

NOUN **2** An **overhaul** is a careful and detailed examination of something in order to repair its faults.

overhead

ADVERB OR ADJECTIVE above your head, or in the sky • *Seagulls flew overhead.* • *The overhead wires were being repaired.*

overhear **overhears, overhearing, overheard**

VERB If you **overhear** someone's conversation, you hear what they are saying to someone else.

overlap **overlaps, overlapping, overlapped**

VERB If one thing **overlaps** another, it covers part of the other thing.

overload **overloads, overloading, overloaded**

VERB If you **overload** someone or something, you give them too much to do or to carry.

overlook **overlooks, overlooking, overlooked**

VERB **1** If a building or window **overlooks** a place, it has a view of it from above.

2 If you **overlook** something, you ignore it or do not notice it.

overnight

ADVERB OR ADJECTIVE **1** during the night
• *We took an overnight flight.*

2 sudden or suddenly • *He seemed to become such a good player overnight.*

A B C D E F G H I J K L M N O P Q R S T U V W X Y Z

overseas

ADJECTIVE OR ADVERB abroad • *We have some* **overseas** *students visiting the school.* • *My brother is going* **overseas** *for a year.*

oversleep **oversleeps, oversleeping, overslept**

VERB If you **oversleep**, you sleep on past the time you intended to wake up.

overtake **overtakes, overtaking, overtook, overtaken**

VERB If you **overtake** someone or something, you pass them because you are moving faster than they are.

overtime

NOUN time that someone works in addition to their normal working hours

overture **overtures**

NOUN the opening piece of music at a concert, show or ballet

overweight

ADJECTIVE People or animals that are **overweight** are too heavy for their size.

overwhelm **overwhelms, overwhelming, overwhelmed**

VERB **1** If something **overwhelms** you, it affects you very strongly.
2 If one group of people **overwhelms** another, they completely defeat them.
3 If you **overwhelm** someone with something, you load them with too much of it. • *He was* **overwhelmed** *with work.*

owe **owes, owing, owed**

VERB **1** If you **owe** someone money, they have lent it to you and you have not yet paid it back.
2 If you **owe** a quality or skill to someone, you only have it because of them. • *He* **owes** *his success as a tennis player to his coach.*

owl **owls**

NOUN a bird of prey that hunts at night. **Owls** have large eyes and short, hooked beaks.

own **owns, owning, owned**

ADJECTIVE OR PRONOUN **1** If something is your **own**, it belongs to you or is associated with you. • *She now has her* **own** *bedroom.*
VERB **2** If you **own** something, it belongs to you.
PHRASE **3** **On your own** means alone.

owner **owners**

NOUN the person to whom something belongs

ox **oxen**

NOUN **Oxen** are cattle used for carrying or pulling things.

oxygen

NOUN a colourless gas that makes up about 21% of the earth's atmosphere. All animals and plants need **oxygen** to live, and fires need it to burn.

oyster **oysters**

NOUN a large, flat shellfish. Some **oysters** can be eaten, and others produce pearls.

ozone

NOUN a form of oxygen that is poisonous and has a strong smell
[from Greek *ozein* meaning smell]

ozone layer

NOUN a layer of the earth's atmosphere that protects living things from the harmful radiation of the sun

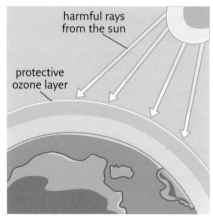

harmful rays from the sun

protective ozone layer

Pp

pace paces, pacing, paced
NOUN **1** the distance you move when you take one step
2 Your **pace** is the speed at which you are walking or running.
VERB **3** If you **pace**, you walk up and down, usually because you are anxious or impatient.

Pacific
NOUN the ocean separating North and South America from Asia and Australia

pacifist pacifists
NOUN someone who is opposed to all violence and war
pacifism NOUN

pacify pacifies, pacifying, pacified
VERB If you **pacify** someone who is angry, you calm them.
pacifier NOUN

pack packs, packing, packed
VERB **1** If you **pack** things, you put them neatly into a container, bag or box.
NOUN **2** a complete set of playing cards
3 a group of wolves or dogs

package packages
NOUN a small parcel

packet packets
NOUN a small box or bag in which something is sold

pact pacts
NOUN a formal agreement or treaty

pad pads
NOUN **1** a set of sheets of paper glued together at one end
2 a thick, soft piece of material
3 one of the soft parts under an animal's paws

paddle paddles, paddling, paddled
NOUN **1** a short pole with a broad blade at one or both ends, used to move a small boat or a canoe
VERB **2** If someone **paddles** a boat, they move it using a paddle.
3 If you **paddle**, you walk in shallow water with bare feet.

paddock paddocks
NOUN a small field where horses are kept

padlock padlocks, padlocking, padlocked
NOUN **1** a special kind of metal lock used to fasten two things together
VERB **2** If you **padlock** something, you lock it with a padlock.

pagan pagans
NOUN **1** someone who does not believe in any of the main religions of the world
ADJECTIVE **2** involving beliefs and worship outside the main religions of the world
• *pagan myths and cults*
paganism NOUN

page pages
NOUN **1** one side of a sheet of paper in a book or magazine • *Turn to page four.*
2 a single sheet of paper

pagoda pagodas
NOUN a tall, elaborately decorated Buddhist or Hindu temple

paid
VERB past tense and past participle of **pay**

pail pails
NOUN a bucket

pain pains
NOUN **1** a feeling of discomfort and hurt in your body, caused by an illness or injury

PHRASE **2** If you are **in pain** you are hurting. [from Latin *poena* meaning punishment]

painful
ADJECTIVE causing emotional or physical pain

painkiller **painkillers**
NOUN a drug that reduces or stops pain

painless
ADJECTIVE Something that is **painless** causes no pain.

paint **paints, painting, painted**
NOUN **1** a coloured liquid used to decorate buildings and make pictures
VERB **2** If you **paint** a picture of something, you make a picture of it using paint.
3 If you **paint** something such as a wall, you cover it with paint.

painting **paintings**
NOUN **1** a picture that someone has created using paints
2 the activity of painting pictures

pair **pairs**
NOUN **1** two things of the same type that are meant to be used together • a **pair** of socks
2 objects that have two main parts of the same size and shape • a **pair** of scissors

✎ Do not confuse *pair* with *pear*.

pal **pals**
NOUN INFORMAL a friend
[from the Romani for brother]

palace **palaces**
NOUN a large, grand house, especially the home of a king or queen

pale **paler, palest**
ADJECTIVE not strong or bright in colour

palette **palettes**
NOUN a board on which an artist mixes colours

palm **palms**
NOUN **1** a tropical tree with no branches and broad, long leaves at the top of its trunk. **Palm** trees often produce fruit, such as coconuts or dates.
2 the flat area on the inside of your hand

pamper **pampers, pampering, pampered**
VERB If you **pamper** someone, you give them a lot of kindness and comfort.

pamphlet **pamphlets**
NOUN a very thin book in paper covers, giving information about something

pan **pans**
NOUN a round metal container with a long handle, used for cooking things

pancake **pancakes**
NOUN a thin, flat piece of fried batter that can be served with savoury or sweet fillings

panda **pandas**
NOUN a large animal, rather like a bear, that lives in China. A giant **panda** has black fur with large patches of white.

pane **panes**
NOUN a sheet of glass in a window or door

panel **panels**
NOUN **1** a group of people who are chosen to discuss or decide something
2 a flat piece of wood, metal or other material that is part of a larger object, such as a door or a wall

panic **panics, panicking, panicked**
NOUN **1** a sudden strong feeling of fear or anxiety
VERB **2** If you **panic**, you become so afraid or anxious that you cannot act sensibly.

panorama **panoramas**
NOUN an extensive view over a wide area of land
panoramic ADJECTIVE

pant **pants, panting, panted**
VERB If you **pant**, you take short, quick breaths through your mouth.

panther **panthers**
NOUN a large wild animal belonging to the cat family, especially the black leopard

pantomime **pantomimes**
NOUN a funny musical play, usually based on a fairy story and performed at Christmas

pants
PLURAL NOUN **1** underpants or knickers
2 another word for **trousers**

paper papers
NOUN **1** a material that you write on or wrap things with
2 a newspaper
[from *papyrus*, the plant from which paper was made in ancient Egypt, Greece and Rome]

paperback paperbacks
NOUN a book with a thin cardboard cover

papier-mâché
Said "pap-yey **mash**-ay" NOUN a mixture of mashed wet paper and glue that can be moulded into shapes, then dried and decorated to make bowls, ornaments and other objects
[from French, meaning chewed paper]

parable parables
NOUN a short story that makes a moral or religious point

parachute parachutes
NOUN a large umbrella-like piece of fabric attached by lines to a person or package so that it can fall safely to the ground from an aircraft
parachuting NOUN

parade parades, parading, paraded
NOUN **1** a line of people or vehicles moving together through a public place in order to celebrate something
VERB **2** When people **parade**, they walk together in a group, usually in front of spectators.

3 When soldiers **parade**, they gather together for inspection.

paradise
NOUN **1** According to some religions, **paradise** is a wonderful place where good people go when they die.
2 Somewhere very beautiful and wonderful in real life can be called **paradise**. ● *Some of the beaches we went to on holiday were **paradise**.*

paraffin
NOUN a strong-smelling liquid used as a fuel

paragraph paragraphs
NOUN a section of a piece of writing. **Paragraphs** begin on a new line.

parallel
ADJECTIVE If two lines or objects are **parallel**, they are the same distance apart along the whole of their length.

parallel lines

parallelogram parallelograms
NOUN a four-sided shape, each side of which is parallel to the opposite side

paralysed
ADJECTIVE If a part of your body is **paralysed**, you cannot move it. ● *Since the accident my uncle has been **paralysed** from the waist down.*
paralyse VERB **paralysis** NOUN

paramedic paramedics
NOUN a person who does some types of medical work, for example for the ambulance service

parasite parasites
NOUN a small animal or plant that lives on or inside a larger animal or plant
[from Greek *parasitos* meaning someone who eats at someone else's table]
parasitic ADJECTIVE

paratroops or paratroopers
PLURAL NOUN soldiers trained to be dropped from aircraft by parachute

a b c d e f g h i j k l m n o p q r s t u v w x y z

A
B
C
D
E
F
G
H
I
J
K
L
M
N
O
P
Q
R
S
T
U
V
W
X
Y
Z

parcel parcels
NOUN something wrapped up in paper

parched
ADJECTIVE **1** very dry and in need of water
• The earth was **parched** during the drought.
2 very thirsty • I was **parched** after the race.

pardon pardons, pardoning, pardoned
PHRASE **1** You say **pardon** or **I beg your pardon** when you want someone to repeat something they have said.
VERB **2** If you **pardon** someone, you forgive or excuse them for something they have done wrong.

parent parents
NOUN Your **parents** are your father and mother.

parish parishes
NOUN an area with its own church and clergyman

park parks, parking, parked
VERB **1** When someone **parks** a vehicle, they drive it into a position where it can be left.
NOUN **2** a public area with grass and trees

parliament parliaments
NOUN the group of people who make or change the laws of a country

parole
NOUN When prisoners are given **parole**, they are released early on condition that they behave well.

parrot parrots
NOUN a brightly coloured tropical bird with a curved beak

parsley
NOUN a herb with curly leaves used for flavouring in cooking

parsnip parsnips
NOUN a long, pointed, cream-coloured root vegetable

part parts, parting, parted
NOUN **1** a piece of something, and not all of it
2 If you have a **part** in a play, you have a role in it.
VERB **3** If you **part** people or things, you separate them.

partial
ADJECTIVE **1** not complete or whole
PHRASE **2** If you are **partial to** someone or something, you like them.
partially ADVERB

participate participates, participating, participated
VERB If you **participate** in an activity, you take part in it or join in with other people.

participle participles
NOUN a word that is formed from a verb and used as part of the verb or as an adjective. For example, eating is the present **participle** of eat, and loaded is the past **participle** of load.

particle particles
NOUN a very small piece of something
• There were **particles** of dust floating in the air.

particular
ADJECTIVE **1** to do with only one person or thing • That **particular** recipe is very easy to make.
2 If you are **particular**, you are fussy and pay attention to detail.
particularly ADVERB

partition partitions
NOUN a screen separating one part of a room or vehicle from another

partly
ADVERB to some extent, but not completely
• It's **partly** my fault.

partner partners
NOUN **1** Someone's **partner** is the person they are married to or living with.
2 one of two people who do something together, such as dancing or running a business

part of speech parts of speech
NOUN one of the groups that words are divided into in grammar, such as a noun or an adjective

partridge **partridges**
NOUN a brown game bird with a round body and a short tail

part-time
ADJECTIVE OR ADVERB involving work for only a part of each normal working day or week

party **parties**
NOUN **1** a social occasion when people meet to enjoy themselves, often in order to celebrate something
2 a group of people who are doing something together • *A party of school children visited the museum.*

pass **passes, passing, passed**
VERB **1** If you **pass** someone or something, you go past them without stopping.
2 If you **pass** something to someone, you give it to them.
3 If you **pass** an examination, you are successful in it.

passage **passages**
NOUN **1** a long, narrow corridor or space that connects two places • *There was a **passage** from the front garden through to the back garden.*
2 a section of a book or piece of music

passenger **passengers**
NOUN a person travelling in a vehicle, aircraft or ship

passion **passions**
NOUN a very strong feeling

passive
ADJECTIVE **1** Someone who is **passive** does not take action or react strongly to things.
NOUN **2** In grammar, the **passive**, or **passive** voice, is the form of the verb in which the person or thing to which an action is being done is the subject of the sentence. For example, the sentence *The burglar was seen by the police* is in the **passive**. For the active, or active voice, the subject of the sentence is the person or thing doing the activity: *The police saw the burglar.*

Passover
NOUN an eight-day Jewish festival held in spring

passport **passports**
NOUN an official document showing your identity and nationality, that you need to show when you enter or leave a country

password **passwords**
NOUN **1** a secret word known to only a few people. It allows people on the same side to recognize a friend.
2 a word you need to know to get into some computer files

past
NOUN **1** the period of time before the present
ADJECTIVE **2** **Past** events are ones that happened or existed before the present.
PREPOSITION OR ADVERB **3** You use **past** to tell the time when it is thirty minutes or less after a particular hour. • *It's ten **past** eleven.*
4 If you go **past** something, you move towards it and continue until you are on the other side. • *An ambulance drove **past**.*
PREPOSITION **5** Something that is **past** a place is situated on the other side of it. • *The farm is just **past** the next village.*

pasta
NOUN a dried mixture of flour, eggs and water, formed into different shapes [an Italian word meaning flour mixture]

paste **pastes, pasting, pasted**
NOUN **1** a soft, sticky mixture that can be spread easily
VERB **2** If you **paste** something somewhere, you stick it there with glue.

pasteurized; also spelt **pasteurised**
Said "**past**-yoor-ized" ADJECTIVE **Pasteurized** milk has been heated by a special process to kill bacteria. [after the French chemist Louis *Pasteur* who invented the process]

pastime **pastimes**
NOUN something that you enjoy doing in your spare time

pastry **pastries**
NOUN **1** a mixture of flour, fat and water that is used for making pies

2 a small cake • *There is a selection of* ***pastries*** *for tea.*

pasture **pastures**
NOUN an area of grass where cows, horses and sheep can graze

pasty **pasties; pastier, pastiest**
Rhymes with "nasty" NOUN **1** a small pie containing meat and vegetables
Rhymes with "tasty" ADJECTIVE **2** Someone who is **pasty** looks pale and unhealthy.

pat **pats, patting, patted**
VERB If you **pat** someone or something, you tap them lightly with an open hand.

patch **patches, patching, patched**
NOUN **1** a piece of material used to cover a hole in something • *She put a* ***patch*** *over the hole in her jeans.*
2 an area of a surface that is different in appearance from the rest • *We want to grow vegetables on that* ***patch*** *of ground.*
VERB **3** If you **patch** something that has a hole in it, you mend it by fixing something over the hole.

patchy **patchier, patchiest**
ADJECTIVE uneven in quantity, quality or both • *We drove through* ***patchy*** *fog.*

pâté **pâtés**
Said "**pa**-tay" NOUN a paste made from meat, fish or vegetables, and spread on toast or biscuits
[from the French word for paste]

patent **patents**
NOUN the official right given to someone to make something they have invented. It stops others from copying it.

paternal
ADJECTIVE relating to or like a father
[from Latin *pater* meaning father]

path **paths**
NOUN **1** a strip of ground for people to walk or ride along
2 the direction in which something travels • *The trail of smoke showed the* ***path*** *of the plane.*

pathetic
ADJECTIVE **1** If something is **pathetic**,

it makes you feel pity.
2 very poor or unsuccessful • *He made a* ***pathetic*** *attempt to swim.*
[from Greek *pathetikos* meaning sensitive]
pathetically ADVERB

patience
NOUN the ability to stay calm in a difficult or irritating situation

patient **patients**
ADJECTIVE **1** If you are **patient**, you stay calm in a difficult or irritating situation.
NOUN **2** a person receiving treatment from a doctor
patiently ADVERB

patio **patios**
NOUN a paved area close to a house

patriot **patriots**
NOUN someone who loves their own country and is very loyal to it
patriotic ADJECTIVE **patriotism** NOUN

patrol **patrols, patrolling, patrolled**
VERB **1** When soldiers, police or guards **patrol** an area, they walk or drive around it to make sure there is no trouble.
NOUN **2** a group of people patrolling an area

patter **patters, pattering, pattered**
VERB **1** If something **patters** on a surface, it makes quick, light, tapping sounds.
• *The rain* ***pattered*** *against the window.*
NOUN **2** a series of light, tapping sounds
• *We could hear the* ***patter*** *of light rain.*

pattern **patterns**
NOUN **1** a design of shapes repeated at regular intervals
2 a drawing that can be copied to make something else, such as clothes

pause **pauses, pausing, paused**
VERB **1** If you **pause**, you stop speaking or doing something for a short time.
NOUN **2** a period when something stops for a short time before continuing

pavement **pavements**
NOUN a raised pathway with a hard surface along the side of a road
[from Latin *pavimentum* meaning hard floor]

pavilion pavilions
NOUN a building at a sports ground, especially a cricket pitch, where players can change

paw paws
NOUN the foot of an animal that has claws and pads

pawn pawns, pawning, pawned
VERB **1** If you **pawn** something, you leave it with someone called a pawnbroker who lends you money. When you repay the money, the pawnbroker will give back the item you **pawned**.
NOUN **2** the smallest and least valuable piece in the game of chess

pay pays, paying, paid
VERB **1** If you **pay** someone, you give them money in exchange for something.
PHRASE **2** If you **pay attention**, you listen carefully to what is being said.

payment payments
NOUN If you make a **payment** for something, you give someone money in exchange for goods or a service.

PC PCs
NOUN **1** the abbreviation of *personal computer*
2 In Britain, **PC** is also the abbreviation of *police constable*.

PE
NOUN an abbreviation of *physical education*, which is the sports that you do at school

pea peas
NOUN a small, round green seed that is eaten as a vegetable

peace
Said "**peess**" NOUN **1** a state of undisturbed calm and quiet
2 If a country is at **peace**, it is not at war.

Do not confuse *peace* with *piece*.

peaceful
ADJECTIVE quiet and calm

peach peaches
NOUN a soft, round fruit with yellow flesh and a yellow and red skin

peacock peacocks
NOUN a large male bird with very long green and blue tail feathers that it can spread out in a fan. The female is called a peahen.

peak peaks
NOUN **1** the highest point of a mountain
2 The **peak** of an activity or process is the point at which it is strongest or most successful.
3 the part of a cap that sticks out over your eyes

peal peals
NOUN the loud musical sound made by bells ringing one after another

peanut peanuts
NOUN a small nut that grows under the ground

pear pears
NOUN a green or yellow fruit that is narrow at the top and wider at the bottom

Do not confuse *pear* with *pair*.

pearl pearls
NOUN a hard, round, creamy-white ball used in jewellery. **Pearls** grow inside the shell of an oyster.

peasant peasants
NOUN a person who works on the land, earning little money

peat
NOUN dark-brown decaying plant material found in cool, wet regions. Dried **peat** can be used as fuel or fertilizer.

pebble pebbles
NOUN a smooth, round stone often found on the beach

peck pecks, pecking, pecked
VERB If a bird **pecks** something, it bites at it quickly with its beak. • *The birds **pecked** at the seeds on the ground.*

peculiar
ADJECTIVE strange and unusual • *She thought the food tasted **peculiar**.*
peculiarly ADVERB peculiarity NOUN

a
b
c
d
e
f
g
h
i
j
k
l
m
n
o
p
q
r
s
t
u
v
w
x
y
z

pedal pedals, pedalling, pedalled
VERB **1** When you **pedal** a bicycle, you push the pedals around with your feet to make it move.
NOUN **2** a control lever that you press with your foot to make a machine or vehicle work

pedestrian pedestrians
NOUN someone who is walking • *Only* **pedestrians** *are allowed down this street.*

pedigree pedigrees
ADJECTIVE **1** A **pedigree** animal is bred from a single breed and its ancestors are known and recorded.
NOUN **2** a list of a person's or an animal's ancestors

peek peeks, peeking, peeked
VERB **1** If you **peek** at something, you have a quick look at it.
NOUN **2** a quick look at something

peel peels, peeling, peeled
NOUN **1** the skin of a fruit or vegetable
VERB **2** When you **peel** fruit or vegetables, you remove the skin.
3 If a layer of something **peels**, it comes off a surface. • *Paint was* **peeling** *off the walls.*

peep peeps, peeping, peeped
VERB **1** If you **peep** at something, you have a quick, secretive look at it, or you look at it through a small opening.
NOUN **2** a quick look at something

peer peers, peering, peered
VERB **1** If you **peer** at something, you look at it very hard. • *He* **peered** *into the dark room.*
NOUN **2** Your **peers** are your equals in age, interests and background.

peg pegs
NOUN **1** a plastic or wooden clip for attaching clothes to a washing line
2 a hook where you can hang things

pelican pelicans
NOUN a large water bird with a pouch beneath its beak in which it stores fish

pellet pellets
NOUN a small ball of food, paper, lead or other material

pelt pelts, pelting, pelted
NOUN **1** the skin and fur of an animal, especially when it is used for making clothes
VERB **2** If you **pelt** someone with something, you throw it at them very hard.
3 If rain **pelts** down, it rains very hard.

pen pens
NOUN **1** an instrument with a pointed end used for writing with ink
2 a small, fenced area where farm animals are kept • *a sheep* **pen**

penalty penalties
NOUN **1** a punishment
2 In sport, a **penalty** is an advantage or point given to one team when their opponents break the rules.

pence
NOUN a plural form of **penny**

pencil pencils
NOUN a small stick of wood with a type of soft mineral called graphite in the centre, used for drawing or writing
[from Latin *pencillus* meaning painter's brush]

pendant pendants
NOUN a piece of jewellery attached to a chain and worn round the neck

penetrate penetrates, penetrating, penetrated
VERB If someone or something **penetrates** an object or area, they succeed in getting into or through it. • *Eventually they* **penetrated** *the forest and found the cabin.*

pen friend pen friends
NOUN someone living in a different place or country whom you write to regularly, although you may never have met each other

penguin penguins
NOUN a black and white bird with webbed feet and small wings like flippers. **Penguins** are found mainly in the Antarctic.

penicillin
NOUN a powerful antibiotic obtained from fungus and used to treat infections

peninsula **peninsulas**
NOUN an area of land almost surrounded by water
[from Latin *paene* + *insula* meaning almost an island]

penis **penises**
NOUN A man's **penis** is the part of the body he uses when urinating.

penknife **penknives**
NOUN a small folding knife

penny **pennies** or **pence**
NOUN a unit of currency in Britain and some other countries. In Britain, there are 100 **pennies** in a pound.

pension **pensions**
NOUN a regular sum of money paid to a retired, widowed or disabled person

pentagon **pentagons**
NOUN a flat shape with five straight sides
pentagonal ADJECTIVE

pentathlon **pentathlons**
NOUN a sports contest in which athletes compete in five different events
[from Greek *pente* meaning five and *athlon* meaning contest]

people
PLURAL NOUN human beings – men, women and children

pepper **peppers**
NOUN **1** a hot-tasting powdered spice used for flavouring in cooking
2 a hollow green, red or yellow vegetable, with sweet-flavoured flesh

peppermint **peppermints**
NOUN **1** a plant with a strong taste. It is used for making sweets and in medicine.
2 a sweet flavoured with peppermint

per
PREPOSITION **Per** means *for each* and is used when speaking about prices, measurements, rates and ratios
• *60 kilometres **per** hour* • *three times **per** year* • *90p **per** kilo*

perceive **perceives, perceiving, perceived**
VERB If you **perceive** something, you see, notice or understand it.

per cent
PHRASE You use **per cent** to show amounts out of a hundred. The symbol for per cent is %. • *She got 98 **per cent** (98%) for her maths test.*
[from Latin **per** meaning each and **centum** meaning hundred]

percentage **percentages**
NOUN an amount or rate expressed as a number of hundredths

perceptive
ADJECTIVE Someone who is **perceptive** notices and understands things more quickly than other people.
SYNONYMS: observant, sharp
perceptively ADVERB

perch **perches, perching, perched**
VERB **1** If you **perch** on something, you sit on the edge of it.
2 When a bird **perches** on something, it stands on it.
NOUN **3** a short rod for a bird to stand on
4 an edible freshwater fish

percussion
NOUN OR ADJECTIVE musical instruments that you hit or shake to produce sounds, such as drums and tambourines
percussionist NOUN

drum

tambourine

triangle

perennial
ADJECTIVE occurring or lasting for many years

perfect **perfects, perfecting, perfected**
*Said "**pur**-fikt"* ADJECTIVE **1** Something that is **perfect** is as good as it possibly can be.

a
b
c
d
e
f
g
h
i
j
k
l
m
n
o
p
q
r
s
t
u
v
w
x
y
z

A
B
C
D
E
F
G
H
I
J
K
L
M
N
O
P
Q
R
S
T
U
V
W
X
Y
Z

Said "pur-**fekt**" VERB **2** If you **perfect** something, you make it as good as it possibly can be.

perform **performs, performing, performed**
VERB **1** If you **perform** a play or piece of music, you do a show of it in front of an audience.
2 If you **perform** a task or action, you do it.
performer NOUN

performance **performances**
NOUN an entertainment provided for an audience • *The orchestra gave an excellent* **performance***.*

perfume **perfumes**
NOUN **1** a pleasant-smelling liquid that people put on their skin
2 a pleasant smell • *These roses have a lovely* **perfume***.*

perhaps
ADVERB You use **perhaps** when you are not sure if something is true or possible.
• **Perhaps** *we could see you tomorrow?*

peril **perils**
NOUN FORMAL great danger
perilous ADJECTIVE **perilously** ADVERB

perimeter **perimeters**
NOUN **1** the distance all the way round the edge of an area
2 the edge or boundary of something

period **periods**
NOUN **1** a particular length of time • *We will be away for a* **period** *of a few months.*
2 A woman's **period** is the monthly bleeding from her womb.
3 In American English, a **period** is a full stop.

periodical **periodicals**
NOUN a magazine that is published regularly

periscope **periscopes**
NOUN a tube with mirrors placed in it so that you can see things that are otherwise out of sight. **Periscopes** are used for seeing out of submarines.

perish **perishes, perishing, perished**
VERB **1** If fruit, rubber or fabric **perishes**, it rots.

2 FORMAL If someone or something **perishes**, they die or are destroyed.
perishable ADJECTIVE

perm **perms**
NOUN If someone has a **perm**, their hair is curled and treated with chemicals to keep the curls for several months.

permanent
ADJECTIVE lasting forever or present all the time

permission
NOUN If you have **permission** to do something, you are allowed to do it.

permit **permits, permitting, permitted**
Said "pur-**mit**" VERB **1** If someone or something **permits** you to do something, they allow it or make it possible. • *We* **permit** *children to ride bicycles to school.*
SYNONYM: give permission
Said "**pur**-mit" NOUN **2** an official document that says that you are allowed to do something

perpendicular
ADJECTIVE A line that is **perpendicular** to another one meets it at a right angle (90°).

perpetual
ADJECTIVE never ending
perpetually ADVERB

perplexed
ADJECTIVE If you are **perplexed**, you are puzzled and do not know what to do.
SYNONYM: confused

persecute **persecutes, persecuting, persecuted**
VERB If someone **persecutes** another person, they continually treat them with cruelty and unfairness, often because of their religious beliefs.
persecution NOUN **persecutor** NOUN

persevere **perseveres, persevering, persevered**
VERB If you **persevere**, you keep trying to do something and do not give up.
perseverance NOUN

persist persists, persisting, persisted

VERB **1** If something **persists**, it continues and will not stop. • The rain **persisted** all day.

2 If you **persist** in doing something, you continue with it in spite of difficulties or opposition.

person people or persons

NOUN **1** a man, woman or child

SYNONYMS: human being, individual

2 In grammar, the first **person** is the speaker (I), the second **person** is the person being spoken to (you), and the third **person** is anyone else being referred to (he, she, they).

PHRASE **3** If you do something **in person**, you do it yourself rather than letting someone else do it for you.

[from Latin persona meaning actor's mask]

The usual plural of person is people. Persons is much less common, and is used only in formal English.

personal

ADJECTIVE **1** belonging or relating to a particular person

SYNONYMS: individual, own

2 **Personal** matters are personal things that you may not wish to discuss with other people. • I cannot tell you for **personal** reasons.

personality personalities

NOUN Your **personality** is your character and nature. • She's got a very lively **personality**.

personally

ADVERB **1** in person • He came to school to thank us **personally** for the money we raised for the charity.

2 You use **personally** to express your own opinion of something. • **Personally**, I don't mind where we go.

personnel

Said "per-son-**nell**" PLURAL NOUN the people who work for an organization

perspective perspectives

NOUN **1** the impression of distance and depth in a picture or a drawing

2 a particular way of thinking about something or looking at something • What is your **perspective** on discipline?

perspire perspires, perspiring, perspired

VERB When people **perspire**, they sweat.

perspiration NOUN

persuade persuades, persuading, persuaded

VERB If you **persuade** someone to do something, or **persuade** them that something is true, you make them do it or believe it by giving them good reasons.

persuasion NOUN **persuasive** ADJECTIVE

pessimism

NOUN the feeling that bad things will always happen

pessimist pessimists

NOUN If you are a **pessimist**, you expect the worst to happen.

ANTONYM: optimist

pessimistic ADJECTIVE

pessimistically ADVERB

pest pests

NOUN **1** an insect or other small animal that damages plants or food supplies

2 someone who keeps bothering or annoying you

pester pesters, pestering, pestered

VERB If you **pester** someone, you keep bothering them or asking them to do something.

pesticide pesticides

NOUN a chemical sprayed onto plants to kill insects and grubs

pet pets

NOUN **1** a tame animal kept at home

2 a person who is treated as a favourite

petal petals

NOUN one of the coloured outer parts of a flower that attract insects. Some **petals** are perfumed.

petition petitions

NOUN a written document, signed by a lot of people, requesting official action be taken on something

A
B
C
D
E
F
G
H
I
J
K
L
M
N
O
P
Q
R
S
T
U
V
W
X
Y
Z

petrified
ADJECTIVE If you are **petrified**, you are very frightened.
SYNONYM: terrified

petrol
NOUN a liquid that is used as a fuel for motor vehicles

petty **pettier, pettiest**
ADJECTIVE trivial and unimportant ● *We should not argue over **petty** things.*

pew **pews**
NOUN a long wooden seat with a back, that people sit on in church

pH
NOUN The **pH** of a solution or of the soil is a measurement of how acid or alkaline it is. Substances with a **pH** above 7 are alkaline and substances with a **pH** below 7 are acid.

phantom **phantoms**
NOUN **1** a ghost
ADJECTIVE **2** imagined or unreal

pharmacy **pharmacies**
NOUN a shop where medicines are sold
SYNONYM: chemists

phase **phases**
NOUN a particular stage in the development of something

pheasant **pheasants**
NOUN a large, long-tailed game bird

phenomenon **phenomena**
NOUN something that happens or exists, especially something extraordinary or remarkable ● *The eclipse was a fascinating **phenomenon**.*
phenomenal ADJECTIVE
phenomenally ADVERB

philosophy **philosophies**
NOUN **1** the study or creation of ideas about humans, their relationship to the universe and beliefs
2 a set of beliefs a person has

phobia **phobias**
NOUN a deep fear or dislike of something
phobic ADJECTIVE

phoenix **phoenixes**
*Said "**fee**-niks"* NOUN an imaginary bird that, according to myth, sets fire to itself every five hundred years, and rises from the ashes

phone **phones, phoning, phoned**
NOUN OR VERB an abbreviation of **telephone**

phoney **phonier, phoniest**; also spelt **phony**
ADJECTIVE false, not genuine, and meant to trick ● *He had a **phoney** passport.*
ANTONYM: genuine

photo **photos**
NOUN an abbreviation of **photograph**

photocopier **photocopiers**
NOUN a machine that makes instant copies of documents

photocopy **photocopies, photocopying, photocopied**
VERB **1** If you **photocopy** a document, you make a copy of it using a photocopier.
NOUN **2** a copy of a document made using a photocopier

photograph **photographs, photographing, photographed**
NOUN **1** a picture taken with a camera and then printed on special paper
VERB **2** If you **photograph** someone or something, you use a camera to take a picture of them.

photography
*Said "fo-**tog**-raff-ee"* NOUN the job or hobby of taking photographs
photographer NOUN

photosynthesis
*Said "fo-toh-**sin**-th-sis"* NOUN the process by which green plants make their own food from carbon dioxide and water in the presence of sunlight

phrase **phrases**
NOUN a short group of words or musical notes

physical
ADJECTIVE concerning the body rather than the mind
[from Greek *phusis* meaning nature]

physical education
NOUN physical exercise and sports that you do at school

physics
NOUN the scientific study of the forces and properties of matter, such as heat, light, sound and electricity

pianist *pianists*
NOUN someone who plays the piano

piano *pianos*
NOUN a large musical instrument with a row of black and white keys. When the keys are pressed, little hammers hit wires to produce different notes.

piccolo *piccolos*
NOUN a high-pitched wind instrument like a small flute

pick *picks, picking, picked*
VERB **1** If you **pick** someone or something, you choose them. • *I **picked** Hannah for my partner.*
2 If you **pick** a flower or a fruit, you break it off from where it is growing.
3 If someone **picks** a lock, they open it with a piece of wire instead of a key.

pick on
VERB If you **pick on** someone, you treat them unkindly and unfairly.

pick up
VERB **1** If you **pick up** someone or something, you lift them.
2 If you **pick up** someone or something from a place, you collect them from there.

picket *pickets, picketing, picketed*
VERB **1** When a group of people **picket** a place of work during a strike, they stand outside and try to persuade other workers not to go in to work.
NOUN **2** someone who is picketing a place

pickle *pickles*
NOUN **Pickles** are vegetables or fruit preserved in vinegar or salt water.

pickpocket *pickpockets*
NOUN a thief who steals things from pockets or bags

picnic *picnics*
NOUN a meal eaten outdoors

pictogram *pictograms*
NOUN a type of graph that uses small pictures to show information

pictorial
ADJECTIVE relating to or using pictures

picture *pictures*
NOUN a drawing, painting, photograph or television image of someone or something

picturesque
ADJECTIVE A place that is **picturesque** is very attractive and unspoiled.
[from Italian *pittoresco* meaning in the style of a painter]

pie *pies*
NOUN a dish of meat, vegetables or fruit covered with pastry

piece *pieces*
*Said "**peess**"* NOUN **1** a portion or part of something
2 an individual thing of a particular kind • *This is a good **piece** of work.*
3 a coin • *a 50 pence **piece***

🖉 Do not confuse *piece* with *peace*.

pie chart *pie charts*
NOUN a circular diagram that is divided into segments to show how a quantity or an amount of something is shared

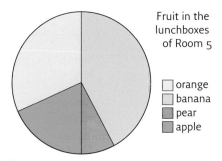

Fruit in the lunchboxes of Room 5

☐ orange
☐ banana
■ pear
■ apple

pier *piers*
NOUN a large structure at the seaside, with a platform built from the shore out into the sea, that people can walk along

pierce *pierces, piercing, pierced*
VERB If a sharp object **pierces** something, it goes through it, making a hole.

A
B
C
D
E
F
G
H
I
J
K
L
M
N
O
P
Q
R
S
T
U
V
W
X
Y
Z

piercing

ADJECTIVE **1** a **piercing** sound is high pitched and sharp, and it hurts your ears
SYNONYM: shrill
2 Someone with **piercing** eyes seems to stare at you intensely.

pig pigs

NOUN a farm animal with pink or black skin, a curly tail and a snout, that is kept for its meat. Pork, ham and bacon all come from **pigs**.

pigeon pigeons

NOUN a grey bird with a small head and large chest, often found in towns and cities

piglet piglets

NOUN a young pig

pigsty pigsties

NOUN **1** a small shelter with an enclosed area where pigs are kept
2 If you say a place is like a **pigsty**, you mean that it is very dirty and untidy.

pigtail pigtails

NOUN a plait of hair • *She wore her hair in **pigtails**.*

pike pikes

NOUN **1** a large freshwater fish with strong, sharp teeth
2 a weapon used in medieval times. A **pike** was a long pole with a spike on the end.

pile piles, piling, piled

NOUN **1** a quantity of things lying on top of one another
VERB **2** If you **pile** things somewhere, you put them on top of one another.

pilgrim pilgrims

NOUN a person who goes on a journey to a holy place for religious reasons

pilgrimage pilgrimages

NOUN a journey to a holy place for religious reasons

pill pills

NOUN a small, round tablet of medicine that you swallow

pillar pillars

NOUN a tall, solid structure like a large post, often made of stone and usually supporting part of a building

pillow pillows

NOUN a large cushion that you rest your head on when you are in bed

pilot pilots

NOUN **1** a person who is trained to fly an aircraft
2 the person who guides a ship into port

pimple pimples

NOUN a small spot on the skin
pimply ADJECTIVE

pin pins, pinning, pinned

NOUN **1** a thin, pointed piece of metal, used to fasten things like paper or cloth together
VERB **2** If you **pin** something, you attach it with a pin.

pincers

PLURAL NOUN **1** The **pincers** of a crab or a lobster are its large front claws.
2 a tool consisting of two pieces of metal hinged in the middle, used for gripping and pulling things

pinch pinches, pinching, pinched

VERB **1** If you **pinch** something, you squeeze it between your thumb and first finger.
2 INFORMAL If someone **pinches** something, they steal it.
NOUN **3** A **pinch** of something is the amount that you can hold between your thumb and first finger. • *Add a **pinch** of salt to the soup.*

pine pines, pining, pined

NOUN **1** an evergreen tree with very thin leaves called needles

needles

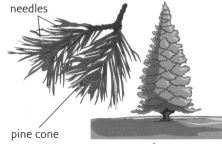

pine cone

pine tree

VERB **2** If you **pine** for something or someone, you feel sad because they are not there.

pineapple **pineapples**
NOUN a large, oval tropical fruit with sweet, yellow flesh and thick, woody skin

pink **pinker, pinkest**
ADJECTIVE pale reddish-white

pint **pints**
NOUN a unit of measurement for liquids equal to about 0.568 litres

pioneer **pioneers**
NOUN one of the first people to go to a place or to do something new

pip **pips**
NOUN **1** the hard seeds in a fruit
2 a short, high-pitched sound

pipe **pipes, piping, piped**
NOUN **1** a long, hollow tube through which liquid or gas can flow
2 an object that is used for smoking tobacco, consisting of a small hollow bowl attached to a thin tube
3 a tube-shaped musical instrument
VERB **4** If liquid or gas is **piped** somewhere, it is transferred there through a pipe.

pipeline **pipelines**
NOUN **1** a large underground pipe that carries oil or gas over a long distance
PHRASE **2** If something is **in the pipeline**, it is already planned or has begun.

pirate **pirates**
NOUN a sailor who attacks and robs other ships

pistol **pistols**
NOUN a small gun held in the hand

pit **pits**
NOUN **1** a large hole in the ground
2 a coal mine

pitch **pitches, pitching, pitched**
NOUN **1** an area of ground marked out for playing a game such as football or cricket
2 The **pitch** of a sound is how high or low it is.
3 a black substance painted onto roofs

and boat bottoms to make them waterproof
VERB **4** If you **pitch** something somewhere, you throw it there with a lot of force.
5 If you **pitch** a tent, you put it up.

pitcher **pitchers**
NOUN a large jug

pitchfork **pitchforks**
NOUN a long-handled fork with two large prongs, used for lifting and moving hay

pitfall **pitfalls**
NOUN one of the difficulties or dangers of a situation

pitta **pittas**
NOUN a flat disc of bread with a hollow inside, that can be filled with food
[from Greek, meaning a cake]

pity **pities, pitying, pitied**
VERB **1** If you **pity** someone, you feel sorry for them.
NOUN **2** a feeling of sadness and concern for someone
3 If you say that something is a **pity**, you mean it is disappointing. • It's a **pity** we couldn't play tennis.

pivot **pivots, pivoting, pivoted**
VERB **1** If something **pivots**, it balances or turns on a central point.
NOUN **2** the central point on which something balances or turns
pivotal ADJECTIVE

pizza **pizzas**
Said "**peet**-sa" NOUN a flat piece of dough usually covered with cheese, tomato and other savoury food and baked in an oven
[an Italian word]

placard **placards**
NOUN a large notice carried at a demonstration or displayed in a public place • The man carried a **placard** advertising the furniture sale.

place **places, placing, placed**
NOUN **1** a particular point, position, building or area • They found a good **place** to camp.
2 a particular position in a race,

competition, or series ● *Last year she finished in third **place**.*

3 If you have a **place** in a team or on a course, you are allowed to join the team or course. ● *I eventually got a **place** at the new school.*

VERB **4** If you **place** something somewhere, you put it there. ● *She **placed** her hand gently on my shoulder.*

PHRASE **5** When something **takes place**, it happens. ● *The competition will **take place** next month.*

placid
ADJECTIVE calm and not easily excited or upset

SYNONYMS: even-tempered, unexcitable

placidly ADVERB

plague plagues, plaguing, plagued
Said "**playg**" NOUN **1** a very infectious disease that kills large numbers of people

2 A **plague** of unpleasant things is a large number of them occurring at the same time.

VERB **3** If you **plague** someone, you keep pestering them.

4 If problems **plague** you, they keep causing you trouble.

plaice
NOUN an edible European flat fish

plaid plaids
Said "**plad**" NOUN woven material with a tartan design

plain plainer, plainest; plains
ADJECTIVE **1** very simple in style, with no pattern or decoration

2 obvious or easy to understand

NOUN **3** a large, flat area of land with very few trees

plait plaits, plaiting, plaited
Said "**plat**" VERB **1** If you **plait** hair or rope, you twist three lengths together in turn to make one thick length.

NOUN **2** a length of hair that has been plaited

plan plans, planning, planned
NOUN **1** a method of achieving something that has been worked out beforehand

VERB **2** If you **plan** something, you decide in detail what you are going to do.

3 If you **plan** to do something, you intend to do it.

plane planes
NOUN **1** an abbreviation of *aeroplane*

2 a tool for smoothing wood

ADJECTIVE **3** A **plane** shape has a flat, level surface. A **plane** mirror is flat and not curved.

planet planets
NOUN a large sphere in space that orbits a sun. The Earth and Mars are both **planets** that revolve around our sun.

plank planks
NOUN a long rectangular piece of wood

plankton
NOUN a layer of tiny plants and animals that live just below the surface of a sea or lake

plant plants, planting, planted
NOUN **1** a living thing that grows in the earth and has a stem, leaves, and roots.

VERB **2** If you **plant** things such as flowers or trees, you put them in the ground so that they will grow.

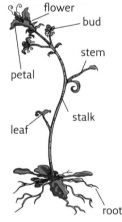

flower
bud
stem
petal
leaf
stalk
root

plantation plantations
NOUN **1** a large area of land where crops such as tea, cotton or sugar are grown

2 a large number of trees planted together

plaque plaques
Said "**plak**" NOUN **1** a flat piece of metal or porcelain, fixed to a wall, with an inscription on it in memory of a famous person or event

2 a substance that forms around your teeth. It is made up of bacteria, saliva and food.

plaster **plasters**
NOUN **1** a paste made of sand, lime and water, that is used to form a smooth surface for inside walls and ceilings
2 a strip of sticky material with a small pad, used for covering cuts on your body
3 Plaster of Paris is a white powder mixed with water, that becomes hard when it dries. It is used for making moulds and for holding broken bones in place while they heal.
plasterer NOUN

plastic **plastics**
NOUN **1** a light synthetic material made from oil by a chemical process. **Plastics** can be moulded into different shapes for many different uses.
ADJECTIVE **2** made of plastic

Plasticine
NOUN TRADEMARK a soft, coloured material like clay, used for making models

plate **plates**
NOUN **1** a flat dish used to hold food
2 a flat piece of hard material such as glass or metal

plateau **plateaus** or **plateaux**
NOUN a large area of high and fairly flat land
[from Old French *platel* meaning a flat piece of metal]

platform **platforms**
NOUN **1** a raised structure on which someone or something can stand
2 the raised area in a railway station where passengers get on and off trains

platinum
NOUN a valuable silver-coloured metal

platypus **platypuses**
NOUN an Australian mammal that lives in rivers. It has brown fur, webbed feet, and a beak like a duck.
[from Greek *platus* meaning flat and *pous* meaning foot]

play **plays, playing, played**
VERB **1** When children **play**, they take part in games or use toys for fun.
2 When you **play** a sport or game, you take part in it.
3 If an actor **plays** a character in a play or film, they perform that role.
4 If you **play** a musical instrument, you produce music from it.
NOUN **5 Play** is the activity of playing a game or sport.
6 a story acted out in the theatre, on the radio or on television
player NOUN

playground **playgrounds**
NOUN a special area for children to play in

playgroup **playgroups**
NOUN an informal group of very young children who play together, supervised by adults

playtime **playtimes**
NOUN the time in a school day when children go out to play

playwright **playwrights**
NOUN a person who writes plays

plea **pleas**
Said "**plee**" NOUN **1** If you make a **plea**, you make an urgent request or an appeal for something.
2 In a law court, a **plea** is someone's statement that they are guilty or not guilty.

plead **pleads, pleading, pleaded**
VERB **1** If you **plead** with someone, you beg them for something. ● *She came to* **plead** *for help.*
2 In a law court, when a person **pleads** guilty or not guilty, they state that they are guilty or not guilty.

pleasant
ADJECTIVE nice, pleasing, enjoyable or attractive in some way

please **pleases, pleasing, pleased**
1 You say **please** when you are asking someone politely to do something. ● *Can you help me,* **please**?
VERB **2** If something **pleases** you, it makes you feel happy and satisfied.

pleasure pleasures
NOUN a feeling of happiness, satisfaction or enjoyment

pleat pleats
NOUN a permanent fold in fabric, made by folding one part over another

pledge pledges, pledging, pledged
NOUN **1** a solemn promise
VERB **2** If you **pledge** something, you promise that you will do it or give it.

plenty
NOUN OR PRONOUN If you have **plenty** of something, you have more than enough for your needs. • We've got **plenty** of time.

pliable
ADJECTIVE If something is **pliable**, you can bend it without breaking it. • This **pliable** material will be easier to work with.
SYNONYM: flexible

pliers
PLURAL NOUN a small tool with metal jaws for gripping small objects such as nails and bending wire

plight plights
NOUN a difficult or dangerous situation • the **plight** of the homeless

plod plods, plodding, plodded
VERB If you **plod**, you walk slowly and heavily. • We **plodded** home through the mud.

plop plops, plopping, plopped
NOUN **1** a gentle sound of something lightweight dropping into a liquid
VERB **2** If something **plops** into a liquid, it drops into it with a gentle sound.

plot plots, plotting, plotted
NOUN **1** a secret plan made by a group of people
2 The **plot** of a film, novel or play is the story.
VERB **3** If people **plot** to do something, they plan it secretly.

plough ploughs, ploughing, ploughed
NOUN **1** a large farming tool that is pulled across a field to turn the soil over before planting seeds
VERB **2** When farmers **plough** land, they use a plough to turn over the soil.

pluck plucks, plucking, plucked
VERB **1** If you **pluck** a fruit or flower, you remove it with a sharp pull.
2 If you **pluck** a dead bird, such as a chicken or a turkey, you pull the feathers off it before cooking it.
3 When you **pluck** a stringed instrument, you pull the strings and let them go.

plug plugs, plugging, plugged
NOUN **1** a device that connects a piece of electrical equipment to an electric socket
2 a thick circular piece of rubber or plastic that you use to block the hole in a sink or bath

plug in
VERB If you **plug in** a piece of electrical equipment, you push its plug into an electric socket.

plum plums
NOUN a small fruit with a smooth red or yellow skin and a stone in the middle

plumage
NOUN a bird's feathers

plumber plumbers
NOUN a person who connects and repairs water pipes

plump plumper, plumpest
ADJECTIVE rounded, or slightly fat

plunge plunges, plunging, plunged
VERB If you **plunge** somewhere, especially into water, you fall or rush there.
SYNONYMS: dive, drop, fall

plural plurals
NOUN the form of a word that is used when referring to more than one person or thing • The usual **plural** of person is people.

plus
PREPOSITION **1** You use **plus** to show that one number is being added to another. • Two **plus** two equals four.
2 You can use **plus** when you mention an additional item. • She gave us our coats, **plus** a blanket.

plywood
NOUN wooden board made from several thin sheets of wood glued together under pressure

p.m.
used to show times between 12 noon and 12 midnight • *I go to bed at 8 **p.m.** on schooldays and 9 **p.m.** at weekends.* [from Latin *post meridiem* meaning after noon]

pneumatic
ADJECTIVE operated by or filled with compressed air • *a **pneumatic** drill*

pneumonia
NOUN a serious disease that affects a person's lungs and makes breathing difficult

poach **poaches, poaching, poached**
VERB **1** If someone **poaches** animals, they hunt them illegally on someone else's land.
2 When you **poach** food, especially fish, or an egg taken out of its shell, you cook it gently in hot liquid.
poacher NOUN

pocket **pockets**
NOUN a small pouch for keeping things in, that forms part of a piece of clothing

pocket money
NOUN an amount of money given regularly to children by their parents

pod **pods**
NOUN a long, narrow seed container that grows on plants such as peas or beans

podcast **podcasts**
NOUN a file similar to a radio broadcast that can be downloaded for listening to on a computer or MP3 player

poem **poems**
NOUN a piece of writing, usually arranged in short rhythmic lines, with words chosen for their sound or impact

poet **poets**
NOUN a person who writes poems

poetry
NOUN poems, considered a form of literature

point **points, pointing, pointed**
VERB **1** If you **point** at or to something, you hold out your finger towards it to show where it is.
NOUN **2** the thin, sharp end of something such as a needle or knife
3 a particular place or time • *At some **point** during the night, the storm began.*
4 a single mark in a competition • *They won by 21 **points** to 18.*
5 the purpose or the most important part of something • *What do you think is the **point** of this exercise?*
6 an opinion or fact expressed by someone • *That's a very good **point**.*
7 In mathematics, the decimal **point** in a number is marked by a dot, as in 5.2.
8 one of the 32 marks on the circumference of a compass to show direction

pointed
ADJECTIVE A **pointed** object has a thin, sharp end.

pointless
ADJECTIVE Something that is **pointless** has no purpose.

point of view **points of view**
NOUN Your **point of view** is your opinion about something or your attitude towards it.

poised
ADJECTIVE If you are **poised** to do something, you are ready to do it at any moment.

poison **poisons, poisoning, poisoned**
NOUN **1** a substance that harms or kills you if you swallow it or absorb it
VERB **2** To **poison** someone means to harm them by giving them poison.

poke **pokes, poking, poked**
VERB If you **poke** someone or something, you give them a push with your finger or a sharp object.

poke out
VERB If something **pokes out** from behind or from underneath another thing, it

a
b
c
d
e
f
g
h
i
j
k
l
m
n
o
p
q
r
s
t
u
v
w
x
y
z

shows. • The label **poked out** from the back of his anorak.

polar
ADJECTIVE relating to the area around the North Pole or the South Pole • the **polar** regions

polar bear polar bears
NOUN a large white bear that lives in the area around the North Pole

pole poles
NOUN **1** a long, slender, rounded piece of wood or metal
2 The earth has two **poles** at the opposite ends of its imaginary axis. • the North and South **Pole**

pole vault
NOUN an athletics event in which contestants jump over a high bar using a long, flexible pole to lift themselves into the air

police
PLURAL NOUN the official organization responsible for making sure that people obey the law

police officer police officers
NOUN a member of the police force

policy policies
NOUN a set of plans and ideas, especially in politics or business • What is their **policy** on education?

polish polishes, polishing, polished
NOUN **1** a substance that you put on an object to clean it and make it shine
VERB **2** If you **polish** something, you put polish on it or rub it with a cloth to make it shine.

polite
ADJECTIVE Someone who is **polite** has good manners and is not rude to other people.
SYNONYM: courteous

political
ADJECTIVE to do with politics and politicians

politician politicians
NOUN a person who is involved in the government of a country

politics
NOUN the activity of governing a country

poll polls
NOUN a survey in which people are asked their opinions about something

pollen
NOUN a fine yellow or orange powder produced by the male part of a flowering plant

pollen

pollinate pollinates, pollinating, pollinated
VERB A plant is **pollinated** when pollen from the male part of another plant lands on its female part. This leads to fertilization and the formation of seeds.

pollination
NOUN the process by which plants are fertilized with pollen

pollute pollutes, polluting, polluted
VERB If water, air or land is **polluted**, it is dirty and dangerous to use or live in.

polo
NOUN a game played between two teams of players on horseback. The players use wooden hammers with long handles to hit a ball.

poltergeist poltergeists
NOUN a noisy, mischievous ghost that moves or throws things around in a house

poly-
PREFIX added to some words to mean many, for example **poly**gons and **poly**hedrons are many-sided shapes

polyester
NOUN a man-made fibre, especially used to make clothes

polygon **polygons**
NOUN any two-dimensional shape whose sides are all straight

polyhedron **polyhedra**
NOUN a solid shape with many faces

polystyrene
NOUN a very light plastic, especially used as insulating material or to make containers

polythene
NOUN a type of plastic that is used to make thin sheets or bags

pompous
ADJECTIVE Someone who is **pompous** behaves in a way that is too serious and self-important.
pomposity NOUN

pond **ponds**
NOUN a small area of water enclosed by land

ponder **ponders, pondering, pondered**
VERB If you **ponder**, you think carefully and seriously about something.

pony **ponies**
NOUN a small horse

ponytail **ponytails**
NOUN a hairstyle in which long hair is scooped up and tied at the back of the head so that it hangs down like a tail

pool **pools**
NOUN **1** a small area of still water, such as a pond or a puddle
2 an abbreviation of *swimming pool*

poor **poorer, poorest**
ADJECTIVE **1** having very little money
2 of a low quality or standard

poorly
ADJECTIVE **1** If you are **poorly**, you feel ill.
ADVERB **2** If something is done **poorly**, it is not done well.

pop **pops, popping, popped**
NOUN **1** modern music, played and enjoyed especially by young people
2 a short, sharp, explosive sound
3 a fizzy, non-alcoholic drink
VERB **4** If you **pop** somewhere, you go

there quickly for a short while. ● *I will* **pop** *in to see you before tea.*

popcorn
NOUN a snack food made from grains of maize that are heated until they puff up and burst

Pope **Popes**
NOUN the head of the Roman Catholic Church

poplar **poplars**
NOUN a type of tall, slender tree

poppadom **poppadoms**
NOUN thin, round, crisp bread, fried or roasted and served with Indian food [from Tamil *pappadam* meaning lentil cake]

poppy **poppies**
NOUN a plant with a large red flower on a hairy stem, that often grows in cornfields and meadows

popular
ADJECTIVE liked or approved of by a lot of people

populated
ADJECTIVE If a place is **populated**, people or animals live there.

population **populations**
NOUN **1** the people who live in a place
2 the number of people living in a place

porch **porches**
NOUN a covered area at the entrance to a building

porcupine **porcupines**
NOUN a large rodent with long spines covering its body
[from Old French *porc d'espins* meaning pig with spines]

pore **pores, poring, pored**
NOUN **1** The **pores** in your skin or on the surface of a plant are very small holes that allow moisture to pass through.
VERB **2** If you **pore** over a piece of writing or a diagram, you study it carefully.

pork
NOUN meat from a pig

a
b
c
d
e
f
g
h
i
j
k
l
m
n
o
p
q
r
s
t
u
v
w
x
y
z

A
B
C
D
E
F
G
H
I
J
K
L
M
N
O
P
Q
R
S
T
U
V
W
X
Y
Z

porous
ADJECTIVE If something is **porous**, it lets water through.

porpoise porpoises
NOUN a sea mammal related to the dolphin
[from Latin *porcus* meaning pig and *piscis* meaning fish]

porridge
NOUN a thick, sticky food made from oats cooked in water or milk

port ports
NOUN **1** a town or area that has a harbour or docks
ADJECTIVE **2** The **port** side of a ship is the left side when you are facing the front.

portable
ADJECTIVE designed to be easily carried

porter porters
NOUN a person employed to carry luggage and other goods at a railway station or in a hotel

porthole portholes
NOUN a small window in the side of a ship or aircraft

portion portions
NOUN **1** a part of something
SYNONYMS: bit, piece
2 an amount of food sufficient for one person

portrait portraits
NOUN a picture or photograph of someone, often of only their head and shoulders

pose poses, posing, posed
NOUN **1** a way of standing, sitting or lying for a photograph to be taken, or a drawing or painting to be made of you
● *Try to hold this **pose** while the others draw it.*
VERB **2** If you **pose** for a photograph or painting, you stay in a particular position so that someone can photograph or paint you.
3 If you **pose** as someone or something, you pretend to be someone or something you are not.

4 If something **poses** a problem or danger, it causes it. ● *This polluted water could **pose** a threat to their health.*

position positions, positioning, positioned
NOUN **1** When someone or something is in a particular **position**, they are sitting or lying in that way. ● *I raised myself to a sitting **position**.*
2 The **position** that you are in is the situation that you are in. ● *Your request puts me in a difficult **position**.*
PHRASE **3** If you are **in position** at the beginning of a race, you are ready to start.
VERB **4** If you **position** something, you put it in place.

positive
ADJECTIVE **1** If something is **positive**, it is certain.
2 If someone is **positive**, they are confident and hopeful.

possession possessions
NOUN a thing that you own, or that you have with you

possessive
ADJECTIVE **1** A **possessive** person wants to keep things for themselves.
NOUN **2** In grammar, the **possessive** is the form of a noun or pronoun used to show possession, for example, *my*, *his*, *theirs*, *Harry's*.

possible
ADJECTIVE If something is **possible**, it can be done or can happen.
possibility NOUN

possum possums
NOUN a nocturnal marsupial with thick fur and a long tail that lives in trees

post posts, posting, posted
NOUN **1** the system by which letters and parcels are collected and delivered
2 letters and parcels that are delivered to you
3 an upright pole fixed into the ground
VERB **4** If you **post** a letter, you send it to someone through the post.

postage
NOUN the money that you pay to send letters and parcels by post • *You will need to send extra money for* **postage** *and packing.*

post box **post boxes**
NOUN a box into which you put letters that are to be sent by post

postcard **postcards**
NOUN a card, often with a picture on one side, that you write on and send to someone without an envelope

postcode **postcodes**
NOUN a short sequence of letters and numbers at the end of an address

poster **posters**
NOUN a large notice, picture or advertisement that you stick on a wall

postman or postwoman
postmen or **postwomen**
NOUN someone who collects and delivers parcels and letters

post office **post offices**
NOUN a building where you can buy stamps and post letters and parcels

postpone **postpones, postponing, postponed**
VERB If you **postpone** an event, you arrange for it to take place at a later time than was originally planned.

potato **potatoes**
NOUN a round, white, root vegetable that has a brown or red skin and grows beneath the ground

potential
ADJECTIVE **1** capable of happening or of becoming a particular kind of person or thing • *He's a* **potential** *world champion.*
NOUN **2** If someone or something has **potential**, they are capable of being successful or useful in the future.

pothole **potholes**
NOUN **1** a hole in the surface of a road caused by bad weather or traffic
2 a deep, natural hole in the ground that often leads to an underground cavern

potion **potions**
NOUN a drink containing medicine, poison or supposed magical powers
[from Latin *potio* meaning a drink]

potter **potters, pottering, pottered**
NOUN **1** a person who makes pottery
VERB **2** If you **potter** about, you pass the time doing pleasant, unimportant things.

pottery
NOUN **1** pots, dishes and other items made from clay and fired in a kiln
2 the craft of making pottery

pouch **pouches**
NOUN **1** a small, soft container with a fold-over top, like a bag or a pocket
2 a pocket of skin in which marsupials carry their young

poultry
NOUN chicken, turkeys and other birds that are kept for their meat or eggs

pounce **pounces, pouncing, pounced**
VERB If a person or other animal **pounces** on something, they jump on it suddenly.

pound **pounds, pounding, pounded**
NOUN **1** the main unit of currency in Britain
2 a unit of weight equal to 16 ounces, or about 0.454 kilograms
VERB **3** If you **pound** something, or **pound** on it, you hit it repeatedly or crush it.
4 If your heart **pounds**, it beats very fast and strongly.
5 If you **pound** somewhere, you run there with loud, heavy footsteps.

pour **pours, pouring, poured**
VERB **1** If you **pour** liquid out of a container, you tip the container until the liquid flows out.
2 If something **pours** somewhere, it flows there quickly and in large quantities.
3 If it is **pouring** with rain, it is raining very heavily.

pout **pouts, pouting, pouted**
VERB If you **pout**, you stick out your lips, or

A
B
C
D
E
F
G
H
I
J
K
L
M
N
O
P
Q
R
S
T
U
V
W
X
Y
Z

your bottom lip, because you are cross or annoyed.

poverty
NOUN the state of being very poor

powder powders
NOUN many tiny particles of a solid, dry substance, such as flour

power powers
NOUN **1** control over people and events
2 physical strength
3 the rate at which energy is changed from one form to another, such as electrical energy changed into light or heat

powerful
ADJECTIVE **Powerful** people or organizations have a great deal of power or influence.
powerfully ADVERB

powerless
ADJECTIVE If you are **powerless**, you are unable to control or influence events.
powerlessly ADVERB

power station power stations
NOUN a building where electricity is produced

practical
ADJECTIVE **1** Someone who is **practical** is efficient and sensible, and good at getting things done.
2 Something that is **practical** is sensible and useful.
3 involving real situations and doing things, rather than ideas or theories • *We will do some **practical** experiments in Science today.*
[from Greek *praktikos* meaning concerned with action]

practical joke practical jokes
NOUN a trick you play on someone

practice practices
NOUN **1** regular training or exercise that you do to improve your skill at something
2 A doctor's or lawyer's **practice** is their business.

🖉 The noun *practice* ends in *ce*.

practise practises, practising, practised
VERB **1** If you **practise** something, you do it regularly in order to do it better.
• *She **practises** every day on the piano.*
2 When people **practise** a religion, custom or craft, they regularly take part in the activities associated with it. • *a custom still **practised** in some areas*
3 If you **practise** medicine or law, you work as a doctor or lawyer.

🖉 The verb *practise* ends in *se*.

prairie prairies
NOUN a large area of flat, grassy land in North America

praise praises, praising, praised
VERB **1** If you **praise** someone or something, you say good things about them, or tell them they have done well.
NOUN **2** what you say or write when you praise someone or something

pram prams
NOUN a small carriage, like a baby's cot on wheels, for pushing a baby around in

prank pranks
NOUN a childish trick

prawn prawns
NOUN a small, edible shellfish with a long tail

pray prays, praying, prayed
VERB When someone **prays**, they speak to God, to give thanks or to ask for help.

prayer prayers
NOUN the activity of praying or the words said when someone prays

pre-
PREFIX added to some words to mean before a particular time or event, for example **pre**school, **pre**war, **pre**history

preach preaches, preaching, preached
VERB When someone **preaches**, they give a short talk on a religious or moral subject. **preacher** NOUN

precarious
ADJECTIVE **1** Someone or something in a **precarious** position is not very safe or secure, and they may fall or fail at any time. • *Her position was **precarious** because she needed only one point to win.*
2 Something that is **precarious** is likely to fall because it is not well balanced or secured.
precariously ADVERB

precaution precautions
NOUN an action that is intended to prevent something unwanted or unpleasant from happening

precede precedes, preceding, preceded
VERB **1** If one event **precedes** another, it happens before it. • *A short film **preceded** the talk about elephants.*
2 If you **precede** someone, you go in front of them.

precinct precincts
NOUN a pedestrian shopping area

precious
ADJECTIVE Something that is **precious** is valuable or important and should be looked after or used carefully.
[from Latin *pretiosus* meaning valuable]

precipice precipices
NOUN a very steep rock face or sheer cliff

precise
ADJECTIVE very accurate • *We will never know the **precise** details of what happened.*
SYNONYM: exact

predator predators
NOUN an animal that kills and eats other animals
predatory ADJECTIVE

predecessor predecessors
NOUN Someone's **predecessor** is the person who used to do their job before them.

predicament predicaments
NOUN a difficult or awkward situation

predict predicts, predicting, predicted
VERB If you **predict** something, you say what you think will happen in the future.

preen preens, preening, preened
VERB When a bird **preens**, it cleans and tidies its feathers using its beak.

preface prefaces
NOUN an introduction at the beginning of a book, explaining what it is about or why it was written

prefect prefects
NOUN a pupil who has special duties at a school
[from Latin *praefectus* meaning someone put in charge]

prefer prefers, preferring, preferred
VERB If you **prefer** one thing to another, you like it better than the other thing.

preferable
ADJECTIVE Something that is **preferable** to something else, is more suitable or you like it better than the other thing. • *We thought that going to the cinema was **preferable** to watching TV.*

prefix prefixes
NOUN a letter or group of letters added to the beginning of a word to make a new word, for example *dis-*, *pre-* and *un-*

pregnant
ADJECTIVE A woman or other female animal who is **pregnant** has a baby developing in their womb.

prehistoric
ADJECTIVE existing at a time in the past before anything was written down

prejudice prejudices
NOUN an unreasonable and unfair dislike of or preference for a particular person or thing
prejudiced ADJECTIVE

A B C D E F G H I J K L M N O **P** Q R S T U V W X Y Z

preliminary
ADJECTIVE **Preliminary** activities take place before something starts and in preparation for it. • *They lost in the **preliminary** rounds of the competition.*

prelude preludes
NOUN **1** something that happens before an event and prepares you for it
2 a short piece of music

premature
ADJECTIVE happening too early, or earlier than expected • *The **premature** baby had to spend time in hospital to gain weight.*
prematurely ADVERB

premier premiers
Said "**prem**-mee-uh" NOUN **1** The leader of a government is sometimes referred to as the **premier**.
2 In Australia, the leader of a State government is called the **Premier**.
ADJECTIVE **3** considered to be the best or most important • *the **premier** department store*
[from Latin *primarius* meaning principal]

premiere premieres
Said "**prem**-mee-er" NOUN the first public performance of a new play or film • *The **premiere** of the new film is in London next week.*
[from French *premier* meaning first]

premises
Said "**prem**-is-iz" PLURAL NOUN buildings and land belonging to an organization

premium premiums
Said "**pree**-mee-um" NOUN **1** an extra sum of money that has to be paid for something
2 money paid regularly to an insurance company

premonition premonitions
NOUN a feeling that something unpleasant is going to happen

preoccupied
ADJECTIVE If you are **preoccupied**, you are deep in thought or totally involved with something, and you do not notice anything else. • *It is difficult to talk to him as he seems so **preoccupied**.*

preparation preparations
NOUN **1 Preparation** is the act of getting things ready.
2 Preparations are all the things you do and the arrangements you make before an event can happen. • *We started making **preparations** for the party by buying some decorations.*

prepare prepares, preparing, prepared
VERB If you **prepare** something, or **prepare** for something, you get it ready or get ready for it.

preposition prepositions
NOUN a word that is used before a noun or pronoun to show how it is connected to other words. For example, in the sentence *I put the book on the table*, the word *on* is the **preposition**.

prescribe prescribes, prescribing, prescribed
VERB If a doctor **prescribes** a medicine for a patient, he or she tells the patient what medicine they need and gives them a prescription.

prescription prescriptions
NOUN a written instruction from a doctor to a chemist, to provide a person with a particular medicine

presence
NOUN the **presence** of a person in a place is the fact that they are there

present presents, presenting, presented
Said "**prez**-ent" ADJECTIVE **1** If someone is **present** at a place or an event, they are there.
2 happening now
SYNONYMS: contemporary, current
NOUN **3** the period of time that is taking place now
4 something that you give to someone for them to keep, especially on their birthday or at Christmas, or on some other special occasion
SYNONYM: gift
Said "pri-**zent**" VERB **5** If you **present** someone with something, or if you

present it to them, you formally give it to them.

presentation presentations

NOUN **1** a talk or a lecture showing or describing something
2 a ceremony where awards or prizes are given
3 The **presentation** of something is the way it looks. • *My teacher was pleased with the presentation of my project.*

presently

ADVERB If something will happen **presently**, it will happen soon. • *I'll finish the job presently.*

preservative preservatives

NOUN a substance or a chemical that stops things such as food from going bad

preserve preserves, preserving, preserved

VERB If you **preserve** something, you make sure that it stays as it is and does not change or end.

president presidents

NOUN The **president** of a country that has no king or queen is the leader of the country. • *the President of the United States*

press presses, pressing, pressed

VERB **1** If you **press** something, you push it or hold it firmly against something else.
2 If you **press** clothes, you iron them.
3 If you **press** someone to do something, you try to make them do it.
NOUN **4** a machine for printing
5 The **press** is a term used for all the newspapers and the journalists who work for them.

pressure pressures

NOUN **1** the amount of force that is pushing on a particular area
2 If there is **pressure** on you to do something, someone is trying to persuade or force you do it.

presume presumes, presuming, presumed

VERB If you **presume** something, you think

that it is probably true without knowing for certain.
SYNONYMS: believe, suppose
presumption NOUN

pretend pretends, pretending, pretended

VERB If you **pretend** that something is the case, you try to make people believe that it is true when it is not.

pretty prettier, prettiest

ADJECTIVE **1** attractive and pleasant
ADVERB **2** INFORMAL quite or rather • *He spoke pretty good English.*

prevent prevents, preventing, prevented

VERB If you **prevent** something, you stop it happening.

preview previews

NOUN a showing of something like a film, play or exhibition before it is shown to the general public

previous

ADJECTIVE A **previous** time or thing is one that occurred before the present one.
• *I'm happier in this class than I was in the previous one.*
previously ADVERB

prey preys, preying, preyed

NOUN **1** an animal that is hunted and eaten by another animal
VERB **2** An animal that **preys** on another animal lives by hunting and eating it.

price prices

NOUN the amount of money that you pay to buy something • *The price of bread has increased significantly.*

priceless

ADJECTIVE Something that is **priceless** is so valuable that it is difficult to work out how much it is worth.

prick pricks, pricking, pricked

VERB If you **prick** something, you stick a sharp object into it.

prickle prickles, prickling, prickled

NOUN **1** a small sharp point or thorn growing on a plant

A
B
C
D
E
F
G
H
I
J
K
L
M
N
O
P
Q
R
S
T
U
V
W
X
Y
Z

VERB **2** If your skin **prickles**, it feels as if a lot of sharp points are being stuck into it.

prickly ADJECTIVE

pride **prides**

NOUN **1** a feeling of satisfaction and pleasure you have when you, or people close to you, have done something well **2** a feeling of dignity and self-respect **3** a group of lions that live together

priest **priests**

NOUN **1** a member of the clergy in some Christian Churches **2** someone who performs religious ceremonies in non-Christian religions

prim **primmer, primmest**

ADJECTIVE Someone who is **prim** always behaves very correctly and is easily shocked by anything rude.

primary

ADJECTIVE extremely important or most important

primary colour **primary colours**

NOUN The **primary colours** are red, yellow and blue. From these all the other colours can be made.

primary school **primary schools**

NOUN a school for children between the ages of 5 and 11

prime

ADJECTIVE **1** main or most important **2** of the best quality [from Latin *primus* meaning first]

prime minister **prime ministers**

NOUN the leader of the government

primitive

ADJECTIVE **1** connected with a society in which people live very simply **2** very simple, basic or old-fashioned • *Their accommodation was **primitive**, but they still enjoyed their trip.*

primrose **primroses**

NOUN a small plant that has pale yellow flowers in spring [from Latin *prima rosa* meaning first rose]

prince **princes**

NOUN a male member of a royal family, especially the son of a king or queen

princess **princesses**

NOUN a female member of a royal family, especially the daughter of a king or queen, or the wife of a prince

principal **principals**

ADJECTIVE **1** main or most important • *He had the **principal** role in the play.*
NOUN **2** the person in charge of a school or college

Do not confuse *principal* with *principle*.

principle **principles**

NOUN **1** a general rule or law about how something works **2** a belief that you have about the way you should behave • *I try to help others as a matter of **principle**.*

Do not confuse *principle* with *principal*.

print **prints, printing, printed**

VERB **1** When words or pictures are **printed**, they are put onto paper in large numbers by a printing machine, for example to make books or newspapers. **2** If you **print** your name, or some other writing, you write letters that are not joined up.
NOUN **3** The letters and numbers on the pages of a book or newspaper are referred to as the **print**. • *The columns of tiny **print** were difficult to read.*

printer **printers**

NOUN **1** a person who prints books and newspapers **2** a machine that prints the data from a computer onto paper

print-out **print-outs**

NOUN a printed copy of information from a computer

priority **priorities**

NOUN something that needs to be dealt with first because it is more urgent or important than other things • *He needed to make his homework a **priority**.*

prism prisms

NOUN **1** In mathematics, a **prism** is any three- dimensional shape that has the same size and shape of face at each end. A **prism** is the same size and shape along its length.
2 a solid piece of clear glass or plastic with flat sides, that can be used to separate light passing through it into the colours of the rainbow

prison prisons

NOUN a building where people who have broken the law are locked up as a punishment

prisoner prisoners

NOUN someone who is kept in prison or held in captivity

privacy

NOUN If you have **privacy**, you have somewhere private where you can be alone without being disturbed.

private privates

ADJECTIVE **1** for the use of only one person or group of people, rather than for the general public • *The hotel had a **private** beach.*
2 meant to be kept secret
NOUN **3** a soldier of the lowest rank

privilege privileges

NOUN a special right or advantage that is given to a person or group

prize prizes

NOUN a reward given to the winner of a competition or game

pro-

PREFIX supporting or being in favour of
• *a **pro**-animal rights march*
ANTONYM: anti-

probability

NOUN the measure of how likely an event is

probable

ADJECTIVE likely to happen or likely to be true

probably

ADVERB likely but not certainly • *I am **probably** having a party for my birthday.*

probation

NOUN **1** a period of time during which a person convicted of a crime is supervised by a social worker called a **probation** officer, instead of being sent to prison
2 a period of time when someone is tried out to see if they are suitable for a particular job

probe probes, probing, probed

VERB **1** If you **probe**, you investigate something, often by asking a lot of questions to discover the facts about it.
2 If you **probe** something, you gently push a long, thin instrument into it, usually to find something.
NOUN **3** a long, thin instrument used to look closely at something
[from Latin *probare* meaning to test]

problem problems

NOUN **1** an unsatisfactory situation that causes difficulties
SYNONYMS: difficulty, predicament
2 a puzzle or question that you solve using logical thought or mathematics

procedure procedures

NOUN a way of doing something, especially the correct or usual way • *The entire **procedure** takes about 15 minutes.*

proceed proceeds, proceeding, proceeded

Said "pro-**seed**" VERB **1** If you **proceed** to do something, you do it after doing something else. • *He then **proceeded** to tell us the story.*

a
b
c
d
e
f
g
h
i
j
k
l
m
n
o
p
q
r
s
t
u
v
w
x
y
z

A
B
C
D
E
F
G
H
I
J
K
L
M
N
O
P
Q
R
S
T
U
V
W
X
Y
Z

2 If you **proceed**, you move in a particular direction. ● We **proceeded** along the corridor.
Said "**pro**-seedz" PLURAL NOUN **3** The **proceeds** of an event are the money that is obtained from it. ● The **proceeds** from the concert will go towards famine relief.
[from Latin pro + cedere meaning to go onward]

process processes, processing, processed
NOUN **1** a series of actions or events that have a particular result
PHRASE **2** If you are **in the process** of doing something, you have started doing it but have not yet finished.
VERB **3** You **process** something when you put it through a series of actions in order to have a particular result. For example, you **process** milk to pasteurize it.

procession processions
NOUN a group of people or vehicles moving together in a line, often as part of a ceremony ● There was a **procession** of musicians along the high street on Sunday.

proclaim proclaims, proclaiming, proclaimed
VERB If someone **proclaims** something, they announce it or make it known publicly.
proclamation NOUN

prod prods, prodding, prodded
VERB If you **prod** something or somebody, you give them a poke with your finger.

produce produces, producing, produced
Said "pro-**dewss**" VERB **1** If someone or something **produces** something, they make it or cause it to happen.
2 If you **produce** something from somewhere, you bring it out so that it can be seen. ● The magician **produced** a rabbit out of the hat.
3 If you **produce** a film, play or other form of entertainment, you are in charge of organizing it.
Said "**prod**-yooss" NOUN **4** food that is grown to be sold

producer producers
NOUN The **producer** of a record, film, play or programme is the person in charge of making it or putting it on. ● a television **producer**

product products
NOUN **1** something that is made or produced to be sold
2 The **product** is the answer to a multiplication sum. ● The **product** of 4 and 6 is 24.

production productions
NOUN **1** the process of manufacturing or growing something in large quantities
2 a version of something such as a play or a film

profession professions
NOUN a job for which you need special training and education ● the medical **profession** ● the teaching **profession**

professional professionals
ADJECTIVE **1** **Professional** is used to describe activities that are done to earn money rather than as a hobby. ● He earns a lot of money as a **professional** footballer.
2 You can use **professional** to describe work that is of a very high standard.
NOUN **3** someone who does a particular type of work to earn money

professor professors
NOUN the most senior teacher in a department of a British university, or a teacher at an American college or university

proficient
ADJECTIVE If you are **proficient** at something, you can do it well. ● I am pleased to see how **proficient** you are in reading.
proficiency NOUN

profile profiles
NOUN the outline of a face seen from the side
[from Italian profilare meaning to sketch lightly]

profit **profits, profiting, profited**
NOUN **1** an amount of money that you gain when you are paid more for something than it cost to buy or make
VERB **2** If you **profit** from something, you gain or benefit from it. ● *I think you will* **profit** *from some extra lessons.*

profound
ADJECTIVE **1** very deep or intense
● *discoveries that have a* **profound** *effect on life today*
2 showing or needing deep thought or understanding ● *He asked a* **profound** *question for someone of his age.*

program **programs, programming, programmed**
NOUN **1** a set of instructions that a computer follows in order to perform particular tasks
VERB **2** When someone **programs** a computer, they prepare a program and put it into the computer.

programme **programmes**
NOUN **1** something that is broadcast on television or radio
2 a planned series of events
3 a booklet giving information about a play, concert or show

progress **progresses, progressing, progressed**
*Said "***proh***-gress"* NOUN **1** the process of gradually improving or getting near to achieving something
*Said "pro-***gress***"* VERB **2** If you **progress**, you become more advanced or skilful at something.
3 to continue or move forward ● *As the trip* **progressed***, I began to feel sick.*

prohibit **prohibits, prohibiting, prohibited**
VERB If someone **prohibits** something, they forbid it or make it illegal. ● *Visitors are prohibited from smoking.*

project **projects, projecting, projected**
*Said "***proj***-ekt"* NOUN **1** a carefully planned task that requires a lot of time or effort
*Said "pro-***jekt***"* VERB **2** If you **project** an image onto a screen, you make it appear there using a projector.
3 If something **projects**, it sticks out.

projector **projectors**
NOUN a piece of equipment that produces a large image on a screen by shining light through a photographic slide or film strip

prologue **prologues**
*Said "***pro***-log"* NOUN a short piece of writing at the beginning of a book, or a speech that introduces a play

prolong **prolongs, prolonging, prolonged**
VERB If you **prolong** something, you make it last longer. ● *We* **prolonged** *the holiday.*

promenade **promenades**
*Said "prom-un-***ahd***"* NOUN a path or road by the sea for walking along

prominent
ADJECTIVE **1** A **prominent** person is important or well known.
2 very noticeable ● *The church is a* **prominent** *landmark.*
[from Latin *prominere* meaning to stick out]

promise **promises, promising, promised**
VERB **1** If you **promise** to do something, you say that you will definitely do it.
NOUN **2** a statement made by someone that they will definitely do something
3 Someone or something that shows **promise** seems likely to be successful in the future.

promising
ADJECTIVE likely to be successful or good

promote **promotes, promoting, promoted**
VERB **1** If someone **promotes** something, they try to make it happen, or become more popular or successful.
2 If someone is **promoted**, they are given a more important job at work.

prompt **prompts, prompting, prompted**
VERB **1** If something or someone **prompts** you to do something, they encourage you or make you decide to do it.

a b c d e f g h i j k l m n o p q r s t u v w x y z

2 If you **prompt** an actor, you remind them of their lines in a play if they forget them.
ADJECTIVE **3** A **prompt** action is done immediately, without any delay.

prone
ADJECTIVE **1** If you are **prone** to something, you have a tendency to be affected by it or to do it. • *I am **prone** to catching colds in the winter.*
2 If you are **prone**, you are lying flat and face downwards.

prong **prongs**
NOUN The **prongs** of a fork are the long pointed parts.

pronoun **pronouns**
NOUN a word that is used to replace a noun. **Pronouns** are used instead of naming a person or a thing. *He, she* and *them* are all examples of **pronouns**.

pronounce **pronounces, pronouncing, pronounced**
VERB **1** When you **pronounce** a word, you say it.
2 When someone **pronounces** something, they state or announce it formally.

pronunciation **pronunciations**
NOUN the way a word is usually said

proof
NOUN If you have **proof** of something, you have evidence which shows that it is true or exists.
SYNONYM: confirmation

prop **props, propping, propped**
VERB **1** If you **prop** an object somewhere, you lean it against something for support.
NOUN **2** an object, such as a piece of wood or metal, used to support something
3 an object or piece of furniture used on stage in the theatre, or on a film set

propaganda
NOUN information, sometimes untrue and often exaggerated, that is used by political groups to influence people

propel **propels, propelling, propelled**
VERB To **propel** something is to push it forward.

propeller **propellers**
NOUN a device on a boat or aircraft with rotating blades, that makes the boat or aircraft move

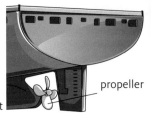
propeller

proper
ADJECTIVE If you do something in the **proper** way, you do it correctly.

properly
ADVERB If something is done **properly**, it is done correctly and to the right standard.

proper noun **proper nouns**
NOUN A proper noun is the name of a person, place or institution, and usually starts with a capital letter. For example, *Mary*, *London* and the *Statue of Liberty* are all **proper nouns**.
See **noun**

property **properties**
NOUN **1** A person's **property** is something, or all the things, that belong to them.
2 A **property** is a building and the land around it.
3 a characteristic that something has • *A **property** of mint is its strong smell.*
[from Latin *proprietas* meaning something personal]

prophet **prophets**
NOUN a person who predicts what will happen in the future

proportion **proportions**
NOUN **1** part of an amount or group
2 The **proportion** of one amount to another is its size in relation to the whole amount, usually expressed as a fraction or percentage. • *The **proportion** of boys in the school is 58%.*

propose **proposes, proposing, proposed**
VERB **1** If you **propose** a plan or idea, you suggest it.
2 If you **propose** to someone, you ask them to marry you.

proprietor **proprietors**
NOUN the owner of a shop or business

prose
NOUN ordinary written language, rather than poetry

prosecute **prosecutes, prosecuting, prosecuted**
VERB If someone is **prosecuted**, they are charged with a crime and put on trial.

prospect **prospects, prospecting, prospected**
NOUN **1** something that may happen in the future
2 Your **prospects** are your chances of being successful in the future. ● *If she works hard at school, her **prospects** are good.*
VERB **3** When people **prospect** for gold, oil or other minerals, they search for them.
prospector NOUN

prosper **prospers, prospering, prospered**
VERB When people or businesses **prosper**, they are successful and make money.
prosperous ADJECTIVE **prosperity** NOUN

protect **protects, protecting, protected**
VERB If you **protect** someone or something, you prevent them from being harmed.

protein **proteins**
NOUN a substance that is found in meat, eggs and milk. It is needed by your body to make you grow and keep you healthy.

protest **protests, protesting, protested**
Said "pro-**test**" VERB **1** If you **protest**, you say or do something to show that you strongly disapprove of something.
Said "**pro**-test" NOUN **2** a demonstration or statement to show that you strongly disapprove of something

Protestant **Protestants**
NOUN someone who belongs to the branch of the Christian Church that separated from the Catholic Church in the sixteenth century

protractor **protractors**
NOUN a flat, semicircular instrument used for measuring angles

protrude **protrudes, protruding, protruded**
VERB FORMAL If something **protrudes** from a surface or edge, it sticks out. ● *The handle of his racket **protruded** from his sports bag.*
protrusion NOUN

proud **prouder, proudest**
ADJECTIVE **1** If you are **proud** of something, you feel satisfaction and pleasure because of something you own or have achieved.
2 Someone who is **proud** has a lot of dignity and self-respect.

prove **proves, proving, proved** or **proven**
VERB If you **prove** that something is true, you show by means of argument or evidence that it is definitely true.
SYNONYMS: confirm, verify

proverb **proverbs**
NOUN a short, well-known saying that gives advice or makes a comment about life. For example, *A stitch in time saves nine.*
proverbial ADJECTIVE

provide **provides, providing, provided**
VERB If you **provide** something for someone, you give it to them or make it available to them.

province **provinces**
NOUN one of the areas into which some large countries are divided ● *Each **province** has its own administration.*

provision **provisions**
NOUN the act of supplying or making something available to people

provisional
ADJECTIVE A **provisional** arrangement is one that has been agreed on for the time being, but has not yet been made definite.

provisions
PLURAL NOUN supplies of food and drink

a
b
c
d
e
f
g
h
i
j
k
l
m
n
o
p
q
r
s
t
u
v
w
x
y
z

provoke provokes, provoking, provoked
VERB **1** If you **provoke** someone, you deliberately try to make them angry.
2 If something **provokes** a reaction or feeling, it causes it.
provocation NOUN provocative ADJECTIVE

prow prows
NOUN the front part of a boat or ship

prowl prowls, prowling, prowled
VERB If a person or animal **prowls** around, they move around quietly and secretly, as if hunting.

proximity
NOUN FORMAL nearness to someone or something ● *I lost my bag in the* **proximity** *of the swimming pool.*

prune prunes, pruning, pruned
NOUN **1** a dried plum
VERB **2** When someone **prunes** a tree or shrub, they cut back some of the branches to make it grow well.

pry pries, prying, pried
VERB If someone **pries**, they try to find out about something secret or private.

PS
PS is written at the end of a letter to give an extra message. It is an abbreviation of *postscript*.
[from Latin *postscribere* meaning to write (*scribere*) after (*post*)]

psalm psalms
NOUN one of the 150 songs, poems and prayers that form the Book of **Psalms** in the Bible
[from Greek *psalmos* meaning song accompanied on the harp]

pseudonym pseudonyms
NOUN a false name an author uses rather than using their real name

psychiatry
Said "sy-**ky**-a-tree" NOUN the branch of medicine concerned with mental illness
[from Greek *psukhē* meaning mind and *iatros* meaning healer]
psychiatrist NOUN psychiatric ADJECTIVE

psychic
ADJECTIVE having unusual mental powers, such as the ability to read people's minds or predict the future

psychology
NOUN the scientific study of the mind and of the reasons for people's behaviour

PTO
an abbreviation of *please turn over*. **PTO** is written at the bottom of a page to show that there is more writing on the other side.

pub pubs
NOUN a place where people go to buy and drink alcoholic and other drinks, and to talk to their friends. **Pub** is an abbreviation of *public house*.

puberty
NOUN the stage when a person's body changes from that of a child into that of an adult

public
NOUN **1** You can refer to people in general as the **public**. ● *The castle is open to the* **public** *on Sundays.*
ADJECTIVE **2** relating to people in general ● **public** *opinion*
3 provided for everyone to use ● *We try to use* **public** *transport whenever possible.*

publication publications
NOUN **1** The **publication** of a book is the act of printing it and making it available.
2 a book, newspaper or magazine

publicity
NOUN information or advertisements about an item or event to attract attention to it

public school public schools
NOUN **1** In England and Wales, a **public school** is a private secondary school that charges fees.
2 In Scotland and America, a **public school** is a state school.

publish publishes, publishing, published
VERB **1** When a company **publishes** a

book, newspaper or magazine, they print copies of it and distribute it.
2 When a newspaper or magazine **publishes** an article or photograph, they print it.

pudding puddings
NOUN **1** a cooked sweet food, often made with flour and eggs, and usually served hot
2 You can refer to the sweet course of a meal as the **pudding**.

puddle puddles
NOUN a small shallow pool of rain water or other liquid

puff puffs, puffing, puffed
VERB **1** If you are **puffing**, you are breathing loudly and quickly with your mouth open.
2 If something **puffs out** or **puffs up**, it swells and becomes larger and rounder.
NOUN **3** a small blast of air, smoke or steam • The car let out a **puff** of smoke before it sped away.

pull pulls, pulling, pulled
VERB **1** If you **pull** something, you get hold of it and move it towards you with force.
2 If a vehicle or an animal **pulls** something, they move it along behind them.
3 When you **pull** the curtains, you move them across a window.
4 If you **pull** a muscle, you damage it temporarily by stretching it too much.
5 If someone **pulls down** a building, they demolish it.
6 If you **pull out** of an activity, you decide not to do it.

pulley pulleys
NOUN a piece of machinery with a wheel and chain or rope over it, used for lifting heavy things

pullover pullovers
NOUN a knitted piece of clothing, put on over your head, that covers the top part of your body

pulpit pulpits
NOUN the small raised platform in a church or cathedral where a member of the clergy stands to preach

pulse pulses
NOUN **1** the regular beating of your heart as it pumps blood through your body. You can feel your **pulse** at your wrists and some other places on your body.
2 Your **pulse** rate is a measure of how fast your heart is beating.

pump pumps, pumping, pumped
NOUN **1** a machine that is used to force a liquid or gas to move in a particular direction
VERB **2** If someone or something **pumps** a liquid or gas somewhere, they force it to flow in that direction, using a pump.

pumpkin pumpkins
NOUN a very large, round, orange vegetable

pun puns
NOUN a clever and amusing use of words so that what you say has two different meanings

punch punches, punching, punched
VERB **1** If you **punch** someone or something, you hit them hard with your fist.
NOUN **2** a hard blow with the fist

punchline punchlines
NOUN The **punchline** of a joke or a story is the last part, that makes it funny.

punctual
ADJECTIVE arriving at the correct time
SYNONYMS: on time, prompt
punctually ADVERB **punctuality** NOUN

punctuation
NOUN the marks in writing that make it easier to understand, such as full stops, question marks and commas

puncture punctures
NOUN a small hole in a car or bicycle tyre, made by a sharp object

pungent
ADJECTIVE having a strong, unpleasant smell or taste
pungency NOUN

punish **punishes, punishing, punished**
VERB To **punish** someone means to make them suffer for doing wrong.
punishment NOUN

puny **punier, puniest**
ADJECTIVE very small and weak

pupa **pupae**
NOUN an insect at the stage of development between a larva and a fully grown adult
SYNONYM: chrysalis

pupil **pupils**
NOUN **1** The **pupils** at a school are the children who attend it.
2 Your **pupils** are the small, round, black holes in the centre of your eyes.

puppet **puppets**
NOUN a doll that can be moved by pulling strings or by putting your hand inside its body

puppy **puppies**
NOUN a young dog

purchase **purchases, purchasing, purchased**
VERB **1** When you **purchase** something, you buy it.
NOUN **2** something that you have bought

pure **purer, purest**
ADJECTIVE **1** Something that is **pure** is not mixed with anything else.
2 clean and free from harmful substances

purify **purifies, purifying, purified**
VERB If someone **purifies** something, they remove all dirty or harmful substances from it.
purification NOUN

purple
ADJECTIVE OR NOUN reddish-blue

purpose **purposes**
NOUN **1** the reason for something
2 the thing that you want to achieve
PHRASE **3** If you do something **on purpose**, you do it deliberately.

purr **purrs, purring, purred**
VERB When a cat **purrs**, it makes a low vibrating sound because it is contented.

purse **purses**
NOUN **1** a container, usually made of leather, plastic or fabric and like a very small bag, for carrying money and credit cards
2 In American English, a **purse** is a handbag.

pursue **pursues, pursuing, pursued**
VERB **1** If you **pursue** someone, you follow them in order to catch them.
2 If you **pursue** an activity or plan, you try to achieve it.

pus
NOUN a thick yellowish liquid that forms in an infected wound or a boil

push **pushes, pushing, pushed**
VERB If you **push** someone or something, you use force to move them away from you.

pushchair **pushchairs**
NOUN a small folding chair on wheels in which a baby or a toddler can be pushed along

put **puts, putting, put**
VERB **1** If you **put** something somewhere, you move it into that position.
2 If you **put** an idea in a particular way, you express it.
PHRASE **3** If you **put off** doing something, you delay it.
4 If you **put out** the light, you switch it off.
5 If you **put up** with something, you let it happen without complaining.

putt **putts**
NOUN In golf, a **putt** is a gentle stroke made when the ball is near the hole.

putty
NOUN a paste used to fix panes of glass into frames

puzzle **puzzles, puzzling, puzzled**
VERB **1** If something **puzzles** you, it confuses you and you do not understand it.

A B C D E F G H I J K L M N O P Q R S T U V W X Y Z

NOUN **2** a game or question that requires a lot of thought to complete or solve

PVC
NOUN a plastic material used for making various things, including clothing, drainpipes and tiles. **PVC** is an abbreviation of *polyvinyl chloride*.

pyjamas
PLURAL NOUN loose trousers and a loose jacket that you wear in bed
[from Persian *pay jama* meaning leg clothing]

pylon **pylons**
NOUN a tall metal structure that carries overhead electricity cables

pyramid **pyramids**
NOUN **1** a three-dimensional shape with a flat base and flat triangular sides sloping upwards to a point
2 an ancient stone structure in this shape, built over the tombs of Egyptian kings and queens

python **pythons**
NOUN a large snake that kills other animals by squeezing them with its body
[from Greek *Puthon*, a huge mythical serpent]

quack **quacks, quacking, quacked**
VERB **1** When a duck **quacks**, it makes a loud harsh sound.
NOUN **2** A **quack** is the sound made by a duck.

quadrangle **quadrangles**
NOUN **1** a courtyard with buildings all round it
2 In geometry, a **quadrangle** is a four-sided shape.

quadrant **quadrants**
NOUN a quarter of a circle

quadrilateral **quadrilaterals**
NOUN a plane shape with four straight sides

quadruplet **quadruplets**
NOUN one of four children born at the same time to the same mother

quail **quails**
NOUN a type of small game bird with a round body and a short tail

quaint **quainter, quaintest**
ADJECTIVE If something is **quaint**, it is attractive and charming in an old-fashioned or unusual way. • *The quaint little village was filled with thatched cottages.*

quake **quakes, quaking, quaked**
VERB **1** If you **quake**, you tremble because you are very frightened.
2 If the ground **quakes**, it moves, usually because of an earthquake.
NOUN **3** an abbreviation of *earthquake*

Quaker **Quakers**
NOUN a member of a Christian group called the Society of Friends, that gathers together for peaceful thought and prayer

a
b
c
d
e
f
g
h
i
j
k
l
m
n
o
p
q
r
s
t
u
v
w
x
y
z

qualification qualifications
NOUN Your **qualifications** are your skills and achievements. You gain **qualifications** by passing tests and examinations.

qualify qualifies, qualifying, qualified
VERB If you **qualify**, you pass examinations and gain qualifications, often for a particular job. ● *After many years of study and training, she **qualified** as a doctor.*

quality
NOUN The **quality** of something is how good it is.

quantity quantities
NOUN an amount that you can measure or count

quarantine
*Said "***kwo**-ran-teen"* NOUN a period of time that a person or animal has to spend apart from others to prevent the possible spread of disease
[from Italian *quarantina* meaning forty days]

quarrel quarrels, quarrelling, quarrelled
NOUN **1** an angry argument
VERB **2** If people **quarrel**, they have an angry argument.

quarry quarries
NOUN a place where stone is removed from the ground by digging or blasting

quart quarts
*Said "***kwort***"* NOUN a unit of liquid volume equal to two pints or about 1.136 litres

quarter quarters
NOUN **1** one of four equal parts of something
2 When you are telling the time, **quarter** means fifteen minutes before or after the hour. ● *The programme starts at a **quarter** to six, and finishes at a **quarter** past.*
3 an American or Canadian coin worth 25 cents, which is a **quarter** of a dollar

quartet quartets
NOUN **1** a group of four musicians who sing or play together
2 a piece of music written for four instruments or singers

quartz
NOUN a type of hard, shiny crystal used in making very accurate watches and clocks

quay quays
NOUN a place where boats are tied up and loaded or unloaded

queasy queasier, queasiest
ADJECTIVE If you feel **queasy**, you feel slightly sick.

queen queens
NOUN a female monarch or a woman married to a king

queer queerer, queerest
ADJECTIVE very strange

quench quenches, quenching, quenched
VERB If you **quench** your thirst, you have a drink so that you are no longer thirsty.

query queries
NOUN a question ● *I cannot answer your **query**.*

quest quests
NOUN a long search for something

question questions, questioning, questioned
NOUN **1** a sentence that asks for information
VERB **2** If you **question** someone, you ask them questions.
PHRASE **3** If something is **out of the question**, it is impossible and not worth considering.

question mark **question marks**
NOUN a punctuation mark (?) used at the end of a question

questionnaire **questionnaires**
NOUN a list of questions that people fill in as part of a survey

queue **queues, queuing** or **queueing, queued**
NOUN **1** a line of people or vehicles that are waiting for something
VERB **2** When people **queue**, or **queue up**, they stand in a line waiting for something.

✏ *Queuing* and *queueing* are both correct spellings.

quibble **quibbles, quibbling, quibbled**
VERB If you **quibble** about something, you argue about something that is not very important.

quiche **quiches**
Said "**keesh**" NOUN a tart with a savoury filling made of eggs

quick **quicker, quickest**
ADJECTIVE If you are **quick**, you move or do things with great speed.

quicksand **quicksands**
NOUN an area of deep, wet sand that you sink into if you walk on it

quid
NOUN INFORMAL In British English, a **quid** is a pound in money.

quiet **quieter, quietest**
ADJECTIVE **1** If someone or something is **quiet**, they are not making much noise, or they are not making any noise at all.
2 A **quiet** place, time or situation is calm and peaceful.
NOUN **3** silence

quill **quills**
NOUN **1** a pen made from a feather
2 A bird's **quills** are the large feathers on its wings and tail.
3 A porcupine's **quills** are its spines.

quilt **quilts**
NOUN a thick, soft, warm cover for a bed, usually padded

quit **quits, quitting, quit**
VERB If you **quit** something, you leave it or stop doing it.

quite
ADVERB fairly but not very ● *She's **quite** old, but not as old as my grandma.*

quiver **quivers, quivering, quivered**
VERB **1** If something **quivers**, it trembles.
● *The leaves on the trees **quivered** in the breeze.*
NOUN **2** a container for carrying arrows

quiz **quizzes**
NOUN a game in which someone tests your knowledge by asking you questions

quota **quotas**
NOUN a number or quantity of something that is allowed by the rules ● *We have already had our **quota** of class outings for this term.*
[from Latin *quot* meaning how many]

quotation **quotations**
NOUN a small part of a piece of writing taken from a book or speech

quotation marks
PLURAL NOUN the punctuation marks (" " ' ') that show where written speech or quotations begin and end

quote **quotes, quoting, quoted**
VERB If you **quote** something that someone has written or said, you repeat their words.

quotient **quotients**
NOUN the number of times one number can be divided into another. For example, in 42 ÷ 6 = 7, 7 is the **quotient**.

Qur'an
NOUN another spelling of **Koran**

Rr

rabbi **rabbis**
NOUN a Jewish religious leader

rabbit **rabbits**
NOUN a small furry rodent with long ears

rabies
NOUN a disease that causes humans and some other animals, especially dogs, to go mad and die

race **races, racing, raced**
NOUN **1** a competition to see who is fastest at something
2 a large group of people who look alike in some way. Different **races** have, for example, different skin colour or differently shaped eyes.
VERB **3** If you **race**, you take part in a race. ● *She has **raced** against some of the best in the world.*
4 If you **race** somewhere, you go there as quickly as possible. ● *He **raced** after the others.*

racehorse **racehorses**
NOUN a horse that is trained to run fast for races

racial
ADJECTIVE to do with the different races that people belong to
racially ADVERB

racism
Said "**ray**-sizm" NOUN **1** hostility shown by one race of people to another
2 believing that one race of people is better than all others
racist NOUN OR ADJECTIVE

rack **racks**
NOUN a piece of equipment for holding things or hanging things on

racket **rackets**
NOUN **1** a bat with an oval frame and strings across and down it, used in games like tennis
2 If someone is making a **racket**, they are making a lot of noise.

radar
NOUN a way of discovering the position or speed of objects, such as ships or aircraft, by using radio signals
[an abbreviation for *radio detecting and ranging*]

radiant
ADJECTIVE **1** shining or sparkling
2 Someone who is **radiant** looks beautiful because they are so happy.

radiate **radiates, radiating, radiated**
VERB **1** Things that **radiate** from something come out in lines from a central point, like the spokes of a wheel or the sun's rays.
2 When a fire or a light **radiates** heat or light, it gives them out.

radiation
NOUN **1** very small particles given out by radioactive substances
2 the heat and light energy given out from a source such as the sun

radiator **radiators**
NOUN **1** a hollow metal device filled with hot water for heating a room
2 the part of a car that is filled with water to cool the engine

radio **radios**
NOUN **1** a system of sending sound over a distance by transmitting electrical signals
2 the broadcasting of programmes for the public to listen to by radio
3 a piece of equipment for listening to radio programmes ● *They are in daily **radio** contact with the expedition.*
4 a piece of equipment for sending and receiving **radio** messages ● *A policeman raised the alarm on his **radio**.*

radioactive
ADJECTIVE **Radioactive** substances give out energy in the form of powerful and harmful rays.

radish **radishes**
NOUN a small salad vegetable with a red skin and white flesh, and with a hot taste

radius **radii**
NOUN **1** a straight line going from the centre of a circle to the outside edge
2 the length of a straight line going from the centre of a circle to the outside edge

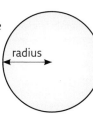
radius

raffle **raffles, raffling, raffled**
NOUN **1** a competition in which people buy numbered tickets and win a prize if their ticket is chosen
VERB **2** If you **raffle** something, you give it as a prize in a raffle.

raft **rafts**
NOUN a floating platform made from long pieces of wood tied together

rafter **rafters**
NOUN the sloping pieces of wood that support a roof

rag **rags**
NOUN **1** a piece of old cloth used to wipe or clean things
2 If someone is dressed in **rags**, they are wearing very old, torn clothes.

rage **rages, raging, raged**
NOUN **1** strong, uncontrollable anger
SYNONYMS: anger, fury, wrath
VERB **2** If something such as a storm or battle **rages**, it continues with great force or violence.

ragged
ADJECTIVE torn or frayed, with rough edges

raid **raids, raiding, raided**
VERB **1** When people **raid** a place, they enter it by force in order to attack it or to look for something or someone.
NOUN **2** a sudden, surprise attack

rail **rails**
NOUN **1** a fixed bar that you can hang things on

2 one of the heavy metal bars that trains run along

railings
PLURAL NOUN a series of metal bars that make up a fence

railway **railways**
NOUN a route along which trains travel on metal tracks

rain **rains, raining, rained**
NOUN **1** water falling from the clouds in small drops
VERB **2** When it **rains**, small drops of water fall from clouds in the sky.

Do not confuse *rain* with *rein* or *reign*.

rainbow **rainbows**
NOUN an arch of different colours that sometimes appears in the sky after it has been raining

raincoat **raincoats**
NOUN a waterproof coat

rainfall
NOUN the amount of rain that falls in one place during a particular period of time

rainforest **rainforests**
NOUN a dense forest of tall trees that grows in a tropical area where there is a lot of rain

raise **raises, raising, raised**
VERB **1** If you **raise** something, you make it higher. • *He raised his hand.*
2 If you **raise** your voice, you speak more loudly.
3 If you **raise** money for something, you get people to give money towards it.

raisin **raisins**
NOUN a dried grape

rake **rakes**
NOUN a garden tool with a row of metal teeth and a long handle, for collecting together dead leaves or cut grass

rally **rallies**
NOUN **1** a competition in which vehicles race along public roads
2 a large public meeting

a
b
c
d
e
f
g
h
i
j
k
l
m
n
o
p
q
r
s
t
u
v
w
x
y
z

3 In tennis or squash, a **rally** is a continuous series of shots exchanged by the players.

ram rams, ramming, rammed

VERB **1** If you **ram** something somewhere, you push it there firmly. • *She rammed her purse into her bag as she ran for the bus.*
2 If one vehicle **rams** another, it crashes into it.
NOUN **3** an adult male sheep

Ramadan

NOUN the ninth month of the Muslim year, during which Muslims eat and drink nothing during daylight
[from Arabic *Ramadan* meaning be hot, as the fasting takes place during a hot month]

ramble rambles, rambling, rambled

NOUN **1** a long walk in the countryside
VERB **2** to go for a ramble
3 If you **ramble**, you talk in a confused way.
rambler NOUN

ramp ramps

NOUN a sloping surface linking two places that are at different levels

rampage rampages, rampaging, rampaged

VERB If you **rampage**, you rush about wildly, causing damage.

rampart ramparts

NOUN an earth bank, often with a wall on top, built to protect a castle or city

ramshackle

ADJECTIVE A **ramshackle** building is in very poor condition.

ran

VERB the past tense of **run**

ranch ranches

NOUN a large farm where cattle or horses are reared, especially in the USA

random

ADJECTIVE OR NOUN Something that is done in a **random** way, or at **random**, is done by chance or without a definite plan.
SYNONYMS: chance, haphazard

rang

VERB the past tense of **ring**

range ranges, ranging, ranged

NOUN **1** a selection or choice of different things of the same kind • *This top is available in a wide range of colours.*
2 a set of values on a scale
3 the maximum distance over which something can reach things or detect things
4 a long line of hills or mountains
VERB **5** When a set of things **ranges** between two points, they vary within these points on a scale.

ranger rangers

NOUN someone whose job is to look after a forest or park

rank ranks

NOUN **1** a position or grade that someone holds in an organization
2 a row of people or things • *We went to the taxi rank outside the station to catch a taxi home.*

ransack ransacks, ransacking, ransacked

VERB If you **ransack** a place, you disturb everything in order to search for or steal something, and leave it in a mess.

ransom ransoms

NOUN money that is demanded by kidnappers to free someone they have taken hostage

rap raps, rapping, rapped

NOUN **1** a quick knock or blow on something • *There was a sharp rap on the door.*
2 a type of music in which the words are spoken in a rapid, rhythmic way
VERB **3** If you **rap** something, or **rap** on it, you hit it with a series of quick blows.

rapid

ADJECTIVE happening or moving very quickly

rapier rapiers

NOUN a long thin sword with a sharp point

rare rarer, rarest

ADJECTIVE **1** Something that is **rare** is not common or does not often happen.
2 Meat that is **rare** is cooked very lightly.

rascal **rascals**
NOUN someone who does naughty or mischievous things

rash **rashes**
NOUN **1** an area of red spots that appear on your skin when you are ill or have an allergy
ADJECTIVE **2** If you are **rash**, you do something without thinking properly about it.

rasher **rashers**
NOUN a thin slice of bacon

raspberry **raspberries**
NOUN a small soft red fruit that grows on a bush

rat **rats**
NOUN a rodent with a long tail, that looks like a large mouse

rate **rates**
NOUN how quickly or slowly, or how often something happens

rather
ADVERB **1** fairly, or to a certain extent
● **rather** large
2 If you would **rather** do one thing than another, you would prefer to do it. ● I don't want to go out. I'd **rather** stay here.

ratio **ratios**
NOUN The **ratio** between two things shows how many times one is bigger than another. A **ratio** is used to compare two or more quantities, for example, if a class has 15 boys and 10 girls, the **ratio** of boys to girls is 15 to 10.

ration **rations, rationing, rationed**
NOUN **1** the amount of something you are allowed to have
VERB **2** When something is **rationed**, you are only allowed a limited amount of it because there is a shortage.
rationing NOUN

rational
Said "**rash**-un-ul" ADJECTIVE well thought out, sensible and reasonable ● It was a **rational** decision.
ANTONYM: irrational

rattle **rattles, rattling, rattled**
VERB When something **rattles**, or when you **rattle** it, it makes short, regular knocking sounds, for example because it is shaking.

rattlesnake **rattlesnakes**
NOUN a poisonous American snake that can rattle its tail

rave **raves, raving, raved**
VERB **1** If someone **raves**, they talk in an excited and uncontrolled way.
2 INFORMAL If you **rave** about something, you talk about it very enthusiastically.
NOUN **3** INFORMAL a large dance event with electronic music

raven **ravens**
NOUN **1** a large black bird with a deep, harsh call
ADJECTIVE **2** **Raven** hair is black and shiny.

ravenous
ADJECTIVE very hungry
ravenously ADVERB

ravine **ravines**
NOUN a deep, narrow valley with steep sides

ravioli
NOUN an Italian dish made of small squares of pasta filled with meat or vegetable paste and served with sauce

raw
ADJECTIVE **1** **Raw** food is uncooked.
2 If part of your body is **raw**, the skin has been rubbed or scraped away.
3 A **raw** substance is in its natural state before being processed.

raw material **raw materials**
NOUN natural substances used to make things

a
b
c
d
e
f
g
h
i
j
k
l
m
n
o
p
q
r
s
t
u
v
w
x
y
z

ray rays
NOUN a beam of light ● *the sun's* **rays**

razor razors
NOUN an instrument that people use for shaving

re-
PREFIX used to form words that show something is being done again. For example, if you **re**use something you use it again, if you read something again you **re**read it, and if you marry for a second time you **re**marry.

reach reaches, reaching, reached
VERB **1** When you **reach** a place, you arrive there.
2 When you **reach** for something, you stretch out your arm to touch or get hold of it. ● *I can't* **reach** *that shelf.*

react reacts, reacting, reacted
VERB When you **react** to something, you behave in a particular way because of it.

reaction reactions
NOUN Your **reaction** to something is what you say, do or feel because of it.

reactor reactors
NOUN a device used to produce nuclear energy

read reads, reading, read
VERB When you **read** something that is written, you look at it and understand or say aloud the words that are there.

reader readers
NOUN The **readers** of a newspaper or magazine are the people who read it regularly.

readily
Said "**red**-ily" ADVERB **1** willingly or eagerly ● *They* **readily** *tidied their bedrooms.*
2 easily or quickly ● *Help was* **readily** *available.*

reading readings
NOUN **1** the act of reading books, newspapers or magazines
2 The **reading** on a meter, gauge or other measuring instrument is the amount it shows.

ready
ADJECTIVE If someone or something is **ready**, they are prepared for doing something.
● *Your glasses will be* **ready** *in a fortnight.*

real
ADJECTIVE **1** actually true and not imagined
2 genuine and not artificial

realistic
ADJECTIVE **1** A **realistic** painting, story or film shows things in a way that is like real life.
2 If you are **realistic** about a situation, you recognize and accept that it is true.

reality
NOUN **1** what is real, and not imagined or invented
SYNONYMS: fact, truth
2 If something has become a **reality**, it has happened. ● *Her dream of being a dancer had become a* **reality**.

realize realizes, realizing, realized; also spelt **realise**
VERB If you **realize** something, you become aware of it or understand it.

really
ADVERB **1** You use **really** to emphasize a point. ● *It is a* **really** *good film.*
2 You use **really** when you are talking about the true facts about something.
● *What was* **really** *going on?*

reap reaps, reaping, reaped
VERB When someone **reaps** a crop, such as corn, they cut and gather it.
reaper NOUN

reappear reappears, reappearing, reappeared
VERB When people or things **reappear**, they can be seen again after they have been out of sight.

rear rears, rearing, reared
NOUN **1** The **rear** of something is the part at the back.
VERB **2** To **rear** children or other young animals means to bring them up until they are able to look after themselves.
3 When a horse **rears**, it raises the front part of its body, so that its front legs are in the air.

rearrange rearranges, rearranging, rearranged
VERB If you **rearrange** something, you organize it or arrange it in a different way.

reason reasons, reasoning, reasoned
NOUN **1** the fact that explains why something happens
VERB **2** to think in a logical way and draw conclusions
3 If you **reason** with someone, you discuss something with them in a sensible way.

reasonable
ADJECTIVE **1** fair and sensible
2 A **reasonable** amount is a fairly large amount.

reassure reassures, reassuring, reassured
VERB If you **reassure** someone, you say or do things to calm their fears or stop them from worrying.

rebel rebels, rebelling, rebelled
Said "**reb**-el" NOUN **1** someone who does not agree with rules, and behaves differently from other people
2 one of a group of people who are fighting against their own country's army in order to change how it is ruled
Said "rib-**el**" VERB **3** When someone **rebels**, they refuse to obey rules, and they behave differently from other people.

rebellious
ADJECTIVE Someone who is **rebellious** breaks rules and refuses to obey orders.
rebellion NOUN

rebound rebounds, rebounding, rebounded
VERB If something **rebounds**, it bounces back after hitting something.

rebuild rebuilds, rebuilding, rebuilt
VERB When something is **rebuilt**, it is built again after being damaged or destroyed.

rebuke rebukes, rebuking, rebuked
VERB If you **rebuke** someone, you tell them off for something wrong that they have done.

recall recalls, recalling, recalled
VERB When you **recall** something, you remember it.

recede recedes, receding, receded
VERB **1** When something **recedes**, it moves away into the distance. • We watched the tide **receding**.
2 When a man's hair **recedes**, he starts to go bald from the front of his head.

receipt receipts
NOUN a piece of paper given to you as proof that you have paid for something or delivered something

receive receives, receiving, received
VERB When you **receive** something, you get it after someone has given or sent it to you.

receiver receivers
NOUN the part of a telephone that you hold near to your ear and your mouth

recent
ADJECTIVE A **recent** event is something that happened a short time ago.

reception receptions
NOUN **1** the place near the entrance of a hotel or office where appointments and enquiries are dealt with
2 a formal party

receptionist receptionists
NOUN In a hotel or office, the **receptionist** is the person who receives and welcomes visitors as they arrive, answers the telephone and arranges appointments.

recipe recipes
NOUN a list of ingredients and instructions for cooking or preparing a particular dish • My grandma gave me her **recipe** for Yorkshire pudding.

recital recitals
NOUN a performance of poetry or music, usually by one person

recite recites, reciting, recited
VERB If you **recite** something such as a poem, you say it aloud.
recitation NOUN

A
B
C
D
E
F
G
H
I
J
K
L
M
N
O
P
Q
R
S
T
U
V
W
X
Y
Z

reckless
ADJECTIVE If you are **reckless**, you do not care about any danger or damage you cause.

reckon reckons, reckoning, reckoned
VERB **1** If you **reckon** an amount, you calculate it.
2 If you **reckon** something is true, you think it is true.

reclaim reclaims, reclaiming, reclaimed
VERB **1** When you **reclaim** something, you fetch it after losing it or leaving it somewhere.
2 If land is **reclaimed**, it is made useable again, for example by draining water from it.

recline reclines, reclining, reclined
VERB to lean or lie back • We **reclined** on deckchairs in the sun.

recognize recognizes, recognizing, recognized; also spelt **recognise**
VERB When you **recognize** someone or something, you realize you know who or what they are.

recoil recoils, recoiling, recoiled
VERB If you **recoil**, you suddenly back away from something, usually because it shocks or horrifies you. • I **recoiled** from the huge spider.

recollect recollects, recollecting, recollected
VERB If you **recollect** something, you remember it.
recollection NOUN

recommend recommends, recommending, recommended
VERB If you **recommend** something to someone, you suggest that they try it because you think it is good.

reconcile reconciles, reconciling, reconciled
VERB When people are **reconciled**, they become friendly again after a quarrel.
reconciliation NOUN

reconstruct reconstructs, reconstructing, reconstructed
VERB To **reconstruct** something that has been damaged means to build it again.
reconstruction NOUN

record records, recording, recorded
Said "**rek**-ord" NOUN **1** a written account of something
2 a round, flat piece of plastic on which music has been recorded
3 an achievement that is the best of its type • He holds the world **record** for the high jump.
Said "ri-**kord**" VERB **4** If you **record** information, you write it down so that it can be referred to later.
5 If you **record** sounds and pictures, you copy them onto a tape or disc so that they can be listened to or watched again.

recorder recorders
NOUN **1** a small woodwind instrument
2 a machine for copying sounds and pictures, such as a tape **recorder** or a video **recorder**

recount recounts, recounting, recounted
Said "ri-**count**" VERB **1** If you **recount** a story, you tell it.
Said "**ree**-count" VERB **2** If you **recount** something such as votes, you count them for a second time.

recover recovers, recovering, recovered
VERB **1** When you **recover**, you get better after being ill.
2 If you **recover** something that has been lost or stolen, you get it back.

recreation recreations
NOUN the things you do for enjoyment in your spare time

recruit recruits, recruiting, recruited
VERB **1** If you **recruit** people, you persuade them to join a group or help with something.
NOUN **2** someone who has joined the

army or some other organization
recruitment NOUN

rectangle **rectangles**
NOUN a four-sided shape with four right
angles
rectangular ADJECTIVE

recuperate **recuperates,
recuperating, recuperated**
VERB When you **recuperate**, you gradually
recover after being ill or injured.
recuperation NOUN

recur **recurs, recurring, recurred**
VERB If something **recurs**, it happens
again.

recycle **recycles, recycling, recycled**
VERB When you **recycle** something, you
use it again for a different purpose.

red **redder, reddest; reds**
NOUN OR ADJECTIVE **1** the colour of blood or of
a ripe tomato
ADJECTIVE **2** **Red** hair is between orange
and brown in colour.

redden **reddens, reddening,
reddened**
VERB If something **reddens**, it becomes
red. ● His face **reddened** with
embarrassment.

red-handed
ADJECTIVE If you catch someone **red-
handed**, you catch them while they are
doing something wrong.

redraft **redrafts, redrafting,
redrafted**
VERB If you **redraft** a piece of writing, you
rewrite it to improve or change it.

reduce **reduces, reducing, reduced**
VERB If you **reduce** something, you make
it smaller in size or amount.
SYNONYMS: cut, decrease

reduction **reductions**
NOUN If there is a **reduction** in
something, it becomes smaller or less.
● There are great **reductions** in prices
during the sales.

redundant
ADJECTIVE **1** When people are made

redundant, they lose their jobs because
there is no more work for them.
2 If something becomes **redundant**, it is
no longer needed or useful.

reed **reeds**
NOUN **1** a hollow-stemmed plant that
grows in shallow water or on wet ground
2 a thin piece of cane or metal inside
some wind instruments, that vibrates and
makes a sound when air is blown over it

reef **reefs**
NOUN a long line of rocks or coral close to
the surface of the sea

reek **reeks, reeking, reeked**
VERB **1** If something **reeks**, it has a strong,
unpleasant smell.
NOUN **2** a strong, unpleasant smell

reel **reels, reeling, reeled**
NOUN **1** a cylindrical object around which
you wrap something such as a fishing
line, a film or thread
2 a fast Scottish dance
VERB **3** If you **reel**, you stagger and look as
if you will fall.

refer **refers, referring, referred**
VERB **1** If you **refer** to someone or
something, you mention them when you
are speaking or writing.
2 If you **refer** to a book or other source of
information, you look at it in order to find
something out.
3 If someone **refers** a problem or a
question to someone else, they pass it on
to them to deal with.

referee **referees**
NOUN the official who controls a sports
match and makes sure that the rules are
not broken

a
b
c
d
e
f
g
h
i
j
k
l
m
n
o
p
q
r
s
t
u
v
w
x
y
z

reference references

NOUN **1** a mention of someone or something in a speech or a piece of writing

2 a document written by someone who knows you, that describes your character and abilities, usually when you are applying for a job

reference book reference books

NOUN a book that you use to get information

referendum referendums or referenda

NOUN a vote in which all the people of voting age in a country are asked to say if they agree with a particular government policy or not

refill refills, refilling, refilled

VERB **1** If you **refill** something, you fill it again.

NOUN **2** a container of something to replace something that is used up • *I need a **refill** for my pen.*

refine refines, refining, refined

VERB If substances such as oil or sugar are **refined**, all the impurities are taken out of them.

refined

ADJECTIVE Someone who is **refined** is very polite and well mannered.

refinery refineries

NOUN a factory where sugar or oil are refined

reflect reflects, reflecting, reflected

VERB **1** When rays of heat or light **reflect** off something, they bounce back from it.

2 When something smooth and shiny, such as a mirror, **reflects** something, it shows an image of it.

3 When you **reflect** on something, you think about it carefully.

reflection reflections

NOUN the image you see when you look in a mirror or in very clear, still water

reflex reflexes

NOUN **1** a sudden uncontrollable movement that you make as a result of pressure or a blow to a particular nerve

2 If you have good **reflexes**, you respond very quickly when something unexpected happens.

reform reforms, reforming, reformed

VERB **1** When organizations or laws are **reformed**, changes are made to them to improve them.

2 When people **reform**, they stop doing bad things such as committing crimes.

refrain refrains, refraining, refrained

VERB **1** FORMAL If you **refrain** from doing something, you do not do it.

NOUN **2** a short, simple part of a song that is repeated

SYNONYM: chorus

refresh refreshes, refreshing, refreshed

VERB If something **refreshes** you, it makes you feel less tired or less thirsty.

refreshing

ADJECTIVE If something is **refreshing**, it makes you cool or less tired after you have been hot or busy. • *We went for a **refreshing** swim after walking along the beach.*

refreshments

PLURAL NOUN drinks and snacks

refrigerator refrigerators

NOUN an electrically cooled container for putting food in to keep it fresh

refuel refuels, refuelling, refuelled

VERB When an aircraft or vehicle is **refuelled**, it is filled with more fuel.

refuge refuges

NOUN a place where you go for safety and protection

SYNONYMS: haven, sanctuary, shelter

[from Latin *refugere* meaning to flee]

refugee refugees

NOUN a person who has been forced to leave their country and live elsewhere, for example because of war, famine or persecution

refund refunds, refunding, refunded
NOUN **1** a sum of money that is paid back to you, for example because you have returned goods to a shop
VERB **2** If someone **refunds** your money, they pay it back to you.

refuse refuses, refusing, refused
Said "ri-**fyooz**" VERB **1** If you **refuse** something, you say no to it, or decide firmly that you will not do it or do not accept it.
Said "**ref**-yooss" NOUN **2** rubbish or waste

regal
ADJECTIVE very grand and suitable for a king or queen

regard regards, regarding, regarded
VERB **1** To **regard** someone or something in a certain way is to think of them in that way. • *We regarded him as a friend.*
2 to look closely at someone or something
NOUN **3** If you have a high **regard** for someone, you have a very good opinion of them.

regarding
PREPOSITION on the subject of • *"I will now answer any questions regarding your homework," said the teacher.*

regardless
PREPOSITION OR ADVERB If you do something **regardless** of what may happen as a result, you do it anyway.

regards
PLURAL NOUN kind wishes or friendly feelings for someone, usually sent in a message
• *Give him my regards when you see him.*

regatta regattas
NOUN a race meeting for sailing or rowing boats

reggae
NOUN a type of music with a strong beat, originally from the West Indies

regiment regiments
NOUN a large group of soldiers commanded by a colonel
regimental ADJECTIVE

region regions
NOUN a large area of a country or of the world

register registers, registering, registered
NOUN **1** an official list that is used to keep a record of things that happen or people who attend an event
VERB **2** When something is **registered**, it is recorded on an official list.

regret regrets, regretting, regretted
VERB **1** If you **regret** something, you wish that it had not happened or you had not done it.
2 You can use **regret** to say you are sorry about something. • *We regret any inconvenience caused to passengers by the delay.*

regretful
ADJECTIVE If you are **regretful**, you are sorry or sad about something.

regular
ADJECTIVE **1** **Regular** events happen at equal or frequent intervals.
2 If you are a **regular** visitor somewhere, you go there often.

regulate regulates, regulating, regulated
VERB If someone or something **regulates** something, they control it. • *My grandad takes tablets to regulate his blood pressure.*

regulation regulations
NOUN an official rule

rehearse rehearses, rehearsing, rehearsed
VERB When people **rehearse** a performance, they practise it in preparation for the actual event.

a
b
c
d
e
f
g
h
i
j
k
l
m
n
o
p
q
r
s
t
u
v
w
x
y
z

reign reigns, reigning, reigned
VERB **1** When a king or queen **reigns**, he or she is the leader of the country.
NOUN **2** The **reign** of a king or queen is the period when they reign.

Do not confuse reign with rain or rein.

rein reins
NOUN one of the thin leather straps that you hold when you are riding a horse

Do not confuse rein with rain or reign.

reindeer
NOUN a deer with large antlers, that lives in northern regions of the world

reinforce reinforces, reinforcing, reinforced
VERB If you **reinforce** something, you strengthen it.

reject rejects, rejecting, rejected
VERB If you **reject** something, you throw it away or refuse to accept it.

rejoice rejoices, rejoicing, rejoiced
VERB If you **rejoice**, you celebrate because you are very pleased about something.

relate relates, relating, related
VERB **1** If one thing **relates** to another, it is concerned or connected with it in some way, or can be compared with it.
2 If you **relate** a story, you tell it.

related
ADJECTIVE If people, animals or plants are **related**, they belong to the same family groups or species.

relation relations
NOUN **1** one of the people who are related to you, such as aunts, uncles and grandparents
2 the way that one thing is connected or compared with another

relationship relationships
NOUN **1** The **relationship** between two people or groups is the way they feel and behave towards each other.
2 a close friendship, especially one involving romantic feelings

relative relatives
ADJECTIVE **1** compared with other things or people of the same kind
NOUN **2** a member of your family

relax relaxes, relaxing, relaxed
VERB **1** When you **relax**, or when something **relaxes** you, you become calm and less worried or tense. • *Massage is used to relax muscles.*
2 If you **relax**, you stop work and rest or enjoy your free time.
SYNONYMS: take it easy, unwind

relay relays, relaying, relayed
VERB **1** If you **relay** something, such as a message, you pass it from one person to the next.
NOUN **2** a race between teams, in which each team member runs one part of the race

release releases, releasing, released
VERB If you **release** someone or something, you set them free or unfasten them.

relent relents, relenting, relented
VERB If someone **relents**, they give in and allow something that they refused to allow before. • *Dad relented and allowed us to stay up late.*

relevant
ADJECTIVE connected with what is being discussed or dealt with

reliable
ADJECTIVE **Reliable** people and things can be trusted and depended upon.

relic relics
NOUN **1** an object or custom that has survived from an earlier time
2 an object regarded as holy because it is thought to be connected with a saint

relief
NOUN If you feel **relief**, you feel glad because something unpleasant is over or has been avoided.

relieve relieves, relieving, relieved
VERB If something **relieves** an unpleasant feeling, it makes it less unpleasant.

relieved

ADJECTIVE If you are **relieved**, you are thankful that something worrying or unpleasant has stopped. • *I was **relieved** when the exams were over.*

religion religions

NOUN **1** belief in a god or gods
2 a particular set of religious beliefs
• *the Christian **religion***

religious

ADJECTIVE to do with religion

relish relishes, relishing, relished

VERB **1** If you **relish** something, you enjoy it very much. • *He **relished** the thought of chocolate cake for tea.*
NOUN **2** enjoyment • *"I'm allowed to stay up as long as like," she said with **relish**.*
3 a savoury pickle

reluctant

ADJECTIVE If you are **reluctant** to do something, you do not want to do it.

rely relies, relying, relied

VERB If you **rely** on someone or something, you trust and depend on them. • *I **relied** on my friends to help me.*

remain remains, remaining, remained

VERB **1** If you **remain** in a particular place, you stay there.
PLURAL NOUN **2** The **remains** of something are the parts that are left after most of it has been destroyed or used.

remainder

NOUN **1** the part of something that is left
2 In arithmetic, the **remainder** is the amount left over when one number cannot be divided exactly by another.

remark remarks, remarking, remarked

VERB **1** If you **remark** on something, you mention it or comment on it.
NOUN **2** a comment you make or something you say

remarkable

ADJECTIVE impressive and noticeable • *Her tennis skills were **remarkable**.*

remedy remedies, remedying, remedied

NOUN **1** a cure for something
2 a way of dealing with a problem
VERB **3** If you **remedy** a problem, you put it right.

remember remembers, remembering, remembered

VERB **1** If you **remember** someone or something from the past, you still have an idea of them and you are able to think about them.
2 If you **remember** to do something, you do it when you intended to.
3 If you **remember** something, it suddenly comes into your mind again.

remind reminds, reminding, reminded

VERB **1** If someone **reminds** you of something, they help you remember it.
2 If someone or something **reminds** you of another person or thing, they are similar to the other person or thing and make you think of them.

remnant remnants

NOUN a small part of something that is left after the rest has been used or destroyed

remorse

NOUN FORMAL a strong feeling of guilt and regret
remorseful ADJECTIVE

remote remoter, remotest

ADJECTIVE **1** far away from where most people live
2 far away in time

remote control

NOUN **1** a system of controlling a machine or vehicle from a distance, using radio or electronic signals
2 a hand-held device for controlling a machine or vehicle from a distance
• *a TV **remote control***

removal removals

NOUN **1** the act of taking something away
• *The house felt very bare after the **removal** of the furniture.*
ADJECTIVE **2** A **removal** company moves furniture from one building to another.

a b c d e f g h i j k l m n o p q r s t u v w x y z

331

remove removes, removing, removed
VERB If you **remove** something, you take it away.

rendezvous
Said "**ron**-day-voo" NOUN a meeting or meeting place
[a French word, meaning present yourselves!]

renew renews, renewing, renewed
VERB **1** If you **renew** something such as a piece of equipment, you replace it or parts of it with a new one or new parts.
2 If you **renew** an activity or relationship, you begin it again.

renewable
ADJECTIVE **1** able to be renewed • *a good source of* **renewable** *energy*
NOUN **2** a renewable form of energy, such as wind power or solar power • *Our energy mix needs more* **renewables**.

renovate renovates, renovating, renovated
VERB If you **renovate** something old, you repair it and restore it to good condition.
renovation NOUN

renowned
ADJECTIVE well known, especially for something good • *She's* **renowned** *for her kindness.*

rent rents, renting, rented
VERB **1** If you **rent** something, you pay the owner a regular sum of money to use it.
NOUN **2** the amount of money you pay regularly to use something that belongs to someone else

rental rentals
NOUN **1** the amount paid as rent
ADJECTIVE **2** to do with rent

repair repairs, repairing, repaired
NOUN **1** something that you do to mend something that is damaged
VERB **2** If you **repair** something that is damaged, you mend it.

repay repays, repaying, repaid
VERB **1** When you **repay** money, you give it back to the person who lent it to you.
2 If you **repay** a favour, you do something to help the person who helped you.
repayment NOUN

repeat repeats, repeating, repeated
VERB **1** If you **repeat** something, you say, write or do it again.
NOUN **2** something that is done again or happens again

repeatedly
ADVERB again and again, several times • *He knocked* **repeatedly** *on the door, but nobody answered.*

repel repels, repelling, repelled
VERB **1** If something **repels** you, it disgusts you.
2 If someone **repels** an attack, they defend themselves successfully against it.
3 If someone or something **repels** something, they push it away. • *True magnets can* **repel** *other magnets.*
repellent ADJECTIVE

repetition
NOUN If there is a **repetition** of something, it happens again or is repeated.

repetitive
ADJECTIVE Something that is **repetitive** is repeated over and over again, and can be extremely boring. • *Fruit picking is a* **repetitive** *job.*

replace replaces, replacing, replaced
VERB **1** If you **replace** something, you put it back.
2 If you **replace** something old, broken or missing, you put another one or a new one in its place. • *Ben* **replaced** *Tina in the team.*

replay replays, replaying, replayed
VERB **1** If you **replay** a tape or a film, you play it again.
NOUN **2** a sports match that is played for a second time

replica replicas
NOUN an accurate copy of something

reply replies, replying, replied
VERB **1** If you **reply** to something, you say or write something as an answer to it.
NOUN **2** what you say or write when you answer someone

report reports, reporting, reported
VERB **1** If you **report** that something has happened, you inform someone about it.
NOUN **2** an account of an event or situation

reporter reporters
NOUN someone who writes news articles or broadcasts news reports

represent represents, representing, represented
VERB If someone **represents** you, they act on your behalf.

representative representatives
NOUN a person who acts on behalf of another person or group of people

reprieve reprieves
NOUN a cancellation or postponement of a punishment, especially the death penalty

reprimand reprimands, reprimanding, reprimanded
VERB If you **reprimand** someone, you officially tell them that they should not have done something.

reproach reproaches, reproaching, reproached
VERB **1** If you **reproach** someone, you blame them for something, or criticize them.
NOUN **2** the act of reproaching someone

reproduce reproduces, reproducing, reproduced
VERB **1** If you **reproduce** something, you make a copy of it.
2 When living things **reproduce**, they produce more of their own kind. • *Rats* ***reproduce*** *up to five times every year.*

reproduction
NOUN the process by which each living thing produces young
reproductive ADJECTIVE

reptile reptiles
NOUN an animal such as a snake, turtle or lizard that has scales on its skin, lays eggs, and is cold-blooded
[from Latin *reptilis* meaning creeping]

snake   lizard

republic republics
NOUN a country that has a president rather than a king or queen

repulsion
NOUN the force pushing two magnets away from each other

repulsive
ADJECTIVE horrible and disgusting

reputation reputations
NOUN the opinion that people have of someone or something

request requests, requesting, requested
VERB **1** If you **request** something, you ask for it politely or formally.
NOUN **2** If you make a **request** for something, you ask for it.

require requires, requiring, required
VERB **1** If you **require** something, you need it.
2 If you are **required** to do something, you have to do it. • *You are* ***required*** *to report to the office at 9 a.m.*

requirement requirements
NOUN something you must have or must do

rescue rescues, rescuing, rescued
VERB **1** If you **rescue** someone, you save them from a dangerous or unpleasant situation.
NOUN **2** an attempt to save someone from a dangerous or unpleasant situation

a
b
c
d
e
f
g
h
i
j
k
l
m
n
o
p
q
r
s
t
u
v
w
x
y
z

research researches, researching, researched
NOUN **1** detailed study to discover facts about something
VERB **2** If you **research** something, you study it carefully to discover facts about it.

resemble resembles, resembling, resembled
VERB If one thing or person **resembles** another, they are similar to each other.

resent resents, resenting, resented
VERB If you **resent** something, you feel bitter and angry about it.

reserve reserves, reserving, reserved
VERB **1** If you **reserve** something, you ask for it to be kept aside or ordered for you, or you keep it for a particular purpose. ● *We have **reserved** this table for someone else.*
NOUN **2** an area of land where animals, birds or plants are officially protected and can safely breed
3 If you are a **reserve** in a team, you play if one of the other team members cannot.

reserved
ADJECTIVE **1** kept for someone ● *All of these tables are **reserved**.*
2 People who are **reserved** are quiet and shy.

reservoir reservoirs
Said "**rez**-uh-vwar" NOUN a lake, often artificial, used for storing water before it is supplied to people

residence residences
NOUN FORMAL Your **residence** is your home.

resident residents
NOUN A **resident** of a house or area is someone who lives there.

resign resigns, resigning, resigned
VERB **1** If you **resign** from your job, you give it up.
2 If you **resign** yourself to an unpleasant situation, you accept it without complaining.
resignation NOUN

resist resists, resisting, resisted
VERB **1** If you **resist** something, you refuse to accept it and try to stop it happening.
2 If you **resist** an attack, you fight back.

resistance
NOUN fighting or taking action against something or someone ● *Her body's **resistance** to disease helped her to get well.*

resolute
Said "**rez**-ul-loot" ADJECTIVE If you are **resolute**, you are determined not to change your mind.
resolutely ADVERB

resolution resolutions
Said "rez-ul-**loo**-shun" NOUN
1 determination
2 If you make a **resolution**, you promise yourself that you will do something.
3 a decision made at a meeting ● *The **resolution** to improve the play area was agreed.*

resolve resolves, resolving, resolved
VERB **1** If you **resolve** a problem, you find a way of sorting it out.
2 If you **resolve** to do something, you make up your mind firmly to do it.
NOUN **3** determination to do something

resort resorts, resorting, resorted
NOUN **1** a place where a lot of people spend their holidays, especially by the sea
VERB **2** If you **resort** to doing something, you do it because everything else has failed and you have no alternative.
PHRASE **3** If you do something **as a last resort**, you do it because you can find no other way of solving a problem.

resource resources

NOUN The **resources** of a country, organization or person are the materials, money or skills they have and can use.

resourceful

ADJECTIVE A **resourceful** person is good at solving problems and finding ways to do things.

respect respects, respecting, respected

VERB **1** If you **respect** someone, you admire and like them.

2 If you **respect** someone's feelings or wishes, you treat them with consideration.

NOUN **3** a feeling of admiration for someone's good qualities or achievements

4 consideration for other people

respectable

ADJECTIVE Someone who is **respectable** behaves in a way that is approved of in the society where they live.

respiration

NOUN breathing • His **respiration** was affected by his cold.

respond responds, responding, responded

VERB If you **respond** to someone or something, you react to them by doing or saying something.

response responses

NOUN a reply or a reaction to something

responsible

ADJECTIVE **1** If you are **responsible** for something, you are in charge of it and must take the blame if it goes wrong. • If we get a pet, you will be **responsible** for looking after it.

2 A **responsible** person is sensible, trustworthy and reliable.

3 If you are **responsible** for something, you are the cause of it. • She was **responsible** for the accident.

responsibility NOUN

rest rests, resting, rested

VERB **1** If you **rest**, you take a break from what you are doing and relax for a while.

2 If you **rest** something against something else, you lean it there.

NOUN **3** The **rest** of something is all the parts that are left or have not been mentioned.

4 If you have a **rest**, you do not do anything active for a while.

5 an object that supports something else, such as a headrest or a footrest

restaurant restaurants

NOUN a place where you can buy and eat a meal • an Italian **restaurant**

restless

ADJECTIVE If you are **restless**, you find it hard to stay still or relaxed because you are bored or impatient.

restlessness NOUN **restlessly** ADVERB

restore restores, restoring, restored

VERB If you **restore** something, you get it back to its original state.

restrain restrains, restraining, restrained

VERB If you **restrain** someone or something, you hold them back or stop them from doing what they want to.

restrict restricts, restricting, restricted

VERB To **restrict** someone or something means to set limits on them. • The police **restricted** parking outside the school.

result results, resulting, resulted

NOUN **1** The **result** of an action or situation is what happens because of it.

2 The **result** of a contest, calculation or exam is the final score, figure or mark at the end of it.

VERB **3** If something **results** from a particular event, it is caused by that event.

resume resumes, resuming, resumed

VERB If you **resume** something, you start doing it again after a break. • After dinner, Dad **resumed** his work on the car.

retail

NOUN the activity of selling goods to the public, usually in small amounts

ANTONYM: wholesale

retailer NOUN

a
b
c
d
e
f
g
h
i
j
k
l
m
n
o
p
q
r
s
t
u
v
w
x
y
z

retain retains, retaining, retained
VERB If you **retain** something, you keep it.

retaliate retaliates, retaliating, retaliated
VERB If you **retaliate**, you do something to harm or upset someone because they have harmed or upset you.
retaliation NOUN

retire retires, retiring, retired
VERB **1** When older people **retire**, they leave their job and stop working.
2 If you **retire** from a race, you withdraw from it.

retort retorts, retorting, retorted
VERB **1** If you **retort**, you reply angrily.
NOUN **2** a short, angry reply

retrace retraces, retracing, retraced
VERB If you **retrace** your steps, you go back exactly the same way you came.

retreat retreats, retreating, retreated
VERB If you **retreat** from someone or something unpleasant or dangerous, you move away from them.

retrieve retrieves, retrieving, retrieved
VERB If you **retrieve** something, you get it back or find it again.

return returns, returning, returned
VERB **1** If you **return** to a place, you go back there.
2 If you **return** something to someone, you give it back to them.
NOUN **3** the act of giving or putting something back
4 a ticket for a journey to a place and back again

reunion reunions
NOUN a meeting or a party at which people who have not seen each other for a long time get together
reunite VERB

rev revs, revving, revved
VERB **1** When someone **revs** an engine, they press the accelerator to increase its speed.
NOUN **2** The speed of an engine is measured in **revs**, which is an abbreviation of *revolutions per minute*.

reveal reveals, revealing, revealed
VERB **1** If you **reveal** something, you tell people about it.
2 If you **reveal** something that has been hidden, you uncover it.

revel revels, revelling, revelled
VERB If you **revel** in a situation, you enjoy it very much.
reveller NOUN   **revelry** NOUN

revenge
NOUN the act of hurting someone who has hurt you

revenue revenues
NOUN money that a government, company or organization receives

Reverend
NOUN a title used before the name of a member of the clergy

reverse reverses, reversing, reversed
VERB **1** If you **reverse** the order of things, you arrange them in the opposite order.
2 When someone **reverses** a car, they drive it backwards.

reversible
ADJECTIVE **Reversible** clothing can be worn with either side on the outside.

review reviews, reviewing, reviewed
NOUN **1** an article in a magazine or newspaper, or a talk on television or radio, giving an opinion of a new book, play, or film
VERB **2** When someone **reviews** a book, play or film, they write an account or have a discussion expressing their opinion of it.

revise revises, revising, revised
VERB If you **revise** for an exam, you go over your work to make sure you know it properly.

revive revives, reviving, revived

VERB When you **revive** someone who has fainted, they become conscious again.

revolt **revolts, revolting, revolted**
NOUN **1** a violent uprising or rebellion against authority
VERB **2** When people **revolt**, they rebel against the system that governs them.
3 If something **revolts** you, it disgusts you.

revolting
ADJECTIVE horrible and disgusting

revolution **revolutions**
NOUN a violent attempt by a large number of people to change the way their country is run

revolutionize **revolutionizes, revolutionizing, revolutionized**
VERB If something is **revolutionized**, it is changed completely, usually for the better. • *Science and technology have **revolutionized** the way we live.*

revolve **revolves, revolving, revolved**
VERB When something **revolves**, it turns in a circle around a central point.
revolving ADJECTIVE

revolver **revolvers**
NOUN a small gun held in the hand

reward **rewards, rewarding, rewarded**
NOUN **1** something you are given because you have done something good
VERB **2** If you **reward** someone, you give them a reward.

rewarding
ADJECTIVE Something that is **rewarding** gives you a lot of satisfaction. • *Nursing is a **rewarding** job.*

rewind **rewinds, rewinding, rewound**
VERB If you **rewind** a cassette or video tape, you wind it back to the beginning.

rewrite **rewrites, rewriting, rewrote, rewritten**
VERB If you **rewrite** something you have written, you write it again to make changes to it and improve it.
SYNONYM: redraft

rhetorical
ADJECTIVE A question that is **rhetorical** is asked in order to make a statement, rather than to get an answer. For example, *What's the world coming to?*

rheumatism
NOUN an illness that makes your joints and muscles stiff and painful
rheumatic ADJECTIVE

rhinoceros **rhinoceroses**
NOUN a large African or Asian mammal with one or two horns on its nose [from Greek *rhin* meaning of the nose and *keras* meaning horn]

rhombus **rhombuses** or **rhombi**
NOUN a plane shape like a diamond, with four equal sides and no right angles

rhubarb
NOUN a plant with long red stems that can be cooked with sugar and eaten

rhyme **rhymes, rhyming, rhymed**
VERB **1** If one word **rhymes** with another, both words have a very similar sound in their final syllable. For example, *Sally* rhymes with *valley*.
NOUN **2** a word that rhymes with another • *He couldn't find a **rhyme** for "orange".*

There is an *h* before the *y* in *rhyme* and *rhythm*.

rhythm **rhythms**
NOUN a regular series of sounds, movements or actions • *The poem was easy to learn because it had a strong **rhythm**.*

rib **ribs**
NOUN Your **ribs** are the curved bones that go from your spine to your chest.

ribbon **ribbons**
NOUN a long, narrow piece of cloth used as a fastening or decoration

rice
NOUN white or brown grains taken from a cereal plant and used for food

rich **richer, richest; riches**
ADJECTIVE **1** Someone who is **rich** has a lot of money or possessions.

a b c d e f g h i j k l m n o p q r s t u v w x y z

337

2 Something that is **rich** in something contains a large amount of it. • *Fruit is rich in vitamins.*

3 Rich food contains a large amount of fat, oil or sugar.

PLURAL NOUN **4 Riches** are valuable possessions or large amounts of money.

rickshaw **rickshaws**
NOUN a two-wheeled, hand-pulled cart used in Asia for carrying passengers

ricochet **ricochets, ricocheting** or **ricochetting, ricocheted** or **ricochetted**
Said "**rik**-oh-shay" VERB When an object **ricochets**, it hits a surface and then bounces away from it.

rid
PHRASE When you **get rid of** something you do not want, you throw it away.

riddle **riddles**
NOUN an amusing or puzzling question, sometimes in rhyme, to which you must find an answer

ride **rides, riding, rode, ridden**
VERB **1** When you **ride** a horse or a bicycle, you sit on it and control it as it moves along.
2 When you **ride** in a car, you travel in it.
NOUN **3** a journey on a horse or bicycle or in a vehicle

ridge **ridges**
NOUN a long, narrow piece of high land

ridicule **ridicules, ridiculing, ridiculed**
VERB **1** If you **ridicule** someone, you make fun of them in an unkind way.
NOUN **2** unkind laughter or teasing

ridiculous
ADJECTIVE very foolish

rifle **rifles**
NOUN a gun with a long barrel

rig **rigs, rigging, rigged**
NOUN **1** a large structure used for taking oil or gas from the ground or the sea bed • *an oil rig*

VERB **2** When someone **rigs** a boat, they fit it with ropes and sails.

right **rights**
NOUN **1** correct behaviour • *At least he knew right from wrong.*
ANTONYM: wrong
2 If you have a **right** to do something, you are allowed to do it.
3 one of two opposite directions, sides or positions. If you are facing north and you turn to the **right**, you will be facing east.
ANTONYM: left
ADJECTIVE OR ADVERB **4** If something is **right**, it is correct.
ANTONYM: wrong
5 on or towards the right of something
ANTONYM: left

right angle **right angles**
NOUN an angle of 90°

90°

rigid
ADJECTIVE A **rigid** object is stiff and does not bend easily.
rigidly ADVERB

rim **rims**
NOUN the outer edge of something such as a bowl or wheel

rind **rinds**
NOUN the skin on bacon, cheese and some fruits

ring **rings, ringing, rang, rung**
VERB **1** If you **ring** someone, you phone them.
2 When a telephone or bell **rings**, it makes a clear, loud sound.
NOUN **3** a small circle of metal that you wear on your finger

ringleader **ringleaders**
NOUN the leader of a group, who leads the others into mischief or crime

rink **rinks**
NOUN a large indoor area for ice skating or roller skating

rinse **rinses, rinsing, rinsed**
VERB When you **rinse** something, you wash it in clean water, without soap.

riot riots, rioting, rioted
NOUN **1** When there is a **riot**, a crowd of people behave violently in a public place.
VERB **2** When people **riot**, they behave violently in a public place.

rip rips, ripping, ripped
VERB If you **rip** something, you tear it.

ripe riper, ripest
ADJECTIVE **Ripe** fruit or grain is fully developed and ready to be eaten.

ripple ripples, rippling, rippled
NOUN **1** a little wave on the surface of calm water
2 If there is a **ripple** of laughter or applause, people laugh or clap their hands gently for a short time.
VERB **3** When the surface of water **ripples**, little waves appear on it.

rise rises, rising, rose, risen
VERB **1** If something **rises**, it moves upwards. • *Wilson watched the smoke* **rise** *from the fire.*
2 When the sun or moon **rises**, it appears from below the horizon.
NOUN **3** When something goes up, it is called a **rise**, for example a **rise** in the land or a **rise** in prices.
VERB **4** When you **rise**, you get out of bed.
5 If something such as a sound, or the level of a liquid or prices **rise**, they become higher.

risk risks, risking, risked
NOUN **1** If there is a **risk** of something unpleasant, it might happen.
2 Someone or something that is a **risk** is likely to cause harm or have bad results.
VERB **3** If you **risk** something, you do something knowing that an unpleasant thing might happen as a result. • *If he doesn't play, he* **risks** *losing his place in the team.*

ritual rituals
NOUN **1** a traditional ceremony
ADJECTIVE **2 Ritual** activities happen as part of a tradition or ritual.

rival rivals
NOUN Someone's **rival** is the person they are competing with.

river rivers
NOUN a large, continuous stretch of fresh water flowing in a channel across land, to a larger **river**, a lake or the sea

road roads
NOUN a long stretch of hard ground built between two places so that people can travel along it easily

roam roams, roaming, roamed
VERB If you **roam** around, you wander around without any particular reason.

roar roars, roaring, roared
VERB **1** If something **roars**, it makes a very loud noise.
NOUN **2** a very loud noise

roast roasts, roasting, roasted
VERB **1** When you **roast** meat or other food, you cook it in an oven or over a fire.
ADJECTIVE **2 Roast** meat or vegetables have been roasted.

rob robs, robbing, robbed
VERB If someone **robs** a person or place, they steal money or property from them.

robe robes
NOUN a long, loose piece of clothing that covers the body

robin robins
NOUN a small bird with a red breast

robot robots
NOUN a machine that moves and does things automatically
[from Czech *robota* meaning work]

rock rocks, rocking, rocked
NOUN **1 Rock** is made up of small pieces of one or more minerals. The earth's surface is made up of **rock**.
2 A **rock** is a piece of rock.
3 music with a strong beat, usually involving electric guitars and drums
4 a hard sweet, usually brightly coloured and shaped like a long stick
VERB **5** When something **rocks**, or when you **rock** it, it moves regularly backwards and forwards or from side to side.

a
b
c
d
e
f
g
h
i
j
k
l
m
n
o
p
q
r
s
t
u
v
w
x
y
z

A
B
C
D
E
F
G
H
I
J
K
L
M
N
O
P
Q
R
S
T
U
V
W
X
Y
Z

rocket **rockets**
NOUN **1** a space vehicle, usually shaped like a long pointed tube
2 an explosive missile

rod **rods**
NOUN a long, thin pole or bar

rode
VERB the past tense of **ride**

rodent **rodents**
NOUN a small mammal with sharp front teeth that it uses for gnawing. Rabbits and mice are **rodents**.
[from Latin *rodere* meaning to gnaw]

rogue **rogues**
NOUN a dishonest or mischievous person

role **roles**
NOUN An actor's **role** is the character that he or she plays in a play or film.

roll **rolls, rolling, rolled**
VERB **1** If something **rolls**, or if you **roll** it, it moves along a surface, turning over many times.
2 If you **roll** something, or **roll it up**, you wrap it around itself so that it has a rounded shape.
NOUN **3** A **roll** of paper or cloth is a long piece of it that has been rolled into a tube.
4 a small, circular loaf of bread

roller coaster **roller coasters**
NOUN a pleasure ride at a fun fair, consisting of a small railway that goes up and down steep slopes and around bends

roller skate **roller skates**
NOUN **Roller skates** are shoes or boots with four small wheels underneath.
roller-skate VERB

ROM
NOUN a computer storage device that holds information that cannot be changed by the programmer. **ROM** is an abbreviation for *read only memory*.

Roman Catholic **Roman Catholics**
NOUN someone who belongs to the branch of the Christian Church that has the Pope in Rome as its leader

romance **romances**
NOUN **1** a love story
2 If two people have a **romance**, they have a romantic relationship.

Romani; also spelt **Romany**
NOUN the language of the Gypsies

Roman numerals
PLURAL NOUN numbers written in the form of letters and used by ancient Romans. For example, I = 1, V = 5, X = 10, L = 50, C = 100, D = 500, M = 1000.

romantic
ADJECTIVE **1** to do with romance and love
2 A **romantic** person is rather emotional and not very realistic about life and love.

roof **roofs**
NOUN the covering on top of a building or vehicle

rook **rooks**
NOUN **1** a large black bird
2 a chess piece that can move any number of squares in a straight but not diagonal line. It is also called a castle.

room **rooms**
NOUN **1** a separate section in a building, divided from other **rooms** by walls
2 If there is **room** for something, there is enough space for it.

roost **roosts, roosting, roosted**
NOUN **1** a place where birds rest or build their nests

VERB **2** When birds **roost**, they settle somewhere for the night.

root roots
NOUN **Roots** are the parts of a plant that usually grow underground. They anchor the plant and carry water from the soil.

root word root words
NOUN a word that you can add a prefix or a suffix to in order to make other words. For example, in the words *unclear*, *clearly* and *cleared*, the **root word** is *clear*.

rope ropes, roping, roped
NOUN **1** a thick, strong cord made by twisting together several thinner cords
VERB **2** If you **rope** one thing to another, you tie them together with rope.

rosary rosaries
NOUN a string of beads that Catholics use for counting prayers

rose roses
NOUN **1** a flower that has a pleasant smell and grows on a bush with thorns
VERB **2** the past tense of **rise**

rosette rosettes
NOUN a large circular badge of coloured ribbons worn as a prize in a competition or to support a political party

Rosh Hashanah; also spelt Rosh Hashana
NOUN the festival celebrating the Jewish New Year

rosy rosier, rosiest
ADJECTIVE **1** reddish-pink ● *Our cheeks were rosy after our walk on the windy beach.*
2 hopeful and positive ● *He always has a rosy outlook on life.*

rot rots, rotting, rotted
VERB When food, wood or other substances **rot**, or when something **rots** them, they decay and fall apart.
SYNONYM: decompose

rotary
ADJECTIVE moving or able to move in a circular direction around a fixed point

rotate rotates, rotating, rotated
VERB When something **rotates**, it turns with a circular movement, like a wheel.

rotation rotations
NOUN **1** a complete circular movement
● the **rotation** of a wheel ● the **rotation** of the earth
PHRASE **2** If you do things **in rotation**, you do them one after the other, and when you finish you start all over again.

rotor rotors
NOUN **1** the part of a machine that turns
2 The **rotors**, or **rotor** blades, of a helicopter are the four long, flat pieces of metal on top of it, that rotate and lift it off the ground.

rotten
ADJECTIVE **1** Something that is **rotten** has decayed.
2 INFORMAL bad, unpleasant or unfair
● *I think it's a rotten idea.*

rough rougher, roughest
ADJECTIVE **1** uneven and not smooth ● *His hands were hard and rough.*
ANTONYM: smooth
2 using too much force ● *Don't be so rough with that toy or you'll break it.*
ANTONYM: gentle
3 approximate ● *At a rough guess, it is five o'clock.*
ANTONYMS: exact, precise

roughly
ADVERB **1** almost or approximately ● *There are roughly 100 marbles in that box.*
2 If you treat someone or something **roughly**, you treat them clumsily or violently.

round rounder, roundest; rounds
ADJECTIVE **1** Something **round** is shaped like a ball or a circle.
PREPOSITION OR ADVERB **2** If something is **round** something else, it surrounds it.
3 If something goes **round**, it moves in a circle. ● *The sails of the windmill went round.*
PREPOSITION **4** If you go **round** something, you go to the other side of it. ● *Suddenly a car came round the corner.*

ADVERB **5** If you turn or look **round**, you turn or look in a different direction.
6 If you move things **round**, you move them so that they are in different places.
7 If you go **round** to someone's house, you visit them.
NOUN **8** one of a series of events, especially in a competition
9 a series of calls or deliveries • *Our house is the last one on the milkman's **round**.*
10 a whole slice of bread, or a sandwich made of two slices
11 a type of song in which people sing the same words but start at different times
rounded ADJECTIVE

roundabout **roundabouts**
NOUN **1** a meeting point of several roads with a circle in the centre that vehicles have to travel around
2 a circular platform that goes round and that children can ride on in a playground
3 a large, circular platform with horses or cars on it, for children to ride on as it goes round and round
SYNONYM: merry-go-round

rounders
NOUN a team game in which players hit a ball with a bat and run round a circuit

rouse **rouses, rousing, roused**
VERB **1** If you **rouse** someone, you wake them up.
2 If you **rouse** yourself, you make yourself get up and do something.
3 If something **rouses** your emotions, it makes you feel those emotions.

rousing
ADJECTIVE Something that is **rousing**, such as a game, speech or song, makes you feel excited and emotional.

route **routes**
NOUN a way from one place to another
• *the most direct **route** to the town centre*

routine **routines**
ADJECTIVE **1 Routine** activities are done regularly.
NOUN **2** the usual way or order in which you do things

row **rows, rowing, rowed**
Rhymes with "snow" VERB **1** When you **row** a boat, you use oars to make it move through the water.

NOUN **2** several objects or people in a line
Rhymes with "cow" NOUN **3** an argument
4 a lot of noise

rowdy **rowdier, rowdiest**
ADJECTIVE rough and noisy
rowdily ADVERB

royal
ADJECTIVE belonging to or involving a queen, a king, or a member of their family

RSVP
RSVP written at the end of a letter or an invitation means please reply.
[an abbreviation for the French expression *Répondez s'il vous plaît* meaning please reply]

rub **rubs, rubbing, rubbed**
VERB If you **rub** something, you move your hand, or a cloth, very firmly backwards and forwards over it.

rubber **rubbers**
NOUN **1** a strong, elastic substance used for making tyres, boots and other products
2 a small piece of rubber or plastic that you use to remove mistakes when writing or drawing with a pencil

rubbish
NOUN **1** unwanted things or waste material
SYNONYMS: garbage, refuse, trash
2 something foolish
3 something of very poor quality

rubble
NOUN bits of old brick and stone

ruby **rubies**
NOUN a type of red jewel

rucksack rucksacks
NOUN a bag with shoulder straps for carrying things on your back

rudder rudders
NOUN a piece of wood or metal at the back of a boat or plane that is moved to make the boat or plane turn

rude ruder, rudest
ADJECTIVE **1** not polite
2 embarrassing or offensive because of reference to body parts or bodily functions

ruff ruffs
NOUN a stiff circular collar with many pleats in it. These collars were very popular in the 16th century.

ruffle ruffles, ruffling, ruffled
VERB **1** If you **ruffle** someone's hair, you move your hand quickly backwards and forwards over their head.
2 If something **ruffles** you, it makes you annoyed or upset.
NOUN **3 Ruffles** are small folds made in a piece of material for decoration.

rug rugs
NOUN **1** a small thick carpet
2 a warm covering for your knees or for sitting on outdoors

rugby
NOUN a game played by two teams, who try to kick or throw an oval ball past a line at their opponents' end of the pitch [named after *Rugby* School where it was first played]

rugged
ADJECTIVE **1** Somewhere **rugged** is rocky, wild and unsheltered.
2 Someone **rugged** is strong and tough.

ruin ruins, ruining, ruined
VERB **1** If you **ruin** something, you destroy or spoil it completely.
NOUN **2** the part that is left after something has been severely damaged

rule rules, ruling, ruled
NOUN **1 Rules** are instructions that tell you what you must do.
VERB **2** When someone **rules** a country or a group of people, they govern it and are in charge of its affairs.

ruler rulers
NOUN **1** a person who rules a country
2 a long, flat object with straight edges, marked with a scale, used for measuring things or drawing straight lines

rum rums
NOUN a strong alcoholic drink made from sugar cane juice

rumble rumbles, rumbling, rumbles
VERB **1** If something **rumbles**, it makes a continuous low sound. • *My stomach is **rumbling** because I am hungry.*
NOUN **2** a continuous deep sound • *There was a **rumble** of thunder.*

rumour rumours
NOUN a piece of information or a story that people are talking about, but which may not be true

run runs, running, ran
VERB **1** When you **run**, you move quickly, with both feet leaving the ground at each stride.
2 If you **run** water, you turn on the tap to let the water flow out.
3 If your nose is **running**, a lot of liquid is coming out of it.
4 If you **run** an activity or a place such as a school or shop, you are in charge of it.
5 If you **run away** from a place, you leave it suddenly and secretly.

run out
VERB If you **run out** of something, you have no more left.

rung rungs
NOUN one of the bars that form the steps of a ladder

runner runners
NOUN **1** a person who runs as a sport, especially in competitions
2 a person who takes messages or runs errands
3 A **runner** on a plant such as a strawberry is a long shoot from which a new plant develops.

A B C D E F G H I J K L M N O P Q R S T U V W X Y Z

runny **runnier, runniest**
ADJECTIVE flowing or moving like liquid

runway **runways**
NOUN a long strip of ground used by aeroplanes for taking off and landing

rural
ADJECTIVE to do with the countryside

rush **rushes, rushing, rushed**
VERB **1** If you **rush** somewhere, or if you are **rushed** there, you go there quickly.
2 If you **rush** something, or if you are **rushed** into something, you do it too quickly.
NOUN **3** a type of plant that grows in or beside fresh water, such as rivers, ponds and lakes

rust **rusts, rusting, rusted**
NOUN **1** a reddish-brown substance that forms on metal when it is exposed to water and the oxygen in the air
VERB **2** When metal **rusts**, it corrodes and a reddish-brown substance is formed. **Rusting** occurs when iron or steel is exposed to water and the oxygen in the air.

rustle **rustles, rustling, rustled**
VERB If something **rustles**, it makes a soft, crisp sound as it moves, like the sound of dry leaves moving.

rusty **rustier, rustiest**
ADJECTIVE **1** covered with rust • *The old bicycle was* ***rusty***.
2 not as good as it once was because of lack of practice • *Dad's maths is a bit* ***rusty***.

rut **ruts**
NOUN a deep, narrow groove in the ground made by the wheels of a vehicle

ruthless
ADJECTIVE very harsh or cruel, and without any pity

rye
NOUN a cereal crop that produces light-brown grain used to make flour

Ss

Sabbath **Sabbaths**
NOUN the day of the week that some religious groups, such as Jews and Christians, use for rest and prayer
[from Hebrew *shabbath* meaning to rest]

sabotage **sabotages, sabotaging, sabotaged**
NOUN **1** the deliberate damaging of machinery and equipment such as railway lines
VERB **2** If something is **sabotaged**, it is deliberately damaged.
saboteur NOUN

sabre **sabres**
NOUN **1** a heavy curved sword
2 a light sword used in fencing

sachet **sachets**
NOUN a small packet containing something like sugar or shampoo

sack **sacks**
NOUN **1** a large bag made of rough material, for carrying such things as potatoes and grain • *a* ***sack*** *of potatoes*
PHRASE **2** INFORMAL If someone **gets the sack**, they are dismissed from their job by their employer.

sacred
ADJECTIVE holy, or connected with religion or religious ceremonies

sacrifice **sacrifices, sacrificing, sacrificed**
VERB If you **sacrifice** something valuable or important, you give it up.

sad **sadder, saddest**
ADJECTIVE If you are **sad**, you feel unhappy.

sadden **saddens, saddening, saddened**
VERB If something **saddens** you,

it makes you feel sad.
saddening ADJECTIVE

saddle **saddles, saddling, saddled**
NOUN **1** a leather seat strapped to an animal's back, for the rider to sit on
2 the seat on a bicycle
VERB **3** If you **saddle** a horse, you put a saddle on it.

safari **safaris**
NOUN an expedition for hunting or observing wild animals
[from Swahili *safari* meaning journey]

safari park **safari parks**
NOUN a large park where wild animals such as lions, giraffes and elephants are free to roam

safe **safer, safest; safes**
ADJECTIVE **1** If you are **safe**, you are not in any danger.
2 Something that is **safe** does not cause harm or danger.
NOUN **3** a strong metal box with special locks, in which you can keep valuable things

safeguard **safeguards, safeguarding, safeguarded**
VERB **1** If you **safeguard** something, you protect it.
NOUN **2** a law or a rule to help protect people or things from harm

safety
NOUN protection, being safe • *child* **safety**
• *We should have* **safety** *in our homes.*

saga **sagas**
NOUN a very long story, usually telling of many different adventures

said
VERB the past tense and past participle of **say**

sail **sails, sailing, sailed**
VERB **1** When a ship **sails**, it moves across water.
2 If you **sail** somewhere, you go there by ship.
NOUN **3** one of the large pieces of material attached to a ship's mast. The wind blows against the **sail** and moves the ship.
4 The arm of a windmill is called a **sail**.

sailor **sailors**
NOUN **1** a member of a ship's crew
2 someone who sails

saint **saints**
NOUN a person who is given a special honour by a Christian Church, after they have died, because they lived a very holy life

sake **sakes**
PHRASE If you do something for someone's **sake**, you do it to help or please them.

salad **salads**
NOUN a mixture of foods eaten cold or warm, and often raw

salami
NOUN a kind of spicy sausage
[Italian plural of *salame*, from *salare* meaning to salt]

salary **salaries**
NOUN a payment made each month to an employee

sale **sales**
NOUN **1** The **sale** of goods is the selling of them.
2 an occasion when a shop sells things at reduced prices

saliva
NOUN the watery liquid in your mouth that softens food, which helps you chew and digest it

salmon **salmons** or **salmon**
NOUN a large, edible, silver-coloured fish with pink flesh

salt
NOUN a white substance used to flavour and preserve food

salute **salutes, saluting, saluted**
NOUN **1** a formal sign of respect. Soldiers give a **salute** by raising their right hand to their forehead.
VERB **2** If you **salute** someone, you give them a salute.

salvage **salvages, salvaging, salvaged**
VERB If you **salvage** things, you save them from, for example, a wrecked ship or a destroyed building.

A
B
C
D
E
F
G
H
I
J
K
L
M
N
O
P
Q
R
S
T
U
V
W
X
Y
Z

same

ADJECTIVE **1** If two things are the **same**, they are like one another.
2 just one thing and not two different ones • *They were born in the* **same** *town.*

sample **samples, sampling, sampled**

NOUN **1** a small amount of something that you can try or test, for example for quality or to find out more about it
VERB **2** If you **sample** something, you try it. • *I* **sampled** *his cooking.*

sanctuary **sanctuaries**

NOUN **1** a place where you are safe from harm or danger
2 a place where wildlife is protected

sand **sands**

NOUN a substance consisting of tiny pieces of stone. Beaches are made of **sand**.

sandal **sandals**

NOUN **Sandals** are light shoes with straps, worn in warm weather.

sandwich **sandwiches**

NOUN two slices of bread with a filling between them

sandy **sandier, sandiest**

ADJECTIVE **1** A **sandy** area is covered with sand.
2 **Sandy** hair is a light orange-brown colour.

sane **saner, sanest**

ADJECTIVE If someone is **sane**, they have a healthy mind.

sang

VERB the past tense of **sing**

sank

VERB the past tense of **sink**

sap **saps, sapping, sapped**

NOUN **1** the juice found in the stems of plants
VERB **2** If something such as an illness **saps** your energy or your strength, it gradually weakens you.

sapling **saplings**

NOUN a young tree

sapphire **sapphires**

NOUN a blue precious stone

sarcastic

ADJECTIVE If someone is **sarcastic**, they say the opposite of what they really mean in order to mock or insult someone.

sardine **sardines**

NOUN a small edible sea fish

sari **saris**

NOUN a piece of clothing consisting of a long piece of material folded around the body, worn especially by Indian women [a Hindi word]

sash **sashes**

NOUN a long piece of cloth worn round the waist or over one shoulder

sat

VERB the past tense and past participle of **sit**

satchel **satchels**

NOUN a leather or cloth bag with a long strap, especially used for carrying books to and from school

satellite **satellites**

NOUN **1** a spacecraft sent into space to orbit the earth, to collect information, or as part of a communications system

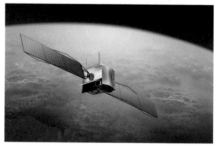

2 a natural object in space that moves round another, larger object, such as a planet or star

satellite dish **satellite dishes**

NOUN a dish-shaped aerial that receives television signals sent by satellite

satellite television

NOUN television programmes received by signals from artificial satellites

satin satins
NOUN a kind of smooth, shiny fabric often made from silk

satisfactory
ADJECTIVE acceptable or adequate
satisfactorily ADVERB

satisfy satisfies, satisfying, satisfied
VERB If you **satisfy** someone, you do something or give them something to make them pleased or contented.

saturated
ADJECTIVE soaking wet

Saturday Saturdays
NOUN the seventh day of the week, coming between Friday and Sunday

sauce sauces
NOUN a liquid eaten with food to add flavour • It's pasta with tomato **sauce** for dinner.

saucepan saucepans
NOUN a deep metal pan with a handle and a lid used for cooking

saucer saucers
NOUN a small curved plate for a cup to stand on

sauna saunas
Said "**saw** -nah" NOUN If you have a **sauna**, you go into a very hot room in order to sweat, then have a cold bath or shower.
[a Finnish word]

saunter saunters, sauntering, sauntered
VERB If you **saunter** somewhere, you walk there slowly and casually.

sausage sausages
NOUN a mixture of minced meat and herbs formed into a tubular shape and served cooked

savage savages, savaging, savaged
ADJECTIVE **1** cruel and violent
SYNONYMS: brutal, vicious
NOUN **2** If you call someone a **savage**, you mean that they are violent and uncivilized.

VERB **3** If an animal **savages** you, it attacks you and bites you.

savannah savannahs
NOUN a grassy plain with few trees in a hot country

save saves, saving, saved
VERB **1** If you **save** someone, you rescue them or help to keep them safe.
2 If you **save** something, you keep it so that you can use it later.
3 If you **save** time, money or effort, you stop it from being wasted.

savings
PLURAL NOUN Your **savings** are money you have saved.

saviour saviours
NOUN **1** a person who saves others from danger or loss
PROPER NOUN **2** In Christianity, the **Saviour** is Jesus Christ.

savoury
ADJECTIVE salty or spicy • Salt and vinegar crisps are my favourite **savoury** snack.

saw saws, sawing, sawed, sawn
NOUN **1** a tool that has a blade with sharp teeth along one edge for cutting wood
VERB **2** If you **saw** something, you cut it with a saw.
3 the past tense of **see**

sawdust
NOUN the fine powder produced when you saw wood

saxophone saxophones
NOUN a curved metal wind instrument often played in jazz bands
[named after Adolphe *Sax* (1814–1894), who invented the instrument]

say says, saying, said
VERB If you **say** something, you speak words.

saying sayings
NOUN a well-known sentence or phrase that tells you something about life

scab scabs
NOUN a hard, dry covering that forms over a wound while it is healing

a
b
c
d
e
f
g
h
i
j
k
l
m
n
o
p
q
r
s
t
u
v
w
x
y
z

scaffolding

NOUN a framework of poles and boards that is used by workmen to stand on while they are working on the outside of a building

scald scalds, scalding, scalded

VERB **1** If you **scald** yourself, you burn yourself with very hot liquid or steam.
NOUN **2** a burn caused by very hot liquid or steam

scale scales

NOUN **1** the size or extent of something
• The **scale** of the building was enormous.
2 a set of marks or numbers used for measuring something
3 The **scale** of something like a map, a plan or a model shows the relationship between the measurements represented and those in the real world. For example, a **scale** of 1:10 tells you that one centimetre on a model represents 10 centimetres in real life.
4 one of the small, hard pieces of skin covering the body of a fish or a reptile
5 a series of musical notes going upwards or downwards in a particular order
PLURAL NOUN **6 Scales** are a piece of equipment used for weighing things or people.

scalene

ADJECTIVE A **scalene** triangle has sides of different lengths.

scalp scalps

NOUN the skin under the hair on your head

scamper scampers, scampering, scampered

VERB If you **scamper**, you run quickly and lightly.

scampi

PLURAL NOUN large prawns, often eaten fried in breadcrumbs

scan scans, scanning, scanned

VERB **1** If you **scan** something, you look at every part of it carefully.
2 If you **scan** a piece of writing, you look at it quickly but not in detail.
3 If a machine **scans** something, it examines it with a beam of light or X-rays.
NOUN **4** an examination of part of the body with X-ray or laser equipment

scandal scandals

NOUN **1** a situation or event that people think is shocking and immoral
2 gossip about bad things that can ruin a person's reputation
scandalous ADJECTIVE

scanner scanners

NOUN a machine that is used to examine, identify or record things by using a beam of light or an X-ray

scapegoat scapegoats

NOUN If someone is made a **scapegoat**, they are blamed for something, although it may not be their fault.

scar scars, scarring, scarred

NOUN **1** a mark left on your skin after a wound has healed
VERB **2** If an injury **scars** you, it leaves a mark on your skin for ever.

scarce scarcer, scarcest

ADJECTIVE If something is **scarce**, there is not very much of it.

scare scares, scaring, scared

VERB **1** If something **scares** you, it frightens you.
NOUN **2** something that gives you a fright

scarecrow scarecrows

NOUN an object shaped like a person and put in a field to scare birds away from the crops

scarf scarfs or scarves

NOUN a piece of cloth worn round your neck or head to keep you warm

scarlet

NOUN OR ADJECTIVE bright red

scary scarier, scariest

ADJECTIVE INFORMAL frightening • The film was so **scary** I hid behind the sofa.

scatter scatters, scattering, scattered

VERB **1** When you **scatter** things, you throw or drop them so they spread over a large area.

2 If a group of people or animals **scatter**, they suddenly move off in different directions.

scavenge scavenges, scavenging, scavenged
VERB If a human or other animal **scavenges** for things, they search for them among waste and rubbish.
scavenger NOUN

scene scenes
NOUN part of a play or film in which a series of events happen in one place

scenery
NOUN **1** In the countryside, you can refer to everything you see as the **scenery**.
2 In a theatre, the **scenery** is the painted cloth on the stage that makes it seem like a particular place.

scent scents
NOUN a smell, especially a pleasant one

sceptic sceptics
Said "**skep**-tik" NOUN someone who does not believe things easily

schedule schedules
NOUN a list of events or things you have to do, and the times at which each thing should be done or will happen

scheme schemes, scheming, schemed
NOUN **1** a plan or arrangement
VERB **2** When people **scheme**, they make secret plans.

scholar scholars
NOUN **1** a person who studies an academic subject and knows a lot about it
2 In South African English, a **scholar** is a school pupil.

scholarship scholarships
NOUN If you win a **scholarship** to a school or university, your studies are paid for by the school or university, or by some other organization.

school schools
NOUN a place where children are educated

science sciences
NOUN the study of living things, materials and physical processes such as forces, electricity, sound and light

science fiction
NOUN stories about travelling through space, and imaginary events happening in the future or in other worlds

scientist scientists
NOUN someone who studies science or is an expert in science

scissors
PLURAL NOUN a cutting tool with two sharp blades

scold scolds, scolding, scolded
VERB If you **scold** someone, you tell them off.

scone scones
NOUN a small cake made from flour and fat, and usually eaten with cream and jam

scoop scoops, scooping, scooped
VERB **1** If you **scoop** something up, you pick it up using a spoon or the palm of your hand.
NOUN **2** an object like a large spoon that is used for picking up food such as ice cream

scooter scooters
NOUN **1** a small, light motorcycle
2 a simple cycle that a child rides, with two wheels and a narrow platform for standing on while pushing the ground with one foot

scope
NOUN **1** the opportunity or freedom to do something
2 the extent of something ● *That subject is beyond the* **scope** *of this lesson.*

scorch scorches, scorching, scorched
VERB If you **scorch** something, you burn it slightly.

score scores, scoring, scored
VERB **1** If you **score** in a game, you get a goal, a run or a point.
NOUN **2** the number of goals, runs or points obtained by the two opponents in a game

349

A B C D E F G H I J K L M N O P Q R S T U V W X Y Z

scornful

ADJECTIVE If you are **scornful** of something or someone, you think very little of them and show very little respect for them.

scorpion scorpions

NOUN an animal that looks like a small lobster. It has a long tail with a poisonous sting on the end.

scour scours, scouring, scoured

VERB **1** If you **scour** a place, you look all over it in order to find something.
2 If you **scour** something like a pan, you clean it by rubbing it hard with something rough.

scout scouts, scouting, scouted

NOUN **1** A **Scout** is a boy who is a member of the **Scout** Association, an organization for boys that aims to develop character and responsibility.
2 someone who is sent on ahead to get information about something
VERB **3** If you **scout** around for something, you look around for it.

scowl scowls, scowling, scowled

VERB **1** If you **scowl**, you frown because you are angry.
NOUN **2** an angry expression

scrabble scrabbles, scrabbling, scrabbled

VERB If you **scrabble** at something, you scrape at it with your hands.

scramble scrambles, scrambling, scrambled

VERB **1** If you **scramble** over something, you climb over it using your hands to help you.
2 When you **scramble** eggs, you mix them up and cook them in a pan.
NOUN **3** a motorcycle race over rough ground

scrap scraps, scrapping, scrapped

NOUN **1** a very small piece of something
2 unwanted or waste material
3 INFORMAL If you get into a **scrap**, you get into a fight.
VERB **4** If you **scrap** something, you get rid of it.

scrapbook scrapbooks

NOUN a book with blank pages that you can fill with photographs or cuttings that interest you

scrape scrapes, scraping, scraped

VERB **1** If you **scrape** something off a surface, you remove it by pulling a rough or sharp object over it.
2 If you **scrape** past something, you pass very close to it.

scratch scratches, scratching, scratched

VERB **1** If you **scratch** something, you make a small cut or mark on it with something sharp.
2 If you **scratch**, you rub your skin with your nails because it is itching.
NOUN **3** a small cut or mark on the surface of something

scrawl scrawls, scrawling, scrawled

VERB **1** If you **scrawl** something, you write it in a careless and untidy way.
NOUN **2** careless and untidy writing

scream screams, screaming, screamed

VERB **1** If you **scream**, you shout or cry in a loud, high-pitched voice.
NOUN **2** a loud, high-pitched cry

screech screeches, screeching, screeched

VERB **1** If a person, animal or machine **screeches**, they make an unpleasant, high-pitched noise.
NOUN **2** an unpleasant, high-pitched noise

screen screens, screening, screened

NOUN **1** a vertical surface on which a picture can be shown, such as a television **screen**
2 a panel used to separate different parts of a room, or to protect or hide something
VERB **3** If a doctor **screens** you for a disease, they test to see if you have it.

screenplay screenplays

NOUN the script of a film

screw screws, screwing, screwed

NOUN **1** a small, sharp piece of metal with

a spiral groove cut into it, used for fixing things together or for fixing something to a wall using a twisting action

VERB **2** If you **screw** something onto something else, you fix it there by twisting it round and round, or by using a screw.
• He **screwed** the top on the ink bottle.

screw up
VERB If you **screw up** paper or cloth, you twist it or squeeze it into a tight ball.

screwdriver
screwdrivers
NOUN a tool for putting in or taking out screws

scribble
scribbles, scribbling, scribbled
VERB **1** If you **scribble** something, you write it quickly and untidily.
2 To **scribble** also means to make meaningless marks. • When Caroline was three she **scribbled** on a wall.

script **scripts**
NOUN the written version of a play or film

scripture **scriptures**
NOUN sacred writings, especially the Bible

scroll **scrolls, scrolling, scrolled**
NOUN **1** a long roll of paper or parchment with writing on it
VERB **2** When you **scroll** text on a computer screen, you move it up or down to see the text that is not visible on the screen.

scrounge **scrounges, scrounging, scrounged**
VERB INFORMAL If you **scrounge** something, you get it by asking for it rather than by earning or buying it.

scrub **scrubs, scrubbing, scrubbed**
VERB **1** If you **scrub** something, you clean it by rubbing it very hard, especially with a brush and water.
NOUN **2** ground covered with bushes and small trees

scruffy **scruffier, scruffiest**
ADJECTIVE untidy

scrum **scrums**
NOUN When rugby players form a **scrum**, they form a group and push against each other with their heads down in an attempt to get the ball.

scuba diving
NOUN the sport of swimming underwater with special breathing equipment [an abbreviation for self-contained underwater breathing apparatus]

scuffle **scuffles, scuffling, scuffled**
VERB **1** When people **scuffle**, they have a short, rough fight.
NOUN **2** a short, rough fight

sculptor **sculptors**
NOUN someone who makes sculptures

sculpture **sculptures**
NOUN a work of art made by shaping or carving stone, clay or wood

scum
NOUN a layer of dirty froth on the surface of a liquid

scurry **scurries, scurrying, scurried**
VERB If you **scurry**, you run with quick, short steps.

scuttle **scuttles, scuttling, scuttled**
VERB **1** If a person or an animal **scuttles**, they run with short, quick steps.
2 To **scuttle** a ship means to sink it deliberately by making holes in the bottom.
NOUN **3** a container for coal

scythe **scythes**
NOUN a tool with a long handle and a curved blade used for cutting grass or grain

sea **seas**
NOUN one of the areas of salty water that cover much of the earth's surface

seafood
PLURAL NOUN fish or shellfish from the sea eaten as food

seagull **seagulls**
NOUN a common, white, grey and black bird that lives near the sea

a
b
c
d
e
f
g
h
i
j
k
l
m
n
o
p
q
r
s
t
u
v
w
x
y
z

seahorse **seahorses**

NOUN a small fish that swims upright, with a head that looks rather like a horse's head

seal **seals, sealing, sealed**

NOUN **1** a fish-eating mammal with flippers, that lives partly on land and partly in the sea

2 something fixed over the opening of a container that prevents anything getting in or out, and which must be broken before the container can be opened

VERB **3** If you **seal** an envelope, you stick down the flap.

seam **seams**

NOUN **1** a line of stitches joining two pieces of cloth

2 a long, narrow layer of coal beneath the ground

search **searches, searching, searched**

VERB **1** If you **search** for something, you look for it very thoroughly.

2 If a person is **searched**, their body and clothing are examined to see if they are hiding anything.

NOUN **3** an attempt to find something
• *I found my purse after a long* **search**.

search engine **search engines**

NOUN a service on the internet which lets you search for information

searchlight **searchlights**

NOUN a light with a powerful beam that can be turned in different directions

seashore

NOUN the land along the edge of the sea

seasick

ADJECTIVE feeling sick because of the movement of a boat

seasickness NOUN

seaside

NOUN a place by the sea, especially where people go on holiday

season **seasons, seasoning, seasoned**

NOUN **1** one of the periods into which a year is divided and which have their own typical weather conditions. The **seasons** are spring, summer, autumn and winter.

2 a period of the year when something usually happens

VERB **3** If you **season** food, you add salt, pepper, herbs or spices to it.

seasoning **seasonings**

NOUN something with a strong taste, like salt, pepper or spices used to add flavour to food

seat **seats**

NOUN something you can sit on

seat belt **seat belts**

NOUN a strap that you put around your body for safety when you are travelling in a car, coach or aircraft

seaweed

NOUN plants that grow in the sea

secluded

ADJECTIVE quiet and hidden from view
• *We found a lovely* **secluded** *beach.*

second **seconds**

NOUN OR ADJECTIVE **1** The **second** or the **second** thing in a series is the one counted as number two.

NOUN **2** one of the sixty parts that a minute is divided into

secondary

ADJECTIVE **1** Something **secondary** is less important than something else.

2 **Secondary** education is education for pupils between the ages of 11 and 18.

secondary school **secondary schools**

NOUN a school for pupils aged between 11 and 18

second-hand

ADJECTIVE OR ADVERB Something that is **second-hand** has already been owned by someone else. • *My brother has a* **second-hand** *car.*

second person

NOUN In grammar, you use the **second person** *you* when you speak or write to someone directly, for example, *you said, you are.*

secret secrets

ADJECTIVE **1** Something that is **secret** is known to only a small number of people and hidden from everyone else. • *a **secret** meeting*

NOUN **2** something known to only a small number of people and hidden from everyone else

secretary secretaries

NOUN a person employed by an organization to keep records, write letters and do office work

secretive

ADJECTIVE **Secretive** people tend to hide their feelings and intentions, and like to keep things secret.

sect sects

NOUN a group of people who have special or unusual religious beliefs

section sections

NOUN one of the parts that something is divided into

secure secures, securing, secured

VERB **1** If you **secure** something, you make it safe or fix it firmly.

ADJECTIVE **2** If something is **secure**, it is safe from harm.

security

NOUN OR ADJECTIVE all the things you do to make sure that you and your property are safe

see sees, seeing, saw, seen

VERB **1** If you **see** something, you look at it or notice it with your eyes.

2 If you **see** something, you understand it or realize what it means. • *I **see** what you mean.*

3 If you **see** that something happens, you make sure that it is done.

seed seeds

NOUN the part of a plant that can grow into a new plant of the same type

seek seeks, seeking, sought

VERB FORMAL If you **seek** something, you try and find it.

seem seems, seeming, seemed

VERB If something **seems** to be the case, it appears to be the case, or you think it is the case.

seen

VERB the past participle of **see**

seep seeps, seeping, seeped

VERB If a liquid or gas **seeps**, it flows very slowly.

seesaw seesaws

NOUN a long plank supported in the middle, so that one person can sit on either end and each can move up and down

seethe seethes, seething, seethed

VERB **1** When a liquid **seethes**, it boils or bubbles.

ADJECTIVE **2** If you are **seething**, you are very angry.

segment segments

NOUN **1** one part of something

2 The **segments** of an orange or grapefruit are the sections you can divide it into.

segregate segregates, segregating, segregated

VERB To **segregate** two groups of people means to keep them apart from each other.

seize seizes, seizing, seized

VERB If you **seize** something, you grab it firmly.

seldom

ADVERB not very often • *They **seldom** watch television.*

select selects, selecting, selected

VERB If you **select** something, you choose it.

self selves

NOUN your own personality or nature that makes you different from anyone else

a
b
c
d
e
f
g
h
i
j
k
l
m
n
o
p
q
r
s
t
u
v
w
x
y
z

self-conscious

ADJECTIVE Someone who is **self-conscious** is easily embarrassed, and worried about what other people think of them. • *She was self-conscious when the teacher asked her to read her poem.*

self-defence

NOUN the use of special physical techniques to protect yourself when someone attacks you

selfie **selfies**

NOUN INFORMAL a photograph taken by pointing a camera at yourself

selfish

ADJECTIVE caring only about yourself, and not about other people

self-service

ADJECTIVE A **self-service** shop or restaurant is one where you serve yourself.

sell **sells, selling, sold**

VERB If you **sell** something, you let someone have it in return for money.

Sellotape

NOUN TRADEMARK a transparent sticky tape

semaphore

NOUN a system of signalling by holding flags out with your arms in different positions to show letters of the alphabet

semi-

PREFIX You add **semi-** to the beginning of a word to mean half or partly. For example, a **semi**circle is half of a circle.

semicircle **semicircles**

NOUN a half of a circle, or something with this shape
semicircular ADJECTIVE

semicolon **semicolons**

NOUN the punctuation mark (;) is used to separate different parts of a sentence or to show a pause

semidetached

ADJECTIVE A **semidetached** house is joined to another house on one side.

semifinal **semifinals**

NOUN one of the two matches or races in a competition that are held to decide who will compete in the final

send **sends, sending, sent**

VERB **1** When you **send** something to someone, you arrange for it to be delivered to them.
2 If a person **sends** someone somewhere, they tell them to go there.

senile

ADJECTIVE If old people become **senile**, they become confused and cannot look after themselves.

senior **seniors**

ADJECTIVE **1** A **senior** official or employee has one of the highest and most important jobs in an organization.
NOUN **2** If you are someone's **senior**, you are older than they are, or in a more important position.

senior citizen **senior citizens**

NOUN an elderly person, especially one receiving a pension

sensation **sensations**

NOUN **1** a feeling that you have
2 If something causes a **sensation**, it causes great interest and excitement.

sensational

ADJECTIVE **1** INFORMAL extremely good • *The concert was sensational.*
2 causing great excitement or interest

sense **senses**

NOUN **1** the physical abilities of sight, hearing, smell, touch and taste • *I have a good sense of smell.*
2 a feeling • *a sense of guilt*
3 the ability to think and behave sensibly
PHRASE **4** If something **makes sense**, you can understand it or it seems sensible.

senseless

ADJECTIVE **1** Something **senseless** has no reason to it. • *The violence of the hooligans was senseless.*
2 If someone is **senseless**, they are unconscious.

sensible

ADJECTIVE showing good sense and judgment

sensitive

ADJECTIVE **1** If you are **sensitive**, you understand other people's feelings.
SYNONYM: perceptive
2 If you are **sensitive** about something, you are easily worried or upset about it.
SYNONYM: touchy
3 easily affected or harmed by something
• My skin is **sensitive** to the sun.

sent

VERB the past tense and past participle of **send**

sentence sentences, sentencing, sentenced

NOUN **1** a group of words that make a statement, question or command. When written down, a **sentence** begins with a capital letter and ends with a full stop.
2 In a law court, a **sentence** is a punishment given to someone who has been found guilty.
VERB **3** When a guilty person is **sentenced**, they are told officially what their punishment will be.

sentimental

ADJECTIVE **1** having an exaggerated feeling of tenderness or sadness
2 having something to do with a person's feelings

sentry sentries

NOUN a soldier who keeps watch and guards a camp or building

separate separates, separating, separated

ADJECTIVE **1** If something is **separate** from something else, the two things are not connected.
VERB **2** If you **separate** people or things, you cause them to be apart from each other.
3 If people or things **separate**, they move away from each other.

There are two as in separate.

September

NOUN the ninth month of the year. **September** has 30 days.
[from the Latin word septem meaning

seven, because it was the seventh month of the Roman calendar]

septic

ADJECTIVE If a wound becomes **septic**, it becomes infected by harmful bacteria.

sequel sequels

NOUN A **sequel** to a book or film is another book or film that continues the story.

sequence sequences

NOUN **1** a number of events coming one after the other
2 the order in which things are arranged or happen • Put the pictures in **sequence** to tell the story.

serene

ADJECTIVE peaceful and calm

sergeant sergeants

NOUN a rank in the police force, the army or the air force

serial serials

NOUN a story that is broadcast or published in a number of parts over a period of time

series

NOUN **1** a number of things coming one after the other
2 A radio or television **series** is a set of programmes with the same title.

serious

ADJECTIVE **1** A **serious** problem or situation is very bad and worrying.
2 **Serious** matters are important and should be thought about carefully.
3 If you are **serious** about something, you really mean it.
4 People who are **serious** are thoughtful, quiet and do not laugh much.

sermon sermons

NOUN a talk on a religious or moral subject given as part of a church service

serpent serpents

NOUN LITERARY a snake

servant servants

NOUN someone who is employed to work in another person's house

a b c d e f g h i j k l m n o p q r s t u v w x y z

355

A
B
C
D
E
F
G
H
I
J
K
L
M
N
O
P
Q
R
S
T
U
V
W
X
Y
Z

serve serves, serving, served

VERB **1** If you **serve** food or drink to people, you give it to them.

2 When someone **serves** customers in a shop, bar or restaurant, they help them and supply them with what they want. • *The shop was very busy so we had to wait for the assistant to* **serve** *us.*

3 In some games, such as tennis, when you **serve** you start the game by hitting the ball to your opponent.

service services

NOUN **1** a system organized to provide something for the public • *The bus* **service** *from our village into town is very good.*

2 Motorway **services** consist of a petrol station, toilets, a shop and a restaurant.

3 If your car has a **service**, it is checked over and repaired if it is broken or damaged.

4 a religious ceremony

session sessions

NOUN the period during which an activity takes place

set sets, setting, set

VERB **1** When something such as jelly or concrete **sets**, it changes from a liquid into a solid.

NOUN **2** a group of things that go together

3 In mathematics, a **set** is a collection of numbers that are treated as a group.

4 In tennis, a **set** is a group of six or more games.

VERB **5** If you **set** your watch or clock, you adjust it for a particular time.

ADJECTIVE **6** If you do something at a **set** time, it is fixed at that time and does not change.

settee settees

NOUN a long comfortable seat for two or three people to sit on

SYNONYM: sofa

setting settings

NOUN The **setting** of something like a play or a story is its surroundings, and where it happens.

settle settles, settling, settled

VERB **1** If you **settle** something, you decide on it or sort it out. • *Let's* **settle** *this argument as quickly as possible.*

2 If you **settle** in a place, you make it your home.

3 If you **settle**, or **settle** down, you relax and make yourself comfortable.

4 If snow or dust **settles**, it sinks slowly down and comes to rest.

settlement settlements

NOUN a place where people have settled and made their homes

seven

NOUN **Seven** is the number 7.

seventh NOUN OR ADJECTIVE

seventeen

NOUN **Seventeen** is the number 17.

seventeenth NOUN OR ADJECTIVE

seventy

NOUN **Seventy** is the number 70.

seventieth NOUN OR ADJECTIVE

sever severs, severing, severed

Rhymes with "never" VERB If you **sever** something, you cut it off or cut right through it.

several

ADJECTIVE OR PRONOUN a small number of people or things

severe

Said "suh-**veer**" ADJECTIVE **1** extremely bad or serious

2 strict or harsh

sew sews, sewing, sewed, sewn

VERB When you **sew** something, you use a needle and thread to make or mend it.

sewage

NOUN dirty water and waste that is carried away in drains from buildings

sewer sewers

NOUN a series of pipes and drains that carries away dirty water and waste from buildings

sex sexes

NOUN **1** one of the two groups, male and female, into which animals, including humans, are divided

2 the physical activity by which people and animals produce young
sexual ADJECTIVE

sexism
NOUN the belief that one gender is less intelligent or less able than the other, or in some way not as good as the other
sexist ADJECTIVE OR NOUN

shabby shabbier, shabbiest
ADJECTIVE Something or someone who is **shabby** looks old and ragged.

shack shacks
NOUN a small, roughly built hut

shade shades, shading, shaded
NOUN **1** an area of darkness and coolness that sunshine does not reach
2 the different forms of a colour. For example, olive green is a **shade** of green.
3 an object that decreases or shuts out light, such as a lampshade
VERB **4** If you **shade** a person or a thing, you protect them from the sun's heat or light.

shadow shadows, shadowing, shadowed
NOUN **1** the dark shape formed when an opaque object stops light from reaching a surface

shadow

VERB **2** When you **shadow** someone, you follow them and watch them closely.

shady shadier, shadiest
ADJECTIVE A **shady** place is sheltered from the sunlight by trees or buildings.

shaft shafts
NOUN **1** A **shaft** in a mine or for a lift is a passage that goes straight down.
2 a beam of light
3 In a machine, the **shaft** is a rod that turns in order to transmit power or movement.

shaggy shaggier, shaggiest
ADJECTIVE covered with thick, long, untidy hair

shake shakes, shaking, shook, shaken
VERB **1** If you **shake** something, you move it quickly from side to side or up and down.
2 If something **shakes**, it moves from side to side or up and down with small, quick movements.
3 When you **shake** your head, you move it from side to side in order to say no.
NOUN **4** If you give something a **shake**, you shake it.
PHRASE **5** When you **shake hands** with someone, you grasp their hand in yours as a way of greeting them.

shaky shakier, shakiest
ADJECTIVE rather weak, shaking and unsteady ● The foal got up on **shaky** legs.

shall should
VERB used with I and we to refer to the future ● I **shall** go shopping tomorrow.
● I **should** wait till next week to open my birthday present.

shallow shallower, shallowest
ADJECTIVE not deep ● The water here is quite **shallow**.

shame
NOUN **1** the feeling of guilt or embarrassment you get when you know you have done something wrong or foolish
2 If you say something is a **shame**, you mean you are sorry about it. ● It's a **shame** you can't come round to tea.

shampoo shampoos
NOUN a soapy liquid used for washing your hair

shamrock shamrocks
NOUN a plant with three round leaves on each stem, which is the national emblem of Ireland
[from Irish Gaelic seamrog meaning little clover]

shanty shanties
NOUN **1** a small, rough hut
2 A sea **shanty** is a song sailors used to sing.

shape shapes

NOUN **1** The **shape** of something is the form or pattern of its outline, for example whether it is round or square. ● *The chocolates came in a box in the* **shape** *of a heart.*

2 something with a definite form, for example a circle or square

share shares, sharing, shared

VERB **1** If two people **share** something, they both use it, do it, or have it. ● *We* **shared** *a bar of chocolate.*

NOUN **2** A **share** of something is a portion of it. ● *I want a fair* **share** *of the cake.*

share out

VERB If you **share out** something, you give it out equally among a group of people. ● *They* **shared out** *the food between them.*

shark sharks

NOUN a large, powerful fish, usually with two fins on its back and rows of sharp teeth

sharp sharper, sharpest

ADJECTIVE **1** A **sharp** object has an edge or point that is good for cutting or piercing things.

2 A **sharp** change is sudden and noticeable. ● *There was a* **sharp** *rise in temperature after the sun came up.*

3 A **sharp** taste is sour.

4 Someone who is **sharp** can pick up ideas very quickly.

5 A **sharp** pain is strong and sudden.

sharpen sharpens, sharpening, sharpened

VERB If you **sharpen** an object such as a knife, you make its edge or point sharper.

shatter shatters, shattering, shattered

VERB If something **shatters**, it breaks into a lot of small pieces. ● *The windows* **shattered** *in the explosion.*

shave shaves, shaving, shaved

VERB When someone **shaves**, they remove hair with a razor from part of their body.

shavings

PLURAL NOUN small, fine pieces of wood that have been cut off a larger piece

shawl shawls

NOUN a large piece of cloth worn round a woman's head or shoulders, or used to wrap a baby in

she

PRONOUN **She** is used to refer to a woman or girl who has already been mentioned.

sheaf sheaves

NOUN **1** a bundle of papers

2 a bundle of ripe corn

shear shears, shearing, sheared, shorn

VERB When someone **shears** a sheep, they cut the wool off it.

shears

PLURAL NOUN **Shears** are a tool like a large pair of scissors, used especially for cutting hedges.

sheath sheaths

NOUN a cover for the blade of a knife or a sword

shed sheds, shedding, shed

NOUN **1** a small building used for storing things, especially in a garden

VERB **2** When an animal **sheds** hair or skin, some of it comes off.

3 If you **shed** tears, you cry.

she'd

a contraction of *she had* or *she would*

sheen

NOUN a gentle shine on the surface of something

sheep

NOUN a mammal kept on farms for its meat and wool

✎ The plural of *sheep* is *sheep*.

sheepdog sheepdogs

NOUN a breed of dog often used for controlling sheep

sheepish

ADJECTIVE If you look **sheepish**, you look shy or embarrassed.

sheer sheerer, sheerest
ADJECTIVE **1** A **sheer** cliff or drop is vertical.
2 complete and total • *sheer exhaustion*
3 Sheer fabrics are very light and delicate.

sheet sheets
NOUN **1** a large rectangular piece of cloth used to cover a bed
2 a rectangular piece of paper

sheikh sheikhs
Rhymes with "make" NOUN an Arab chief or ruler
[from Arabic *shaykh* meaning old man]

shelf shelves
NOUN a flat piece of wood, metal or glass fixed to a wall or a cabinet or cupboard and used for putting things on

shell shells
NOUN **1** the hard covering of an egg or nut
2 the hard, protective covering on the back of a tortoise, snail or crab

she'll
a contraction of *she will* or *she shall*

shellfish shellfish or shellfishes
NOUN a small sea creature with a shell

shelter shelters, sheltering, sheltered
NOUN **1** a small building made to protect people from bad weather or danger • *We waited in the bus **shelter**.*
2 If a place gives **shelter**, it protects you from bad weather or danger.
VERB **3** If you **shelter** in a place, you stay there and are safe and protected.
4 To **shelter** someone or something means to protect them from bad weather or danger.

shepherd shepherds
NOUN a person who looks after sheep

sheriff sheriffs
NOUN **1** in America, a person elected to enforce the law in a county
2 in Scotland, the senior judge of a county or district
3 in Australia, an officer of the Supreme Court who does certain paperwork

sherry sherries
NOUN a kind of strong wine

she's
a contraction of *she is* or *she has*

shield shields, shielding, shielded
NOUN **1** a large piece of a strong material like metal or plastic that soldiers or policemen carry to protect themselves
VERB **2** If you **shield** someone or something, you protect them from something. • *He **shielded** his eyes from the sun with his hand.*

shift shifts, shifting, shifted
VERB **1** If you **shift** something, you move it.
2 If something **shifts**, it moves.
NOUN **3** a set period during which people work • *the night **shift***

shilling shillings
NOUN a coin that was once used in Britain, Australia and New Zealand. There were 20 **shillings** in a pound.

shimmer shimmers, shimmering, shimmered
VERB **1** If something **shimmers**, it shines with a faint, flickering light.
NOUN **2** a faint, flickering light

shin shins
NOUN the front part of your leg between your knee and your ankle

shine shines, shining, shone or shined
VERB **1** When something **shines**, it is bright because it gives out or reflects light.
2 If you **shine** a torch or lamp somewhere, you point it there so that it becomes light.
3 If you **shine** your shoes, you polish them.

shingle
NOUN small pebbles on the seashore

shingles
PLURAL NOUN a disease that causes a painful red rash, especially around the waist

a
b
c
d
e
f
g
h
i
j
k
l
m
n
o
p
q
r
s
t
u
v
w
x
y
z

shiny shinier, shiniest

ADJECTIVE **Shiny** things are bright and look as if they have been polished.

ship ships, shipping, shipped

NOUN **1** a large boat that carries passengers or cargo

VERB **2** If people or things are **shipped** somewhere, they are transported there by ship.

shipwreck shipwrecks; shipwrecked

NOUN **1** When there is a **shipwreck**, a ship is destroyed in a storm or an accident at sea.

2 the remains of a ship that has been damaged or sunk

ADJECTIVE **3** If someone is **shipwrecked**, they survive a shipwreck and manage to reach land.

shipyard shipyards

NOUN a place where ships are built and repaired

shirk shirks, shirking, shirked

VERB If you **shirk** a task, you try to avoid doing it.

shirt shirts

NOUN a piece of clothing with a collar, sleeves and buttons down the front, worn on the upper part of the body

shiver shivers, shivering, shivered

VERB When you **shiver**, you tremble slightly because you are cold or scared.

shoal shoals

NOUN a large group of fish swimming together

shock shocks, shocking, shocked

NOUN **1** a sudden upsetting experience

VERB **2** If something **shocks** you, it upsets you because it is unpleasant and unexpected.

shocking

ADJECTIVE **1** Something that shocks people is **shocking**.

2 INFORMAL very bad • *The weather has been shocking.*

shoddy shoddier, shoddiest

ADJECTIVE badly made or done

shoe shoes

NOUN a strong covering for each of your feet. **Shoes** cover most of your foot, but not your ankle.

shoelace shoelaces

NOUN a cord for fastening a shoe

shone

VERB the past tense and past participle of **shine**

shook

VERB the past tense of **shake**

shoot shoots, shooting, shot

VERB **1** If someone **shoots** a person or an animal, they injure or kill them by firing a gun at them.

2 When a film is **shot**, it is filmed.

shooting star shooting stars

NOUN a meteor

shop shops, shopping, shopped

NOUN **1** a place where things are sold

2 a place where a particular type of work is done • *a bicycle repair shop*

VERB **3** When you **shop**, you go to the shops to buy things.

shopkeeper shopkeepers

NOUN someone who owns or manages a small shop

shopping

NOUN Your **shopping** is the goods you have bought in a shop.

shore shores

NOUN the land along the edge of a sea, lake or wide river

short shorter, shortest

ADJECTIVE **1** not lasting very long

2 small in length, distance or height

3 If you are **short** of something, you do not have enough of it.

A B C D E F G H I J K L M N O P Q R S T U V W X Y Z

4 If a name is **short** for another name, it is a quick way of saying it. ● *her friend Kes* (**short** *for Kesewa*)

shortage **shortages**
NOUN If there is a **shortage** of something, there is not enough of it.

shortcut **shortcuts**
NOUN **1** a quicker way of getting somewhere than the usual route
2 a quicker way of doing something than the usual way

shorten **shortens, shortening, shortened**
VERB If you **shorten** something, you make it shorter.

shorthand
NOUN a way of writing in which signs represent words or syllables. It is used to write down quickly what someone is saying.

shortly
ADVERB soon ● *I'll be there* **shortly**.

shorts
PLURAL NOUN trousers with legs that stop at or above the knee

short-sighted
ADJECTIVE If you are **short-sighted**, you cannot see things clearly when they are far away.

shot **shots**
VERB **1** the past tense of **shoot**
NOUN **2** the act of firing a gun
3 In football, golf, tennis and other ball games, a **shot** is the act of kicking or hitting the ball.
4 a photograph or short film sequence

should
VERB **1** You use **should** to say that something ought to happen. ● *Kylie* **should** *have done better.*
2 You also use **should** to say that you expect something to happen.
● *We* **should** *have heard by now.*
3 **Should** is used in questions where you are asking someone for advice about what to do. ● **Should** *we tell her about it?*

shoulder **shoulders**
NOUN Your **shoulders** are the parts of your body between your neck and the tops of your arms.

shouldn't
VERB a contraction of *should not*

shout **shouts, shouting, shouted**
NOUN **1** a loud call or cry
VERB **2** If you **shout** something, you say it very loudly.

shove **shoves, shoving, shoved**
VERB **1** If you **shove** someone or something, you push them roughly.
NOUN **2** a rough push

shovel **shovels, shovelling, shovelled**
NOUN **1** a tool like a spade, with the sides curved up, used for moving earth or snow
VERB **2** If you **shovel** earth or snow, you move it with a shovel.

show **shows, showing, showed, shown**
VERB **1** If you **show** someone something, you let them see it.
2 If you **show** someone how to do something, you demonstrate it to them. ● *Jake* **showed** *me how to make a chocolate cake.*
3 If something **shows**, you can see it.
4 If you **show** someone to a room or seat, you lead them there.
NOUN **5** a form of entertainment at the theatre or on television ● *My favourite talk* **show** *is on TV tonight.*
6 a display or exhibition ● *a flower* **show**

show off
VERB INFORMAL If someone is **showing off**, they are trying to impress people.

shower **showers, showering, showered**
NOUN **1** a device that sprays you with water so that you can wash yourself
2 If you have a **shower**, you wash yourself by standing under a **shower**.
3 a short period of rain

VERB **4** If you are **showered** with a lot of things, they fall on you like rain.

showroom showrooms
NOUN a shop where goods such as cars or electrical items are displayed for customers to look at

shrank
VERB the past tense of **shrink**

shrapnel
NOUN small pieces of metal scattered from an exploding shell
[named after General Henry *Shrapnel* (1761–1842), who invented it]

shred shreds, shredding, shredded
VERB **1** If you **shred** something, you cut or tear it into very small pieces.
NOUN **2** a small, narrow piece of paper or material

shrew shrews
NOUN a small mouse-like mammal with a long pointed nose

shrewd shrewder, shrewdest
ADJECTIVE Someone who is **shrewd** makes good judgments and uses their common sense.

shriek shrieks, shrieking, shrieked
NOUN **1** a high-pitched cry or scream
VERB **2** If you **shriek**, you make a high-pitched cry or scream.

shrill shriller, shrillest
ADJECTIVE A **shrill** sound is unpleasantly high-pitched and piercing.
shrilly ADVERB

shrimp shrimps
NOUN a small edible shellfish with a long tail and many legs

shrine shrines
NOUN a place of worship connected with a sacred person or object

shrink shrinks, shrinking, shrank, shrunk
VERB If something **shrinks**, it becomes smaller.

shrinkage
NOUN the amount by which something shrinks

shrivel shrivels, shrivelling, shrivelled
VERB When something **shrivels**, it becomes dry and withered.

shrub shrubs
NOUN a bushy plant with woody stems

shrug shrugs, shrugging, shrugged
VERB If you **shrug** your shoulders, you raise them slightly as a sign that you do not know or do not care about something.

shrunk
VERB the past participle of **shrink**

shudder shudders, shuddering, shuddered
VERB **1** If you **shudder**, you tremble with fear or horror.
2 If a machine or vehicle **shudders**, it shakes violently.
NOUN **3** a shiver of fear or horror

shuffle shuffles, shuffling, shuffled
VERB **1** If you **shuffle**, you walk without lifting your feet off the ground properly, so that they drag.
2 If you **shuffle** a pack of cards, you mix them up before you begin a game.

shut shuts, shutting, shut
VERB **1** If you **shut** something, you close it.
ADJECTIVE **2** If something is **shut**, it is closed.

shutter shutters
NOUN **1** a screen that can be closed over a window
2 the device in a camera that opens and closes to let light onto the film

shuttle shuttles
ADJECTIVE **1** A **shuttle** service is an air, bus or train service that makes frequent journeys between two places.
NOUN **2** a type of American spacecraft

shuttlecock
shuttlecocks
NOUN the feathered object that players hit over the net in the game of badminton

shy **shyer, shyest**
ADJECTIVE A **shy** person is quiet and uncomfortable in the company of other people.

sibling **siblings**
NOUN FORMAL Your **siblings** are your brothers and sisters.
[from Old English *sibling* meaning relative]

sick **sicker, sickest**
ADJECTIVE **1** If you are **sick**, you are ill.
2 If you feel **sick**, you feel as if you are going to vomit.
3 If you are **sick**, you vomit.

sickness **sicknesses**
NOUN an illness or disease

side **sides, siding, sided**
NOUN **1** a position to the left or right of something • *There were trees on both **sides** of the road.*
2 The **sides** of something are its outside surfaces, or edges, that are not at the top, bottom, front or back. • *There is a label on the **side** of the box.*
3 The **sides** of an area, surface or object are its different surfaces or edges. • *Write on one **side** of the paper.*
4 Your **sides** are the parts of your body from your armpits down to your hips.
5 The two **sides** in a war, argument or relationship are the two people or groups involved. • *Whose **side** are you on?*
ADJECTIVE **6** situated on a side of a building or vehicle • *the **side** door*
VERB **7** If you **side** with someone, you support them in a quarrel or an argument.

sideways
ADVERB moving or facing towards one side • *I took a step **sideways**.*

siding **sidings**
NOUN a short railway track beside the main tracks, where engines and carriages are left when not in use

siege **sieges**
NOUN a military operation in which an army surrounds a place to stop food or help from reaching the people inside

sieve **sieves, sieving, sieved**
NOUN **1** a tool made of mesh, used for sifting or straining things
VERB **2** If you **sieve** a powder or liquid, you pass it through a sieve to get rid of lumps and make it smooth.

sift **sifts, sifting, sifted**
VERB If you **sift** a powdery substance like flower or sugar, you pass it through a sieve to remove lumps.

sigh **sighs, sighing, sighed**
VERB When you **sigh**, you let out a deep breath, usually because you are tired, sad or relieved.

sight **sights**
NOUN **1** being able to see
2 something you see • *The sunset was a beautiful **sight**.*
PLURAL NOUN **3** **Sights** are interesting places that tourists visit.

sightseeing
NOUN visiting the interesting places that tourists usually visit

sign **signs, signing, signed**
NOUN **1** a mark or symbol that always has a particular meaning, for example in mathematics or music • *a plus **sign***
2 a board or notice with words, a picture or a symbol on it, giving information or a warning • *a stop **sign***
VERB **3** If you **sign** a document, you write your name on it by hand, in the way you usually write it.

signal **signals**
NOUN **1** a gesture, sound or action that is meant to give a message to someone
2 A railway **signal** is a piece of equipment beside the track that tells train drivers whether or not to stop.

signature **signatures**
NOUN If you write your **signature**, you write your name by hand in the way you usually write it.

significant
ADJECTIVE **1** A **significant** amount is large enough to be noticed and to matter. • *A **significant** number of people can't read.*

2 Something that is **significant** is important and means something.

sign language
NOUN a way of communicating using your hands, used especially by deaf people

signpost signposts
NOUN a road sign with information on it, such as the name of a town and how far away it is

Sikh Sikhs
NOUN a person who believes in Sikhism, an Indian religion that separated from Hinduism in the 16th century and which teaches that there is only one God

silence
NOUN When there is **silence**, there is no sound.
SYNONYM: quietness

silent
ADJECTIVE **1** If you are **silent**, you are not saying anything.
2 When something is **silent**, it makes no noise.

silhouette silhouettes
NOUN the dark outline of a shape against a light background
silhouetted ADJECTIVE

silicon
NOUN an element found in sand, clay and stone. It is used to make glass and parts of computers.

silk silks
NOUN fine, soft cloth made from threads produced from silkworm cocoons

sill sills
NOUN a strip of stone, wood or metal underneath a window or a door

silly sillier, silliest
ADJECTIVE foolish or childish

silver
NOUN a valuable greyish-white metal used for making jewellery and ornaments

similar
ADJECTIVE If one thing is **similar** to another, they are quite like each other.

simile similes
NOUN an expression in which a person or thing is described as being similar to someone or something else. Examples of **similes** are *she runs like a deer* and *he's as white as a sheet.*

simmer simmers, simmering, simmered
VERB When food **simmers**, it cooks gently, just below boiling point.

simple simpler, simplest
ADJECTIVE **1** Something that is **simple** is easy to understand or do.
2 plain in style

simplify simplifies, simplifying, simplified
VERB If you **simplify** something, you make it simple or easy to understand.

simply
ADVERB in a simple way

simultaneous
ADJECTIVE Things that are **simultaneous** happen at the same time.
simultaneously ADVERB

sin sins, sinning, sinned
NOUN **1** wicked behaviour, particularly if it breaks a religious or moral law
VERB **2** To **sin** means to do something wicked.

since
PREPOSITION, CONJUNCTION OR ADVERB **1** from a particular time until now • *I've been waiting **since** half past three.*
2 because • *I had a drink, **since** I was feeling thirsty.*

sincere
ADJECTIVE If you are **sincere**, you are genuine and truly mean what you say.

sing sings, singing, sang, sung
VERB **1** When you **sing**, you make musical sounds with your voice, usually with words that fit a tune.
2 When birds or insects **sing**, they make pleasant and tuneful sounds.

singe singes, singeing, singed
VERB If you **singe** something, you burn it

slightly so that it goes brown but does not catch fire.

single singles
ADJECTIVE **1** only one and not more ● A **single** shot was fired.
2 People who are **single** are not married.
3 A **single** bed or bedroom is for one person.
NOUN **4** A **single**, or a **single** ticket, is a ticket for a journey to a place but not back again.
5 a recording of one or two short pieces of music on a small record, CD or cassette

singular
NOUN In grammar, the **singular** is the form of a word that means just one person or thing.
ANTONYM: plural

sinister
ADJECTIVE Something or someone **sinister** seems harmful or evil.
[from Latin sinister meaning left-hand side, because the left side was considered unlucky]

sink sinks, sinking, sank, sunk
NOUN **1** a fixed basin with taps supplying water, usually in a kitchen or bathroom
VERB **2** If something **sinks**, it moves downwards, especially through water.

sip sips, sipping, sipped
VERB If you **sip** a drink, you take small mouthfuls.

sir
NOUN **1** FORMAL a polite way to address a man
2 **Sir** is the title of a knight or baronet.

siren sirens
NOUN a warning device, for example on an ambulance, that makes a loud, wailing noise ● The fire engines switched on their **sirens** as they raced to the fire.

sister sisters
NOUN Your **sister** is a girl or woman who has the same parents as you.

sister-in-law sisters-in-law
NOUN Someone's **sister-in-law** is the wife of their brother, the sister of their husband or wife, or the woman married to their wife's or husband's brother.

sit sits, sitting, sat
VERB When you **sit**, you rest your bottom on something such as a chair or the floor. ● We **sat** on the bench at the bus stop.

site sites
NOUN a piece of ground where something happens or will happen ● the **site** for the fairground

sitting room sitting rooms
NOUN a room with comfortable chairs for relaxing in

situated
ADJECTIVE in a particular place ● The cottage was **situated** on the edge of a forest.

situation situations
NOUN **1** what is happening in a particular place at a particular time
2 The **situation** of a town or a building is its surroundings and its position.

six
NOUN **Six** is the number 6.
sixth NOUN OR ADJECTIVE

sixteen
NOUN **Sixteen** is the number 16.
sixteenth NOUN OR ADJECTIVE

sixty
NOUN **Sixty** is the number 60.
sixtieth NOUN OR ADJECTIVE

size sizes
NOUN **1** The **size** of something is how big it is.
2 a standard measurement for clothes, shoes and other objects

sizzle sizzles, sizzling, sizzled
VERB If something **sizzles**, it makes a hissing sound. ● The sausages **sizzled** in the frying pan.

skate skates, skating, skated
NOUN **1** **Skates** are ice **skates** or roller **skates**.
VERB **2** If you **skate**, you move about wearing skates.

skateboard skateboards
NOUN a narrow board on wheels, that you stand on and ride for fun
skateboarder NOUN skateboarding NOUN

skeleton
skeletons

NOUN the framework of bones in your body

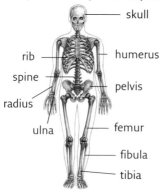

skull
rib
humerus
spine
radius
pelvis
ulna
femur
fibula
tibia

sketch sketches, sketching, sketched

NOUN **1** a quick, rough drawing
VERB **2** If you **sketch** something, you draw it quickly and roughly.

sketchy sketchier, sketchiest

ADJECTIVE If something is **sketchy**, it has little detail. • *The map showing how to get to the new house was **sketchy**.*

ski skis, skiing, skied

NOUN **1 Skis** are long pieces of wood, metal or plastic that you fasten to special boots so you can move easily on snow.
VERB **2** When you **ski**, you move on snow wearing skis, especially as a sport. [from Old Norse *skith* meaning snowshoes]

skid skids, skidding, skidded

VERB **1** If someone or something **skids**, they slide accidentally.
NOUN **2** a skidding movement

skilful

ADJECTIVE having a lot of skill
skilfully ADVERB

skill skills

NOUN **1** the knowledge and ability that enable you to do something well
2 a type of work or technique that needs special training and knowledge • *I would like to learn some new **skills**.*

skim skims, skimming, skimmed

VERB **1** If you **skim** something from the surface of a liquid, you remove it.
2 If something **skims** a surface, it moves lightly, smoothly and quickly over it.
• *seagulls **skimming** the waves*

skin skins

NOUN **1** the natural covering of a person or animal
2 the outer covering a fruit or vegetable

skinny skinnier, skinniest

ADJECTIVE thin

skip skips, skipping, skipped

VERB **1** When you **skip**, you jump lightly from one foot to the other, often over a rope.
2 If you **skip** something, you miss it out.
• *Amy **skipped** the part with the long words.*

skipper skippers

NOUN INFORMAL the captain of a ship or boat

skirt skirts

NOUN a piece of clothing that fastens at a woman's or girl's waist and hangs down over her legs

skittle skittles

NOUN **1** a wooden or plastic object, shaped like a bottle, that people try to knock down with a ball
2 Skittles is a game in which players roll a ball and try to knock down objects called skittles.

skull skulls

NOUN the bony part of your head that surrounds your brain

skunk skunks

NOUN a small black and white animal from North America that gives off an unpleasant smell if it is frightened

sky skies

NOUN the space around the earth that you can see when you look upwards

skyscraper skyscrapers

NOUN a very tall building

slab slabs

NOUN a thick, flat piece of something, such as stone

slack slacker, slackest
ADJECTIVE Something that is **slack** is loose and not firmly stretched or pulled tight.

slam slams, slamming, slammed
VERB If you **slam** something, such as a door, or if it **slams**, it shuts with a loud bang.

slang
NOUN very informal words and expressions

slant slants, slanting, slanted
VERB **1** If something **slants**, it slopes.
NOUN **2** a slope or a leaning position

slap slaps, slapping, slapped
VERB **1** If you **slap** someone, you hit them with the palm of your hand.
NOUN **2** If you give someone a **slap**, you slap them.

slash slashes, slashing, slashed
VERB **1** If someone **slashes** something, they make a long, deep cut in it.
NOUN **2** a long, deep cut

slate slates
NOUN **1** a dark grey rock that splits easily into thin layers
2 **Slates** are small, flat pieces of slate used for covering roofs.

slaughter slaughters, slaughtering, slaughtered
VERB **1** To **slaughter** farm animals means to kill them for meat.
2 To **slaughter** animals or people means to kill a large number of them unjustly or cruelly.
NOUN **3** the killing of many people or animals

slave slaves, slaving, slaved
NOUN **1** someone who is owned by another person and must work for them
VERB **2** If you **slave** over something, you work very hard at it.

slay slays, slaying, slew, slain
VERB LITERARY To **slay** someone means to kill them.

sledge
sledges
NOUN a vehicle on runners used for travelling over snow

sledgehammer sledgehammers
NOUN a large, heavy hammer

sleek sleeker, sleekest
ADJECTIVE If something such as hair is **sleek**, it is smooth and shiny.

sleep sleeps, sleeping, slept
VERB When you **sleep**, you close your eyes and your whole body rests.

sleepless
ADJECTIVE unable to sleep or without sleep
• I had a **sleepless** night last night.

sleepy sleepier, sleepiest
ADJECTIVE tired and feeling like sleeping
sleepily ADVERB   sleepiness NOUN

sleet
NOUN a mixture of rain and snow

sleeve sleeves
NOUN The **sleeves** of a piece of clothing are the parts that cover your arms.
• a shirt with long **sleeves**

sleigh sleighs
NOUN a sledge pulled by animals

slender
ADJECTIVE slim

slept
VERB the past tense and past participle of **sleep**

slice slices, slicing, sliced
NOUN **1** A **slice** of cake, bread or other food is a piece of it cut from a larger piece.
VERB **2** If you **slice** food, you cut it into thin pieces.
3 To **slice** through something means to cut or move through it quickly, like a knife. • The ship **sliced** through the water.

slick slicker, slickest; slicks
ADJECTIVE **1** A **slick** action is done quickly and smoothly.
NOUN **2** An oil **slick** is a layer of oil floating on the surface of the sea or a lake.

slide slides, sliding, slid
VERB When something **slides**, it moves smoothly over or against something else.
• She **slid** the door open.

slight slighter, slightest
ADJECTIVE **1** small in amount • a **slight** dent in the car
2 A **slight** person has a slim, small body.

slim slimmer, slimmest
ADJECTIVE **1** A **slim** person is thin.
2 A **slim** object is fairly thin. • a **slim** book
3 If there is only a **slim** chance that something will happen, there is only a small chance that it will happen.

slime
NOUN an unpleasant, thick, slippery substance

sling slings, slinging, slung
VERB **1** INFORMAL If you **sling** something somewhere, you throw it there.
2 If you **sling** a rope between two points, you attach it so that it hangs loosely between them.
NOUN **3** a piece of cloth tied round a person's neck to support a broken or injured arm

slip slips, slipping, slipped
VERB **1** If you **slip**, you accidentally lose your balance.
2 If you **slip** somewhere, you go there quickly and quietly.
NOUN **3** a small mistake
4 a small piece of paper

slipper slippers
NOUN **Slippers** are loose, soft shoes that you wear indoors.

slippery
ADJECTIVE smooth, wet or greasy, and difficult to hold or walk on

slit slits
NOUN a long cut or narrow opening

slither slithers, slithering, slithered
VERB To **slither** somewhere means to move there by sliding along the ground in an uneven way. • The snake **slithered** into the water.

sliver slivers
NOUN a small, thin piece of something

slog slogs, slogging, slogged
VERB **1** If you **slog** at something, you work hard at it.
NOUN **2** a piece of hard work or effort

slogan slogans
NOUN a short, easily-remembered phrase used in advertising or by a political party
SYNONYMS: catch phrase, motto

slope slopes, sloping, sloped
NOUN **1** a flat surface that is at an angle, so that one end is higher than the other
VERB **2** If a surface **slopes**, it is at an angle.

sloppy sloppier, sloppiest
ADJECTIVE **1** liquid and spilling easily
2 careless or badly done
3 sentimental
sloppily ADVERB   **sloppiness** NOUN

slot slots
NOUN a narrow opening in a machine or container for pushing something into
• She put the coin in the **slot**.

sloth sloths
NOUN **1** a South and Central American animal that moves very slowly and hangs upside down from the branches of trees
2 FORMAL laziness
slothful ADJECTIVE

slouch slouches, slouching, slouched
VERB If you **slouch**, you stand or sit with your shoulders and head drooping forwards.

slow slower, slowest; slows, slowing, slowed
ADJECTIVE **1** moving, happening or doing something with very little speed
2 If a clock or watch is **slow**, it shows a time earlier than the correct one.
VERB **3** If something **slows**, or you **slow** it, it moves or happens more slowly.

slow down
VERB If something **slows down** or something **slows** it **down**, it moves or happens more slowly.

slug slugs
NOUN a small, slow-moving animal with a slimy body, like a snail without an outer shell

sluggish
ADJECTIVE moving slowly and without much energy

slum slums
NOUN a poor, run-down area of a city or town

slumber slumbers, slumbering, slumbered
NOUN **1** LITERARY sleep
VERB **2** LITERARY When you **slumber**, you sleep.

slump slumps, slumping, slumped
VERB If you **slump** somewhere, you fall or sit down heavily.

slush
NOUN melting snow

sly slyer or slier, slyest or sliest
ADJECTIVE **1** A **sly** person is cunning and good at deceiving people.
2 A **sly** expression or remark shows that you know something other people do not know.

smack smacks, smacking, smacked
VERB **1** If you **smack** someone, you hit them with your open hand.
NOUN **2** If you give someone a **smack**, you smack them.

small smaller, smallest
ADJECTIVE not large in size, number or amount

smart smarter, smartest
ADJECTIVE **1** A **smart** person is clean and neatly dressed.
2 clever ● *That's a **smart** idea.*

smartphone smartphones
NOUN a mobile phone that can send e-mails and access the internet

smash smashes, smashing, smashed
VERB **1** If you **smash** something, you break it into a lot of pieces by hitting it or dropping it.
2 If someone or something **smashes** through something, such as a fence, they go through it by breaking it.
3 To **smash** against something means

to hit it with great force. ● *A huge wave **smashed** against the boat.*

smear smears, smearing, smeared
NOUN **1** a dirty, greasy mark on a surface
VERB **2** If something **smears** something else, it leaves a dirty or greasy mark by rubbing against it.

smell smells, smelling, smelled or smelt
VERB **1** When you **smell** something, you notice it with your nose.
2 If something **smells**, it gives out an odour that people notice.
NOUN **3** Your sense of **smell** is your ability to smell things.
4 an odour or scent, especially an unpleasant one

> 🖊 You can write either *smelled* or *smelt* as the past form of *smell*.

smile smiles, smiling, smiled
VERB When you **smile**, you are happy. Your lips curve upwards at the edges and open a little.

smirk smirks, smirking, smirked
VERB When you **smirk**, you smile in a sneering, unpleasant way.

smog
NOUN a mixture of smoke and fog that occurs in some industrial cities
[from a combination of *smoke* and *fog*]

smoke smokes, smoking, smoked
NOUN **1** a mixture of gases and small bits of solid material sent into the air when something burns
VERB **2** If something is **smoking**, smoke is coming from it.
3 When someone **smokes** a cigarette, cigar or pipe, they suck smoke from it into their mouth and blow it out again.

smooth smoother, smoothest; smooths, smoothing, smoothed
ADJECTIVE **1** A **smooth** surface has no roughness and no holes in it.
2 A **smooth** liquid or mixture has no lumps in it.
VERB **3** If you **smooth** something, you move your hands over it to make it smooth and flat.

a
b
c
d
e
f
g
h
i
j
k
l
m
n
o
p
q
r
s
t
u
v
w
x
y
z

smother smothers, smothering, smothered

VERB **1** If you **smother** a fire, you cover it with something to put it out.

2 To **smother** a person means to cover their face with something so that they cannot breathe.

smoulder smoulders, smouldering, smouldered

VERB When something **smoulders**, it burns slowly, producing smoke but no flames.

smudge smudges, smudging, smudged

NOUN **1** a dirty or blurred mark or a smear on something

VERB **2** If you **smudge** something, you make it dirty or messy by touching it or rubbing it.

smug smugger, smuggest

ADJECTIVE Someone who is **smug** is very pleased with how good or clever they are, and is self-satisfied in an unpleasant way.

smugly ADVERB

smuggle smuggles, smuggling, smuggled

VERB To **smuggle** goods means to take them in or out of a country secretly and against the law.

snack snacks

NOUN **1** a small, quick meal

2 something eaten between meals

snag snags, snagging, snagged

NOUN **1** a small problem

VERB **2** If you **snag** your clothes, you catch them on something sharp.

snail snails

NOUN a small, slow-moving animal with a long, shiny body and a shell on its back

snake snakes

NOUN a long, thin reptile with scales and no legs

snap snaps, snapping, snapped

VERB **1** If something **snaps**, it breaks suddenly with a sharp noise.

2 If an animal **snaps** at you, it shuts its jaws together quickly as if it is going to bite you.

NOUN **3** an informal photograph

snare snares, snaring, snared

NOUN **1** a trap for catching birds or small animals

VERB **2** To **snare** an animal or bird means to catch it using a snare.

snarl snarls, snarling, snarled

VERB **1** When an animal **snarls**, it bares its teeth and makes a fierce, growling noise.

2 If you **snarl**, you say something in a fierce, angry way.

NOUN **3** the noise an animal makes when it snarls

snatch snatches, snatching, snatched

VERB **1** If you **snatch** something, you reach out for it quickly and grab it.

NOUN **2** A **snatch** of conversation or song is a very small piece of it.

sneak sneaks, sneaking, sneaked

VERB If you **sneak** somewhere, you go there quietly, trying not to be seen or heard.

sneaky sneakier, sneakiest

ADJECTIVE dishonest or deceitful

sneer sneers, sneering, sneered

VERB If you **sneer** at someone or something, you show by what you say that you think they are stupid or inferior.

sneeze sneezes, sneezing, sneezed

VERB **1** When you **sneeze**, you suddenly take a breath and blow it noisily down your nose, because there is a tickle in your nose or you have a cold.

NOUN **2** the action or sound of sneezing

sniff sniffs, sniffing, sniffed

VERB When you **sniff**, you breathe in air through your nose hard enough to make a sound.

snigger sniggers, sniggering, sniggered

VERB If you **snigger**, you laugh quietly and disrespectfully.

snip snips, snipping, snipped
VERB If you **snip** something, you make small, quick cuts in it or through it.

sniper snipers
NOUN a person who shoots at people from a hiding place

snivel snivels, snivelling, snivelled
VERB When someone **snivels**, they cry and sniff in an irritating way.

snob snobs
NOUN **1** someone who admires people considered to be socially superior and looks down on people considered to be socially inferior
2 someone who believes that they are better than other people
snobbery NOUN

snooker
NOUN a game played on a large table covered with smooth, green cloth. Players score points by hitting differently coloured balls into pockets using a long stick called a cue.

snoop snoops, snooping, snooped
VERB INFORMAL If you **snoop**, you secretly look round a place to find out things.

snooze snoozes, snoozing, snoozed
VERB **1** INFORMAL If you **snooze**, you sleep lightly for a short time, especially during the day.
NOUN **2** INFORMAL a short, light sleep

snore snores, snoring, snored
VERB When a sleeping person **snores**, they make a loud noise each time they breathe.

snorkel snorkels, snorkelling, snorkelled
NOUN **1** a tube you can breathe through when you are swimming just under the surface of the sea
VERB **2** If you **snorkel**, you swim underwater using a snorkel.
snorkelling NOUN

snout snouts
NOUN An animal's **snout** is its nose.

snow snows, snowing, snowed
NOUN **1** soft, white flakes of ice that fall from the sky in cold weather

VERB **2** When it **snows**, snow falls from the sky.

snowball snowballs
NOUN a ball of snow for throwing

snowboard snowboards
NOUN a board you stand on to slide across snow
snowboarding NOUN

snowflake snowflakes
NOUN a flake of snow

snowman snowmen
NOUN a pile of snow shaped like a person

snowstorm snowstorms
NOUN a storm with snow falling

snub snubs, snubbing, snubbed
VERB **1** If you **snub** someone, you behave rudely towards them, especially by making an insulting remark or ignoring them.
ADJECTIVE **2** A **snub** nose is short and turned-up.

snug
ADJECTIVE **1** A **snug** place is warm and comfortable.
2 If you are **snug**, you are warm and comfortable.
3 If something is a **snug** fit, it fits very closely.
snugly ADVERB

snuggle snuggles, snuggling, snuggled
VERB If you **snuggle** somewhere, you cuddle up more closely to something or someone.

so
ADVERB **1** also ● *She laughed, and* ***so*** *did the teacher.*
2 very ● *You are* ***so*** *funny.*
CONJUNCTION **3** therefore, for that reason
● *I was cold,* ***so*** *I put on a coat.*

soak soaks, soaking, soaked
VERB **1** If you **soak** something, or leave it to **soak**, you put it in a liquid and leave it there for some time.
2 When a liquid **soaks** something, it makes it very wet.
3 When something **soaks** up a liquid,

A B C D E F G H I J K L M N O P Q R S T U V W X Y Z

the liquid is drawn up into it. ● *The cloth* ***soaked*** *up the spilt milk.*

soap **soaps**
NOUN a substance used with water for washing yourself ● *a bar of* **soap**

soap opera **soap operas**
NOUN a popular television drama serial about people's daily lives
[so called because soap manufacturers were often sponsors of these]

soar **soars, soaring, soared**
VERB If something **soars** into the air, it rises high into it.
soaring ADJECTIVE

sob **sobs, sobbing, sobbed**
VERB When someone **sobs**, they cry noisily, gulping in short breaths.

sober **soberer, soberest**
ADJECTIVE **1** not drunk
2 serious and thoughtful

soccer
NOUN a game played by two teams of eleven players kicking a ball in an attempt to score goals

sociable
ADJECTIVE **Sociable** people are friendly and enjoy talking to other people.
SYNONYM: friendly

social
ADJECTIVE **1** to do with society or life within a society ● *women from similar* **social** *backgrounds*
2 to do with leisure activities that involve meeting other people ● *We should organize more* **social** *events.*

social networking site **social networking sites**
NOUN a website that lets people connect, chat and share photographs, videos, etc

society **societies**
NOUN **1** the community of people in a particular country or region
2 an organization for people who have the same interests

sock **socks**
NOUN a piece of clothing that covers your foot and ankle

socket **sockets**
NOUN **1** a place on a wall or on a piece of electrical equipment into which you can put a plug or bulb
2 any hollow part of something, or an opening into which another part fits ● *eye* **sockets**

sofa **sofas**
NOUN a long comfortable seat, with a back and arms, for two or more people
[from Arabic *suffah* meaning an upholstered raised platform]

soft **softer, softest**
ADJECTIVE **1** not hard, stiff or firm ● *a* **soft** *towel*
2 very gentle ● *a* **soft** *breeze*

soften **softens, softening, softened**
VERB When you **soften** something, you make it softer.

software
NOUN computer programs

soggy **soggier, soggiest**
ADJECTIVE unpleasantly wet

soil **soils, soiling, soiled**
NOUN **1** the top layer of the land surface of the earth, in which plants can grow
VERB **2** If you **soil** something, you make it dirty.

solar
ADJECTIVE to do with the sun ● **solar** *energy*

solar system
NOUN the sun and all the planets, comets and asteroids that orbit round it

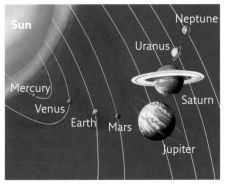

sold
VERB the past tense and past participle of **sell**

soldier soldiers
NOUN a person in an army

sole soles
NOUN The **sole** of your foot or shoe is the underneath part.

solemn
ADJECTIVE serious rather than cheerful

solicitor solicitors
NOUN a lawyer who gives legal advice and prepares legal documents and cases

solid solids
NOUN **1** a substance that is not a liquid or gas
2 an object that is hard or firm
ADJECTIVE **3** You say that something is **solid** when it does not have any space in it. • a **solid** steel bar
4 A **solid** shape is a three-dimensional shape such as a cylinder or a cone.

solidify solidifies, solidifying, solidified
VERB If something **solidifies**, it changes from a liquid into a solid.

solitary
ADJECTIVE alone

solo solos
NOUN **1** a piece of music played or sung by one person alone
ADJECTIVE **2** A **solo** performance or activity is done by one person alone.
ADVERB **3** alone • to sail **solo** around the world

solstice solstices
NOUN one of two times in the year when the sun is at its furthest point south or north of the equator

soluble
ADJECTIVE able to be dissolved in a liquid
• **soluble** aspirin

solution solutions
NOUN **1** a way of dealing with a problem or difficult situation
2 the answer to a riddle or a puzzle

3 a liquid in which a solid substance has been dissolved

solve solves, solving, solved
VERB If you **solve** a problem or a question, you find a solution or answer to it.
SYNONYM: work out

sombre
ADJECTIVE **1 Sombre** colours are dark and dull.
2 A **sombre** person is serious, sad or gloomy.

some
ADJECTIVE OR PRONOUN You use **some** to refer to a quantity or number when you are not stating the exact quantity or number.
• There's **some** money on the table.

somebody
PRONOUN some person
See **someone**

somehow
ADVERB **1** You use **somehow** to say that you do not know how something was done or will be done. • You'll find a way of doing it **somehow**.
2 You use **somehow** to say that you do not know the reason for something.
• **Somehow** it didn't feel quite right.

someone
PRONOUN You use **someone** to refer to a person without saying exactly who you mean. • I need **someone** to help me.

somersault somersaults, somersaulting, somersaulted
NOUN **1** a forwards or backwards roll in which the head is placed on the ground and the body is brought over it
VERB **2** If you **somersault**, you perform a somersault.

something
PRONOUN You use **something** to refer to anything that is not a person, without saying exactly what it is. • There was **something** wrong.

sometimes
ADVERB occasionally, rather than always or never

a
b
c
d
e
f
g
h
i
j
k
l
m
n
o
p
q
r
s
t
u
v
w
x
y
z

somewhere
ADVERB **1 Somewhere** is used to refer to a place without stating exactly where it is.
• *a flat **somewhere** in the city*
2 Somewhere is used when giving an approximate amount, number or time.
• *It was **somewhere** between four and five o'clock.*

son sons
NOUN a person's male child

song songs
NOUN **1** a piece of music with words that are sung to the music
2 singing • *I was woken by the bird **song** early in the morning.*

sonnet sonnets
NOUN a poem with 14 lines that rhyme according to fixed patterns

soon sooner, soonest
ADVERB If something is going to happen **soon**, it will happen in a very short time.

soot
NOUN black powder that rises in the smoke from a fire
sooty ADJECTIVE

soothe soothes, soothing, soothed
VERB **1** If you **soothe** someone who is angry or upset, you make them calmer.
2 Something that **soothes** pain makes the pain less severe.

sophisticated
ADJECTIVE **1** A **sophisticated** person is experienced in social situations and able to talk easily about anything.
SYNONYMS: cultured, urbane
2 Something **sophisticated** is made using advanced and complicated methods, or is able to do advanced and complicated things. • *a **sophisticated** new telescope*
SYNONYM: highly developed

sorcerer sorcerers
NOUN someone in stories who performs magic by using the power of evil spirits

sore sorer, sorest; sores
ADJECTIVE **1** If part of your body is **sore**, it causes you pain and is uncomfortable.
• *I have a cough and a **sore** throat.*
SYNONYMS: painful, sensitive, tender
NOUN **2** a painful place where your skin has become infected

sorrow sorrows
NOUN deep sadness or regret

sorry sorrier, sorriest
ADJECTIVE If you are **sorry** about something, you feel sadness, regret or sympathy because of it.

sort sorts, sorting, sorted
NOUN **1** Different **sorts** of something are different types of it.
SYNONYM: kind
VERB **2** If you **sort** things, you arrange them into different groups.

sort out
VERB If you **sort out** a problem or misunderstanding, you find a solution to it.

SOS
NOUN a signal appealing urgently for help from someone whose life is in danger. **SOS** stands for Save Our Souls.

sought
VERB the past tense and past participle of **seek**

soul souls
NOUN the spiritual part of a person that some people think continues after the body is dead

sound sounds, sounding, sounded
NOUN **1 Sound** is everything that can be heard.
2 something particular that you hear
• *the **sound** of a door opening*
VERB **3** If something **sounds**, or if you **sound** it, it makes a noise. • *He **sounded** his horn to warn them.*

sound effect sound effects
NOUN **Sound effects** are added to films or plays to make them sound more life-like.

soundproof soundproofs, soundproofing, soundproofed
ADJECTIVE **1** If a room is **soundproof**,

sound cannot get into it or out of it.
VERB **2** To **soundproof** something means to make it soundproof.

soup soups
NOUN liquid food made by boiling meat, fish or vegetables in water

sour
ADJECTIVE **1** If something is **sour**, it has a sharp, acid taste like lemons or vinegar.
2 If milk is **sour**, it is no longer fresh.

source sources
NOUN The **source** of something is the person, place or thing that it originally comes from. • the **source** of the river

south
NOUN one of the four main points of the compass. If you face the point where the sun rises, **south** is on your right. The abbreviation for **south** is S.

south-east
NOUN, ADJECTIVE OR ADVERB midway between south and east. The abbreviation for **south-east** is SE.

southern
ADJECTIVE in or from the south

south-west
NOUN, ADJECTIVE OR ADVERB midway between south and west. The abbreviation for **south-west** is SW.

souvenir souvenirs
NOUN something you keep to remind you of a holiday, place or event

sovereign sovereigns
NOUN **1** a king, queen or royal ruler of a country
2 In the past, a **sovereign** was a British gold coin worth one pound.

sow sows, sowing, sowed, sown
Rhymes with "cow" NOUN **1** a female pig
Rhymes with "go" VERB **2** If you **sow** seeds, you put them in the ground so they can grow.

soya
NOUN a protein derived from **soya** beans. **Soya** beans are used to make **soya** flour, margarine, oil and milk.

space spaces
NOUN **1** the area that is empty or available in a place, building or container
2 the area beyond the earth's atmosphere surrounding the stars and planets
3 a gap between two things

spacecraft spacecraft
NOUN a vehicle for travelling in outer space

spaceship spaceships
NOUN a spacecraft

spacesuit spacesuits
NOUN protective clothing that astronauts wear in outer space

spacious
ADJECTIVE having or providing a lot of space

spade spades
NOUN **1** a tool with a flat metal blade and a long handle used for digging
2 Spades is one of the four suits in a pack of playing cards. It is marked by a black symbol in the shape of a heart-shaped leaf with a stem.

spaghetti
NOUN long, thin pieces of pasta [the plural of the Italian word *spaghetto* meaning string]

span spans, spanning, spanned
NOUN **1** a period of time • *looking back over a **span** of 40 years*
2 the total length of something from one end to the other • *Seagulls have a large wing **span**.*
3 Your **span** is the distance from the top of your thumb to the top of your little finger when your hand is stretched.
VERB **4** If something **spans** a particular length of time, a distance or a gap, it stretches across it. • *The bridge **spanned** the width of the river.*

spaniel spaniels
NOUN a breed of dog with long ears and silky fur

spank spanks, spanking, spanked
VERB If a child is **spanked**, it is punished by being slapped, usually on the leg or bottom.

A
B
C
D
E
F
G
H
I
J
K
L
M
N
O
P
Q
R
S
T
U
V
W
X
Y
Z

spanner spanners
NOUN a tool with a specially shaped end that fits round a nut to turn it

spare spares, sparing, spared
ADJECTIVE **1** extra, or kept to be used when it is needed • *There is a **spare** tyre in the boot of the car.*
VERB **2** If you **spare** something for a particular purpose, you make it available. • *Can you **spare** the time to help me later?*
3 If someone is **spared** an unpleasant experience, they are prevented from suffering it.

spark sparks
NOUN a tiny, bright piece of burning material thrown up by a fire

sparkle sparkles, sparkling, sparkled
VERB If something **sparkles**, it shines with a lot of small, bright points of light.
SYNONYMS: glitter, twinkle

sparrow sparrows
NOUN a common, small bird with brown and grey feathers

sparse sparser, sparsest
ADJECTIVE small in number or amount and spread out over an area

spatter spatters, spattering, spattered
VERB If something **spatters** a surface, it covers it with small drops of liquid.

spawn spawns, spawning, spawned
NOUN **1** a jelly-like substance containing the eggs of fish or amphibians
VERB **2** When fish or amphibians **spawn**, they lay their eggs.

speak speaks, speaking, spoke, spoken
VERB **1** When you **speak**, you use your voice to say words.
SYNONYMS: say, talk, utter
2 If you **speak** a foreign language, you know it and can use it.

speaker speakers
NOUN **1** a person who is speaking or making a speech
2 the part of a radio or stereo system from which the sound comes

spear spears, spearing, speared
NOUN **1** a weapon consisting of a long pole with a sharp point
VERB **2** To **spear** something means to pierce it with a spear or other pointed object.

special
ADJECTIVE Someone or something **special** is different from other people or things, often in a way that makes it more important or better than others.

specialist specialists
NOUN an expert in a particular subject

species
NOUN a group of plants or animals that have the same main features and are able to breed with each other

The plural of *species* is *species*.

specimen specimens
NOUN an example or small amount of something that gives an idea of what the whole is like • *a **specimen** of your writing*

speck specks
NOUN **1** a very small stain
2 a very small amount of something

speckled
ADJECTIVE Something that is **speckled** is covered in small marks or spots.

spectacle spectacles
NOUN **1** a grand and impressive event or performance
PLURAL NOUN **2** Someone's **spectacles** are their glasses.

spectacular
ADJECTIVE very impressive or dramatic

spectator spectators
NOUN a person who watches an event or a show

spectrum spectra or spectrums
NOUN the range of different colours

produced when light passes through a prism or a drop of water. A rainbow shows the colours in a **spectrum**.

speech speeches
NOUN **1** the ability to speak or the act of speaking
2 a formal talk given to an audience

speech bubble speech bubbles
NOUN a line around words, used in comic strips or cartoons to show what characters are saying

speechless
ADJECTIVE unable to speak

speech marks
PLURAL NOUN punctuation marks (" " ' ') used in written texts to show when someone is speaking

speed speeds, speeding, sped or speeded
NOUN **1** the rate at which something moves or happens
2 very fast movement or travel
VERB **3** If you **speed** somewhere, you move or travel there quickly.
4 Someone who is **speeding** is driving a vehicle faster than the legal speed limit.

speedboat speedboats
NOUN a fast motorboat

spell spells, spelling, spelt or spelled
VERB **1** When you **spell** a word, you name or write its letters in order.
NOUN **2** a short period of something
• We expect a **spell** of good weather.
3 words or rhymes used to perform magic

You can write either *spelt* or *spelled* as the past form of *spell*.

spellbound
ADJECTIVE If you are **spellbound**, you are so fascinated by something that you cannot think of anything else.

spellcheck spellchecks, spellchecking, spellchecked
VERB If you **spellcheck** a document, you run a program over it to find any words that have not been spelt correctly.

spelling spellings
NOUN the correct order of letters in a word

spend spends, spending, spent
VERB **1** When you **spend** money, you buy things with it.
2 If you **spend** time or energy, you use it.

sphere spheres
NOUN a perfectly round object, such as a ball

sphinx sphinxes
NOUN In mythology, the **sphinx** was a monster with a person's head and a lion's body.

spice spices
NOUN a substance obtained from a plant, often in the form of a powder or a seed, and added to food to give it flavour

spicy spicier, spiciest
ADJECTIVE strongly flavoured with spices

spider spiders
NOUN a small animal with eight legs. Some **spiders** spin webs to catch insects for food, others hunt.

spike spikes
NOUN something long and sharply pointed. Runners often have **spikes** on the soles of their shoes to stop them slipping.

spill spills, spilling, spilled or spilt
VERB If you **spill** something, or if it **spills**, it accidentally falls or runs out of a container.

You can write either *spilled* or *spilt* as the past form of *spill*.

spin spins, spinning, spun
VERB **1** If someone or something **spins**, it turns quickly around a central point.
• The earth **spins** on its own axis.
NOUN **2** a rapid turn around a central point

spinach
NOUN a vegetable with large green leaves

spine spines
NOUN **1** the row of bones down the middle of your back
SYNONYM: backbone
2 a spike on a plant or an animal

• *Porcupines are covered in **spines**.*
3 the part of a book where the pages are joined together

spiral **spirals**
NOUN **1** a continuous curve that winds round and round, with each curve moving further out or further up
ADJECTIVE **2** in the shape of a spiral

spire **spires**
NOUN the pointed structure on top of a steeple

spirit **spirits**
NOUN **1** the part of you that is not physical and that is connected with the way you are
2 a ghost or supernatural being
3 liveliness, energy and self-confidence

spiritual
ADJECTIVE **1** to do with people's thoughts and beliefs, rather than their bodies and physical surroundings
2 to do with people's religious beliefs

spit **spits, spitting, spat**
VERB **1** If you **spit**, you forcefully send saliva out of your mouth.
NOUN **2** saliva
3 a long piece of metal or wood that you push through meat so that it can be hung over a fire to cook
4 a long, flat, narrow piece of land sticking out into the sea

spite
NOUN **1** the desire to deliberately hurt or upset somebody
PHRASE **2 In spite of** is used to begin a statement that makes the rest of what you are saying seem surprising. • *In spite of the rain, they watched the fireworks outside.*

spiteful
ADJECTIVE A **spiteful** person does or says nasty things to people to hurt them.
spitefully ADVERB

splash **splashes, splashing, splashed**
VERB **1** If you **splash** around in water, you make the water fly around in a noisy way.
NOUN **2** the sound made when something hits or falls into water

splendid
ADJECTIVE very good or very impressive

splint **splints**
NOUN a straight piece of metal or wood that is tied to a broken arm or leg to stop it moving

splinter **splinters, splintering, splintered**
NOUN **1** a thin, sharp piece of wood or glass that has broken off a larger piece
VERB **2** If something **splinters**, it breaks into thin, sharp pieces.

split **splits, splitting, split**
VERB If something **splits**, or if you **split** it, it divides into two or more parts.

split second **split seconds**
NOUN an extremely short period of time

splutter **splutters, spluttering, spluttered**
VERB **1** If you **splutter**, you speak in a confused way because you are embarrassed or angry.
2 If someone or something **splutters**, they make a series of short, coughing, spitting noises.

spoil **spoils, spoiling, spoiled** or **spoilt**
VERB **1** To **spoil** something means to damage it or stop it being successful or satisfactory. • *My holiday was **spoiled** by rain.*
2 To **spoil** children means to give them everything they want, making them selfish.

You can write either *spoiled* or *spoilt* as the past form of *spoil*.

spoilsport **spoilsports**
NOUN someone who spoils other people's fun

spoke **spokes**
NOUN **1** The **spokes** of a wheel are the

bars that connect the hub to the rim.
VERB **2** the past tense of **speak**

spoken
VERB the past participle of **speak**

sponge **sponges**
NOUN **1** a soft, natural or man-made material with lots of small holes, used for washing yourself
2 an animal found in the sea that has a body made up of many cells
3 a soft, light cake or pudding
spongy ADJECTIVE

sponsor **sponsors, sponsoring, sponsored**
VERB **1** If an organization **sponsors** something, such as an event or someone's training, it gives money to pay for it.
2 If you **sponsor** someone who is doing something for charity, you agree to give them a sum of money for the charity if they manage to do it.
NOUN **3** a person or organization that sponsors something or someone

spontaneous
ADJECTIVE something that is not planned or arranged
spontaneously ADVERB

spooky **spookier, spookiest**
ADJECTIVE frightening and creepy

spoon **spoons**
NOUN an object shaped like a small shallow bowl with a long handle, used for eating, stirring and serving food

sport **sports**
NOUN games and other enjoyable activities that need physical effort and skill

spot **spots, spotting, spotted**
NOUN **1** a small, round, coloured area on a surface
2 a pimple on a person's skin
3 a small amount of something
4 a particular place
VERB **5** If you **spot** something, you suddenly see it.
PHRASE **6** If you do something **on the spot**, you do it immediately.

spotless
ADJECTIVE perfectly clean

spotlight **spotlights**
NOUN a powerful light that can be directed to light up a small area • stage **spotlights**

spotty **spottier, spottiest**
ADJECTIVE marked with spots

spouse **spouses**
NOUN Someone's **spouse** is the person they are married to.

spout **spouts, spouting, spouted**
VERB **1** When liquid or flame **spouts** out of something, it shoots out in a long stream.
NOUN **2** a tube or opening from which liquid can pour
VERB **3** When someone **spouts** what they have learned, they say it in a boring way.

sprain **sprains, spraining, sprained**
VERB **1** If you **sprain** a joint, you accidentally damage it by twisting it violently.
NOUN **2** the injury caused by spraining a joint

sprang
VERB the past tense of **spring**

sprawl **sprawls, sprawling, sprawled**
VERB **1** If you **sprawl** somewhere, you sit or lie there with your legs and arms spread out. • She **sprawled** on the bed reading her book.
2 A place that **sprawls** is spread out over a large area.

spray **sprays, spraying, sprayed**
NOUN **1** many small drops of liquid splashed or forced into the air
2 a liquid kept under pressure in a container
VERB **3** If you **spray** a liquid over something, you cover it with drops of the liquid. • We **sprayed** the dry lawn with water from the hose pipe.

spread **spreads, spreading, spread**
VERB **1** If you **spread** a substance on a surface, you put a thin layer of it on the surface. • **Spread** the butter on the bread before you make the sandwich.

379

2 If you **spread** something out, you open it out or arrange it so that it can be seen or used easily. • He **spread** the map out on his knees.

3 If something **spreads**, it gradually reaches more people. • The news **spread** quickly.

sprightly **sprightlier, sprightliest**
ADJECTIVE lively and active

spring **springs, springing, sprang, sprung**
NOUN **1** the season between winter and summer, when most plants start to grow
2 a coil of wire that returns to its original shape after being pressed or pulled
3 a place where water naturally comes up through the ground
VERB **4** If you **spring**, you jump upwards or forwards.

springboard **springboards**
NOUN a springy board on which a gymnast or diver jumps to gain height

springbok **springboks**
NOUN a small South African antelope that moves in leaps

sprinkle **sprinkles, sprinkling, sprinkled**
VERB If you **sprinkle** a liquid or powder over something, you scatter it over it.

sprint **sprints, sprinting, sprinted**
NOUN **1** a short, fast race
VERB **2** If you **sprint**, you run fast over a short distance.

sprout **sprouts, sprouting, sprouted**
VERB **1** When something **sprouts**, it starts to grow.
2 If things **sprout** up, they appear very quickly.
NOUN **3** an abbreviation of Brussels sprout

sprung
VERB the past participle of **spring**

spun
VERB the past tense and past participle of **spin**

spur **spurs, spurring, spurred**
VERB **1** If you **spur** someone on, you encourage them.

NOUN **2** a sharp device worn on the heel of a rider's boot to urge the horse to go faster

spurt **spurts, spurting, spurted**
NOUN **1** a jet of liquid or flame
2 a sudden increase in speed
VERB **3** If a liquid **spurts**, it gushes in a sudden stream. • Water **spurted** out of the hose.

spy **spies, spying, spied**
NOUN **1** a person sent to find out secret information about a country or organization
VERB **2** Someone who **spies** tries to find out secret information about another country or organization.
3 If you **spy** on someone, you watch them secretly.

squabble **squabbles, squabbling, squabbled**
VERB **1** When people **squabble**, they quarrel about something unimportant.
NOUN **2** a quarrel

squad **squads**
NOUN a small group of people chosen to do a particular activity

squadron **squadrons**
NOUN a section of one of the armed forces, especially the air force
[from Italian squadrone meaning soldiers drawn up in a square formation]

squalid
ADJECTIVE dirty, untidy and in bad condition

squander **squanders, squandering, squandered**
VERB If you **squander** money or resources, you waste them.

square **squares**
NOUN **1** a plane shape with four equal sides and four right angles
2 In a town or city, a **square** is a flat, open area with buildings or streets around the edge.
ADJECTIVE **3** shaped like a **square**
[from Latin quadra meaning square]

squash squashes, squashing, squashed
VERB If you **squash** something, you press it so that it becomes flat or loses its shape.

squat squats, squatting, squatted; squatter, squattest
VERB **1** If you **squat** down, you crouch, balancing on your feet with your legs bent.
2 A person who **squats** in an unused building lives there without permission and without paying.
ADJECTIVE **3** short and thick

squawk squawks, squawking, squawked
VERB **1** When a bird **squawks**, it makes a loud, harsh noise.
NOUN **2** a loud, harsh noise made by a bird

squeak squeaks, squeaking, squeaked
VERB **1** If something or someone **squeaks**, they make a short, high-pitched sound.
NOUN **2** a short, high-pitched sound

squeal squeals, squealing, squealed
VERB **1** When things or people **squeal**, they make long, high-pitched sounds.
NOUN **2** a long, high-pitched sound

squeamish
ADJECTIVE easily upset by unpleasant sights or situations

squeeze squeezes, squeezing, squeezed
VERB **1** When you **squeeze** something, you press it firmly from two sides.
2 If you **squeeze** somewhere, you force yourself into a small space or through a gap.
3 If you **squeeze** something somewhere, you force it into a small space.

squelch squelches, squelching, squelched
VERB If something **squelches**, it makes a wet, sucking sound.

squid squids
NOUN an animal that lives in the sea, with a long, soft body and ten limbs

squiggle squiggles
NOUN a wiggly line

squint squints, squinting, squinted
VERB **1** If you **squint**, you screw up your eyes to look at something.
NOUN **2** If someone has a **squint**, their eyes look in different directions from each other.

squirm squirms, squirming, squirmed
VERB If you **squirm**, you wriggle and twist your body about, usually because you are nervous or embarrassed.

squirrel squirrels
NOUN a small, furry rodent with a long, bushy tail

squirt squirts, squirting, squirted
VERB **1** If a liquid **squirts**, or you **squirt** it, it comes out of a narrow opening in a thin, fast stream.
NOUN **2** a thin, fast stream of liquid

stab stabs, stabbing, stabbed
VERB To **stab** someone means to wound them by pushing a knife into their body.

stable stables
NOUN **1** a building in which horses are kept
ADJECTIVE **2** Something that is **stable** cannot be moved or shaken.
3 If someone is **stable**, they are level-headed and dependable.

stack stacks, stacking, stacked
NOUN **1** a pile of things, one on top of the other
VERB **2** If you **stack** items, you pile them up neatly.

stadium stadiums
NOUN a sports ground with rows of seats around it for spectators

staff **staffs**

NOUN the people who work for an organization

stag **stags**

NOUN an adult male deer

stage **stages, staging, staged**

NOUN **1** In a theatre, the **stage** is the raised platform where the actors or entertainers perform.

VERB **2** If someone **stages** a play or event, they organize it or present it.

stagger **staggers, staggering, staggered**

VERB **1** If you **stagger**, you walk unsteadily, for example because you are ill.

2 If something **staggers** you, it amazes you.

3 If events are **staggered**, they are arranged so that they do not all happen at the same time.

stagnant

ADJECTIVE **Stagnant** water is still rather than flowing, and is often smelly and dirty.

stain **stains**

NOUN a mark on something that is difficult or impossible to clean off

stair **stairs**

NOUN one of a set of steps, usually inside a building going from one floor to another

staircase **staircases**

NOUN a set of stairs

stake **stakes, staking, staked**

PHRASE **1** If something is **at stake**, it might be lost or damaged if something else is not successful. • *The cup was at stake if he missed the goal.*

VERB **2** If you say you would **stake** your money, life or reputation on the result of something, you mean you would risk it.

stalactite **stalactites**

NOUN a stony spike hanging down like an icicle from the ceiling of a cave

stalagmite **stalagmites**

NOUN a pointed piece of rock standing on the floor of a cave

stalactites and stalagmites in a cave

stale **staler, stalest**

ADJECTIVE **Stale** food or air is no longer fresh.

SYNONYMS: fusty, musty, old

stalk **stalks, stalking, stalked**

NOUN **1** The **stalk** of a flower or leaf is its stem.

VERB **2** To **stalk** a person or an animal means to follow them quietly in order to catch, kill or observe them. • *The cat is stalking the bird in the garden.*

stall **stalls, stalling, stalled**

NOUN **1** a large table displaying goods for sale or information

PLURAL NOUN **2** In a theatre, the **stalls** are the seats at the lowest level, in front of the stage.

VERB **3** When a vehicle **stalls**, the engine suddenly stops.

stallion **stallions**

NOUN an adult male horse that can be used for breeding

stamen **stamens**

NOUN the part of a flower that produces pollen

stamina

NOUN the physical or mental energy needed to do something for a very long time • *Running a marathon takes determination and stamina.*

stammer stammers, stammering, stammered

VERB **1** When someone **stammers**, they speak with difficulty, repeating words and sounds and hesitating.

NOUN **2** Someone who has a **stammer** tends to stammer when they speak.

stamp stamps, stamping, stamped

NOUN **1** a small piece of paper that you stick on a letter or parcel before posting it, to prove that you have paid the postage

VERB **2** To **stamp** a piece of paper means to make a mark on it using a small block with a pattern cut into it. • *He stamped her passport.*

3 If you **stamp**, you lift your foot and put it down hard on the ground.

stamp out

VERB To **stamp out** something means to put an end to it. • *We must try to stamp out this kind of behaviour.*

stampede stampedes, stampeding, stampeded

VERB **1** When a group of animals **stampede**, they rush forward in a wild, uncontrolled way.

NOUN **2** a group of animals stampeding

stand stands, standing, stood

VERB **1** If you are **standing**, you are upright with your weight on your feet.

2 If something **stands** somewhere, that is where it is. • *The house stands on top of a hill.*

3 If you cannot **stand** someone or something, you do not like them at all.

4 If you **stand** in an election, you are a candidate.

NOUN **5** A **stand** at a sports ground is a building where people can watch what is happening.

stand up

VERB When you **stand up**, you get into a standing position.

standard standards

NOUN **1** how good something is

2 an officially agreed level against which things can be measured or judged

standstill

NOUN a complete stop

stank

VERB the past tense of **stink**

stanza stanzas

NOUN a verse of a poem

staple staples, stapling, stapled

NOUN **1** a small piece of wire that holds sheets of paper firmly together. You insert it with a device called a stapler.

VERB **2** If you **staple** sheets of paper, you fasten them together with staples.

star stars

NOUN **1** a large ball of burning gases in space that appears as a point of light in the sky at night. Our sun is a **star**.

2 a shape with several points, usually five or six, sticking out in a regular pattern

3 a famous actor, sports player or musician

starboard

ADJECTIVE OR NOUN The **starboard** side of a ship is the right-hand side when you are facing the front.

starch starches

NOUN **1** a substance found in foods such as bread, rice, pasta and potatoes that gives you energy

2 a substance used for stiffening fabric

stare stares, staring, stared

VERB **1** If you **stare** at something, you look at it for a long time.

NOUN **2** a long, fixed look at something

starfish starfishes or starfish

NOUN a star-shaped animal found in the sea that has five pointed limbs

starling starlings

NOUN a common European bird with shiny dark feathers

start starts, starting, started

VERB **1** If you **start** something, you begin it.

NOUN **2** The **start** of something is the point or time at which it begins.

a
b
c
d
e
f
g
h
i
j
k
l
m
n
o
p
q
r
s
t
u
v
w
x
y
z

A
B
C
D
E
F
G
H
I
J
K
L
M
N
O
P
Q
R
S
T
U
V
W
X
Y
Z

startle **startles, startling, startled**
VERB If something sudden and unexpected **startles** you, it surprises you and give you a slight fright.

starve **starves, starving, starved**
VERB If people are **starving**, they are suffering from a serious lack of food and are likely to die.

state **states, stating, stated**
NOUN **1** The **state** of something or someone is their condition, or how they are.
2 Some countries are divided into regions called **states** that make some of their own laws.
3 You can call the government and the officials of a country the **state**. • Carmen received a pension from the **state**.
VERB **4** If you **state** something, you say it or write it clearly, especially in a formal way. • Please **state** your name and address.

statement **statements**
NOUN something you say or write that gives information in a formal way

static
ADJECTIVE **1** never moving or changing • The temperature is fairly **static**.
NOUN **2** an electrical charge caused by friction

station **stations**
NOUN **1** a building where trains or buses stop to let passengers on and off
2 A building that is used by people such as the police and fire brigade. • police **station**

stationary
ADJECTIVE not moving • a **stationary** car
SYNONYM: motionless

stationery
NOUN paper, pens and other writing equipment

statistics
PLURAL NOUN facts worked out by looking at information that is given in numbers • They gathered **statistics** about journeys to school.

statue **statues**
NOUN a sculpture, often of a person

stay **stays, staying, stayed**
VERB **1** If you **stay** in one place, you do not move away from it.
2 If you **stay** with a friend, you spend time with them as a visitor.

steady **steadier, steadiest**
ADJECTIVE firm and not moving about • She made sure the ladder was **steady** before she climbed up it.
SYNONYMS: firm, secure, stable

steak **steaks**
NOUN a large, good-quality piece of beef or fish

steal **steals, stealing, stole, stolen**
VERB If someone **steals** something, they take it without permission and without meaning to return it.

steam
NOUN the hot vapour formed when water boils

steam-engine **steam-engines**
NOUN any engine that is powered by steam

steel
NOUN a very strong metal made mainly from iron

steel band **steel bands**
NOUN a group of people who play music on special metal drums

steep **steeper, steepest**
ADJECTIVE A **steep** slope rises sharply and is difficult to go up.

steeple **steeples**
NOUN a tall, pointed structure above a church roof

steer **steers, steering, steered**
VERB When someone **steers** a vehicle or boat, they control it so that it goes in the direction they want.

stem **stems**
NOUN the thin, usually upright, part of a plant that grows above the ground and on which the leaves and flowers grow

stencil **stencils, stencilling, stencilled**
NOUN **1** a thin sheet of card, metal or plastic with a pattern cut out of it. The pattern can be copied onto another surface by painting over the **stencil**.
VERB **2** If you **stencil** a design onto a surface, you create it using a stencil.

step **steps, stepping, stepped**
NOUN **1** the movement of lifting your foot and putting it down again when you are walking, running or dancing
2 one of the places at different levels that you put your feet on when you go up and down a ladder or stairs
VERB **3** If you **step** in a particular direction, you take a step there.

stepbrother **stepbrothers**
NOUN the son of someone's stepmother or stepfather

stepchild **stepchildren**
NOUN a stepdaughter or stepson

stepdaughter **stepdaughters**
NOUN someone's daughter by their wife's or husband's previous marriage

stepfather **stepfathers**
NOUN a man who is married to your mother but who is not your natural father

stepmother **stepmothers**
NOUN a woman who is married to your father but who is not your natural mother

stepsister **stepsisters**
NOUN the daughter of someone's stepmother or stepfather

stepson **stepsons**
NOUN someone's son by their wife's or husband's previous marriage

stereo **stereos**
NOUN a piece of equipment that reproduces sound from records, tapes or CDs, directing the sound through two speakers

stereotype **stereotypes**
NOUN a simplified way people think of a particular type of person or thing
• the **stereotype** of the polite, industrious Japanese

sterile
ADJECTIVE **1** clean and free from germs
2 unable to have children or reproduce
sterility NOUN

sterling
NOUN the money system of Great Britain

stern **sterner, sternest**
ADJECTIVE very serious and strict

stethoscope **stethoscopes**
NOUN a device used by doctors to listen to a patient's heart and breathing, made of earpieces connected to a hollow tube and a small disc

stew **stews, stewing, stewed**
NOUN **1** a dish of small pieces of savoury food cooked together slowly in a liquid
VERB **2** If you **stew** meat, vegetables or fruit, you cook them slowly in a liquid. [from Middle English *stuen* meaning to take a very hot bath]

steward **stewards**
NOUN **1** a person who works on a ship or plane looking after passengers and serving meals
2 a person who helps to direct the public at events such as a race or a concert

stick **sticks, sticking, stuck**
NOUN **1** a long, thin piece of wood

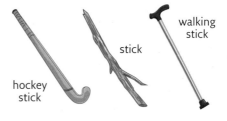
walking stick
hockey stick
stick

VERB **2** If you **stick** a long or pointed object into something, you push it in.
3 If you **stick** one thing to another, you attach it with glue or tape.
4 If something **sticks**, it becomes fixed or jammed.

stick out
VERB If something **sticks out**, it projects from something else.

stick up for
VERB INFORMAL If you **stick up for** someone or something, you support or defend them.

sticker stickers
NOUN a label with words or pictures on it for sticking on something

sticky stickier, stickiest
ADJECTIVE If something is **sticky**, it is covered with a substance that can stick to other things.

stiff stiffer, stiffest
ADJECTIVE **1** Something that is **stiff** is firm and not easily bent. • *a* **stiff** *piece of card*
2 If you feel **stiff**, your muscles or joints ache when you move.
3 Stiff behaviour is formal, and not friendly or relaxed.
4 difficult or severe • *It was a* **stiff** *competition.*

stifle stifles, stifling, stifled
VERB **1** If you feel **stifled**, you feel you cannot breathe properly.
2 If you **stifle** something, you stop it happening. • *She* **stifled** *a yawn.*
ADJECTIVE **3 Stifling** heat is very hot and makes it difficult to breathe. • *The atmosphere in the greenhouse was* **stifling**.

stile stiles
NOUN a step built in a hedge or wall so that people can climb over or through it

still stiller, stillest
ADVERB OR ADJECTIVE **1** If someone or something is **still**, they stay in the same position without moving.
2 You say **still** when something is the same as it was before. • *I've* **still** *got a headache.*
3 When the air is **still**, there is no wind.
4 A **still** drink is not fizzy.
5 even then • *I've worked all day and there's* **still** *more to do.*

stilts
PLURAL NOUN **1** long poles on which people balance or walk
2 long poles on which houses are sometimes built

stimulate stimulates, stimulating, stimulated
VERB **1** To **stimulate** something means to encourage it to begin or develop.
• *to* **stimulate** *interest*
SYNONYM: inspire
2 If something **stimulates** you, it interests and excites you.
SYNONYM: inspire

sting stings, stinging, stung
VERB **1** If an animal or plant **stings** you, it pricks your skin and hurts.
2 If a part of your body **stings**, you feel a sharp, tingling pain there.

stink stinks, stinking, stank, stunk
VERB **1** Something that **stinks** smells very unpleasant.
NOUN **2** a very unpleasant smell

stir stirs, stirring, stirred
VERB **1** When you **stir** a liquid, you move it around using a spoon or a stick.
2 If someone **stirs**, they move slightly, or start to move after sleeping or being still.
• *It was very noisy but the baby didn't* **stir**.

stirrup stirrups
NOUN one of the two metal loops hanging by leather straps from a horse's saddle, that you put your feet in when riding

stitch stitches, stitching, stitched
VERB **1** When you **stitch** pieces of material together, you use a needle and thread to sew them together.
NOUN **2** one of the pieces of thread that can be seen where material has been sewn
3 one of the pieces of thread that can be seen where skin has been sewn together to heal a wound • *He had eleven* **stitches** *in his lip.*
4 a sharp pain you feel in your side after running

stoat stoats
NOUN a small wild mammal with a long body, brown fur and a black-tipped tail

stock stocks
NOUN **1** the total amount of goods a shop has for sale
2 If you have a **stock** of things, you have a supply ready for use.

stocking **stockings**
NOUN one of a pair of long pieces of fine, stretchy fabric that cover a woman's leg and foot

stole **stoles**
VERB **1** the past tense of **steal**
NOUN **2** a shawl to cover a woman's shoulders

stolen
VERB the past participle of **steal**

stomach **stomachs**
NOUN **1** the organ inside your body where food is digested

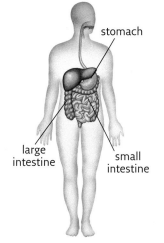

stomach

large intestine

small intestine

2 the front part of your body below your waist

stone **stones**
NOUN **1** the hard solid substance found in the ground and used for building
2 a small piece of rock
3 a unit of weight equal to 14 pounds or about 6.35 kilograms

stony **stonier, stoniest**
ADJECTIVE **Stony** ground has many stones in it.

stood
VERB the past tense and past participle of **stand**

stool **stools**
NOUN a seat with legs but no back or arms

stoop **stoops, stooping, stooped**
VERB **1** If you **stoop**, you bend your body forwards.
2 If you would not **stoop** to something, you would not disgrace yourself by doing it.

stop **stops, stopping, stopped**
VERB **1** If you **stop** doing something, you no longer do it.
2 If an activity **stops**, it comes to an end.
3 If you **stop** something, you prevent it from happening or continuing.
4 If people or things that are moving **stop**, they no longer move.
NOUN **5** a place where a bus, train or other vehicle stops to let passengers on and off

stopwatch **stopwatches**
NOUN a watch that can be started and stopped, that is used to time things such as races

storage
NOUN the keeping of something somewhere until it is needed

store **stores, storing, stored**
NOUN **1** a shop
2 a supply of something that is kept until it is needed
3 a place where things are kept while they are not used
VERB **4** When you **store** something somewhere, you keep it there until it is needed.

storey **storeys**
NOUN one of the floors or levels of a building

stork **storks**
NOUN a very large white and black bird with long red legs and a long bill. **Storks** live mainly near water in Eastern Europe and Africa.

storm **storms, storming, stormed**
NOUN **1** a period of bad weather, when there is heavy rain, a strong wind and often thunder and lightning
VERB **2** If soldiers **storm** a defended place, they make a surprise attack on it.
NOUN **3** If there is a **storm** of protest, many people complain loudly.

a b c d e f g h i j k l m n o p q r s t u v w x y z

A
B
C
D
E
F
G
H
I
J
K
L
M
N
O
P
Q
R
S
T
U
V
W
X
Y
Z

story **stories**
NOUN a telling of events, real or imaginary, spoken or written

stout **stouter, stoutest**
ADJECTIVE **1** rather fat
2 thick, strong and sturdy • *stout walking shoes*

stove **stoves**
NOUN a piece of equipment for heating a room or for cooking • *She warmed the milk on the stove.*

straddle **straddles, straddling, straddled**
VERB If you **straddle** something, you stand or sit with your legs either side of it.

straight **straighter, straightest**
ADJECTIVE OR ADVERB **1** continuing in the same direction without curving or bending
2 honest and direct • *a straight answer*
ADVERB **3** immediately and directly • *We will go straight to school.*
4 If you stand up **straight**, you stand upright.

straighten **straightens, straightening, straightened**
VERB If you **straighten** something, you make it straight.

straightforward
ADJECTIVE **1** easy to understand
2 honest and truthful

strain **strains, straining, strained**
ADJECTIVE **1** If you feel **strained**, you feel tense and anxious.
NOUN **2** If a **strain** is put on something, it is affected by a strong force that may damage it.
VERB **3** If you **strain** a muscle, you use it too much and injure it so that it is painful.
4 If you **strain** food or a mixture, you separate the solid parts from the liquid parts, for example by putting it through a sieve.

strait **straits**
NOUN a narrow strip of sea between two pieces of land, that connects two larger areas of sea

stranded
ADJECTIVE If someone or something is **stranded**, they are stuck somewhere and cannot leave. • *stranded on the rocks*

strange **stranger, strangest**
ADJECTIVE **1** unusual or unexpected
• *a strange dream*
2 not known, seen or experienced before
• *She was all alone in a strange country.*

stranger **strangers**
NOUN someone you have never met before

strangle **strangles, strangling, strangled**
VERB To **strangle** someone means to kill them by squeezing their throat to stop them breathing.

strap **straps**
NOUN a narrow piece of leather or cloth, used to fasten or hold things together

strategy **strategies**
NOUN a plan for achieving something

straw **straws**
NOUN **1** a hollow tube of paper or plastic that you use to suck a drink into your mouth
2 the dry, yellowish stalks of some crops

strawberry **strawberries**
NOUN a small red fruit with tiny seeds in its skin

stray **strays, straying, strayed**
VERB **1** When people or animals **stray**, they wander away from where they should be.
2 If your thoughts **stray**, you stop concentrating.
ADJECTIVE **3** A **stray** dog or cat is one that has wandered away from its home.
NOUN **4** a stray dog or cat

streak **streaks**
NOUN a long, narrow mark or stain

stream **streams, streaming, streamed**
NOUN **1** a small river
2 You can refer to a steady flow of something as a **stream**. • *a constant stream of children*

VERB **3** If something **streams**, it flows fast, without stopping. ● *Rain **streamed** down the windscreen.*

streamer **streamers**
NOUN a long piece of paper or ribbon used as a decoration

street **streets**
NOUN a road in a town or village, usually with buildings along it

strength
NOUN how strong or powerful someone or something is
SYNONYMS: might, force, power

strenuous
ADJECTIVE involving a lot of effort or energy

stress **stresses, stressing, stressed**
NOUN **1** worry and nervous tension
SYNONYMS: anxiety, pressure, strain
VERB **2** If you **stress** a point, you emphasize it and draw attention to how important it is.

stretch **stretches, stretching, stretched**
VERB **1** If you **stretch** something soft or elastic, you pull it to make it longer or bigger.
2 Something that **stretches** over an area covers the whole of that area.
● *Forests **stretched** the length of the valley.*
3 When you **stretch**, you move part of your body as far away from you as you can.
NOUN **4** an area of something ● *This is a quiet **stretch** of beach.*

stretcher **stretchers**
NOUN a long piece of material with a pole along each side, used to carry an injured person

strict **stricter, strictest**
ADJECTIVE **1** Someone who is **strict** controls other people very firmly.
2 exact or complete ● *We were given **strict** instructions.*

stride **strides, striding, strode, stridden**
VERB **1** If you **stride** along, you walk

quickly with long steps.
NOUN **2** a long step

strike **strikes, striking, struck**
VERB **1** If you **strike** something, you hit it with a lot of force.
2 If workers **strike**, they refuse to work because they want better working conditions or more money.
3 If you **strike** a match, you make a flame by rubbing it against something rough.

striking
ADJECTIVE very noticeable because of being unusual or attractive

string **strings**
NOUN **1** thin rope made of twisted threads
2 a row or series of similar things
● *a **string** of islands*

strip **strips, stripping, stripped**
NOUN **1** a long, narrow piece of something
VERB **2** If you **strip**, you take off all your clothes.

stripe **stripes**
NOUN a long, thin line of colour

strode
VERB the past tense of **stride**

stroke **strokes, stroking, stroked**
VERB **1** If you **stroke** something, you move your hand smoothly and gently over it.
NOUN **2** The **strokes** of a brush or pen are the movements that you make with it.
3 If someone has a **stroke**, a blood vessel in the brain bursts or gets blocked, possibly causing death or paralysis.
4 a style of swimming ● *My best **stroke** is the front crawl.*

stroll **strolls, strolling, strolled**
VERB **1** If you **stroll** along, you walk slowly in a relaxed way.
SYNONYMS: amble, saunter
NOUN **2** a slow, pleasurable walk
SYNONYMS: amble, saunter

strong **stronger, strongest**
ADJECTIVE **1** Someone who is **strong** has a lot of physical power.
2 You also say that someone is **strong**

a
b
c
d
e
f
g
h
i
j
k
l
m
n
o
p
q
r
s
t
u
v
w
x
y
z

389

when they are confident and have courage.

3 Strong objects are able to withstand rough treatment, and are not easily damaged.

4 great or intense ● *a strong wind*

struck

VERB the past tense and past participle of **strike**

structure structures

NOUN **1** The **structure** of something is the way it is made, built or organized.

2 something that has been built or put together

struggle struggles, struggling, struggled

VERB **1** If you **struggle** to do something difficult, you try hard to do it.

2 When people **struggle**, they twist and move violently to get free of something or someone.

NOUN **3** Something that is a **struggle** is difficult to achieve and takes a lot of effort.

stubble

NOUN **1** the short stalks remaining in the ground after a crop is harvested

2 If a man has **stubble** on his face, he has very short hair growing there because he has not shaved recently.

stubborn

ADJECTIVE Someone who is **stubborn** is determined not to change the way they think or how they do things.

SYNONYM: obstinate

stuck

ADJECTIVE **1** If something or someone is **stuck**, they cannot be moved.

2 If you are **stuck**, you cannot go on with your work because you are finding it too difficult.

VERB **3** the past tense and past participle of **stick**

stud studs

NOUN **1** a small piece of metal, or other material, fixed into something ● *Rachel wore gold studs in her ears.*

2 A male horse or other animal that is kept

for **stud** is kept for breeding purposes.

3 a place where horses are kept and bred

student students

NOUN a person studying at a university, college or school

studio studios

NOUN **1** a room where an artist works

2 a room containing special equipment where records, films, or radio or television programmes are made

studious

ADJECTIVE Someone who is **studious** studies hard or is fond of studying.

study studies, studying, studied

VERB **1** If you **study** a particular subject, you spend time learning about it.

2 If you **study** something, you look at it carefully.

NOUN **3** a room for studying or working in

stuff stuffs, stuffing, stuffed

NOUN **1** You can refer to a substance or a group of things as **stuff**. ● *She spread out her stuff on top of the table.*

VERB **2** If you **stuff** something somewhere, you push it there quickly and carelessly.

3 If you **stuff** something, you fill it with something else. ● *Mum stuffed the turkey.*

stuffy stuffier, stuffiest

ADJECTIVE **1** If it is **stuffy** in a room, there is not enough fresh air.

2 boring and old-fashioned

stumble stumbles, stumbling, stumbled

VERB **1** If you **stumble** while you are walking or running, you trip and nearly fall.

2 If you **stumble** when you are speaking, you hesitate or make mistakes.

stump stumps, stumping, stumped

NOUN **1** a small part of something that is left when the rest has gone ● *a tree stump*

2 In cricket, the **stumps** are the three upright wooden sticks that support the bails, forming the wicket.

VERB **3** If a question or problem **stumps** you, you cannot think of an answer or solution.

stun stuns, stunning, stunned
VERB **1** If you are **stunned**, or something **stuns** you, you are very shocked by it.
2 If something **stuns** a person or an animal, it knocks them unconscious.

stung
VERB the past tense and past participle of **sting**

stunk
VERB the past participle of **stink**

stunt stunts
NOUN an unusual or dangerous and exciting thing that someone does to get publicity or as part of a performance

stupid stupider, stupidest
ADJECTIVE If you are **stupid**, you are not sensible and do not make wise decisions.

sturdy sturdier, sturdiest
ADJECTIVE strong, firm and well built

stutter stutters, stuttering, stuttered
NOUN **1** Someone who has a **stutter** finds it difficult to speak smoothly and often repeats the beginning of words.
VERB **2** When someone **stutters**, they hesitate or repeat sounds when speaking.

sty sties
NOUN a hut with a yard where pigs are kept on a farm

style styles
NOUN **1** how something is done, made, said or written • *The food was cooked in Cantonese* **style**.
2 A person or place that has **style** is smart, elegant and fashionable.

sub-
PREFIX You add **sub-**to the beginning of a word to mean below or beneath. For example, something that is **sub**standard is below the required standard, and a **sub**heading comes somewhere below a main heading.

subheading subheadings
NOUN a title to a part of a larger section of a book. A chapter may have several sections in it, each with a **subheading**.

subject subjects, subjecting, subjected
*Said "***sub***-jekt" NOUN* **1** The **subject** of a book, programme or conversation is the thing or person it is about. • *Horses are the* **subject** *of this book.*
2 something that you learn about • *Maths is my favourite* **subject**.
3 The **subjects** of a country are the people who live there.
4 In grammar, the **subject** is the word or words representing the person or thing doing the action. For example, in the sentence *My cat keeps catching birds*, *my cat* is the **subject**.
*Said "***sub***-jekt" VERB* **5** If you **subject** someone to something, you make them experience it.

submarine submarines
NOUN a type of ship that can travel beneath the surface of the sea

submerge submerges, submerging, submerged
VERB To **submerge** means to go beneath the surface of a liquid, or to push something beneath the surface of a liquid.

submit submits, submitting, submitted
VERB **1** If you **submit** to something or someone, you give in to them.
2 If you **submit** something like a report or an essay, you hand it in.

subscribe subscribes, subscribing, subscribed
VERB If you **subscribe** to something, you regularly pay a sum of money to be a member of something or to receive a magazine.

subside subsides, subsiding, subsided
VERB **1** If something **subsides**, it sinks.
2 To **subside** is to become quiet or back to normal after a fuss.

a
b
c
d
e
f
g
h
i
j
k
l
m
n
o
p
q
r
s
t
u
v
w
x
y
z

A
B
C
D
E
F
G
H
I
J
K
L
M
N
O
P
Q
R
S
T
U
V
W
X
Y
Z

substance substances

NOUN anything that is a solid, a powder, a liquid or a paste

SYNONYM: material

substantial

ADJECTIVE **1** very large in degree or amount **2** large and strongly built

substitute substitutes, substituting, substituted

VERB **1** If you **substitute** one thing for another, you use it instead of the other thing.

NOUN **2** If one thing is a **substitute** for another, it is used instead of it or put in its place.

SYNONYMS: alternative, replacement

subtitle subtitles

NOUN A film or television programme with **subtitles** has the speech, or a translation of it, printed at the bottom of the screen.

subtle subtler, subtlest

ADJECTIVE very fine, delicate or small in degree

subtract subtracts, subtracting, subtracted

VERB If you **subtract** one number from another, you take away the first number from the second.

suburban

ADJECTIVE to do with the outskirts of a town or city

subway subways

NOUN **1** a footpath that goes underneath a road

2 an underground railway

succeed succeeds, succeeding, succeeded

VERB **1** If you **succeed**, you manage to do what you are trying to do.

2 If one person **succeeds** another, they come after them and take their place.

success successes

NOUN the achievement of something you have been trying to do

successful

ADJECTIVE having success

succession successions

NOUN **1** a number of things happening one after the other

2 When someone becomes the next person to have an important position, you can call this event their **succession**.

such

ADVERB **1** You can use **such** to emphasize something. ● *He's* **such** *a nice boy.*

ADJECTIVE **2** the same kind or similar ● *I have never seen* **such** *flowers.*

PHRASE **3** You can use **such as** to introduce examples of something. ● *There were trees* **such as** *oak, ash and elm.*

suck sucks, sucking, sucked

VERB If you **suck** something, you hold it in your mouth and pull at it with your cheeks and tongue, usually to get liquid out of it.

sudden

ADJECTIVE happening quickly and unexpectedly ● *We heard a* **sudden** *cry.*

sue sues, suing, sued

VERB To **sue** someone means to start a legal case against them, usually to claim money from them.

suede

NOUN a thin, soft leather with a velvety surface

suffer suffers, suffering, suffered

VERB If you **suffer**, you feel pain or sadness.

sufficient

ADJECTIVE If an amount is **sufficient**, there is enough of it available.

suffix suffixes

NOUN a group of letters that is added to the end of a word to form a new word, for example *-ness* or *-ship*, which would make *good* into *goodness* and *friend* into *friendship*

suffocate suffocates, suffocating, suffocated

VERB If someone **suffocates**, they die because they have no air to breathe.

sugar
NOUN a sweet substance obtained from some plants and used to sweeten food and drinks

suggest **suggests, suggesting, suggested**
VERB When you **suggest** something, you offer it as an idea.

suicide
NOUN People who commit **suicide** deliberately kill themselves.

suit **suits, suiting, suited**
NOUN **1** a matching jacket and trousers or skirt
VERB **2** If an arrangement **suits** you, it is convenient and suitable for you.
3 If a piece of clothing or a colour **suits** you, you look good when you are wearing it.
NOUN **4** A **suit** in a pack of cards is one of the sets of diamonds, clubs, hearts or spades.

suitable
ADJECTIVE right or acceptable for a certain person, occasion, time or place • *Many roads are not **suitable** for cycling.*

suitcase **suitcases**
NOUN a case in which you carry your belongings when you are travelling

suite **suites**
NOUN **1** a set of rooms in a hotel
2 a set of matching furniture or bathroom fittings

sulk **sulks, sulking, sulked**
VERB If you **sulk**, you show your annoyance by being silent and moody.

sullen
ADJECTIVE behaving in a bad-tempered and disagreeably silent way

sulphur
NOUN a yellow chemical used in industry and medicine. **Sulphur** burns with a very unpleasant smell.

sultana **sultanas**
NOUN a dried, seedless grape

sum **sums**
NOUN **1** an amount of money
2 the total of numbers added together

summarize **summarizes, summarizing, summarized**; also spelt **summarise**
VERB If you **summarize** something, you give a short account of its main points.

summary **summaries**
NOUN a short account of the main points of something said or written

summer **summers**
NOUN the warmest season of the year, between spring and autumn

summit **summits**
NOUN the top of a mountain • *The view from the **summit** was spectacular.*

summon **summons, summoning, summoned**
VERB If someone **summons** you, they order you to go to them.

sun
NOUN **1** the star in our solar system around which the earth and other planets travel, and that gives us heat and light
2 the heat and light from the sun

sunbathe **sunbathes, sunbathing, sunbathed**
VERB When you **sunbathe**, you sit in the sun to get brown.

A

sunburn
NOUN sore red skin due to being in the sun for too long

B

Sunday Sundays
NOUN the first day of the week, coming before Monday

C

D

sunflower sunflowers
NOUN a tall flower with a very large, round yellow head

E

F

sung
VERB the past participle of **sing**

G

sunglasses
PLURAL NOUN dark glasses worn to protect your eyes from the sun

H

I

sunk
VERB the past participle of **sink**

J

K

sunlight
NOUN the light from the sun

L

sunny sunnier, sunniest
ADJECTIVE having lots of sunshine

M

N

sunrise sunrises
NOUN the time in the day when the sun first appears

O

sunset sunsets
NOUN the time when the sun goes down

P

sunshine
NOUN warmth and light that come from the sun

Q

R

super
ADJECTIVE excellent, very good

S

superb
ADJECTIVE very good indeed

T

superficial
ADJECTIVE only on the surface

U

superior
ADJECTIVE **1** better or of higher quality than other similar things
2 in a more important position than another person

V

W

X

superlative superlatives
ADJECTIVE **1** of the highest quality, the best
NOUN **2** the form of an adverb or adjective that expresses *most*. For example, the

Y

Z

superlative of *hot* is *hottest*, and the **superlative** of *easy* is *easiest*.

supermarket supermarkets
NOUN a very large self-service shop that sells food and household goods

supernatural
ADJECTIVE Something that is **supernatural**, such as ghosts or witchcraft, cannot be explained by natural, scientific laws.

supersonic
ADJECTIVE faster than the speed of sound [from Latin *super* + *sonus* meaning above sound]

superstar superstars
NOUN a very famous entertainer or sportsperson

superstitious
ADJECTIVE People who are **superstitious** believe in things like magic and powers that bring good or bad luck.

supervise supervises, supervising, supervised
VERB If you **supervise** someone, you check what they are doing to make sure that they do it correctly.

supper suppers
NOUN a meal eaten in the evening or a snack eaten before you go to bed

supple
ADJECTIVE able to bend and move easily
● *Gymnasts are usually very* **supple**.

supplement supplements, supplementing, supplemented
VERB **1** To **supplement** something means to add something to it to improve it.
● *Many villagers* **supplemented** *their food supply by fishing for salmon.*
NOUN **2** something that is added to something else to improve it

supply supplies, supplying, supplied
VERB **1** If you **supply** someone with something, you provide them with it.
PLURAL NOUN **2 Supplies** are food and equipment for a special purpose. ● *His medical* **supplies** *were running low.*

support supports, supporting, supported

VERB **1** If something **supports** an object, it is underneath it and holding it up.

2 If you **support** a sports team, you are a fan.

3 If you **support** someone, you give them money, help or encouragement.

NOUN **4** If you give **support** to someone, you are kind, encouraging and helpful to them.

5 something that supports an object

suppose supposes, supposing, supposed

VERB If you **suppose** that something is so, you think that it is likely.

suppress suppresses, suppressing, suppressed

VERB If an army or government **suppresses** something, it stops people doing it.

supreme

ADJECTIVE greatest, best or most important

sure surer, surest

ADJECTIVE **1** If you are **sure** about something, you know you are right.

2 If something is **sure** to happen, it will definitely happen.

surf surfs, surfing, surfed

NOUN **1** the white foam that forms on the top of waves when they break near the shore

VERB **2** When you **surf**, you ride towards the shore on top of a wave, on a special board called a surfboard.

3 When you **surf** the Internet, you go from website to website reading the information.

surface surfaces

NOUN the top or outside area of something ● The wind ruffled the **surface** of the lake.

surge surges, surging, surged

NOUN **1** a sudden great increase in the amount of something ● After the rain there was a **surge** of water down the river.

VERB **2** If someone or something **surges**, they move suddenly and powerfully. ● The crowd **surged** forward.

surgeon surgeons

NOUN a doctor who performs operations

surgery surgeries

NOUN **1** medical treatment in which part of the patient's body is cut open ● He had to have **surgery** to repair his knee.

2 a room where doctors or dentists see their patients

surname surnames

NOUN your last name. Members of the same family usually have the same **surname**.

surplus surpluses

NOUN If there is a **surplus** of something, there is more of it than is needed.

surprise surprises, surprising, surprised

NOUN **1** an unexpected event

2 the feeling caused when something unexpected happens

VERB **3** If something **surprises** you, it gives you a feeling of surprise.

surrender surrenders, surrendering, surrendered

VERB If someone **surrenders**, they admit that they are defeated.

surround surrounds, surrounding, surrounded

VERB To **surround** someone or something means to be situated all around them. ● The house is **surrounded** by a high fence.

surroundings

PLURAL NOUN the things and conditions around a person or place

a
b
c
d
e
f
g
h
i
j
k
l
m
n
o
p
q
r
s
t
u
v
w
x
y
z

A
B
C
D
E
F
G
H
I
J
K
L
M
N
O
P
Q
R
S
T
U
V
W
X
Y
Z

survey **surveys, surveying, surveyed**
Said "sur-vey" VERB **1** If you **survey** something, you look carefully at the whole of it. • *They stood back and surveyed the scene.*
2 to make a detailed inspection of something
Said "sur-vey" NOUN **3** A **survey** of something, such as people's habits, is a detailed examination of it, often in a report.

survive **survives, surviving, survived**
VERB To **survive** means to continue to live or exist in spite of danger or difficulties.

suspect **suspects, suspecting, suspected**
Said "sus-spekt" VERB **1** If you **suspect** something, you think that it might be true.
2 If you **suspect** someone of doing something wrong, you think that they have done it.
Said "suss-pekt" NOUN **3** someone who is thought to be guilty of a crime

suspend **suspends, suspending, suspended**
VERB **1** to hang something up
2 to delay something for a time

suspense
NOUN the feeling of excitement or fear when you are waiting for something to happen

suspicion **suspicions**
NOUN the feeling of not trusting someone or that something is wrong

suspicious
ADJECTIVE **1** If you are **suspicious** of someone, you do not trust them.
2 If something is **suspicious**, it causes suspicion.

swallow **swallows, swallowing, swallowed**
VERB If you **swallow** something, you make it go down your throat and into your stomach.

swam
VERB the past tense of **swim**

swamp **swamps, swamping, swamped**
NOUN **1** an area of permanently wet land
VERB **2** If something is **swamped**, it is covered or filled with water.
3 If you are **swamped** by things, you have more than you can manage.

swan **swans**
NOUN a large, usually white, bird with a long neck that lives on rivers or lakes

swap **swaps, swapping, swapped**
Rhymes with "stop" VERB If you **swap** one thing for another, you replace the first thing with the second.
SYNONYM: exchange

swarm **swarms, swarming, swarmed**
NOUN **1** a large group of insects flying together
VERB **2** When bees or other insects **swarm**, they fly together in a large group.
3 If a place is **swarming** with people, it is crowded with people.

swat **swats, swatting, swatted**
VERB If you **swat** an insect, you hit it quickly to kill it.

sway **sways, swaying, swayed**
VERB If something or someone **sways**, they lean or swing slowly from side to side.

swear **swears, swearing, swore, sworn**
VERB **1** If you **swear**, you use very rude words.
2 If you **swear** to do something, you promise that you will do it.

sweat **sweats, sweating, sweated**
NOUN **1** the salty liquid that comes through your skin when you are hot or afraid
VERB **2** When you **sweat**, sweat comes through your skin.

sweater **sweaters**
NOUN a knitted piece of clothing covering your upper body and arms

sweatshirt sweatshirts
NOUN a piece of clothing made of thick cotton, covering your upper body and arms

swede swedes
NOUN a large round root vegetable with yellow flesh and a brownish-purple skin

sweep sweeps, sweeping, swept
VERB **1** If you **sweep** the floor, you use a brush to gather up dust or rubbish from it.
2 If you **sweep** things off a surface, you push them all off with a quick, smooth movement.
3 If something **sweeps** from one place to another, it moves there very quickly.
• *The boat* **swept** *down the river with the outgoing tide.*

sweet sweeter, sweetest; sweets
ADJECTIVE **1** tasting of sugar or honey
2 A **sweet** sound is gentle and tuneful.
3 attractive and delightful • *He's such a* **sweet** *little baby.*
NOUN **4** small pieces of sweet food, such as toffees, chocolates and mints
5 something sweet that you eat at the end of a meal
SYNONYM: dessert

sweetcorn
NOUN a long stalk covered with juicy yellow seeds that can be eaten as a vegetable

sweetheart sweethearts
NOUN You can call someone you are very fond of **sweetheart**.

swell swells, swelling, swelled, swollen
VERB If something **swells**, it becomes larger and rounder.

sweltering
ADJECTIVE If the weather is **sweltering**, it is very hot.

swept
VERB the past tense and past participle of **sweep**

swerve swerves, swerving, swerved
VERB If someone or something **swerves**, they suddenly change direction to avoid colliding with something.

swift swifter, swiftest; swifts
ADJECTIVE **1** happening or moving very quickly
NOUN **2** a bird with narrow crescent-shaped wings

swim swims, swimming, swam, swum
VERB When you **swim**, you move through water by making movements with your arms and legs.

swimming
NOUN the act of moving through water using your arms and legs

swimming costume swimming costumes
NOUN a garment you wear while swimming

swimming pool swimming pools
NOUN an area of water made for swimming, usually a large hole that has been tiled and filled with water

swimsuit swimsuits
NOUN a one-piece swimming costume

swindle swindles, swindling, swindled
VERB **1** If someone **swindles** someone else, they trick them to obtain money or property.
NOUN **2** a trick in which someone is cheated out of money or property

swine swine
NOUN OLD-FASHIONED a pig

The plural of *swine* is *swine*.

swing swings, swinging, swung
VERB **1** If something **swings**, or if you **swing** it, it moves repeatedly from side to side or backwards and forwards from a fixed point.
NOUN **2** a seat hanging from a frame or a branch, that moves backwards and forwards when you sit on it

a
b
c
d
e
f
g
h
i
j
k
l
m
n
o
p
q
r
s
t
u
v
w
x
y
z

swipe swipes, swiping, swiped

VERB **1** If you **swipe** at something, you try to hit it with a curved swinging movement. **2** If a credit card is **swiped**, it is put though an electronic machine to read it when paying. **3** INFORMAL If someone **swipes** something, they steal it.

switch switches, switching, switched

NOUN **1** a device used to control an electrical device or machine. When the **switch** is on, or closed, it completes the circuit and electricity can flow. **2** a change

VERB **3** To **switch** to a different task or topic means to change to it.

switch off

VERB If you **switch off** a light or a machine, you stop it working by pressing a switch.

switch on

VERB If you **switch on** a light or a machine, you start it working by pressing a switch.

switchboard switchboards

NOUN a panel with switches on for connecting telephone lines

swivel swivels, swivelling, swivelled

VERB **1** to turn round on a central point

ADJECTIVE **2** A **swivel** chair or lamp is made so that you can move the main part of it while the base remains in a fixed position.

swollen

ADJECTIVE **1** Something that is **swollen** has swelled up.

SYNONYMS: enlarged, puffed up

VERB **2** the past participle of **swell**

swoop swoops, swooping, swooped

VERB To **swoop** is to move downwards through the air in a fast curving movement.

swop swops, swopping, swopped

VERB to swap

sword swords

NOUN a weapon consisting of a very long blade with a short handle

swum

VERB the past participle of **swim**

swung

VERB the past tense and past participle of **swing**

sycamore sycamores

NOUN a tree that has large leaves with five points, and winged seed cases

syllable syllables

NOUN a part of a word that contains a single vowel sound and is said as one unit ● "Book" has one **syllable** and "reading" has two.

syllabus syllabuses or syllabi

NOUN the subjects that are studied for a particular course or examination

symbol symbols

NOUN a shape, design or idea that is used to represent something ● Apple blossom is a Chinese **symbol** of peace and beauty.

symmetrical

ADJECTIVE **Symmetrical** objects can be divided in half so that both halves match, with one half like a reflection of

a symmetrical pattern

the other.

symmetry

NOUN If something has **symmetry**, it is the same in both halves.

sympathetic

ADJECTIVE feeling sympathy or understanding for someone

sympathy

NOUN an understanding of people's feelings and opinions, especially someone who is in difficulties

SYNONYM: compassion

symphony **symphonies**
NOUN a piece of music for an orchestra, usually in four parts called movements

symptom **symptoms**
NOUN something wrong with your body that is a sign of illness

synagogue **synagogues**
NOUN a building where Jewish people meet for worship and religious instruction

synonym **synonyms**
NOUN two words that have the same or a very similar meaning • *Speak is a* **synonym** *for talk.*

synthetic
ADJECTIVE made from artificial substances rather than natural ones

syringe **syringes**
NOUN a hollow tube with a plunger, used for drawing up or pushing out liquids. Doctors and vets use them to give injections.

syrup **syrups**
NOUN a thick, sweet liquid made by boiling sugar with water
[from Arabic *sharab* meaning drink]

system **systems**
NOUN an organized way of doing or arranging something according to a fixed plan or set of rules

Tt

tab **tabs**
NOUN a small extra piece that is attached to something and sticks out, for example a sticky marker that you put in a book to mark your place

table **tables**
NOUN **1** a piece of furniture with a flat top supported by one or more legs
2 a set of facts or figures arranged in rows or columns

tablecloth **tablecloths**
NOUN a cloth used to cover a table and to keep it clean

tablespoon **tablespoons**
NOUN **1** a large spoon used for serving food
2 the amount that a **tablespoon** contains • *For this recipe you need two* **tablespoons** *of caster sugar.*

tablet **tablets**
NOUN **1** medicine in a small, solid lump that you swallow
SYNONYM: pill
2 a flat piece of stone with words carved on it
3 a small mobile personal computer with a screen that you tap or swipe

table tennis
NOUN a game for two or four people who use bats to hit a small ball over a net across the middle of the table

tabloid **tabloids**
NOUN a newspaper with small pages, short news stories, and lots of photographs

tack **tacks, tacking, tacked**
NOUN **1** a short nail with a flat top
2 If you change **tack**, you find a different way of doing something.
VERB **3** If you **tack** something to a surface, you fix it there with a tack.

4 If you **tack** in a boat, you sail in a zigzag course to catch the wind.

5 If you **tack** a piece of fabric, you sew it with long, loose stitches.

NOUN **6** equipment for horses, such as bridles, saddles and harnesses

tackle tackles, tackling, tackled

VERB **1** If you **tackle** a difficult task, you start dealing with it.

2 If you **tackle** someone in a game such as hockey or soccer, you try to get the ball away from them.

NOUN **3** an attempt to get the ball away from your opponent in certain sports

tact

NOUN the ability to deal with people without upsetting or offending them
tactless ADJECTIVE   tactlessly ADVERB

tactful

ADJECTIVE Someone who is **tactful** has the ability to deal with people without upsetting or offending them.
tactfully ADVERB

tactic tactics

NOUN one of the methods you use in order to achieve what you want

tadpole tadpoles

NOUN a young frog or toad. **Tadpoles** are black with round heads and long tails, and live in water.
[Middle English *tadde* meaning toad and *pol* meaning head]

tag tags, tagging, tagged

NOUN **1** a small label made of cloth

2 a game in which one person chases the other people who are playing

VERB **3** If you **tag along** behind someone, you follow and try to keep up.

tail tails

NOUN **1** The **tail** of an animal is the part extending beyond the end of its body. For example, a fox has a bushy **tail**.

2 the end part of something

ADJECTIVE OR ADVERB **3** When you toss a coin, the **tails** side is the one that does not have a person's head on it.

🖊 Do not confuse *tail* with *tale*.

tailor tailors

NOUN a person who makes, alters and repairs clothes, especially for men

take takes, taking, took, taken

VERB **1** If you **take** someone or something to a place, you get them there. ● *She **took** the cat to the vet.*

2 Take is used to show what activity is being done. ● *Sam **took** a shower.*

3 If you **take** a pill or some medicine, you swallow it.

4 When you **take** one number from another, you subtract it.

5 If you **take** a photograph, you use a camera to produce it.

take after

VERB If you **take after** a member of your family, you are like them in some way.

take off

VERB When a plane **takes off**, it goes into the air.

takeaway takeaways

NOUN **1** a shop or restaurant that sells hot, cooked food to be taken away and eaten elsewhere

2 a hot cooked meal bought from a takeaway restaurant

talcum powder

NOUN a soft, perfumed powder to put on the skin to dry it

tale tales

NOUN a story

🖊 Do not confuse *tale* with *tail*.

talent talents

NOUN the ability to do something very well

talk talks, talking, talked

VERB **1** When you **talk**, you say things to someone.

NOUN **2** a conversation or discussion

3 an informal speech about something

talkative

ADJECTIVE If you are **talkative**, you talk a lot.
SYNONYM: chatty

tall taller, tallest

ADJECTIVE **1** If you are **tall**, you are more than the average height.
2 having a particular height • *How tall are you?*

tally tallies

NOUN an informal record that you keep as you count objects

Talmud

NOUN a collection of books of the ancient Jewish ceremonies and laws

talon talons

NOUN a sharp, hooked claw, especially of a bird of prey

tambourine tambourines

NOUN a percussion instrument made of a skin stretched tightly over a circular frame. It has small round pieces of metal around the edge that jangle when the **tambourine** is beaten or shaken. [from Old French *tambourin* meaning little drum]

tame tamer, tamest; tames, taming, tamed

ADJECTIVE **1** A **tame** animal is not afraid of people.
VERB **2** If you **tame** a wild animal, you train it not to be afraid of humans.

tamper tampers, tampering, tampered

VERB If you **tamper** with something, you interfere with it.

tan tans, tanning, tanned

NOUN **1** a suntan
2 a yellowish-brown colour
VERB **3** If your skin **tans**, it goes brown in the sun.
4 When an animal's skin is **tanned**, it is turned into leather by treating it with chemicals.

tang tangs

NOUN a strong flavour or smell

tangerine tangerines

NOUN **1** a type of small sweet orange that is easy to peel
NOUN OR ADJECTIVE **2** reddish-orange

tangle tangles, tangling, tangled

NOUN **1** a mass of things, such as hairs or fibres, that are twisted together and difficult to separate
VERB **2** If you **tangle** something, you twist it into knots.

tank tanks

NOUN **1** a large container for storing liquid or gas
2 an armoured military vehicle that moves on tracks and has guns or rockets

tanker tankers

NOUN a ship or lorry designed to carry large quantities of gas or liquid

tantrum tantrums

NOUN a noisy and sometimes violent outburst of bad temper, especially by a child

tap taps, tapping, tapped

NOUN **1** a device for controlling the flow of gas or liquid from a pipe
VERB **2** If you **tap** something, you hit it lightly and quickly.
NOUN **3** a light hit, or its sound

tape tapes, taping, taped

NOUN **1** a long plastic ribbon covered with a magnetic substance and used to record sounds, pictures and computer information
2 a cassette with magnetic **tape** wound round it • *video tape*
3 a strip of sticky plastic used for sticking things together
VERB **4** If you **tape** sounds or television pictures, you record them using a tape recorder or a video recorder.

tape measure tape measures

NOUN a long, narrow tape marked with centimetres or inches, and used for measuring

taper tapers, tapering, tapered

VERB Something that **tapers** becomes thinner towards one end.

tape recorder tape recorders

NOUN a machine that records sounds onto a special magnetic tape that can be played back later

a
b
c
d
e
f
g
h
i
j
k
l
m
n
o
p
q
r
s
t
u
v
w
x
y
z

tapestry **tapestries**
NOUN a piece of heavy cloth with designs embroidered on it
[from Old French *tapisserie* meaning carpeting]

tar
NOUN a thick, black, sticky substance that is used in making roads

tarantula **tarantulas**
NOUN a large, hairy, poisonous spider

target **targets**
NOUN something you aim at when firing a weapon

tarmac
NOUN a mixture of tar and crushed stones, used for making road surfaces
[short for *tarmacadam*, from the name of John *McAdam*, the Scottish engineer who invented it]

tarnish **tarnishes, tarnishing, tarnished**
VERB If metal **tarnishes**, it becomes stained and loses its shine.
tarnished ADJECTIVE

tarpaulin **tarpaulins**
NOUN a sheet of heavy waterproof material used as a protective covering

tart **tarts**
NOUN **1** a pastry case, usually filled with something sweet such as fruit or jam
ADJECTIVE **2** Something **tart** has a sharp or sour taste.

tartan **tartans**
NOUN a coloured, woollen fabric from Scotland, with a special pattern of checks and stripes, depending on which clan it belongs to

task **tasks**
NOUN any piece of work that has to be done
SYNONYMS: chore, duty, job

tassel **tassels**
NOUN a tuft of loose threads tied by a knot and used for decoration

taste **tastes, tasting, tasted**
NOUN **1** Your sense of **taste** is your ability to recognize the flavour of things in your mouth.
2 The **taste** of something is its flavour.
3 your own particular choice of things such as clothes, music and food ● *Jenny and I have the same* **taste** *in music.*
VERB **4** When you can **taste** something in your mouth, you know what its flavour is like.
5 If food or drink **tastes** of something, it has that flavour.

tasty **tastier, tastiest**
ADJECTIVE Something that is **tasty** has a pleasant flavour.

tattered
ADJECTIVE ragged and torn

tattoo **tattoos, tattooing, tattooed**
VERB **1** If someone is **tattooed**, they have a design drawn on their skin by pricking little holes and filling them with coloured dye.
NOUN **2** a picture or design tattooed on someone's body

taught
VERB the past tense and past participle of **teach**

taunt **taunts, taunting, taunted**
VERB If you **taunt** someone, you tease them about their weaknesses or failures in order to make them angry or upset.

taut
ADJECTIVE Something that is **taut** is stretched very tight.

tawny
ADJECTIVE brownish-yellow

tax **taxes, taxing, taxed**
NOUN **1** an amount of money that people

have to pay to the government so that it can provide public services such as health care and education

VERB **2** If a sum of money is **taxed**, a certain amount of it is paid to the government.

3 If something **taxes** you, it exhausts you and drains your energy.

taxi taxis
NOUN a car with a driver that you hire, usually for a short journey

tea teas
NOUN **1** the dried leaves of a shrub found in Asia

2 a drink made by soaking the leaves of the tea plant in hot water

3 a meal taken in the late afternoon or early evening

tea bag tea bags
NOUN a small paper packet with tea leaves in it, that you use to make a drink of tea

teach teaches, teaching, taught
VERB If someone **teaches** you something, they help you learn about it or show you how to do it.

SYNONYMS: educate, instruct, train

teacher teachers
NOUN someone who teaches at a school or college

teak
NOUN a hard wood that comes from a large Asian tree

team teams
NOUN a group of people who play together against another group in a sport or game

teapot teapots
NOUN a container in which tea is made. It has a handle, a spout and a lid.

tear tears, tearing, tore, torn
Rhymes with "fear" NOUN **1** a drop of liquid that comes out of your eyes when you cry

Rhymes with "hair" NOUN **2** a hole or rip that has been made in something ● *There was a **tear** in the curtain.*

VERB **3** If you **tear** something, you damage it by pulling so that a hole or rip appears in it.

tearful
ADJECTIVE If you are **tearful**, you cry easily or you are crying.

tease teases, teasing, teased
VERB If someone **teases** you, they deliberately make fun of you or embarrass you.

teaspoon teaspoons
NOUN **1** a small spoon used for stirring drinks

2 the amount that a **teaspoon** holds

● *I have two **teaspoons** of sugar in my coffee.*

teat teats
NOUN **1** a nipple on a female animal

2 a piece of rubber or plastic that is shaped like a nipple and fitted to a baby's feeding bottle

technical
ADJECTIVE If something is **technical**, it is to do with machines, the way things work, and materials used in industry, transport and communications.

technique techniques
Said "tek-**neek**" NOUN a particular way of doing something

technology
NOUN practical things that have come about because of a greater understanding of science ● *New **technology** has helped us develop faster computers.*

teddy bear teddy bears
NOUN a soft, furry toy bear

tedious
ADJECTIVE boring and lasting for a long time

teenager teenagers
NOUN a person aged between 13 and 19 years old

teeth
PLURAL NOUN the plural of **tooth**

tele-
PREFIX You add **tele-**to the beginning of a word to mean at or over a distance.

● *telephone*

[from the Greek *tele* meaning far]

A B C D E F G H I J K L M N O P Q R S T U V W X Y Z

telecommunications

NOUN the science and activity of sending signals and messages over long distances, for example by radio and telephone

telegram **telegrams**

NOUN a message sent by telegraph to an office, and then delivered by hand to a person's home • *He received many letters and **telegrams** of congratulations when he won the race.*

telegraph

NOUN a system of sending messages over long distances using electrical or radio signals

telephone **telephones, telephoning, telephoned**

NOUN **1** a piece of electrical equipment for talking directly to someone who is in a different place

VERB **2** If you **telephone** someone, you speak to them using a telephone.

telescope

telescopes

NOUN a long instrument, shaped like a tube, that contains lenses. When you look through it with one eye, distant objects appear larger and nearer.

televise **televises, televising, televised**

VERB If an event is **televised**, it is filmed and shown on television.

television **televisions**

NOUN a piece of electronic equipment that receives pictures and sounds transmitted over a distance

tell **tells, telling, told**

VERB **1** If you **tell** someone something, you let them know about it.

2 If you **tell** someone to do something, you order them to do it.

telly **tellies**

NOUN an abbreviation of *television*

temper

NOUN **1** Your **temper** is the mood you are in and the way you are feeling, whether you are irritable and angry or calm and peaceful. • *I started the day in a bad **temper**.*

PHRASE **2** If you **lose your temper**, you become very angry.

temperamental

ADJECTIVE Someone who is **temperamental** changes their mood often and suddenly.

temperature **temperatures**

NOUN **1** how hot or cold something is • *There was a sudden drop in **temperature** once the sun had gone down.*

2 Your **temperature** is the temperature of your body. The normal body **temperature** for humans is 37°C. • *His **temperature** continued to rise.*

temple **temples**

NOUN **1** a building used for the worship of a god in various religions

2 the part on either side of your head between your forehead and your ear

tempo **tempos** or **tempi**

NOUN TECHNICAL The **tempo** of a piece of music is its speed.

temporary

ADJECTIVE lasting for only a short time

tempt **tempts, tempting, tempted**

VERB **1** If you **tempt** someone, you try to persuade them to do something by offering them something they want.

ADJECTIVE **2** If something is **tempting**, it is attractive and difficult to resist.

ten

NOUN **Ten** is the number 10.

tenth NOUN OR ADJECTIVE

tenant **tenants**

NOUN someone who pays rent for the place they live in, or for land or buildings that they use

tenancy NOUN

tend **tends, tending, tended**

VERB **1** If something **tends** to happen, it usually happens.

2 If you **tend** something or someone, you look after them. ● *Bob **tended** the plants.*

tendency tendencies

NOUN the way a person or a thing is likely to behave or has a habit of behaving ● *She has a **tendency** to write messily.*

tender tenderer, tenderest

ADJECTIVE **1** Someone who is **tender** is gentle and caring.

SYNONYMS: affectionate, gentle, loving

2 Tender food is easy to cut and chew.
3 If a part of your body is **tender**, it is painful and sore.

tendon tendons

NOUN **Tendons** are like strong cords. They hold your muscles and bones together.

tennis

NOUN a game played by two or four players on a rectangular court. The players hit a ball over a central net.

tense tenser, tensest; tenses, tensing, tensed

ADJECTIVE **1** If you are **tense**, you feel worried and unable to relax.
NOUN **2** The **tense** of a verb shows whether it is in the past, present or future.
VERB **3** If you **tense** your muscles, you tighten them up.

tension tensions

NOUN the feeling of nervousness or worry that you have when something dangerous or important is happening

tent tents

NOUN a shelter made of fabric held up by poles and pinned down at the bottom with pegs and ropes

tentacle tentacles

NOUN the long, bending parts of an animal, such as an octopus, that it uses to feel and hold things

tepid

ADJECTIVE **Tepid** liquid is only slightly warm.

term terms

NOUN **1** one of the periods of time that each year is divided into at a school or college
2 Terms are words that relate to a

particular subject, for example, medical **terms**, legal **terms** and scientific **terms**.
3 Terms are the conditions of an agreement. ● *He made a list of **terms** for doing the job.*
4 If you are on good **terms** with someone, you get on well with them.

terminal terminals

NOUN **1** a place where vehicles, passengers or goods begin or end a journey
2 a keyboard and screen connected to a main computer
ADJECTIVE **3** A **terminal** illness or disease cannot be cured and gradually causes death.
[from Latin *terminus* meaning end]

terminate terminates, terminating, terminated

VERB When you **terminate** something, or it **terminates**, it stops or ends.

terrace terraces

NOUN **1** a row of houses joined together
2 a flat area of stone next to a building, where people can sit

terrapin terrapins

NOUN a small North American freshwater turtle
[an American Indian word]

terrible

ADJECTIVE **1** serious and unpleasant ● *He had a **terrible** illness.*
2 very bad or of poor quality ● *That is a **terrible** haircut.*

terrier terriers

NOUN a breed of small dog
[from Old French *chien terrier* meaning earth dog, because they were originally bred to hunt animals living in holes in the ground, such as rabbits and badgers]

terrific

ADJECTIVE **1** very pleasing or impressive ● *That was a **terrific** film.*
2 very great or strong ● *There is a **terrific** wind blowing down on the beach.*

terrify terrifies, terrifying, terrified

VERB If something **terrifies** you, it makes you feel extremely frightened.

a
b
c
d
e
f
g
h
i
j
k
l
m
n
o
p
q
r
s
t
u
v
w
x
y
z

A
B
C
D
E
F
G
H
I
J
K
L
M
N
O
P
Q
R
S
T
U
V
W
X
Y
Z

territory **territories**
NOUN The **territory** of a country is the land that it controls.

terror **terrors**
NOUN great fear or panic

terrorism
NOUN the use of violence for political purposes

test **tests, testing, tested**
VERB **1** When you **test** something, you try it to find out what it is, what condition it is in, or how well it works.
2 To **test** someone means to ask them questions to find out how much they know.
NOUN **3** a set of questions or tasks given to someone to find out what they know or can do

test tube **test tubes**
NOUN a small cylindrical glass container that is used in chemical experiments

tetanus
NOUN a painful infectious disease caused by germs getting into wounds

tether **tethers, tethering, tethered**
VERB **1** If you **tether** an animal, you tie it to something such as a post.
NOUN **2** a rope for tying an animal to something such as a post

tetrahedron
tetrahedrons or **tetrahedra**
NOUN a solid shape with four triangular faces

text **texts, texting, texted**
NOUN **1** the written part of a book, rather than the pictures or the index
2 short for **text message**
VERB **3** If you **text** someone, you send them a text message.

textbook **textbooks**
NOUN a book about a particular subject for students to use

textile **textiles**
NOUN a woven cloth or fabric

text message **text messages**
NOUN a written message sent using a mobile phone

texture **textures**
NOUN the way something feels when you touch it • *Silk has a very smooth, soft* ***texture***.

than
CONJUNCTION OR PREPOSITION You use **than** when you compare one thing with another. • *She is bigger* ***than*** *her sister.*

thank **thanks, thanking, thanked**
VERB When you **thank** someone, you show that you are pleased or grateful for something that they have done for you.

thank you
EXCLAMATION You say **thank you** to show that you are grateful to someone for something.

that **those**
ADJECTIVE OR PRONOUN **1 That** is used when you are referring to someone or something you have already mentioned. • ***That*** *is the film I want to see.*
CONJUNCTION **2 That** is used to introduce a fact, a statement or a result. • *His writing was so bad* ***that*** *nobody could read it.*

thaw **thaws, thawing, thawed**
VERB **1** When snow or ice **thaws**, it melts.
2 When you **thaw** frozen food, or when it **thaws**, it defrosts.

the
ADJECTIVE called the definite article. You use **the** in front of a noun when you are referring to something in particular. • *That's* ***the*** *chair I bought yesterday.*

theatre **theatres**
NOUN **1** a building where plays and other shows are performed on a stage
2 a room in a hospital where operations are carried out

theft **thefts**
NOUN the crime of stealing
SYNONYM: robbery

their
ADJECTIVE **Their** refers to something belonging to people or things, other than

yourself or the person you are talking to, that have already been mentioned. • *The children had been playing football, and **their** shirts were dirty.*

🖊 Do not confuse *their* with *there* or *they're.*

theirs

PRONOUN **Theirs** refers to something belonging to people or things, other than yourself or the person you are talking to, that have already been mentioned. • *The children said that the ball that came over the wall was **theirs**.*

them

PRONOUN **Them** refers to things or people, other than yourself or the person you are talking to, that have already been mentioned. • *She took her gloves off and put **them** in a drawer.*

theme themes

NOUN a main idea in a piece of writing, painting, film or music • *The main **theme** of the book is growing up.*

themselves

PRONOUN **Themselves** is used when people, other than yourself or the person you are talking to, do an action and are affected by it. • *They enjoyed **themselves** at the fair.*

then

ADVERB after that; next • *He put on his shoes and **then** went for a walk.*

theology

NOUN the study of religion and God

theory theories

NOUN an idea or set of ideas that is meant to explain something

therapy

NOUN the treatment of a mental or physical illness
therapist NOUN

there

ADVERB in that place or to that place • *He's sitting over **there**.*

🖊 Do not confuse *there* with *their* or *they're.*

therefore

ADVERB as a result • *I worked hard and **therefore** I won a prize.*

thermal

ADJECTIVE **1** to do with or caused by heat
2 Thermal clothing is specially designed to keep you warm in cold weather.

thermometer thermometers

NOUN an instrument for measuring the temperature of a room or a person's body

Thermos

NOUN TRADEMARK a container used to keep drinks hot or cold

thermostat thermostats

NOUN a device used to control temperature, for example on a central heating system

thesaurus thesauruses

NOUN a reference book in which words with similar meanings are grouped together

these

ADJECTIVE OR PRONOUN the plural of **this**

they

PRONOUN **They** refers to people or things that have already been mentioned. • *I saw Tom and Ben. **They** were looking in a shop window.*

they'd

a contraction of *they had* or *they would*

they'll

a contraction of *they will* or *they shall*

they're

a contraction of *they are*

🖊 Do not confuse *they're* with *their* or *there.*

they've

a contraction of *they have*

thick thicker, thickest

ADJECTIVE **1** Something **thick** has a large distance between its two sides. • *I'd like a **thick** slice of bread and butter.*
ANTONYM: thin
2 If you want to know how **thick** something is, you want to know the measurement between its two sides.

- How **thick** is this wall?

ANTONYM: thin

3 close together and in a large number
- She has **thick**, dark hair.

4 Thick liquids contain little water and do not flow easily. • *The **thick** soup was very filling.*

ANTONYM: thin

thicken thickens, thickening, thickened

VERB If you **thicken** something, or if it **thickens**, it becomes thicker. • *Stir the custard in the pan until it **thickens**.*

thickness thicknesses

NOUN how thick something is

thief thieves

NOUN a person who steals

thigh thighs

NOUN the top part of your leg, between your knee and your hip

thimble thimbles

NOUN a small metal or plastic cap that you put on the end of your finger to protect it from the needle when you are sewing

thin thinner, thinnest

ADJECTIVE **1** Something that is **thin** is much narrower than it is long.

ANTONYM: thick

2 A **thin** person or animal has very little fat on their body.

3 Thin liquids contain a lot of water and flow easily.

ANTONYM: thick

thing things

NOUN an object rather than a plant, animal or person

think thinks, thinking, thought

VERB **1** When you **think** about ideas or problems, you use your mind to sort them out.

2 If you **think** something, you believe it is true. • *I **think** she's got a bike for her birthday.*

3 If you **think** of something, you remember it or it comes into your mind.

4 If you are **thinking** of doing something, you might do it.

third thirds

NOUN OR ADJECTIVE **1** The **third** or the **third** thing in a series is the one counted as number three.

NOUN **2** one of three equal parts into which something can be divided

third person

NOUN In grammar, the **third person** is *he, she, it* or *they*.

thirst

NOUN If you have a **thirst**, you feel the need to drink something.

thirsty thirstier, thirstiest

ADJECTIVE If you are **thirsty**, you feel as if you need to drink something.
thirstily ADVERB

thirteen

NOUN **Thirteen** is the number 13.
thirteenth NOUN OR ADJECTIVE

thirty

NOUN **Thirty** is the number 30.
thirtieth NOUN OR ADJECTIVE

this those

ADJECTIVE OR PRONOUN **This** means the one here, not a different one. • ***This** food looks nice.*

thistle thistles

NOUN a wild plant with prickly-edged leaves and purple flowers

thorn thorns

NOUN one of many sharp points growing on the stems of some plants. For example, brambles have many **thorns**.

thorough

ADJECTIVE done very carefully and completely
thoroughly ADVERB

those

ADJECTIVE OR PRONOUN the plural of **that**

though

Rhymes with "show" CONJUNCTION **1** despite the fact that • *She felt better, **though** her cough was still bad.*

2 You can use **though** to mean if.
- *Try to look as **though** you're working.*

thought **thoughts**
VERB **1** the past tense and past participle of **think**
NOUN **2** the activity of thinking • *She was lost in* **thought**.

thoughtful
ADJECTIVE **1** If you are **thoughtful**, you are quiet and serious.
2 A **thoughtful** person thinks of what other people need and what they would like.
thoughtfully ADVERB

thoughtless
ADJECTIVE A **thoughtless** person does not care or think about other people's needs.
thoughtlessness NOUN
thoughtlessly ADVERB

thousand **thousands**
NOUN A **thousand** is the number 1000.
thousandth NOUN OR ADJECTIVE

thrash **thrashes, thrashing, thrashed**
VERB **1** To **thrash** someone is to beat them by hitting them with something like a stick or a whip.
2 If you **thrash** someone in a contest or fight, you defeat them completely.
3 If you **thrash**, or **thrash** about, you move about wildly and violently.

thread **threads**
NOUN a long, fine piece of cotton, silk, nylon or wool

threadbare
ADJECTIVE Fabric or clothes that are **threadbare** are old and worn thin.

threat **threats**
NOUN **1** a warning that someone will harm you if you do not do what they want
2 a danger or something that might cause harm

threaten **threatens, threatening, threatened**
VERB If you **threaten** someone, you tell them that you intend to harm them in some way.

three
NOUN **Three** is the number 3.

three-dimensional
ADJECTIVE A **three-dimensional** object or shape is not flat, but has height or depth as well as length and width.

threw
VERB the past tense of **throw**

thrill **thrills, thrilling, thrilled**
NOUN **1** a sudden feeling of great excitement, pleasure or fear
VERB **2** If something **thrills** you, it gives you a feeling of great pleasure and excitement.
thrilled ADJECTIVE   **thrilling** ADJECTIVE

thriller **thrillers**
NOUN a book, film or play that tells an exciting story about dangerous or mysterious events

thrive **thrives, thriving, throve** or **thrived**
VERB to grow strongly and healthily, or to prosper

throat **throats**
NOUN **1** the back of your mouth and the top part of the tubes inside your neck that lead to your stomach and lungs
2 the front part of your neck

throb **throbs, throbbing, throbbed**
VERB If something **throbs**, it beats or vibrates with a strong, regular rhythm.
• *My finger* **throbbed** *after I trapped it in the door.*

throne **thrones**
NOUN a ceremonial chair used by a king or queen on important official occasions

throng **throngs, thronging, thronged**
NOUN **1** a large crowd of people • *There was a* **throng** *of fans waiting at the stage door.*
VERB **2** If people **throng** somewhere, or **throng** a place, they go there in great numbers. • *Hundreds of royal admirers* **thronged** *to see the procession.*

throttle **throttles, throttling, throttled**
VERB If a person **throttles** someone, they

kill or injure them by squeezing their throat.

SYNONYM: strangle

through

PREPOSITION If you move **through** something, you go from one side of it to the other. ● *We followed the path* **through** *the woods.*

throughout

PREPOSITION OR ADVERB all the way through

throw **throws, throwing, threw, thrown**

VERB When you **throw** something you let it go with a quick movement of your arm, so that it moves through the air.

SYNONYMS: chuck, fling, toss

throw away

VERB If you **throw away** something that you do not want, you get rid of it, usually by putting it in the rubbish bin.

thrush **thrushes**

NOUN a small brown songbird

thrust **thrusts, thrusting, thrust**

VERB If you **thrust** something somewhere, you move or push it there quickly and with a lot of force.

thud **thuds, thudding, thudded**

VERB **1** to fall heavily
NOUN **2** the dull sound of something heavy falling

thug **thugs**

NOUN a very rough and violent person
[from Hindi *thag* meaning thief]

thumb **thumbs**

NOUN the short, thick, jointed part on the side of your hand, similar to a finger but lower down

thump **thumps, thumping, thumped**

VERB **1** If you **thump** someone or something, you hit them hard with your fist.
2 When your heart **thumps**, it beats strongly and quickly.
NOUN **3** a hard hit
4 a fairly loud, dull sound

thunder

NOUN the loud, rumbling noise that you hear from the sky during some storms, often after a flash of lightning

thunderstorm **thunderstorms**

NOUN a storm with thunder and lightning

Thursday

NOUN the fifth day of the week, coming between Wednesday and Friday
[from Old English *Thursdæg* meaning Thor's day; Thor was the Norse god of thunder]

tick **ticks, ticking, ticked**

NOUN **1** a written mark to show that something is correct
VERB **2** If you **tick** something written on a piece of paper, you put a tick next to it.
3 When a clock **ticks**, it makes a regular clicking noise as it works.

ticket **tickets**

NOUN a piece of paper or card which shows that you have paid for a journey or have paid to go into a place ● *Don't lose your bus* **ticket***.*

tickle **tickles, tickling, tickled**

VERB When you **tickle** someone, you move your fingers lightly over their body in order to make them laugh.

tide **tides**

NOUN the regular change in the level of the sea on the shore

tidy **tidier, tidiest; tidies, tidying, tidied**

ADJECTIVE **1** Something that is **tidy** is neat and arranged in an orderly way.
2 Someone who is **tidy** always keeps their things neat.
VERB **3** If you **tidy** a place, you make it neat by putting things in their proper place.

tie **ties, tying, tied**

VERB **1** If you **tie** one thing to another, you fasten it using cord of some kind.
2 If you **tie** a piece of cord or cloth, you fasten the ends together in a knot or bow.
NOUN **3** a long, narrow piece of cloth worn around the neck under a shirt collar, and tied in a knot at the front

A B C D E F G H I J K L M N O P Q R S T U V W X Y Z

tiger tigers
NOUN a large wild cat that has an orange-coloured coat with black stripes

tight tighter, tightest
ADJECTIVE **1** If clothes are **tight**, they fit you very closely.
ADVERB **2** If you hold **tight**, you hold on very firmly.

tighten tightens, tightening, tightened
VERB **1** If you **tighten** something like a rope or a chain, you pull it until it is straight and firmly stretched.
2 If you **tighten** something like a screw or a knot, you fasten or fix it more firmly.

tightrope tightropes
NOUN a tightly-stretched rope on which an acrobat balances and performs tricks

tights
PLURAL NOUN a piece of clothing made of thin, stretchy material that fits closely round a person's hips, legs and feet

tile tiles, tiling, tiled
NOUN **1** a flat, rectangular piece of something, such as slate, carpet or baked clay, that is used to cover surfaces
VERB **2** If you **tile** a surface, you fix tiles to it.

till tills, tilling, tilled
NOUN **1** a drawer or box in a shop where money is kept, usually in a cash register
PREPOSITION OR CONJUNCTION **2** up to a certain time • *You can stay up **till** nine o'clock.*
VERB **3** If someone **tills** the soil, they plough it.

tiller tillers
NOUN a handle fixed to the top of the rudder on a boat. It turns the rudder and steers the boat.

tilt tilts, tilting, tilted
VERB If you **tilt** an object, you move it so that one end or side is higher than the other.

timber timbers
NOUN **1** wood that has been cut and prepared ready for building and making furniture

2 The **timbers** of a ship or house are the large pieces of wood that have been used to build it.

time times, timing, timed
NOUN **1** what we measure in minutes, hours, days, weeks and years
2 a particular point in the day • *What **time** is it?*
3 a particular period in history
VERB **4** If you **time** something like a race, you measure how long it takes.

times
PLURAL NOUN multiplied by • *Two **times** three is six ($2 \times 3 = 6$).*

timetable timetables
NOUN **1** a plan of the times when particular activities or jobs should be done
2 a list of the times when particular trains, boats, buses or aircraft arrive and depart

timid
ADJECTIVE If you are **timid**, you are shy and lacking in confidence.
ANTONYM: bold
timidly ADVERB

tin tins
NOUN **1** a soft, silvery-white metal
2 a metal container that is filled with food and then sealed in order to keep the food fresh
3 a small metal container that may have a lid

tingle tingles, tingling, tingled
VERB When a part of your body **tingles**, you feel a slight prickling sensation there.
tingling NOUN OR ADJECTIVE

tinkle tinkles, tinkling, tinkled
VERB Something that **tinkles** makes a light, ringing sound.

tinsel
NOUN long threads with strips of shiny paper attached, used as a decoration at Christmas

tint tints
NOUN a shade of a particular colour, particularly a pale one

a
b
c
d
e
f
g
h
i
j
k
l
m
n
o
p
q
r
s
t
u
v
w
x
y
z

411

tiny *tinier, tiniest*
ADJECTIVE extremely small

tip *tips, tipping, tipped*
NOUN **1** the point or the very end of something
2 a small gift of money given to someone like a waiter, who has done a service for you
3 a place where rubbish is left
4 a piece of useful information or advice
VERB **5** If you **tip** something, you tilt or overturn it. ● *When he jumped up, he **tipped** the chair over.*
6 If you **tip** something somewhere, you pour it quickly and carelessly, or you empty it from a container. ● *When they had finished the washing up, they **tipped** the water out of the bowl.*

tiptoe *tiptoes, tiptoeing, tiptoed*
VERB If you **tiptoe** somewhere, you walk there very quietly on your toes.

tire *tires, tiring, tired*
VERB **1** If something **tires** you, it makes you use a lot of energy so that you want to rest or sleep afterwards.
2 If you **tire** of something, you become bored with it.
tired ADJECTIVE **tiredness** NOUN

tissue *tissues*
NOUN a small piece of soft paper that you use as a handkerchief

title *titles*
NOUN the name of something such as a book, play, film or piece of music

to
PREPOSITION **1** towards
2 used to compare units ● *There are 100 centimetres **to** a metre.*
3 compared with or rather than ● *I prefer fruit **to** chocolate.*
4 used to indicate the limit of something ● *I am allowed to spend up **to** an hour watching television each night.*
ADVERB **5** if you push something like a door **to**, you close it but do not shut it completely

🖉 Do not confuse *to* with *too* or *two*.

toad *toads*
NOUN an animal similar to a frog, but with drier skin and living more on land and less in the water

toadstool *toadstools*
NOUN a type of fungus similar to a mushroom and often poisonous

toast *toasts, toasting, toasted*
NOUN **1** slices of bread made brown and crisp by cooking them at a high temperature
VERB **2** If you **toast** bread, you cook it at a high temperature so that it becomes brown and crisp.

toaster *toasters*
NOUN an electrical device for toasting bread

tobacco
NOUN the dried leaves of a plant called **tobacco**. People smoke it in pipes, cigarettes and cigars.

toboggan *toboggans, tobogganing, tobogganed*
NOUN **1** a flat seat with two wooden or metal runners, used for sliding over the snow
SYNONYM: sledge
VERB **2** If you **toboggan**, you use a toboggan to slide over the snow.
SYNONYM: sledge

today
NOUN OR ADVERB the day that is happening now

toddler *toddlers*
NOUN a small child who has just learned to walk

toe *toes*
NOUN **1** one of the five movable parts at the end of your foot
2 the part of a shoe or sock that covers the end of your foot

toffee *toffees*
NOUN a sticky, chewy sweet made by boiling sugar and butter together with water

toga **togas**

NOUN a long, loose robe worn in ancient Rome

together

ADVERB **1** If people do something **together**, they do it with each other.
2 If two things happen **together**, they happen at the same time.
3 If things are joined, mixed or fixed **together**, they are put with each other.

toil **toils, toiling, toiled**

VERB **1** If you **toil**, you work very hard.
NOUN **2** very hard work

toilet **toilets**

NOUN **1** a large bowl, connected to the drains, which you use to get rid of waste from your body
SYNONYM: lavatory
2 a small room containing a toilet
SYNONYM: lavatory

token **tokens**

NOUN **1** a piece of paper or card that is worth a particular amount of money and can be exchanged for goods • *I got a book* **token** *for my birthday.*
2 a flat round piece of metal or plastic that can sometimes be used instead of money • *Some of the telephones only take* **tokens**.
3 a sign or symbol of something • *We bought her some flowers as a* **token** *of our thanks.*

told

VERB the past tense and past participle of **tell**

tolerate **tolerates, tolerating, tolerated**

VERB If you **tolerate** something, you put up with it even though you do not like it.

tomato **tomatoes**

NOUN a small, round, red fruit used as a vegetable and eaten cooked or raw

tomb **tombs**

NOUN a large grave where one or more people are buried

tomorrow

NOUN OR ADVERB the day after today

🖋 *Tomorrow* has one *m* and two *r*s.

ton **tons**

NOUN a unit of weight equal to 2240 pounds or about 1016 kilograms

tone **tones**

NOUN **1** a particular quality that a sound has • *the clear* **tone** *of the bell*
2 a shade of a colour

tongs

PLURAL NOUN two long, narrow pieces of metal joined together at one end. You press the pieces together to pick up objects.

tongue **tongues**

NOUN the soft part in your mouth that you can move and use for tasting, licking and speaking

tongue twister **tongue twisters**

NOUN a sentence or a rhyme that is very difficult to say

tonight

ADVERB OR NOUN the evening or night that will come at the end of today

tonne **tonnes**

NOUN a unit of weight equal to 1000 kilograms

tonsil **tonsils**

NOUN one of the two small, soft lumps at the back of your throat

tonsillitis

NOUN a painful swelling of your tonsils caused by an infection

too

ADVERB **1** also or as well • *She was there* **too**.
2 **Too** shows that there is more of something than you want. • *I've had* **too** *much to eat.*

🖋 Do not confuse *too* with *to* or *two*.

took

VERB the past tense of **take**

tool tools

NOUN any hand-held piece of equipment that you use to help you do a particular kind of work

tooth teeth

NOUN one of the hard, white bony parts in your mouth that you use for biting and chewing food

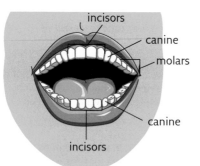

incisors

canine

molars

canine

incisors

toothache

NOUN a pain in one of your teeth

toothbrush toothbrushes

NOUN a brush for cleaning your teeth

toothpaste

NOUN the substance that you use with a toothbrush to clean your teeth

top tops

NOUN **1** the highest point of something
• *There was snow on the mountain top.*
2 the upper side of something • *There was a vase of flowers on the table top.*
3 a piece of clothing that you wear on the top half of your body
4 a toy that can be made to spin
ADJECTIVE **5** The **top** thing of a series of things is the highest one. • *the top floor of the building*

topic topics

NOUN a particular subject that you write about or discuss

topical

ADJECTIVE to do with things that are happening now

Torah

NOUN Jewish law and teaching

torch torches

NOUN a small electric light carried in the hand and powered by batteries
[from Old French *torche* meaning handful of twisted straw, which was set on fire and held up to provide light]

tore

VERB the past tense of **tear**

torment torments, tormenting, tormented

NOUN **1** great pain or unhappiness
VERB **2** If something **torments** you, it causes you great unhappiness.
3 If someone **torments** you, they keep deliberately annoying you.

torn

VERB the past participle of **tear**

tornado tornadoes or tornados

NOUN a violent storm with strong circular winds around a funnel-shaped cloud

torpedo torpedoes, torpedoing, torpedoed

NOUN **1** a tube-shaped bomb that travels underwater and explodes when it hits a target
VERB **2** If a ship is **torpedoed**, it is hit, and usually sunk, by a torpedo.

torrent torrents

NOUN a very strong stream or fall of water
• *The rain fell in a torrent.*

torrential

ADJECTIVE **Torrential** rain pours down very fast and in great quantities.

tortoise tortoises

NOUN a slow-moving reptile with a hard shell over its body into which it can pull its head and legs for protection

torture tortures, torturing, tortured

VERB If someone **tortures** another person, they deliberately cause them great pain, usually as a punishment or to get information from them.

toss tosses, tossing, tossed

VERB **1** If you **toss** something somewhere, you throw it there lightly and carelessly.
2 If you **toss** a coin, you decide

something by throwing a coin into the air and guessing which side will face upwards when it lands.

total **totals, totalling, totalled**
NOUN **1** the number you get when you add several numbers together
VERB **2** If you **total** amounts, you add them together to find the total.
ADJECTIVE **3** complete

toucan **toucans**
NOUN a large tropical bird with a large, colourful beak

touch **touches, touching, touched**
VERB **1** If you **touch** something, you put your fingers or hand on it.
2 When two things **touch**, they come into contact.
3 If something **touches** you, it affects your emotions. ● *The sad story **touched** us all.*
NOUN **4** Your sense of **touch** is your ability to feel things by touching them.

touchdown **touchdowns**
NOUN the landing of an aircraft or spacecraft

touchy **touchier, touchiest**
ADJECTIVE sensitive and easily offended

tough **tougher, toughest**
ADJECTIVE **1** A **tough** person is strong and able to put up with things that are difficult.
2 Something that is **tough** is strong and difficult to break or damage.
3 **Tough** food is difficult to cut and chew. ANTONYM: tender

tour **tours, touring, toured**
NOUN **1** a long journey during which you visit several places
2 a short trip round a place such as a city or a famous building
VERB **3** If you **tour** a place, you go on a journey or a trip round it.

tourist **tourists**
NOUN someone who is travelling on holiday

tournament **tournaments**
NOUN a competition in which many players

or teams compete in a series of games or contests

tow **tows, towing, towed**
VERB **1** If a vehicle **tows** another vehicle, it pulls it along behind it.
NOUN **2** To give a vehicle a **tow** is to pull it along behind.

towards
PREPOSITION If you go **towards** something, you move in its direction.

towel **towels**
NOUN a piece of thick, soft cloth that you use to dry yourself with

tower **towers**
NOUN a tall, narrow building, sometimes attached to a larger building such as a castle or church

town **towns**
NOUN a place with many streets and buildings where people live and work

toxic
ADJECTIVE poisonous

toy **toys**
NOUN something to play with

trace **traces, tracing, traced**
VERB **1** If you **trace** something like a drawing, you copy it by drawing on thin paper over the top, which you can see through.
2 If you **trace** something, you find it after looking for it. ● *Scientists **traced** the origin of the disease.*
NOUN **3** a tiny amount of something or a small mark

track **tracks, tracking, tracked**
NOUN **1** a narrow road or path
2 a strip of ground with rails on it that a train travels along
3 a piece of ground, shaped like a ring, that horses, cars or athletes race around
VERB **4** If you **track** someone or something, you follow them by following the marks they leave as they pass.

tracksuit **tracksuits**
NOUN a loose, warm suit of trousers and a top, worn for outdoor sports

tractor tractors

NOUN a vehicle with large rear wheels, that is used on farms for pulling machinery and other heavy loads

trade trades

NOUN the activity of buying, selling or exchanging goods or services between people or countries

SYNONYM: business

trademark trademarks

NOUN a name or symbol that a manufacturer always uses on its products. **Trademarks** are usually protected by law so that no one else can use them.

trade union trade unions

NOUN an organization of workers that tries to improve the pay and conditions of its members

tradition traditions

NOUN a custom or belief that has existed for a long time and been passed down through the generations without changing [from Latin *traditio* meaning a handing down]

traditional

ADJECTIVE **1** passed down from one generation to the next

2 having existed or gone on for a long time

traffic

NOUN all the vehicles, ships, aircraft or people moving along a route at a particular time

traffic lights

PLURAL NOUN a set of lights used to control traffic at road junctions

traffic warden traffic wardens

NOUN an official whose job is to make sure that vehicles are not parked in the wrong place or for longer than is allowed

tragedy tragedies

NOUN **1** a very sad or disastrous event or situation, especially one in which people are killed

2 a serious story or play that usually ends with the death of the main character

tragic

ADJECTIVE very sad and distressing, usually involving death, destruction or disaster

trail trails

NOUN **1** a rough path across open country or through forests

2 a series of marks or other signs left by someone or something as they move along • *He left a **trail** of mud behind him.*

trailer trailers

NOUN **1** a small vehicle that can be loaded with things and pulled behind a car or lorry

2 a series of short pieces taken from a film or television programme in order to advertise it

train trains, training, trained

NOUN **1** a number of carriages or trucks that are pulled by a railway engine along railway lines

VERB **2** If you **train**, you learn how to do a particular job.

3 If you **train**, or someone **trains** you, for a sports match or a race, you prepare for it by doing exercises.

trainers

PLURAL NOUN special shoes worn for running and other sports

traitor traitors

NOUN someone who betrays their country or the group that they belong to

tram trams

NOUN a passenger vehicle that runs on rails along the street and is powered by electricity from an overhead wire

tramp **tramps, tramping, tramped**
NOUN **1** a person who has no home, no job, and very little money
2 a long country walk
VERB **3** If you **tramp** from one place to another, you walk with slow, heavy footsteps.

trample **tramples, trampling, trampled**
VERB If you **trample** on something, you tread heavily on it so that it is damaged.

trampoline **trampolines**
NOUN a piece of gymnastic equipment made of a large piece of strong cloth held tight by springs in a frame, on which a gymnast bounces

trance **trances**
NOUN If someone is in a **trance**, they seem to be asleep, but they can still see, hear, answer questions and obey orders.

trans-
PREFIX You add **trans-** to a word to mean across, through or beyond. For example, **trans**atlantic means across or beyond the Atlantic Ocean.

transaction **transactions**
NOUN a business deal that involves buying and selling something

transatlantic
ADJECTIVE used to describe something that crosses the Atlantic Ocean or is on the other side of it

transfer **transfers, transferring, transferred**
VERB **1** If you **transfer** something from one place to another, you move it there.
NOUN **2** a piece of paper with a design or drawing on one side that can be ironed or pressed onto another surface, such as cloth, paper or china

transform **transforms, transforming, transformed**
VERB If you **transform** something, or it **transforms**, it changes completely.

transfusion **transfusions**
NOUN a process in which blood donated by a healthy person is injected into the body of another person who needs it because they are badly injured or ill

transistor **transistors**
NOUN **1** a small electrical device in something such as a television or radio, which is used to control electric currents
2 a small portable radio

translate **translates, translating, translated**
VERB If you **translate** something that someone has said or written, you say it or write it in a different language.

translucent
ADJECTIVE If something is **translucent**, it allows the light to shine through and appears to glow.

transmit **transmits, transmitting, transmitted**
VERB **1** When a message or an electronic signal is **transmitted**, it is sent by radio waves.
2 If you **transmit** something, you send it to a different place.
3 If you **transmit** a disease, you pass it on to other people.

transmitter **transmitters**
NOUN a device for sending radio messages

transparent
ADJECTIVE If an object or substance is **transparent**, you can see through it.
SYNONYMS: clear, see-through

transplant **transplants, transplanting, transplanted**
VERB **1** To **transplant** something living, like a plant or an organ, means to remove it from one place and put it in another.
NOUN **2** an operation where an organ, such as a heart or a kidney, is taken from one person and put into another

transport **transports, transporting, transported**
VERB **1** If you **transport** someone or something, you take them from one place to another.
NOUN **2** the name for vehicles you travel in
• Cars and planes are forms of **transport**.

trap **traps, trapping, trapped**

NOUN **1** a piece of equipment or a hole that is dug to catch animals

2 a plan to trick, capture or cheat a person

VERB **3** If you **trap** animals, you catch them using a trap.

4 If you **trap** someone, you trick, capture or cheat them.

trapeze **trapezes**

NOUN a bar hanging from two ropes on which acrobats and gymnasts swing and perform skilful movements

trash

NOUN rubbish

traumatic

ADJECTIVE A **traumatic** experience is very upsetting and causes great stress.

travel **travels, travelling, travelled**

VERB **1** If you **travel**, you go from one place to another.

NOUN **2** the journeys that people make

trawler **trawlers**

NOUN a fishing boat that pulls a wide net behind it to catch fish

tray **trays**

NOUN a flat piece of wood, metal or plastic used for carrying things on

treacherous

ADJECTIVE **1** disloyal and untrustworthy

2 dangerous or unreliable

treacle

NOUN a thick, sweet syrup used to make cakes and toffee

tread **treads, treading, trod, trodden**

VERB **1** If you **tread** on something, you walk on it or step on it.

NOUN **2** The **tread** of a tyre or shoe is the pattern of ridges on it that stops it slipping.

3 the part of a staircase or ladder that you put your foot on

treason

NOUN the crime of betraying your country, for example by helping its enemies

treasure **treasures, treasuring, treasured**

NOUN **1** a collection of gold, silver, jewels or other precious objects, especially one that has been hidden

2 a valuable object, such as a work of art

VERB **3** If you **treasure** something, you look after it carefully because it is important to you. ● *She **treasured** the shells she had collected on her holiday.*

treasury **treasuries**

NOUN **1** a place where treasure is stored

2 The **Treasury** is the government department that looks after a country's finances.

treat **treats, treating, treated**

NOUN **1** If you give someone a **treat**, you buy or arrange something special for them that they will enjoy.

VERB **2** When a doctor **treats** a patient or an illness, he or she gives them medical care and attention.

3 If you **treat** someone or something in a particular way, you behave that way towards them.

treaty **treaties**

NOUN a written agreement between countries, in which they agree to do something or to help each other

treble **trebles, trebling, trebled**

VERB **1** If something **trebles**, or is **trebled**, it becomes three times greater in number or amount.

NOUN **2** **Treble** the amount of something is three times the amount.

tree **trees**

NOUN a large plant with a hard trunk, branches and leaves

trek **treks, trekking, trekked**

VERB **1** If you **trek** somewhere, you go on a long and difficult journey to get there.

NOUN **2** a long and difficult journey, especially one made on foot
[an Afrikaans word]

tremble **trembles, trembling, trembled**

VERB If you **tremble**, you shake slightly,

usually because you are frightened or cold.

tremendous
ADJECTIVE **1** large or impressive ● *It was a **tremendous** performance.*
2 INFORMAL very good or pleasing ● *The game was **tremendous** fun.*

tremor **tremors**
NOUN **1** a small earthquake
2 a slight, uncontrollable shaking movement

trench **trenches**
NOUN a long narrow channel or ditch dug into the ground

trend **trends**
NOUN **1** a general direction in which something is moving
2 a fashion

trendy **trendier, trendiest**
ADJECTIVE INFORMAL fashionable

trespass **trespasses, trespassing, trespassed**
VERB If you **trespass** on someone's land or property, you go onto it without their permission.

trial **trials**
NOUN **1** a legal process in which a court listens to evidence to decide whether a person is innocent or guilty of a crime
2 a type of experiment in which someone or something is tested to see how well they perform

triangle **triangles**
NOUN **1** a plane shape with three straight sides
2 a percussion instrument consisting of a thin steel bar bent in the shape of a triangle. It produces a note when struck with a small metal rod.
triangular ADJECTIVE

tribe **tribes**
NOUN a group of people of the same race, who have the same customs, religion, beliefs, language or land
tribal ADJECTIVE

tributary **tributaries**
NOUN a stream or river that flows into a larger river

tribute **tributes**
NOUN something said or done to show admiration and respect for someone

trick **tricks, tricking, tricked**
VERB **1** If someone **tricks** you, they deceive you.
NOUN **2** an action done to deceive someone
3 a clever or skilful action that is done in order to entertain people ● *a card **trick***

trickle **trickles, trickling, trickled**
VERB When a liquid **trickles**, it flows slowly in a thin stream.

tricky **trickier, trickiest**
ADJECTIVE difficult to do or deal with

tricycle **tricycles**
NOUN a vehicle similar to a bicycle but with three wheels, two at the back and one at the front

tried
VERB the past tense and past participle of **try**

trifle **trifles**
NOUN **1** a cold pudding made of layers of sponge cake, fruit, jelly and custard
2 something unimportant or of little value

trigger **triggers**
NOUN the small lever on a gun that is pulled in order to fire it

trim **trims, trimming, trimmed; trimmer, trimmest**
VERB **1** If you **trim** something, you cut small amounts off it to make it more tidy.
ADJECTIVE **2** neat and tidy
NOUN **3** If something is given a **trim**, it is cut a little.
4 a decoration along the edges of something ● *a coat with a velvet **trim***

trinket **trinkets**
NOUN a cheap ornament or piece of jewellery

trio trios

NOUN **1** a group of three musicians who sing or play together
2 a piece of music written for three instruments or singers

trip trips, tripping, tripped

NOUN **1** a journey made to a place
VERB **2** If you **trip**, or **trip over**, you catch your foot on something and fall over.
3 If you **trip** someone, or **trip** them up, you make them fall over by making them catch their foot on something.

triple triples, tripling, tripled

ADJECTIVE **1** made of three things or three parts
VERB **2** If you **triple** something, or if it **triples**, it becomes three times greater in number or size.

triplet triplets

NOUN one of three children born at the same time to the same mother

tripod tripods

NOUN a stand with three legs used to support something like a camera or telescope

triumph triumphs, triumphing, triumphed

NOUN **1** a great success or achievement
2 a feeling of great satisfaction when you win or achieve something
VERB **3** If you **triumph**, you win a victory or succeed in overcoming something.

triumphant

ADJECTIVE If you are **triumphant**, you feel very happy because you have won a victory or achieved something.

trivial

ADJECTIVE unimportant

trod

VERB the past tense of **tread**

trodden

VERB the past participle of **tread**

troll trolls

NOUN an imaginary creature in Scandinavian mythology, that is either a dwarf or a giant and lives in caves or mountains

trolley trolleys

NOUN **1** a basket or cart on wheels, in which you can carry your shopping or luggage
2 a small table on wheels, used to serve food and drink

trombone trombones

NOUN a brass wind instrument with a U-shaped tube that you slide to produce different notes

troop troops, trooping, trooped

PLURAL NOUN **1 Troops** are soldiers.
NOUN **2** A **troop** of people or animals is a group of them.
VERB **3** If people **troop** somewhere, they go there in a group.

trophy trophies

NOUN a cup or shield given as a prize to the winner of a competition

tropic tropics

NOUN The **tropics** are the hottest regions of the world, that lie on either side of the equator.

Tropic of Cancer
Equator
Tropic of Capricorn

tropical

ADJECTIVE belonging to or typical of the tropics

trot trots, trotting, trotted

VERB **1** When a horse **trots**, it runs with short steps, lifting its feet quite high off the ground.
2 If you **trot**, you run slowly with small steps.

trouble troubles, troubling, troubled

NOUN **1** a difficulty or problem
SYNONYM: worry
PHRASE **2** If you are **in trouble**, someone is angry with you because of something you have done wrong.
VERB **3** If something **troubles** you, it worries or bothers you.
4 If you **trouble** someone, you worry or bother them.

trough troughs

NOUN a long, narrow container from which animals drink or feed

trousers

PLURAL NOUN a piece of clothing for the lower half of your body, from the waist down, covering each leg separately

trout

NOUN a type of edible freshwater fish

trowel trowels

NOUN **1** a garden tool like a small spade, used for planting or weeding
2 a small, flat spade used by builders for spreading cement and mortar

truant truants

NOUN a child who stays away from school without permission

truce truces

NOUN an agreement between two people or groups to stop fighting for a short time

truck trucks

NOUN a large motor vehicle used for carrying heavy loads

trudge trudges, trudging, trudged

VERB **1** If you **trudge**, you walk with slow, heavy steps.
NOUN **2** a slow, tiring walk

true truer, truest

ADJECTIVE **1** A **true** story or statement is based on facts and is not invented.
SYNONYMS: accurate, correct, factual
PHRASE **2** If something **comes true**, it actually happens. ● *I hope your wish comes true*.

trumpet trumpets

NOUN a wind instrument made of a narrow brass tube that widens at the end into a bell-like shape

truncheon truncheons

NOUN a short, thick stick that policemen carry as a weapon

trunk trunks

NOUN **1** the main stem of a tree from which the branches and roots grow
2 the long, flexible nose of an elephant
3 a large, strong case or box with a hinged lid, used for storing things
4 In American English, the **trunk** of a car is the boot, a covered space at the back or front that is used for luggage.
5 the main part of your body, excluding your arms, legs and head
PLURAL NOUN **6** A man's **trunks** are his bathing pants or shorts.

trust trusts, trusting, trusted

VERB **1** If you **trust** someone, you believe that they are honest and reliable, and will treat you fairly.
2 If you **trust** someone to do something, you believe they will do it.
NOUN **3** the feeling that someone can be trusted
4 the responsibility you have to people who trust you

trustworthy

ADJECTIVE A **trustworthy** person is responsible and reliable, and you know that they will do what they say they will do.

truth truths

NOUN the facts about something, rather than things that are imagined or invented

truthful

ADJECTIVE A **truthful** person is honest and tells the truth.

a
b
c
d
e
f
g
h
i
j
k
l
m
n
o
p
q
r
s
t
u
v
w
x
y
z

try **tries, trying, tried**
VERB **1** If you **try** to do something, you make an effort to do it.
2 If you **try** something, you use it, taste it or experiment with it to see how good or suitable it is.
3 When a court **tries** a person, they listen to evidence to decide if that person is guilty of a crime.
4 A person who **tries** your patience is extremely irritating and difficult.
NOUN **5** an attempt to do something
6 A **try** in rugby is when a player scores by carrying the ball over the opponents' goal line and putting it on the ground.

try on
VERB If you **try on** a piece of clothing, you wear it to see if it fits you or if it looks nice.

T-shirt **T-shirts**; also spelt **tee shirt**
NOUN a simple short-sleeved cotton shirt with no collar

tub **tubs**
NOUN a wide, circular container

tuba **tubas**
NOUN a large brass musical instrument that can produce very low notes

tube **tubes**
NOUN a hollow cylinder made of metal, plastic, rubber or other material

tuck **tucks, tucking, tucked**
VERB **1** If you **tuck** a piece of fabric into or under something, you push the loose ends inside or under it to make it tidy.
2 If you **tuck** into a meal, you eat eagerly and with pleasure.
3 If you **tuck** someone up in bed, you put the bedclothes snugly round them.

Tuesday
NOUN the third day of the week, coming between Monday and Wednesday
[an Anglo-Saxon name honouring the god of war called *Tiw*, said *tue*]

tuft **tufts**
NOUN A **tuft** of something, such as hair or grass, is a bunch of it growing closely together.

tug **tugs, tugging, tugged**
VERB **1** If you **tug** something, you give it a quick, hard pull.
NOUN **2** a small, powerful boat that tows large ships

tulip **tulips**
NOUN a brightly coloured spring flower [from Turkish *tulbend* meaning turban, because of the flower's shape]

tumble **tumbles, tumbling, tumbled**
VERB If you **tumble**, you fall with a rolling or bouncing movement.

tumbler **tumblers**
NOUN **1** a drinking glass with no handle or stem
2 an acrobat

tumour **tumours**
NOUN an abnormal growth in the body

tuna
NOUN a large, edible fish that lives in warm seas

tune **tunes**
NOUN a series of musical notes arranged in a particular way

tunnel **tunnels**
NOUN a long underground passage
• *a railway* **tunnel**

turban **turbans**
NOUN a long piece of cloth worn wound round the head, especially by a Hindu, Muslim or Sikh man

turbine **turbines**
NOUN a machine or engine powered by a stream of air, gas, water or steam [from Latin *turbo* meaning whirlwind]

turf
NOUN short, thick, even grass and the layer of soil beneath it

turkey turkeys
NOUN a large bird kept for its meat

turn turns, turning, turned
VERB **1** When you **turn**, you move so that you are facing or going in a different direction.
2 When you **turn** something, or when it **turns**, it moves so that it faces in a different direction or is in a different position. • She **turned** the key in the lock.
3 When something **turns**, or **turns into** something else, it becomes something different, or has a different appearance or quality. • The leaves **turned** brown in autumn.
NOUN **4** If it is your **turn** to do something, you do it next.
VERB **5** If you **turn down** something, you refuse it. • I was not hungry, so I **turned down** the chips.
6 If you **turn up** the television, for example, you increase the volume.
7 If someone **turns up**, they arrive.

turnip turnips
NOUN a round root vegetable with a white or yellow skin

turquoise
NOUN **1** light bluish-green
2 A light bluish-green stone used in jewellery.

turret turrets
NOUN a small, narrow tower on top of a larger tower or other building, such as a castle

turtle turtles
NOUN a large reptile with flippers for swimming and a thick shell covering its body. It lays its eggs on land but lives the rest of its life in the sea.
See **reptile**

tusk tusks
NOUN one of the pair of long, curving, pointed teeth of an elephant, wild boar or walrus

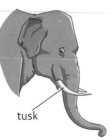

tusk

tutor tutors
NOUN a private teacher or a teacher at a college or university

TV
NOUN an abbreviation of *television*

tweed tweeds
NOUN a thick woollen cloth. Someone wearing **tweeds** is wearing a **tweed** suit.

tweezers
PLURAL NOUN a small tool with two arms that can be closed together to grip something. **Tweezers** are used for pulling out hairs or picking up small objects.

twelve
NOUN **Twelve** is the number 12.
twelfth NOUN OR ADJECTIVE

twenty
NOUN **Twenty** is the number 20.
twentieth NOUN OR ADJECTIVE

twice
ADVERB two times

twiddle twiddles, twiddling, twiddled
VERB If you **twiddle** something, you turn it quickly round and round or over and over.

twig twigs
NOUN a small branch on a tree or bush

twilight
NOUN the time after sunset when it is just getting dark

twin twins
NOUN If two people are **twins**, they have the same mother and were born on the same day.

twinkle twinkles, twinkling, twinkled
VERB Something that **twinkles** shines with little flashes of light.
SYNONYMS: glitter, sparkle

twirl twirls, twirling, twirled
VERB If you **twirl** something, you make it spin round quickly.

twist twists, twisting, twisted
VERB **1** When you **twist** something, you

A
B
C
D
E
F
G
H
I
J
K
L
M
N
O
P
Q
R
S
T
U
V
W
X
Y
Z

turn the two ends in opposite directions. **2** If you **twist** part of your body, you injure it by turning it too sharply or in an odd direction.

two

NOUN **Two** is the number 2.

Do not confuse two *with* to *or* too.

two-dimensional

ADJECTIVE A **two-dimensional** object or shape is flat.

tying

VERB the present participle of **tie**

type **types, typing, typed**

NOUN **1** If something is the same **type** as something else, they belong to the same group and have many things in common.

SYNONYMS: kind, sort

VERB **2** If you **type** something, you use a typewriter or computer to write it.

typewriter **typewriters**

NOUN a machine with keys that are pressed to write numbers and letters on a page

typhoon **typhoons**

NOUN a very violent tropical storm [from Chinese *tai fung* meaning great wind]

typical

ADJECTIVE Something that is **typical** of a person or animal is usual and what is to be expected of them.

tyrannosaurus **tyrannosauruses**

NOUN a very large meat-eating dinosaur that walked upright on its back legs

tyrant **tyrants**

NOUN a person who treats the people they have power over with cruelty

tyre **tyres**

NOUN a thick ring of rubber fitted round each wheel of a vehicle and filled with air

Uu

udder **udders**

NOUN the bag-like part of a cow, goat or ewe from which milk comes

UFO **UFOs**

NOUN an abbreviation of *unidentified flying object*. **UFOs** are objects seen in the skies, which some people believe come from other planets because they cannot be identified.

ugly **uglier, ugliest**

ADJECTIVE very unattractive or unpleasant

ulcer **ulcers**

NOUN a sore area on the skin or inside the body, that can take a long time to heal

ultimate

ADJECTIVE **1** final

NOUN **2** the best example of something

ultraviolet light

NOUN **Ultraviolet light** is not visible to the human eye. It is a form of radiation that causes your skin to tan in sunlight.

umbrella **umbrellas**

NOUN a folding frame covered in fabric and attached to a long stick, which you can open over you to protect you from the rain

umpire **umpires, umpiring, umpired**

NOUN **1** The **umpire** in a cricket or tennis match is the person who makes sure that the game is played fairly and the rules are not broken.

VERB **2** If a person **umpires** a game, they are the umpire.

un-

PREFIX You add **un-** to the beginning of a word to mean not. For example, **un**common means not common, and **un**likely means not likely.

unable
ADJECTIVE If you are **unable** to do something, you cannot do it.

unanimous
Said "yoo-**nan**-nim-mus" ADJECTIVE A **unanimous** decision or vote has the agreement of everyone involved.

unaware
ADJECTIVE not aware

unbearable
ADJECTIVE Something **unbearable** is so painful or upsetting that you feel that you cannot bear or endure it.

unbelievable
ADJECTIVE **1** very surprising or wonderful **2** so unlikely that it is hard to believe

uncanny
ADJECTIVE strange and mysterious

uncertain
ADJECTIVE If you are **uncertain** about something, you are not sure about it.
SYNONYM: doubtful
uncertainty NOUN

uncle **uncles**
NOUN the brother of your mother or father, or the husband of your aunt
[from Latin *avunculus* meaning mother's brother]

uncomfortable
ADJECTIVE **1** If you are **uncomfortable**, your body is not relaxed or comfortable. **2** If something like a chair or a piece of clothing is **uncomfortable**, it is not comfortable to sit in or to wear. **3** If you feel **uncomfortable** in a situation, you feel worried or nervous.

uncommon
ADJECTIVE not common

unconscious
ADJECTIVE If someone is **unconscious**, they are unable to see, feel or hear anything that is going on. This is usually because they have fainted or been badly injured.

uncover **uncovers, uncovering, uncovered**
VERB **1** to take the cover off something **2** to find out a secret or discover something

under
PREPOSITION **1** below or beneath **2** less than • *children **under** the age of 14* **3** controlled or ruled by • *The soldiers were **under** his command.* **4** If something like a building is **under** construction, or **under** repair, it is in the process of being built or repaired.

under-
PREFIX You add **under-** at the beginning of a word to mean beneath or below. For example, if you **under**estimate an amount, you estimate it below what it really is.

undercarriage **undercarriages**
NOUN the part of an aircraft, including the wheels, that supports the aircraft when it is on the ground

underestimate **underestimates, underestimating, underestimated**
VERB **1** If you **underestimate** someone, you do not realize how much they can do. **2** If you **underestimate** something, you do not realize how big it is or how long it will take.

undergo **undergoes, undergoing, underwent, undergone**
VERB If you **undergo** something, you experience it or are subjected to it.
• *She **underwent** an operation to remove her tonsils.*

underground
ADJECTIVE **1** below the surface of the ground
NOUN **2** a railway system in which trains travel in tunnels below the ground

a
b
c
d
e
f
g
h
i
j
k
l
m
n
o
p
q
r
s
t
u
v
w
x
y
z

undergrowth
NOUN small plants growing under trees

underline underlines, underlining, underlined
VERB If you **underline** a word or sentence, you draw a line under it.

undermine undermines, undermining, undermined
VERB **1** If you **undermine** a person's efforts or plans, you weaken them.
2 To **undermine** something is to make a hollow or tunnel beneath it. When the sea **undermines** a cliff, for example, it gradually wears away the base and weakens it.

underneath
PREPOSITION OR ADVERB below or beneath

underpants
PLURAL NOUN a piece of men's underwear worn under trousers

underpass underpasses
NOUN a place where one road or path goes under another

underprivileged
ADJECTIVE **Underprivileged** people have less money and fewer opportunities than other people.

understand understands, understanding, understood
VERB **1** If you **understand** what someone says, or what you read, you know what it means.
2 If you **understand** how something works, you know how it works.
3 If you **understand** someone, you know them well and think you know why they behave the way they do.

understudy understudies
NOUN someone who has learnt the lines of a part in a play, and plays the part when the main actor or actress cannot perform

undertake undertakes, undertaking, undertook, undertaken
VERB If you **undertake** to do something, you agree to do it.

undertaker undertakers
NOUN someone whose job is to prepare bodies for burial and arrange funerals

underwater
ADVERB OR ADJECTIVE below the surface of the water

underwear
NOUN Your **underwear** is the clothing you wear next to your skin under your other clothes.

undo undoes, undoing, undid, undone
VERB **1** If you **undo** something like a knot, you loosen or unfasten it.
2 If you **undo** something that has been done, you reverse or remove the effects of it.

undress undresses, undressing, undressed
VERB If you **undress**, you take your clothes off.

unearth unearths, unearthing, unearthed
VERB If you **unearth** something, you dig it up or discover it.

uneasy uneasier, uneasiest
ADJECTIVE anxious or worried

unemployed
ADJECTIVE An **unemployed** person has no job.

uneven
ADJECTIVE An **uneven** surface is not level or smooth.

unexpected
ADJECTIVE Something **unexpected** is surprising because it was not thought likely to happen.

unfair
ADJECTIVE Something **unfair** does not seem right, reasonable or fair.

unfold unfolds, unfolding, unfolded
VERB **1** If you **unfold** something that is folded, such as a map, you open it out.
2 When a story **unfolds**, it gradually becomes clear.

unfortunate
ADJECTIVE unlucky

unfriendly
ADJECTIVE not friendly

ungrateful
ADJECTIVE not grateful

unhappy unhappier, unhappiest
ADJECTIVE sad, not happy

unhealthy
ADJECTIVE not healthy

unicorn unicorns
NOUN an imaginary animal that looks like a white horse with a straight horn growing from its forehead
[from Latin *unicornis* meaning having one horn]

uniform uniforms
NOUN a special set of clothes worn by people at work or school
[from Latin *uniformis* meaning of one kind]

unify unifies, unifying, unified
VERB If several things, especially countries, are **unified**, they join together to make one.

uninhabited
ADJECTIVE An **uninhabited** place is a place where nobody lives.

union unions
NOUN an organization of workers that aims to improve the working conditions, pay and benefits of its members

unique
ADJECTIVE Something that is **unique** is the only one of its kind.
[from Latin *unicus* meaning one and only]

unisex
ADJECTIVE designed to suit either men or women

unison
NOUN If a group of people does something in **unison**, they all do it together at the same time.
[from Latin *unisonus* meaning making the same musical sound]

unit units
NOUN **1** one single, complete thing
2 a term used to describe a fixed quantity or measurement • *A centimetre is a **unit** of length.*

unite unites, uniting, united
VERB If a number of people **unite**, they join together and act as a group.

universal
ADJECTIVE concerning or relating to everyone and everything

universe universes
NOUN everything that exists, including the whole of space, all the stars and the planets
[from Latin *universum* meaning whole world]

university universities
NOUN a place where students study for degrees

unkempt
ADJECTIVE untidy and not looked after properly
[from Old English *uncembed* meaning not combed]

unkind
ADJECTIVE rather cruel, not kind

unknown
ADJECTIVE If someone or something is **unknown**, people do not know about them or have not heard of them.

unleaded
ADJECTIVE **Unleaded** petrol does not contain any lead, and is less harmful to the atmosphere than petrol that does contain lead.

unless
CONJUNCTION You use **unless** to introduce the only circumstances in which something may or may not happen or is not true.
• *The team will play tomorrow **unless** it is raining.* • *I won't go **unless** you ask me.*

unlike
ADJECTIVE **1** If one thing is **unlike** another, the two things are different.
PREPOSITION **2** not like • *Unlike me, she hates chocolate.*

unlikely unlikelier, unlikeliest
ADJECTIVE not likely to happen or be true

a b c d e f g h i j k l m n o p q r s t u v w x y z

unload **unloads, unloading, unloaded**
VERB to take things out of or off a container, a vehicle or a trailer

unlock **unlocks, unlocking, unlocked**
VERB When you **unlock** something, you open it by turning a key in the lock.

unlucky **unluckier, unluckiest**
ADJECTIVE If you are **unlucky**, you are unfortunate and have bad luck.
ANTONYMS: fortunate, lucky

unnatural
ADJECTIVE not natural or normal

unnecessary
ADJECTIVE not necessary

unoccupied
ADJECTIVE A house that is **unoccupied** has no one living in it.

unpack **unpacks, unpacking, unpacked**
VERB When you **unpack**, you take everything out of a suitcase, bag or box.

unpleasant
ADJECTIVE **1** Something **unpleasant** is not enjoyable and may make you uncomfortable or upset.
2 An **unpleasant** person is unfriendly or rude.

unplug **unplugs, unplugging, unplugged**
VERB If you **unplug** something, you take the plug out of the socket to disconnect it from the electricity supply.

unpopular
ADJECTIVE not liked very much

unravel **unravels, unravelling, unravelled**
VERB **1** If you **unravel** threads that are knitted or tangled, you undo or untangle them.
2 If you **unravel** a mystery, you solve it.

unreal
ADJECTIVE existing only in the imagination, not real

unreasonable
ADJECTIVE not reasonable or fair

unroll **unrolls, unrolling, unrolled**
VERB If you **unroll** something that has been rolled up, you open it and make it flat.

unruly
ADJECTIVE badly behaved and difficult to control

unsafe
ADJECTIVE not safe

unscrew **unscrews, unscrewing, unscrewed**
VERB If you **unscrew** something, you remove it by turning it or by removing the screws that are holding it.

unselfish
ADJECTIVE An **unselfish** person is not selfish and is concerned about other people's needs.

unsteady
ADJECTIVE If you are **unsteady**, you are not steady and have difficulty balancing.

unsuccessful
ADJECTIVE If you are **unsuccessful**, you do not manage to succeed in what you are trying to do.

unsuitable
ADJECTIVE Things that are **unsuitable** are not right or suitable for a particular purpose.

untidy **untidier, untidiest**
ADJECTIVE not tidy

untie **unties, untying, untied**
VERB If you **untie** something that has been tied, you unfasten or undo it.

until
PREPOSITION OR CONJUNCTION **1** If something happens **until** a particular time, it happens before that time and stops at that time. ● *The shops stay open **until** eight o'clock on Thursdays.*
2 If something does not happen **until** a particular time, it does not happen before that time and only starts happening at that time. ● *It didn't rain **until** the middle of the afternoon.*

untrue
ADJECTIVE not true

unusual
ADJECTIVE Something that is **unusual** is not usual and does not happen very often.

unwell
ADJECTIVE If you are **unwell**, you are ill.

unwilling
ADJECTIVE If you are **unwilling** to do something, you do not want to do it.
unwillingly ADVERB

unwind **unwinds, unwinding, unwound**
VERB **1** If you **unwind** something that was wound into a ball or around something else, you undo it.
2 If you **unwind** after working hard, you relax.

unwrap **unwraps, unwrapping, unwrapped**
VERB If you **unwrap** something, you take off the paper or other wrapping that is around it.

up
ADVERB OR PREPOSITION **1** towards or in a higher place • *They went **up** the stairs to bed.*
ADVERB **2** If an amount of something goes **up**, it increases.
PREPOSITION **3** If you go **up** the road, you go along it.
ADJECTIVE **4** If you are **up**, you are not in bed.

upbringing
NOUN the way you have been brought up, and how your parents have taught you to behave

upheaval **upheavals**
NOUN a sudden big change that causes a lot of disturbance

uphill
ADVERB If you go **uphill**, you go up a hill or a slope.

upholstery
NOUN the soft covering on chairs and sofas that makes them comfortable
upholstered ADJECTIVE

upload **uploads, uploading, uploaded**
VERB When you **upload** a computer file or program, you put it onto a computer or the internet.

upon
PREPOSITION on or on top of

upper
ADJECTIVE The **upper** of two things is the top or higher one. • *the **upper** deck of the bus*

upper-case
ADJECTIVE **Upper-case** letters are written as capitals. For example, A, H, L and P are all **upper-case** letters.

upright
ADJECTIVE OR ADVERB **1** Something or someone that is **upright**, is standing up straight or vertically, rather than bending or lying down.
2 An **upright** person is decent and honest.

uproar
NOUN a lot of shouting and noise, often because people are angry
SYNONYMS: commotion, pandemonium
[from Dutch *oproer* meaning revolt]

upset **upsets, upsetting, upset**
ADJECTIVE **1** unhappy and disappointed
VERB **2** If something **upsets** you, it makes you feel worried or unhappy.
3 If you **upset** something, you knock it over or spill it accidentally.
NOUN **4** A stomach **upset** is a slight stomach illness.

upside down
ADJECTIVE **1** the wrong way up • *She was **upside down** on the climbing frame.*

2 If a place is **upside down**, it is very untidy.

a b c d e f g h i j k l m n o p q r s t u v w x y z

upstairs
ADVERB OR ADJECTIVE up to or on a higher floor

up-to-date
ADJECTIVE If something is **up-to-date**, it is modern or is the newest thing of its kind.

upwards
ADVERB going towards a higher place

uranium
NOUN a radioactive metallic element used to make nuclear energy and weapons

urban
ADJECTIVE to do with towns or cities rather than the country
[from Latin *urbs* meaning city]

urge urges, urging, urged
NOUN **1** If you have an **urge** to do something, you very much want to do it.
VERB **2** If you **urge** someone to do something, you try to persuade and encourage them to do it.

urgent
ADJECTIVE If something is **urgent**, it needs to be dealt with immediately.

urine
NOUN the waste liquid that you get rid of from your body when you go to the toilet

URL URLs
NOUN A website's **URL** is its address on the internet. **URL** is an abbreviation for *uniform resource locator.*

us
PRONOUN A speaker or writer uses **us** to mean himself or herself and one or more other people.

use uses, using, used
Said "**yooz**" VERB **1** If you **use** something, you do something with it that helps you to do a job or sort out a problem.
Said "**yooss**" NOUN **2** the purpose or value of something, and the way it is used

used
Said "**yoosst**" VERB **1** If something **used to** happen, it happened before but does not happen now. • *We **used to** fish in this stream.*
ADJECTIVE **2** If you are **used to** something,

you are familiar with it and have often experienced it.
Said "**yoozd**" VERB **3** the past tense and past participle of **use**
ADJECTIVE **4** A **used** item has already belonged to someone else.

useful
ADJECTIVE If something is **useful**, you can use it to help you in some way.

useless
ADJECTIVE Something that is **useless** is no good for anything.

user-friendly
ADJECTIVE If something is **user-friendly**, it is easy to understand and use. • *the most **user-friendly** camera available*

usher ushers
NOUN a person who shows people where to sit at the theatre or cinema

usual
ADJECTIVE **1** Something **usual** is expected and happens often.
PHRASE **2** If something happens **as usual**, it happens as you would expect, and is not surprising because it often happens that way.

utensil utensils
NOUN a tool • *A whisk is a kitchen **utensil**.*

utility utilities
NOUN a service that is useful for everyone, such as water and gas supplies

utter utters, uttering, uttered
VERB **1** When you **utter** sounds, you make or say them.
ADJECTIVE **2** complete or total • *This is **utter** nonsense.*

Vv

vacant
ADJECTIVE If something is **vacant**, it is not being used or no one is in it. ● *I couldn't find a **vacant** seat on the train.*

vacation vacations
NOUN a holiday

vaccinate vaccinates, vaccinating, vaccinated
*Said "**vak**-si-nayt"* VERB If someone **vaccinates** you, they give you an injection to protect you against a disease.

vacuum vacuums, vacuuming, vacuumed
NOUN **1** a completely empty space containing no matter, solid, liquid or gas
VERB **2** If you **vacuum** something, you clean it using a vacuum cleaner.
[from Latin *vacuum* meaning empty space]

vacuum cleaner vacuum cleaners
NOUN an electrical device that sucks up dust and dirt from the floor

vagina vaginas
NOUN A woman's **vagina** is the passage that leads from the outside of her body to her womb.

vague vaguer, vaguest
*Said "**vayg**"* ADJECTIVE not clear, definite or certain ● *They could see the **vague** outline of the mountains in the distance.*
SYNONYM: unclear
vaguely ADVERB **vagueness** NOUN

vain vainer, vainest
ADJECTIVE **1** A **vain** person is too proud of their looks, intelligence or other good qualities.
2 A **vain** attempt to do something is an unsuccessful attempt.

valentine valentines
NOUN **1** someone you love and send a card to on Saint **Valentine's** Day, February 14th
2 a card you send to someone you love on Saint **Valentine's** Day
[Saint *Valentine* was a third-century martyr]

valiant
ADJECTIVE brave and courageous

valid
ADJECTIVE A **valid** ticket or document is legal and accepted by people in authority.

valley valleys
NOUN a long stretch of land between hills, often with a river flowing through it

valuable
ADJECTIVE of great worth or very important ● *The diamond ring was very **valuable**.*

value values, valuing, valued
NOUN **1** the importance or usefulness of something
2 the amount of money that something is worth
VERB **3** If you **value** something, you think it is important and valuable.

valve valves
NOUN **1** a device attached to a pipe or tube that controls the flow of gas or liquid
2 a small flap in your heart or in a vein that controls the flow and direction of blood

vampire vampires
NOUN In horror stories, **vampires** come out of graves at night and suck people's blood.

a
b
c
d
e
f
g
h
i
j
k
l
m
n
o
p
q
r
s
t
u
v
w
x
y
z

van **vans**

NOUN a vehicle for carrying goods

vandal **vandals**

NOUN someone who deliberately damages or destroys things, particularly public property

vandalize or vandalise VERB

vandalism NOUN

vanilla

NOUN a flavouring used in food such as ice cream. It comes from the pod of a tropical plant.

vanish **vanishes, vanishing, vanished**

VERB If something **vanishes**, it disappears or does not exist any more.

vapour

NOUN a mass of tiny drops of water or other liquids in the air, which looks like mist

[from Latin *vapor* meaning steam]

variety **varieties**

NOUN a number of different kinds of similar things • *There was a **variety** of food from different countries on the menu.*

SYNONYMS: assortment, range

various

ADJECTIVE of several different types • *trees of **various** sorts*

SYNONYMS: different, miscellaneous

varnish **varnishes, varnishing, varnished**

NOUN **1** a liquid which, when painted onto a surface such as wood, gives it a hard, clear, shiny finish

VERB **2** If you **varnish** something, you paint it with varnish.

vary **varies, varying, varied**

VERB If something **varies**, it changes and is not always the same.

vase **vases**

NOUN a jar or other container for putting cut flowers in

vast

ADJECTIVE extremely large

vastly ADVERB vastness NOUN

vat **vats**

NOUN a large container used for storing liquids

VAT

NOUN an abbreviation of *value-added tax*, which is a tax you pay on things you buy

vault **vaults, vaulting, vaulted**

NOUN **1** a strong secure room where valuables are stored, often underneath a building, or where people are buried underneath a church

2 an arched roof, often found in churches

VERB **3** If you **vault** over something, you jump over it using your hands or a pole to help.

VDU

NOUN an abbreviation of *visual display unit*, which is a monitor screen for computers

veal

NOUN the meat from a calf

Veda

NOUN the collection of ancient sacred writings of the Hindu religion

vegetable **vegetables**

NOUN **Vegetables** are plants or parts of plants that can be eaten. Peas, carrots, cabbage and potatoes are **vegetables**.

vegetarian **vegetarians**

NOUN a person who does not eat meat, poultry or fish

vegetation

NOUN the plants growing in a particular area

vehicle **vehicles**

NOUN a machine, often with an engine, such as a car, bus or lorry, used for moving people or goods from one place to another

veil **veils**

NOUN a piece of thin, soft cloth that women sometimes wear over their heads and faces

vein **veins**

NOUN Your **veins** are the tubes in your body through which your blood flows to your heart.

See **artery**

A B C D E F G H I J K L M N O P Q R S T U V W X Y Z

velvet
NOUN a very soft material that has a thick layer of short threads on one side

vengeance
NOUN the act of harming someone because they have harmed you

venison
NOUN the meat from a deer

Venn diagram **Venn diagrams**
NOUN a diagram using circles to show how sets of things relate to each other. **Venn diagrams** are used in mathematics.

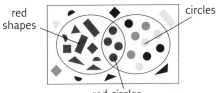

red shapes — circles — red circles

venom
NOUN the poison of a snake, scorpion or spider
[from Latin *venenum* meaning love potion or poison]
venomous ADJECTIVE **venomously** ADVERB

vent **vents**
NOUN an opening in something, especially to let out smoke or gas

ventilate **ventilates, ventilating, ventilated**
VERB If you **ventilate** a place, you allow fresh air to move freely through it.

venture **ventures, venturing, ventured**
NOUN **1** something new that you do which involves some sort of risk
VERB **2** If you **venture** somewhere that might be dangerous, you go there.

veranda **verandas**; also spelt **verandah**
NOUN a platform with a roof that is fixed to the outside wall of a house at ground level. It is often made of wood.

verb **verbs**
NOUN In grammar, a **verb** is a word that expresses actions and states, for example *be*, *become*, *take* and *run*.

verbal
ADJECTIVE spoken rather than written
verbally ADVERB

verdict **verdicts**
NOUN In a law court, a **verdict** is the decision reached by the judge or jury about whether a prisoner is guilty or not guilty.

verge **verges**
NOUN the narrow strip of grassy ground at the side of a road • We walked along the *verge*.

verify **verifies, verifying, verified**
VERB If you **verify** something, you check that it is true or correct.
verifiable ADJECTIVE **verification** NOUN

verruca **verrucas**
NOUN a small, hard, infectious growth that you can get on the sole of your foot

versatile
ADJECTIVE If someone or something is **versatile**, they have many different skills or uses.
versatility NOUN

verse **verses**
NOUN **1** another word for **poetry**
2 one part of a poem, song or chapter of the Bible

version **versions**
NOUN A **version** of something is a form of it that is different in some way from earlier or later forms.

versus
PREPOSITION **Versus** means against, and is used to show that two people or teams are competing against each other.

vertebra **vertebrae**
NOUN one of the bones that make up your backbone

vertebrate **vertebrates**
NOUN an animal with a backbone

vertex **vertices**
NOUN the highest point of a hill, or a corner of a two-dimensional or three-dimensional shape
See **apex**

vertical
ADJECTIVE Something that is **vertical** is in an upright position or points straight up.

very
ADVERB **Very** is used before words to emphasize them. • *I had a **very** bad dream.*
SYNONYMS: extremely, greatly, really

vessel **vessels**
NOUN **1** a ship or large boat
2 a container for liquids
3 one of the tubes in an animal or a plant that carries blood or other liquid around the body

vest **vests**
NOUN a piece of underwear worn on the top half of the body for warmth
[from Latin *vestis* meaning clothing]

vet **vets**
NOUN a doctor for animals. **Vet** is an abbreviation of *veterinary surgeon*.

veteran **veterans**
NOUN **1** a person with a lot of experience of something, or who has been involved in something for a long time
2 someone who has served in the armed forces, particularly during a war • *My uncle is a Gulf War **veteran**.*

via
PREPOSITION If you go to one place **via** another, you travel through that other place to get to your destination.
[from Latin *via* meaning way or road]

viaduct **viaducts**
NOUN a high bridge that carries a road or railway across a valley

vibrate **vibrates, vibrating, vibrated**
VERB If something **vibrates**, it moves a tiny amount backwards and forwards very quickly.
vibration NOUN

vicar **vicars**
NOUN a priest in the Church of England

vice **vices**
NOUN a bad habit, such as being greedy or smoking

vice versa
ADVERB the other way around

vicinity **vicinities**
NOUN an area round something • *She was seen in the **vicinity** of the school.*

vicious
ADJECTIVE cruel and violent

victim **victims**
NOUN someone who has been harmed or injured by someone or something

victor **victors**
NOUN the winner of a contest or battle

victory **victories**
NOUN a success in a battle or competition
SYNONYMS: conquest, triumph, win

video **videos, videoing, videoed**
NOUN **1** a sound and picture recording that can be played back on a television set
2 the recording and showing of films and events using a **video** recorder, tape and a television set
3 a video recorder • *Set the **video** to record a programme at eight o'clock.*
VERB **4** If you **video** something, you record it on video tape to watch later.
[from Latin *videre* meaning to see]

video game **video games**
NOUN a game that can be played by using an electronic control to move symbols on a screen

view **views**
NOUN everything you can see from a particular place

viewer **viewers**
NOUN one of the people who watch something, especially a television programme

viewpoint **viewpoints**
NOUN Your **viewpoint** is your attitude towards something.

vigilant
ADJECTIVE careful and alert to danger or trouble
vigilance NOUN   vigilantly ADVERB

vigorous
ADJECTIVE energetic or enthusiastic
vigorously ADVERB

villa villas
NOUN a house, especially a pleasant holiday home in a country with a warm climate

village villages
NOUN a collection of houses and other buildings in the countryside
[from Old French *ville* meaning farm]

villain villains
NOUN someone who harms others or breaks the law
SYNONYMS: criminal, rogue

vine vines
NOUN a climbing plant, especially one that produces grapes

vinegar
NOUN a sharp-tasting liquid made from sour wine and used for flavouring food
[from French *vin aigre* meaning sour wine]

vineyard vineyards
NOUN an area of land where grapes are grown for making wine

vintage
ADJECTIVE **1** A **vintage** wine is a good quality wine made in a particular year.
2 A **vintage** car is one made between 1918 and 1930.

vinyl
NOUN a strong plastic used to make things such as furniture and floor coverings

viola violas
NOUN a musical instrument like a violin, but larger and with a lower pitch

violence
NOUN **1** behaviour that is intended to hurt or kill
2 force that does harm or damage ● *The* **violence** *of the storm surprised everyone.*
violent ADJECTIVE   violently ADVERB

violet violets
NOUN **1** a plant with dark purple flowers
NOUN OR ADJECTIVE **2** bluish purple

violin violins
NOUN a musical instrument with four strings that is held under the chin and played with a bow

VIP
NOUN an abbreviation of *very important person* ● *The* **VIPs** *had the best seats at the concert.*

viper vipers
NOUN a type of poisonous snake

virtual
ADJECTIVE almost exactly the same as the real thing

virtual reality
NOUN an environment or image that has been created by a computer and looks real to the person using it

virtue virtues
NOUN **1** moral goodness
2 a good quality in someone's character

virus viruses
NOUN **1** a tiny organism that can cause disease
2 A disease caused by a virus can be called a **virus**.
3 a program that damages the information stored in a computer system

visible
ADJECTIVE able to be seen

vision visions
NOUN **1** the ability to see
2 a picture of something in your mind or imagination

visit visits, visiting, visited
VERB **1** If you **visit** someone, you go to see them and spend time with them.

2 If you **visit** a place, you go to see it.
NOUN **3** a trip to see a person or place

visor visors

NOUN **1** a transparent, movable shield attached to a helmet, which can be pulled down to protect the eyes or face
2 a shade to protect your eyes from the sun

visual

ADJECTIVE to do with sight and seeing

vital

ADJECTIVE necessary or very important
SYNONYM: essential

vitality

NOUN People who have **vitality** are energetic and lively.

vitamin vitamins

NOUN one of a group of substances you need to have in your diet in order to stay healthy. For example, **vitamin** C is found in oranges.

vivid

ADJECTIVE very bright in colour or clear in detail

vivisection

NOUN the use of living animals for medical research

vixen vixens

NOUN a female fox

vocabulary vocabularies

NOUN **1** the total number of words someone knows in a particular language
2 all the words in a language

vocal

ADJECTIVE to do with or involving the use of the human voice
vocalist NOUN vocally ADVERB

vocation vocations

NOUN **1** If you have a **vocation**, you want very much to do a particular job, especially one that involves helping other people.
2 a profession or career

voice voices

NOUN Your **voice** is what you hear when you speak or sing.

void voids

NOUN a very large empty space or deep hole

volcano volcanoes

NOUN a mountain with an opening at the top called a crater, from which lava, gas and ash sometimes erupt
[named after *Vulcan*, the Roman god of fire]

vole voles

NOUN a small mammal like a mouse with a short tail, which lives in fields and near rivers

volley volleys

NOUN **1** A **volley** of shots or missiles is a lot of them fired or thrown at the same time.
2 In tennis, a **volley** is a stroke in which the player hits the ball before it bounces.

volleyball

NOUN a game in which two teams hit a ball back and forth over a high net with their hands. The ball is not allowed to bounce on the ground.

volt volts

NOUN the unit used to measure the voltage of a battery
[named after Alessandro *Volta* who invented the electric battery]

voltage voltages

NOUN the measure of how much electrical current a battery can push through an electric circuit

volume volumes

NOUN **1** the amount of space something contains or occupies
2 The **volume** of a radio, TV or record player is how loud it is.
3 a book, or one of a series of books

voluntary

ADJECTIVE Something **voluntary** is done because you want to do it, not because you are paid or told to do it.
voluntarily ADVERB

volunteer volunteers, volunteering, volunteered

NOUN **1** someone who does work that they are not paid for

VERB 2 If you **volunteer** to do something, you offer to do it without expecting any reward.

vomit **vomits, vomiting, vomited**
VERB If you **vomit**, food and drink comes back up from your stomach and out through your mouth.

vote **votes, voting, voted**
NOUN 1 Someone's **vote** is their choice in an election, or at a meeting where decisions are taken.
VERB 2 When people **vote**, they show their choice or opinion, usually by writing on a piece of paper or by raising their hand.

voucher **vouchers**
NOUN a piece of paper that can be used instead of money to pay for something

vow **vows, vowing, vowed**
VERB 1 If you **vow** to do something, you make a promise to do it.
NOUN 2 a promise

vowel **vowels**
NOUN 1 a sound made without your tongue touching the roof of your mouth or your teeth
2 In the English language the letters a, e, i, o and u are **vowels**.

voyage **voyages**
NOUN a long journey on a ship or in a spacecraft

vulgar
ADJECTIVE rude or offensive

vulnerable
ADJECTIVE without protection and easily hurt or damaged
SYNONYM: defenceless

vulture **vultures**
NOUN a large bird that lives in hot countries and eats the flesh of dead animals

Ww

waddle **waddles, waddling, waddled**
VERB to walk with short, quick steps, swaying slightly from side to side • *A duck **waddled** past.*

wade **wades, wading, waded**
VERB If you **wade**, you walk through water or mud.

wafer **wafers**
NOUN a thin, crisp biscuit, often eaten with ice cream

waffle **waffles, waffling, waffled**
VERB 1 When someone **waffles**, they talk or write a lot without being clear or without saying anything of importance.
NOUN 2 a thick, crisp pancake with squares marked on it, often eaten with syrup poured over it

wag **wags, wagging, wagged**
VERB 1 When a dog **wags** its tail, it shakes it repeatedly from side to side.
2 If you **wag** your finger, you move it repeatedly up and down.

wage **wages**
NOUN the regular payment made to someone each week for the work they do

wagon **wagons**; also spelt **waggon**
NOUN a strong four-wheeled cart for carrying heavy loads. **Wagons** are usually pulled by horses or tractors.

wail **wails, wailing, wailed**
VERB If a person or an animal **wails**, they cry or moan loudly.

waist **waists**
NOUN the middle part of your body where it narrows slightly above your hips

waistcoat **waistcoats**
NOUN a sleeveless piece of clothing, usually worn over a shirt and under a jacket

A
B
C
D
E
F
G
H
I
J
K
L
M
N
O
P
Q
R
S
T
U
V
W
X
Y
Z

wait **waits, waiting, waited**
VERB **1** If you **wait**, you spend time in a place or a situation, usually doing little or nothing, before something happens.
2 to serve people food and drinks as a waiter or waitress
NOUN **3** A **wait** is a period of time before something happens.

waiter **waiters**
NOUN a man who works in a restaurant, serving people with food and drink

waitress **waitresses**
NOUN a woman who works in a restaurant, serving people with food and drink

wake **wakes, waking, woke, woken**
VERB When you **wake**, or when something **wakes** you, you become conscious again after being asleep.

walk **walks, walking, walked**
VERB **1** When you **walk**, you move along by putting one foot in front of the other on the ground.
NOUN **2** If you go for a **walk**, you go from one place to another on foot.

wall **walls**
NOUN **1** a narrow structure of brick or stone built round a garden or building
2 one of the four sides of a room

wallaby **wallabies**
NOUN a marsupial that looks like a small kangaroo
[from *wolaba*, an Australian Aboriginal word]

wallet **wallets**
NOUN a small, flat, folding case made of leather or plastic, used for holding paper money and sometimes credit cards

wallpaper **wallpapers**
NOUN thick coloured or patterned paper that comes in rolls, for pasting onto the walls of rooms to decorate them

walnut **walnuts**
NOUN **1** a nut that you can eat. It has a wrinkled shape and a hard, round, light-brown shell.

2 the tree on which walnuts grow. The wood from these trees is often used for making expensive furniture.

walrus **walruses**
NOUN an animal that lives in the sea. It looks like a large seal with a tough skin, coarse whiskers and two tusks.

waltz **waltzes, waltzing, waltzed**
NOUN **1** a dance that has a rhythm of three beats to the bar
VERB **2** If you **waltz** with someone, you dance a waltz with them.

wand **wands**
NOUN a long, thin rod used by magicians when they perform magic tricks, and by fairies in stories

wander **wanders, wandering, wandered**
VERB If you **wander** in a place, you walk around in a casual way.

want **wants, wanting, wanted**
VERB **1** If you **want** something, you feel that you would like to have it or do it.
2 to need something

wanted
ADJECTIVE being looked for, especially by the police as a suspected criminal

war **wars**
NOUN a period of fighting between countries or states, when weapons are used and many people may be killed

ward **wards**
NOUN **1** a long room with beds in for patients in a hospital
2 a child who is looked after by a guardian rather than their parents

warden **wardens**
NOUN **1** a person in charge of a place like a park or a block of flats, or an institution like a prison or a hostel
2 an official who makes sure that certain laws or rules are obeyed

wardrobe **wardrobes**
NOUN a tall cupboard in which you can hang your clothes
[from Old French *warder* meaning to guard robes and *robes* meaning clothing]

warehouse **warehouses**
NOUN a large building where goods are stored

warm **warmer, warmest; warms, warming, warmed**
ADJECTIVE **1** Something that is **warm** has some heat, but not enough to be hot.
2 Warm clothes or blankets are made of material that protects you from the cold.
VERB **3** If you **warm** something, you heat it up gently so that it stops being cold.

warn **warns, warning, warned**
VERB If you **warn** someone, you tell them that they may be in danger or in trouble.

warning **warnings**
NOUN something said or written to warn someone of a possible danger or problem

warp **warps, warping, warped**
VERB If something **warps**, or is **warped**, it becomes bent and twisted, usually because of heat or dampness.

warrant **warrants**
NOUN a special document that gives someone permission to do something
• The police had a **warrant** to search the house for evidence.

warren **warrens**
NOUN an area of ground where there are many rabbit burrows

warrior **warriors**
NOUN a fighting man or soldier

wart **warts**
NOUN a small, hard growth on the skin

wary **warier, wariest**
ADJECTIVE If you are **wary** of something or someone, you are not sure about them, so you are cautious.

was
VERB a past tense of **be**

wash **washes, washing, washed**
VERB **1** If you **wash** something, you clean it with water and soap.
2 If you **wash**, you clean yourself using soap and water.

wash up
VERB If you **wash up**, you wash the dishes, pans and cutlery used in preparing and eating a meal.

washable
ADJECTIVE able to be washed without being damaged

washing
NOUN clothes that need to be washed or that have been washed

washing machine **washing machines**
NOUN a machine for washing clothes

washing-up
NOUN the task of washing plates, cutlery and pots after a meal

wasp **wasps**
NOUN a flying insect with yellow and black stripes across its body, which can sting

waste **wastes, wasting, wasted**
VERB **1** If you **waste** time, money or energy, you use too much of it on something that is not important or that you do not need.
NOUN **2** using more money or some other resource than you need to
3 rubbish or other material that is no longer wanted, or that is left over

watch **watches, watching, watched**
NOUN **1** a small clock, usually worn on a strap on a person's wrist
VERB **2** If you **watch** something, you look at it for some time and pay attention to what is happening.

watch out
VERB **1** If you **watch out** for something or someone, you keep alert to see if they are near you.
2 If you tell someone to **watch out**, you are warning them to be careful.

water **waters, watering, watered**
NOUN **1** a clear, colourless, tasteless liquid that falls from clouds as rain
VERB **2** If you **water** a plant, you pour water into the soil around it.
3 If your eyes or mouth **water**, they

a
b
c
d
e
f
g
h
i
j
k
l
m
n
o
p
q
r
s
t
u
v
w
x
.

produce tears or saliva. ● *My mouth started **watering** when I smelled Mum's baking.*

watercolour **watercolours**

NOUN **1** a type of paint that is mixed with water and used for painting pictures
2 a picture that has been painted using watercolours

waterfall **waterfalls**

NOUN water from a stream or river as it flows over rocks or the edge of a steep cliff and falls to the ground below

Victoria Falls, Zimbabwe

waterlogged

ADJECTIVE Something that is **waterlogged** is so wet that it cannot soak up any more water.

watermark **watermarks**

NOUN **1** a mark showing the level of water
2 a faint design in some types of paper which you can see if you hold it up to the light

waterproof

ADJECTIVE Something that is **waterproof** does not let water pass through it.
● *We put on our **waterproof** jackets as it was raining.*

watertight

Something that is **watertight** allow water to pass in or out.

orks

ace where the public supply of red and cleaned, and from upplied to our homes

watt **watts**

Said "**wot**" NOUN a unit of measurement of electrical power
[Named after James *Watt* (1736–1819) who invented the steam engine]

wave **waves, waving, waved**

VERB **1** If you **wave** your hand, you move it from side to side, usually to say hello or goodbye.
2 If you **wave** something, you hold it up and move it from side to side. ● *People in the crowd were **waving** flags.*
NOUN **3** a ridge of water on the surface of the sea caused by wind or by tides
4 the form in which some types of energy, such as heat, light or sound, travel

wax **waxes**

NOUN **1** a solid, slightly shiny substance made of fat or oil, that melts easily and is used to make candles and polish
2 the sticky yellow substance in your ears

way **ways**

NOUN **1** The **way** of doing something is how you do it.
2 The **way** to a place is how you get there.

WC **WCs**

NOUN an abbreviation of *water closet*. It is used on plans and signs to show where the toilet is located.

we

PRONOUN **We** refers to the person writing or talking and one or more other people.

weak **weaker, weakest**

ADJECTIVE If someone is **weak**, they do not have much strength or energy.

wealth

NOUN a large amount of money or property that someone owns

wealthy **wealthier, wealthiest**

ADJECTIVE Someone who is **wealthy** has a lot of money.

weapon **weapons**

NOUN an object used to hurt or kill people in a fight or war

wear wears, wearing, wore, worn
VERB When you **wear** something, such as clothes, make-up or jewellery, you have them on your body or face.

wear out
VERB When something **wears out**, or when you **wear** it **out**, it is used so much that it becomes thin, weak and no longer usable.

weary wearier, weariest
ADJECTIVE If you are **weary**, you are very tired.
wearily ADVERB **weariness** NOUN

weasel weasels
NOUN a small wild mammal with a long, thin body and short legs

weather
NOUN the conditions of sunshine, rain, wind or snow at a particular time in a particular place

weave weaves, weaving, wove, woven
VERB **1** If you **weave** something like cloth or a basket, you make it by crossing threads or grasses over and under each other. Cloth is often **woven** using a machine called a loom.
2 If you **weave** your way, you move from side to side past people and other obstacles.

web webs
NOUN a fine net of threads that a spider makes from a sticky substance that it produces in its body

Web
NOUN short for **World Wide Web**

webbed
ADJECTIVE **Webbed** feet have skin joining the toes together, like ducks' feet.

webcam webcams
NOUN a camera that sends pictures over the internet

website websites
NOUN a place on the internet where you can find out about a particular subject or person

we'd
a contraction of *we had* or *we would*

wedding weddings
NOUN a marriage ceremony

wedge wedges, wedging, wedged
VERB **1** If you **wedge** something somewhere, you make it stay there by holding it tightly, or by fixing something next to it to stop it from moving.
NOUN **2** a piece of something such as wood, metal or rubber with one thin edge and one thick edge, used to hold something still • *I put a **wedge** under the door to keep it open.*
3 a piece of something that has a thick triangular shape • *I cut a **wedge** of cheese.*

Wednesday
NOUN the fourth day of the week, coming between Tuesday and Thursday [Wednesday was the day the Anglo-Saxons honoured their god *Odin* or *Woden*]

weed weeds, weeding, weeded
NOUN **1** a wild plant growing somewhere it is not wanted
VERB **2** If you **weed** an area of ground, you remove the weeds from it.

week weeks
NOUN **1** a period of seven days, especially one beginning on a Sunday and ending on a Saturday
2 the part of a week that does not include Saturday and Sunday

weekday weekdays
NOUN any day except Saturday and Sunday

weekend weekends
NOUN Saturday and Sunday.

weekly
ADJECTIVE OR ADVERB happening or appearing once every week

441

A
B
C
D
E
F
G
H
I
J
K
L
M
N
O
P
Q
R
S
T
U
V
W
X
Y
Z

weep **weeps, weeping, wept**
VERB If someone **weeps**, they cry.

weigh **weighs, weighing, weighed**
VERB **1** If something **weighs** a particular amount, that is how heavy it is.
2 If you **weigh** something, you find out how heavy it is by using scales.

weight **weights**
NOUN the heaviness of something

weir **weirs**
NOUN a low dam built across a river to raise the water level, control the flow of water, or change the direction of the water [from Old English *wer* meaning river-dam or enclosure for fish]

weird **weirder, weirdest**
ADJECTIVE strange or odd

welcome **welcomes, welcoming, welcomed**
VERB **1** If you **welcome** a visitor, you greet them in a friendly way when they arrive.
EXCLAMATION **2 Welcome** can be said as a greeting to a visitor who has just arrived.
ADJECTIVE **3** If someone is **welcome** at a place, they will be accepted there in a friendly way.
[from Old English *wilcuma* meaning welcome guest]

weld **welds, welding, welded**
VERB If you **weld** two pieces of metal together, you join them by heating their edges and pressing them together so that when they cool they harden into one piece.
welder NOUN

welfare
NOUN The **welfare** of a person or group is their health, comfort and happiness.

welfare state
NOUN a system in which the government uses money from taxes to provide health care and education services, and to give benefits to people who are old, unemployed or sick

well **better, best; wells**
ADJECTIVE **1** If you are **well**, you are healthy.
ADVERB **2** If you do something **well**, you do it to a high standard.

NOUN **3** a hole in the ground with water or oil at the bottom

we'll
a contraction of *we will* or *we shall*

wellington **wellingtons**
NOUN a long waterproof rubber boot [named after the Duke of *Wellington*]

went
VERB the past tense of **go**

wept
VERB a past tense and past participle of **weep**

were
VERB a past tense of **be**

we're
a contraction of *we are*

west
NOUN one of the four main points of the compass. The sun sets in the **west**. The abbreviation for **west** is W.

western **westerns**
ADJECTIVE **1** in or from the west
NOUN **2** a film or book about the west of America in the nineteenth and early twentieth centuries

wet **wetter, wettest; wets, wetting, wet** or **wetted**
ADJECTIVE **1** covered or soaked with water or other liquid
2 Wet weather is rainy.
VERB **3** If you **wet** something, you make it wet.

we've
a contraction of *we have*

whale **whales**
NOUN a very large sea mammal that breathes out water through a hole on the top of its head

wharf **wharves** or **wharfs**
NOUN a platform beside a river or the sea, where ships load and unload

what
ADJECTIVE **1 What** is used in questions.
• *What time is it?*

2 You use **what** to emphasize a comment. • *What excellent work!*

PHRASE **3** You use **what about** to show that you are making a suggestion or a question. • *What about the homework from last night?*

PRONOUN **4** refers to information about something • *I really have no idea what you mean.*

whatever

PRONOUN **1** anything or everything of a particular type

CONJUNCTION **2** You use **whatever** to mean no matter what. • *I will go whatever happens.*

wheat

NOUN a cereal plant grown for its grain that is used to make flour

wheel **wheels, wheeling, wheeled**

NOUN **1** a circular object that turns on a rod attached to its centre. **Wheels** are fixed underneath vehicles so that they can move along.

VERB **2** If you **wheel** something somewhere, you push it along on wheels.

wheelbarrow **wheelbarrows**

NOUN a small cart with a single wheel at the front, pushed along by two handles at the back. It is used by people such as gardeners and builders.

wheelchair **wheelchairs**

NOUN a chair with large wheels, for use by people who find walking difficult or impossible

wheeze **wheezes, wheezing, wheezed**

VERB If someone **wheezes**, they breathe with difficulty, making a whistling sound.

when

ADVERB **1** You use **when** to ask at what time something will happen or how long ago it has happened. • *When shall I see you?*

CONJUNCTION **2** You use **when** to refer to a certain time. • *I had fun when I was on holiday.*

whenever

CONJUNCTION at any time, or every time that something happens • *I go to the park whenever I can.*

where

ADVERB **1** You use **where** to ask which place something is in, is from, or is going to. • *Where are we?*

CONJUNCTION **2** You use **where** to refer to a place in which something or someone is. • *You do not know where we live.*

wherever

CONJUNCTION in, at or to any place or situation • *Alex heard the same thing wherever he went.*

whether

CONJUNCTION You use **whether** when you are talking about two or more things to choose from. • *I don't know whether that's true or false.*

which

ADJECTIVE OR PRONOUN **1** You use **which** to ask about alternatives. • *Which girl is your sister?*

2 Which shows the thing you are talking about or gives more detail about it. • *The book which is on the table is mine.*

whichever

PRONOUN OR ADJECTIVE You use **whichever** when talking about different possibilities. • *You can have cake or chocolate, whichever you prefer.*

whiff **whiffs**

NOUN a slight smell of something • *I caught a whiff of her perfume as she passed.*

while

CONJUNCTION **1** If something happens **while** something else is happening, the two things happen at the same time. • *Mum went to the café while I had my lesson.*

2 While can be used to mean but or although. • *I like dogs, while my brother prefers cats.*

NOUN **3** a period of time • *a little while earlier*

whim **whims**

NOUN a sudden wish or desire

SYNONYM: impulse

whimper whimpers, whimpering, whimpered

VERB When children or animals **whimper**, they make soft, low, unhappy sounds.

whine whines, whining, whined

VERB **1** If a person or an animal **whines**, they make a long, high-pitched noise, especially one that sounds sad or unpleasant.

2 If someone **whines** about something, they complain about it in an annoying way.

whip whips, whipping, whipped

NOUN **1** a long, thin piece of leather or rope attached to a handle, which is used for hitting people or animals

VERB **2** To **whip** a person or animal means to hit them with a whip.

whirl whirls, whirling, whirled

VERB When something **whirls**, or when you **whirl** it round, it turns or spins round very fast.

whirlpool whirlpools

NOUN a small area in a river or the sea where the water is moving quickly round and round in a circle so that objects floating near it are pulled into its centre

whirlwind whirlwinds

NOUN a tall column of air that spins round and round very fast

whirr whirrs, whirring, whirred

VERB When something like a machine **whirrs**, it makes a continuous buzzing sound.

whisk whisks, whisking, whisked

VERB **1** If you **whisk** eggs or cream, you stir air into them quickly.

2 If you **whisk** something somewhere, you move it there quickly.

NOUN **3** a kitchen utensil for whisking things

whisker whiskers

NOUN **1** The **whiskers** of an animal such as a cat are the long, stiff hairs near its mouth.

2 You can refer to the hair on a man's face, especially on his cheeks, as his **whiskers**.

whisky whiskies

NOUN a strong alcoholic drink made from grain such as barley

whisper whispers, whispering, whispered

VERB When you **whisper**, you talk very quietly and softly.

whistle whistles, whistling, whistled

VERB **1** When you **whistle**, you make a high-pitched sound by forcing your breath out between your lips. ● He **whistled** a tune.

2 If something **whistles**, it makes a loud, high sound. ● The kettle **whistled**.

NOUN **3** a small metal tube that you blow into to produce a whistling sound

white whiter, whitest; whites

NOUN OR ADJECTIVE **1** the lightest possible colour, like milk or fresh snow

2 **White** coffee contains milk or cream.

NOUN **3** The **white** of an egg is the clear liquid around the yolk.

whiteboard whiteboards

NOUN **1** a shiny white board that you can write on and then wipe clean

2 a large screen that shows computer images which can be moved or altered by a pen, a finger or a stylus

who

PRONOUN **1** You use **who** when you are asking about someone's identity. ● **Who** are you?

2 You use **who** to refer to the person you are talking about. ● I know you are the one **who** was in trouble yesterday.

whoever

PRONOUN **Whoever** means the person who. ● **Whoever** wants to can go on the excursion.

whole wholes

NOUN OR ADJECTIVE **1** The **whole** of something is all of it.

ADVERB **2** in one piece ● He swallowed the sweet **whole**.

wholemeal

ADJECTIVE **Wholemeal** flour is made from the whole grain of the wheat plant, including the husk.

wholesale

ADJECTIVE OR ADVERB If a shopkeeper buys his or her goods **wholesale**, he or she buys large amounts of them cheaply before selling them on to his or her customers.

ANTONYM: retail

wholesome

ADJECTIVE healthy or good for you

who's

a contraction of *who is* or *who has*

Do not confuse *who's* with *whose*.

whose

PRONOUN **1** You use **whose** to ask who something belongs to. • **Whose** *shoe is this?* **2 Whose** gives information about something belonging to the person or things just mentioned. • *She is the pupil* **whose** *poem won the prize.*

Do not confuse *whose* with *who's*.

why

ADVERB OR PRONOUN You use **why** when you are talking about the reason for something. • **Why** *did you do that?* • *I wondered* **why** *he did that.*

wick wicks

NOUN the cord that burns in the middle of a candle

wicked

ADJECTIVE **1** very bad
SYNONYMS: evil, sinful
2 mischievous in an amusing or attractive way
[from Old English *wicca* meaning witch]
wickedly ADVERB **wickedness** NOUN

wicker

NOUN things made of reed or cane woven together, such as baskets or furniture

wicket wickets

NOUN **1** one of the two sets of stumps and bails at which the bowler aims the ball in cricket

2 The grass between the **wickets** in cricket is also called the **wicket**.

wide wider, widest

ADJECTIVE **1** measuring a large distance from one side to the other
2 measuring a certain amount from one side to the other • *The pool is 10 metres* **wide**.
3 If there is a **wide** variety, range or selection of something, there are many different kinds of it.
ADVERB **4** If you open or spread something **wide**, you open it as far as you can. • *Open your mouth* **wide**.

widow widows

NOUN a woman whose husband has died

widower widowers

NOUN a man whose wife has died

width widths

NOUN The **width** of something is how wide it is from one side to the other.

wife wives

NOUN A man's **wife** is the woman he is married to.

Wi-Fi

NOUN a system of accessing the internet from machines such as laptop computers that are not physically connected to a network

wig wigs

NOUN a covering of artificial hair worn over someone's own hair to change their appearance or to hide their baldness
[short for *periwig*, from Italian *perrucca* meaning wig]

wiggle wiggles, wiggling, wiggled

VERB If you **wiggle** something, you move it up and down or from side to side with small, jerky movements.
wiggly ADJECTIVE

wigwam wigwams

NOUN a kind of tent used by Native Americans
[from American Indian *wikwam* meaning their house]

wild wilder, wildest; wilds

ADJECTIVE **1 Wild** animals and plants live and grow in natural surroundings and are not looked after by people.

2 Wild land is natural and not used for farming.

3 Wild behaviour is excited and uncontrolled.

NOUN **4** a free and natural state of living
• *There are very few tigers left in the **wild**.*

wilderness wildernesses
NOUN an area of natural land that is not cultivated

wildlife
NOUN wild animals and plants

wilful
ADJECTIVE **1** Someone who is **wilful** is determined to get their own way.
SYNONYMS: headstrong, stubborn
2 Something that is **wilful** is done or said deliberately. • *wilful damage*
wilfully ADVERB

will wills
VERB **1** You use **will** to form the future tense. • *I will do the washing up after dinner.*
NOUN **2** the determination to do something
3 a legal document in which people say what they want to happen to their money and property when they die
4 what you choose or want to do • *Don't make them do it against their **will**.*

willing
ADJECTIVE If you are **willing**, you are glad and ready to do what is wanted or needed.

willow willows
NOUN a tree with long, thin branches and narrow leaves that often grows near water

wilt wilts, wilting, wilted
VERB If a plant **wilts**, it droops because it needs more water or is dying.

wily wilier, wiliest
ADJECTIVE clever and cunning

wimp wimps
NOUN INFORMAL someone who is feeble and timid

win wins, winning, won
VERB **1** If you **win** a fight, game or argument, you defeat your opponent.

2 If you **win** a prize, you receive it as a reward for succeeding in something.

winch winches, winching, winched
NOUN **1** a machine used to lift or pull heavy objects. It consists of a cylinder or wheel around which a rope or cable is wound.
VERB **2** If you **winch** an object or person somewhere, you lift, lower or pull them using a winch.

wind winds, winding, wound
Rhymes with "mind" VERB **1** If a road or river **winds**, it is not straight, but twists and turns.
2 When you **wind** something round something else, you wrap it round it several times.
3 When you **wind** a clock or machine, or **wind** it up, you turn a key or handle several times to make it work.
Rhymes with "tinned" NOUN **4** a current of air that moves across the land and sea
ADJECTIVE **5** A **wind** instrument is a musical instrument that you play by blowing into it.

windmill windmills
NOUN a machine in a special building, for generating electricity, grinding grain or pumping water. It is powered by long arms called sails that are turned by the wind.

window windows
NOUN a space in a wall or roof or in the side of a vehicle, usually with glass in it so that light can pass through and people can see in or out

windpipe windpipes
NOUN the tube through which air travels in and out of your lungs when you breathe

A B C D E F G H I J K L M N O P Q R S T U V W X Y Z

withdraw

windscreen windscreens
NOUN the glass at the front of a vehicle through which the driver looks

windsurfing
NOUN the sport of moving over the surface of the sea or a lake on a board with a sail fixed to it
windsurfer NOUN

windy windier, windiest
ADJECTIVE If it is **windy**, there is a lot of wind.

wine wines
NOUN an alcoholic drink usually made from grapes

wing wings
NOUN **1** A bird's or insect's **wings** are the parts of its body that it uses for flying.
2 An aeroplane's **wings** are the long, flat parts on each side that support it while it is in the air.

wink winks, winking, winked
VERB When you **wink**, you close and open one eye very quickly, often to show that something is a joke or a secret.

winner winners
NOUN someone who wins something

winter winters
NOUN the coldest season of the year, between autumn and spring

wipe wipes, wiping, wiped
VERB If you **wipe** something, you rub its surface lightly with a cloth or your hand to clear off dirt or liquid.

wire wires, wiring, wired
NOUN **1** long, thin, bendy metal that can be used to make or fasten things, or to conduct an electric current
VERB **2** If someone **wires** something, or **wires** it up, they connect it so that electricity can pass through it.

wireless wirelesses
ADJECTIVE **1** If a computer network is **wireless**, it is connected by radio signals rather than cables.
NOUN **2** OLD-FASHIONED another word for **radio**

wisdom
NOUN a person's ability to use the things they have done and learned to give good advice or make good decisions

wise wiser, wisest
ADJECTIVE Someone who is **wise** can use their experience and knowledge to make sensible decisions and judgements.

wish wishes, wishing, wished
NOUN **1** something that you want very much
2 the act of wishing for something
VERB **3** If you **wish** something for someone, you hope that they will have it.
• I **wished** her good luck in her exams.
4 If you **wish** to do something, you want to do it.
5 If you **wish** something was true, you would like it to be, but know it is not very likely.

wisp wisps
NOUN A **wisp** of something such as smoke or hair is a small, thin, streak or bunch of it. • A **wisp** of hair fell over her eyes.
wispy ADJECTIVE

wit wits
NOUN the ability to use words or ideas in an amusing and clever way

witch witches
NOUN a woman who claims to have magic powers and to be able to use them for good or evil. **Witches** are often characters in fairy stories.
[from Old English *wicca* meaning witch]

witchcraft
NOUN the skill or art of using magic powers, especially evil ones

with
PREPOSITION If you are **with** someone, you are in their company. • We went **with** Mum to the shops.

withdraw withdraws, withdrawing, withdrew, withdrawn
VERB **1** If you **withdraw** something, you take it out. • He **withdrew** the money from his bank.
2 If you **withdraw** from something, you do not continue with it. • She **withdrew** from the race because of injury.

447

A
B
C
D
E
F
G
H
I
J
K
L
M
N
O
P
Q
R
S
T
U
V
W
X
Y
Z

wither **withers, withering, withered**
VERB If a plant **withers**, it wilts or shrivels up and dies.

within
PREPOSITION OR ADVERB **1** inside, not going outside certain limits ● Stay **within** the school grounds.
2 before a period of time has passed ● Bring back the book **within** three weeks.

without
PREPOSITION **1** not having, not feeling or not showing something ● They went out **without** coats as it was a warm, dry day.
2 If you do something **without** someone else, they are not with you when you do it. ● He went **without** me.

witness **witnesses**
NOUN **1** someone who has seen an event, such as an accident, and can describe what happened
2 someone who appears in a court of law to say what they know about a crime or other event

witty **wittier, wittiest**
ADJECTIVE amusing in a clever way

wizard **wizards**
NOUN a man in a fairy story who has magic powers

wobble **wobbles, wobbling, wobbled**
VERB If something **wobbles**, it shakes or moves from side to side because it is loose or unsteady.

wok **woks**
NOUN a large bowl-shaped pan used for Chinese cooking

woke
VERB the past tense of **wake**

woken
VERB the past participle of **wake**

wolf **wolves; wolfs, wolfing, wolfed**
NOUN **1** a wild animal related to the dog. **Wolves** hunt in packs and kill other animals for food.
VERB **2** INFORMAL If you **wolf** food, or **wolf** it down, you eat it up quickly and greedily.

woman **women**
NOUN an adult female human being

womb **wombs**
NOUN A woman's **womb** is the part inside her body where her unborn baby grows.

won
VERB the past tense and past participle of **win**

wonder **wonders, wondering, wondered**
VERB **1** If you **wonder** about something, you think about it and try to guess or understand more about it.
2 If you **wonder** at something, you are amazed by it.
NOUN **3** a feeling of amazement and admiration

wonderful
ADJECTIVE marvellous or impressive

won't
VERB a contraction of will not

wood **woods**
NOUN **1** the substance that forms the trunks and branches of trees
2 a large area of trees growing near each other

wooden
ADJECTIVE Something **wooden** is made of wood.

woodland **woodlands**
NOUN land that is mostly covered with trees

woodlouse **woodlice**
NOUN a small animal with seven pairs of legs, that lives in damp soil and rotten wood

woodpecker **woodpeckers**
NOUN a climbing bird with a long, sharp beak that it uses to drill holes in trees to find the insects that live in the bark

woodwind
ADJECTIVE **Woodwind** instruments are musical instruments such as flutes, oboes, clarinets and bassoons, made of wood or metal. They are played by being blown into.

woodwork

NOUN **1** the activity of making things out of wood
2 the parts of a building that are made of wood

woof woofs

NOUN the sound a dog makes

wool wools

NOUN **1** the hair that grows on sheep and some other animals
2 thread or cloth made from the wool of animals, and used to make clothes, blankets and carpets

woollen

ADJECTIVE made of wool

woolly

ADJECTIVE made of wool, or looking like wool

word words

NOUN **1** a single unit of language in speech or writing which has a meaning. *Bird*, *hot* and *sing* are all **words**.
PLURAL NOUN **2** The **words** of a play or song are the words you say or sing.
NOUN **3** If you give someone your **word** about something, you promise to do it.
4 If you ask for a **word** with someone, you want to say something briefly to them.

wore

VERB the past tense of **wear**

work works, working, worked

VERB **1** People who **work** have a job that they are paid to do.
2 When you **work**, you spend time and energy doing something useful.
3 If something **works**, it does what it is supposed to do.
PHRASE **4** If something **works its way** into a certain position, it moves itself there gradually.
5 If you **work out** an answer to a problem, you solve it.

workout workouts

NOUN a session of exercise or training for the body

workshop workshops

NOUN a room or building that has tools or machinery in it that are used for making or repairing things

world worlds

NOUN **1** the planet we live on
2 A person's **world** is the life they lead and the people they know.
3 a particular field of activity • *He is a top player in the rugby* **world**.
PHRASE **4** If you **think the world** of someone, you like or admire them very much.

World Wide Web

NOUN The **World Wide Web** is a system of linked documents accessed via the internet.

worm worms

NOUN a small, thin animal without bones or legs, especially an earthworm

worn

VERB **1** the past participle of **wear**
ADJECTIVE **2** looking old or exhausted

worry worries, worrying, worried

VERB **1** If you **worry**, you feel anxious about a problem or about something that might happen.
NOUN **2** a problem, or something that makes you worry

worse

ADJECTIVE OR ADVERB less good or less well. The comparative form of *bad* and *badly*.
• *The team's results are* **worse** *this year than they were last year.*
ANTONYM: better

worship worships, worshipping, worshipped

VERB If you **worship** a god, you show your love and respect by praying or singing hymns.

worst

ADJECTIVE the least well or the least good. The superlative form of *bad* and *badly*.
• *It was the* **worst** *meal I have ever eaten.*
ANTONYM: best

worth

ADJECTIVE **1** If something is **worth** a sum of money, it has that value.

A
B
C
D
E
F
G
H
I
J
K
L
M
N
O
P
Q
R
S
T
U
V
W
X
Y
Z

2 If something is **worth** doing, it deserves to be done.

worthless

ADJECTIVE Something that is **worthless** has no use or no value.

worthwhile

ADJECTIVE If something is **worthwhile**, it is important enough to spend time or effort doing it.

would

VERB **1** the past tense of **will**. You use **would** to talk about something that was in the future the last time you were talking about it. • *We were sure it* ***would*** *be a success.*
2 You use **would** in polite questions. • ***Would*** *you like some lunch?*

wouldn't

VERB a contraction of *would not*

wound wounds, wounding, wounded

Rhymes with "sound" VERB **1** the past tense and past participle of **wind**
Said "**woond**" NOUN **2** an injury to part of a person's or an animal's body, especially a cut
VERB **3** If someone or something **wounds** a person or an animal, they injure them, especially with a cut.

wove

VERB the past tense of **weave**

woven

VERB the past participle of **weave**

wrap wraps, wrapping, wrapped

VERB If you **wrap** something, you fold cloth or paper around it.

wrapping wrappings

NOUN material used to wrap something, such as a present

wrath

NOUN great anger

wreath wreaths

NOUN an arrangement of flowers and leaves, often in the shape of a circle, which is put on a grave to remember someone who has died

wreck wrecks, wrecking, wrecked

VERB **1** To **wreck** something means to break it, destroy it or spoil it completely.
NOUN **2** a vehicle or ship that has been badly damaged, usually in an accident
wreckage NOUN

wren wrens

NOUN a small, brown songbird

wrench wrenches, wrenching, wrenched

VERB **1** If you **wrench** something, you give it a sudden and violent twist or pull.
2 If you **wrench** a limb or a joint, you twist and injure it.
NOUN **3** a wrenching movement
4 a tool for gripping or tightening nuts and bolts

wrestle wrestles, wrestling, wrestled

VERB If you **wrestle** someone, or **wrestle** with them, you fight them by holding or throwing them, but not hitting them.
wrestler NOUN

wretched

ADJECTIVE very unhappy or unfortunate

wriggle wriggles, wriggling, wriggled

VERB **1** If a person or an animal **wriggles**, they twist and turn their body in a lively and excited way.
2 If you **wriggle** out of doing something that you do not want to do, you manage to avoid doing it.

wring wrings, wringing, wrung

VERB When you **wring** a wet cloth, or **wring** it out, you squeeze the water out of it by twisting it.

wrinkle wrinkles, wrinkling, wrinkled

NOUN **1** a soft fold or crease in something, especially a person's skin as they grow older
VERB **2** If something **wrinkles**, folds or creases develop in it.

wrinkled

ADJECTIVE Something that is **wrinkled** has wrinkles in it.

wrist **wrists**
NOUN the part of your body between your hand and your arm, which bends when you move your hand

wrist
arm
hand

wristwatch **wristwatches**
NOUN a watch you wear on your wrist

write **writes, writing, wrote, written**
VERB **1** When you **write**, you use a pen or pencil to form letters, words or numbers on a surface. ● *I have **written** my name in the front of my book.*
2 If you **write** something such as a poem, a book or a piece of music, you think of the words or notes for yourself.
3 When you **write** to someone, you send them a letter.

writer **writers**
NOUN **1** a person who writes books, stories or articles as a job
2 The **writer** of something is the person who wrote it.

writhe **writhes, writhing, writhed**
VERB If you **writhe**, you twist and turn your body, often because you are in pain.

writing **writings**
NOUN **1** something that has been written or printed
2 Your **writing** is the way you write with a pen or pencil.

written
VERB the past participle of **write**

wrong
ADJECTIVE **1** If there is something **wrong** with an object, it is not working properly or has a fault. ● *There must be something **wrong** with the car as it will not start.*
2 If something is **wrong**, it is not correct or truthful.

3 An action that is **wrong** is bad or against the law.

wrote
VERB the past tense of **write**

wrung
VERB the past tense and past participle of **wring**

a
b
c
d
e
f
g
h
i
j
k
l
m
n
o
p
q
r
s
t
u
v
w
x
y
z

A
B
C
D
E
F
G
H
I
J
K
L
M
N
O
P
Q
R
S
T
U
V
W
X
Y
Z

Xx

X-ray X-rays, X-raying, X-rayed
NOUN **1** a type of radiation that can pass through some solid materials. **X-rays** are used by doctors to examine the bones or organs inside a person's body.
2 a picture made by sending X-rays through someone's body in order to examine the inside of it
VERB **3** If someone **X-rays** something, they make a picture of the inside of it by passing X-rays through it.

xylophone xylophones
Said "**ziy**-lu-fohn" NOUN a musical instrument made of a row of wooden bars of different lengths. It is played by hitting the bars with special hammers.

Yy

yacht yachts
NOUN a boat with sails or an engine, used for racing or for pleasure trips

yak yaks
NOUN a type of long-haired ox with long horns, found mainly in the mountains of Tibet

yam yams
NOUN a root vegetable that grows in tropical regions

yard yards
NOUN **1** a unit of length equal to 36 inches or about 91.4 centimetres
2 a paved space with walls around it, next to a building
3 a place where certain types of work are carried out, such as a ship**yard** or a builder's **yard**

yarn yarns
NOUN **1** thread used for knitting or making cloth
2 INFORMAL a story that someone tells, often with invented details to make it more interesting or exciting

yawn yawns, yawning, yawned
VERB When you **yawn**, you open your mouth wide and take in more air than usual, often when you are tired or bored.

year years
NOUN **1** a period of twelve months or 365 days (366 days in a leap year), usually measured from the first of January to the thirty-first of December. It takes a **year** for the earth to orbit the sun.
2 the part of a year during which something happens or is organized
• *the school **year***

yeast
NOUN a type of fungus used in baking and in making beer

yell yells, yelling, yelled
VERB **1** If you **yell**, you shout loudly, usually because you are angry, excited or in pain.
NOUN **2** a loud shout

yellow yellower, yellowest
NOUN OR ADJECTIVE the colour of buttercups, egg yolks or lemons

yelp yelps, yelping, yelped
VERB **1** When people or animals **yelp**, they give a sudden cry.
NOUN **2** a sudden cry

yes
EXCLAMATION You say **yes** to agree with someone, to say that something is true or to accept something.
ANTONYM: no

yesterday
NOUN OR ADVERB the day before today

yet
ADVERB **1** If something has not happened **yet**, you expect it to happen in the future. **2** If something should not be done **yet**, it should be done later. ● *Don't switch it off* **yet***.*
CONJUNCTION **3** You use **yet** to introduce something that is rather surprising. ● *He doesn't like maths,* **yet** *he always does well.*

yew yews
NOUN an evergreen tree with bright red berries

yodel yodels, yodelling, yodelled
VERB When someone **yodels**, they sing normal notes with high quick notes in between. You can hear this style of singing in the Swiss and Austrian Alps.

yoga
NOUN a Hindu form of exercise that develops the body and the mind, making you relaxed and fit

yogurt yogurts; also spelt **yoghurt**
NOUN a slightly sour, thick, liquid food made from milk that has had bacteria added to it

yoke yokes
NOUN a wooden bar laid across the necks of animals such as oxen to hold them together when they pull a plough or a cart

yolk yolks
NOUN the yellow part in the middle of an egg

Yom Kippur
NOUN an annual Jewish religious holiday, which is a day of fasting and prayers. It is also called the Day of Atonement. [from Hebrew *yom* meaning day and *kippur* meaning atonement]

you
PRONOUN **You** refers to the person or people you are talking or writing to.

you'd
a contraction of *you had* or *you would*

you'll
a contraction of *you will* or *you shall*

young younger, youngest
ADJECTIVE **1** A **young** person, animal or plant has not lived very long and is not yet mature.
PLURAL NOUN **2** The **young** of an animal are its babies.

your
ADJECTIVE belonging to you

you're
a contraction of *you are*

yours
PRONOUN belonging to you

yourself yourselves
PRONOUN you and only you ● *Have you hurt* **yourself***?*

youth youths
NOUN **1** Someone's **youth** is the time of their life before they are a fully mature adult.
2 a boy or young man
3 young people in general

you've
a contraction of *you have*

yo-yo yo-yos
NOUN a round wooden or plastic toy attached to a string. You play by making the **yo-yo** move up and down the string.

a
b
c
d
e
f
g
h
i
j
k
l
m
n
o
p
q
r
s
t
u
v
w
x
y
z

A
B
C
D
E
F
G
H
I
J
K
L
M
N
O
P
Q
R
S
T
U
V
W
X
Y
Z

zany **zanier, zaniest**
ADJECTIVE odd in a funny way
[from Italian *zanni* meaning clown]

zap **zaps, zapping, zapped**
VERB INFORMAL If you **zap** someone or something in a computer game, you get rid of them.

zeal
NOUN eagerness and enthusiasm

zebra **zebras**
NOUN a type of African wild horse with black and white stripes

zebra crossing **zebra crossings**
NOUN part of a road marked with broad black and white stripes, where pedestrians can cross

zero
NOUN nought. The sign for zero is 0.

zest
NOUN **1** a feeling of great enjoyment and enthusiasm
2 The **zest** of a citrus fruit such as an orange or lemon is the outside of the peel, used to flavour food and drinks.
zestful ADJECTIVE **zestfully** ADVERB

zigzag **zigzags, zigzagging, zigzagged**
NOUN **1** a line that has a series of sharp, angular bends to the right and left

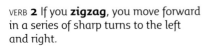

VERB **2** If you **zigzag**, you move forward in a series of sharp turns to the left and right.

zinc
NOUN a bluish-white metal used to coat other metals to stop them rusting

zip **zips, zipping, zipped**
NOUN **1** a fastener used on clothes and bags, with two rows of metal or plastic interlocking teeth that separate or fasten together as you pull a small tag along them
VERB **2** When you **zip** something, or **zip** it up, you fasten it using a zip.

zodiac
NOUN a diagram used by astrologers to represent the movement of the stars. It is divided into 12 sections, each with a special name and symbol. ● *"Capricorn", "Gemini", "Taurus" and "Pisces" are all signs of the **zodiac**.*
[from the Greek *zōidiakos kuklos* meaning "circle of signs"]

zone **zones**
NOUN an area of land or sea that is considered different from the areas around it, or is separated from the areas around it in some way

zoo **zoos**
NOUN a place where live animals are kept so that people can look at them

zoology
NOUN the scientific study of animals
zoological ADJECTIVE **zoologist** NOUN

zoom lens **zoom lenses**
NOUN A **zoom lens** on a camera helps the photographer to take close-up pictures from far away.

zucchini
PLURAL NOUN small vegetable marrows with dark green skin. They are also called courgettes.
[from Italian plural of *zucchino* meaning gourd]

Word Wizard

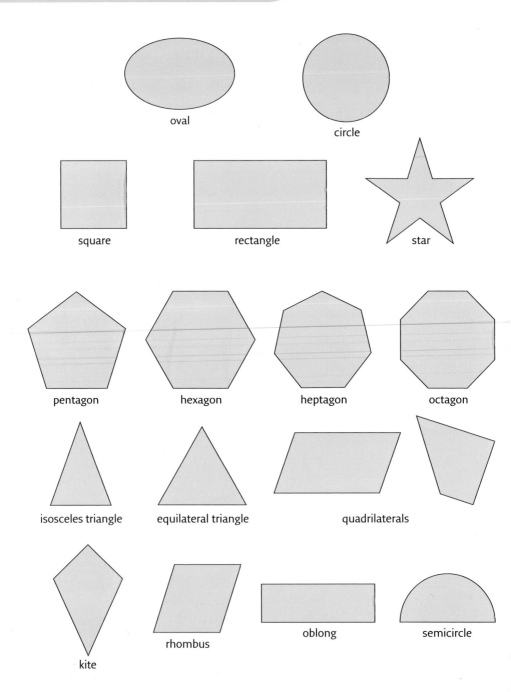

oval

circle

square

rectangle

star

pentagon

hexagon

heptagon

octagon

isosceles triangle

equilateral triangle

quadrilaterals

kite

rhombus

oblong

semicircle

3D shapes

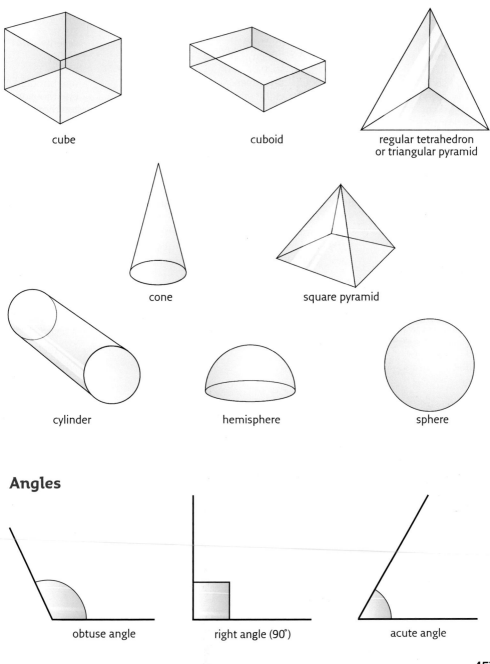

cube

cuboid

regular tetrahedron
or triangular pyramid

cone

square pyramid

cylinder

hemisphere

sphere

Angles

obtuse angle

right angle (90°)

acute angle

Numbers and fractions

Numbers

1	one	12	twelve	50	fifty
2	two	13	thirteen	60	sixty
3	three	14	fourteen	70	seventy
4	four	15	fifteen	80	eighty
5	five	16	sixteen	90	ninety
6	six	17	seventeen	100	one hundred
7	seven	18	eighteen	1000	one thousand
8	eight	19	nineteen	10 000	ten thousand
9	nine	20	twenty	1 000 000	one million
10	ten	30	thirty	10 000 000	ten million
11	eleven	40	forty		

1st	first	7th	seventh	13th	thirteenth	19th	nineteenth
2nd	second	8th	eighth	14th	fourteenth	20th	twentieth
3rd	third	9th	ninth	15th	fifteenth	21st	twenty-first
4th	fourth	10th	tenth	16th	sixteenth	22nd	twenty-second
5th	fifth	11th	eleventh	17th	seventeenth		
6th	sixth	12th	twelfth	18th	eighteenth		

Roman numerals

I	1	V	5	IX	9	D	500
II	2	VI	6	X	10	M	1000
III	3	VII	7	L	50	MCMXCVI	1996
IV	4	VIII	8	C	100	MM	2000

Fractions

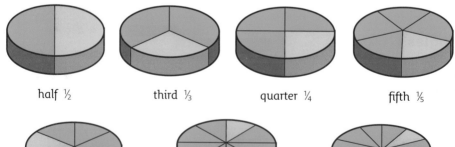

half ½   third ⅓   quarter ¼   fifth ⅕

sixth ⅙   eighth ⅛   tenth ¹/₁₀

Telling the time

a.m.   half past   watch   analogue
p.m.   quarter past   timer   digital
o'clock   quarter to   clock

11:55

eleven fifty-five

five to twelve

Measuring time
second
minute
hour
day
week
fortnight
month
year
leap year
decade
century
millennium

Times of day
dawn
sunrise
morning
midday
noon
afternoon
dusk
twilight
sunset
evening
night
midnight

breakfast time
breaktime
playtime
lunchtime
dinnertime
suppertime
bedtime

When/how often?
never
once
twice
rarely
occasionally
from time to time
sometimes
often
soon
frequently
usually
always

Days
Monday
Tuesday
Wednesday
Thursday
Friday
Saturday
Sunday

Months
January
February
March
April
May
June
July
August
September
October
November
December

Seasons
spring
summer
autumn
winter

More time words
yesterday
today
tomorrow

calendar
date
weekend
holiday
birthday
term

Noun

A **noun** is a person, place, thing, or idea. There are different types of noun.

A noun can be **singular**, which means one ...   ... or **plural**, which means more than one.

book

books

Common nouns name people, places, things, or ideas in general. For example, "boy", "dog", "school", "computer", and "happiness" are common nouns.

Proper nouns are the names of particular people, places, or things. They start with a capital letter. For example, "Ben", "France", and "Buckingham Palace" are proper nouns.

Collective nouns

A **collective noun** names a group of things.

a **clutch** of eggs
a **flock** of sheep
a **pack** of wolves
a **litter** of puppies
a **herd** of cows
a **swarm** of bees
a **school** of dolphins

a **shoal** of fish

a **bunch** of grapes

a **pride** of lions

Pronoun

A **pronoun** is used to replace a noun.

I	me	mine	myself
you	you	yours	yourself, yourselves
he, she, it	him, her, it	his, hers, its	himself, herself, itself
we	us	ours	ourselves
they	them	theirs	themselves

Personal pronouns are used for a person or thing that has already been named, for example "me", "her", "you", "it". *John jumped for the ball. He caught it!*

Possessive pronouns show that a noun belongs to a person or thing that has already been named, for example, "mine", "theirs", "his", "ours". *That pencil isn't his. It's mine.*

Adjective

An **adjective** describes a noun. For example, "tall", "happy", and "lucky" are all adjectives.

Some adjectives have a **comparative** and a **superlative** form. In most cases, these forms are made by adding **-er** or **-est** to the adjective.

adjective	comparative (more)	superlative (most)
tall	taller	tallest
hot	hotter	hottest
good	better	best
lucky	luckier	luckiest

Verb

A **verb** is an action word. It tells you what people and things do. For example, "sleep", "think", and "play" are all verbs.

Verbs have different forms called **tenses**. A tense shows whether you are talking about the past, present, or future.

past	present	future
I played	*I play*	*I will play*
	I am playing	

Adverb

An **adverb** tells you more about a verb. For example, "shyly", "brightly", and "happily" are all adverbs. Many adverbs end in the suffix **-ly**.

How did Mary and Brian talk? *They talked loudly.*

Other adverbs tell you where, when, or how often something happens.

where: outside, inside, here, there
when: today, soon, immediately
how often: never, frequently, often, always

Prepositions

Prepositions link two nouns or pronouns, to show how they are connected to each other.

- Prepositions may tell you the **place** of something in relation to another thing:

  *She found the book **on** the table.*
  *We saw the ball **beneath** the bush.*

- Prepositions may indicate **movement**:

  *The dog ran **towards** us.*
  *They walked **along** the beach.*

- Prepositions may indicate **time**:

  *I got to stay up **until** ten o'clock.*
  *We went on holiday **for** a week.*

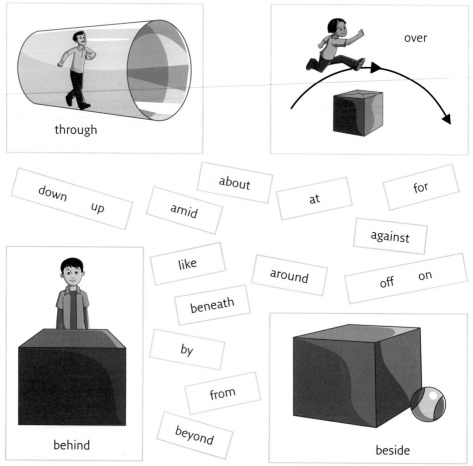

through

over

down   up

about

amid

at

for

against

like

around

off   on

beneath

by

from

beyond

behind

beside

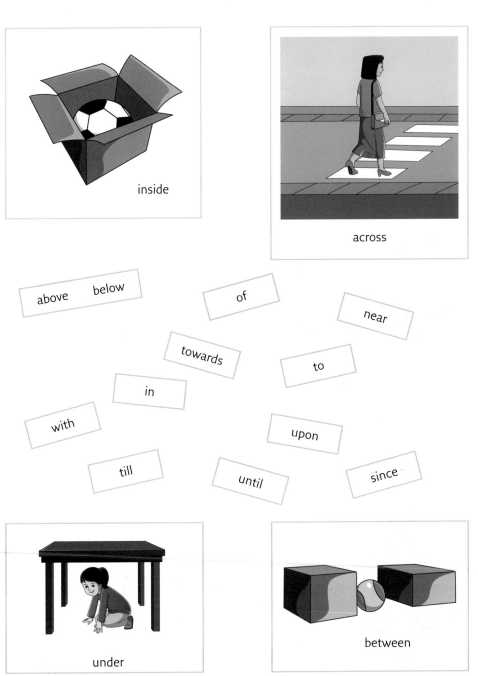

inside

across

above   below

of

near

towards

to

in

with

upon

till

until

since

under

between

Prefixes

A **prefix** is a group of letters added to the beginning of a word. It changes or adds to the meaning of the word: **tele**scope, **mis**understand, **semi**circle.

Prefix	Meaning	Example
anti-	opposite of, against	anticlockwise
arch-	chief	archbishop
auto-	self	autobiography
co-	together	cooperate
com-	together	compare
contra-	against	contradict
de-	take away	defrost
dis-	opposite of	disappear
em-	in	embark
ex-	former	ex-partner
extra-	more	extraordinary
fore-	before, in front of	forecast
il-, im-, in-, ir-	not	illegal, impossible, inaccurate, irrational
inter-	between	international
micro-	very small	microscope
mid-	middle	midday
mini-	smaller	minibus
mis-	wrong	misspell
mono-	one	monologue
multi-	many	multitude
non-	not	nonfiction
over-	too much	overgrown
poly-	many	polygon
post-	after	post-war
pre-	before	prehistoric
pro-	supporting	pro-European
re-	again	reappear
semi-	half	semicircle
sub-	below	submarine
super-	over, more than	supersonic
tele-	at a distance	telephone
trans-	across	transport
ultra-	beyond	ultraviolet
un-	not	unkind
under-	under, not enough	underestimate

A **suffix** is a letter or group of letters added to the end of a word. It can change the tense of a verb from present to past, as in *talk* to *talked*.

Suffixes can also:

- change nouns into other nouns: child – child**hood**; friend – friend**ship**; art – art**ist**.
- change nouns into verbs: length – length**en**; fright – fright**en**.
- change nouns or verbs into adjectives: drink – drink**able**; use – use**ful**; harm – harm**less**.
- change adjectives into adverbs: slow – slow**ly**; happy – happi**ly**; quick – quick**ly**.
- change verbs or adjectives into nouns: happy – happi**ness**; enjoy – enjoy**ment**; invite – invit**ation**.
- change nouns to be feminine: lion – lion**ess**; prince – princ**ess**.
- change a noun to a diminutive (a word that shows something is small): kitchen – kitchen**ette**; pig – pig**let**.

Suffix	Meaning	Example
-able, -ible, -uble	able to be	enjoyable, edible, soluble
-ant, -ent	a doer	attendant, resident
-dom	condition, rank, territory	freedom, earldom, kingdom
-ee	one who is	employee
-er	a doer	farmer, miner, teacher
-er	more	higher, lower
-ess	used to make the feminine	goddess, princess
-est	most	hardest, lightest
-ful	full of	truthful
-hood	state of	childhood
-ic	belonging to	prehistoric
-ish	like	boyish
-ism	belief	Judaism, Buddhism
-ist	a doer	artist
-itis	inflammation of	appendicitis
-ize, ise	used to make verbs	realize, advertise
-less	free from	thoughtless, smokeless
-let	small	booklet, piglet
-ly	used to make adverbs	hotly, sleepily
-ment	used to make nouns	pavement
-ness	state of being	kindness
-oid	like	cuboid
-ology	study of	biology
-or	a doer	sailor, actor
-ous	used to make adjectives	dangerous
-ship	state of being	friendship
-some	tending to	tiresome
-ty	showing condition	cruelty
-wards	in a direction	southwards

Days of the week

Most of the days of the week were named by the Saxons. The Saxons came from Denmark and Germany to live in Britain over 1500 years ago.

Sunday is named after the **sun**.

Monday is named after the **moon**.

Tuesday is named after **Tiu**, the Saxon god of war and of the sky.

Wednesday is named after **Woden**, leader of the Viking gods.

Thursday is named after **Thor**, the Saxon god of thunder and lightning.

Friday is named after **Frigga**. She was the goddess of marriage, and sat on a throne beside her husband, Woden.

Saturday is named after **Saturn**, the Roman god of farmers and farming.

Months of the year

The months of the year were given their names by the Romans.

January is named after **Janus**, the Roman god of doorways and beginnings.

February is named after **Februa**, a Roman festival when people were purified.

March is named after **Mars**, the Roman god of war.

April's name comes from the Latin word **aperire**, meaning "to open". Spring is when the year "opens".

May is named after **Maia**, a Roman goddess connected with growth.

June is named after the Roman goddess **Juno**, queen of the gods.

July was named after **Julius Caesar**, army general and ruler of Ancient Rome.

August was named after the Roman emperor **Augustus**.

September comes from the Latin word **septem**, meaning "seven". The Roman year used to begin in March, so September was their seventh month.

October comes from the Latin word **octo**, meaning "eight". October was once the eighth month.

November comes from the Latin word **novem**, meaning "nine". November was once the ninth month.

December comes from the Latin word **decem**, meaning "ten". December was once the tenth month.

Words from other languages

Many words we use today come from other languages. Here are some examples.

Latin: adolescent, adverb, benefit, calculate, castle, evaporate, human, industry, literature, manual, observe, square, video.

Greek: acrobat, autograph, colossal, history, hour, ozone, pathetic, telephone.

French: banquet, café, chef, oboe, tapestry, torch, vinegar.

Old English: barn, beetle, bless, cluster, daisy, Easter, ooze, sibling, Thursday, welcome.

Arabic: genie, kebab, sofa, syrup.

Hindi: bungalow, juggernaut, jungle, thug, yoga.

Spanish: alligator, cockroach, crusade, grenade.

Italian: ballet, brave, macaroni, pasta, picturesque, profile, quarantine, spaghetti, squadron, zany.

Here are a few more words from other languages, with an explanation of how they got their names! Look up the words in the dictionary, and then read the explanations below.

appendix
This word comes from the Latin for "the part that hangs". Your appendix hangs at the end of your large intestine. The appendices of this book come at the end.

biscuit
The old French word for twice is *bis*, and the old French for cooked is *cuit*. Put them together and you get biscuit, which meant "cooked twice". Food was cooked like this to make it crisp.

essay
The French word *essayer* means "to try". When someone writes an essay, they are trying to put their ideas down in writing.

hazard
The Arabic word *az-zahr* means "the dice", and the word *hazard* was once used to mean all games played with dice. It came to have a different meaning because games of dice were associated with the dangers of gambling and losing money.

ketchup
Ke-tsiap was a sauce originally invented by the Chinese. It was made of fish and spices. Over time, people added tomatoes and changed the recipe to the sauce that we know today.

Tips for tricky words

Sometimes thinking of a silly phrase or sentence can help you remember how to spell tricky words. Here are some examples:

beautiful

Big elephants are useful.

qu words (q is always followed by u)

The Queen always carries an umbrella.

See how many of these you can remember. Then see if you can think up some of your own!

all right
It's either all right or all wrong.

believe
Believe has a lie in it.

piece
Have a piece of pie.

February
You say "br" in February because it's cold.

receive
R-e-c-e is very easy.

different
One thing differs from another.

hear
You hear with your ear.

separate
Separate has a rat in it.

library
Look into books. Reach and read yours.

friend
I'm seeing my friend on Friday, which comes at the end of the week.

necessary
Necessary has one collar and two socks (one **c** and two **s**'s!).

there
There is a place like here.

weather
We eat in all kinds of weather.

whose
Whose hose is that?

because
Ben eats cake and uses six eggs.

Sound it out!

Another good way to remember the spelling of some words is to sound out their different parts. Try these!

answer	cupboard	Wednesday	together
ans-wer	cup-board	Wed-nes-day	to-get-her

Look, say, cover, write, check!

- **Look** at the word in the dictionary and point to it.
- **Say** the word out loud, and then spell it out.
- **Cover** the word up, remembering what it looks like.
- **Write** the word down on a piece of paper and say it out loud again.
- **Check** your spelling against the dictionary.
- If you got it wrong, cover the page again and **try again!**

Tricky words to learn

The words on this list are tricky, so learn all of them to be a top speller!

address	certain	rhyme
among	course	scissors
autumn	definite	
awful	does	
balloon	everybody	
	exciting	
	exercise	sentence
	guess	straight
	interest	through
	necessary	trouble
beginning	people	until
breakfast	really	usually
build	remember	whole
careful		

Punctuation

ABC	A **capital letter** is used at the beginning of a sentence and for proper nouns.	*My brother Jim lives in New Zealand.*
.	You put a **full stop** at the end of a sentence.	*This is a sentence.*
?	You put a **question mark** at the end of a question.	*Can you come to my party?*
,	You use a **comma** to separate parts of a sentence or items on a list.	*She brought sandwiches, crisps, apples, and juice to the picnic.*
!	You use an **exclamation mark** at the end of a sentence to show a strong feeling.	*Wow!*
'	An **apostrophe** is used in contractions and to show belonging.	*I didn't mean to break my brother's toy.*
" " ' '	**Speech marks** show where speech begins and ends.	*"I like your hair," she said.*
-	You use a **hyphen** to join together words or parts of words.	*I'm left-handed.*
( )	**Brackets** are used to show that something is not part of the main text.	*My cousin (the one from America) is coming to stay.*
—	A **dash** can be used instead of brackets, or to show a change of subject.	*My best friend — besides you — is George.*
:	You can use a **colon** for several things, for example in front of a list.	*You will need the following: strong walking boots, a map, and a compass.*
;	A **semicolon** is used to separate different parts of a sentence or list, or to show a pause.	*The pizza choices are: cheese; onions, peppers, and mushrooms; ham and pineapple; pepperoni; or sausage.*

The Earth and Space

The Solar System

Earth, our planet, is one of eight planets that travel around the Sun. These planets make up the Solar System. The path that a planet follows around the Sun is called its orbit, and the Sun's gravity keeps the planets in their orbits. The planets are all at different distances from the Sun and take different lengths of time to orbit it.

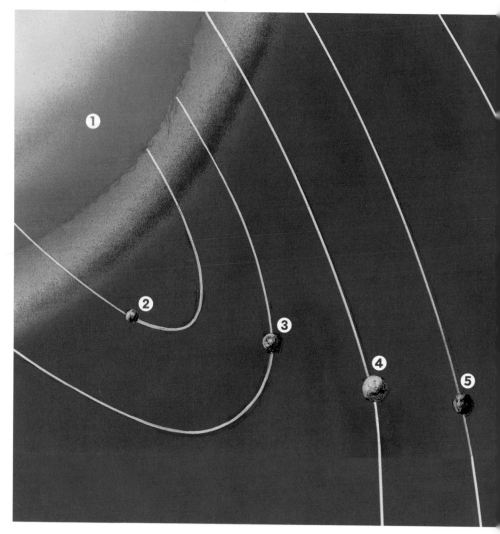

❶ The **Sun** is the fiery centre of our Solar System.

❷ **Mercury** is a small, hot, rocky planet with a very thin atmosphere. It takes 88 days to orbit the Sun.

❸ **Venus** is slightly smaller than the Earth, and is extremely hot and covered in thick clouds of acid. It takes 225 days to orbit the Sun.

5 **Mars** is a rocky planet, sometimes called the Red Planet because it is covered in iron oxide dust. It takes 687 days to orbit the Sun.

6 **Jupiter** is the largest of the planets. It is a huge ball of gases that takes 12 years to orbit the Sun.

7 **Saturn** is an enormous, bright planet surrounded by rings made up of small pieces of ice. It takes nearly 30 years to orbit the Sun.

8 **Uranus** is huge ball of gas covered in blue-green clouds. It has rings around it that may be made of pieces of ice. It takes 84 years to orbit the Sun.

9 **Neptune** is a large, bluish ball of gas. It has a ring system, and is orbited by at least thirteen moons. It takes 165 years to orbit the Sun.

4 **Earth** has breathable air in its atmosphere, temperatures that are not too extreme, and plenty of water, all of which mean that we can live here. It takes just over 365 days (one year) to orbit the Sun.

The Earth

Earth is the only planet in the Universe known to support life! It is a living planet, with plently of water, trees, plants, and breathable air, protected by its atmosphere. It is the third planet from the Sun and is the largest of the four rocky inner planets. Oceans, at least 4 kilometres deep, cover nearly 70 per cent of the Earth's surface. It has one moon, which is the only other place to be visited by people from Earth. It takes the Earth 365 days and 6 hours (one year) to orbit the Sun.

A satellite view of the Earth

A cross-section of the Earth

The Earth was formed around 4600 million years ago. In the beginning it was not solid, but molten. Over time the outside has cooled to form a hard, rock **crust**.

Beneath the crust is another layer of rock called the **mantle**. The mantle is very hot but does not melt completely because of great pressure.

At the centre of the Earth is the **core**. The **outer core** is liquid, but it is thought that the **inner core** is solid.

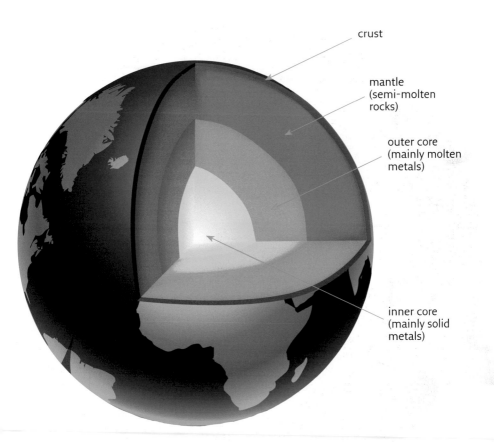

crust

mantle (semi-molten rocks)

outer core (mainly molten metals)

inner core (mainly solid metals)

The Moon

The Moon is Earth's only natural satellite. It is the second brightest object in the sky after the Sun and is thought to have formed from the debris when a planet-sized object collided with Earth billions of years ago. It is the only object, other than Earth, that human beings have set foot on. Although the Moon's appearance changes because of its phases, you are only ever able to see one side of it, as it always faces Earth.

There are a lot of dark patches on the Moon, which are flat areas of old lava flows which look like seas. The surface is very mountainous and there are peaks nearly as high as Mount Everest (the highest mountain on Earth). The surface also has a lot of craters, such as Plato, Copernicus, and Tycho.

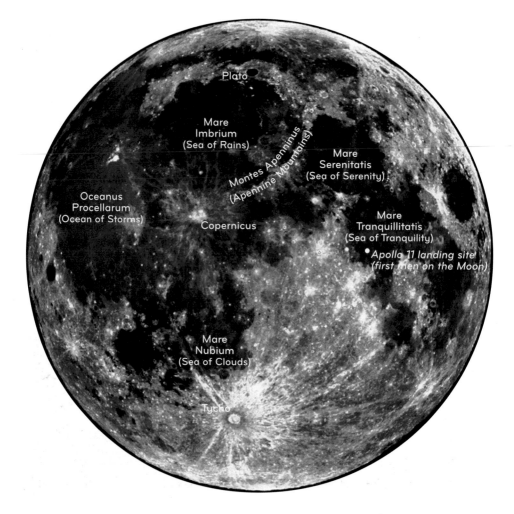

Plato

Mare Imbrium (Sea of Rains)

Montes Apenninus (Apennine Mountains)

Mare Serenitatis (Sea of Serenity)

Oceanus Procellarum (Ocean of Storms)

Copernicus

Mare Tranquillitatis (Sea of Tranquility)

Apollo 11 landing site (first men on the Moon)

Mare Nubium (Sea of Clouds)

Tycho

Phases of the Moon

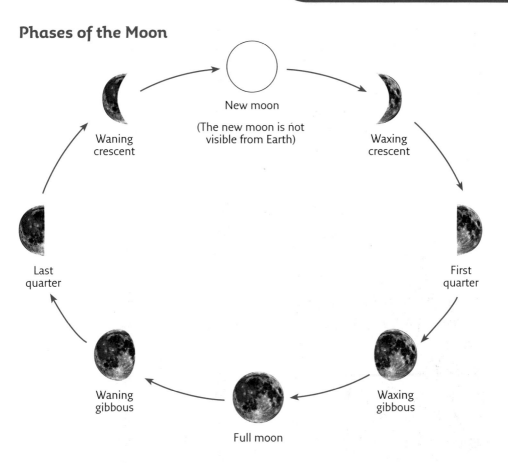

New moon

(The new moon is not visible from Earth)

Waning crescent

Waxing crescent

Last quarter

First quarter

Waning gibbous

Full moon

Waxing gibbous

What is an eclipse?

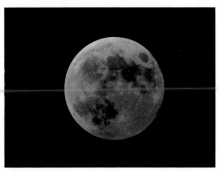

A lunar eclipse occurs when the Earth passes between the Sun and the Moon.

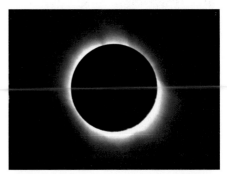

A solar eclipse occurs when the Moon passes between the Sun and the Earth.

477

Continents

These globes show the seven continents: North America, South America, Antarctica, Europe, Asia, Africa, and Oceania. Globes are the only way to show the true size and shape of the continents. However, flat maps are often more convenient.

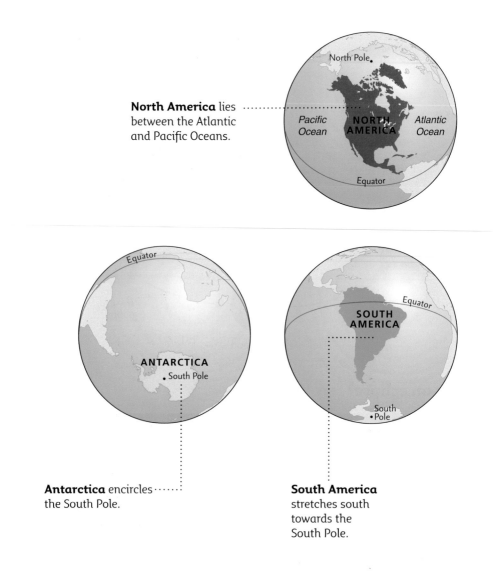

North America lies between the Atlantic and Pacific Oceans.

North Pole
Pacific Ocean
NORTH AMERICA
Atlantic Ocean
Equator

Equator
ANTARCTICA
• South Pole

SOUTH AMERICA
Equator
South • Pole

Antarctica encircles the South Pole.

South America stretches south towards the South Pole.

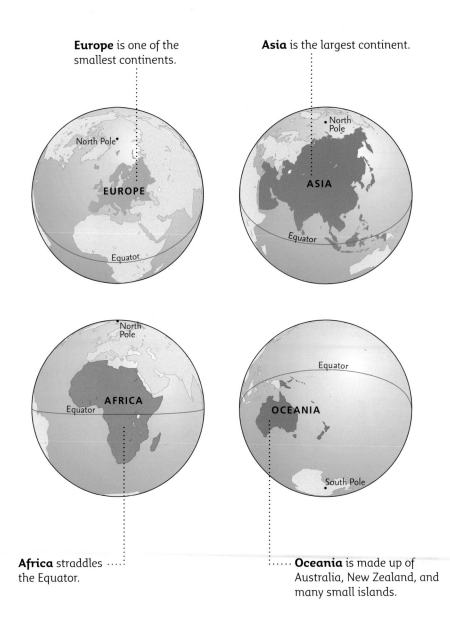

Europe is one of the smallest continents.

Asia is the largest continent.

North Pole

EUROPE

Equator

North Pole

ASIA

Equator

North Pole

AFRICA

Equator

Equator

OCEANIA

South Pole

Africa straddles the Equator.

Oceania is made up of Australia, New Zealand, and many small islands.

Mountains, rivers, and oceans

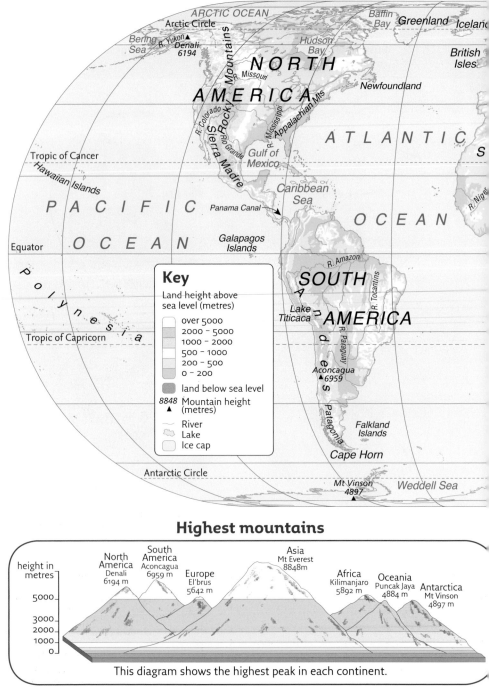

Highest mountains

This diagram shows the highest peak in each continent.

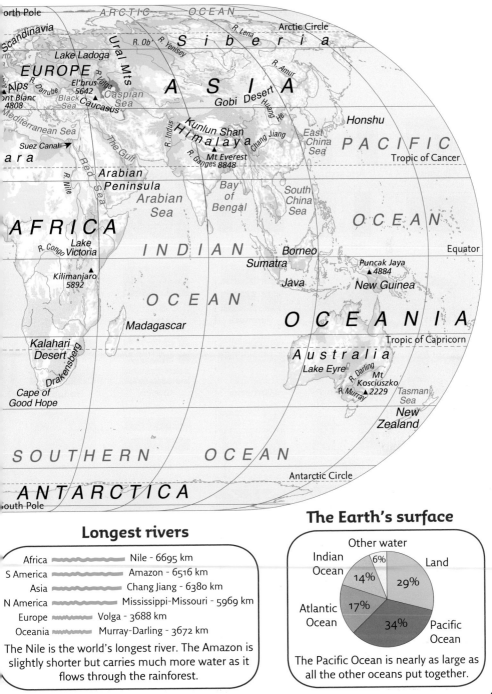

Longest rivers

Africa		Nile - 6695 km
S America		Amazon - 6516 km
Asia		Chang Jiang - 6380 km
N America		Mississippi-Missouri - 5969 km
Europe		Volga - 3688 km
Oceania		Murray-Darling - 3672 km

The Nile is the world's longest river. The Amazon is slightly shorter but carries much more water as it flows through the rainforest.

The Earth's surface

Other water 6%
Indian Ocean 14%
Land 29%
Atlantic Ocean 17%
Pacific Ocean 34%

The Pacific Ocean is nearly as large as all the other oceans put together.

Flags of the world

Here is a selection of flags from around the world:

EUROPE

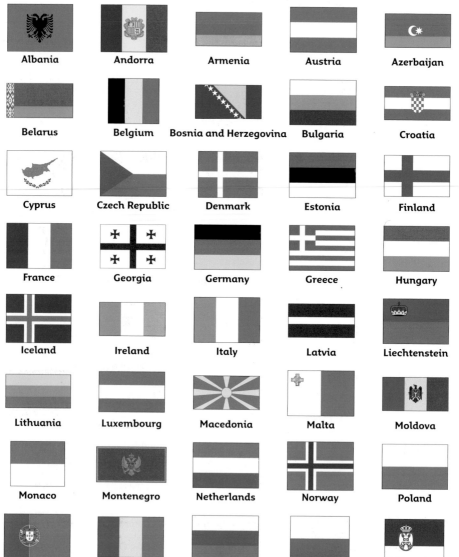

Albania	Andorra	Armenia	Austria	Azerbaijan
Belarus	Belgium	Bosnia and Herzegovina	Bulgaria	Croatia
Cyprus	Czech Republic	Denmark	Estonia	Finland
France	Georgia	Germany	Greece	Hungary
Iceland	Ireland	Italy	Latvia	Liechtenstein
Lithuania	Luxembourg	Macedonia	Malta	Moldova
Monaco	Montenegro	Netherlands	Norway	Poland
Portugal	Romania	Russia	San Marino	Serbia

Slovakia

Slovenia

Spain

Sweden

Switzerland

Ukraine

United Kingdom

Vatican City

AFRICA

Algeria

Angola

Benin

Botswana

Burkina

Burundi

Cameroon

Cape Verde

Central African Rep.

Chad

Comoros

Congo

Congo, Dem. Rep. of

Côte d'Ivoire

Djibouti

Egypt

Equatorial Guinea

Eritrea

Ethiopia

Gabon

The Gambia

Ghana

Guinea

Guinea-Bissau

Kenya

Lesotho

Liberia

Libya

Madagascar

Malawi

Mali

Mauritania

Mauritius

Morocco

Mozambique

Flags of the world

Namibia

Niger

Nigeria

Rwanda

São Tomé and Príncipe

Senegal

Seychelles

Sierre Leone

Somalia

South Africa

South Sudan

Sudan

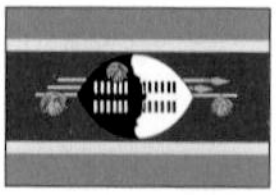

Swaziland

Tanzania

Togo

Tunisia

Uganda

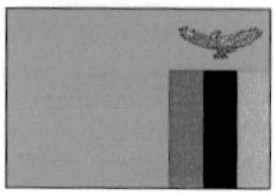

Zambia

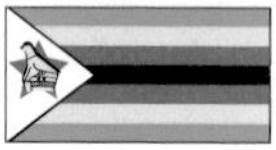

Zimbabwe

ASIA

Afghanistan

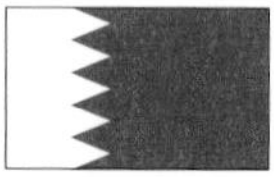

Bahrain

Bangladesh

Bhutan

Brunei

Cambodia

China

East Timor

India

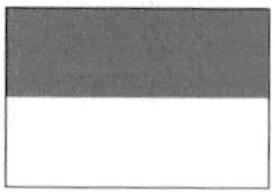

Indonesia

Iran

Iraq

Israel

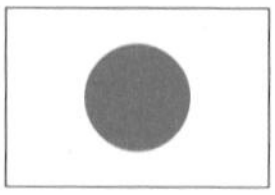

Japan

Jordan

Kazakhstan

Kuwait

Kyrgyzstan

Laos

Lebanon

Flags of the world

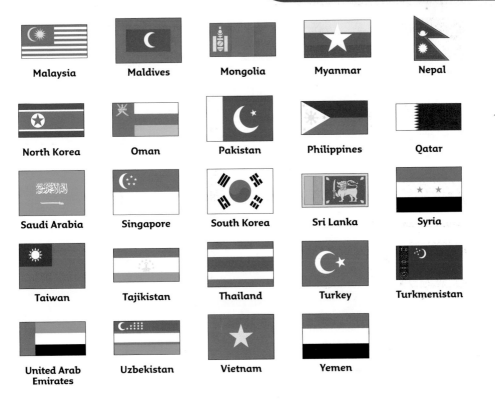

Malaysia	Maldives	Mongolia	Myanmar	Nepal
North Korea	Oman	Pakistan	Philippines	Qatar
Saudi Arabia	Singapore	South Korea	Sri Lanka	Syria
Taiwan	Tajikistan	Thailand	Turkey	Turkmenistan
United Arab Emirates	Uzbekistan	Vietnam	Yemen	

NORTH AMERICA

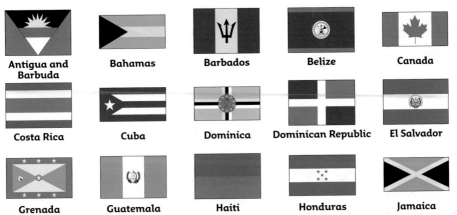

Antigua and Barbuda	Bahamas	Barbados	Belize	Canada
Costa Rica	Cuba	Dominica	Dominican Republic	El Salvador
Grenada	Guatemala	Haiti	Honduras	Jamaica

Flags of the world

Mexico

Nicaragua

Panama

St Kitts and Nevis

St Lucia

St Vincent and
the Grenadines

Trinidad and
Tobago

United States
of America

SOUTH AMERICA

Argentina

Bolivia

Brazil

Chile

Colombia

Ecuador

Guyana

Paraguay

Peru

Suriname

Uruguay

Venezuela

OCEANIA

Australia

Fiji

Kiribati

Marshall Islands

Micronesia,
Fed. States of

Nauru

New Zealand

Palau

Papua New Guinea

Samoa

Solomon Islands

Tonga

Tuvalu

Vanuatu

Picture credits

Photo credits

P8 © clivewa* , P18 © Vitalii Hulai* (newt), P18 © picturepartners* (frog), P20 © Hurst Photo*, P23 © Andreas Zerndl*, P28 © JIANG HONGYAN*, P35 © Dmitry Skutin*, P38 © padu_foto*, P45 © dgcampillo*, P46 © trusjom*, P48 © Lisa S.*, P51 © Oliver Wilde*, P55 © Lightspring*, P57 © Dan Breckwoldt*, P65 © Seregam*, P67 © Pozezan*, P71 © Hurst Photo*, P74 © mama_mia*, P88 © Andaman*, P92 © Drew Rawcliffe*, P95 © Marcos Mesa Sam Wordley*, P100 © SurangaSL*, P106 © Josef Hanus*, P108 © CraigBurrows*, P120 © Venus Angel* (double bass), © vnlit* (dragonfly), P125 © Bas Meelker* (dyke), P126 © Juergen Faelchle*, P130 © Eric Isselee*, P135 © andrea crisante*, P146 © ladyphoto*, P154 © KIM NGUYEN* (both photos), P158 © Sombra*, P161 © Karramba Production*, P163 © Alex Mit*, P167 © Denis Kichatof*, P169 © Blue Marble: Next Generation. NASA's Earth Observatory, P171 © JLR Photography*, P177 © Lebedinski Vladislav*, P190 © Africa Studio*, P193 © Harvepino*, P195 © Denis Burdin*, P205 © Eric Isselee*, P217 © Kbiros*, P218 © takayuki*, P220 © Andy Lidstone*, P221 © howamo*, P226 © Berents*, P241 © Anan Kaewkhammul*, P245 © MAHATHIR MOHD YASIN*, P249 © Mehmet Cetin*, P256 © defpicture*, P259 © Jose Ignacio Soto* (mummy), P265 © Vishnevskiy Vasily*, P270 © Matthias G. Ziegler*, P281 © Nid santana*, P283 © Alexey U*, P300 © de2marco*, P304 © kavram*, P309 © Mmaxer*, P317 © WitR*, P318 © muratart*, P323 © fivespots*, P327 © BlueOrange Studio*, P329 © Pal Teravagimov*, P334 © Dan Schreiber*, P340 © bom*, P346 © puchan*, P353 © Nattika*, P360 © Finomax*, P362 © natrot*, P367 © Sashkin*, P376 © Sirichai Puangsuwan*, P382 © Santi Rodriguez*, P391 © xavier gallego morell*, P393 © Brovkina*, P395 © EpicStockMedia*, P402 © jorisvo*, P408 © Richard Griffin*, P412 © Michiel de Wit*, P416 © Sergey Dzyuba*, P422 © holbox*, P425 © Jaromir Chalabala*, P431 © ChrisVanLennepPhoto*, P435 © Bildagentur Zoonar GmbH*, P440 © InnaFelker*, P441 © Carlos Romero*, P446 © JeniFoto*, P451 © ILYA AKINSHIN*, P459 © funkypoodle* (left), © Pressmaster* (right), P460 © LanKS* (book), © rzstudio* (books), © EM Arts* (grapes), © Rich Carey* (fish), © EastVillage Images* (lions), P467 © Garsya*, P469 © Viet Gallery* (balloons), P474 © NASA, P476 © Lick Observatory, P477 © Lick Observatory (Moon), © Primo_Cigler* (lunar eclipse), © Vladimir Wrangel* (solar eclipse)

Artwork credits

P187 © artform*, P268 © gst*, P398 © velirina*, P475 © Webspark*

Artwork on pages 21, 25, 30, 34, 37, 60, 68, 80, 81, 86, 97, 99, 111, 125, 141, 173, 184, 209, 212, 232, 236, 259 (muscle), 271, 278, 290, 293, 321, 337, 338, 366, 378, 387, 406, 419, 420, 433, 456, and 457 appeared in the first edition of the Collins Primary Illustrated Dictionary. The illustrators for the first edition were Tim Archbold, Cy Baker, Simone Boni, Maggie Brand, Tamsin Cook, Joanne Cowne, Luigi Crittone, William Donohoe, Richard Draper, Luigi Gallante, Jeremy Gower, Nick Harris, Christian Hook, Felicity House, Hans Jenssen, Sharon MacCausland, John Mack, Kevin Maddison, Tony Morris, Pat Murray, Chris Orr Associates, Malcolm Porter, Sebastian Quigley, Steve Roberts, Mike Saunders, Peter Scott, Siena Artworks, Hayley Simmons, Gill Thomblin, Phil Weare, Steve Weston, Sarah Wimperis, Ann Winterbotham, and Sue Woollatt.

Artwork on pages 196, 229, 264, 289, and 326 Emily Skinner

Cover artwork and artwork on pages 11, 14, 41, 52, 56, 62, 69, 78, 112, 116, 119, 123, 133, 136, 148, 150, 162, 170, 180, 189, 198, 203, 215, 225, 235, 237, 248, 251, 254, 269, 272, 275, 280, 287, 294, 296, 312, 333, 342, 351, 357, 361, 370, 385, 400, 404, 414, 423, 429, 438, 444, 452, 453, 458, 462, 463, 466, 468, and 469 by Q2A Media Services Private Limited

*from Shutterstock.com